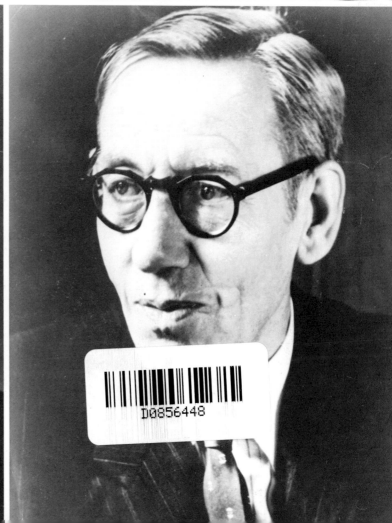

# German Fiction Writers, 1914-1945

# Dictionary of Literary Biography

## Documentary Series

## Yearbooks

## Concise Series

# German Fiction Writers, 1914-1945

Edited by
James Hardin
*University of South Carolina*

A Bruccoli Clark Layman Book

Gale Research Company • Book Tower • Detroit, Michigan 48226

Manufactured by Edwards Brothers, Inc.
Ann Arbor, Michigan
Printed in the United States of America

Copyright © 1987
GALE RESEARCH COMPANY

**Library of Congress Cataloging-in-Publication Data**

German fiction writers, 1914-1945.

(Dictionary of literary biography; v. 56)
"A Bruccoli Clark Layman book."
Includes index.
1. German fiction—20th century—Bio-bibliography.
2. Novelists, German—20th century—Biography—Dic-
tionaries. 3. German fiction—20th century—History and
criticism. I. Hardin, James N. II. Series.
PT772.G39  1987  833'.912'09  [B]  87-216
ISBN 0-8103-1734-6

CARA

*For Tim, Maxie,*
*Jim and Will*

# Contents

# Plan of the Series

*. . . Almost the most prodigious asset of a country, and perhaps its most precious possession, is its native literary product—when that product is fine and noble and enduring.*

Mark Twain*

The advisory board, the editors, and the publisher of the *Dictionary of Literary Biography* are joined in endorsing Mark Twain's declaration. The literature of a nation provides an inexhaustible resource of permanent worth. It is our expectation that this endeavor will make literature and its creators better understood and more accessible to students and the literate public, while satisfying the standards of teachers and scholars.

To meet these requirements, *literary biography* has been construed in terms of the author's achievement. The most important thing about a writer is his writing. Accordingly, the entries in *DLB* are career biographies, tracing the development of the author's canon and the evolution of his reputation.

The publication plan for *DLB* resulted from two years of preparation. The project was proposed to Bruccoli Clark by Frederick G. Ruffner, president of the Gale Research Company, in November 1975. After specimen entries were prepared and typeset, an advisory board was formed to refine the entry format and develop the series rationale. In meetings held during 1976, the publisher, series editors, and advisory board approved the scheme for a comprehensive biographical dictionary of persons who contributed to North American literature. Editorial work on the first volume began in January 1977, and it was published in 1978.

In order to make *DLB* more than a reference tool and to compile volumes that individually have claim to status as literary history, it was decided to organize volumes by topic or period or genre. Each of these freestanding volumes provides a biographical-bibliographical guide and overview for a particular area of literature. We are convinced that this organization—as opposed to a single alphabet method—constitutes a valuable innovation in the presentation of reference material. The volume

plan necessarily requires many decisions for the placement and treatment of authors who might properly be included in two or three volumes. In some instances a major figure will be included in separate volumes, but with different entries emphasizing the aspect of his career appropriate to each volume. Ernest Hemingway, for example, is represented in *American Writers in Paris, 1920-1939* by an entry focusing on his expatriate apprenticeship; he is also in *American Novelists, 1910-1945* with an entry surveying his entire career. Each volume includes a cumulative index of subject authors and articles. The final *DLB* volume will be a comprehensive index to the entire series.

With volume ten in 1982 it was decided to enlarge the scope of *DLB*. By the end of 1986 twenty-one volumes treating British literature had been published, and volumes for Commonwealth and Modern European literature were in progress. The series has been further augmented by the *DLB Yearbooks* (since 1981) which update published entries and add new entries to keep the *DLB* current with contemporary activity. There have also been occasional *DLB Documentary Series* volumes which provide biographical and critical background source materials for figures whose work is judged to have particular interest for students. One of these companion volumes is entirely devoted to Tennessee Williams.

The purpose of *DLB* is not only to provide reliable information in a convenient format but also to place the figures in the larger perspective of literary history and to offer appraisals of their accomplishments by qualified scholars.

We define literature as the *intellectual commerce of a nation:* not merely as belles lettres but as that ample and complex process by which ideas are generated, shaped, and transmitted. *DLB* entries are not limited to "creative writers" but extend to other figures who in this time and in this way influenced the mind of a people. Thus the series encompasses historians, journalists, publishers, and screenwriters. By this means readers of *DLB* may be aided to perceive literature not as cult scripture in the keeping of cultural high priests but as at the center of a nation's life.

*DLB* includes the major writers appropriate to each volume and those standing in the ranks immediately behind them. Scholarly and critical coun-

*From an unpublished section of Mark Twain's autobiography, copyright © by the Mark Twain Company.

sel has been sought in deciding which minor figures to include and how full their entries should be. Wherever possible, useful references are made to figures who do not warrant separate entries.

Each *DLB* volume has a volume editor responsible for planning the volume, selecting the figures for inclusion, and assigning the entries. Volume editors are also responsible for preparing, where appropriate, appendices surveying the major periodicals and literary and intellectual movements for their volumes, as well as lists of further readings. Work on the series as a whole is coordinated at the Bruccoli Clark editorial center in Columbia, South Carolina, where the editorial staff is responsible for the accuracy of the published volumes.

One feature that distinguishes *DLB* is the illustration policy—its concern with the iconography of literature. Just as an author is influenced by his surroundings, so is the reader's understanding of the author enhanced by a knowledge of his environment. Therefore *DLB* volumes include not only drawings, paintings, and photographs of authors, often depicting them at various stages in their careers, but also illustrations of their families and places where they lived. Title pages are regularly reproduced in facsimile along with dust jackets for modern authors. The dust jackets are a special fea-

ture of *DLB* because they often document better than anything else the way in which an author's work was launched in its own time. Specimens of the writers' manuscripts are included when feasible.

A supplement to *DLB*—tentatively titled *A Guide, Chronology, and Glossary for American Literature*—will outline the history of literature in North America and trace the influences that shaped it. This volume will provide a framework for the study of American literature by means of chronological tables, literary affiliation charts, glossarial entries, and concise surveys of the major movements. It has been planned to stand on its own as a vade mecum, providing a ready-reference guide to the study of American literature as well as a companion to the *DLB* volumes for American literature.

Samuel Johnson rightly decreed that "The chief glory of every people arises from its authors." The purpose of the *Dictionary of Literary Biography* is to compile literary history in the surest way available to us—by accurate and comprehensive treatment of the lives and work of those who contributed to it.

The *DLB* Advisory Board

# Foreword

*German Fiction Writers, 1914-1945* treats twentieth-century German and Swiss authors whose first significant prose work appeared in or after 1914 and whose chief literary activity took place between the world wars. While any such demarcation is arbitrary (and in this case underscores the tragic nature of the period), this periodization—from the outbreak of the Great War to the end of World War II—has a certain logic. No one can deny the complete break with the political past in both parts of Germany in 1945—and the break was not just a political one. The year 1914 likewise marked the end of an epoch; it can be argued that no one writing after the events of Sarajevo and the inevitable outbreak in August 1914 wrote as he did before the war. On the other hand, it is quite true that the sense of imminent disaster pervading much early expressionist poetry anticipated the events of 1914. But dates must be chosen and we have made a decision that provides the present volume a necessary structure.

This book will be followed by a companion volume treating twentieth-century writers who began their literary careers *before* 1914 and by volumes on German-Swiss prose fiction writers after 1945. A final volume in the series will include Austrian authors from 1900 to the present.

The focus of the articles in all volumes is prose fiction, but we also include figures primarily known as poets or dramatists who happened also to write significant prose fiction works. Perhaps the most striking example is Rainer Maria Rilke, with his *Aufzeichnungen des Malte Laurids Brigge* (1910), but there are also—among many others—the examples of the poet Else Lasker-Schüler and the dramatist Fritz von Unruh. In such cases, the other genres are discussed insofar as they are relevant to the prose works.

Every effort has been made to be as inclusive as possible. As the volumes aim for objectivity, no criteria could be allowed that would exclude a writer because of philosophical or political convictions or on the basis of unsavory personal associations. Thus, we have included not only the figures who appear in virtually every literary history (writers of unquestionable literary significance or those who are notable for their influence, for good or evil, on contemporary writers and the broad public,

and also lesser talents who are especially typical of a given movement or tendency) but also unjustly neglected writers who may have been "discovered" only in recent years. The result of this open approach was enlightening. Some of the most interesting articles deal with figures who, for whatever reason, have received little critical attention for decades. Many Germanists, even those who specialize in literature of the twentieth century, have not had the time to actually *read* the works of writers such as Hermann Stehr, Clara Viebig, Hans Henny Jahnn, Paul Ernst, Gustav Meyrink, Kurt Martens, Franziska zu Reventlow, or Lou Andreas-Salomé, who are familiar to most of us by name only. I think that some of these articles will be a revelation, since the scholars who wrote them have gone *ad fontes*, as it were, and have read or reread books that had lain unopened in great libraries for half a century. These scholars attempted a fresh look at all the figures and succeeded in avoiding the historically sanctioned, dismissive "one-liners" granted peripheral figures in most literary histories. And so, as a result of the hard work of the contributors to our volumes, even the specialist will find information previously unavailable in any book in English or German.

The volumes are unique in their emphasis on the *lives* of the writers and in their attempt to make the entries comprehensible to individuals from an entirely different culture. The series as a whole will cover in several volumes German, Austrian, and Swiss prose fiction of the twentieth century. We are acutely aware of the lacunae in this work, which is, after all, but one piece in the mosaic we intend to prepare, and plan to fill these gaps in future *DLB* volumes concentrating on German-language poetry and drama of the same period. Other volumes on the Age of Goethe are in preparation. Our goal, in the fullness of time, is to treat the entirety of German literature from 1700 to the present.

We have tried to present the articles in such a way that they will be understandable and useful for Americans. We are assuming that most readers will have little knowledge of German, and for that reason the contributors have provided translations of titles of works mentioned and passages quoted in their entries. The bibliographies of the subjects' writings include English translations, where these exist. Secondary literature in both English and German has been included in the reference section at the end of each entry. The location of the letters and other papers (the *Nachlaß*, to use the more specific German word) has been given in all cases where it is known. Any serious study of the writer in question would have to include a careful evaluation of those materials.

—*James Hardin*

# Acknowledgments

This book was produced by Bruccoli Clark Layman, Inc. Karen L. Rood is senior editor for the *Dictionary of Literary Biography* series. Philip B. Dematteis was the in-house editor.

Art supervisor is Pamela Haynes. Copyediting supervisor is Patricia Coate. Production coordinator is Kimberly Casey. Typesetting supervisor is Laura Ingram. Lucia Tarbox is editorial assistant. The production staff includes Rowena Betts, David R. Bowdler, Mary S. Dye, Charles Egleston, Kathleen M. Flanagan, Joyce Fowler, Karen Fritz, Judith K. Ingle, Judith E. McCray, Janet Phelps, and Joycelyn R. Smith. Jean W. Ross is permissions editor. Joseph Caldwell, photography editor, and Joseph Matthew Bruccoli did photographic copy work for the volume.

Walter W. Ross and Rhonda Marshall did the library research with the assistance of the staff at the Thomas Cooper Library of the University of South Carolina: Lynn Barron, Daniel Boice, Connie Crider, Kathy Eckman, Michael Freeman, Gary Geer, David L. Haggard, Jens Holley, Marcia Martin, Dana Rabon, Jean Rhyne, Jan Squire, Ellen Tillett, and Virginia Weathers.

Special thanks are due to the Lilly Library, Indiana University, for assistance with illustrations for this volume.

Thanks are also extended to Uta Friedlein and Renate Wilson, who are native speakers of German as well as students of German language and literature, for their careful proofreading of the entries in the volume.

# German Fiction Writers, 1914-1945

# Ernst Barlach
*(2 January 1870-24 October 1938)*

Ursula R. Mahlendorf
*University of California, Santa Barbara*

BOOKS: *Figuren-Zeichnen* (Strelitz: Hittenkofer, 1895);

*Der tote Tag: Drama in fünf Akten* (Berlin: Cassirer, 1912);

*Der arme Vetter: Drama* (Berlin: Cassirer, 1918);

*Die echten Sedemunds: Drama* (Berlin: Cassirer, 1920);

*Der Findling: Ein Spiel in drei Stücken* (Berlin: Cassirer, 1922);

*Die Wandlungen Gottes: Sieben Holzschnitte* (Berlin: Cassirer, 1922);

*Die Sündflut: Drama in fünf Teilen* (Berlin: Cassirer, 1924);

*Der blaue Boll: Drama* (Berlin: Cassirer, 1926);

*Ein selbsterzähltes Leben* (Berlin: Cassirer, 1928);

*Die gute Zeit: Zehn Akte* (Berlin: Cassirer, 1929);

*Zeichnungen*, introduction by Paul Fechter (Munich: Piper, 1935);

*Fries der Lauschenden*, introduction by Hugo Körtzinger (Othmarschen: Privately printed, 1936);

*Fragmente aus sehr früher Zeit* (Berlin: Riermerschmidt, 1939);

*Der gestohlene Mond: Roman. Nach Ernst Barlachs nachgelassener Handschrift*, edited by Friedrich Droß (Berlin & Frankfurt am Main: Suhrkamp, 1948);

*Seespeck: Nach Ernst Barlachs nachgelassener Handschrift*, edited by Droß (Berlin & Frankfurt am Main: Suhrkamp, 1948);

*Sechs Kleine Schriften zù besonderen Gelegenheiten*, edited by F. Schult (Bremen: Heye, 1950);

*Fragmente* (Güstrow: Schult, 1950);

*Der Graf von Ratzeburg: Drama. Nach Ernst Barlachs nachgelassener Handschrift*, edited by Schult (Hamburg: Grillen-Presse, 1951);

*Güstrower Fragmente* (Bremen: Ernst Barlach-Gesellschaft, 1951);

*Drei Pariser Fragmente* (Bremen: Ernst Barlach-Gesellschaft, 1952);

*Kunst im Krieg*, edited by Droß (Bremen: Ernst Barlach-Gesellschaft, 1953);

*Zwischen Erde und Himmel: 45 Handzeichnungen,* edited by Carl Georg Heise (Munich: Piper, 1953);

*Werkverzeichnis,* compiled by Schult, 2 volumes (Hamburg: Hauswedell, 1958-1960);

*Plastik,* compiled by Wolf Stubbe, photos by Friedrich Hewicker (Munich: Piper, 1959);

*Two Acts from The Flood; A Letter on Kandinsky; Eight Sculptures; Brecht: Notes on the Barlach Exhibition* (Northampton: Printed at the Gehenna Press for *The Massachusetts Review,* 1960);

*Eine Steppenfahrt,* edited by Werner Timm (Leipzig: Graphische Kunstanstalt, 1961);

*Zeichnungen,* compiled by Stubbe, photos by Hewicker (Munich: Piper, 1961);

*The Transformations of God: Seven Woodcuts by Ernst Barlach with Selections from His Writings in Translation by Naomi Jackson Groves* (Hamburg: Christians, 1962);

*Das schlimme Jahr,* text by Franz Fühmann (Rostock: Hinstorff, 1965);

*Ernst Barlach Fragmente* (Hamburg: Ernst Barlach-Gesellschaft, 1970);

*Ernst Barlach, das Wirkliche und Wahrhaftige: Briefe, Grafik, Plastik, Dokumente,* edited by Fühmann, photos by Gisela Pätsch (Rostock: Hinstorff, 1970);

*Fulfilled Moments on a Higher Plane: From the German of Ernst Barlach, Glücksmomente im höheren Reich,* translated by Groves (Hamburg: Ernst Barlach Haus, Hermann F. Reemtsma Foundation, 1971);

*35* (Munich: Piper, 1974);

*Güstrower Tagebuch,* edited by Elmar Jansen (Berlin: Union, 1978).

**Collections:** *Das dichterische Werk,* volume 1: *Die Dramen,* edited by Klaus Lazarowicz and Friedrich Droß (Munich: Piper, 1956); volume 2: *Die Prosa 1,* edited by Droß (Munich: Piper, 1958); volume 3: *Die Prosa II,* edited by Droß, Afterword by Walter Muschg (Munich: Piper, 1959);

*Three Plays,* translated by Alex Page (Minneapolis: University of Minnesota Press, 1964).

When plays of the expressionist Ernst Barlach were first performed in the 1920s in major cities of the Weimar Republic, no less a critic than Thomas Mann compared Barlach favorably to the young playwright Bertolt Brecht, then much in vogue, and praised the folk-song-like, dark power of Barlach's *Der tote Tag* (The Dead Day, 1912). Barlach's reputation as the most interesting playwright of the expressionist movement is attested to

*Charcoal self-portrait of Barlach, drawn in Paris in 1895*

by the fact that more studies were devoted to his work than to that of Carl Sternheim, Georg Kaiser, or Ernst Toller. During the 1920s, two of his plays, *Die echten Sedemunds* (1920; translated as *The Genuine Sedemunds* in *Three Plays,* 1964) and *Der blaue Boll* (1926; translated as *The Blue Boll* in *Three Plays*), had successful, long runs in the expressionist staging of Jürgen Fehling and Leopold Jeßner. While the playwright's achievements have not been questioned by literary critics, the prose writer's have. Published only posthumously, his two volumes of prose with diaries "Russisches Tagebuch" (Russian Diary) and "Güstrower Tagebuch" (Güstrow Diary—both published in *Das dichterische Werk* [The Literary Work, 1956-1959]); his novelistic fragments "Die Reise des Humors und des Beobachtungsgeistes" (The Travels of Humor and the Spirit of Observation, published in *Das dichterische Werk*) and *Seespeck* (1948); and his one completed novel, *Der gestohlene Mond* (The Stolen Moon, 1948), have had a mixed reception. *Der gestohlene Mond,* to Barlach enthusiast Walter Muschg, is comparable to Franz Kafka's *Das Schloß* (1926; translated as *The Castle,* 1930), Alfred Döblin's *Berlin Alexanderplatz*

(1929), Robert Musil's *Der Mann ohne Eigenschaften* (1952; translated as *The Man without Qualities*, 1953), or Hermann Broch's *Die Schlafwandler* (1931-1932; translated as *The Sleepwalkers*, 1947). Barlach's biographer Hans Franck, on the other hand, though appreciative of the novel fragments and diaries, finds the novel confused, abstract, and abstruse. To understand Barlach's greatness as a writer and artist, his art, his prose, and his drama must be evaluated together. They are different aspects of a single concern, each aspect illuminating the others. The basic, expressive forms of his drawings and sculptures—for instance, his self-portrait of 1928 and the *Blind Man* of 1935—are abstracted from the figures of his environment or from his own face. They show superb craftsmanship and compassion for suffering humanity, as in such war memorials as the angel of Güstrow Cathedral with the face of the artist Käthe Kollwitz. As a writer, Barlach sought clarification of pressing personal problems through novelistic and dramatic representation. The personal beginning, however, leads to broader ethical questions and finally to a search for the ultimate meaning of human existence. Barlach shares the basic themes of his expressionist contemporaries: criticism of contemporary bourgeois society, the struggle between generations, the search for transcendence and transformation, the apocalypse. He modulates these themes, however, to his own vision of the world. Unlike other writers of expressionism, for instance, he centers in his plays on the father figure and the son's search for the father rather than on the rebel son. Moreover, beginning with *Seespeck*, he increasingly portrayed memorably individualized characters who do not fit the expressionistic mold. Barlach does not revel in expressionistic pathos and rhetoric. His narratives and dramas are earthy, grotesquely humorous, and scatological but also abound with the abstractions and paradoxes of mysticism. Prose and plays begin in naturalistic, often autobiographical reality of character and situation and then develop into exploration of the inner meaning of events through the characters' relationships to each other and their moments of epiphany as well as through their metaphysical questioning, through myth and symbol.

Born in Wedel in 1870, Ernst Heinrich Barlach was the first of four sons of a north German country doctor, Georg Barlach, who took the boy along on his visits to the sick, giving him, as he wrote in *Ein selbsterzähltes Leben* (A Self-Told Life, 1928), "das beste Beispiel nützlichen Tuns" (the best example of useful activity) and early knowl-

edge of sickness, suffering, and death. His parents' marriage was troubled: the doctor was a poor manager and his wife, Luise Vollert Barlach, was emotionally ill. When Barlach was thirteen, his mother entered a psychiatric clinic. A year later she reappeared, abruptly and unexpectedly, and soon afterwards his father died of pneumonia. A recurring theme in his work, the yearning for a spiritual father's guidance, has its roots here. The family was left unprovided for, and only Barlach was able to finish high school. He enrolled at the Hamburg Gewerbeschule, but art school was a disappointment. Barlach turned to sculpture and transferred to the Dresden Academy of Fine Arts, but remained unsatisfied. His interest in art and writing, his increasing technical skill in both, and his capacity for friendship earned him assistance and intellectual encouragement from such friends as Carl Garbers, for whom he worked on Hamburg public sculpture projects; Friedrich Düsel, a future literary critic and editor in chief of *Westermanns Monatshefte;* and Reinhard Piper, a future publisher. These friendships resulted in some of the finest letters of the twentieth century. After graduating from Dresden in 1895, Barlach studied in Paris for a few months. The novel fragment "Reise des Humors und des Beobachtungsgeistes" gives an exuberant, satirical account of his reaction to French art and of Germans studying in Paris. With its playful grotesque personifications of human faculties and ideas (Mr. Belief-in-Authority, Miss Idée Fixe), the fragment shows young Barlach's closeness to the Jugendstil (Youth Style—the ornamental, decorative style of art that prevailed in Germany from 1898 to 1910). Exposure to French art had no impact on him, and for the next eleven years he moved about restlessly, experimented in art and writing to try to find his own voice, and increasingly despaired of success.

He was thirty-five when two events brought decisive changes in his art and life. During a trip to Russia in 1906 his experience of the beggars and peasants of the vast steppes as symbols of the human condition gained him the insight that "du darfst alles Deinige, das Äußerste, das Innerste, Gebärde der Frömmigkeit und Ungebärde der Wut, ohne Scheu wagen" (you can express everything that is truly yours, external and innermost, the gesture of piety as well as the disfigurement of rage, without embarrassment). He restricted his figures to one expressive gesture and finally saw his work recognized at the 1907 exhibit of the Berlin Secession, a group of artists (later called expressionists) who had split off from the naturalists in

*Sculptures by Barlach*

Part of a page from the manuscript for Barlach's novel fragment Seespeck, *published posthumously in 1948*
(*Barlach-Archiv, Güstrow*)

1898. A contract with the Berlin art dealer and publisher Paul Cassirer assured him a monthly salary so that he could devote himself to his work. Equally important was the birth in 1906 of his illegitimate son, Klaus, for whose custody he won a struggle with the boy's mother in 1908. He studied Italian art on a fellowship in Florence in 1909, and in 1910 he settled down with his mother and Klaus at Güstrow, near Lübeck. Being responsible for a new life, he felt a need to resolve his relationships with his own parents and with his son's mother. The result of this self-confrontation was his symbolic first drama, *Der tote Tag*, portraying the unsuccessful struggle of a fatherless boy to free himself from his mother's stifling dominance so as to follow his spiritual father's call toward self-realization.

The play *Der arme Vetter* (The Poor Cousin, 1918), written between 1911 and 1916, describes a son's quest for spirituality out of revulsion from material existence. Partly Easter resurrection play and partly naturalistic, north German small-town farce, the work pits Hans Iver, a young, suicidal visionary, against the worldly businessman Siebenmark. But Siebenmark's is the inner dramatic conflict, as Barlach concerned himself increasingly with realistically drawn, carnal-minded characters rather than spiritual son-figures like Iver. The change in emphasis appears in the contemporaneous novel fragment *Seespeck*, based on Barlach's return home to Wedel from art school, in which his protagonist experiences the everyday difficul-

ties of establishing himself in a business and stumbling through the family lives of his brother and his friends. In contrast to his earlier allegorical prose, this work shows Barlach a keen observer of his fellow men, skilled in revealing their essence through gesture and image.

At the outbreak of World War I, Barlach shared the nationalism of many of his countrymen. The Güstrow diaries give a vivid, day-by-day account of the patriot's changing view of the war. Too old to fight, he volunteered for home service and worked in a children's nursery. When the army needed more soldiers in 1916, he was called up and received basic training. Soon disillusioned by the army, the suffering of the home front, and the needless slaughter, he wrote *Die echten Sedemunds*. The play criticizes the pretentious respectability, self-indulgent power hunger, and secret criminality of Wilhelminian society which he held responsible for the war. This play is Barlach's only comedy; its action moves between carnival fairground, insane asylum, and cemetery. Scenes of a dance of life change to scenes of a dance of death. The confrontation between young radical Sedemund and his callous, Karamazov-like father over the suicide of Mrs. Sedemund exposes old Sedemund's duplicity and his son's ineffective, arrogant idealism. In his main characters, Barlach succeeded in drawing vital comic types comparable to Wedekind's or Brecht's, while the metaphor of the asylum as a place of sanity foreshadows the theater of the absurd. The preoccupation with suicide in

*Barlach self-portrait, 1928 (by permission of the Estate of Ernst Barlach)*

sibility of personal change. Calan's insights reflect the mysticism mediated to Barlach through the writings of Jakob Böhme. Though the play was not a theatrical success, its ideas, the beauty of its language, and the power of its character portrayal won critical acclaim, as witnessed by the award of the Kleist prize in 1924. As the pleasure-seeking 1920s roared on, Barlach's concern about personal transformation as antidote to social chaos grew more urgent. In his most successful play, *Der blaue Boll*, this concern is projected into a small-town milieu and is even reflected in his protagonist's physical condition. Another play, *Die gute Zeit (The Good Age,* 1929), satirizes the society of the 1920s bent, in Barlach's view, on destruction by heedless self-indulgence.

Barlach's autobiography, the finest of expressionist self-portrayals, appeared in 1928 as an introduction to a retrospective volume of his artistic work. With sharp self-awareness and humor, Barlach traces his spiritual development from childhood, through years of perplexity and

Barlach's plays and prose probably derives from the fact that his mother had been suicidal since his childhood. She finally drowned herself in 1920.

Like many contemporary writers Barlach responded to postwar misery with a passion play. *Der Findling (The Foundling,* 1922) was intended to express his hope for a better future. Overburdened with symbolism and sentiment, the play, though Barlach's favorite, was performed only once and never gained an audience. His next play, *Die Sündflut* (1924; translated as *The Flood* in *Three Plays*), concerns a confrontation between a traditional, almost bourgeois Judaic-Christian view of God as represented by Noah and a Nietzschean, mystical view represented by Noah's antagonist Calan, a desert nomad. Here Barlach dramatizes his skepticism about the apocalypse as the cause of man's transformation; his expressionist contemporaries saw the end of their bourgeois world as a chance for social and personal renewal. In portraying the Flood and the reactions of the characters to it, Barlach shows through Noah's family that there will be no new society. In the person of Calan, however, he affirms his belief in the need for and the pos-

*Title page by Barlach for his 1929 ten-act play satirizing German society of the 1920s*

experimentation, to the time of finding his own style as a writer and artist. The visions to which his characters are prone here appear as early as the twelve-year-old boy's being overcome by an awareness "eines Wirklichen ohne Darstellbarkeit" (of something real that cannot be portrayed) for which he thenceforth felt compelled to find adequate form. While he was, like many young artists of the 1880s and 1890s, uninterested in social and political issues, he early sought the subjects for his art in the urban streets among the people, astonished and nauseated by "den Unsinn eines solchen Seins" (the nonsense of such an existence).

It is the novel *Der gestohlene Mond*, written during 1936 and 1937, the worst year of personal intimidation, defamation, and destruction of his art by the Nazis, which shows him at his finest as storyteller and visionary. It is not character development that interests the narrator conscious of his craft: "Nichts, was zu einem guten und gerechten Bündel von Romankapiteln gehört, wird verheißen" (nothing like a good and just bundle of chapters of a novel is promised). Gone is Barlach's earlier concern with transcendence and transformation. Rather, seemingly gratuitous events reveal the relationships of figures to one another; test the mettle of each; and crush, bend, and destroy some while passing others by. Barlach works by gradual disclosure of ever new realities behind ever new facades in ever changing configurations: friends are actually enemies, persecutors are actually victims. The protagonist Wau, a publican, and his friend and enemy Wahl, an up-and-coming businessman of the wheeler-dealer type, are seen as aspects of contemporary bourgeois man. Behind Wau's facade of an educated, broad-minded, philosophical attitude to life hides a man haunted by singular, Jean Paul-like visions of terror (chapter eleven) or of a shadow cast over the world (chapter fourteen). Behind Wahl's facade of lust for wealth and show lurks a ruthlessness that persecutes those who get in his way to their very deaths. To be sure, Wau has that insight into his visions and personal relationships that assures him the reader's sympathy; he knows, for instance, that Wahl manipulates him, that the shadow over the world is his own, and that his marriage has become an empty form. Yet he fails to respond to his insights with that responsible involvement which might save his marriage and his wife's life or help the most innocent of Wahl's victims, a pregnant servant girl. As the action progresses into the lower-class world of Wahl/Wau's victims, the narrator reveals—behind the victims' small-town clinging to the shreds

of respectability—their greed for easy profit, their vicious backbiting, and their servile betrayal of each other. Except in Wahl's case, the narrator has compassion for his characters' humanity and suffering even in their degradation, just as Barlach the sculptor has compassion for the lowest of his creatures (as in *Freezing Woman*, 1937).

At the beginning of the novel, the narrator forecasts Wau's tragic failure. Yet Wau survives the scandal of his involvement in the death of the pregnant servant girl and his resignation from office. He even reconciles himself with Wahl. Critics, such as Franck, who read this ending as a true reconciliation fail to note that Wau is not Barlach and that Barlach's irony shapes the ending. Wahl and the powers he commands (the corruptibility of officialdom and the people) restore a morally bankrupt Wau to the lethargy which he (and the naive reader) mistook for the contemplative life. Barlach's earlier humor has turned to dark irony. The subtle use of narrative perspective, the keen penetration into inner and complex dynamics of individuals and of a society undergoing profound

*Barlach, age sixty-five, in front of the south door of the Gertrude Chapel in Güstrow (Berthold Kegebein, Güstrow)*

social changes make this work comparable to Broch's *Die Schlafwandler*, Hans Henny Jahnn's *Fluß ohne Ufer* (River without Banks, 1949-1950, 1961), or Döblin's *Berlin Alexanderplatz*. The violent action, the degradation experienced by his characters, their passivity in the face of destructive powers reflect much of Barlach's own experience of Nazi Germany. Like Wau, Barlach went through a vicious defamation campaign; like Wau, Barlach, through no fault of his own, was indebted beyond his earning power.

Since 1930 a campaign of character assassination because of his pacifist war memorials had been under way from the political right. A few days before Hitler came to power, Barlach in a courageous radio broadcast spoke out against rightist political and racial intolerance. A last honor came to him in February 1933 when, with the backing of Kollwitz, he received the Ritter der Friedensklasse des Ordens pour le mérite. When Kollwitz and Heinrich Mann were ousted from the Prussian Academy of Arts that month, Barlach, doubting the official announcement of their voluntary resignations, naively asked the academy's president if his own presence in the academy had political implications. (The president's answer is not known, but Barlach remained in the academy.) Politically unsophisticated and unaffiliated, isolated by his individualism, Barlach suffered without protest the gradual removal of all his art works from public squares and museums, the confiscation or banning of his publications, and the cancellation of commissions and performances of his plays. Retrospectively, the inclusion of his sculptures in the 1937 exhibition of "Decadent Art" can be seen as an honor. But the piecemeal dismantling of his life's work, threats of house searches, and the expectation of being forbidden to sculpt and write finally undermined his health, and he died of pneumonia in the Rostock clinic in October 1938.

With the rediscovery of expressionism after the collapse of the Third Reich, Barlach's art and writing experienced a renaissance. The artist fared better than the writer, for his sculptures, woodcuts, and drawings became immensely popular. A Barlach society was formed; his only art patron during the Nazi years, the cigarette manufacturer Reemtsma, founded a Barlach Museum in Hamburg; his childhood home in Ratzeburg/Holstein became a memorial; his house at Güstrow in the German Democratic Republic was made a Barlach archive; in 1986 the house of his birth at Wedel was made the home of Barlach archives of the Federal Republic of Germany. But except for performances given out of respect for the neglected expressionist tradition, Barlach's plays and especially his prose remained the province of historians and students of literature. They deserve better, for Barlach the writer found memorable formulations for modern man's perplexities and ethical dilemmas. Barlach himself had rejected the performance of his plays and their interpretation as expressionist works as too stylized. Mysticism being the most obvious characteristic of his writing, his audiences and readers have been slow to appreciate its criticism of his age and his society, its surrealism and humor. Barlach has also been counted as a writer of the Inner Emigration, those intellectuals who remained in the country and silently opposed Nazism. Because of his regional rootedness in northern Germany, a part of the country extolled by the Nazis for its racial purity, he has even been counted as a proto-fascist. The latter judgment neglects the facts of his life and the meaning of his literary and artistic work.

**Letters:**
*Die Briefe I: 1888-1938*, edited by Friedrich Droß, 2 volumes (Munich: Piper, 1968-1969).

**Biographies:**
Paul Schurek, *Begegnungen mit Barlach: Ein Erlebnisbericht* (Augsburg: List-Bücher, 1949);

Hans Franck, *Ernst Barlach: Leben und Werk* (Stuttgart: Kreuz, 1961);

Henning Falkenstein, *Ernst Barlach* (Berlin: Colloquium, 1978).

**References:**
Heinz Beckmann, "Die metaphysische Tragödie in Ernst Barlachs Dramen," *Veröffentlichungen der Ernst Barlach Gesellschaft* (1964-1965): 338-358;

Wolfgang Brekle, "Die antifaschistische Literatur in Deutschland (1933-1945)," *Weimarer Beiträge: Zeitschrift für Literaturwissenschaft, Aesthetik und Kulturtheorie*, 16, no. 6 (1970): 6, 67-128;

Edson M. Chick, *Ernst Barlach* (New York: Twayne, 1967);

Helmut Dohle, *Das Problem Barlach: Probleme, Charaktere seiner Dramen* (Köln: Verlag Christoph Czwiklitzer, 1957);

Manfred Durzak, *Das expressionistische Drama; Ernst Barlach, Ernst Toller, Fritz von Unruh* (Munich: Nymphenburger Verlagshandlung, 1979);

Willi Flemming, *Ernst Barlach: Wesen und Werk* (Bern: Sammlung Dalp, 1958);

Karl Graucob, *Ernst Barlachs Dramen* (Kiel: Mühlau, 1969);

Margarethe Heukäufer, *Sprache und Gesellschaft im dramatischen Werk Ernst Barlachs* (Heidelberg: Winter, 1985);

Elmar Jansen, "Barlachs *Ein Selbsterzähltes Leben*," *Marginalien: Zeitschrift für Buchkunst und Bibliophilie*, 52 (1973): 1-15;

Jansen, ed., *Ernst Barlach: Werk and Wirkung. Berichte, Gespräche, Erinnerungen* (Frankfurt am Main: Athenäum, 1972);

Klaus Günther Just, "Ernst Barlach," in *Deutsche Dichter der Moderne*, edited by Benno von Wiese (Berlin: Schmidt, 1975), pp. 456-475;

Herbert Kaiser, *Der Dramatiker Ernst Barlach* (Munich: Fink, 1972);

Helmut Krapp, "Der allegorische Dialog," *Akzente*, 1 (1954): 3, 210-219;

Otto Mann, "Ernst Barlach," in *Expressionismus: Gestalten einer literarischen Bewegung*, edited by Herrmann Friedmann and Otto Mann (Heidelberg: Rothe, 1956), pp. 296-313;

Walter Muschg, "Ein Opfer. Ernst Barlachs Briefe" and "Der Dichter Ernst Barlach," in his *Die Zerstörung der deutschen Literatur* (Bern: Francke, 1958), pp. 84-109, 231-261;

Muschg, "Ernst Barlach als Erzähler," in his *Von Trakl zu Brecht. Dichter des Expressionismus* (Munich: Piper, 1963), pp. 244-263;

Wolfgang Paulsen, *Deutsche Literatur des Expressionismus* (Frankfurt am Main: Lang, 1983);

Paulsen, "Zur Struktur von Barlachs Dramen," in *Aspekte des Expressionismus*, edited by Paulsen (Heidelberg: Winter, 1968), pp. 103-132;

Ernst Piper, *Ernst Barlach und die nationalsozialistische Kunstpolitik. Eine dokumentarische Darstellung zur 'entarteten Kunst'* (Munich & Zurich: Piper, 1984);

Wolfgang Rothe, "Ernst Barlach," in *Christliche Dichter im 20. Jahrhundert*, edited by Mann (Bern: Francke, 1970), pp. 269-285;

Friedrich Schult, *Barlach im Gespräch* (Wiesbaden: Insel, 1948);

Heinz Schweitzer, *Ernst Barlachs Roman "Der gestohlene Mond"* (Bern: Francke, 1959);

Hans Schwerte, "Über Barlachs Sprache," *Akzente*, 1 (1954): 3, 219-225;

Ilhi Synn, "*Culpa Patris* in Barlach's Dramas," *Literatur in Wissenschaft und Unterricht*, 4 (1972): 158-166;

Synn, "The Language in Barlach's Dramas," *Revue des Langes Vivantes*, 37 (1971): 723-730.

**Papers:**

Some of Barlach's literary remains, manuscripts, unpublished works, diaries, and letters are located at the Archive of the Ernst Barlach Haus, Stiftung Hermann F. Reemtsma, Jenisch Park, Hamburg, and at the Barlach memorial in Ratzeburg, Federal Republic of Germany; the largest collection of Barlach manuscripts is available in the Barlach Museum at 26 Güstrow, Heidberg, German Democratic Republic.

# Gottfried Benn
## *(2 May 1886-7 July 1956)*

### Gerlinde F. Miller
*University of Illinois at Chicago*

BOOKS: *Morgue und andere Gedichte* (Berlin-Wilmersdorf: Meyer, 1912);

*Söhne: Neue Gedichte* (Berlin-Wilmersdorf: Meyer, 1913);

*Gehirne: Novellen* (Leipzig: Wolff, 1916);

*Fleisch: Gesammelte Lyrik* (Berlin-Wilmersdorf: Aktion, 1917);

*Diesterweg: Eine Novelle* (Berlin-Wilmersdorf: Aktion, 1918);

*Etappe* (Berlin-Wilmersdorf: Aktion, 1919);

*Ithaka: Dramatische Szene* (Berlin-Wilmersdorf: Aktion, 1919);

*Der Vermessungsdirigent: Erkenntnistheoretisches Drama* (Berlin-Wilmersdorf: Aktion, 1919);

*Das moderne Ich* (Berlin: Reiss, 1920);

*Die gesammelten Schriften* (Berlin: Reiss, 1922);

*Schutt* (Berlin-Wilmersdorf: Meyer, 1924);

*Betäubung: Fünf neue Gedichte* (Berlin-Wilmersdorf: Meyer, 1925);

*Die Dänin: Ein Gedicht* (Potsdam: Weitbrecht, 1925);

*Spaltung: Neue Gedichte* (Berlin: Meyer, 1925);

*Gesammelte Gedichte* (Stuttgart & Berlin: Deutsche Verlagsanstalt, 1927);

*Gesammelte Prosa* (Berlin: Kiepenheuer, 1928);

*Fazit der Perspektiven* (Berlin: Kiepenheuer, 1930);

*Das Unaufhörliche: Oratorium*, text by Benn, music by Paul Hindemith (Mainz: Schott, 1931);

*Nach dem Nihilismus* (Berlin: Kiepenheuer, 1932);

*Der neue Staat und die Intellektuellen* (Stuttgart: Deutsche Verlagsanstalt, 1933);

*Kunst und Macht* (Stuttgart: Deutsche Verlagsanstalt, 1934);

*Ausgewählte Gedichte, 1911-1936* (Stuttgart: Deutsche Verlagsanstalt, 1936);

*Zweiundzwanzig Gedichte: 1936-1943* (Berlin: Privately printed, 1943);

*Statische Gedichte* (Zurich: Arche, 1948);

*Ausdruckswelt: Essays und Aphorismen* (Wiesbaden: Limes, 1949);

*Trunkene Flut: Ausgewählte Gedichte* (Wiesbaden: Limes, 1949; enlarged, 1952);

*Goethe und die Naturwissenschaften* (Zurich: Arche, 1949);

*Drei alte Männer: Gespräche* (Wiesbaden: Limes, 1949);

*Der Ptolemäer* (Wiesbaden: Limes, 1949);

*Doppelleben: Zwei Selbstdarstellungen* (Wiesbaden: Limes, 1950);

*Frühe Prosa und Reden*, introduction by Max Bense (Wiesbaden: Limes, 1950);

*Essays* (Wiesbaden: Limes, 1951);

*Fragmente: Neue Gedichte* (Wiesbaden: Limes, 1951);

*Probleme der Lyrik: Vortrag in der Universität Marburg am 21. August 1951* (Wiesbaden: Limes, 1951);

*(Ullstein)*

12

*Frühe Lyrik und Dramen* (Wiesbaden: Limes, 1952);

*Die Stimme hinter dem Vorhang* (Wiesbaden: Limes, 1952);

*Destillationen: Neue Gedichte* (Wiesbaden: Limes, 1953);

*Monologische Kunst: Ein Briefwechsel zwischen Alexander Lernet-Holenia und Gottfried Benn. Im Anhang: Nietzsche nach fünfzig Jahren* (Wiesbaden: Limes, 1953);

*Altern als Problem für Künstler: Vortrag im Süddeutschen Rundfunk am 7. März 1954 und in der Bayerischen Akademie der Schönen Künste am 8. März 1954* (Wiesbaden: Limes, 1954);

*Aprèslude* (Wiesbaden: Limes, 1955);

*Provoziertes Leben: Eine Auswahl aus den Prosaschriften* (Berlin: Ullstein, 1955);

*Reden* (Munich: Langen-Müller, 1955);

*Gesammelte Gedichte 1912-1956* (Wiesbaden: Limes, 1956);

*Soll die Dichtung das Leben bessern?*, by Benn and Reinhold Schneider (Wiesbaden: Limes, 1956);

*Über mich selbst: 1886-1956* (Munich: Langen-Müller, 1956);

*Dr. Rönne: Frühe Prosa*, edited by E. Neff (Zurich: Arche, 1957);

*Primäre Tage: Gedichte und Fragmente aus dem Nachlaß* (Wiesbaden: Limes, 1958);

*Roman des Phänotyp: Landsberger Fragment, 1944* (Frankfurt am Main: Insel, 1961).

**Collections:** *Gottfried Benn: Gesammelte Werke in vier Bänden*, edited by Dieter Wellershoff, 4 volumes (Wiesbaden: Limes, 1959-1961);

*Primal Vision: Selected Writings of Gottfried Benn*, edited by E. B. Ashton (Norfolk, Conn.: Laughlin, 1960);

*Gottfried Benn: Medizinische Schriften*, edited by Werner Rübe (Wiesbaden: Limes, 1965);

*Das Gottfried Benn-Buch: Eine innere Biographie in Selbstzeugnissen*, edited by Max Niedermayer and Marguerite Schlüter (Frankfurt am Main & Hamburg: Fischer, 1968);

*Gottfried Benn*, edited by Edgar Lohner (Wiesbaden: Limes, 1969);

*Das Gottfried-Benn-Brevier: Aphorismen, Reflexionen, Maximen aus Werken und Briefen*, edited by Jürgen P. Wallmann (Munich: Limes, 1979).

OTHER: *Heinrich Mann: Fünf Reden und eine Entgegnung zum sechzigsten Geburtstag*, contribution by Benn (Berlin: Kiepenheuer, 1931);

W. H. Auden, *Das Zeitalter der Angst: Ein barockes Hirtengedicht*, introduction by Benn (Wiesbaden: Limes, 1953);

*Lyrik des expressionistischen Jahrzehnts: Von den Wegbereitern bis zum Dada*, edited by Benn (Wiesbaden: Limes, 1955).

PERIODICAL PUBLICATIONS: "Goethe und die Naturwissenschaften," *Neue Rundschau* (1932);

"Berliner Brief," *Merkur* ( January 1949).

Even today, thirty years after his death, Gottfried Benn is one of the most controversial figures of modern German literature. Arguments over his literary and political positions continue to spark debate. As Benn himself stated in 1948, he was denounced in the course of the previous fifteen years by all factions of the political and ideological spectrum: by the Nazis, the Communists, and the Democrats, as well as by various proponents of religion and humanism. Opposing evaluations of Benn's person and work extend also into the realm of literary criticism. Walter Muschg accused Benn of frivolously destroying the essence of the German literary tradition, while Ernst Robert Curtius claimed that all of German literature since George and Hofmannsthal sinks into oblivion in the face of Benn's prose. Reinhold Grimm ranked Benn among the foremost European lyric poets. Edgar Lohner considered Benn an equal of T. S. Eliot in scrupulousness of style, of Ezra Pound in scope, of W. H. Auden in formal invention and use of the vernacular, and of Wallace Stevens in ideas on the value of poetry and expression. Benn epitomized the avant-garde that challenged German literary tradition in the first decades of the twentieth century; for many critics he remained the "unreconstructed expressionist." Both within Germany and abroad, Benn has been interpreted as an exemplary figure of the most recent intellectual and political history of his country. Indeed, he has remained a significant phenomenon within twentieth-century German literature because he embodies in his person and his work nearly all of the contradictions inherent in literary modernism.

The second of eight children, Benn was born on 2 May 1886 in the small village of Mansfeld, about halfway between Berlin and Hamburg. Benn loved these eastern plains, which have belonged to Poland since 1945, and for the rest of his life he referred to them as his true home. His father, Gustav Benn, was a Lutheran minister; Prussia's lower nobility stood under his pastoral care. As Benn reflected later, his father exercised a strong influence in these aristocratic circles. His mother came from the French-speaking part of Switzerland and all of her life had problems with the pronunciation of German. With great pride Benn pointed to his parentage as a combination of the two significant components of European culture, the French and the German. Equally proudly, he noted that the Protestant parsonage had brought forth a greater portion of culturally distinctive persons than any other milieu in Europe by fostering a unique combination of intellectual and poetic gifts.

Benn's childhood and early schooling took place among the village youth, with some private instruction at the home of Count Finkenstein. Since Benn belonged neither to the nobility nor the peasantry, much has been made of his early experiences as an outsider, although his own description of his early years shows no signs of alienation. From 1896 to 1903 he attended the Gymnasium at Frankfurt an der Oder, living in the same boardinghouse as Count Finkenstein and, later, the poet Klabund. At that time the debate on Ernst Haeckel's interpretation of Darwin's theory of evolution was raging. To prevent the replacement of religious instruction with the science-based monism propounded by Haeckel, biology courses were eliminated from the upper-class curriculum in Prussia. Benn secretly read Haeckel's forbidden *Welträtsel* (1899; translated as *The Riddle of the Universe at the Close of the Nineteenth Century*, 1900), which proclaimed a mechanistic progressive Darwinism as the new foundation of science and society.

In 1903 Benn entered the University of Marbach and studied, in accordance with his father's expectations, theology and philosophy. The following year he switched to the University of Berlin as a student of philology and finally obtained his father's permission to enter medical school. Benn was accepted in 1905 at the Kaiser Wilhelm Akademie, established in conjunction with the University of Berlin to educate medical personnel for the armed forces. Instruction was almost free of charge to the students, who had to commit themselves to one year of military service for each semester of study. Students were also introduced to the etiquette of the officer's corps and were obligated to attend special lectures on literature and history.

In the first decade of the twentieth century the University of Berlin enjoyed international acclaim; it was considered to be at the forefront of scientific study and research. Positivism combined with a progressive optimism permeated the atmosphere. Darwinism dominated in the biological sciences and social Darwinism influenced the social and medical sciences. In his autobiography Benn claimed that his scientific education was the basis

for his existence, not only because it taught him to provide and demand factual verification of data, but more importantly because it instilled the merciless self-criticism and profound skepticism which characterize his work.

During his student years Benn wrote neo-romantic poetry, of which very little remains. In "Gespräch" (Dialogue) he professed to be a disciple of the Danish poet Jens Peter Jacobsen, vowing to create poetic works that embody all the evolutionary possibilities inherent in a person. In 1910 and 1911 Benn published three scientific articles that contributed to debates on the development of modern science, psychiatry, and 'brain physiology. He primarily supported positions taken by Theodor Ziehen, professor of psychiatry and neurology, under whom Benn worked as an intern. His study "Ätiologie der Pubertätsepilepsie" (Etiology of Epilepsy during Puberty) earned him the first prize, the Golden Medal of the University of Berlin, but he chose to convert it into the Copper Medal plus a cash award to augment his meager finances.

In 1912 fundamental changes took place in Benn's life and writings. On 24 February he received his doctorate. His thesis was "Über die Häufigkeit des Diabetes mellitus im Heer" (On the Incidence of Diabetes Mellitus in the Army), a statistical evaluation of army records, the very type of work he would later ridicule in *Das moderne Ich* (The Modern I, 1920). Shortly afterwards Benn was assigned to active military duty. When he fell ill after strenuous exercises on horseback, a congenital defect (a floating kidney) was discovered that prevented him from full participation in basic training.

In a kind of trance due to exhaustion after an autopsy course, he had written *Morgue*, a cycle of poems in unrhymed free verse or very free rhymes, combining crude naturalistic images with the cynical jargon of medical students and Berlin slang. These elements constitute the unique style of his early poetry. Instantly Benn achieved fame and notoriety. His poems began to appear regularly in expressionist journals dominated by a forcefully emerging avant-garde that had already begun to challenge the "romantic" perception of poetry held by the educated public. Thus the pamphlet *Morgue und andere Gedichte* (Morgue and Other Poems), published in March 1912 by A. R. Meyer while Benn was still in the military, aroused a flood of condemnations and reproaches. Only a few critics, such as Ernst Stadler, recognized the intense sympathy behind the seemingly detached accounts of human suffering and mortality and praised the poetic force that had produced these haunted visions.

On 9 April Benn's mother died of breast cancer. Due to the rigorous religious beliefs of his father, Benn was not permitted to ease her suffering with morphine injections. Poems expressing intense hatred of his father, such as "Pastorensohn," show the deep rift that existed for several years between father and son.

Also in 1912 Benn entered into an intimate relationship with the expressionist poet Else Lasker-Schüler, whose nonconformist life-style, extravagant appearance, and unique poetry fascinated him. He dedicated *Söhne* (Sons), his second collection of expressionist poems, to her in 1913. Although the nature of their friendship changed about a year later, they always respected each other's poetic accomplishments.

Honorably discharged from the military because of his health problems, Benn worked from October 1912 until December 1913 as an assistant at the Pathological Institute of the Westend Hos-

pital, performing 297 autopsies. For the first three months in 1913 he was also the director of a small pathology station; he quit this job for unknown reasons. It is not possible to ascertain the duration of Benn's employment as an assistant in psychiatry at the hospital under Karl Bonhoeffer, who had replaced Ziehen in May 1912. Sometime in 1913 Bonhoeffer dismissed Benn from his position, presumably because he had failed to maintain case histories as required. Only from Benn's own accounts is it known that he was then suffering from depersonalization, a mental disorder defined as the experience of remoteness from one's own feelings and body functions as well as from the surrounding world. Such conditions can last for years, totally incapacitating the afflicted, or they may occur and recur for days or even hours. The extent to which Benn suffered from this illness is not documented.

As a ship's physician, Benn sailed across the Atlantic in the spring of 1913. During the five-day

*Dust-jacket illustration by Ludwig Meidner for Benn's second volume of poems, 1913*

*Cover for Benn's third collection of poems, published in 1917 (Lilly Library, Indiana University)*

The first line of the most famous, "Gesänge I" (Songs I), praises the primordial condition of life as the ideal one: "O daß wir unsere Ururahnen wären" (Oh if only we were our primeval ancestors), because the natural functions of birth and death would then be carried out without any self-awareness and therefore without pain. The poem also demonstrates Benn's ambivalent attitude toward evolutionary processes: he acknowledges them as irreversible, but he laments this progressive differentiation because long before the emergence of man, the evolutionary process had resulted in physiological complexities that lead to the experience of pain even in such lowly creatures as dragonflies and seagulls.

In March 1919 *Ithaka*, Benn's first experiment in dramatic writing, was published. In this sketch the father-son conflict, typical of expressionist theater, was transferred into the university milieu and intensified through a ferocious protest against the empiricism of modern science. The spokesman for the student rebellion, Dr. Rönne, the assistant in pathology, is suffering from depersonalization. Rönne is no longer capable of writing a research paper based on the autopsy of an infant. Since Benn himself had actually published such a report, the autobiographical aspects of the Rönne figure must be downplayed. Of great importance, however, is the clear evidence of Nietzsche's influence on Benn when Rönne calls for Dionysian ecstasy as a means of overcoming man's estrangement from the world, caused by the rationalistic approach to and utilitarian exploitation of the environment by science and technology. Regardless of the degree of personal reference in *Ithaka*, the figure of Dr. Rönne embodied the sentiment of the expressionist generation and anticipated the precarious existential situation of postwar German youth.

In the early summer of 1914, on the resort island Hiddensee, Benn met Edith Brosin, an elegant actress from a wealthy patrician family. After several weeks as a locum tenens in a tuberculosis sanatorium near Bayreuth, Benn married her on 30 July. Later he adopted her son, Andreas, from a previous marriage. Benn's only child—a daughter, Nele—was on 8 September 1915.

On 1 August 1914 Benn had to report for military duty as World War I began. Although he served in the medical corps, he actively participated in the conquest of Antwerp and received the Iron Cross, Second Class for his valor. From October 1914 until the summer of 1917 Benn lived in Brussels as a military doctor in charge of a hospital for

layover in New York, he left the ship only to hear Caruso sing at the Metropolitan Opera. Because of his proneness to seasickness, he did not pursue this career. (This decision was fortunate, for the ship to which he had been assigned sank without survivors.) Instead, Benn returned to his position at the Pathological Institute in Berlin. The theme of the morgue continues to dominate Benn's poetry, which appeared in various journals; the third collection, *Fleisch* (Flesh), was published in 1917. Dissected and decaying bodies rise up to challenge the Christian-bourgeois perception of man's essence and destiny—in particular, the belief in an immortal soul. Provocative lines such as "Die Krone der Schöpfung, der Mensch, das Schwein" (The Crown of Creation, Man, the Swine) are intended to shake people out of a false notion that all is well with the human condition. But the collection also contains poems full of melancholy and resignation over the fact that there is no relief from suffering.

prostitutes. He did not have to wear a military uniform and could stroll about the occupied city observing the hostility of the populace toward the German troops. Later Benn described these years as perhaps his greatest phase of visionary creativity. He wrote poems probing the meaning of human existence and evoking creative possibilities dormant within the psyche, including "Karyatide" (Caryatid), "O Nacht" (O Night), "Kokain" (Cocaine), and "Ikarus."

In his dramatic writings of the Brussels years Benn treats different topics from those in his poems. In *Etappe* (Home Front) he chastises corruption in occupied territories with biting sarcasm. In 1915 Benn sent the drama to Switzerland for publication in *Die Weissen Blätter,* but it was confiscated by the army and did not appear in print until 1919. Benn uses a totally different approach to the dramatic form in the epistemological drama *Der Vermessungsdirigent* (The Surveyor, 1919). Pameelen, the main figure, attempts to "survey"—reassess—the human personality and discovers that neither the form established by nineteenth-century idealism and expected by bourgeois culture nor the one assembled under the auspices of scientific research exists any longer: "Das Ich ist ein Phantom. Kein Wort gibt es, das seine Existenz verbürgte, keine Prüfung, keine Grenze" (The I is a phantom. There is no word that verifies its existence, no test, no limitation).

Benn's best-known writings of the years in Brussels are the works known as the "Rönne novellas": "Gehirne" (Brains), "Die Eroberung" (Conquest), "Die Reise" (Journey), "Die Insel" (Island), and "Der Geburtstag" (Birthday), were published in 1916 under the title *Gehirne* by Kurt Wolff of Leipzig. Dr. Rönne, a former pathologist, is the main character in all five novellas. He is suffering from depersonalization in its various stages but is slowly attaining the ability to cope with his problems. The material for the stories is taken from case histories on the disorder; the frequently stated interpretation that the novellas represent Benn's state of mind in Brussels must be rejected. Not only did close personal friends such as Thea and Carl Sternheim, Carl Einstein, and Otto Flake discount the notion that Benn had been particularly disoriented and unhappy there but, in the professional deliberations on this disease and its treatment based on Husserl's theory of the stratified psyche, the creative process is considered the greatest hope for overcoming the illness. Producing a work of art—unlike any other human endeavor—brings about a state of ecstasy that loosens rational control to allow emotional and visionary impulses to emerge from the innermost stratum of the psyche. Thus, the act of creating art unifies all levels of the psyche, which had been disjointed due to the unyielding grip of the outer layer, dominated either by a science-based rationalist approach to self and world or by rigid social conventions. Although the specific details in these novellas are not autobiographical, Benn did depict his own situation in them. His creative drive was his "salvation" from a frightfully debilitating disease, brought on by his other self, the scientist Benn, who was fascinated by verifiable facts and statistical evaluations. To Benn's initial surprise, however, Rönne was interpreted as an exemplary figure of the postwar generation. Rönne's efforts to become a whole person and to find a community that would accept him epitomized the existential situation that was so extensively debated by philosophers in the 1920s. The Rönne novellas also earned critical acclaim because of Benn's unique prose style, in which associative and visionary elements merge to the exclusion of descriptive, psychologically oriented narrative. Therefore they were praised as the best example of the avant-garde precept of "absolute prose."

Another novella, begun in Brussels, was published in 1918: *Diesterweg* probes the model of a stratified psyche more deeply, exploring situations in which the archetypal stratum bursts through the rationalist crust. Diesterweg, an army doctor experiencing the disintegration of his personality, is sent back to Berlin on a medical discharge. This incident has led many critics to assume that Benn's return to Berlin more than a year before the armistice was due to a mental disorder. The facts appear to be otherwise. Benn had written a research paper during his two and a half years in Brussels, carefully documenting reactions and side effects on patients during and after injections with Arthigon, a medication for gonorrhea advocated by Edmund Lesser, professor of venereal and skin diseases in Berlin. Benn had sent Lesser his paper supporting this much-criticized treatment. He returned to Berlin in the summer of 1917 hoping to continue his research as one of Lesser's assistants, but in the fall Lesser died suddenly from food contamination. Three weeks later, on 10 November, Benn opened a private practice as a specialist in skin and venereal diseases. He continued collecting data and evaluating statistical results, without ever attaining the scientific research position he had hoped for. His sarcastic assessment of the intellectual accomplishments of scientists may reflect his professional disappointment, but it should also be seen as self-critical irony.

The essay *Das moderne Ich*, a fictitious speech addressing postwar medical students, introduces a different aspect of Benn's thinking. He takes issue with positivism, utilitarianism, and Darwinism, especially with the image of man propounded in these theories. He deplores the reduction of man to a mere commodity manipulated by politicians and exploited in the labor market and implores the young to cast aside the mechanistic interpretation of man and world in favor of an experiment in creativity. With great eloquence Benn turns against those who hold some historical necessity responsible for Germany's defeat in World War I. He rejects both the Hegelian and Marxist theories of the historical process and opts for Hans Driesch's notion of "cumulative" history, which replaces inevitable development with a series of more or less accidental events. Causes and effects are ascertained in hindsight from accumulated evidence, as in geology. In the 1930s Benn replaced the cumulative view of history with Kurt Breysig's application of typology to the historical process.

Despite these theoretical statements denying man a comfortable faith in a meaningful existence, Benn never failed to take seriously the suffering of an individual. He even volunteered for medical duty during the street battles between right- and left-wing revolutionaries in Berlin in the postwar years, when medical supplies and doctors were scarce. Since Benn treated patients regardless of their ability to pay, his practice was not a financial success. In addition to financial difficulties, Benn suffered a severe personal loss when Edith died on 19 November 1922 after a gall bladder operation he had counseled her against. Benn could no longer afford the luxury apartment his family had lived in and had to make the painful decision to send Andreas to boarding school and the seven-year-old Nele to Denmark, where she lived with the opera singer Ellen Overgaard and her husband. Benn moved into a room behind his medical office.

In the early 1920s Benn wrote two prose works in which he celebrates creativity while condemning the rationalist approach as an aberration that has led mankind to a dead end. "Der Garten von Arle" (The Garden of Arles) praises the creative genius of van Gogh, who did not copy nature but instead invented a new reality. Kant, on the other hand, he chastises, because he sees Kant's rationalism as having led to the advancement of the noncreative, average person who dominates the world through technology. The creative sphere is

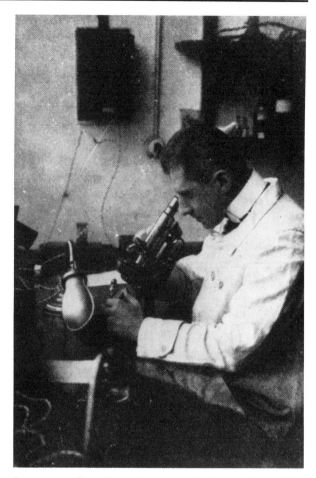

*Benn as a military doctor in charge of a Brussels hospital for prostitutes in 1916*

even more intensely invoked in "Das letzte Ich" (The Last I). The innermost stratum of the psyche with its inherited mythical remnants is contrasted to the outer, superficial stratum that makes up the human personality, which is the result of education and scientific training. Both pieces contain pessimistic, satirical criticism of modern man in general and German society in particular. Both were included in *Die gesammelten Schriften* (The Collected Works), which was published in 1922 but had to be withdrawn because of a dispute over publication rights with the Wolff firm, which had published the Rönne novellas. For this edition Benn wrote his first autobiographical work, "Epilog." Here he seems to have reached a state of exhaustion. Denying the notion that development brings forth innovation, he upholds visionary introspection as the prerequisite for artistic production. In 1927, however, Benn expanded on his autobiographical statement in "Lyrisches Ich" (Lyrical I), which counters this seeming end to his creative endeavor with a perception of his artistic abilities. Benn defines the "lyrische Ich" as an entity separate from himself which emerges only to construct poems and thus interrupts his personal continuity.

On his fortieth birthday in 1926, Benn totaled his earnings from his creative writings; they averaged four and a half marks a month. Yet Benn was among the most widely discussed expressionist poets in Germany. Moreover, translations of his poems had appeared in numerous European anthologies and in Japan. The international P.E.N. Club accepted Benn as a member in 1928.

The mid 1920s was a time of reorientation for Benn. He studied Lucien Lévy-Bruhl's interpretation of the primitive mind, which approaches the self and the world through mystical participation and prelogical thinking. Although Benn does not call for regression to primitivism, he acknowledges in these psychological reactions modern man's ancestral patterns which facilitate the creative process: "Es gibt nur den Einsamen und seine Bilder seit kein Manitou mehr zum Clan erlöst. Vorbei die mystiche Partizipation, durch die saughaft und getränkeartig die Wirklichkeit genommen und in Träumen und Ekstasen abgegeben wurde, aber ewig die Erinnerung an ihre Totalisation" (Only the hermit and his images exist, since manitou no longer delivers into the clan. Gone the mystical participation through which reality was absorbed like a drink and shared in dreams and ecstatic trances, but eternal remains the memory of its totalization).

In 1924 and 1925 three collections of Benn's poems were published: *Schutt* (Debris, 1924), *Betäubung* (Intoxication, 1925), and *Spaltung* (Fission, 1925). Long poems in traditional, classic forms with three to six eight-line stanzas dominate. Most are rhymed; very few are in free verse. Primitive societies conjuring up visions through mystical participation, drugs, and rhythmic dances are frequent topics, as well as modern man's attempts to awaken within himself archetypal elements and primeval fragments.

Inspired by Max Scheler's suggestion that a new image of man must be constructed from the most recent scientific data available, Benn expanded his knowledge in paleontology and anthropology. By the end of the 1920s he was pouring his new insights into speeches and the fourteen essays he wrote from 1926 to 1932. He discovered new theories of the relationship of body and mind in biological, medical, and psychological works. He was fascinated by the theory of the collective unconscious as defined by C. G. Jung. He opposed Darwinism because, as the theory was then taught,

it could not account for sudden mutations or for any unique, creative element as a contributing factor in the evolutionary ascent of man. The summary of his extensive readings on the mind-body problem is found in "Der Aufbau der Persönlichkeit" (The Structure of the Personality), which arrives at the conclusion that despite massive scientific research the relationship between body and mind has remained the ultimate mystery.

Benn's own emphasis was on the body: "Der Leib transzendiert die Seele" (The body transcends the soul). Studies on the interconnection of body structure, blood chemistry, and personality type led him to delve into relations between the types of creative ability and the body types of artists, whom he grouped into "zyklothym" and "schyzothym." He found himself in the latter group with its tensions between strict adherence to form and total shapelessness, between lyrical expression—up to and including banal sentimentality—and crass cynicism. Through these efforts Benn constructed a theory which does not restrict the artistic drive to a mechanistically defined progression of emotional tensions or to a sublimation of unfulfilled sexual drives, but ties it to the genetic basis of the individual, who must express his inborn urge to create art. In this context Benn also discusses "Genie und Gesundheit" (Genius and Health) in two publications. While disagreeing with the argument that the genius is insane, he claims in these essays that a certain defect within the personality structure facilitates artistic production. Benn's "Zur Problematik des Dichterischen" (On the Problem of the Poetic) is directed against the claim that poetry lacks a social base in modern times and that therefore true art has to be politically oriented and has to assist the disadvantaged in obtaining justice. In response, Benn defends the notion that poetry has a more important mission: it influences the genetic basis of man and thus provokes possibilities for expanding human capabilities.

This position led to a falling-out with writers and poets from Marxist literary circles. The expressionist poet Johannes R. Becher ridiculed Benn as a "schöne Seele" (beautiful soul), out of step with the times. Benn's difficulties with the left intensified in 1931 after he delivered a speech honoring Heinrich Mann on his sixtieth birthday as "der Meister, der uns alle schuf" (the master who created us all), thus celebrating Mann's artistic genius without mentioning Mann's active political engagement in the Weimar Republic. Subsequently Benn was attacked by a left-wing journalist, who had never read any of Mann's novels, as a fascist. A right-wing paper denounced Benn simultaneously as a degenerate indulging in aestheticism. In responding to both sides Benn tried to maintain an anti-ideological viewpoint that stands above party quarrels. In the midst of these turbulent exchanges Benn was struck by another personal tragedy when his intimate friend, the actress Lilli Breda, committed suicide by jumping out of her fifth-floor window after Benn tried on the telephone to talk her out of doing so.

Political controversies notwithstanding, Benn continued to gain recognition as a writer. At the invitation of the composer, Benn wrote the text for Paul Hindemith's oratorio *Das Unaufhörliche* (The Unceasing, 1931). Its world premiere on 22 November 1931 was performed by the Berlin Philharmonic Orchestra under the direction of Otto Klemperer. Although pessimism and criticism of modern civilization permeate Benn's text, the main focus is on the creative transformation in which man mysteriously partakes. Both Hindemith's music and Benn's text achieved great critical acclaim.

The following year, Benn wrote the essay *Nach dem Nihilismus* (After Nihilism), which contains a new theory of the creative process: "der konstruktive Geist." This theory employs the intellect, the rational faculty of man in the artistic endeavor, as a countermeasure to all forms of materialism. The "constructive spirit" constitutes the guiding principle in the creative process by consciously setting a new reality that supersedes the two precepts that confront modern man: nihilism and "progressive Zerebration" (progressive cerebration), an inevitable increase in the size of the cerebrum and as a consequence in man's capacity for rational thought. Benn proclaims the onset of the final epoch of mankind, the "Epoche eines großartig halluzinatorisch-konstruktiven Stils" (epoch of a grand hallucinatory-constructive style). Thus the antagonistic relationship between the innermost creative substance and the trained rational thought process which characterized Benn's expressionist years is transformed into a complementary one, as Benn explicated further in the speech he delivered on accepting his election to the Prussian Academy of Art in 1932. Benn now sees the challenge of the artist who must face up to the "formfordernde Gewalt des Nichts" (the form-demanding force of nothingness) in the creative process as the ultimate challenge to mankind: "Der sich durch Formung von Bildern und Gestalten vom Chaos differenzierende Mensch" (the human being who differentiates himself from chaos by creating images and figures) ultimately validates humanity

as the only metaphysical being in a physical form. This conviction remained the cornerstone of both Benn's anthropology and his poetic theory.

The prestigious issue of *Neue Rundschau* commemorating the 100th anniversary of Goethe's death in 1832 contained Benn's most famous essay of the early 1930s: "Goethe und die Naturwissenschaften" (Goethe and the Natural Sciences). Benn praises Goethe's pioneer work in developing morphology as the new comparative method for establishing evolutionary interconnections. Goethe's precise but skeptical employment of experimentation, according to Benn, preempted twentieth-century criticisms of the positivist misuse of the experimental method. Benn upholds Goethe's approach to nature as more encompassing than that of positivist science, which, despite Goethe's unceasing reproaches, has dominated subsequent generations. This significant essay led to Benn's friendship with F. W. Oelze, who became the poet's spiritual-intellectual companion and mentor.

Publication of the essay on Goethe together with the writings of the most distinguished representatives of German and European literature and culture, including Thomas Mann, André Gide, and José Ortega y Gasset, indicated acceptance and recognition of the chronic outsider Benn and at the same time challenged his isolationist views with regard to modern civilization. Furthermore, his membership in the Prussian Academy of Arts gave him for the first time a sense of official responsibility.

When Hitler was appointed to head the German government in 1933, Benn was embroiled in a controversy over a reactionary history of literature written by Paul Fechter. Benn wrote the official response of the academy to Fechter, repudiating both left- and right-wing attempts at subjugating art to politics. But when Heinrich Mann, the president of the literary section of the academy, signed a publicly displayed call for a Socialist-Communist union to overthrow the Hitler regime, Benn took the side of the "legal" government. Mann was expelled from the academy; his brother Thomas and many others resigned rather than sign a pledge in support of the Nazi regime written by Benn. On 5 May 1933 Benn was appointed kommisarischer Leiter (acting chairman) of the literary section. Four days later Klaus Mann wrote to Benn, questioning his cooperation with the new regime. Benn, perceiving this as an affront to his position in the academy, answered in a radio address, "Antwort an die literarischen Emigranten" (Answer to the Literary Émigrés). As in an earlier radio address, *Der neue Staat und die Intellektuellen* (The New Government and the Intellectuals, 1933), Benn's main concern is the issue of an anthropological transformation which he sees taking place. Basing his position on Breysig's application of typology to history, Benn interprets the totalitarian state as a necessary consequence of the disintegrating Weimar Republic, the primary feature of which had been identified by Breysig as the isolated, self-centered individual interested mainly in material success. Now a new type of human being seems to have emerged, willing to devote himself to the community and capable of acknowledging his metaphysical origin. Democracy and the inviolable dignity and freedom of the individual represent only a failed past which Benn does not consider worth upholding. He argues that it is not governmental forms that are really at issue, but rather the emergence of a new creative epoch for mankind. Benn had predicted the previous year that a rebirth of artistic abilities was dependent upon getting in touch with one's mythological roots; he now mistook the Nazi propaganda of a new youth in touch with its regional customs and rituals for such a return to Teutonic tribal origins. Benn seemed to be so infatuated with the notion that his artistic theory had become political reality that he convinced himself that he was experiencing a major turning point of history; he brushed aside as irrelevant arguments concerning details of brutal tactics during the Nazi takeover. Until the end of May 1933 Benn believed that his participation would influence the direction in which the new state was going, despite the fact that the people in charge did not really measure up to his expectations. But on 7 June the expressionist poet Hanns Johst was appointed president of the literary section when the academy was reorganized by the Nazis. Left without any official function, Benn began to examine the actual political situation.

In the fall of 1933 Benn elaborated in his radio address "Zucht und Zukunft" (Breeding and Future) on the idea that not only physical but also mental features can be inherited; he referred to families of geniuses, such as the Bachs, in which a certain capability dominated over several generations. With special pride he pointed to the milieu of Protestant parsonages, which for centuries brought forth persons of extraordinary intellectual and poetic abilities in Germany and northern Europe, and identified himself as one such offspring.

Around that time the German members of the international P.E.N. Club left the organization; a few months later they formed the Union national-

aler Schriftsteller, eventually electing Benn as its vice president. In this capacity he welcomed the Italian Futurist Emilio Marinetti to Berlin. In his welcoming speech Benn referred to Hitler with the much-quoted phrase "Führer, den wir alle unentwegt verehren" (leader, whom we all unceasingly honor), while celebrating the Futurists' political success that had helped shape fascism in Italy. At the same time Benn was publicly denounced as a Jew and was required to disclose his ancestry to prove otherwise.

Meanwhile, Benn was forbidden to issue certain health certificates because he was suspected of being Jewish. With his medical practice in jeopardy, he rejoined the army medical corps in 1935. Because the Prussian lower nobility and not the Nazi party dominated the army, Benn called his enlistment the "aristokratische Form der Emigrierung" (aristocratic form of emigration). He was assigned to the north German town of Hannover. With his departure from Berlin, Benn left behind his activities at the academy, hoping to remove himself from all political connections. But when a new edition of his poems, *Ausgewählte Gedichte, 1911-1936*, appeared in honor of his fiftieth birthday in 1936, Benn was viciously attacked by the SS paper *Das Schwarze Korps* and the article was reprinted in several Nazi journals. Despite the political clout of these papers, Johst, the president of the Reichsschrifttumskammer (Department of Literature in the Reich) wrote a supportive letter for Benn. Moreover, Benn's superior, a general of the old school, read a number of non-Nazi reviews of Benn's work and decided that Benn could remain in the military and thus be protected from the Nazi party. Shortly thereafter, Rudolf Hess, Hitler's deputy, wrote an intimidating letter to Benn's publisher which forced the withdrawal of the *Ausgewählte Gedichte* and the publication of a "cleansed" edition in December 1936. But the attacks on Benn did not subside.

On 1 July 1937 Benn was transferred to Berlin, where he was assigned to work at army headquarters on problems of compensation for injuries. His political troubles followed him: he was attacked by Wolfgang Wilrich, a mediocre painter and a member of the SS, whose book *Säuberung des Kunsttempels* (Cleansing the Temple of Art) appeared in July 1937. After some difficult weeks Johst provided a letter which not only protected Benn but contained a statement by Heinrich Himmler, leader of the SS, that the SS would not persecute Benn but would leave the matter to Johst. Benn was not ousted from the military, as he had feared he would be. Meanwhile, he continued to write poems, such as "Astern," "Die weißen Segel" (The White Sails), "Das Ganze" (The Whole), and "Ach, das Erhabene" (Oh, the Sublime), which are among his best-known lyrics. He also completed the prose piece "Weinhaus Wolf," which is based on the atmosphere in Hannover. There Benn asserts the existence of two spheres: "Geist" (Spirit) and "Leben" (Life). The human being, alone of all creatures, has a choice where he will belong. Benn opts for Geist, which encompasses art but not politics and history. His retreat from any political involvement could not be expressed more decisively. The piece was not published until 1949.

On 22 January 1938 Benn married Herta von Wedemeyer, who was twenty-one years younger than he, impeccable in social skills but otherwise totally uneducated. It was not a passionate relationship, but one of friendship and trust. Benn enjoyed introducing her to the works of various literary giants, such as Shakespeare, which she read with great enthusiasm.

To his surprise Benn received a letter dated 18 March 1938 which officially excluded him from membership in the Reichsschrifttumskammer and threatened him with penalties should he continue to write. Benn had had nothing published since January 1937, when six poems had appeared in the journal *Literatur*. Again, Benn had to submit the matter to his military superiors, who decided, even without support from Johst, to retain him within their ranks. He was, however, excluded from active duty or promotion. As a result, Benn was not affected by the outbreak of World War II in September 1939. He continued to write guidelines for compensation of medical disabilities. During this time he fought the military medical hierarchy on the issue of suicide, which he proved to be the result of depression rather than an act of cowardice. As a consequence, regular death benefits were paid to the families of soldiers who killed themselves.

Meanwhile, Benn's friend Oelze had set up an archive in Bremen for Benn's unpublished writings. At the height of Hitler's popularity due to the victory over France in 1940, Benn wrote one of his most significant recantations of his earlier beliefs and hopes: "Züchtung II" (Breeding II). He criticizes Nietzsche's vision of breeding, which had been perverted by the Nazis: "Rassenzüchtung als Politik ist die Kinderliebe von Kidnappern" (Racial breeding as politics is the kidnapper's love of children). Against the political misuse of Nietzsche Benn maintains a different viewpoint: "Was bleibt, ist das zu Bildern verarbeitete Sein" (What remains, is ex-

istence assimilated in images). A year later Benn wrote "Kunst und Drittes Reich" (Art and the Third Reich), in which biting sarcasm and extreme criticism of the current cultural situation dominate. He wants to be understood as making the Gegenäußerung der Kunst (counterstatement of art) against the topics of Nazi-approved art, which include "die Fresse von Cäsaren und das Gehirn von Troglodyten, die Moral des Protoplasmas und das Ehrgefühl von Hotelratten" (the mug of Caesars and the brain of troglodytes, the morality of protoplasm and a hotel rat's sense of humor). Benn's disgust with the cultural aspects of the Third Reich is also expressed in the poem "Monolog," contained in the privately printed *Zweiundzwanzig Gedichte, 1936-1943* (Twenty-two Poems, 1936-1943, 1943) which he sent to a few trustworthy friends.

Due to the intensity of bombing attacks on Berlin by American and British forces, Benn's office was relocated to Landsberg an der Warthe on 14 August 1943. From this small town in the east Benn had to make weekly trips to Berlin on trains packed with refugees from eastern Europe and Prussia's eastern provinces who were fleeing the approaching Russian army. Benn lived in barracks on a hill high above the town, had little actual work due to the disorganization of the office, observed the hasty training of the last German troops, and wrote poems and the "Roman des Phänotyp" (Novel of the Phenotype), which he describes as an "anti-novel" without a central character who undergoes psychological or historical development. Instead, it seeks to identify "Schnittpunkte" (points of interaction) between the person and history which reveal essential positions and existential insights into the human condition.

Benn managed to bring his wife to Landsberg and eventually to have her assigned as his secretary, thus avoiding the problem of having an outsider know the nature of his writings. Shortly before the Russian army overran the town, Benn sent Herta, who suffered from arthritis, back to Berlin on a truck, the only means of transportation out of the panic-stricken town. Then he shipped all his writings, labeled as the property of one Dr. Rönne who had died in Stalingrad, by military mail to Oelze in Bremen. The following day, 28 January 1945, Benn and the rest of the military personnel stationed in Landsberg fled on foot in a snowstorm. For thirty kilometers they marched alongside the highway clogged with the horse-drawn wagons of refugees, whose frozen children had been thrown into the ditches. Finally they reached a functioning railroad station where they were loaded onto open animal wagons for the ride of sixty kilometers to bombed-out Berlin. Benn found his wife in their old apartment, which had no windows or furniture. They slept on the floor, covered only with Benn's army overcoat, when they did not spend the night in bomb shelters. All civilian order broke down; the dead were left lying on the sidewalks to be covered with snow. Some of these gruesome scenes Benn was to use in his postwar novella *Der Ptolemäer* (The Ptolemean, 1949). On 5 April Herta left for a village on the river Elbe which was expected to be in the American occupation zone. Benn intended to join her but had to wait for relocation orders for his office. On 8 May Germany surrendered unconditionally. Shortly thereafter Benn tried to have his wife brought back to Berlin, but failed to reach her. On 2 July she committed suicide after she was left behind when the American troops withdrew to turn the village over to the Russians. When Benn learned of her death weeks later, he fell into a deep depression. In the poem "Orpheus Tod" (Death of Orpheus) he expresses his sorrow.

Germany and, separately, Berlin were initially divided into four occupation zones ruled by Allied forces. Cultural decisions were to a great extent in the hands of the émigrés who had returned with the foreign troops. Everywhere Benn's position of 1933 was well remembered; his later difficulties under the Nazi regime, however, were disregarded. Therefore, Benn was not permitted to publish what he had written since 1937. On his sixtieth birthday in May 1946 he seemed to be a forgotten man. On 18 December 1946 Benn entered into his third marriage. Dr. Ilse Kaul, a dentist, was a generation younger than he; but according to his daughter Nele, she was the only one of his wives who understood his writings and was his intellectual equal.

During the precarious time of the Berlin blockade in 1947 Benn wrote his famous and provocative "Berliner Brief" (Berlin Letter) to Hans Paeschke, the editor of the newly established *Merkur, Zeitschrift für europäisches Denken*, in which he claimed that the downfall of Western civilization was due not to the Nazis or the Communists but to the "hündisches Kriechen seiner Intelligenz vor den politischen Begriffen" (the dog-like crawling of its intellectuals before political concepts). Due to financial difficulties, the *Merkur* could not publish its Benn issue—containing, in addition to the letter, excerpts from "Roman des Phänotyp" and Max Bense's study on Benn—until January 1949.

Meanwhile, Benn's literary comeback was facilitated by the publisher Peter Schifferli in Switzer-

GOTTFRIED
BENN

DER
PTOLEMÄER

.. *von deutscher Seite aus der erste international zu wertende Beitrag, der in ganz selbständiger Form einen Zeit-Bezug über die Zeit erhebt* ...
Alfred Richard Meyer

LIMES·VERLAG

*Dust jacket for Benn's 1949 prose collection which included the title novella along with "Roman des Phänotyp" and "Weinhaus Wolf" (Lilly Library, Indiana University)*

land, who did not have to bow to the Allies' political regulations and therefore published *Statische Gedichte* (Static Poems, 1948), which contained most of Benn's poems written between 1936 and 1947 and brought him instant fame. Eventually the Limes publishing house in Wiesbaden, run by Max Niedermayer, was able to obtain the license to print Benn's writings in Germany. Around Christmas 1948 the dialogue *Drei alte Männer* (Three Old Men, dated 1949) appeared, resulting in controversy over the statement "Sich irren und doch seinem Inneren weiter glauben schenken müssen, das ist der Mensch, und jenseits von Sieg und Niederlage beginnt sein Ruhm" (To err and yet to be forced to have faith in one's innermost self, that is the human being, and beyond victory and defeat his glory begins). To Benn's dismay, this statement was interpreted by many as an excuse for political crimes. In February 1949 the prose volume *Der Ptolemäer* followed; in addition to the novella of that name, the book contained "Roman des Phänotyp" and "Weinhaus Wolf." When the volume *Ausdruckswelt* (World of Expression), in which Benn's essays from 1940 to 1944 were printed for the first time, appeared in June 1949, the poet had already become the subject of discussion beyond literary circles. At Oelze's urging the essay "Zum Thema Geschichte" was withheld and not published until 1959. There Benn indicts as sources of National Socialism not only the German bourgeois tradition but also widely held cultural and intellectual tenets, such as Darwinism: "Gedanken töten" (thoughts kill).

Another volume of recent poems, *Trunkene Flut* (Intoxicated Flood), came out in October 1949 and made Benn even more popular among young aspiring poets, literary critics, and the general public, despite vicious attacks from the Marxist camp. In March 1950 Limes published Benn's autobiography, *Doppelleben* (Double Life), which spawned further debate on Benn's writings as well as on his political and intellectual positions. In the 1950 radio address "Nietzsche nach fünfzig Jahren" (Nietzsche after Fifty Years) Benn celebrates Nietzsche as the propagator of pure expression and as the greatest German stylistic genius since Luther. Benn was disappointed by the response to his speech, which was criticized for not addressing the political implications of the Nazis' misuse of Nietzsche. In November 1950 Limes began to introduce Benn's readers to his early prose works, among which the Rönne novellas drew the greatest attention. At the same time Benn's productivity continued at an amazing rate. In the summer of 1951 another collection of poems, *Fragmente*, was published. A few weeks later Benn gave one of his most discussed speeches, *Probleme der Lyrik*, which was considered the bible of the new generation of poets by critics and poets alike. Although Benn's deliberations on the monologue poem and the criteria for identifying it were not entirely original, he clearly stood in the tradition of Western modernism with his definitions and descriptions of present-day poetry. In Darmstadt in October 1951 Benn received the Georg Büchner Prize which represented acceptance and recognition despite Benn's insistence on his outsider positions.

The dramatic dialogue *Die Stimme hinter dem Vorhang* (The Voice behind the Curtain) appeared in December 1951 (1952 is the date given on the title page). It is dedicated to Benn's third wife, "eine Generation jünger als ich, die mit zarter und kluger Hand die Stunden und die Schritte und in den Vasen die Astern ordnet" (a generation younger than I, who orders with a tender and wise hand my hours, my steps, and the asters in the vases). The dialogue concerns a "creator" whose children try to make sense out of life by reading the Sunday paper and asking him questions, despite his impatient and often shocking answers.

Benn's recognition as a great poet was further enhanced when he received the Bundesverdienstkreuz erster Klasse (Order of Merit First Class of the Federal Republic) on 5 September 1952. A few days later he traveled to Knokke in Belgium to deliver a speech in French on modern poetry, in which he repeated the most important points from *Probleme der Lyrik*. In 1953 Benn was chosen as a member of an international jury selecting the work for the prize for literature of the European Center in Geneva. In April 1953 another collection of poems, *Destillationen* (Distillations), was published. In July Benn gave up his medical practice after thirty-six years, both because his wife's dental practice was doing well and because Benn for the first time in his life had a substantial income from his literary work. During this year Benn lived in fear of somehow losing his third wife, since both his first and second wives had died in their seventh year of marriage.

In March 1954 Benn presented the speech *Altern als Problem für Künstler* (Aging as a Problem for Artists) at the prestigious Bavarian Academy of Fine Arts. He points to a health-giving function of art by noting the great number of very old artists throughout the centuries. At the same time he questions a number of popular ideas, in particular the notion of a development of an artist toward a higher maturity and perfection in old age.

Benn met many leading artists and thinkers during his last years, including W. H. Auden and Theodor Adorno, with whom he planned a radio discussion on the subject of engaged art; the discussion, however, did not take place. In 1955 Benn edited the volume *Lyrik des expressionistischen Jahrzehnts* (Poetry of the Expressionist Decade). In September Benn's last collection of poems, *Aprèslude*, appeared; it brought him much criticism, especially from the younger generation, which accused him of having become soft and sentimental. Nevertheless, Benn was invited to make a lecture tour of West Germany in October 1955. He was very impressed with the Catholic poet Reinhold Schneider, with whom he held a radio discussion, *Soll die Dichtung das Leben bessern?* (Should Poetry Improve Life?, 1956). Benn again argues against useful po-

*Benn in 1956 (Ullstein)*

etry, but insists that poetry changes man at the genetic level, which causes a different kind of person to emerge.

Benn's seventieth birthday in 1956 was celebrated in grand style, beginning with an official ceremony at the Berlin Senate and ending with a private reception. Telegrams and greetings came from all over the world. Benn was, however, very ill. Various attempts to diagnose the problem and provide relief from his horrendous pain remained unsuccessful. Not until the day before his death was an advanced cancer of the spine identified. In the presence of his wife Benn died on 7 July 1956. He was eulogized as one of Germany's greatest poets of the twentieth century.

**Letters:**
*Gottfried Benn: Ausgewählte Briefe* (Wiesbaden: Limes, 1957);
*Gottfried Benn: Briefe an F. W. Oelze,* edited by Harald Steinhagen and Jürgen Schröder, 3 volumes (Wiesbaden: Limes, 1977-1980);
*Gottfried Benn: Briefwechsel mit Hindemith,* edited by Ann Clark Fehn (Wiesbaden: Limes, 1978).

**Bibliographies:**
Edgar Lohner, "Gottfried Benn-Bibliographie 1912-1955," *Philobiblon: Eine Vierteljahrsschift für Buch- und Graphik-Sammler,* 1 (1957): 59-70;
Peter Schönemann and Oskar Sahlberg, "Bibliographie Gottfried Benn," *Text und Kritik,* 44 (1985): 156-166.

**References:**
Reinhard Alter, "Gottfried Benn zwischen Weimarer Republik und Bundesrepublik," in *Die Mühen der Ebenen: Kontinuität und Wandel in der deutschen Literatur und Gesellschaft. 1945-49,* edited by Bernd Hüppauf (Heidelberg: Winter, 1981), pp. 331-359;
Alter, "The Outsider as Insider: Gottfried Benn's Letters to F. W. Oelze 1932-56," *German Life and Letters,* 38 (1984-1985): 83-95;
Alfred Behrmann, "Katabasis: Zu Gottfried Benns Gedicht 'Sieh die Sterne, die Fänge,' " *Zeitschrift für deutsche Philologie,* 103 (1984): 563-576;
Peter Bürger, " 'Punktuelle Perspektiven': Benn und die Wiederkehr der 50er Jahre," *Merkur,* 39 (1985): 157-161;
Reinhold Grimm, *Gottfried Benn: Die farbliche Chiffre in der Dichtung* (Nuremberg: H. Carl, 1958);
Bruno Hillebrand, ed., *Gottfried Benn* (Darmstadt: Wissenschaftliche Buchgesellschaft, 1979);
Peter Uwe Hohendahl, ed., *Benn—Wirkung wider Willen: Dokumente zur Wirkungsgeschichte Benns* (Frankfurt am Main: Athenäum, 1971);
Brian Holbeche, "Die Lyrik Gottfried Benns im westdeutschen literarischen Leben der 50er Jahre—Rezeption und Einfluß," in *Die Mühen der Ebenen: Kontinuität und Wandel in der deutschen Literatur und Gesellschaft. 1945-49,* edited by Hüppauf (Heidelberg: Winter, 1981), pp. 307-330;
Erich Huber-Thoma, *Die triadische Struktur in der Lyrik Gottfried Benns* (Würzburg: Königshausen & Neumann, 1983);
Dietrich Krusche, "Palau—Verführung der Ferne: Zu dem Motivkomplex 'Außer-Europa' in der Lyrik Gottfried Benns," *Jahrbuch Deutsch als Fremdsprache,* 10 (1984): 33-44;
Edgar Lohner, "The Development of Gottfried Benn's Idea of Expression as Value," *German Quarterly,* 26 (1953): 39-54;
Lohner, *Passion und Intellekt: Die Lyrik Gottfried Benns* (Neuwied, Berlin-Spandau: Luchterhand, 1961);

Walter Müller-Seidel, "Goethes Naturwissenschaft im Verständnis Gottfried Benns: Zur geistigen Situation am Ende der Weimarer Republik," in *Die Zeit der Moderne: Zur deutschen Literatur von der Jahrhundertwende bis zur Gegenwart,* edited by Hans-Henrik Krummacher (Stuttgart: Kröner, 1984), pp. 25-53;

Anton Reininger, "Regressive Sehnsucht und ihre sprachliche Manipulation. Benns Lyrik der 20er Jahre," *Annali Sezione Germanica, Studi Tedeschi,* 27 (1984): 135-198;

J. M. Ritchie, *Gottfried Benn: The Unreconstructed Expressionist* (London: Wolff, 1972);

Oskar Sahlberg, "Gottfried Benns Psychotherapie bei Hitler," in *Literaturpsychologische Studien und Analysen,* edited by Walter Schöngau (Amsterdam: Rodopi, 1983), pp. 221-247;

Sahlberg, "Die Wiedergeburt Gottfried Benns aus dem Geiste des Faschismus," in *Freiburger Literaturpsychologische Gespräche, 3,* edited by Johannes Cremerius and Wolfram Mauser (Würzburg: Konigshausen & Neumann, 1984), pp. 101-112;

Harald Steinhagen, "Gottfried Benn, 1933," in *Literatur und Germanistik nach der "Machtübernahme." Colloquium zur 50. Wiederkehr des 30. Januar 1933,* edited by Beda Allemann (Bonn: Bouvier, 1983), pp. 28-51;

Steinhagen, *Die Statischen Gedichte von Gottfried Benn* (Stuttgart: Klett, 1969);

Benno von Wiese, "Gottfried Benn als Literaturkritiker, insbesondere in seinem Briefwechsel mit F. W. Oelze," in *Die Zeit der Moderne. Zur deutschen Literatur von der Jahrhundertwende bis zur Gegenwart,* edited by Krummacher (Stuttgart: Kröner, 1984), pp. 55-71.

# Werner Bergengruen

*(16 September 1892-4 September 1964)*

Gerhard H. Weiss
*University of Minnesota*

BOOKS: *Das Gesetz des Atum: Roman* (Munich: Drei Masken, 1923);

*Rosen am Galgenholz: Geschichten vom anderen Ufer* (Berlin: Dom, 1923);

*Schimmelreuter hat mich gossen: Drei Erzählungen* (Munich: Drei Masken, 1923);

*Das Brauthemd: Drei Novellen* (Frankfurt am Main: Iris, 1925);

*Der Retter des Zaren: Komödie,* by Bergengruen and Wilhelm Meyer-Förster (Berlin: Vertriebsstelle de Verbandes deutscher Bühnenschriftsteller, 1925);

*Das große Alkahest: Roman* (Berlin: Wegweiser, 1926); republished as *Der Starost: Roman* (Hamburg: Hanseatische Verlagsanstalt, 1938);

*Das Kaiserreich in Trümmern: Roman* (Leipzig: Koehler, 1927);

*Das Buch Rodenstein* (Frankfurt am Main: Iris, 1927; revised and enlarged, Zurich: Arche, 1950);

*Capri* (Berlin: Meyer, 1930);

*Herzog Karl der Kühne oder Gemüt und Schicksal: Roman* (Munich: Drei Masken, 1930; revised, Hamburg: Deutsche Hausbücherei, 1943);

*Der tolle Mönch: Zwanzig Novellen* (Berlin: Frundsberg, 1930);

*Die Woche im Labyrinth: Roman* (Stuttgart: Engelhorns, 1930);

*Der goldene Griffel: Roman* (Munich: Müller, 1931);

*Zwieselchen im Warenhaus* (Stuttgart: Thienemann, 1931);

*Zwieselchen im Zoo* (Stuttgart: Thienemann, 1931);

*Baedeker des Herzens: Ein Reiseverführer* (Berlin: Kolk, 1932); republished as *Badekur des Herzens: Ein Reiseverführer* (Leipzig: Breitkopf & Haertel, 1933; revised, Zurich: Arche, 1956);

*Der Wanderbaum: Gedichte* (Berlin: Die Rabenpresse, 1932);

*Zwieselchen und der Osterhas* (Stuttgart: Thienemann, 1932);

*Zwieselchen und Turu-Me* (Stuttgart: Thienemann, 1932);

*Stecowa: Phantastisches und Übersinnliches aus dem Weltkrieg* (Berlin: Kolk, 1932);

*(Ullstein)*

*Die Feuerprobe: Novelle* (Leipzig: Reclam, 1933);

*Die Ostergnade: Novellen* (Berlin: Die Rabenpresse, 1933);

*Der Teufel im Winterpalais und andere Erzählungen* (Leipzig: Hesse & Becker, 1933);

*Zwieselchens große Reise* (Stuttgart: Thienemann, 1933);

*Des Knaben Plunderhorn* (Berlin: Vorhut, 1933,);

*Deutsche Reise* (Berlin: Drei Masken, 1934; revised, Zurich: Arche, 1959);

*Begebenheiten: Geschichten aus einem Jahrtausend* (Berlin: Eckart, 1935);

*Der Großtyrann und das Gericht* (Hamburg: Hanseatische Verlagsanstalt, 1935); translated by Norman Cameron as *A Matter of Conscience* (London & New York: Thames & Hudson, 1952);

*Die Schnur um den Hals: Novellen* (Berlin: Buch- und Tiefdruck-Gesellschaft, 1935); republished as *Die Heiraten von Parma: Novellen* (Hamburg: Hanseatische Verlagsanstalt, 1940);

*Die Rose von Jericho: Gedichte* (Berlin: Die Rabenpresse, 1936);

*Die Drei Falken: Novelle* (Dresden: Heyne, 1937);

*Der ewige Kaiser: Gedichte,* anonymous (Graz: Schmidt-Dengler, 1937; republished, as Bergengruen, with new postscript, 1951);

*Die verborgene Frucht: Gedichte* (Berlin: Die Rabenpresse, 1938);

*Zwieselchen* (Stuttgart: Thienemann, 1938; enlarged, 1950);

*E. T. A. Hoffmann* (Stuttgart: Cotta, 1939);

*Die Leidenschaftlichen: Novellen* (Hamburg: Hanseatische Verlagsanstalt, 1939);

*Der Tod von Reval: Kuriose Geschichten aus einer alten Stadt* (Hamburg: Hanseatische Verlagsanstalt, 1939);

*Am Himmel wie auf Erden: Roman* (Hamburg: Hanseatische Verlagsanstalt, 1940);

*Der spanische Rosenstock: Novelle* (Tübingen: Wunderlich, 1940);

*Das Spielzeug der Komteß, und andere Novellen* (Leipzig: Beyer, 1940);

*Schatzgräbergeschichte* (Gütersloh: Bertelsmann, 1942);

*Das Hornunger Heimweh: Erzählung* (Leipzig: Reclam, 1943);

*Lebensgeschichte Pfeffermanns des Jüngeren* (Gütersloh: Bertelsmann, 1944);

*Dies Irae: Eine Dichtung* (Munich: Zinnen, 1945);

*Ballade vom Wind: Die Geisse Gaugeloren* (Olten: Vereinigung Oltner Bücherfreunde, 1946);

*Das Beichtsiegel: Novelle* (Innsbruck: Tyrolia, 1946);

*Lobgesang* (Basel: Linder, 1946);

*Der hohe Sommer: Gedichte* (Olten: Vereinigung Oltner Bücherfreunde, 1946);

*Die Sultansrose und andere Erzählungen* (Basel: Schwabe, 1946);

*Zauber- und Segenssprüche: Gedichte* (Zurich: Arche, 1947);

*Jungfräulichkeit: Novelle* (Olten: Vereinigung Oltner Bücherfreunde, 1947);

*Pelageja: Erzählung* (Zurich: Arche, 1947);

*Sternenstand: Novellen* (Zurich: Arche, 1947);

*Im Anfang war das Wort: Vortrag* (Freiburg: Albers, 1948);

*Die Hände am Mast: Erzählung* (Zurich: Arche, 1948);

*Dir zu gutem Jahrgeleit: Eine Glückwunschgabe* (Zurich: Arche, 1949);

*Römisches Erinnerungsbuch* (Freiburg & Vienna: Herder, 1949); translated by Roland Hill as *Rome Remembered* (New York: Herder & Herder, 1968);

*Das Feuerzeichen: Roman* (Munich: Nymphenburger Verlagshandlung, 1949);

*Rede über Goethe* (Marburg: Simons, 1949);

*Drei Novellen: Schatzgräbergeschichte; Die Hände am Mast; Die wunderbare Schreibmaschine,* edited by S. P. Wolfs (Amsterdam: Meulenhoff, 1950);

*Die letzte Reise: Novelle* (Zurich: Arche, 1950);

*Das Tempelchen: Erzählung* (Zurich: Arche, 1950);

*Die heile Welt: Gedichte* (Zurich: Arche, 1950);

*Lombardische Elegie* (Zurich: Arche, 1951);

*Erlebnis auf einer Insel: Eine Novelle* (Zurich: Arche, 1952);

*Das Geheimnis verbleibt,* preface by Ida Friederike Görres (Munich: Nymphenburger Verlagshandlung, 1952);

*Nachricht vom Vogel Phönix: Erzählung* (Zurich: Arche, 1952);

*Der letzte Rittmeister* (Munich: Nymphenburger Verlagshandlung, 1952); translated by Eric Peters as *The Last Captain of Horse: A Portrait of Chivalry* (London & New York: Thames & Hudson, 1953);

*Der Pfauenstrauch: Eine Novelle* (Zurich: Arche, 1953);

*Die Flamme im Säulenholz: Novellen* (Passau: Privately printed, 1953; expanded, Munich: Nymphenburger Verlagshandlung, 1955);

*Die Sterntaler: Eine Novelle* (Zurich: Arche, 1953);

*Der Kaiser im Elend* (Gütersloh: Rufer, 1954);

*Die Rittmeisterin: Wenn man so will, ein Roman* (Zurich: Arche, 1954);

*Nie noch sang ich ein Lied, das die Heimkehr preise* (Offenbach: Kumm, 1955);

*Die Zwillinge aus Frankreich: Erzählungen,* afterword by Reinhold Schneider (Frankfurt am Main: Goldene Vlies, 1955);

*Die Zigeuner und das Wiesel: Geschichten* (Gütersloh: Rufer, 1955);

*Die Kunst, sich zu vereinigen: Erzählung* (Zurich: Arche, 1956);

*Das Netz: Novelle* (Zurich: Arche, 1956);

*Privilegien des Dichters* (Mainz: Akademie der Wissenschaften und der Literatur, 1956; expanded, with a foreword by Schneider, Zurich: Arche, 1962);

*Mit tausend Ranken: Gedichte* (Zurich: Arche, 1956);

*Hubertusnacht: Erzählung* (Olten: Vereinigung Oltner Bücherfreunde, 1957);

*Suati: Novelle* (Flensburg: Feldt, 1957);

*Figur und Schatten: Gedichte* (Zurich: Arche, 1958);

*Glückwunschgabe mit einem Zuspruch auf alle Fest-, Pest-, Jahres- und Wochentage* (Zurich: Arche, 1958);

*Zur heiligen Nacht* (Zurich: Arche, 1958);

*Gesammelte Gedichte*, 2 volumes (Munich: Nymphenburger Verlagshandlung, 1958);

*Bärengeschichten* (Zurich: Arche, 1959);

*Otto von Taube: Rede zu seinem 80. Geburtstag* (Munich: Cranach, 1959);

*Zorn, Zeit und Ewigkeit: Erzählungen* (Zurich: Arche, 1959);

*Titulus. Das ist: Miszellen, Kollektaneen und fragmentarische, mit gelegentlichen Irrtümern durchsetzte Gedanken zur Naturgeschichte des deutschen Buchtitels; oder, Unbetitelter Lebensroman eines Bibliotheksbeamten* (Zurich: Arche, 1960);

*Rückblick auf einen Roman* (Mainz: Akademie der Wissenschaften und der Literatur, 1961);

*Vater Jewgenij* (Olten: Vereinigung Oltner Bücherfreunde, 1961);

*Schreibtischerinnerungen* (Munich: Nymphenburger Verlagshandlung, 1961);

*Der Rittmeister und sein Tessin* (Zurich: Arche, 1962); expanded as *Lob des Tessins* (Zurich: Arche, 1972);

*Der dritte Kranz* (Munich: Nymphenburger Verlagshandlung, 1962);

*Mündlich gesprochen* (Zurich: Arche, 1963);

*Der Wahrheit Stimme* (Freiburg: Herder, 1963);

*Die Schwestern aus dem Mohrenland: Erzählung* (Zurich: Arche, 1963);

*Räuberwunder: Erzählungen* (Zurich: Arche, 1964);

*Herbstlicher Aufbruch: Gedichte* (Zurich: Arche, 1965);

*Dichtergehäuse: Aus den autobiographischen Aufzeichnungen*, edited by Charlotte Bergengruen (Zurich: Arche, 1966);

*Pferdegruß Erzählungen und Gedichte von Pferd und Reiter*, edited by Charlotte Bergengruen (Munich: Nymphenburger Verlagshandlung, 1967);

*Die Glückliche: Zwei Erzählungen* (Zurich: Arche, 1968);

*Der Kranke* (Zurich: Arche, 1969);

*Kern der Welt: Gedenkband*, edited by Herbert Gorski (Leipzig: Benno, 1969);

*Das Karnevalsbild und andere Erzählungen* (Basel: Gute Schriften, 1971);

*Und dein Name ausgelöscht: Erzählungen* (Zurich: Arche, 1971);

*Geliebte Siebendinge: Aus den nachgelassenen Aufzeichnungen*, edited by Charlotte Bergengruen (Zurich: Arche, 1972);

*Spuknovellen*, edited by Charlotte Bergengruen (Zurich: Arche, 1973);

*Kindheit am Wasser: Erzählungen* (Zurich: Arche, 1976);

*Magische Nacht* (Zurich: Arche, 1978);

*Leben eines Mannes* (Zurich: Arche, 1982).

RECORDINGS: *Werner Bergengruen spricht einige Werke. Aus: Die heile Welt—Zauber- und Segenssprüche—Die Sultansrose und andere Erzählungen—Die verborgene Frucht* (Hamburg: Telefunken, 1959);

*Werner Bergengruen spricht: Der Herzog und sein Bär—Die verborgene Frucht* (Freiburg: Herder, 1959);

*Werner Bergengruen liest zwei Rodensteingeschichten. "Der Mann aus der Haal"—"Die Zigeuner und das Wiesel"* (Freiburg: Herder, 1963);

*Werner Bergengruen spricht: Das Netz* (Freiburg: Herder, n.d.).

TRANSLATIONS: Leo Tolstoy, *Chadshi-Murat: Ein Roman aus den Kaukasuskämpfen*, translated from Russian by Bergengruen (Berlin: Loewenbruck, 1924);

Tolstoy, *Die Kosaken: Ein Roman aus dem Kaukasus*, translated from Russian by Bergengruen (Berlin: Loewenbruck, 1924);

Ivan Turgenev, *Väter and Söhne*, translated from Russian by Bergengruen (Leipzig: List, 1925);

Fyodor Dostoyevski, *Schuld and Sühne: Roman*, translated from Russian by Bergengruen (Berlin: Knaur, 1928);

Semyon Rosenfeld, *Rußland vor dem Sturm: Roman*, translated from Russian by Bergengruen (Berlin: Bücherkreis, 1933);

Dostoyevski, *Der Traum eines lächerlichen Menschen: Phantastische Geschichte*, translated from Russian by Bergengruen (Horgen & Zurich: Holunderpresse, 1947);

Tolstoy, *Krieg und Frieden*, translated from Russian by Bergengruen (Munich: List, 1953).

OTHER: *Baltisches Dichterbrevier*, edited, with contributions, by Bergengruen (Berlin: Neuner, 1924);

*Baltische Blätter, vereinigt mit den Baltischen Nachrichten*, edited by Bergengruen (Berlin: Baltischer Verlag, 1925);

Fyodor Dostoyevski, *Der Idiot: Eine Erzählung*, translated from Russian by H. von Hoerschelmann, afterword by Bergengruen (Leipzig: List, 1925);

E. T. A. Hoffmann, *Märchen*, edited by Bergengruen (Vaduz: Liechtenstein-Verlag, 1947);

Rudolf Pechel, *Zwischen den Zeilen*, introduction by Bergengruen (Wiesentheid: Droemer, 1948);

Bruno Goetz, *Der Gott und die Schlange: Balladen*, introduction by Bergengruen (Zurich: Bellerive, 1949);

Hoffmann, *Die Elixiere des Teufels: Nachgelassene Papiere des Bruders Medardus, eines Kapuziners*, edited by Bergengruen (Vaduz: Liechtenstein-Verlag, 1949);

Reinhold Schneider, *Der christliche Protest*, introduction by Bergengruen (Zurich: Arche, 1954);

Joseph Freiherr von Eichendorff, *Erzählungen*, edited by Bergengruen (Zurich: Manesse, 1955);

Eichendorff, *Gedichte: Ahnung und Gegenwart*, edited by Bergengruen (Zurich: Manesse, 1955);

Hermann Kunisch, *Der andere Bergengruen*, reply by Bergengruen (Zurich: Arche, 1958);

Schneider, *Pfeiler im Strom*, introduction by Bergengruen (Wiesbaden: Insel, 1958);

Schneider, *Winter in Wien: Aus meinen Notizbüchern 1957/58*, with funeral oration for Schneider by Bergengruen (Freiburg: Herder, 1958);

Otto Gillen, *Alles Schöne ist ein Gleichnis*, introduction by Bergengruen (Zurich: Aldus Manutius, 1959).

Werner Bergengruen was one of the most prominent and widely acclaimed German authors of the 1940s and 1950s, a writer with impeccable anti-Nazi credentials who offered comfort and hope to a demoralized people. The conservative, strongly Christian tone of his works was not threatening to anyone. While others began to question middle-class values and spoke of a disintegrating, senseless, and absurd world, Bergengruen proclaimed a "heile Welt" (sound, uninjured world) in which disorder and chaos were only transitory—testing man's strengths and weaknesses, confronting him with his fate, but in the end leading him to the ultimate recognition of a divine order. If Bergengruen had written *Waiting for Godot*, Mr. Godot would surely have appeared in the end. Bergengruen did not, however, offer simple answers to complex issues; his concept of a heile Welt has nothing to do with a cheap happy ending. His view of the world is best summarized in his poem "Frage und Antwort" (Question and Answer) in the an-thology *Die heile Welt* (1950): "Was aus Schmerzen kam, war Vorübergang. Und mein Ohr vernahm nichts als Lobgesang" (What came from pain was transitory. And my ear perceived nothing but songs of praise). The novel *Pelageja* (1947) ends: "Das ist Gottes Gewohnheit; er führt in die Hölle und wieder hinaus" (This is God's custom: He leads us into hell, and He leads us out of it again).

Bergengruen's popularity began to fade when younger, more politically engaged, and more "modern" authors appeared on the scene. In the company of Günter Grass, Heinrich Böll, Siegfried Lenz, and others who began to excite the literary world of the 1950s and 1960s, Bergengruen seemed out of place. During the last years of his life he became, like his own creation der letzte Rittmeister (the last captain of horse), a relic from the past, looked upon with mild condescension as "typically nineteenth-century." Today his works are seldom read, and they certainly are no longer in the mainstream of critical discussion. Recent literary histories, if they cite Bergengruen at all, usually devote only a few lines to him as a historical phenomenon of no great consequence. This neglect is a pity because some of his books deserve more attention. In addition, his writings and their reception offer valuable clues to the reading tastes of those Germans who were offended by the works of the dominant Nazi writers during the Third Reich. Reading Bergengruen was a mild form of protest, a refuge from the obscenities of the time.

Bergengruen was born in Riga on the Baltic Sea, which was then (as it has been again since 1945) part of Russia. He grew up in a typical middle-class Baltic-German family—his father, Paul Bergengruen, was a doctor; his mother, Helene von Boetticher Bergengruen, was descended from the local nobility—steeped in German culture but also exposed to the traditions and customs of the indigenous Latvian population and of the Russian aristocracy and officialdom in Riga and the surrounding countryside. His youth was shaped by these three cultural entities, for which he developed great love and admiration. He speaks at length about his feelings in the chapter "Verlust der Heimat" (Loss of the Homeland) in the posthumous collection of essays *Dichtergehäuse* (The Poet's Outer Shell, 1966). Bergengruen left Riga in 1903 to become a student at the Gymnasium Katharineum in Lübeck; his parents wanted to give him a good German education rather than an inferior Russian one. He studied from 1911 to 1914 at the universities of Marburg, Munich, and Berlin without any specific academic goal, returning to

Riga only for brief visits. In 1914 he volunteered for military service on the German side; his love for his Baltic homeland, however, remained. In 1919 he served briefly in the Baltic National Guard as first lieutenant, defending his homeland against the threat of the advancing Russian Revolution. One of his first books, *Baltisches Dichterbrevier* (Breviary of Baltic Poets, 1924), is an anthology of poetry by contemporary Baltic writers, including himself. His novels and his novellas, from *Das Gesetz des Atum* (The Law of Atum, 1923) to the Rittmeister collections of the late 1950s and the 1960s, again and again evoke the mood of the land he had known as a child and for which he remained nostalgic throughout his life. These works are, as Bergengruen proclaims in an early autobiographical sketch, "ein Bekenntnis zur Höhle" (a witness to [his] point of origin). Coupled with his love for the Baltic lands was his affection for Russia and for Russian literature. His translations of major works by Dostoyevski, Tolstoy, and Turgenev attest to this affection.

In 1919 Bergengruen married Charlotte Hansel of Berlin. She became his faithful companion for life, assisting him in many ways and even collaborating with him in the preparation of some of his books. She was responsible for the superb illustrations in *Römisches Erinnerungsbuch* (1949; translated as *Rome Remembered*, 1968), and after his death she edited some of the unpublished works he had left behind. The Bergengruens had a son and two daughters. In 1920 Bergengruen moved to Berlin, where he worked as a journalist for the magazine *Ostinformation* from 1920 to 1922 and the newspaper *Baltische Blätter* in 1925. The first years in Berlin were difficult ones. *Das Gesetz des Atum* was serialized in the *Frankfurter Zeitung* in 1922 and appeared as a book during the following year with a blurb on the jacket saying that it was a good story "um das Gruseln zu lernen" (to give [the reader] the creeps). The book was largely ignored by reviewers, although Wilhelm Hegeler commented tersely that it was a "Harmlosigkeit von 300 Seiten" (a 300-page piece of naiveté) in which one "nicht Gruseln, wohl aber Geduld lernen kann, Lammsgeduld" (could learn not horror but patience, the patience of a lamb). The novel is a Gothic tale, much indebted to the romantics and especially to E. T. A. Hoffmann, whom Bergengruen admired and whose biography he wrote in 1939.

Subsequent publications were more successful, but even so, Bergengruen and his young family had to subsist on a modest income. His first collection of novellas, *Schimmelreuter hat mich gossen*

(Schimmelreuter Has Molded Me, 1923), was greeted with greater respect as a work that could serve as a model for modern raconteurs. His first historical novel, *Das Kaiserreich in Trümmern* (The Empire in Ruins, 1927), which describes the struggle between Odoacer and Theodoric in the dying days of the Roman Empire, was damned with faint praise as a not insignificant work from a publishing house that usually printed worse.

To supplement his income, Bergengruen wrote book reviews for the respected journal *Deutsche Rundschau*, whose editor, Rudolf Pechel, became the author's good friend for life. Bergengruen was a regular contributor to the journal from 1928 to 1941. Writing reviews sharpened his critical acumen and contributed to an increased self-discipline in his own literary works. In the collection of essays *Das Geheimnis verbleibt* (The Mystery Remains, 1952), Bergengruen reflects on his early writings; he confesses that it took him a long time to learn that language has to be concise and that his temptation had always been toward verbosity rather than precision. The result of this reappraisal was that Bergengruen disavowed some of his earliest works, including *Das Gesetz des Atum* and *Rosen am Galgenholz* (Roses on the Gallows-Wood, 1923), saying that they deserved to be out of print, burned, and forgotten. He drastically revised some of his later writings before publishing them; he totally rewrote the novel *Das grosse Alkahest* (The Great Alkahest, 1926) and had it published twelve years later under the title *Der Starost*. A close examination of the revised novel reveals in matters of both style and emphasis the considerable maturation process Bergengruen had undergone. The same is true for the novel *Herzog Karl der Kühne* (Duke Charles the Bold), which was originally published in 1930 and revised in 1943. Many of Bergengruen's novellas underwent similar changes, sometimes extensive ones. This practice has created a problem for Bergengruen bibliographers because works reappear in different collections or as new editions, and one is not always sure whether the work at hand is an original or a revised publication.

The late 1920s and the 1930s were years of increasing success. In 1927 Bergengruen was able to buy a small townhouse in the recently completed garden colony of Onkel Toms Hütte, a suburb of Berlin. It was here that he completed many of his novellas (at least one was published each year) and some of the novels that made him famous. In addition he wrote the "Zwieselchen" stories for children and composed lighthearted travel books, including *Badekur des Herzens* (My Heart Goes to

## Eximia perennant.

Gott hat den Sommer lieb, drum hat er nicht gewollt,
daß er in Regenflut und Trübsal altern sollt.
Mit aller Lieblichkeit und Fülle ausgeschmückt
hat er ihn gnadenvoll der argen Zeit entrückt.
Trug eine Schwalbe ihn hoch durch beglänzte Lüfte?
Ward ihm zur Schlummerstatt die Pyramidengruft?
Wie Noah mit Getier und Kind zur Arche schritt,
so gab dem Sommer Gott die werten Gaben mit:
ein Tröpfchen Honigseim, ein Fädchen Sonnenschein
und eine Ähre Brot und eine Beere Wein.
Von keinem Frost versehrt, vom Nebel nicht benetzt,
so bleibt er alterslos erhalten unverletzt.
Erkenne, wenn die Welt zersplittert und vereist,
das herrlichste Gesetz, das Überdauern heißt.
Brich auf und gehe still in deine Heimlichkeit,
denn allenthalben gilt die vorbemessne Zeit.

Das Kostbare nimm mit, so wird die edle Art
in heller Sommerkraft der Künftigkeit gespart.
Verlob dich der Geduld und traue unverzagt.
Mensch, der zu Grabe fährst: dies ist auch dir gesagt.

*Manuscript for a poem by Bergengruen ( from Carl J. Burkhardt, Über Werner Bergengruen)* the Spa, 1933)—originally published in 1932 as *Baedeker des Herzens* (Baedeker of the Heart); the title change was the result of legal action by the Baedeker publishers—and *Deutsche Reise* (German Travels, 1934). He also contributed short pieces to magazines and newspapers. The important harvest of that time includes the novels *Herzog Karl der Kühne, Der goldene Griffel* (The Golden Stylus, 1931)—a story set in inflation-plagued Berlin immediately after World War I—and the novel that firmly established his name, *Der Großtyrann und das Gericht* (The Tyrant and the Court, 1935). In addition, he had begun writing his most significant work, *Am Himmel wie auf Erden* (In Heaven as It Is on Earth), which was not published until 1940. It was also at this time, in 1936, that he officially converted to Catholicism, to which he had been attracted since his youth. Bergengruen reflects on his conversion in his essay "Glaube und Konversion" (Faith and Conversion) in *Dichtergehäuse*. He was attracted to Catholicism, he says, not only because of his religious convictions but also because the church represented a continuum of ancient cultural traditions. The church was the link between the present and the past, and it nurtured his belief in the wholeness and sanctity of the world.

Bergengruen's conservative Christian views were bound to collide with the policies of the National Socialist Reichsschrifttumskammer (Writers' Guild), from which he was expelled in 1937 because he was considered unfit "durch schriftstellerische Veröffentlichungen am Aufbau der deutschen Kultur mitzuarbeiten" (to contribute through his writings to the reconstruction of German culture). Amazingly, however, the work to which the Nazis most objected at that time, *Der Großtyrann und das Gericht,* continued to be published during the war and by 1943 had achieved sales of 155,000 copies. In spite of a paper shortage, and although other Bergengruen works were encountering difficulties, *Der Großtyrann und das Gericht* was even issued as a Feldpostausgabe (paperback edition for soldiers).

Bergengruen's novels are overgrown novellas; they deal with human situations, not with human development; characters do not evolve, they are revealed. These qualities are particularly obvious in *Der Großtyrann und das Gericht,* which is based on the fairy-tale motif of a sultan who orders his vizier to solve a mysterious murder. If he cannot do so within three days, the vizier himself will be executed. The situation suggested in this theme is one that always fascinated Bergengruen: how does a man react when confronted with a "test situation"; how does he react to the question of might

versus right, moral principle versus self-preservation? Bergengruen calls this situation the confrontation with fate, the entering into the "house of fate." If man learns to accept his fate, he will survive and come out of his trial wiser and better; if he fights his fate, he will succumb to it and perish. In *Der Großtyrann und das Gericht,* the ruler of the city-state of Cassano, a fictitious principality in Renaissance Italy, orders Nespoli, his chief of security, to solve the murder of a monk who had served as the ruler's secret messenger. Should he be unable to do so within the allotted time, Nespoli will have to pay with his life. Thereupon is set in motion a chain reaction of fear, accusations, intrigue, and lies which soon envelops the entire city and threatens to destroy it. Cosmos turns into chaos. In typical Bergengruen fashion, events on earth are accompanied by corresponding signs from heaven. Poisonous winds, stifling heat, and explosive thunderstorms reflect the turmoil of the world below. Finally, in one of the grand judicial scenes that the author often employs, the tyrant confesses that he himself had killed the monk for reasons of state; the rest had been simply a game to test the loyalty of his subjects. But the game had become serious. In the end the participants all agree that they had been led into temptation, and that only honesty, love, and forgiveness can prevent their ultimate destruction. Bergengruen calls the story a report of the "temptation of the mighty and the susceptibility of the weak and threatened." Fear and the instinct of self-preservation corrupt the low; the mighty are even more vulnerable than the lowly, for they are tempted to play the role of God: that was the tyrant's offense. The novel is really a parable: as realistic as some of the individual scenes are, there always remains something archetypal about the story. The book received a mixed reaction. To some Nazis (including Alfred Rosenberg and a reviewer in the *Völkische Beobachter*), the work seemed to confirm the leader concept. Others, who could read more closely, saw in the book a veiled protest against the corruption of justice in the Nazi state and a reminder that no human being has the right to consider himself above the law. Yet the tyrant is in no way a Hitler because in the end he learns his lesson and repents. As a conservative, Bergengruen does not question the social order he has established in his little commonwealth of Cassano, but he believes that the rulers and the ruled, the mighty and the weak, are bound together by a contract of trust and mutual loyalty that forbids any abuse of power.

In 1937 Bergengruen's cycle of poems *Der ewige Kaiser* (The Eternal Emperor) was published anonymously in Graz, Austria. These poems are the expression of a European Christian view. The "eternal emperor" is the mysterious Christian ruler, the ideal "imperator" depicted by Bergengruen in the figures of Emperor Friedrich in *Herzog Karl der Kühne*, the elector Joachim of Brandenburg in *Am Himmel wie auf Erden*, and others. He is a truly "*Holy* Roman Emperor" who presides over the ideal kingdom of decency, freedom, and justice. He is the eternal ruler, protecting the sacred order of the world. The language of the poems is hymnic, reminiscent of Hölderlin and Trakl.

His growing success as a writer made it possible in 1937 for Bergengruen to purchase a larger house in Solln, near Munich, a home and study that he fondly remembers in *Schreibtischerinnerungen* (Memories from My Desk, 1961). The delightful genealogy of his new-old desk in "Pettenkofer und sein Schreibtisch" (Pettenkofer and his Desk) is again evidence of how much he treasured every link with the past. A desk that has a history and tradition established by a previous owner is the appropriate working place for a writer who believes in the permanence of things. Bergengruen never revealed why he chose to move to Munich. He had certainly been fond of Berlin, and *Am Himmel wie auf Erden* (completed at the Pettenkofer desk in Munich) testifies to how involved he had become with the history and life of that city. Munich, on the other hand, never plays a role in his writings.

In Munich Bergengruen came in contact with the academic resistance group Die weiße Rose (The White Rose). At night he and his wife would type letters the members of the group had composed; in the morning he would bicycle to Munich and drop them randomly into mailboxes.

After he had settled in Munich, Bergengruen published some of his best novellas, some individually and others in collections. "Jakubsons Zuflucht" (Jakubson's Refuge), in the collection *Der Tod von Reval: Kuriose Geschichten aus einer alten Stadt* (The Death of Reval: Curious Stories from an Old Town, 1939), is a frivolous story set in the milieu of Reval's German-Russian culture. Jakubson, the town drunk, finds refuge one night in the bed of the widow Heydenacker, a miserly and spinsterish woman who had often chased him from her door; he does not realize that she has just died. In the morning he is surprised by the widow's relatives, who accuse him of having violated the poor woman. He makes his escape but feels so close to the de-

ceased that he attends her funeral "to thank her for her hospitality." Bergengruen weaves the widow tale and the town-drunk tale into one and ties it with a humorous knot. He embellishes the story with witty aperçus and creates a funny but also very realistic picture of nineteenth-century Reval. The town drunk is the classic picaro who gets kicked and pushed, but who is always able to duck. He, too, enters his "house of fate"; he neither accepts his fate nor rejects it but weasels his way out of it. The lighthearted language reinforces the humor of the tale, in which the pompous and sanctimonious meet their match and the little fellow prevails. The story would have been appropriate for a Charlie Chaplin film.

*Der spanische Rosenstock* (The Spanish Rosebush, 1940), Bergengruen's best-known novella, follows strictly classical lines. Written in a highly stylized language, it is a tale within a tale. Fabeck, a young poet, tells a story to his beloved Christine during the last moments before a long separation.

*Reinhold Schneider, Bergengruen's closest friend from the early 1930s until Schneider's death in 1958*

The tale Fabeck relates is a parable for the situation in which the lovers find themselves: Lysander and Octavia are about to be separated, and a rosebush becomes the symbol of their affection. As long as the bush prospers, their love will prosper; if the bush wilts, their love is in danger. Old fairy-tale motifs, such as the bush finally growing around the waiting princess in a protective embrace, are interwoven with biblical concepts, such as a seven-year wait. The language is deliberately archaic; the images are taken from Baroque tapestries. The novella is a sentimental love story in which the actors are prototypes. In spite of its obvious artificiality, the work became an immediate success. First published in 1940, it went through sixteen editions during the first ten years, eight of which came out during the war when paper was scarce and Bergengruen was considered a suspect author by the Nazis. The book, however, with all its faults, spoke to many Germans. Separation from loved ones was a common experience during the war, and in the ugliness and misery of everyday life the stylized beauty of the story was an escape that could afford some relief. The Protestant theologian Helmut Gollwitzer reported in his memoirs that whenever he offered to read a story to German soldiers in Russian prison camps, they asked for Bergengruen's book: "Unübertroffen aber blieb der Eindruck von Bergengruens *Spanischem Rosenstock*, der immer wieder verlangt wurde" (Unsurpassed, however, remained the impression of Bergengruen's *Spanish Rosebush*, which was called for again and again).

The novel *Am Himmel wie auf Erden* deals with an actual event: the flight of the elector Joachim von Brandenburg from Berlin on 15 July 1524 to escape the predicted recurrence of the biblical deluge. As in *Der Großtyrann und das Gericht*, Bergengruen confronts the mighty and the weak with an approaching judgment day and examines their reactions and fears. Bergengruen frequently used historical settings, which allowed him to reflect on human issues of archetypal significance in the controlled environment of the past. By selecting topics from history, Bergengruen was also able to demonstrate the permanence of all things human. *Am Himmel wie auf Erden* is a much more dynamic novel than *Der Großtryann und das Gericht*, and it offers a great variety of perspectives. Bergengruen subtly weaves together several themes: the growing fear of the coming flood, the tensions between the German-Christian and the Slavic-pagan elements in Brandenburg, the conflict between the old established families and the Hohenzollerns, the threat of disease spreading from the leper colony, the

growing unrest in the city, the dangers of a land that is mostly swamp or sand, and the moral decay at court and in town. The multitude of themes is brought together through the figure of Dr. Carion, the court astrologer. He is the "wise man" often found in Bergengruen's novels who serves the double role of participant and commentator. *Am Himmel wie auf Erden* is a book about fear and lurking dangers which threaten the very fiber of the community. From where will the destruction come? From the heavens above, from the hidden waters below, from tensions on earth? Bergengruen again places man in his "house of fate." Those who learn to accept their fate and who regain their faith in the ultimate order of things will prevail in the end. Among them are Dr. Carion, and—in spite of his failings—the elector. They are humbled, but they emerge from the ordeal wiser and better. Others get caught up in the turmoil and are destroyed. The novel begins with the motto "Be Not Afraid," and it proceeds to demonstrate the destructive power of fear.

Bergengruen had begun writing *Am Himmel wie auf Erden* in 1931 and completed it in 1940, a time when fear had gripped many Germans and the coming of a judgment day was not just a remote possibility. The work, then, spoke with great immediacy to many, who read it as a Schlüsselroman (roman à clef) in which the past stood for the present. The authorities officially forbade the book in 1941 although it continued to be read and was even available in rental libraries.

In 1942 Bergengruen's house was destroyed during an air raid. He found temporary shelter in Achensee in the Tyrol and in 1946 was given permission to move to Zurich—at that time a rare distinction for a German citizen and evidence that even outside the borders of his own country he was known to be untainted by Nazism. In Zurich he established a close friendship with Peter Schifferli, the owner of the Verlag der Arche, which, together with the Nymphenburger Verlagshandlung in Munich, became Bergengruen's postwar publisher. It was in Zurich that he completed the major novel *Das Feuerzeichen* (The Beacon, 1949).

*Das Feuerzeichen* is the story of the innkeeper Hahn, a respected owner of a resort on the Baltic Sea, who is known to everyone as a just man. During a sudden storm he lights a fire on the beach to save some of his guests who have been caught at sea and have lost their way. Subsequently he is charged with a crime, because the law forbids the setting of fires along the coast. The theme is a Prussian, Kleistian one: the conflict between the law and the acts of the individual. The situation is a Kafkaesque one in which the hero wakes up one morning and finds himself the accused; but different from Kafka is the assurance that while the law may find the hero guilty, his noble act would certainly warrant a pardon. Hahn, however, cannot accept this solution. He fights the fate that has suddenly confronted him, and in the end he sets fire to his house and commits suicide. He wanted absolute justice, not mercy: Hahn is a modern Michael Kohlhaas. The novel is tightly woven and moves between the life-saving fire in the beginning and the destructive fire in the end. There is very little action; the pages are filled with discussions about justice and the universality of law. No one questions the correctness of Hahn's actions in saving his hotel guests; on the other hand, can one simply ignore the law, which was also created to protect and save? Can an individual—even with the best of intentions—be above the law? Would that not be anarchy? Bergengruen's answer is clear: the law must be observed; otherwise the divine order of things would be violated. But justice must also be tempered with mercy through the provision of the pardon. Bergengruen's novel is a parable of his religious view of justice and grace. Those around Hahn learn from his example where the rejection of grace can lead. Düweken Schröder, wife of the wise district judge, comments at the end: "Glaube mir, Lieber, . . . die Welt ist heil, bei allem Kummer und Jammer, der über einen kommen kann" (Believe me, my dear . . . the world is intact, in spite of all the grief and misery that can come over one). Judge Schröder replies: "Vielleicht müßte man gar sagen, damit die Welt richtig sei, könne ein Mensch wie unser armer Hahn ihre Richtigkeit nicht anerkennen dürfen, sonst wäre er selbst nicht in seiner Art richtig" (Perhaps one even would have to say that in order to accept the world as just, a man like our poor Hahn would have to reject it, otherwise Hahn himself would not be consistent in his own ways).

*Das Feuerzeichen* is more a novella than a novel. It presents a confrontation with the classic "extraordinary event," Bergengruen's "house of fate." Bergengruen found it difficult to differentiate between novel, novella, and short story (Erzählung), forms which he considered too much in flux to be accurately defined. He readily admitted that occasionally purely quantitative considerations may have led him to assign a work to one category or the other. A long novella thus may be called a "Roman," a short "Roman" may be called a "Novelle."

While living in Zurich, Bergengruen wrote the first two Rittmeister volumes, *Der letzte Rittmeister* (1952; translated as *The Last Captain of Horse*, 1953) and *Die Rittmeisterin* (The Captain of Horse's Lady, 1954). The latter work is subtitled *Wenn man so will, ein Roman* (If You Wish, a Novel), but both are actually collections of novellas, short stories, and anecdotes. Many of these pieces had been published before, but they are now placed into a frame story: the conversations of the narrator with two delightful companions, an old czarist cavalry officer in exile and his lady friend. These volumes show Bergengruen at his narrative best. He proves himself a master raconteur, able to spin a delightful yarn, reminiscent of Theodor Fontane. Into the character of the old Rittmeister he pours all his love for the slightly old-fashioned, the quixotic, the human.

During the immediate postwar years Bergengruen became one of the most prominent men of letters in Germany; his books sold by the millions

*Bergengruen in 1958*

and he was a frequent speaker and reader at official gatherings. He had become a symbol of comfort and reassurance, a man of integrity who did not have to hide his past, and who at the same time did not condemn those who had been weak. While in some of his poems he spoke of the day of reckoning that had come, he also proclaimed the divine "metanoeite," the forgiveness implied in genuine penance and "turning around" (*Dies Irae*, 1945). In the traumatic conditions of postwar Germany, the message of the heile Welt was soothing for many. Bergengruen also offered an escape from the problems of the present by presenting a simple and romanticized world that still held firm values.

In 1958 Bergengruen moved back to Germany to be near Reinhold Schneider, his friend since the early 1930s. He had built a house at Zeppelinstraße 34, on the outskirts of Baden-Baden, and was looking forward to settling down in a town that he had fondly described in some of his travel books—a town of memories and quiet grandeur, a town made for the Rittmeister, his alter ego. His arrival in Baden-Baden was marred, however, by the death of Schneider, a loss he found it difficult to overcome. The closeness of the two friends is reflected in testimonials they gave each other at birthdays and similar celebrations, and most clearly in their letters.

Bergengruen received many honors, among them an honorary doctorate from the University of Munich and the Order Pour le mérite, both in 1958. His literary production during the Baden-Baden years consisted of reminiscences and essays. *Schreibtischerinnerungen* contains essays reflecting on his work as a writer during the 1930s; *Mündlich gesprochen* (Spoken Orally, 1963) is a collection of speeches, lectures, and radio addresses of both literary and general content delivered between 1946 and 1962. He also produced an amusing volume called *Titulus* (1960), subtitled "*Unbetitelter Lebensroman eines Bibliotheksbeamten*" (Untitled Biographical Novel of a Library Official). This book is anything but a novel. The fictitious author, "aus der unteren, mittleren oder höheren Bibliothekarslaufbahn" (from the lower, intermediate or higher librarian ranks), is a "friedfertiger Mann" (peaceable man) who collects book titles because he is intrigued by their cadences, their topical suggestions and implications, and their invitations to playfulness. The result is a "Naturgeschichte des deutschen Buchtitels" (a natural history of German book titles).

During these last years of his life, Bergengruen completed the third volume of his Rittmeist-er series, *Der dritte Kranz* (The Third Garland, 1962), which, like the previous ones, contained several revised or reissued novellas. In contrast to the first two volumes, *Der dritte Kranz* was not a major success; it lacked the immediacy and charm of the earlier books. Other stories appeared, some in attractive bibliophile editions by the Arche Verlag. They, too, were largely reissues of earlier works.

Times had changed in Germany. The economic miracle, the revival of self-confidence, the hectic materialism and increased political involvement of readers and writers in the early 1960s made Bergengruen's work appear old-fashioned and out of touch with reality. His readership dropped drastically; his disciples dispersed. Still, when Bergengruen died on 4 September 1964, there were many who remembered and mourned him. He was buried in the Stadtfriedhof (city cemetery) of Baden-Baden, just a few steps away from his friend Schneider. Another good friend, Emil Staiger, characterized Bergengruen at his funeral as "ein Mann, ja, um das einzig richtige Wort zu gebrauchen: ein Edelmann, sans tache et sans reproche, ein christlicher Ritter ohne Furcht und Tadel" (a man, indeed, to use the only proper word: a nobleman, without stain and without blame, a Christian knight without fear and fault).

While Bergengruen's human qualities are beyond question, his accomplishments as a writer demand a more critical stance. For a number of reasons, he has not weathered well. A man steeped in the past, he wrote in the style of the past. His often archaic language and his frequent use of pathos give many of his works an artificial ring. They read like vintage nineteenth-century writings, reminiscent of those of Heinrich von Kleist, while his form strikes one as a revival of Paul Heyse. Many of his novellas are charming, but even they appear naive to the contemporary reader. Bergengruen's impact on the reading public was confined to the period between 1935 and 1955. Those were critical years, and his books offered comfort and reassurance to many of that troubled generation. He had a loyal group of followers and disciples who admired him for what he was and what he stood for but who were not very critical in a sophisticated literary sense. That, too, was a sign of the time. Today, his works no longer have the resonance they had for a previous generation. Bergengruen wrote for his time and wrote well. A new generation and new conditions have passed him by.

**Letters:**

*Werner Bergengruen—Reinhold Schneider: Briefwechsel,* edited by N. Luise Hackelsberger-Bergengruen (Freiburg, Basel & Vienna: Herder, 1966).

**References:**

Hans Bänziger, *Werner Bergengruen, Weg und Werk,* revised edition (Bern: Francke, 1961);

Ingrid Bode, *Schriftenverzeichnis Werner Bergengruen. Bibliothek des Deutschen Literaturarchivs im Schiller-Nationalmuseum* (Marbach: Nationalmuseum, 1965);

Otto Friedrich Bollnow, "Friedrich Georg Jünger—Werner Bergengruen, zwei Dichter der neuen Geborgenheit," *Zeitschrift für Religions- und Geistesgeschichte,* 3 (1951): 229-246;

Elisabeth Brock-Sulzer, "Zur Novellistik Werner Bergengruens," *Monatsschrift für das deutsche Geistesleben,* 43 (1941): 135-142;

M. W. F. Brown, "Werner Bergengruen," *Modern Languages,* 37 (December 1955): 135-142;

Wolfgang Emmerich, "Die Literatur des antifaschistischen Widerstandes in Deutschland," in *Die deutsche Literatur im Dritten Reich,* edited by Horst Denkler and Karl Prümm (Stuttgart: Reclam, 1976);

Helmut Gollwitzer, *. . . Und führen wohin du nicht willst* (Munich: Kaiser, 1951);

Ida Friederike Görres, "Die Rose von Jericho: Aus einem Versuch über Werner Bergengruen," *Deutsche Rundschau,* 78 (September 1952): 926-939;

Wilhelm Grenzmann, *Dichtung und Glaube,* second edition (Bonn: Athenäum, 1952);

Erich Hofacker, "Bergengruen's *Das Feuerzeichen* and Kleist's *Michael Kohlhaas,*" *Monatshefte,* 47 (November 1955): 349-357;

Theoderich Kampmann, *Die Welt Werner Bergengruens* (Warendorf: Schnell, 1952);

Lida Kirchberger, "Werner Bergengruen's Novel of the Berlin Panic," *Monatshefte,* 46 (April 1954): 199-206;

Günther Klemm, *Werner Bergengruen,* second edition (Wuppertal-Barmen: Müller, 1954);

Hermann Kunisch, *Der andere Bergengruen: Rede gehalten anläßlich der Verleihung der Ehrendoktorwürde der Ludwig-Maximilians-Universität München an Werner Bergengruen am 24. Juni 1958* (Zurich: Arche, 1958);

Helmut Motekat, "*Am Himmel wie auf Erden,* Roman von Werner Bergengruen," *Jahrbuch der Albertus Universität Königsberg/Pr.,* 3 (1953): 128-147;

David J. Parent, *Werner Bergengruens "Ungeschriebene Novelle"* (Bonn: Bouvier, 1974);

Eric Peters, "Werner Bergengruen—Realist and Mystic," *German Life and Letters,* 2 (April 1949): 179-187;

Peter Schifferli, ed., *Dank an Werner Bergengruen* (Zurich: Arche, 1962);

Gerhard Weiss, "Das Haus des Schicksals als Ausgangspunkt in den Prosawerken Werner Bergengruens," *Monatshefte,* 53 (November 1961): 291-297;

Weiss, "Die Prosawerke Werner Bergengruens," Ph.D. dissertation, University of Wisconsin, 1956;

Werner Wilk, *Werner Bergengruen* (Berlin: Colloquium, 1968).

**Papers:**

Werner Bergengruen's papers are in the Schiller Nationalmuseum, Marbach, West Germany.

# Bertolt Brecht

## Siegfried Mews
### *University of North Carolina at Chapel Hill*

BIRTH: Augsburg, 10 February 1898, to Berthold Friedrich and Sofie Brezing Brecht.

EDUCATION: Munich University, 1917-1921.

MARRIAGES: 3 November 1922 to Marianne Zoff; child: Hanne Hiob. 10 April 1929 to Helene Weigel; children: Stefan, Marie Barbara.

DEATH: East Berlin, 14 August 1956.

SELECTED BOOKS: *Baal* (Potsdam: Kiepenheuer, 1922); translated by Eric Bentley as *Baal* in *Baal, A Man's a Man, and The Elephant Calf* (New York: Grove Press, 1966);

*Trommeln in der Nacht: Drama* (Munich: Drei Masken, 1922; edited by Volkmar Sander, Waltham, Mass., Toronto & London: Blaisdell, 1969); translated by Anselm Hollo and others as *Drums in the Night* in *Jungle of Cities and Other Plays* (New York: Grove Press, 1966);

*Leben Eduards des Zweiten von England: Nach Marlowe. Historie*, by Brecht and Lion Feuchtwanger (Potsdam: Kiepenheuer, 1924); translated by Bentley as *Edward II: A Chronicle Play* (New York: Grove Press, 1966);

*Taschenpostille: Mit Anleitungen, Gesangsnoten und einem Anhange* (Potsdam: Privately printed, 1926);

*Im Dickicht der Städte: Der Kampf zweier Männer in der Riesenstadt Chicago. Schauspiel* (Berlin: Propyläen, 1927); translated by Hollo as *Jungle of Cities* in *Jungle of Cities and Other Plays*;

*Hauspostille: Mit Anleitungen, Gesangsnoten und einem Anhang* (Berlin: Propyläen, 1927); translated by Bentley as *Manual of Piety: A Bilingual Edition* (New York: Grove Press, 1966);

*Mann ist Mann: Die Verwandlung des Packers Galy Gay in den Militärbaracken von Kilkoa im Jahre 1925: Lustspiel* (Berlin: Propyläen, 1927); translated by Bentley as *A Man's a Man* in *Baal, A Man's a Man, and The Elephant Calf*;

*Drei angelsächsische Stücke*, by Brecht and Feuchtwanger (Berlin: Propyläen-Verlag, 1927);

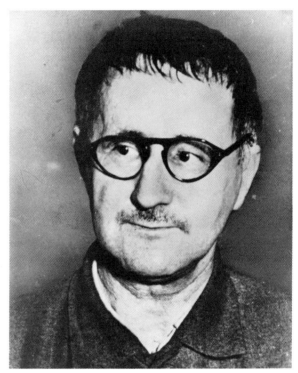

*Bertolt Brecht (Ullstein)*

*Aufstieg und Fall der Stadt Mahagonny: Oper in drei Akten*, text by Brecht, music by Kurt Weill (Vienna & Leipzig: Universal-Edition, 1929); translated by Guy Stern as *Rise and Fall of the City of Mahagonny* (brochure accompanying recorded version, Columbia K3L 243, 1959);

*Die Dreigroschenoper*, text translated from John Gay's *The Beggar's Opera* by Elisabeth Hauptmann, rewritten by Brecht, music by Weill (Vienna: Universal-Edition, 1929; London: Malik, 1938); translated by Bentley and Desmond Vesey as *The Threepenny Opera* (New York: Grove Press, 1964);

*Versuche*, volume 1: *Der Flug der Lindberghs; Radiotheorie; Geschichten vom Herrn Keuner; Fatzer, 3*, edited by Elisabeth Hauptmann (Berlin: Kiepenheuer, 1930);

*Versuche*, volume 2: *Aufstieg und Fall der Stadt Mahagonny: Über die Oper: Aus dem Lesebuch für*

*Städtebewohner: Das Badener Lehrstück vom Einverständnis*, edited by Hauptmann (Berlin: Kiepenheuer, 1930);

*Versuche*, volume 3: *Die Dreigroschenoper; Die Beule: Ein Dreigroschenfilm; Der Dreigroschenprozeß*, edited by Hauptmann (Berlin: Kiepenheuer, 1931);

*Versuche*, volume 4: *Der Jasager und der Neinsager: Schulopern; Die Maßnahme: Lehrstück*, edited by Hauptmann (Berlin: Kiepenheuer, 1931): *Die Maßnahme* translated by Carl L. Mueller as *The Measures Taken* in *The Measures Taken and Other Lehrstücke* (London: Methuen, 1977);

*Versuche*, volume 5: *Die heilige Johanna der Schlachthöfe: Schauspiel; Geschichten vom Herrn Keuner*, edited by Hauptmann (Berlin: Kiepenheuer, 1932); *Die heilige Johanna der Schlachthöfe* translated by Frank Jones as *Saint Joan of the Stockyards* (Bloomington: Indiana University Press, 1969);

*Versuche*, volume 6: *Die drei Soldaten: Ein Kinderbuch*, edited by Hauptmann (Berlin: Kiepenheuer, 1932);

*Versuche*, volume 7: *Die Mutter; Geschichte aus der Revolution*, edited by Hauptmann (Berlin: Kiepenheuer, 1933); *Die Mutter* translated by Lee Baxandall as *The Mother* (New York: Grove Press, 1965);

*Ballade vom armen Stabschef + 30: Juni 1934* (N.p., 1934);

*Dreigroschenroman* (Amsterdam: Albert de Lange, 1934); translated by Vesey and Christopher Isherwood as *A Penny for the Poor* (London: R. Hale, 1937); translation republished as *Threepenny Novel* (New York: Grove Press, 1956; London: Granada, 1981);

*Lieder Gedichte Chöre*, text by Brecht, music by Hanns Eisler (Paris: Editions du Carrefour, 1934);

*Gesammelte Werke*, 2 volumes (London: Malik, 1938);

*Svendborger Gedichte; Deutsche Kriegsfibel; Chroniken: Deutsche Satiren für den deutschen Freiheitssender* (London: Malik, 1939);

*Furcht und Elend des III. Reiches* (Moscow: Meshdunarodnaja Kniga, 1941; New York: Aurora, 1945); translated by Bentley as *The Private Life of the Master Race* (New York: New Directions, 1944);

*Herr Puntila und sein Knecht: Nach Erzählungen der Hella Wuolijoki. Volksstück in 9 Bildern* (Munich: Desch, 1948); republished as *Herr Puntila und sein Knecht Matti*, edited by Margaret Mare (London: Methuen, 1962); translated by John

Willett as *Mr. Puntila and His Man Matti* (London: Methuen, 1977);

*Kalendergeschichten* (Halle/Saale: Mitteldeutscher Verlag, 1948); translated by Yvonne Kapp and Michael Hamburger as *Tales from the Calendar* (London: Methuen, 1961);

*Versuche*, volume 9: *Mutter Courage und ihre Kinder: Eine Chronik aus dem Dreißigjährigen Krieg; Anmerkungen; Fünf Schwierigkeiten beim Schreiben der Wahrheit*, edited by Hauptmann (Berlin & Frankfurt am Main: Suhrkamp, 1949); *Mutter Courage und ihre Kinder* translated by Bentley as *Mother Courage and Her Children* (New York: Grove Press, 1966);

*Das Zukunftslied: Aufbaulied der FDJ*, text by Brecht, music by Paul Dessau (Weimar: Thüringer Volksverlag, 1949);

*Antigonemodell 1948; Die Antigone des Sophokles, nach der Hölderlinschen Übertragung für die Bühne, bearbeitet* (Berlin: Weiss, 1949);

*Versuche*, volume 10: *Herr Puntila und sein Knecht Matti; Chinesische Gedichte; Die Ausnahme und die Regel*, edited by Hauptmann (Berlin & Frankfurt am Main: Suhrkamp, 1950);

*Versuche*, volume 11: *Der Hofmeister*, by Jacob Michael Reinhold Lenz, revised by Brecht; *Studien: Neue Technik der Schauspielkunst; Übungsstücke für Schauspieler; Das Verhör des Lukullus*, by Brecht and Margarete Steffin; *Anmerkungen über die Oper "Die Verurteilung des Lukullus,"* edited by Hauptmann (Berlin: Suhrkamp, 1951); *Das Verhör des Lukullus* translated by H. R. Hays as *The Trial of Lucullus* (New York: New Directions, 1943);

*Offener Brief an die deutschen Künstler und Schriftsteller* (Berlin, 1951);

*Die Erziehung der Hirse. Nach dem Bericht von G. Fisch: Der Mann, der das Unmögliche wahr gemacht hat* (Berlin: Aufbau, 1951);

*Hundert Gedichte, 1918-1950* (Berlin: Aufbau, 1951);

*An meine Landsleute* (Leipzig: VEB Offizin Haag-Drugulin, 1951);

*Das Verhör des Lukullus: Oper in 12 Bildern*, text by Brecht, music by Dessau (Berlin: Aufbau, 1951);

*Die Verurteilung des Lukullus: Oper*, text by Brecht, music by Dessau (Berlin: Aufbau, 1951);

*Versuche*, volume 12: *Der gute Mensch von Sezuan; Kleines Organon für das Theater; Über reimlose Lyrik mit unregelmäßigen Rhythmen; Geschichten vom Herrn Keuner*, edited by Hauptmann (Berlin & Frankfurt am Main: Suhrkamp, 1953); *Der gute Mensch von Sezuan* translated by Bentley as *The Good Woman of Setzuan* in *Parables for the Theatre: Two Plays by Bertolt Brecht* (Minneapolis: University of Minnesota Press, 1948); translation revised as *The Good Woman of Setzuan* (New York: Grove Press, 1966); *Kleines Organon für das Theater* translated by Willett as "A Short Organum for the Theatre" in *Brecht on Theatre* (New York: Hill & Wang, 1964);

*Versuche*, extra volume: *Die Gewehre der Frau Carrar; Der Augsburger Kreidekreis; Neue Kinderlieder*, edited by Hauptmann (Berlin: Aufbau, 1953);

*Versuche*, volume 13: *Der kaukasische Kreidekreis*, by Brecht and Ruth Berlau; *Weite und Vielfalt der realistischen Schreibweise; Buckower Elegien*, edited by Hauptmann (Berlin & Frankfurt am Main: Suhrkamp, 1954); *Der kaukasische Kreidekreis* translated by Bentley and Maja Apelman as *The Caucasian Chalk Circle* in *Parables for the Theatre: Two Plays by Bertolt Brecht*;

*Versuche*, volume 14: *Leben des Galilei; Gedichte aus dem Messingkauf; Die Horatier und die Kuratier*, edited by Hauptmann (Berlin: Suhrkamp, 1955); *Leben des Galilei* translated by Vesey as *The Life of Galileo* (London: Methuen, 1963); translated by Charles Laughton as *Galileo* (New York: Grove Press, 1966);

*Gedichte*, edited by S. Streller (Leipzig: Reclam, 1955);

*Kriegsfibel*, edited by Berlau (Berlin: Eulenspiegel, 1955);

*Gedichte und Lieder*, edited by P. Suhrkamp (Berlin & Frankfurt am Main: Suhrkamp, 1956);

*Die Geschäfte des Herrn Julius Cäsar: Romanfragment* (Berlin: Aufbau, 1957);

*Lieder und Gesänge* (Berlin: Henschel, 1957);

*Versuche*, volume 15: *Die Tage der Commune; Die Dialektik auf dem Theater; Zu "Leben des Galilei"; Drei Reden; Zwei Briefe*, edited by Hauptmann (Berlin & Frankfurt am Main: Suhrkamp, 1957);

*Schriften zum Theater: Über eine nicht-aristotelische Dramatik*, edited by S. Unseld (Berlin & Frankfurt am Main: Suhrkamp, 1957);

*Stücke aus dem Exil; Die Rundköpfe und die Spitzköpfe; Furcht und Elend des Dritten Reiches; Die Gewehre der Frau Carrar; Mutter Courage und ihre Kinder; Das Verhör des Lukullus; Leben des Galilei; Der gute Mensch von Sezuan; Herr Puntila und sein Knecht Matti; Der aufhaltsame Aufstieg des Arturo Ui; Die Geschichte der Simone Machard; Schweyk im zweiten Weltkrieg; Der kaukasische Kreidekreis; Die Tage der Commune*, 5

volumes (Frankfurt am Main: Suhrkamp, 1957); *Die Rundköpfe und die Spitzköpfe* translated by N. Goold-Verschoyle as *Roundheads and Peakheads* in *Jungle of Cities and Other Plays;*

*Geschichten vom Herrn Keuner* (Berlin: Aufbau, 1958);

*Brecht: Ein Lesebuch für unsere Zeit*, edited by Hauptmann & Benno Slupianek (Weimar: Volksverlag Weimar, 1958);

*Mutter Courage und ihre Kinder: Text; Aufführung; Anmerkungen* (Berlin: Henschel, 1958);

*Versuche*, volumes 5-8: *Die heilige Johanna der Schlachthöfe; Die drei Soldaten; Die Mutter; Die Spitzköpfe und die Rundköpfe*, 1 volume (Berlin & Frankfurt am Main: Suhrkamp, 1959);

*Der gute Mensch von Sezuan: Parabelstück*, by Brecht, Berlau, and Steffin, music by Dessau (Berlin & Frankfurt am Main: Suhrkamp, 1959; edited by Margaret Mare, London: Methuen, 1960);

*Schweyk im Zweiten Weltkrieg* (Berlin & Frankfurt am Main: Suhrkamp, 1959);

*Die sieben Todsünden der Kleinbürger* (Frankfurt am Main: Suhrkamp, 1959);

*Bearbeitungen: Die Antigone des Sophokles; Der Hofmeister; Coriolan; der Prozeß der Jeanne d'Arc zu Rouen 1431; Don Juan; Pauken und Trompeten*, 2 volumes (Frankfurt am Main: Suhrkamp, 1959);

*Kleines Organon für das Theater: Mit einem "Nachtrag zum Kleinen Organon"* (Frankfurt am Main: Suhrkamp, 1960);

*Flüchtlingsgespräche* (Berlin: Suhrkamp, 1961);

*Me-ti; Buch der Wendungen-Fragment*, edited by Uwe Johnson (Frankfurt am Main: Suhrkamp, 1965);

*Gesammelte Werke*, 22 volumes (Frankfurt am Main: Suhrkamp, 1967-1969): volumes 1-7, *Stücke*, translation edited by Willett and Ralph Manheim as *Collected Plays*, 9 volumes (London: Methuen, 1971-1973; New York: Random House, 1971-1973); volumes 8-10, *Gedichte*, translated by Willett and Manheim as *Poems 1913-1956* (New York: Methuen, 1976); volume 11, *Prosa I*, translated by Willett and Manheim as *Short Stories 1921-1946* (New York: Methuen, 1983); volumes 15-17, *Schriften zum Theater*, translated by Willett as *Brecht on Theatre* (New York: Hill & Wang, 1964);

*Turandot oder Der Kongreß der Weißwäscher* (Frankfurt am Main: Suhrkamp, 1968);

*Arbeitsjournal 1938 bis 1955*, 3 volumes (Frankfurt am Main: Suhrkamp, 1973);

*Tagebücher 1920-1922: Autobiographische Aufzeich-
nungen 1920-1954,* edited by Herta Ramthun
(Frankfurt am Main: Suhrkamp, 1975); translated by Willett as *Diaries 1920-1922* (New
York: St. Martin's Press, 1979).

OTHER: M. Andersen-Nexö, *Die Kindheit: Erinnerungen,* translated by Brecht (Zurich: Vereinigung "Kultur & Volk," 1945);
Lion Feuchtwanger, *Auswahl,* contributions by
Brecht (Rudolstadt: Greifen, 1949);
T. Otto, *Nie wieder: Tagebuch in Bildern,* foreword
by Brecht (Berlin: Verlag Volk & Welt, 1950);
*Wir singen zu den Weltfestspielen: Herrnburger Bericht,*
edited by Brecht and Paul Dessau (Berlin:
Verlag Neues Leben, 1951);
*Theaterarbeit: Sechs Aufführungen des Berliner Ensem-
bles,* edited by Brecht, Ruth Berlau, C. Hubalek, and others (Dresden: Dresdner Verlag,
1952).

PERIODICAL PUBLICATION: "Die Ausnahme
und die Regel," *Internationale Literatur:
Deutsche Blätter* (Moscow), 7 (9 September
1937): 3-18; translated by Eric Bentley as
"The Exception and the Rule," *Chrysalis,* 14,
no. 68 (1961).

Bertolt Brecht's status as one of the major
playwrights of the twentieth century is largely un-
contested. In addition to writing a significant body
of plays that are performed all over the world,
Brecht also developed in a number of theoretical
writings his theory of "epic" or "dialectic" theater
that he applied to the "model" productions of his
own plays in the early 1950s. Furthermore, practically from the beginning of his literary career
Brecht has been considered a poet of considerable
power and originality; more recently, his prose
fiction has attracted increased attention—although
Brecht the prose fiction writer has not yet been fully
recognized.

It is hardly an exaggeration, then, when Martin Esslin, author of the influential study *Brecht: A
Choice of Evils* (1959) writes: "There can be little
doubt that Bertolt Brecht is one of the most significant writers of this century." Esslin points out
that Brecht had to overcome a special handicap
owing to the fact that "German literature, unlike
that of France, Italy, pre-revolutionary Russia, or
Scandinavia, is on the whole so remote from the
taste and the aesthetic conventions of the English-
speaking world that its influence does not often
make itself felt." Brecht, however, according to Ess-

lin, is one of those rare cases of a writer from the
German-speaking countries who has left a lasting
impression; in fact, Brecht's "influence on the theatre may well prove as powerful as that of Kafka
on the novel."

The curiosity that Brecht and his work
aroused and the renown they have achieved cannot
be exclusively attributed to literary factors; rather,
Brecht's political and ideological persuasion and his
stance as a committed writer contributed consid-
erably to his reputation. Esslin puts the "curious
paradox" of Brecht in a nutshell: "Brecht was a
Communist, he was also a great poet. But while the
West liked his poetry and distrusted his Communism, the Communists exploited his political convictions while they regarded his artistic aims and
achievements with suspicion."

Eugen Berthold Brecht was born in Augsburg
on 10 February 1898. Augsburg, located about
forty miles northwest of Munich, had lost its em-
inence as a mercantile center and was then a provincial city. Brecht's father, Berthold Friedrich, a
Catholic, had come to Augsburg in the early 1890s
as a clerk in a paper mill of which he eventually
became manager. Brecht was brought up in the
Protestant faith of his mother, Sofie, to whom he
felt a special affinity. Brecht's schooling followed
conventional lines; after four years of attending a
Protestant elementary school, he went to a Realgymnasium (secondary school).

Thus Brecht grew up in a solidly and respect-
ably middle-class atmosphere; later he was to dis-
avow his sheltered upbringing in his famed
autobiographical poem "Vom armen B.B." (Of
Poor B.B., 1927). Even as a youth Brecht showed
signs of rebellion against the bourgeois life that he
seemed destined to enter; above all, at an early age
his literary activities began to take precedence over
assignments for school. In 1913 he wrote "Die Bi-
bel," a one-act play that attests to the great and
lasting impression Luther's German Bible made
upon him; the play was published in the school
newspaper. In 1914 Brecht's first contribution appeared in the *Augsburger Neueste Nachrichten,* the
local newspaper. Some of his pieces, such as "Der
Freiwillige" (The Volunteer), a 1914 short story in
which a father restores his imprisoned son's honor
by joining the army, exhibit the patriotism and even
chauvinism rampant at the beginning of World
War I. But in 1916 he was almost expelled from
school on account of a "defeatist" essay that took
issue with the Horatian motto "Dulce et decorum
est pro patria mori" (It is sweet and proper to die
for the fatherland). On account of World War I,

*Brecht with Paula (Bi) Banholzer, who bore his illegitimate son, Frank, in 1919 (courtesy of Werner Frisch, Augsburg)*

he left the Realgymnasium in 1917 with the Not-abitur (emergency school-leaving certificate). Although Brecht may have exaggerated the gruesomeness of his experiences as an orderly in the venereal disease ward of an Augsburg military hospital in 1918, his abhorrence of war became intense, as can be seen in the antimilitaristic, bitterly satirical poem "Legende vom toten Soldaten" (Legend of the Dead Soldier), in which the emperor orders the resurrection of a dead soldier because he needs additional cannon fodder.

At the same time, Brecht's last years in Augsburg were by no means devoid of lighter moments. Taking the balladeer and playwright Frank Wedekind as his model, he propagated antibourgeois sentiments among his friends and followers by singing songs of his own composition, accompanying himself on the guitar; attended the local fair, the Plärrer; and lived a comparatively carefree existence that involved several youthful erotic entanglements—one of which resulted in Paula (Bi) Banholzer's giving birth in 1919 to Brecht's illegitimate son, Frank. Although, strictly speaking, his first published play, *Baal* (1922), is not autobiographical, the protagonist is a poet-genius who re-

sembles Brecht in leading a completely unfettered life, engaging in alcoholic and sexual excesses in defiance of bourgeois morality.

After the death of his mother in 1920, Brecht's ties to his family and his hometown began to weaken. Since 1917 he had been studying literature and medicine in desultory fashion at the University of Munich; in 1921 he gave up his studies without having obtained a degree. In the same year, the aspiring writer attracted the attention of critics and publishers when a short story written in 1919, "Bargan läßt es sein: Eine Flibustiergeschichte" (translated as "Bargan Gives Up: A Pirate Story," 1983), appeared in the Munich magazine *Der Neue Merkur*. The story exhibits some of the hallmarks that are also characteristic of Brecht's early plays and poetry, such as depiction of a non-bourgeois life-style, exoticism, and the theme of homoerotic love. Bargan, the captain of a pirate vessel, gives up his position and everything he has accomplished on account of his inexplicable love for Croze, an extremely ugly, clubfooted, and intensely disliked member of his crew. There is clear evidence of Croze's treachery; yet, when confronted by his men and asked to get rid of Croze,

*Cover for Brecht's first published play, the story of a hedonistic poet-genius (Lilly Library, Indiana University)*

Bargan refuses. In the end the narrator permits Bargan and Croze to escape from the ship in a small boat in which they will presumably perish.

Homoeroticism is to be found in both *Baal* and *Im Dickicht der Städte* (1927; translated as *Jungle of Cities*, 1966); in the latter play, homoerotic love serves as a means of overcoming the individual's isolation and alienation in the big, cold city of Chicago. In "Bargan läßt es sein" this alienation is to be found among the male members of the society of pirates—women are treated as sex objects and are not even given names—who are only held together by their activities of pillaging, plundering, and raping that require coordinated efforts under capable leadership; there are no emotional ties of any sort that could provide a common bond. The quasi-objective mode of narration and the cynicism with which the narrator describes the gruesome events during and after the capture of a Chilean city are indicative of a high degree of individual isolation on his and his fellow pirates' part—precisely the state that Bargan seeks to overcome by

his unconditional love for the lowliest and most despicable among the pirates.

In other stories of his Munich period Brecht turned to the present. "Ein gemeiner Kerl" (1922; translated as "A Mean Bastard," 1983) attacks bourgeois sexual taboos by dispassionately displaying the secret wishes and desires of a respectable woman. The story relates, in a factual style that shuns sensationalism and titillation, the intrusion of a disreputable male into the private sphere of the widow Marie Pfaff who, after feeble protests, abandons all pretense of propriety and "ergab sich mit Leib und Seele" (surrendered herself . . . body and soul) to a complete stranger owing to the unexpected liberation of her long-suppressed lust.

In Munich Brecht made friends with the older, established writer Lion Feuchtwanger, who became his mentor and collaborator; occasionally, Brecht appeared on stage with the Munich folk comedian Karl Valentin. Yet the young writer considered the Bavarian capital merely a stepping stone on his way to Berlin, which in the 1920s was to become a literary and theatrical metropolis whose significance was by no means confined to Germany. After some unsuccessful attempts to gain a foothold, Brecht settled in Berlin in the fall of 1924 and remained there until 1933, the beginning of his exile.

Brecht adapted easily to the "Asphaltstadt" (asphalt city), as he called it in "Vom armen B.B." But Berlin also provided Brecht with a heightened awareness of social forces and social processes. Baal in the play of the same name and Kragler in *Trommeln in der Nacht* (1922; translated as *Drums in the Night*, 1966), who abandons the revolution in favor of domestic bliss, act according to their individualistic impulses. In *Mann ist Mann* (1927; translated as *A Man's a Man*, 1966), a comedy that premiered in 1926, Brecht posits the social determinism of human nature, albeit in a fanciful, vaguely Kiplingesque setting. Brecht's probing of the functions of individuals in specific social contexts resulted in 1926 in his beginning the study of Marxism. Brecht's turning to Marxism has elicited much comment by critics and biographers. Esslin provides a psychological explanation, speaking of Brecht's "divided nature" that alternated "between anarchy and discipline," that is, between anarchy in *Baal* on the one hand and stern, authoritarian party discipline on the other. Esslin's thesis of the "choice of evils" that Brecht was supposedly facing has been echoed by other critics, but it has not remained unchallenged. Biographer Klaus Völker suggested in 1976 that Brecht turned to Marxism-Leninism because he realized that this theory would impart a new quality to his writing and enable him to render social processes more effectively. In fact, Brecht's study of Marxism coincided more or less with his criticism of contemporary theater productions and staging techniques that gradually evolved into his theory of epic theater with its famed Verfremdungseffekt (estrangement effect; often inaccurately translated as "alienation effect"). Verfremden (making strange) is a set of techniques used by playwright, director, and actor in order to achieve Historisierung (historization), a manner of presentation that displays the underlying causes of events and social interactions by removing them from their familiar context so that the spectators' critical awareness will be increased and they will be disposed toward action against injustices.

Paradoxically, in 1928 Brecht achieved his greatest success with a work that clearly belongs to a category of plays that he termed "kulinarisch" (culinary), that is, plays that have the same numbing effect as a lavish meal eaten in a good restaurant. *Die Dreigroschenoper* (1929; translated as *The Threepenny Opera*, 1964), a collaborative effort with the composer Kurt Weill, owes its international acclaim to its catchy tunes rather than to its unfocused indictment of capitalist practices. The fact that *Die Dreigroschenoper* was a free adaptation of John Gay's *The Beggar's Opera* (1728) with interspersed verses by François Villon motivated one critic to accuse Brecht of plagiarism—a charge that Brecht countered—but did not really refute—with his intentionally provocative statement concerning his "Laxheit in Dingen geistigen Eigentums" (laxity in matters of intellectual property). In the powerful and complex *Die heilige Johanna der Schlachthöfe* (1932; translated as *Saint Joan of the Stockyards*, 1969), a play about a modern-day Joan of Arc in the stockyards of Chicago that is indebted to Upton Sinclair's novel *The Jungle* (1906), Brecht's Marxism asserts itself more vigorously than in his previous dramas. Marxist tendencies are also quite pronounced in the Lehrstücke (plays for learning) that Brecht wrote during the late 1920s and early 1930s, such as *Das Badener Lehrstück vom Einverständnis* (The Baden Play for Learning, 1930); the controversial *Die Maßnahme* (1931; translated as *The Measures Taken*, 1977), a play that seemed to advocate human sacrifice for the sake of political expediency; and "Die Ausnahme und die Regel" (1937;

*Brecht (second from left) in the "orchestra" of the Munich folk comedian Karl Valentin in the early 1920s*

*Brecht with his first wife, Marianne Zoff, in 1923 (courtesy of Werner Frisch, Augsburg)*

translated as "The Exception and the Rule," 1961).

Before the stunning success of *Die Dreigro-schenoper*, Brecht had been busily writing short stories. After the expiration in 1925 of his contract as a dramaturge at the Deutsches Theater of the famed director Max Reinhardt he needed an income, and during 1925 and 1926 fourteen of his short prose pieces were published in newspapers, magazines, and journals. In 1928 his narrative "Die Bestie" (translated as "The Monster," 1983) won first prize in the short story competition of the magazine *Berliner Illustrierte Zeitung*. Brecht was not only motivated by financial considerations; there was also, as the critic Jan Knopf suggests, a desire on the young author's part to capture the new reality that was familiar to his city-dwelling readers by means of a style to which they could respond. This new reality found its artistic expression in the so-called Neue Sachlichkeit (New Objectivity), the dominant artistic and literary movement from approximately 1924 to the beginning of the 1930s. The adherents of the New Objectivity did away with expressionism's idealistic visions and dreams of man's moral and spiritual regeneration; instead, they opted for the description in a factual, repor-

torial style of the real world of objects that was governed by technological innovations and was reflected in the rational, nonemotional forms of communication among the members of modern mass society. The United States provided the model for much-admired advances in technology and patterns of behavior—hence the vogue of Americanism in life-styles and art in Germany in the 1920s.

Brecht's short prose pieces from the Berlin period employ an unemotional language and objective narrative stance that show thematic parallels to texts of the New Objectivity without conforming to all of its tenets and presuppositions. In one of his rare historical tales from the 1920s, "Der Tod des Cesare Malatesta" (1924; translated as "The Death of Cesare Malatesta," 1983), which takes place during the Italian Renaissance, Brecht posits a modern problem, the weakening and disappearance of the individual's autonomy. "Gespräch über die Südsee" (1926; translated as "Conversations about the South Seas," 1983) takes place in an exotic milieu that is no longer the adventurous world of the pirates in "Bargan läßt es sein" and of escapism; rather, the South Seas appear as a place in which there is nothing meaningful to do, a place that does not offer a significant alternative to Europe. "Schlechtes Wasser" (1926; translated as "Bad Water," 1983) is even more pointed in its dismissal of exotic places that have been invaded by commerce and exploitation of the natives.

"Brief über eine Dogge" (1925; translated as "Letter about a Mastiff," 1983) may be read, as one critic asserts, as a realistic parable about the rich man's futile claim to the souls of the poor. San Francisco seems to have been chosen as the setting on account of its earthquake rather than with the intent of portraying something specifically American in the fashion of the New Objectivity. Both the social dimension and the American milieu of Chicago, for whose depiction Brecht was indebted to *The Jungle*, are more in evidence in "Das Paket des lieben Gottes" (1926; translated as "The Good Lord's Package," 1983). In "Eine kleine Versicherungsgeschichte" (1926; translated as "A Little Tale of Insurance," 1983), set in Berlin, the exploitation of the poor by the wealthy is depicted more realistically.

Boxing gained in popularity during the 1920s due to the vicarious thrills it provided the spectators and to the clear outcome it offered to those faced with the complex issues of mass society in

*Finale of the premiere of* Die Dreigroschenoper, *31 August 1928 at the Theater am Schiffbauerdamm, Berlin. Left to right: Erich Ponto as Peachum, Roma Bahn as Polly, Harald Paulsen as Macheath, Kurt Gerron as Police Commissioner Brown.*

which the individual—unlike the victorious boxer—had largely lost the ability to determine his fate. Brecht's fascination with the sport is reflected in both "Der Kinnhaken" (1926; translated as "Hook to the Chin," 1983) and "Der Lebenslauf des Boxers Samson Körner" (translated as "Life Story of the Boxer Samson Körner," 1983), an unfinished fictional autobiography of a boxer that appeared in serialized form in a Berlin magazine in 1926. Brecht's matter-of-fact account of the boxer's gradual and adventurous rise from the bottom by dint of his physical prowess ran counter to the tradition of the Bildungsroman (psychological novel) that extolled the spiritual and intellectual development of the individual. Brecht touches upon the subject of sports as big business in "Vier Männer und ein Pokerspiel" (1926; translated as "Four Men and a Poker Game," 1983).

The stories that take place in America exhibit few of those features that were admired by many of Brecht's contemporaries in the middle and late 1920s. Similarly, some stories that have Germany

*Brecht at home in 1927 (Ullstein)*

*Painting of Brecht in 1928 by Rudolf Schlichter*

or, more specifically, Berlin as their setting take issue with the new trends and achievements that were being touted by the followers of the New Objectivity. In "Nordseekrabben" (1927; translated as "North Sea Shrimps," 1983) Brecht pokes fun at those who have succumbed to the utilitarian aesthetics of the most influential artistic movement of the Weimar Republic, the Bauhaus. Under the influence of alcohol the narrator's companion demolishes a friend's modernistic apartment and rearranges the furniture in order to make it more "habitable," that is, more like the dwellings of ordinary, less privileged people.

In "Müllers natürliche Haltung" (1926; translated as "Müller's Natural Attitude,"1983), Brecht casts doubt on the unquestioning reliance on technical innovations. The engineer Müller, a man of common sense, characterizes his partner's unthinking fearlessness during a flight as a lack of "jenes primitive Mißtrauen" (the primitive minimum of mistrust) that is necessary for survival and dissolves their partnership. The short piece "Barbara"

(1927) is in a more satirical vein; initially the narrator, a passenger in the big American automobile of a friend who does not know anything besides how to drive a car, seems destined to become a victim of the friend's speeding. But in the end the car runs out of gas; a tragedy has been averted and the machine-obsessed and machinelike friend, faced with the limits of technology, becomes human again.

There is a general consensus among critics that "Die Bestie" marks Brecht's highest achievement in prose fiction during the Berlin period. Muratov, the former governor of a province in czarist Russia and now a destitute old man, shows up unrecognized in a Soviet film studio that is producing a film about the pre-World War I pogroms in South Russia for which Muratov was chiefly responsible. On account of his uncanny resemblance to the historical Muratov the old man is given a screen test. But Muratov is unable to project a convincing monster, showing that art—not mere physical resemblance—is required to create the impression of authentic bestiality. The film staff is not trying to achieve a mimetic representation of reality but wants to convey its own notion of that reality in a theatrical fashion in order to achieve popular success. Conversely, Brecht surely did not wish to advocate the merely "naturgetreu" (naturalistic) representation that is evident in Muratov's first screen test. Jewish survivors of the massacre, who have been hired as extras, recall that it was Muratov's routinely bureaucratic manner that made their experience so terrifying. Muratov, who was engaged in what Hannah Arendt has called the "banality of evil," may thus be considered a minor precursor of Hitler's bureaucratic annihilator of Jews, Adolf Eichmann. The question that the story poses is, then, how that which so vividly and terrifyingly impressed itself upon the victims can be rendered adequately and convincingly to uninvolved persons via new art forms.

Around 1926 Brecht had begun to write "Geschichten vom Herrn Keuner" (Anecdotes of Mr. Keuner), the first two series of which were published in 1930 and 1932 in volumes one and five of his *Versuche*. Ultimately, Brecht was to write nearly ninety of the tales. Since the writing of the first Keuner stories coincides with the beginning of Brecht's study of Marxism, the Keuner character is essentially a creation of the Marxist Brecht and reflects attitudes and positions that he held after 1926. Mr. Keuner was originally intended to be used in some of Brecht's plays for learning to provide the spectators with the correct critical attitude with which to view the plays and the ideologically correct interpretation of the plays.

There are various theories concerning the origin of the name Keuner. Both its derivation from the German word *Keiner* (nobody) and that from the Greek *koiné*, signifying colloquial speech and general comprehensibility, have been suggested. Mr. Keuner does, indeed, embody the quality of unheroic unpretentiousness as well as the ability to formulate his ideas concisely and in a way that can be generally understood. In fact, conciseness is a characteristic feature of the Keuner stories, which range in length from less than twenty words to less than two pages. The pithy sayings of Mr. Keuner are intended to make a point that is not necessarily evident at first hearing or reading. The text of the extremely short "Das Wiedersehen" (translated as "On Meeting Again," 1961) may serve as an example: "Ein Mann, der Herrn K. lange nicht gesehen hatte, begrüßte ihn mit den Worten: 'Sie haben sich gar nicht verändert.'/'Oh!' sagte Herr K. und erbleichte." (A man who had not seen Mr. K. for a long time greeted him with the words: "You haven't changed at all."/"Oh!" said Mr. K. and turned pale.) Brecht, by having Keuner react in an unexpected fashion, exposes the polite colloquial phrase as a meaningless cliché that conceals

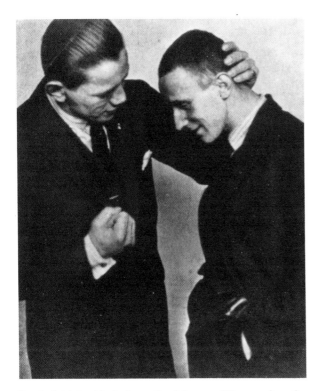

*Brecht (right) with the boxer Paul Samson-Körner, whose fictionalized autobiography he wrote in 1926*

the fact that people do change. More important, Mr. Keuner's unconventional and negative reaction causes the reader to reflect upon the desirability of change, since the inability to change is tantamount to thwarting progress.

Although translated as "Anecdotes of Mr. Keuner," the Keuner stories are not anecdotal in the sense of relating entertaining happenings of a personal or biographical nature. Nor are they parabolic in the sense of conveying moral lessons. Rather, as Esslin puts it, Brecht's Keuner stories are "witty, concise, paradoxical, and profound"— they defy easy definition in terms of genre.

When Hitler came to power on 30 January 1933, Brecht had good reason to be apprehensive. Ever since the publication of "Legende vom toten Soldaten" Brecht had been on the blacklist of the Nazis for desecrating the honor of the German soldier; his turning to Marxism-Leninism was bound to make matters worse. On 27 February 1933 the Reichstag building in Berlin was burned and the Communists were blamed. The fire is generally believed to have been set by the Nazis themselves so that it could be used as a pretext for the wholesale arrest of Communists and other opponents, among them writers and intellectuals. One day after the burning of the Reichstag, Brecht, his wife Helene Weigel, whom he had married in 1929 after his 1927 divorce from Marianne Zoff, and their son, Stefan, left Berlin for Prague—beginning an exile that was to last until 1947. During these years, as Brecht stated with little exaggeration, he, his family, and his collaborators were engaged in "öfter die Länder als die Schuhe wechselnd" (changing countries more often than shoes).

Among other hardships, exile meant a severe curtailment of publishing outlets and stage productions. Hence, the exile years were a "Schlechte Zeit für Lyrik" (Bad Time for Poetry), as Brecht put it in a poem of that title written in 1939. Yet he continued to write; and surprisingly, he did not confine himself to plays with a decidedly anti-Nazi, topical emphasis such as *Furcht und Elend des III. Reiches* (Fear and Misery in the Third Reich, 1941; translated as *The Private Life of the Master Race*, 1944). Beginning in 1937, those plays that are considered to be among his best were written in quick succession: *Der gute Mensch von Sezuan* (1953; translated as *The Good Woman of Setzuan*, 1948), *Leben des Galilei* (1955; translated as *The Life of Galileo*, 1963), *Herr Puntila und sein Knecht* (1948; translated as *Mr. Puntila and His Man Matti*, 1977), and *Mutter Courage und ihre Kinder* (1949; translated as *Mother*

*Brecht in 1931 (Ullstein)*

*Courage and Her Children,* 1966). In addition, Brecht completed his major collection of poetry, *Svendborger Gedichte* (1939; translated as "Svendborg Poems," 1976), and wrote some of his best-known stories. These stories were subsequently published in his only major prose fiction anthology, *Kalendergeschichten* (1948; translated as *Tales from the Calendar,* 1961), a West German edition of which sold more than half a million copies between 1952 and 1975.

Brecht's first major project in exile, however, was a novel, a genre that did not require the medium of the stage to reach its public; it was the only novel Brecht ever completed. For his subject matter Brecht returned to the materials of his greatest

theatrical success, *Die Dreigroschenoper. Dreigroschenroman* was published in Amsterdam in 1934; in 1937 an English translation appeared under the title of *A Penny for the Poor.* Events such as the Wall Street crash, the widespread joblessness in Germany, the attendant intensification of social and political conflicts, and the Nazis' rise to power persuaded Brecht to take a more committed stand against the evils of capitalism than is evident in the play. In a film treatment entitled *Die Beule* (The Welt, or Bruise) that preceded the novel Brecht elaborated on the rhetorical question asked by Macheath in *Die Dreigroschenoper,* "Was ist ein Einbruch in eine Bank gegen die Gründung einer Bank?" (What is the burgling of a bank [compared] to the founding of a bank?), by having Macheath, the former burglar, robber, and murderer, attain bourgeois respectability when he takes over a bank by legitimate means. The producers of the film, who had expected a treatment along the "culinary" lines of *Die Dreigroschenoper* and not a work with a pronounced political and social slant, rejected Brecht's work and produced a film that was not based on his script. Brecht sued the producers for breach of contract; in December 1930 he settled out of court for a large sum. He afterwards asserted in a lengthy essay that he had only engaged in the lawsuit to exhibit the flaws of the bourgeois judicial system that had disregarded his individual and artistic rights in the face of the economic power of the film company—surely a curious stance for a writer who

had professed his own "laxity in matters of intellectual property."

*Dreigroschenroman*, unlike a traditional novel, does not concentrate on individual conflicts and states of mind; rather, the chief ingredients of its two separate and intermittently intertwining plots are business deals, and suspense is created by the constant reversals of fortune in the economic realm that seriously affect the protagonists. The novel is set in London, then the financial capital of the world, during the Boer Wars around the turn of the century.

The first plot revolves around Macheath, now an ostensibly legitimate businessman with a slightly shady reputation, who has established a chain of B-stores—the name is derived from both *Billigkeit*

*Charles Laughton in Brecht's* Life of Galileo (Leben des Galilei) *at the Coronet Theater, Hollywood, in 1947*

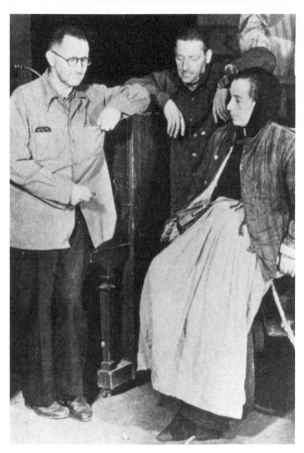

*From left: Brecht, the composer Paul Dessau, and Brecht's second wife, the actress Helene Weigel, during rehearsals for* Mutter Courage und ihre Kinder *at the Berliner Ensemble, 1949*

(cheapness) and *Betrug* (cheating)—in order to sell goods stolen by his gang directly to the public at reduced prices, eliminating the need for fences. In need of capital for the revitalization of his languishing business, he turns his attention to Polly Peachum. Polly's business sense prevails over her sensuality when she secretly marries the middle-aged, seemingly respectable Macheath instead of a young, impecunious clerk by whom she is pregnant. Complications arise when Polly's father wants to use the youth and beauty of his daughter in his own financial schemes. But in a murderous competition with two other store chains Macheath ultimately prevails; he reestablishes his authority over his gang, fuses his stores and those of his competitors into one big superchain, and becomes director of a bank. The fierce price war has resulted in the establishment of a monopoly; consumers will have to pay higher prices and the owners of B-store franchises will have to work even harder. Under such

conditions Peachum can no longer withhold his financial and moral support from his son-in-law, whom he meets for the first time at the end of the novel.

Peachum is in the center of the second plot. His organization functions as a monopoly in that he employs beggars as salaried employees and provides them with their means of production such as tattered clothes, artificial limbs, and the like; without his permission no poor devil can hope to obtain even a few coins. The enterprise has been rationalized to the point where large profits are no longer to be expected; hence the usually cautious and distrustful Peachum embarks upon a venture with the broker Coax, involving the purchase and resale of rotten ships to the government at a sizable profit. Peachum gradually realizes that Coax is planning to cheat him and his partners. He endeavors to get Coax on his side by proposing that he marry Polly; but she is already married to Macheath. Peachum has Macheath jailed on a trumped-up murder charge so that the latter will agree to a divorce from Polly. But Coax is not interested in marrying Polly anyway; he has already been intimate with her, and her father's poor financial condition makes her even less desirable. Peachum hires the invalid ex-soldier Fewkoombey, who is dependent on him for his meager livelihood, to kill Coax. Adapting Karl von Clausewitz's famous statement that war is a continuation of politics by different means, Peachum blandly tells Fewkoombey that murder is "*die Fortführung eines Geschäfts mit anderen Mitteln*" (the conduct of business by other means). Peachum acquires Coax's government contracts; but his profit is threatened one last time when one of the three vessels carrying troops to South Africa sinks in calm seas with no survivors. Instead of the profiteer Peachum and corrupt government officials being blamed, the Communists are accused of sabotaging the ships—a patriotic explanation that will enable Peachum, now allied with Macheath, to continue making profitable deals.

Farfetched as the plot of selling unfit ships to the government may seem, Brecht had read about similar incidents in a German translation of Gustavus Myers's three-volume *History of the Great American Fortunes* (1910). He employed a wide array of sources ranging from Greek and Roman antiquity to modern writers such as Arthur Conan Doyle and H. G. Wells. An avid reader of detective stories, Brecht used Conan Doyle for the creation of his London milieu. But a quotation from Rudyard Kipling's novel *The Light That Failed* (1890), "the sick man dies and the strong man fights," serves as a leitmotiv for Macheath, the ruthless entrepreneur who ultimately emerges victorious from the ferocious battles in the capitalist jungle. At the same time, Macheath is equated with Napoleon Bonaparte—an indication that for Brecht business and politics are not substantially different. More important, Macheath is described as a "geborener Führer" (born leader): he expresses a preference for strong men who are above politics and invokes the Nazis' "Schicksalsverbundenheit von Führer und Geführten" (the mutual attachment between a leader and his followers) that is designed to distract attention from class distinctions and the class struggle. Despite its historical guise, then, the novel makes pointed references to the situation at the time of its composition around 1933.

Brecht reserves his final thrust against capitalism for the epilogue, entitled "Das Pfund der Armen" (The Pound of the Poor). Fewkoombey dreams of a Last Judgment in which he is the presiding judge and Jesus Christ stands accused as the originator of the parable of the pounds from the gospels according to St. Luke and St. John. Whereas the bishop had used the parable to justify the "sacrificial death" of the drowned soldiers, who

were actually victims of profiteering and corruption, Fewkoombey wishes to find out what precisely the pound is that enabled the rich to become even richer and the poor to remain poor. He finally hits upon the solution: "Der Mensch [ist] des Menschen Pfund" (Man [is] the pound of man!). Whereupon Fewkoombey condemns to death Jesus Christ and all those who have spread the parable—including himself because he had done nothing to expose the falsehood that veiled the exploitation of man by man. Fewkoombey's dream of justice that exposes the Bible as an ideological prop of a society divided into classes of haves and have-nots is followed by a rude awakening that confirms the prevailing system of injustice: he is arrested and sentenced to be hanged—not for killing Coax but for a murder he did not commit.

*Dreigroschenroman* may not be, as is sometimes claimed, a thorough fictional analysis of capitalism. It nevertheless offers keen insight into human actions, which are depicted in behavioristic terms without psychologizing and with techniques that owe much to the medium of film, and it depicts the effects of economic factors in a society in which

*A scene from G. W. Pabst's 1931 film version of* Die Dreigroschenoper: *Macheath courts Polly in a café*

*Caricature of Brecht by B. F. Dolbin (Georg Müller Verlag)*

the power and wealth of the few are a result of the misery of the many.

Two lengthy short stories from the beginning of Brecht's exile were written in 1933 but only appeared in print posthumously—an indication of his reduced possibilities of publishing during his exile. They concern social themes with which Brecht had already dealt in Berlin. The story with the ironic English title "Safety First" takes place among sailors for whom economic necessity prevails over adventure—but a happy ending ensues. "Der Arbeitsplatz" (The Job) uses an ironic inversion of the precept from Genesis that one should earn one's bread by the sweat of one's brow to demonstrate the catastrophic effects of the Great Depression upon workers. Forced by hunger and desperation, a woman disguised as a man accepts a job in the place of her dead husband. Within a short time she acquires "male" qualities such as courage, determination, and presence of mind, showing that sex roles are determined by social and economic factors rather than by biology. The woman loses her job when she is found out. The story is an indictment

of the conditions that make such deception necessary.

Living abroad sharpened Brecht's perception for typically German traits and social behavior. Although written in Scandinavian exile, "Ein Irrtum" (1965; translated as "A Mistake," 1983) and "Eßkultur" (1943; translated as "A Question of Taste," 1983) contrast German and French customs and habits. The fragmentary "Die Geschichte des Giacomo Ui" (The History of Giacomo Ui, 1965) is a satire on the rise of a leader in Renaissance Italy. Told fifty years after the dictator's death, the story implies that the people who are preoccupied with the "lowly" task of making ends meet will eventually thwart the heroic ambitions of great men. Brecht used the name Ui again for the main figure in *Der aufhaltsame Aufstieg des Arturo Ui* (1957; translated as *The Resistible Rise of Arturo Ui*, 1976), a parable play about the rise to power of a Hitler-like gangster in Chicago.

The only collection of prose fiction to appear in Brecht's lifetime, *Kalendergeschichten* (1948; translated as *Tales from the Calendar*, 1961), comprises eight stories: "Der Augsburger Kreidekreis" (The Augsburg Chalk Circle), "Die zwei Söhne" (Two Sons), "Das Experiment" (The Experiment), "Der Mantel des Ketzers" (The Heretic's Coat), "Cäsar und sein Legionär" (Caesar and His Legionary), "Der Soldat von La Ciotat" (The Soldier of La Ciotat), "Der verwundete Sokrates" (Socrates Wounded), and "Die unwürdige Greisin" (The Unseemly Old Lady). Most of the stories pose the kinds of questions that are raised in the poem "Fragen eines lesenden Arbeiters" (Questions from a Worker Who Reads), which is also included in the anthology: "Cäsar schlug die Gallier./Hatte er nicht wenigstens einen Koch bei sich?" (Caesar beat the Gauls./Did he not even have a cook with him?) Such questioning suggests that history has been written from the viewpoint of the rulers and great men; the suffering of those who helped them achieve victories and accomplish great deeds has been ignored. In reviving the popular genre of Kalendergeschichten, which had flourished particularly during the nineteenth century, Brecht wished to introduce an alternative reading of history without offering learned historiography. Heroes either do not appear in the stories or their roles are subject to close scrutiny; their willing and unwilling tools and victims tend to be the center of interest. In "Der Soldat von La Ciotat" the narrator observes in a small southern French town a statue of a French soldier that, it turns out, is really a motionless human being covered by a coat of bronze paint.

As a result of having been buried alive at Verdun during World War I, the soldier has acquired an "inexplicable disease" that enables him to make his living by posing as a motionless statue. In reflecting upon the matter, the narrator envisions the soldier as an embodiment of all the latter's predecessors throughout the millennia who have made wars and conquests possible through their acceptance of sacrifice. The narrator ends his reflections by asking whether the terrible affliction of the soldier—both his motionlessness and his willingness to suffer stoically—cannot be cured after all.

Caesar himself appears in "Cäsar und sein Legionär"; in his downfall he contributes to the ruin of his faithful legionary and his family. "Die Trophäen des Lukullus" (1967; translated as "Lucullus's Trophies," 1983), a story that was not incorporated in *Kalendergeschicten* but was more fully developed in the various versions of the play *Das Verhör des Lukullus* (1951; translated as *The Trial of Lucullus*, 1943), features a fictitious dialogue between the Roman general Lucullus and the poet Lucretius, author of the philosophical poem *De rerum natura* (On the Nature of Things). Lucretius settles the issue of Lucullus's fame and accomplishments by pointing to a cherry tree that the general had imported to Europe from Asia, his one deed that is beneficial to mankind.

In contrast to the protagonist's stoic—but ultimately mindless—courage in "Der Soldat von La Ciotat," in the humorous "Der verwundete Sokrates" Socrates, a reluctant draftee and pacifist, is prevented from fleeing from a battle with the Persians when a thorn lodges in his foot so that he is unable to walk. In desperation he begins to defend himself vigorously; the Athenians rally around him and are ultimately victorious. Socrates is declared the hero of the battle but refuses all honors because he then would have to limp in public and reveal the unheroic source of his brave stand. In the end, he summons courage and confesses—whereupon the Athenian general Alcibiades congratulates him for special bravery. Socrates has shown the stature of a great teacher and thinker whose true courage has nothing whatever to do with heroic exploits on the battlefield. "Der Mantel des Ketzers," an episode from Giordano Bruno's incarceration by the Venetian inquisition in the 1590s, complements "Der verwundete Sokrates." Bruno requires all his energies to fight his extradition to Rome, where he will be burned at the stake. Yet he still makes serious efforts to pay a poor tailor for his overcoat. In contrast to the protagonist of *Leben des Galilei*, who is indifferent toward his fellow men and re-

cants his heliocentric theory, the "heretic" Bruno combines social compassion with dedication to truth. In "Das Experiment" a clear distinction is made between Francis Bacon the unsavory politician, on the one hand, and Bacon the eminent scientist, on the other. Only in the latter capacity is Bacon an admirable figure as herald of the new scientific age and transmitter of inquisitiveness and knowledge to an underprivileged stable boy. Brecht later used Bacon's anti-Aristotelian *Novum Organum* as the model for his *Kleines Organon für das Theater* (1953; translated as "A Short Organum for the Theatre," 1964).

The memorable mother figures in Brecht's plays resulted from his conviction that mothers are more interested than fathers in the future of their children and, hence, in a just social order without war and exploitation. Several stories in *Kalendergeschichten* have mothers as their protagonists, notably "Der Augsburger Kreidekreis," a preliminary stage of *Der kaukasische Kreidekreis* (1954; translated as *The Caucasian Chalk Circle*, 1948), one of Brecht's best-known plays. The play begins with a prologue that takes place in the Soviet Union at the end of World War II, then moves backward in time to feudal Georgia; for the setting of his story, however, Brecht chose his hometown during the Thirty Years' War. A Protestant tanner is killed when the Catholic troops of the emperor occupy the Free City of Augsburg. His wife spends so much time packing her dresses and jewelry that she barely manages to escape the soldiers and forgets to take her baby along. The child is rescued by the woman's servant girl, who has no reason to be charitable because of the bad treatment she has received from her mistress. When peace is established between Catholics and Protestants, the natural mother reclaims the child, who is heir to her dead husband's considerable estate. The servant girl, who has made many sacrifices for the child, goes to court and is fortunate in having her case heard by a learned and popular judge. His decision is based on a test, derived from an ancient Chinese play, in which the child is placed in a chalk circle drawn on the floor. The mothers are to try to pull him out of the circle to prove the strength of their love. The wily judge awards the child to the servant girl because she lets go of the child's arm for fear of hurting him when the real mother starts violently pulling his other arm. Thus the judge proceeds from the child's interests and implicitly postulates a new definition of motherhood that is based on the bondage created by work and suffering rather than on biological factors. In *Der kaukasische Kreidekreis* this new definition of motherhood is expanded to promote a new kind of thinking with regard to property rights.

In the chronologically last story of *Kalendergeschichten*, "Die zwei Söhne," written around 1946, a German peasant woman notices a striking similarity between a Russian prisoner of war and her son. The uncanny resemblance enables her to perceive the suffering of the undernourished Russian, who is working as forced labor on the farm. This emotional identification enables her to act in a truly humanitarian fashion in violation of Nazi ideology and regulations prohibiting aid to "subhumans." When her son, who is completely indoctrinated by Nazi propaganda, returns from the front and is determined to continue the savage fighting, she delivers him bound with ropes to the Russians in order to save his life—just as she had saved the life of her "second" son, the Russian, by enabling him to flee. That there are limits to the sacrifices that may be expected of mothers and of women in general is evident in "Die unwürdige Greisin." The narrator expresses approval of the unorthodox life-style that his grandmother belatedly enjoyed after having spent most of her life as a virtual servant of her husband and children, in accordance with the accepted role of women in the early twentieth century.

Brecht reacted to private as well as political events by writing short prose pieces and reflections for the collection *Me-ti: Buch der Wendungen* (Me-ti: The Book of Twists and Turns) from approximately 1934 to 1950; the book was only published after his death. The "Chinese style" of the collection is attributable to Brecht's reading a German translation of the writings of the fifth-century B.C. Chinese philosopher Me-ti or Mo Ti and also to the title of the Confucian *I-Ching* or *Book of Changes*. But apart from endowing the collection with the aura of ancient wisdom, Brecht made comparatively little use of his Chinese sources. The Chinese-sounding names only thinly disguise the identities of philosophers and thinkers, such as Karl Marx (Karmeh) and Friedrich Engels (Eh-fu, Fu-en, En-fu); twentieth-century politicians, such as Lenin (Mi-en-leh) and Stalin (Ni-en); and Brecht himself (Kin-jeh and other names). Thematically, the pieces primarily revolve around the "Große Methode" (great method), a materialistic, dialectical way of thinking, and the "Große Ordnung" (great order), a socialist organization of the economy and society. Great method and great order correspond to each other; in the absence of the former the latter cannot be fully achieved. Hence the social

practice of the Soviet Union (Su), with its lack of freedom of expression and assembly, and the arbitrariness of its authorities, is far removed from the envisioned future society in which such virtues as heroism and sacrifice can be dispensed with and the "Verpflichtung des Einzelnen gegenüber dem Staat" (the obligation of the individual toward the state) is minimal.

Much of Brecht's criticism of the Soviet Union is focused on Stalin's baleful influence. Brecht never spoke out publicly against Stalin's regime of terror for fear of providing ammunition to the enemies of the only socialist country during a time of Nazi aggression. In view of the disappearance in the Soviet Union of some of his friends, such as the actress Carola Neher, one cannot discount concern for his own personal safety as another motive for Brecht's silence. Even in the then unpublished *Me-ti* Brecht's occasional criticism of Stalin is muted by apologetic tones. Perhaps, as Knopf suggests, the aphoristic and unsystematically composed *Me-ti* remained a fragment on account of Brecht's somewhat uncritical portrayal of the great order that did not at all correspond to the Stalinist reality of the Soviet Union before the outbreak of World War II.

Brecht, ordinarily reticent about his private life, devoted "Geschichten von Lai-tu" (Stories about Lai-tu) in *Me-ti* to his relationship with Ruth Berlau, a Danish actress he met in the fall of 1934 after he and his family settled near Svendborg on the Danish isle of Fyn, where they lived from December 1933 to April 1939. Berlau became his mistress, collaborator, and lifelong companion, a relationship that she depicted subsequently in *Brechts Lai-tu* (1985). Although the Lai-tu stories are somewhat autobiographical, Brecht portrayed his relationship with Berlau, which was often stormy, as completely harmonious in accordance with the new kinds of social and personal interaction that the great method anticipated. Love, then, is no longer primarily an expression of subjective feelings or of sexual desires; rather, it is an act in which the partners cooperate in order to attain a friendly disposition toward that which is socially productive. Brecht was, of course, still married to Helene Weigel, who not only tolerated—albeit grudgingly—Brecht's polygamy but in some instances attempted to discreetly facilitate Brecht's relations with other women. But in the end she triumphed over her rivals; Esslin relates an anecdote told him by one of Brecht's closest friends about Brecht's funeral: "There were five widows, all in black. Four were crying. One was laughing:

*Brecht receiving the Stalin Freedom Prize in Moscow, 1955*

Helene Weigel, the legitimate one who inherited the mantle of the great man's fame."

A projected major novel, *Die Geschäfte des Herrn Julius Cäsar* (The Business Dealings of Mr. Julius Caesar, 1957), occupied Brecht from approximately 1937 to 1939 but remained a fragment—albeit a substantial one—and was not published until after his death. Like other exiled writers, Brecht regarded the historical novel as a vehicle for alluding to and taking a stand on contemporary events. Brecht's purpose in the novel is to show Caesar as the protypical dictator whose rise to power in the class-ridden society of Rome can be explained in terms of economic interests. But Brecht does not engage in a facile equation of Hitler's dictatorship with that of Caesar; unlike most other exiled writers of historical novels, Brecht insisted on factual accuracy in his work and perused a host of sources from Roman antiquity, including the writings of Caesar, Cicero, Plutarch, and Suetonius. In seeking to expose the inner workings of political processes Brecht took issue with one of his chief sources, the historian Theodor Mommsen's influential *Römische Geschichte* (Roman History, 1854-1856). Mommsen had depicted Caesar as the only creative genius that the ancient world had produced—precisely the kind of historiographical hero worship that Brecht aimed to abolish.

Brecht depicts Caesar from a perspective designed to destroy all illusions of his greatness. A young historian reports on his visit to the estate of the banker Mummlius Spicer in 24 B.C., twenty years after Caesar's death. He wishes to gather materials for a biography of the great politician, and Spicer is in possession of the diaries of Caesar's secretary, the slave Rarus. Although the historian is aware that the legend surrounding Caesar will be difficult to penetrate and that Caesar had written books with the aim of deceiving posterity, he is amazed when he learns the full extent of Caesar's business dealings from Spicer; from others who had known Caesar; and from the diaries, which he reproduces without comment. These accounts reveal a corrupt Caesar who, constantly beset by huge debts, used politics to promote the business interests of his creditors—the bankers, merchants, and owners of shipping lines who were engaged in a struggle for a larger share of profits with the old aristocracy, the landowning senatorial class of which Caesar was actually a member. Although the people were entitled to vote, they usually sold their vote to the highest bidder and were not an independent political force.

Brecht's relentless concentration on economics and politics caused even his friends Walter Benjamin and Fritz Sternberg, with whom he discussed the novel, to object to the lack of "human interest" and the employment of a valet's perspective. (According to the philosopher Hegel, there are no heroes for a valet because he himself is not a hero but a valet.) But such criticism misses the mark in that Brecht was not intent on writing a traditional psychological novel; rather, he wanted to draw attention to the economic determinants of political life in a quasi-documentary, objective mode that, like a film, presented the protagonist from the outside.

After the German invasion of Denmark and Norway in April 1940, Brecht, his family, and Margarete Steffin, a collaborator from Berlin who had become Brecht's mistress, left Sweden, where they had spent about a year, for Finland. The last major prose project that Brecht undertook in Europe was *Flüchtlingsgespräche* (Conversations of Refugees), on which he worked from October through December 1940. The series of dialogues involves two German refugees in Helsinki, the bourgeois physicist Ziffel

*Martin Florchinger (left) and Hermann Hiesgen in a scene from Brecht's play* Schweyk im zweiten Weltkrieg *at the Berliner Ensemble*

and the worker Kalle, who reflect on the state of the world with considerable grim humor. The work remained unfinished and was published posthumously in 1961. Whereas the experiences reflected in the conversations, such as the beginning of a scarcity of food, are largely autobiographical, the form—a kind of epic Socratic dialogue—is indebted to Diderot's novel *Jacques le fataliste et son maître* (1796). Diderot's work also contributed to Brecht's exploration of the dialectics inherent in the relationship of master and servant in *Herr Puntila und sein Knecht* (1948; translated as *Mr. Puntila and His Man Matti*, 1977), a play that Brecht began writing in Finland. In the refugee conversations the master-servant relationship has been retained in modified fashion in the relationship of bourgeois intellectual and worker. But in contrast to *Herr Puntila und sein Knecht* the physicist becomes class-conscious and approaches the position of the worker. Far from being an ideological tract, however, the conversations are infused with the tone and idiosyncratic diction of Jaroslaw Hašek's immortal character Schweik in *The Good Soldier Schweik* (1920-1923), about whom Brecht wrote his play *Schweyk im Zweiten Weltkrieg* (Schweik in the Second World War, 1957). Schweik's uncanny ability to state the obvious without regard to obfuscating conventions is evident, for example, in Kalle's wistful remark that passports are the noblest part of human beings on account of their paramount importance for those in exile.

Brecht himself was anxiously waiting for the passports that would enable him and his entourage to enter the United States. America beckoned since, after the outbreak of World War II in 1939, Europe increasingly had begun to resemble a trap for the exiles. One might have expected Brecht to prefer the Soviet Union to the United States, but Brecht—who, according to Esslin, showed "uncanny shrewdness" in matters of survival—was not going to take any risks by settling in Stalin's Soviet Union, whose artistic climate was inimical to his literary pursuits. Brecht's stylized theater ran counter to the brand of realism propagated in Moscow by the literary historian Georg Lukács and other exiled Communist writers. Hence, after the passports finally arrived, Brecht's party left Finland in May 1941 and traveled via Moscow to Vladivostok in Siberia, the embarkation point for the West Coast of the United States. In Moscow Brecht had to leave Steffin behind; she died of consumption shortly afterwards.

After arriving in California, Brecht settled in Santa Monica. Although he despised the unadul-

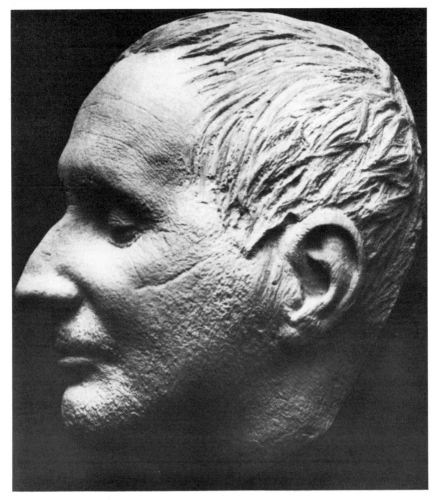

*Death mask of Brecht (Ullstein)*

terated commercialism of the film industry, the necessity of making a living left him with little choice but to try to sell his film treatments to the studios. Unexpectedly, he found himself in a position akin to that of his character Tui, whose name is an abbreviation of *Tellekt-uell-ins* (actually *Intellektuelle* or intellectuals) and signifies those who "lend" their intellects to the highest bidder at a time when everything has become a saleable commodity. Brecht had been planning to write a novel about Tuis since the 1930s; yet unlike the substantial Julius Caesar fragment, the Tui project never progressed significantly beyond the conceptual stage and the collection of materials. Eventually Brecht wrote a play, *Turandot oder Der Kongreß der Weißwäscher* (Turandot or the Congress of Whitewashers, 1968) that is based on some of the Tui materials. It is set in a mythical China and satirizes the intellectuals who too willingly serve as apologists for the prevailing, unjust order.

In California Brecht studied the behavior of his fellow exiles Theodor W. Adorno, Max Horkheimer, and Herbert Marcuse, all of whom he considered Tuis. But Brecht believed that in America the Tui novel would lose its satirical thrust because the public sale of opinions and theories went on there without pretense of intellectual independence; hence the unmasking of the intellectuals' dependence on the buyers of their products would be superfluous. In the trenchant and wistful poem "Hollywood" (1951) Brecht expressed his ambivalent feelings about his situation: "Jeden Morgen, mein Brot zu verdienen/Gehe ich auf den Markt, wo Lügen gekauft werden./Hoffnungsvoll/Reihe ich mich ein zwischen die Verkäufer." (Every day, to earn my daily bread/I go to the market where lies are bought/ Hopefully/I take up my place among the sellers.) Despite Brecht's genuine interest in film, a medium to which he had devoted considerable attention in Germany, he found the

59

subordinate role of the writer in the film industry insufferable; his only major contribution was a collaboration with the director Fritz Lang and the writer John Wexley on the outline and screenplay for the anti-Nazi film *Hangmen also Die* (1943). The collaboration ended on a discordant note: although Brecht was paid for his work, he did not receive the credit he had wanted.

The end of World War II opened the door for Brecht to return to Europe. After an appearance before the House Committee on Un-American Activities in Washington, D.C., on 30 October 1947, in which Brecht craftily dispelled the committee members' suspicions about his Communist leanings, he left the United States—for all practical purposes, unknown and unrecognized. Only after his death did his plays and other works begin to be widely known in the United States, establishing his reputation as one of the most influential practi-

*Brecht's grave in the Dorotheen Cemetery, East Berlin*

tioners and theoreticians of the theater in modern times.

Brecht's decision to settle in East Berlin, which in 1949 became the capital of the German Democratic Republic (GDR), was no doubt influenced by the opportunities offered him there—notably the chance to stage his own plays in his "epic" style in a theater of his own. Although he was not always appreciated in the GDR, Brecht made the Berliner Ensemble, a troupe that was nominally headed by his wife, world famous. Beyond producing his own plays, Brecht rebuilt the theater's repertory by adapting plays by Shakespeare and Molière, among others. The playwright's politics continued to be of interest: Brecht's ambivalent attitude toward the workers' uprising in East Berlin and the GDR on 17 June 1953 rekindled the debate about his beliefs.

Brecht's health was beginning to deteriorate; he developed heart trouble, and in the spring of 1955 he suffered a serious illness. After attending a rehearsal on 10 August 1956, he began feeling very tired; during the night of 13-14 August his condition became critical, and he died of a coronary thrombosis shortly before midnight on 14 August. Even after his death Brecht continued to be a provocation. When the Berlin Wall was erected in August 1961, Brecht's plays were temporarily banned in a number of theaters in the Federal Republic of Germany—an ineffectual attempt to blame the playwright for the policies of the GDR.

Brecht's prose work, which encompasses four volumes in the twenty-two-volume edition of his works (1967-1969), is clearly overshadowed by his plays and poetry. Yet in recent years some detailed studies dealing with the prose fiction have been published, notably those by Klaus-Detlef Müller (1980), Wolfgang Jeske (1984), and Jan Knopf (1984). As of 1986 these studies are only available in German; in fact, not all of Brecht's prose fiction has been translated into English. Although there is a substantial body of secondary literature on Brecht in English, such works tend either to be biographical or to concentrate on analyses of the plays. Inasmuch as the industry of scholarly writings on Brecht shows no sign of abating, it is to be expected that Brecht's prose fiction will be discovered by critics writing in English in the not too distant future.

**Letters:**

*Briefe,* edited by Günter Glaeser, 2 volumes (Frankfurt am Main: Suhrkamp, 1981).

**Bibliographies:**

Klaus-Dietrich Petersen, *Bertolt-Brecht-Bibliographe* (Bad Homburg: Gehlen, 1968);

Reinhold Grimm, *Bertolt Brecht,* third edition (Stuttgart: Metzler, 1971);

Jan Knopf, *Bertolt Brecht. Ein Kritischer Forschungsbericht* (Frankfurt am Main: Athenäum Taschenbuchverlag, 1974);

Stephan Bock, *Brecht, Bertolt. Auswahl- und Ergänzungs- bibliographie* (Bochum: Brockmeyer, 1979).

**Biographies:**

Frederic Ewen, *Bertolt Brecht: His Life, His Art and His Times* (New York: Citadel Press, 1967);

Klaus Völker, *Bertolt Brecht: Eine Biographie* (Munich: Hanser, 1976); translated by John Nowell as *Brecht: A Biography* (New York: Seabury Press, 1978);

James K. Lyon, *Bertolt Brecht in America* (Princeton: Princeton University Press, 1980);

Ronald Hayman, *Brecht: A Biography* (New York: Oxford University Press, 1983);

Bruce Cook, *Brecht in Exile* (New York: Holt, Rinehart & Winston, 1983);

Ruth Berlau, *Brechts Lai-tu: Erinnerungen und Notate,* edited by Hans Bunge (Darmstadt: Luchterhand, 1985).

**References:**

Eric Bentley, *The Brecht Commentaries, 1943-1980* (New York: Grove Press, 1981);

Kirsten Boie-Grotz, *Brecht—Der unbekannte Erzähler: Die Prosa 1913-1934* (Stuttgart: Klett-Cotta, 1978);

Keith A. Dickson, *Towards Utopia: A Study of Brecht* (Oxford: Clarendon Press, 1978);

Martin Esslin, *Brecht: A Choice of Evils* (London: Eyre & Spottiswoode, 1959); republished as *Brecht: The Man and His Work* (Garden City: Doubleday, 1960);

Claude Hill, *Bertolt Brecht* (Boston: Twayne, 1975);

Wolfgang Jeske, *Bertolt Brechts Poetik des Romans* (Frankfurt am Main: Suhrkamp, 1984);

Jan Knopf, *Brecht-Handbuch: Lyrik, Prosa, Schriften* (Stuttgart: Metzler, 1984);

Siegfried Mews and Herbert Knust, eds., *Essays on Brecht: Theater and Politics* (Chapel Hill: University of North Carolina Press, 1974; New York: AMS Press, 1979);

Klaus-Detlef Müller, *Brecht-Kommentar zur erzählenden Prosa* (Munich: Winkler, 1980);

Patty Lee Parmalee, *Brecht's America* (Columbus: Ohio State University Press, 1981);

David Pike, *Lukács and Brecht* (Chapel Hill: University of North Carolina Press, 1985);

Antony Tatlow, *The Mask of Evil. Brecht's Response to the Poetry, Theatre, and Thought of China and Japan* (Bern: Peter Lang, 1977);

Betty Nance Weber and Hubert Heinen, eds., *Bertolt Brecht: Political Theory and Literary Practice* (Athens: University of Georgia Press, 1980).

**Papers:**

Brecht's papers are housed in the Bertolt-Brecht-Archiv, 104 (East) Berlin, Chausseestraße 125. An inventory of the papers is provided in Hertha Ramthun, ed., *Bertolt-Brecht-Archiv. Bestandsverzeichnis des literarischen Nachlasses,* 4 volumes (Berlin: Aufbau Verlag, 1969-1973).

# Willi Bredel

## (2 May 1901-27 October 1964)

Richard H. Lawson
*University of North Carolina at Chapel Hill*

BOOKS: *Marat der Volksfreund* (Hamburg: Neuer Verlag für revolutionäre Literatur, 1924);

*Maschinenfabrik N & K: Ein Roman aus dem proletarischen Alltag* (Berlin: Internationaler Arbeiter-Verlag, 1930);

*Rosenhofstraße: Roman einer Hamburger Arbeiterstraße* (Berlin: Internationaler Arbeiter-Verlag, 1931);

*Paragraf v zashchitu sobstvennosti* (Moscow: Gosudarstvennoe izdatel'stvo khudozhestvennoi literatury, 1933); translated into German by Regina Czora as *Der Eigentumsparagraph: Roman* (Berlin: Dietz, 1961);

*Die Prüfung: Roman aus einem Konzentrationslager* (London: Malik, 1934);

*Der Antifaschist Edgar André vom Tode bedroht* (Strasbourg: Éditions Prométhée, 1936?);

*Vor den Kulissen* (Moscow: Verlagsgenorenschaft ausländischer Arbeiter, 1936);

*Der Regimentskommandeur: Nikolai Schtschors: Ein Held im Kampf gegen deutsche Okkupanten* (Engels: Deutscher Staats-Verlag, 1936);

*Der Spitzel und andere Erzählungen* (London: Malik, 1936);

*Dein unbekannter Bruder: Roman aus dem III. Reich* (London: Malik, 1937);

*Begegnung am Ebro: Aufzeichnungen eines Kriegskommissars* (Paris: Editions du 10. Mai, 1939; revised, Berlin: Lied der Zeit-Verlagsgellschaft, 1948);

*Nach dem Sieg* (Moscow: Mezhdunarodnaja kniga, 1939); revised as *Sieger ohne Sieg: Eine Erzählung um Gneisenau* (Weimar: Thüringer Volksverlag, 1953);

*Der Kommissar am Rhein: Historische Erzählungen* (Moscow: Mezhdunarodnaja kniga, 1940); revised as *Der Kommissar am Rhein und andere historische Erzählungen* (Berlin: Aufbau, 1946);

*Pater Brakel und andere Erzählungen* (Kiev: Ukrgosnatsmenizdat, 1940);

*Scharnhorst, Gneisenau, Clausewitz und die bürgerliche Revolution von 1789* (Moscow: Mezhdunarodnaja kniga, 1940);

*Portrait of Willi Bredel by Bert Heller*

*Der Auswanderer: Der Tod des Siegfried Allzufromm: Zwei Erzählungen über die Judenverfolgungen im faschistischen Deutschland* (Moscow: Mezhdunarodnaja kniga, 1941);

*Der Moorbauer: Antifaschistische Kurzgeschichten* (Moscow: Mezhdunarodnaja kniga, 1941);

*Kurzgeschichten aus Hitlerdeutschland* (Moscow: Verlag für fremdsprachige Literatur, 1942);

*Das Vermächtnis des Frontsoldaten: Novelle* (Moscow: Verlag für fremdsprachige Literatur, 1942; Ludwigslust: Sauerland, 1945);

*Verwandte und Bekannte: Roman* (Moscow: Verlag für fremdsprachige Literatur, 1943; republished as *Verwandte und Bekannte*, volume 1: *Die Väter* (Berlin: Aufbau, 1948);

*Der Sonderführer: Erzählung* (Moscow: Verlag für fremdsprachige Literatur, 1944; Ludwigslust: Sauerland, 1946);

*Um Deutschlands Zukunft: Rede über den Nürnberger Prozeß vor der Lehrerschaft Schwerins* (Schwerin: Verlag demokratischer Erneuerung, 1946);

*Ernst Thälmann: Ein Beitrag zu einem politischen Lebensbild* (Berlin: Dietz, 1948);

*Verwandte und Bekannte*, volume 2: *Die Söhne* (Berlin: Aufbau, 1949; revised and expanded, 1951; revised again, 1960);

*Das Schweigende Dorf, und andere Erzählungen.* (Rostock: Hinstorff, 1949);

*Die kulturelle Verantwortung der Arbeiterklasse: Vier Referate von W. Bredel, W. Girnus, S. Heymann, W. Maschke aus Anlaß der Weimartage der Aktivisten vom 9.-12. VI. 1949* (Berlin: Die freie Gewerkschaft Verlags-Gesellschaft, 1949);

*Fünfzig Tage* (Berlin: Neues Leben, 1950);

*Sieben Dichter* (Schwerin: Petermänkin, 1950; revised, 1952);

*Die Vitalien-Brüder: Ein historischer Roman für die Jugend* (Schwerin: Petermänkin, 1950);

*Über die Aufgaben der Literatur und Literaturkritik: Vortrag auf dem 3. Deutschen Schriftstellerkongreß in Berlin, Mai 1952* (Berlin: Deutscher Schriftstellerverband, 1952);

*Verwandte und Bekannte*, volume 3: *Die Enkel* (Berlin: Aufbau, 1953);

*Ernst Thälmann: Literarisches Szenarium*, by Bredel and Michael Tschesno-Hell, 2 volumes (Berlin: Henschel, 1953-1955);

*Vom Ebro zur Wolga: Drei Begegnungen* (Berlin: Aufbau, 1954);

*Die Fahne der Solidarität (Auszüge)* (Berlin: Ministerium des Innern, 1955);

*Here is the "Lincoln"* (Berlin: Ministerium des Innern, 1955);

*Marcel, der junge Sansculotte* (Berlin: Ministerium des Innern, 1955);

*Das Gastmahl im Dattelgarten* (Berlin: Aufbau, 1956);

*Der rote General* (Berlin: Ministerium für Nationale Verteidigung, 1956);

*Auf den Heerstraßen der Zeit: Erzählungen* (Berlin: Aufbau, 1957);

*Für dich—Freiheit! Kurzgeschichten, Skizzen und Anekdoten* (Berlin: Ministerium für Nationale Verteidigung, 1959);

*Ein neues Kapitel* (Berlin: Aufbau, 1959; revised and expanded, 1961);

*Unter Türmen und Masten: Geschichte einer Stadt in Geschichten* (Schwerin: Petermänkin, 1960; revised and expanded, 1961);

*Willi Bredel: Dokumente seines Lebens* (Berlin: Aufbau, 1961);

*The Death of General Moreau and Other Stories*, translated by Joan Becker (Berlin: Seven Seas, 1962);

*Ein neues Kapitel: Chronik einer Wandlung*, 2 volumes (Berlin: Aufbau, 1964);

*Frühlingssonate: Erzählungen* (Berlin: Aufbau, 1971);

*Der Generalintendant des Königs und andere Erzählungen* (Berlin: Aufbau, 1974);

*Publizistik: Zur Literatur und Geschichte* (Berlin: Aufbau, 1976);

*Spanienkrieg*, edited by Manfred Hahn, 2 volumes (Berlin: Aufbau, 1977);

*Erzählungen*, 2 volumes (Berlin: Aufbau, 1981).

OTHER: *Päpste, Pfaffen und Mönche im Spiegel der Literatur: Ausgewählt und mit Anmerkungen versehen*, edited by Bredel (Kiev: Staatsverlag der nationalen Minderheiten der UdSSR, 1940);

Charles Dickens, *Oliver Twist*, introduction by Bredel (Potsdam: Märkischer Druck & Verlag, 1949);

*Bibliothek fortschrittlicher deutscher Schriftsteller*, edited by Bredel (Berlin & Leipzig: Volk & Wissen, 1950);

S. Wygodski, *Im Kessel*, introduction by Bredel (Berlin: Lied der Zeit, 1950);

J. Izcaray, *Casto Garcia Roza: Geschichte eines spanischen Helden*, translated from Spanish by E. Klemperer, introduction by Bredel (Berlin: Dietz, 1952);

M. Andersen-Nexö, *Erinnerungen*, translated from Danish by E. Harthern, afterword by Bredel (Berlin: Aufbau, 1953);

Erich Weinert, *Memento Stalingrad: Frontnotizbuch. Worte als Partisanen. Aus dem Bericht über dem Nationalkomitee "Freies Deutschland,"* edited by Bredel (Berlin: Volk & Welt, 1957);

*Erich Weinert: Eine Auswahl. Gedichte. Erzählungen, Skizzen, Reden*, edited by Bredel (Berlin: Ministerium für nationale Verteidigung, 1958);

*Erich Weinert: Ein Dichter unserer Zeit. Aufsätze aus drei Jahrzehnten. Mit Zwischentexten*, edited by Bredel (Berlin: Volk & Welt, 1958);

*Neunhundert Tage: Zeugnisse von der heldenhaften Verteidigung Leningrads im Großen Vaterländischen Krieg*, foreword by Bredel (Berlin: Dietz, 1959).

To paraphrase the self-appointed preceptor of German Communist authors, Georg Lukács (before he ceased including Bredel in his purview), Willi Bredel was a highly talented writer capable of artistic growth. He conceived all-embracing epic frames; but there was an unresolved conflict between Bredel's concepts and his narrative style, for the latter was more appropriate to press releases than to art. In Lukács's 1931 six-page critique of Bredel's earliest novels the critic faulted the proletarian author further for the absence of "living men and vibrant, changing, fluid relationships between human beings" as well as for the failure to apply "dialectics in literary representation." Bredel's marginal importance in the West probably lies in his role as a Communist literary practitioner of genuine working-class origin; he was not, as were Lukács and Bertolt Brecht, a convert from the more privileged classes. In the Communist bloc Bredel is of fundamental importance as an extremely popular proselytizer and a practitioner of an eclectic—and frequently criticized—socialist realism.

Most of Bredel's fiction has an autobiographical or historical background. His prevalent theme is the exaltation of the Communist party as the champion of the German working class, or at least the exaltation of the party line of the moment, even when he surely knew it to be based on falsehood. For example, the party persisted in the comforting illusion that Hitler's Germany was fairly crawling with Communist resistance—an illusion (or propaganda strategy) unsupported by facts. When the party, already fully in the embrace of Stalinism, called on the emigrant authors to glorify this all but nonexistent resistance, Bredel dutifully complied by delivering *Dein unbekannter Bruder* (Your Unknown Brother, 1937).

Bredel, the son of a tobacconist, was born in Hamburg on 2 May 1901. At the age of fifteen he left school and became an apprentice lathe operator in an armature factory and a member of the Young Socialist Workers. In 1919 he was one of the first members of the Communist Party of Germany. He studied Marxism-Leninism and read Shakespeare, Tolstoy, Ibsen, Strindberg, Balzac, Victor Hugo, and Georg Büchner. For participating in the October 1923 rebellion in Hamburg he was sentenced to two years' imprisonment. In his cell he secretly wrote his first published work, a study of the French revolutionary Jean-Paul Marat (1924).

*Bredel during his 1930-1932 imprisonment for writing exposés for Communist journals*

After a brief period as a journalist Bredel went to sea as a machinist's assistant and leader of the Communist cell on the motorship *Barbara*. Back ashore and working as a lathe operator at the Nagel & Kaemp machine factory, he wrote exposés for Communist journals, one of which brought him another two-year prison sentence. Again he wrote while imprisoned, this time his first two novels. *Maschinenfabrik N & K* (The N & K Machine Factory, 1930) thematically and structurally prefigures most of his subsequent work. His theme is the revolutionary struggle by the Communist party on behalf of the workers, in this case against the backsliding of the Social Democrats and the older workers in the factory. The structure of the novel is highly episodic; and in some fifty episodes centered almost exclusively on the factory, the young Communist zealot Alfred Melmster reveals to the younger workers—there is where the future lies—

the gross inequities of the workplace and agitates for a strike.

In *Rosenhofstraße* (Rose Court Street, 1931), Bredel switches his focus from the factory to the life of the workers at home. But here again Communist agitation plays the central thematic role. The young Communist Fritz Burmester's agitation culminates in a rent strike. Already in his second novel Bredel brings his collective hero, the tightly organized street cell, into confrontation with fascism.

Released from prison in 1932, Bredel undertook his first trip to the Soviet Union. The third book of what Bredel termed "a little trilogy from the birth-years of proletarian-revolutionary literature" is *Paragraf v zashchitu sobstvennosti*, first published in Moscow in a Russian translation in 1933. The title, which means "The Property Paragraph," refers to that paragraph in the Nazi program recognizing "honorably acquired" private property. The property of the laundry owner Volkmar, however, has been acquired through exploitation of female workers, including the young Communist Lieschen Gebbert. When one of Gebbert's cowork-

*Dust jacket for the Moscow edition of Bredel's novel based on his experiences in a concentration camp in 1933-1934*

ers, Olli Kunze, is fired, a strike is orchestrated by the Communist functionary Ernst Helming. The murder of Helming by the Nazis provides a symbol for the embattled proletarians, whose ultimate victory is assured. *Paragraf v zashchitu sobstvennosti*, whose theme is essentially that of its predecessors, could, of course, not be published in Germany after the Nazi seizure of power; it first saw print in German in 1961 as *Der Eigentumsparagraph*, a back translation of the Russian version of 1933.

In Hamburg in March 1933 Bredel was arrested again and served thirteen months in a concentration camp, an experience reflected in his best-known novel, *Die Prüfung* (The Test, 1934). *Die Prüfung* is Bredel's semifictionalized but basically honest account of what he saw, heard, thought, and endured during his incarceration in the camp. More than simply chronicling the horrors, Bredel tries to uncover the motives that lie behind the actions and reactions of the Nazi jailers and their victims. *Die Prüfung* was translated into seventeen languages and is said to have attained a printing of 800,000 copies in the Soviet Union alone.

On being released Bredel fled to Czechoslovakia and from there to the Soviet Union, where, beginning in 1936, he edited with Bertolt Brecht and Lion Feuchtwanger the German-language literary propaganda monthly *Das Wort*. In the Spanish civil war he served in one of the many international brigades as a battalion political officer and interim commander.

*Dein unbekannter Bruder*, Bredel's fictional account of the scarcely less fictional Communist resistance movement two years after Hitler's seizure of power, centers on the young Communist zealot Arnold Clasen. In concert with other Communist stereotypes and in opposition to Nazi terror and to Nazi spies among the workers, Clasen conducts resistance first in Hamburg, then with a new circle of comrades in Berlin. Among the latter is Renate Stammberger, with whom he falls in love. Already a marked man owing to previous incarceration by the Nazis, Clasen, back in Hamburg, is denounced by a Nazi spy and remanded to a concentration camp. At the end Bredel, showcasing his pervasive theme, the indomitability of the Communist party, adjures the imprisoned Arnold Clasen to be of courage, as he is a comrade in "the most powerful army in the world."

*Begegnung am Ebro* (Encounter on the Ebro, 1939), about a military confrontation at the Ebro River in Spain, is quite likely Bredel's most effective piece of reportage. It derives from his experience as the political officer of the Thälmann Battalion in the Spanish civil war, fighting on the side of the Spanish Republic against the mercenaries of General Franco and their fascist supporters from Germany and Italy. Not writing to a fictional formula, Bredel emerges as a competent—if hardly unbiased—and reflective journalist, horrified at the brutalities of war (without exception committed by the fascists), disgusted at the unmasking of the battalion liaison officer as a Gestapo agent, and rising to the occasion when the military command of the battalion is precipitately thrust upon him.

Before the outbreak of World War II Bredel made his way back to the Soviet Union, where the sudden Hitler-Stalin alliance made emigrant Communist writers and artists distinctly uncomfortable—indeed, disposable. Bredel survived, however. *Der Kommissar am Rhein* (The Commissar on the Rhine, 1940) is typical of his penchant for tales based loosely on history, frequently on the events of the French Revolution susceptible to propagandistic interpretation. The officer in the title is Louis Antoine de Saint-Just, dispatched by the Convention in Paris as a plenipotentiary to the Army of the Rhine to preserve the integrity of the revolution against treason and weakness, as well as the danger of German military intervention. The fictionalized Saint-Just executes his charge with vision and decisiveness. The German military, both in 1795 and in 1940, is the chief enemy of the people's revolution.

After Hitler's surprise invasion of the Soviet Union, Bredel served the Russians at the Battle of Stalingrad, attempting to encourage desertion by the soldiers of the doomed German Sixth Army. He returned in May 1945 to Soviet-occupied East Germany to become an honored—but not uncriticized—writer, as well as a functionary and medal recipient of the state. After one outburst befitting a veteran revolutionary, followed by appropriate reprimand, he seems not to have dared raise his voice again. He continued writing—and, when attacked by party critics, rewriting—finding on the whole a quiet modus vivendi with the regime and its frequently shabby treatment of his more outspoken colleagues. Still, he distinguished himself from the party hacks by his good nature, his sense of humor, and his lack of cynicism.

After 1949 or 1950 his uncomplicated and increasingly monotonous propagandistic purpose so prevailed over his material that one may hardly speak of artistic literature. The only partial exception lies in his historical fiction, which only by carefully if perhaps unnecessarily pointed out

parallelism fulfilled the purpose of propaganda.

Perhaps Bredel's most effective novel, in which he endows his stereotypes with a measure of complexity, is *Die Väter* (The Fathers, 1948), the first book of a transgenerational trilogy entitled *Verwandte und Bekannte* (Relatives and Acquaintances). The central figure of *Die Väter* is not that of the familiar young Communist zealot. Further, evidently as a result of Bredel's continued study of the Russian masters, his canvas, while embracing the familiar Hamburg working-class precincts, is less parochial than in his earlier novels. The iron-founder Johann Hardekopf is a convinced and politically active Social Democrat at the turn of the century who sees his party leadership betray its working-class constituency. The leaders subscribe to Wilhelm II's imperialism and support militarism and World War I. Hardekopf, moreover, has to see his children—all but one—variously betray their Social Democratic heritage. The exception is his daughter Frieda, who becomes the wife of Carl Brenten. Brenten, after undergoing a period of personal doubt and even apostasy, is determined to make a new socialist beginning in the tradition of his wife's heritage.

From the title, one might expect that Carl Brenten would be the central figure in the second book of the trilogy, *Die Söhne* (The Sons, 1949); but that role is played by Carl and Frieda's son Walter. Soviet criticism of Bredel's depiction of the German political situation during and after World War I was so severe that he was moved to rewrite the novel twice. The result is the substantial abandonment of the family-generational structuring principle and theme, and the depiction, in the persona of Walter Brenten, of a pastiche of Bredel's own life as a Communist fighter for the working class. The reader witnesses the development of Walter Brenten into a dedicated and courageous Communist, but as a developed character he is no more interesting than the stereotypes of Bredel's earlier novels.

Walter remains the central figure in the third book of the trilogy, *Die Enkel* (The Grandsons, 1953). It is a tired and disorganized novel covering the period 1933 to 1948, full of unintegrated description and retaining only occasional vestiges of the family structure and theme. The family ties disintegrate narratively as well as structurally and thematically, to be episodically revived, as Walter heroically confronts the Nazis and the Gestapo, travels to Spain and the Soviet Union, and, with the victorious entry of the Red Army into Berlin, is enabled to return to his homeland.

*Bredel (left) with the Russian novelist Mikhail A. Sholokhov (Zentralbild/Hochneder, Berlin)*

The beneficent and humanizing influence of the Red Army in the immediate postwar reconstruction of the Soviet-occupied zone is the theme of the symbolically titled novel *Ein neues Kapitel* (A New Chapter, 1959). The Communist writer Peter Boisen, recently returned from exile—clearly another fictional persona of Bredel himself—to the city of Rostock, comes to perceive in a series of episodes that Colonel Pernikov and Lieutenant Colonel Kovalenko of the occupying Red Army have also suffered personal loss in the war and that they are now truly concerned, as friends of the Germans, to assist in a Communist reconstruction of the city, its politics, and its society. This novel, too, underwent revision after Soviet criticism, presumably to bring it even more in line with the unique Soviet view of events in the occupation zone during the first five months of peace in 1945.

East German sources scarcely mention Bredel's family life; he seems to have been married twice and to have had at least one son. He died of a heart attack in East Berlin on 27 October 1964. His works have been translated into Russian, Bulgarian, Czech, Polish, Hungarian, Chinese, Georgian, and Ossetic, but only rarely into Western languages; *Die Prüfung* was translated into French and Dutch. Only a handful of stories have appeared in English. His works are hardly less unknown in West Germany, although they continue to be reprinted in East Germany.

**References:**

Lilli Bock, *Willi Bredel: Leben und Werk* (Berlin: Volk & Wissen, 1967);

Georg Lukács, "Willi Bredels Romane," *Die Linkskurve,* no. 11 (1931): 22-27;

Marcel Reich-Ranicki, *Deutsche Literatur in West und Ost* (Reinbek: Rowohlt, 1970);

*Sinn und Form; Beiträge zur Literatur*, special Bredel issue (Berlin: Rütten & Loening, 1965).

# Bernard von Brentano

*(15 October 1901-29 December 1964)*

## Hans-Christian Oeser
*University College, Dublin*

BOOKS: *Gedichte* (Freiburg: Urban, 1923);

*Geld: Komödie in fünf Aufzügen* (Freiburg: Urban, 1924);

*Die Gedichte an Ophelia* (Paderborn: Schöningh, 1925);

*Über den Ernst des Lebens* (Berlin: Rowohlt, 1929);

*Kapitalismus und schöne Literatur* (Berlin: Rowohlt, 1930);

*Der Beginn der Barbarei in Deutschland* (Berlin: Rowohlt, 1932);

*Berliner Novellen* (Zurich: Oprecht & Helbling, 1934);

*Theodor Chindler: Roman einer deutschen Familie* (Zurich: Oprecht, 1936);

*Prozeß ohne Richter: Roman* (Amsterdam: Querido, 1937);

*Phädra: Schauspiel in fünf Aufzügen* (Zurich & New York: Oprecht, 1939; revised, Wiesbaden: Limes, 1948);

*Die ewigen Gefühle: Roman* (Amsterdam: Querido, 1939);

*Tagebuch mit Büchern* (Zurich: Atlantis, 1943);

*August Wilhelm Schlegel: Geschichte eines romantischen Geistes* (Stuttgart: Cotta, 1943; revised, 1949);

*Franziska Scheler: Roman einer deutschen Familie* (Zurich: Atlantis, 1945);

*Goethe und Marianne von Willemer: Die Geschichte einer Liebe* (Zurich: Classen, 1945); revised as *Daß ich eins und doppelt bin: Marianne von Willemer und Goethe* (Wiesbaden: Limes, 1961);

*Das unerforschliche Gefecht: Eine Erzählung in Versen* (Zurich: Classen, 1946); revised as *Martha und Maria: Eine Erzählung in Versen* (Wiesbaden: Limes, 1949);

*Streifzüge: Tagebuch mit Büchern: Neue Folge* (Zurich: Classen, 1947);

*Die Schwestern Usedom: Roman* (Zurich: Classen, 1948);

*Sophie Charlotte und Danckelmann: Eine preußische Historie* (Wiesbaden: Limes, 1949);

*Bücher unserer Zeit: Festvortrag, gehalten auf der Morgenfeier des Burgvereins 1952, veranstaltet am 10. August vom Burgverein Eltville, Gutenberg-Ge-* denkstätte, für seine Mitglieder und Freunde (Eltville: Burgverein, 1952);

*Du Land der Liebe: Bericht von Abschied und Heimkehr eines Deutschen* (Tübingen: Wunderlich/Stuttgart: Leins, 1952);

*Die geistige Situation der Kunst in der Gesellschaft der Jahre 1900-1950* (Bad Homburg: Gehlen, 1954);

*Das Menschenbild in der modernen Literatur: Vortrag, gehalten auf der Tagung der hessischen Hochschulwochen in Bad Wildungen* (Bad Homburg: Gehlen, 1958);

*Literatur: Vortrag, gehalten am 25. April 1958 bei den Hochschulwochen für staatswissenschaftliche Fort-*

*Bernard von Brentano (Ullstein)*

68

*bildung in Bad Wildungen* (Bad Homburg: Gehlen, 1958);

*Die öffentliche Meinung aus der Sicht eines Schriftstellers: Vortrag, gehalten am 4. Oktober 1960 bei den Hochschulwochen für staatswissenschaftliche Fortbildung in Bad Wildungen* (Bad Homburg: Gehlen, 1960);

*Medien der öffentlichen Meinung. Literatur und öffentliche Meinung: Vortrag, gehalten am 27. November 1962 bei den Hochschulwochen für staatswissenschaftliche Fortbildung in Bad Nauheim* (Bad Homburg: Gehlen, 1962);

*Schöne Literatur und öffentliche Meinung: Literarische Essays* (Wiesbaden: Limes, 1962);

*Erzählungen* (Darmstadt: Roether, 1965);

*Drei Prälaten: Essays*, edited by Konrad Feilchenfeldt (Wiesbaden: Limes, 1974);

*Wo in Europa ist Berlin? Bilder aus den zwanziger Jahren* (Frankfurt am Main: Insel, 1981).

OTHER: *Weg mit dem Schmutz- und Schundgesetz! Protest-Kundgebung gegen den Gesetzentwurf zur Bewahrung der Jugend vor Schmutz- und Schundschriften am 10. IX. 1926 im Plenarsaal des ehemaligen Herrenhauses Berlin,* preface by Brentano (Berlin: Vereinigung linksgerichteter Verleger, 1926);

*Die schönsten Gedichte von Gottfried Keller,* edited by Brentano and Manuel Gasser (Zurich: Manuel, 1938);

*Das Schönste von Matthias Claudius,* edited by Brentano (Zurich: Classen, 1944).

During the 1930s Bernard von Brentano gained some prominence both in the Weimar Republic and in his Swiss exile. He had been critical of the psychological novel for its reliance on "characters" and for its political abstinence, and he favored the Neue Sachlichkeit (New Objectivity) because it tended to confront social conditions and ideological patterns by means of reportage rather than imagination and of montage rather than imitation. But under the influence of Marxism, Brentano went beyond the passive registering of reality advocated by the adepts of the "Neue Sachlichkeit," and in his own work of sociopolitical reportage, *Der Beginn der Barbarei in Deutschland* (The Beginning of Barbarism in Germany, 1932), he combined descriptive methods and theoretical elements to produce a piece of "operative" literature which would have a positive function in class warfare.

*Theodor Chindler* (1936), Brentano's first novel and by far his most widely read work, is an application of some of these principles to fiction, guided by Bertolt Brecht's theory of the "epical" and by his own insight that "denn sagen lassen sich die Menschen nichts; aber erzählen lassen sie sich alles" (people won't listen unless you tell them a story). With his historical novel, Brentano responded to the demands of the antifascist struggle and "twinned," in Walter Benjamin's terminology, his political and artistic tendencies to form a unified whole. *Theodor Chindler* is one of the first works of fiction to deal with the politics of the Great War rather than with its physical horror. This emphasis on the social causes and political function of war and its disorganizing effect on the fabric of bourgeois society will secure the book a firm place in German literature. Combining a social analysis of Germany during World War I with an acute indictment of the parent generation, the novel is compatible with current literary efforts to come to an understanding of the past in terms of a quest for the father or an examination of childhood. In the late 1970s, when the focus of literary attention had shifted from the political to the personal, from the public to the private, Brentano's work enjoyed a sudden if small-scale revival as some of his books were republished or serialized for television.

Prior to that time Brentano's exile and his about-face from an antifascist to a covertly profascist stance had resulted in his being largely ignored by the public. However much Brentano's reacquired conservatism might have suited the cultural climate of postwar West Germany, the fact that he had emigrated and had addressed the historical and political issues of war, revolution, and dictatorship was sufficient to deny him recognition. On the other hand, his ignominious conduct in Switzerland had isolated him from those with whom he had had contact in the Weimar Republic. His publisher, Max Niedermayer, told of how an irate Brentano paced his office during the 1940s shouting, "Ihr habt doch mich, aber die Deutschen kümmern sich nicht um mich, sie schwärmen von allerlei fragwürdigem Übersetzungsdreck . . . das ist der letzte Dreck!" (Why, you have got me! But the Germans don't care about me, they rave about all sorts of dubious filth translated into German . . . it's junk!).

Brentano's personal tragedy can be defined using Robert Neumann's term *doppelter Salto mortale* (double somersault)—he was a conservative gone full circle, having flirted with both communism and fascism. Rather than face up to his erratic development within the space of less than a decade, Brentano would deny, in turn, his involvement with the Communist party in the 1930s (a betrayal of his own class) and his submission to the Nazis in the 1940s (a betrayal of the ethos of exile). His dubious political physiognomy is indicative of the precarious position of the bourgeois intellectual in the no-man's-land between social camps and political firelines. Brentano's self-justification by partial self-abnegation had a telling effect on his literary production; the novelist in him could no longer carry out what his political bias would require him to do, or, as Franz Theodor Csokor wrote in 1947 in *Der Turm,* "der schwache Mensch hat über den starken Dichter gesiegt" (the weak man has conquered the strong poet). After *Die Schwestern Usedom* (The Sisters Usedom, 1948), a hardly noteworthy attempt to grapple with the mechanics of married life, Brentano published no more fiction.

Eugen Ludwig Franz Bernard Maria von Brentano di Tremezzo was born in Offenbach in Hessen, one of six children of Otto von Brentano, a notary, and Lilla Schwerdt-von Brentano. His full name reveals not only two patents of nobility (according to Max Fürst, his appearance did resemble that of "ein gepflegter Landedelmann mit einem Schuß Turgeniew" [a well-groomed country squire with a touch of Turgenev about him]) but also his descent from highly intellectual Rhenish Hessian stock. Derived from one of four branches of an aristocratic Lombard family named de Brenta with an ancestral seat near Lake Como and based since 1730 in Frankfurt, the Brentanos had brought forth, within four generations, the romantic poets Clemens and Bettina, the philosopher and psychologist Franz, the economist and "professorial socialist" Lujo, and the leading member of the Zentrumspartei, Brentano's father, Otto, a deputy to the Reichstag and later minister of justice and of the interior in Hessen. The literary and political strands in that remarkable family tradition manifested themselves in Brentano's own generation, with Bernard opting early for a career as a writer, whereas his younger brother Heinrich was to become the second foreign minister of the Federal Republic of Germany. Brentano's parents instilled in him a Catholicism and conservatism onto which his subsequent political beliefs were, to a degree, only grafted.

Brentano began his literary career at age seventeen by editing, with Walter Rumpf and Alfred Selzer, the journal *Neuland,* which provided the first platform for his poetry. After moving to Darmstadt with his parents in 1920, he went to Freiburg to study German and philosophy with Edmund Husserl. He continued his studies in Munich and Frankfurt without obtaining a degree. In November 1922, apparently in accordance with the requirements of his social rank, he married Baroness Marie Elisabeth von Esebeck. Through the good offices of Franz von Papen, later to be chancellor in the Third Reich, Brentano was given work with the paper *Germania,* the organ of the Zentrumspartei, and in 1923 he moved to Berlin. In the spring of 1925 the Austrian writer Joseph Roth, seeking to free himself of the burdens of everyday journalism, offered Brentano his post as special correspondent for the renowned left-of-center daily *Frankfurter Zeitung.* By then Brentano had had two volumes of poetry published and had seen his comedy *Geld* (Money, 1924) premiered in Darmstadt; apparently he had also begun work on a novel. After some hesitation he accepted Roth's proposition, and his regular feuilletons signed "bB, Berlin"—some of which were published in a posthumous collection as late as 1981—facilitated his becoming acquainted with most of the celebrities of literary and cultural life in Berlin, including Brecht, Benjamin, Gottfried Benn, Arnolt Bronnen, Alfred Döblin, Ernst Glaeser, and Herbert Ihering. Between 1926 and 1930 he visited Paris, London, Vienna, Rome, Prague, Poland, the Baltic states, and the Soviet Union (where he had a chance encounter with Stalin).

A member of both the P.E.N. Club and the Schutzverband Deutscher Schriftsteller (Protective Association of German Writers), Brentano underwent a rapid political radicalization at what he called the "zeitgenössische Hochschule" (contemporary university) which the cultural capital of Germany—indeed, of Europe—offered him. In 1927 he became a member of the editorial board of the *Neue Bücherschau,* a left-wing periodical, and in 1928, it can be assumed, a founder of the Communist-inspired Bund Proletarisch-Revolutionärer Schriftsteller (League of Proletarian-Revolutionary Authors). After divorcing his wife in February 1929, in September he married Margot Gerlach, with whom he had two sons, Georg Michael (born in 1933) and Peter Christian (born in 1935). When his newspaper changed its political orientation, he quit his post and set himself up as a free-lance publicist, working for the *Berliner Tageblatt* and other papers. In 1930-1931 Brentano, together with Brecht and Benjamin, planned the launching of *Krisis und Kritik,* a revolutionary journal which was to destroy false consciousness by initiating fruitful debate among intellectuals not only about the subject matter of their fields but also about their social situation and their methods and techniques.

The project failed when Brecht, Benjamin, and Brentano clashed with representatives of the Communist party of Germany over the format the journal was to take. Nevertheless, freed from the ties to his bourgeois newspaper, Brentano moved further toward the left and joined the Communist party in 1931. While publishing in *Die Rote Fahne* of the Communist party and *Die Linkskurve* of the Bund Proletarisch-Revolutionärer Schriftsteller, however, Brentano continued to be attacked by his fellow Communists in the same periodicals for his liberal vacillations, such as his support for Chancellor Heinrich Brüning. Significantly, it was in Brecht's famous study group on critical Marxism, centering around the "renegade" Karl Korsch, that he deepened his knowledge of dialectical materialism.

When political power was handed over to Hitler on 30 January 1933, Brentano took part in the attempt to unify and organize the intellectual opposition by means of meetings and leaflets. On his invitation, Brecht, Glaeser, Heinrich Mann, Johannes R. Becher, Leonhard Frank, and Hermann Kesten met in his flat in Berlin to discuss the possibility of writers putting up resistance against the fascist takeover. After the Reichstag blaze of March 1933 Brentano felt compelled to go into exile; via Munich he traveled to Vienna, where the satirist Karl Kraus welcomed him and Brecht with the words, "Die Ratten betreten das sinkende Schiff" (The rats are boarding the sinking ship). How well advised Brentano had been to flee from Nazi Germany was demonstrated to him when his *Der Beginn der Barbarei in Deutschland* was burned in the Nazi bonfires of 10 May 1933 and all his books were placed on the index of banned writings. In 1934, having been granted political asylum in Switzerland, he moved into a home close to Thomas Mann's residence in Küsnacht, near Zurich.

Brentano's first piece of fiction was *Berliner Novellen* (1934), a collection of three short stories which he began writing in 1928. The main story, "Rudi," retells and refutes a Nazi newspaper report on a small boy who was killed while hiding hand grenades for his mother's friend, who had gone underground. Written in terse and, according to Brecht, Tacitus-like prose and interspersed with commentaries and lyrics, the story details a depressing proletarian milieu in Berlin, which causes deprivation and despair at the same time as it gives rise to an insatiable love for life on the part of the boy. While praising the boy's courage, the story demonstrates the political fickleness of the proletariat: "Aber in das schöne rote Tuch hatten die Bewohner das Kreuz eingenäht, an das sie nun geschlagen waren" (But the residents had sewn onto the fine red cloth [the red flag] the very cross [the swastika] to which they were now nailed).

The curse of Cain—exile—proved to be the acid test in Brentano's life. After the crushing defeat of the Communists by the Nazis he questioned not only the party's leadership but the role and structure of the party itself, as well as the trustworthiness of its "masterminds" in the Soviet Union. Brentano's correspondence with Brecht concerning the dialectic of democracy and dictatorship reveals a deep distrust and contempt for the party at a time when he was still a member and was participating in its antifascist and trade union activities. His last connections with the party were severed when he was expelled for breach of discipline in September 1933. Moreover, the physical and political separation from his own country and people led him to doubt the moral justification of being in exile in the first place. It is true that in 1934 he became a founder of the German P.E.N. Club in Exile; that he continued to contribute to émigré periodicals such as *Die Sammlung, Maß und Wert*, and *Die neue Weltbühne* and to frequent meeting places for exiles such as the Rabenhaus; that he was actively involved in Carl Meffert's campaign for higher wages for office employees; and that he donated royalties to persecuted intellectuals. Yet the seeds of his subsequent ideological and political volte-face had already been sown. Thomas Mann, with whom he discussed political matters in Küsnacht, sensed in Brentano's nationalism the beginning of a political reaffiliation as early as 1936, when *Theodor Chindler* was published: "Am besten ginge der junge Mann nach Deutschland" (It would be best if the young man went back to Germany). Together with another ex-Communist, Ignazio Silone, Brentano was classed as belonging to the École de Zurich, whose members differed from the antifascist emigrants by their neutral position toward Germany and by their method of writing, a combination of critical reflection and poetic spontaneity which Jean Paul Samson described as "création critique." Brentano began to frequent the Freitagsrunde, a circle of conservative writers, at the Café Odeon.

*Theodor Chindler*, Brentano's ambitious attempt "die Geschichte meiner Zeit zu erzählen" (to tell the story of my times), can be ranked among the novels of importance to have come out of exile. Contrary to Thomas S. Hansen's claim in 1982 that it marked Brentano's "Abkehr von der antifaschistischen Opposition" (turning away from the antifascist opposition), the work belongs, both in form and content, to the "aesthetic of resistance" mapped out by Werner Mittenzwei in 1981. It forms the first part of a planned trilogy which was to give a panoramic overview of bourgeois society from World War I to the collapse of Germany in 1945, mirrored in the microcosm of a patrician Catholic family. Brentano's project of a political family saga set during wartime dated back to 1929, when, in *Über den Ernst des Lebens* (On the Seriousness of Life), he analyzed the self-deceiving letters of patriotic students fighting at the front and argued that it was the isolation of the individual in civil life which made intellectuals crave for the collective and communal experience of the trenches. In *Theodor Chindler* Brentano probes into, on the one hand, the political strife behind the front lines and, on the other, the family divisions caused by the war. It is not the title character who is at the center of the novel but rather two passive corporate heroes: the Zentrumspartei, of which Chindler is a member, and the bourgeois family, which breaks up under the strains of war and revolution. The various members of the Chindler household represent different aspects of life: Theodor, the political; his wife Elisabeth, the religious; their sons Karl and Ernst, the military; their daughter-in-law Lilli, the erotic; and their son Leopold, the artistic.

The secret heroine of the novel, however, is Theodor and Elisabeth's only daughter, Maggie, who, by allying herself with the rising though divided working-class movement out of love for the revolutionary Dr. Caspar Koch, points the way out of the political crisis: the fight against militarism and capitalism. Hence the Buddenbrookian conflict between the generations, as witnessed in the relationships between Theodor and Leopold—the burgher and the artist—or between Elisabeth and Lilli—the bigoted and the emancipated—takes on the dimensions of class antagonism. Maggie, the strongest character in the book and the only one to undergo a genuine transformation, acquires the ability to act upon her reflections and to reflect upon her actions and thus secures her intellectual and moral independence, while her father is the one who most lacks strength and convictions. Although skeptical about the objectives and prospects of the war as well as opposed to the tactic of U-boat warfare, he has neither the political principles nor the political will to turn his defense of constitutionalism into a forceful assault on the political system itself. Instead, under the influence of his mother, he disowns his daughter and is opportunistic enough to place himself at the disposal of the

Social Democratic state government, which puts down the revolution and arrests his daughter. The story of his political career is an argument against bourgeois politicking.

*Theodor Chindler*, X-raying a society of the past in which both parliament and public are politically ignorant, is a historical novel which undertakes to explain the rise of fascism by implicitly linking two decisive dates in German history: 1914 and 1933. Its author tacitly draws parallels between the abdication of the bourgeoisie during World War I, when political power was yielded to the supreme command of the Reichswehr, and the events of January 1933, when it was handed over to a social movement outside the traditional bounds of the bourgeoisie. Thus the novel indirectly upholds the theory of Bonapartism by pointing out the weaknesses of both the bourgeoisie and the proletariat: the cowardice and cunning of the former and the disunity and ineffectuality of the latter. Autobiographical though it is, the novel does not serve, as Robert Minder claimed in 1972 in his essay *Geist und Macht* (Spirit and Power), as "ein Beitrag zur Chronik der BRENTANO-Sippe und ihren Zerwürfnissen während des ersten Weltkriegs" (a contribution to the chronicle of the Brentano clan and their dissensions during World War I), but rather as the first installment of a national portrait of an entire epoch.

*Prozeß ohne Richter* (Trial without Judge, 1937) bears greater resemblance to a novella than to a novel owing to its stringent composition, sharp focus, brevity, and concentration on plot rather than character or milieu. The apolitical Klitander, professor of mathematics, is called upon by an authoritarian government to give, along with his colleagues Alzest and Oront, his expert opinion on school examinations; but he reports in accordance with his findings rather than in accordance with what he believes to be the requirements of the authorities. His attempt to assert his innocence and integrity fails in the face of a power which can turn his every act or omission into a crime against the state. In the end he is sent to a concentration camp, where he commits suicide. The destruction of humanity by despotism does not stop short of a hapless man who is an opponent of the regime only insofar as he is thoughtful; otherwise he is perfectly loyal to the state. Although Brentano merely sketches the political environment of Klitander and gives no clues as to the time and place of the action or the political nature of the repressive system, he captures the claustrophobic atmosphere of dictatorship and reveals the machinations of tyranny.

As the stylized names of the three male characters, borrowed from Molière's *The Misanthrope*, suggest, the story is a parable about political pressure and personal paranoia. Klitander, in a hallucination of Kafkaesque proportions, stages a self-trial in which he condemns himself for his share of guilt resulting from his secret connivance with the system.

While most emigrants, even though they may have criticized Brentano for his reluctance to specify, held *Prozeß ohne Richter* to be an indictment of fascist Germany, Brentano himself, in a letter to the German authorities, referred to Stalin's Soviet Union. This interpretation would transform what Hansen describes as the book's "Allegorisierung des Faschismus" (allegorization of fascism) into what Jethro Bithell calls an "attack on totalitarian tyranny"—an equivocation between communism and National Socialism. Abstraction from concrete historical detail permitted Brentano to express his political ambiguities, distance himself from contemporary events, and emphasize the universal applicability of his warning. As Döblin pointed out in *Pariser Tageszeitung*, Brentano, by reducing the political realities of the time to their human essence, succeeded in showing "eine furchtbar reale Welt im Spiegel eines Wassertropfens" (a terribly real world in the mirror of a drop of water).

*Die ewigen Gefühle* (The Eternal Feelings) received the International Award for the Best European Book for 1939. Written in the classic realistic vein of Theodor Fontane, the novel is a fictional rendering of the maxim uttered by one of its characters: "In einer moralischen Zeit kann man unmoralisch sein, in einer unmoralischen Zeit wie der unsrigen muß man moralisch sein" (In moral times one can afford to be immoral; in amoral times such as ours one must be moral). It tells the story of the solicitor Elshaltz's passionate and happy love for Sabine Haffner. After much meandering, however, Elshaltz is forced to recognize that there are other values equally worth pursuing, such as the faith, duty, and sincerity owed to his wife and child, and that one can suffer from erotic adventures just as much as from the tedium of everyday life. Under a social order which has conventionalized all forms of human life, marriage and adultery are structurally identical: both are contractual and symbiotic. The moral of this novel of adultery—which, according to Benjamin, examines the "historische Konditionen der Liebe" (historical conditions of love)—is that eternal feelings are neither eternal nor do they elevate the lovers from the "irdisches Gewühle" (worldly bustle) of the Goethe poem from which the title of the novel is taken; love,

passion, and desire have been streamlined so as to interfere as little as possible with the social laws of twentieth-century bourgeois society. Resignation and renunciation are the inescapable results of sexual politics.

At the outbreak of World War II Brentano joined the German colony at Zurich and requested repatriation on the condition that he be given permission to continue to write. In a letter of application of August 1940 to the German General Consulate he stated that he was an Aryan, a patriot, and a passionate German and "froh, daß das Buch durch die Einstampfung aus der Welt geschafft ist" (glad that the book [*Der Beginn der Barbarei in Deutschland*] has been pulped, never to be seen again). Rather than allegiance to his people or a desire for physical proximity to his family, it was probably Hitler's blinding military successes which motivated Brentano to succumb. The notion of the German nation at war seems to have reconciled him to the fascist state, even though he claimed not to equate Germany and National Socialism.

Brentano was allowed to visit Germany in 1940. Three years later he was given permission to have *August Wilhelm Schlegel* (1943), the first biography of the romantic poet, critic, and scholar, published by the Cotta firm of Stuttgart; but it is proof of the far from monolithic character of the Nazi regime that his application for repatriation failed, while his book was confiscated immediately after publication. Even though Brentano successfully fought a Swiss expulsion order in 1944 and won a libel suit against his erstwhile friend Manuel Gasser, who had denounced him as a Nazi and an anti-Semite, his attitudes and allegiances remained unclear.

*Franziska Scheler* (1945), the sequel to *Theodor Chindler*, offers evidence of Brentano's change of perspective in exile. Of the two characters in the earlier novel with whom the reader could identify, Maggie is downgraded to a marginal figure and presented as a bourgeois gone astray; whereas Leopold, now a successful journalist who is writing the biography of Friedrich von Gentz, embodies the aesthetic qualities which Brentano presents as the counterpoise to the economic and political chaos following the Wall Street crash. This reinterpretation of positive characters implies a revaluation of the function of history within fiction as well as in real life. As the emphasis is shifted from the political to the artistic and scholarly, history is no longer the antecedent to be questioned in order to understand the present; it is a refuge from the present. The preoccupation of the liberal Leopold with the reactionary politician Gentz, frowned upon by democrats and reactionaries alike, is a reflection of Brentano's own newfound preference for history and biography as literary genres, which was manifested in his monographs on Schlegel, Goethe and Marianne von Willemer (1945), and Danckelmann and Sophie Charlotte (1949). Brentano now trusts literature to institute comforting bonds between congenial minds rather than to be instrumental in political and social change. In Ulrike Hessler's view literature, in this novel as well as in Brentano's literary journals, is promoted to an "Ersatz, mehr noch . . . Produzent von Wirklichkeit" (substitute for, and indeed . . . producer of reality).

As a colorful kaleidoscope of Berlin and a picture of bourgeois and aristocratic morals, *Franziska Scheler* no longer examines the political and economic genesis of the German catastrophe but, according to François de Bury in his review in *Schweizer Rundschau*, the "Zusammenstoß des deutschen Menschen mit dem europäischen Geist" (clash between the German character and the European mind). The historical approach is replaced by a metaphysical appraisal of the German people's "Abkehr von Gott" (renunciation of God) and their "Verhaftung an die Firmen Satan, Mammon, Nietzsche & Co." (addiction to the enterprises Satan, Mammon, Nietzsche & Co.)—the diabolical attempt to idealize and justify economic activities with Nietzsche's theory of the superman. The social background of newspapers, publishing houses, private clubs, and parliamentary debates serves as a foil for the story of an intellectual who sees the necessity for writing in order to teach self-observation and self-awareness to his nation. The novel's thematic scope is much narrower than that of its forerunner, since a love story ranks above the family chronicle and the social canvas: an automobile journey to Poland provides the setting for the unfolding of an intimate relationship between Leopold and his old sweetheart, Franziska. As Samson remarked in his review in *Neue Schweizer Rundschau*, however, the novel fails to be "der echte Roman einer Leidenschaft" (a genuine novel of passion) but instead merely conveys "Ansichten über die Liebe" (views on love). Accordingly, the dialogue, in *Theodor Chindler* a medium for political argument, becomes merely a vehicle for aphorisms. After World War II Brentano sensed that, as he had almost reversed his original political and artistic positions, his three-part "Roman einer deutschen Familie" (novel of a German family)

would lack inner unity. Consequently, he discontinued the trilogy.

In 1949 Brentano finally returned to West Germany and settled in Wiesbaden. While ignored by the public, he was honored by conservative groups and by the state: he was admitted to the Deutsche Akademie für Sprache und Dichtung in Darmstadt and the Akademie der Wissenschaften und der Literatur in Mainz and was awarded the Hessian Goethe-Plakette and the Bundesverdienstkreuz. In his autobiography, *Du Land der Liebe* (You Land of Love, 1952), Brentano seeks to demonstrate a continuity and coherence in his life which are lacking in his work. The apology had the dual function of explaining to those who stayed at home the moral necessity of emigration and to the exiles his yearning for a premature return to Germany. Written in an attempt to reenter West German public life after the war, it may be classified as Brentano's last piece of fiction. After long suffering, Brentano died in 1964 of multiple sclerosis and tuberculosis.

**References:**

Franz Theodor Csokor, "Der Prozeß Brentano," *Der Turm*, 2, no. 9/10 (1947): 334-335;

Konrad Feilchenfeldt, "Nachwort," in *Drei Prälaten: Essays*, edited by Feilchenfeldt (Wiesbaden: Limes, 1974), pp. 133-180;

Otto Forst de Battaglia, "Bernard von Brentano: Zum Tode eines großen Schriftstellers und bedeutenden, liebenswerten Menschen," *Begegnung*, 20, no. 3 (1965): 71-74;

Max Fürst, *Talisman Scheherezade: Die schwierigen zwanziger Jahre* (Munich: Hanser, 1976);

Martin Gregor-Dellin, "Nachwort," in Bernard von Brentano, *Prozeß ohne Richter: Roman*, revised edition (Frankfurt am Main: Suhrkamp, 1978), pp. 107-114;

Thomas S. Hansen, "Bernard von Brentanos 'Doppelter Salto Mortale' im Exil," in *Das Exilerlebnis: Verhandlungen des vierten Symposiums über deutsche und österreichische Exilliteratur*, edited by Donald D. Daviau and Ludwig M. Fischer (Columbia, S.C.: Camden House, 1982), pp. 253-264;

Hansen, "The 'Deutschlandroman' in Exile: Antifascist Criticism in the Political Prose of Klaus Mann, Walter Mehring, Bernard von Brentano, and Gustav Regler," Ph.D. dissertation, Harvard University, 1977;

Ulrike Hessler, *Bernard von Brentano: Ein deutscher Schriftsteller ohne Deutschland. Tendenzen des Romans zwischen Weimarer Republik und Exil*

(Frankfurt am Main & Basel: Lang, 1984);

Karl August Horst, "Begegnung mit Bernard von Brentano: Zum 60. Geburtstag des Dichters," *Der Literat*, 4, no. 9 (1961): 108-109;

Oskar Jancke, "Über das Werk Bernard von Brentanos," *Das literarische Deutschland*, 2, no. 10 (1951): 4;

Fritz Knöller, "Bernard von Brentano," *Welt und Wort*, 8 (1953): 113-115;

Robert Minder, *Geist und Macht oder Einiges über die Familie Brentano* (Mainz: Akademie der Wissenschaften und der Literatur, 1972);

Werner Mittenzwei, *Exil in der Schweiz* (Frankfurt am Main: Röderberg, 1979), pp. 110-120;

Helmut Mörchen, "Nachwort," in *Fazit: Ein Querschnitt durch die deutsche Publizistik*, edited by Ernst Glaeser (Kronberg: Scriptor, 1977), pp. 317-333;

Hans-Christian Oeser, "Nachdenken brennt wie Feuer": The Aesthetic of Resistance in Bernard von Brentano's Theodor Chindler," in *Neglected German Progressive Writers (2): Galway Colloquium 1985* (Galway: German Department, University College Galway, 1986), pp. 119-141;

Max Rychner, "A. W. Schlegel, der Romantiker. Zu Bernard von Brentano: 'August Wilhelm Schlegel,' " in his *Zeitgenössische Literatur: Charakteristiken und Kritiken* (Zurich: Manesse, 1947), pp. 201-215;

Rychner, "Literatursoziologie der Linken," in his *Zur Europäischen Literatur zwischen den zwei Weltkriegen* (Zurich: Atlantis, 1953), pp. 313-332;

Fritz Usinger, "Gedenkwort für Bernard von Brentano," *Jahrbuch der Deutschen Akademie für Sprache und Dichtung* (1964): 198-200.

**Papers:**

The Bertolt-Brecht-Archiv, East Berlin, holds the letters between Bernard von Brentano and Bertolt Brecht. The Deutsches Literaturarchiv, Marbach, West Germany, has a collection of letters between Brentano and Gottfried Benn, Hermann Beuttenmüller, Karl Friedrich Borée, Joachim Günther, Wilhelm Hausenstein, Bernt von Heiseler, Max Hermann-Neisse, Hermann Hesse, Hannes Küpper, Thomas Mann, Karl August Horst, Benno Reiffenberg, and Friedrich Sieburg. Brentano's literary manuscripts are in the possession of Frau Margot von Brentano, Wiesbaden.

# Kasimir Edschmid
## (Eduard Hermann Wilhelm Schmid)
### (5 October 1890-31 August 1966)

Robert G. Sullivan
*McGill University*

BOOKS: *Verse, Hymnen und Gesänge,* as Ed Schmid (Munich: Bonsels, 1911);

*Bilder: Lyrische Projektionen,* as Schmid (Darmstadt: Hohmann, 1913);

*Die sechs Mündungen: Novellen* (Leipzig: Wolff, 1915);

*Das rasende Leben: Zwei Novellen* (Leipzig: Wolff, 1915);

*Timur: Novellen* (Leipzig: Wolff, 1916);

*Die Karlsreis* (Darmstadt: Dachstube, 1918);

*Die Fürstin* (Weimar: Kiepenheuer, 1918);

*Stehe von Lichtern gestreichelt: Gedichte* (Hannover: Steegemann, 1919);

*Über den Expressionismus in der Literatur und die neue Dichtung,* volume 1 of *Tribüne der Kunst und Zeit* (Berlin: Reiss, 1919);

*Die doppelköpfige Nymphe: Aufsätze über Literatur und die Gegenwart* (Berlin: Cassirer, 1920);

*Die achatnen Kugeln: Roman* (Berlin: Cassirer, 1920);

*In memoriam Lisl Steinrück* (Darmstadt: Dachstube, 1920);

*Kean: Schauspiel in fünf Akten nach Alexandre Dumas* (Berlin: Reiss, 1921);

*Frauen* (Berlin: Cassirer, 1922);

*Hamsun, Flaubert: Zwei Reden* (Hannover: Adam, 1922);

*Rede an einen Dichter* (Hamburg: Harms, 1922);

*Das Bücher-Dekameron: Eine Zehn-Nächte-Tour durch die europäische Gesellschaft und Literatur* (Berlin: Reiss, 1923);

*Die Engel mit dem Spleen* (Berlin: Tillgner, 1923);

*Zur Naturgeschichte der Antilopen* (Darmstadt: Dachstube, 1923);

*Yousouf—Über die dichterische deutsche Jugend,* foreword by A. Happ (Regensburg: Habbel & Naumann, 1924);

*Bullis und Pekingesen* (Darmstadt: Dachstube, 1925);

*Die gespenstigen Abenteuer des Hofrat Brüstlein: Roman* (Vienna: Zsolnay, 1926); revised as *Pourtalès Abenteuer: Roman* (Munich: Desch, 1947);

*Der Russen-Zoo* (Darmstadt: Dachstube, 1926);

*Basken, Stiere, Araber: Ein Buch über Spanien und Marokko* (Frankfurt am Main: Frankfurter Verlagsanstalt, 1927);

*Luxus-Hunde* (Darmstadt: Darmstädter Verlag, 1927);

*Das große Reisebuch: Von Stockholm bis Korsika, von Monte Carlo bis Assisi* (Berlin: Deutsche Buchgemeinschaft, 1927);

*Die neue Frau* (Berlin: Deutsche Buchgemeinschaft, 1927);

*Sport um Gagaly: Roman* (Vienna: Zsolnay, 1928);

*Tiere, Mädchen und Antilopenjagd am Nil* (Darmstadt: Darmstädter Verlag, 1928);

*Lord Byron: Roman einer Leidenschaft* (Vienna: Zsolnay, 1929); translated by Eveline Bennett as

*Kasimir Edschmid (Ullstein)*

76

*Lord Byron: The Story of a Passion* (London: Toulmin, 1930); translated by Whittaker Chambers as *The Passionate Rebel: The Life of Lord Byron* (New York: Boni, 1930);

*Geschichte von den Suahelimädchen und den schwarzen Kriegern* (Darmstadt: Darmstädter Verlag, 1929);

*Afrika, nackt und angezogen* (Frankfurt am Main: Frankfurter Societäts-Druckerei, 1929; revised and enlarged, Munich: Desch, 1951);

*Hallo Welt! Sechzehn Erzählungen* (Vienna: Zsolnay, 1930);

*Bildhauer Bernhard Hoetger,* by Edschmid, Georg Biermann, and others, edited by A. Theile (Bremen: Angelsachsen-Verlag, 1930);

*Feine Leute; oder, Die Großen dieser Erde: Roman. Chronik der zwanziger Jahre* (Vienna: Zsolnay, 1931);

*Indianer* (Darmstadt: Darmstädter Verlag, 1931);

*Exotische Tiergeschichten* (Darmstadt: Darmstädter Verlag, 1931);

*Glanz und Elend Süd-Amerikas: Roman eines Erdteils* (Frankfurt am Main: Societätsverlag, 1931); translated by Oakley Williams as *South America: Lights and Shadows* (New York: Viking, 1932); translation republished as *South America: A Continent of Contrasts* (London: Butterworth, 1934);

*Deutsches Schicksal: Roman* (Vienna: Zsolnay, 1932);

*Südamerika wird photographiert* (Bielefeld & Leipzig: Velhagen & Klasing, 1932);

*Zauber und Größe des Mittelmeers* (Frankfurt am Main: Societätsverlag, 1932);

*Das Südreich: Roman der Germanenzüge* (Vienna: Zsolnay, 1933);

*Im Spiegel des Rheins: Westdeutsche Fahrten* (Frankfurt am Main: Societätsverlag, 1933);

*Italien: Lorbeer, Leid und Ruhm* (Frankfurt am Main: Societätsverlag, 1935);

*Das Drama von Panama* (Darmstadt: Darmstädter Verlag, 1936); republished as *Lesseps: Das Drama von Panama* (Wiesbaden: Grief, 1947);

*Italien: Gärten, Männer und Geschicke* (Frankfurt am Main: Societätsverlag, 1937);

*Der Liebesengel: Roman einer Leidenschaft* (Vienna: Zsolnay, 1937);

*Auto-Reisebuch: Fünfzehn Ferienreisen durch deutsche Flußtäler und Gebirge* (Darmstadt: Wittich, 1938);

*Erika: Erzählung* (Vienna: Zsolnay, 1938);

*Italien: Inseln, Römer und Cäsaren* (Frankfurt am Main: Societätsverlag, 1939);

*Italien: Hirten, Helden und Jahrtausende* (Frankfurt am Main: Societätsverlag, 1941);

*Das gute Recht: Roman* (Munich: Desch, 1946);

*Im Diamantental: Vier Erzählungen* (Munich: Desch, 1947);

*Italienische Gesänge* (Darmstadt: Darmstädter Verlag, 1947);

*Bunte Erde: Gewesenes und Gewandeltes* (Kassel: Schleber, 1948); republished as *Europäisches Reisebuch* (Vienna: Zsolnay, 1953);

*Italien Seefahrt, Palmen und Unsterblichkeit* (Düsseldorf: Bagel, 1948);

*Albert Schweitzer: Kleine Biographie* (Düsseldorf: Bagel, 1949);

*Denkwürdiges Darmstadt: Ein Bildbuch,* by Edschmid and Marie Fröhlich (Darmstadt: von Liebig, 1949);

*Der Zauberfaden: Roman einer Industrie* (Munich: Desch, 1949);

*Wenn es Rosen sind werden sie blühen: Roman über Georg Büchner* (Munich: Desch, 1950);

*Der Bauchtanz: Exotische Novellen* (Vienna: Zsolnay, 1952);

*Der Hauptmann und die Furt* (Freiburg: Klemm, 1953);

*Der Marschall und die Gnade: Der Roman des Simón Bolivar* (Munich: Desch, 1954);

*Italien zwischen Alpen und Apennin* (Stuttgart: Kohlhammer, 1956);

*Italien zwischen Apennin und Abruzzen* (Stuttgart: Kohlhammer, 1956);

*Côte d'Azur: Sonnenland am Mittelmeer,* by Edschmid and René Jacques (Munich & Vienna: Andermann, 1957);

*Frühe Manifeste: Epochen des Expressionismus* (Hamburg: Wegner, 1957);

*Die italienische Riviera* (Munich & Ahrbeck: Knorr & Hirth, 1957);

*In memoriam Dr. Otto Röhm: Zum 50jährigen Bestehen der chemischen Fabrik Röhm & Haas, Darmstadt* (Darmstadt: Hoppenstedts Wirtschaftsarchiv, 1957);

*Zauber der Ferne: 130 internationale Fotos illustrieren eine Weltreise,* edited by E. G. Schleinitz (Stuttgart: Belser, 1957);

*Drei Häuser am Meer: Roman* (Munich, Vienna & Basel: Desch, 1958);

*Drei Kronen für Rico: Ein Stauferroman* (Gütersloh: Bertelsmann, 1958);

*Stürme und Stille am Mittelmeer: Ein Rundblick* (Stuttgart: Goverts, 1959);

*Tagebuch, 1958-1960* (Munich: Desch, 1960);

*Lebendiger Expressionismus: Auseinandersetzungen, Gestalten, Erinnerungen* (Munich: Desch, 1961);

*Vom Mittelmeer zum Nordkap* (Munich: Andermann, 1961);

*Yugoslavia: Dalmatian Coast*, translated by Gladys Wheelhouse (Munich: Andermann, 1961);

*Porträts und Denksteine* (Munich: Desch, 1962);

*Vom Bodensee zur Nordsee: Fahrten im Westen* (Stuttgart: Goverts, 1963);

*Whisky für Algerien? Roman* (Vienna: Desch, 1963);

*Ishia: Die immergrüne Insel* (Zurich: Classen, 1964);

*Die frühen Erzählungen* (Neuwied & Berlin: Luchterhand, 1965);

*Hessen: Porträt eines Landes* (Hannover: Fackelträger, 1967);

*Frühe Schriften*, edited by Ernst Johann (Neuwied & Berlin: Luchterhand, 1970).

OTHER: *Galerie Erich Cüpper—Aachen: Die Sammlung der Werke von Bernhard Hoetger*, introduction by Edschmid (Leipzig & Munich: Wolff, 1916);

*Tribüne der Kunst und Zeit: Eine Schriftensammlung*, edited by Edschmid, 29 volumes (Berlin: Reiss, 1919-1922);

Bernhard Hoetger, *Erster Mappe*, introduction by Edschmid (Düsseldorf: Flechtheim, 1921);

W. Kern, *Davos, die Sonnenstadt im Hochgebirge*, introduction by Edschmid (Zurich: Orell Füssli, 1932);

J. H. Riedesel Freiherr zu Eisenbach, *Reise nach Italien und Großgriechenland*, volume 1: *Sendschreiben über seine Reise nach Sizilien und Großgriechenland*, introduction by Edschmid (Darmstadt: Gesellschaft Hessischer Bücherfreunde, 1939);

Georg Büchner, *Gesammelte Werke*, edited by Edschmid (Munich: Desch, 1948);

Joseph von Eichendorff, *Werke*, edited by Edschmid (Munich, Vienna & Basel: Desch, 1955);

Werner Lenz, *Europa: Das Gesicht seiner Städte und Landschaften*, introduction by Edschmid (Gütersloh: Bertelsmann, 1957);

Karl Sardemann, *Wie sie entkamen: Abenteuerliche und denkwürdige Fluchten*, introduction by Edschmid (Düsseldorf & Cologne: Diederichs, 1957);

*Odenwald: Landschaft und Städte*, introduction by Edschmid (Frankfurt am Main: Weidlich, 1958);

Doré Ogrizek, *Die heiligen Stätten: Jordanien—Syrien—Libanon—Israel*, introduction by Edschmid (Munich: Desch, 1958);

Arno Wrubel, *Capri*, introduction by Edschmid (Munich & Vienna: Andermann, 1958);

Georg Richter, *Vom Main zum Bodensee: Die Landschaft Badens*, introduction by Edschmid (Karlsruhe: Braun, 1959);

Anna Gabriele Therese von Sydow, *Gabriele von Bülow, Tochter Wilhelm von Humboldts: Ein Lebensbild aus den Familienpapieren Wilhelm von Humboldts und seiner Kinder 1791-1887*, introduction by Edschmid (Darmstadt: Toeche-Mittler, 1959);

*Immortal Europe, from the Bosphorus to the North Cape*, introduction by Edschmid (Munich: Andermann, 1961);

*Aktzeichnung großer Meister*, edited by Edschmid (Vienna: Desch, 1963);

*Briefe der Expressionisten*, edited by Edschmid (Frankfurt am Main: Ullstein, 1964);

*150 Jahre deutsche Freiheitsrufe: Vom Wiener Kongreß 1815 bis zu Bundespräsident Heuß* (Frankfurt am Main & Berlin: Ullstein, 1965).

Although his reputation as the creator of expressionist prose has been called into question, Kasimir Edschmid's early novellas and manifestos maintain a secure place in the expressionist canon. In 1950 Frank Thieß wrote in a special volume celebrating Edschmid's sixtieth birthday that few readers of Edschmid's books would know that their author was once the leading revolutionary expressionist; today few readers of Edschmid's expressionist works are aware that he ever wrote anything else.

The bulk of Edschmid's work, however, can scarcely be called expressionist. The most complete bibliography of his writings lists over ninety stories, novels, collections, and travelogues written after the mid 1920s, by which time Edschmid had clearly distanced himself from his earlier expressionist style. Literary histories scarcely mention Edschmid's postexpressionist works, which at best are called "gehobene Unterhaltungsliteratur" (sophisticated light literature). Edschmid the sportsman and gentleman author, whom Thieß praised, has slowly disappeared. Only the expressionist rebel remains.

Eduard Hermann Wilhelm Schmid was born in Darmstadt in 1890 to Bruno Franz Frederick and Bertha Bommersheim Schmid. The Schmids seem to have been a solid middle-class family, firmly anchored in the academic world. Bruno Schmid, who had studied under Wilhelm Röntgen, was a physics teacher at the local Gymnasium. Eduard's grandfather had been a teacher of theology and had written a textbook on botany and edited some poetry anthologies. As a boy, Schmid read by candlelight the exotic accounts of Baker's, Stanley's, and Livingstone's travels and dreamed of becoming a sailor. When he realized that a sailor's life offered little freedom and was less glamorous than he had imagined, he decided upon a university career.

After graduating from the Ludwig-Georgs Gymnasium, Schmid went to Munich to study French literature. Although he had no contact with the expressionist writers whose works Heswarth Walden began publishing in his journal *Der Sturm* in 1910, he did show a great interest in avant-garde artists such as Vasily Kandinsky and Franz Marc.

Around 1909 Schmid went to Paris, where he studied at the Sorbonne and the École de Chartres, visited the art galleries, and wrote conventional poetry. His first book, *Verse, Hymnen und Gesänge* (Verses, Hymns and Songs, 1911), was published under the name Ed Schmid, as was his second, *Bilder: Lyrische Projektionen* (Pictures: Lyrical Projections, 1913), a collection of poems inspired by the paintings of Monet, Manet, Van Gogh, and Picasso. Neither volume attracted much attention.

In 1910 Schmid transferred to Strasbourg, where he studied under Ernst Stadler and became acquainted with René Schickele: Stadler and Schickele were the leading writers of the Alsatian avant-garde. In Strasbourg he began to write prose pieces under the influence of Arnold Zweig and Frank Wedekind. "Der Lazo" (The Lasso), his first published story, appeared in the journal *Licht und Schatten* in 1912.

Schmid had in the meantime transferred to the University of Gießen, where he wrote a dissertation on the dramatic style of Alfred de Musset under the conservative Romanist Dietrich Behrens. By 1913, however, he had lost interest in a university career. He later wrote that it was chance that led him to become a writer, but his autobiographical writings are often contradictory and envelop his expressionist years in myths and distortions. The facts indicate that he was a skillful and deliberate promoter of his work; his career as a writer was anything but haphazard. While cultivating the friendship of the influential editor of the liberal *Frankfurter Zeitung*, Heinrich Simson, who published his more conventional stories, Schmid wrote stories in an ecstatic and modern style for avant-garde journals such as Schickele's *Die weißen Blätter* and Hans Pfempfert's *Die Aktion*. In his edition of Edschmid's *Frühe Schriften* (Early Writings, 1970), Ernst Johann gives an example of Edschmid's ability to write simultaneously in two styles: a winter scene depicted in a realistic and

conversational style for the *Frankfurter Zeitung* was written at the same time as an effusive and intense sketch on the same theme for *Die weißen Blätter*.

Some of Schmid's stories came to the attention of the prominent expressionist publisher Kurt Wolff, who wrote in December 1913 asking if he had anything else available for publication. The two met in early 1914. While Wolff rejected Schmid's traditional stories, he expressed an interest in the "modern" ones and asked Schmid to write some more along the same lines, avoiding psychological analysis and emphasizing adventure and outrageousness. Schmid quickly complied and the result was the collection *Die sechs Mündungen* (The Six Estuaries), publication of which was delayed until 1915 by the outbreak of World War I. The book was published under the pseudonym Kasimir Edschmid, which became the author's legal name in 1947.

*Die sechs Mündungen* is usually hailed as the first example of expressionist prose, but this claim is somewhat exaggerated and is perhaps more due to Edschmid's and his publisher's propaganda than to the inherent novelty of the stories. Heinrich Mann and Alfred Döblin were as much responsible for the expressionist prose style as was Edschmid; Edschmid's stories, however, were unique in their radicalism. As in his later expressionist works, the locales are always exotic and emphatically masculine: America's Wild West, Spain, or medieval France. Some of the plots are conventional; others are grotesquely violent, betraying the influence of Flaubert's *Salammbô* (1862). Edschmid's style, a radical version of the styles of Mann and Döblin, was extremely compressed and elliptical, frantically rushing from one image to the next, and emphasizing action rather than static description. In tone as well as in ethos, Edschmid's early stories are thoroughly Nietzschean: the protagonists are beyond conventional morality and live only to exercise their wills. As Edschmid developed, the style became more ecstatic and the abundance of action more inflated to the point that his last expressionist works were almost self-parodies.

In the preface to *Die sechs Mündungen*, Edschmid explains the work's title: "Diese Novellen, die sechs Mündungen heißen, weil sie von verscheidenen Seiten einströmen in den unendlichen Dreiklang unsrer endlichsten Sensationen: des Verzichts—der tiefen Trauer—und des grenzenlosen Todes . . ." (These novellas are called the six estuaries because they flow into the unending triad of our most finite sensations: renunciation—profound sorrow—and boundless death . . .). Death and renunciation are the only boundaries which confine Edschmid's Nietzschean heroes. For example, in the second story of the collection, "Der aussätzige Wald" (The Leprous Forest), the trouvère Jehan Bodel is attacked in a forest in medieval France by a band of leprous robbers whose state of decomposition is vividly described. Bodel hacks off his mule's leg, which he then uses as a club to fend off the robbers. There is no trace of psychological analysis; Edschmid's protagonists do not think—they act. Bodel's only feelings are disgust for his attackers and anger that he did not have time to kill his mule before removing its leg. He acts and fights: "Jehan floh nicht" (Jehan never fled). Bodel goes on to a town, where he buys a Byzantine slave girl, Beautrix. He falls in love with her, but the encounter with the lepers has left Bodel himself contaminated. Despite Beautrix's vows of loyalty, he leaves her and returns to the forest.

The almost exclusive concentration on action is mirrored in Edschmid's style. For example, in the first story, "Der Lazo," a revised version of his first published story, the feverish pace of action is propelled by the short and often elliptical sentences. Raoul Perten, disgusted with the conventions of middle-class life, suddenly decides to seek adventure in America: "Er kam auf die Straße. Da stand eine Laterne, die einmal ein betrunkener Fahrer umgeworfen hatte. Er schritt an ihr vorbei. Ging immer weiter" (He came to the street. There was a lantern which a drunken driver had knocked over. He walked past it. And went on).

The frantic tempo is common to all six novellas. Reading Edschmid is like watching a film in fast motion. Exotic characters—pirates, flagellants, and cowboys—rush by, leaving the reader no chance to catch his breath. *Das rasende Leben* (The Frantic Life, 1915), the title of Edschmid's second collection of stories, serves well as a motto for all his expressionist works.

The circumstances surrounding the publication and reception of *Die sechs Mündungen* are revealing. Wolff and his assistant, Georg Heinrich Meyer, were pioneers in the aggressive promotion of literature. They advertised their works in newspapers and journals, as well as on posters in the streets. They were also among the first German publishers to utilize advertising copy on their book jackets: the anonymous blurb for *Die sechs Mündungen*, which may have been written by Edschmid himself, announced: "Die Kunst dieses neuen Dichters hat keine Ahnen und Vorläufer, ist in den Mitteln ihres Ausdrucks neuartig. . . . Die kom-

*Etching of Edschmid by Max Beckmann, 1917*

mende Generation unserer deutschen Dichtung kündigt sich bedeutend an. Die ersten Vorposten sind gestellt. Kasimir Edschmid ist unter ihnen" (This new author's art is without precedence or ancestry, in its expressive means entirely novel. . . . The new generation of German literature has an impressive herald. The outposts are in place. Kasimir Edschmid is among them). The excessive claims of Edschmid's novelty annoyed some contemporary critics: Hans Siemsen, for example, wrote in the *Zeit-Echo* that to say that Edschmid's work was without ancestry was "haltlose Verleumdung" (groundless slander), and Franz Herwig objected in *Hochland* to the publisher's assertions of Edschmid's uniqueness. But many reviews were positive. The most favorable one was written by Joachim Benn, Gottfried Benn's cousin; it appeared in the *Frankfurter Zeitung*, to whose publisher, Simson, Edschmid had dedicated the book. Benn's judgment that "die Geschichten Kasimir Edschmids sind Musterbeispiele des literarischen Expressionismus, ja, die ersten, die es bisher gab" (Kasimir Edschmid's stories are exemplary models of literary expressionism, indeed, they are the first to exist) has become a topos of literary historians. Benn died shortly after writing this review, and his position as literary critic for the *Frankfurter Zeitung* was taken over by Edschmid himself.

Wolff followed *Die sechs Mündungen* with the publication of *Das rasende Leben*. The first story, "Das beschämende Zimmer" (The Humiliating Room), tells of the narrator's friend's secret gallery: the pictures evoke experiences and adventures the friend has had. The intensity of his reminiscences, however, leads to the friend's mental breakdown. The narrator coldly observes his collapse and draws a moral for himself: "Denn der Genuß des Abenteuers ist das ungewiß Beschwebende: Wissen, vieles Bunte getan zu haben, aber eine Luft hinter sich zu fühlen ohne Halt und ohne Farbe. *Tosendes . . . rasendes Leben . . .—So ist es*" (For the pleasure of adventure is an uncertain hovering: to know that one has done varied things but also to feel a breeze behind one's self without support or color. *Raging . . . frantic life . . .—That is the way it is*). The story is an obvious parable of Edschmid's ideal: a self-conscious and reflective life is decidedly rejected for the *vita activa*. *Das rasende Leben* was less popular than *Die sechs Mündungen*.

Edschmid's next book, *Timur*, published by Wolff in 1916, contains Edschmid's best expressionist stories. Edschmid's stylistic devices and expressionist ideals reach their high point in the story "Der Bezwinger" (The Conqueror). The hero, the fourteenth-century Mongolian-Turkish warrior Timur, represents Edschmid's version of Nietzsche's Übermensch (overman), placed in a setting reminiscent of *Salammbô*. At the end of the story the power-hungry ruler, whose will to power has manifested itself in victory in battle, kills his mistress and drinks her blood. The book received mixed reviews. Hans Johst, who would later play a leading role in the literary bureaucracy of the Nazi government, criticized *Timur* in *Das literarische Echo* for its violence and excesses.

In 1914 Edschmid volunteered for the army, was rejected because of an appendectomy scar dating from his student days in Munich, and was relegated to hospital duty in Darmstadt for a year and a half. Also in 1914 he came close to notoriety through his incidental involvement in a scandal concerning a blasphemous poem that Hugo Ball had written for *Die Aktion*. Edschmid had translated a mildly erotic old French poem for the same issue in which Ball's poem appeared; unlike Ball and Pfempfert, however, he was acquitted.

Throughout World War I, Edschmid continued to write for the *Frankfurter Zeitung, Die weißen Blätter,* and other journals and papers. His nonfiction pieces were generally written in a feuilletonistic style, far removed from the exaggeration and excesses of his fiction. He was well read in modern literature and wrote reviews of works by Arnold Zweig, Heinrich Mann, Döblin, Franz Kafka, and Carl Sternheim. In his role as literary critic for the influential *Frankfurter Zeitung* he became a spokesman for expressionist literature. In December 1917 he was asked to speak before the Deutsche Gesellschaft 1914, a government-sponsored group in Berlin. Edschmid's presentation, "Über den dichterischen Expressionismus" (On Literary Expressionism), is his most famous contribution to the theory of expressionism and has been reprinted numerous times. Edschmid characterizes the true expressionist: "Er sieht nicht, er schaut. Er schildert nicht, er erlebt. Er gibt nicht wider, er gestaltet. Er nimmt nicht, er sucht. Nun gibt es nicht mehr die Kette der Tatsachen: Fabriken, Häuser, Krankheit, Huren, Geschrei und Hunger. Nun gibt es ihre Vision. . . . Der Kranke ist nicht nur der Krüppel, der leidet. Er wird die Krankheit selbst, das Leid der ganzen Kreatur scheint aus seinem Leib und bringt das Mitleid herab von dem Schöpfer" (He does not merely notice, he looks. He sketches nothing, he experiences. He does not imitate, he forms. He does not take, he seeks. No longer is there a chain of facts: factories, houses, sickness, whores, screaming and hunger. Now there is their vision. . . . The sick man is not only the suffering cripple. He becomes sickness itself. The whole creature's suffering shines forth from his body and calls down the creator's pity).

In addition to propagating an ideal, Edschmid attempts to situate expressionism historically. He surveys the literary movements which led to it, such as naturalism and impressionism, and characterizes expressionism as an existential attitude which, arising from the rejection of the introspective confines of middle-class society, embraces the world and life. Written in the same ecstatic and rhetorical style as his fiction, Edschmid's speech is perhaps less valuable as an analysis of a literary movement than as a historical testament of the expressionist movement itself; the yearning and extravagant claims of many of his contemporaries find a memorable echo in the manifesto.

In early 1918 Edschmid was asked by the German foreign office to deliver a series of lectures in Sweden. Edschmid's lecture on Germany's young writers, "Über die dichterische deutsche Jugend" (On the literary German youth), is his second important manifesto on expressionism. It is a paean to German youth and their ideals: "Donnender schallt ihnen als die Kanonen der größten Offensiven das Wort der Zusammengehörigkeit unter den Menschen. Ist Kampf, sei er von Geist. Sie wollen Gerechtigkeit, aber nicht von der Macht, ungeistig wie nur eine, sondern Gerechtigkeit der Tat und Liebe" (The slogan of human solidarity sounds to them with more thunder than the cannons of the greatest offensives. If there is a struggle, then it should be spiritual. They want justice; but not through power, which is as unspiritual as can be, but rather a justice of action and love). Edschmid renounces the extremes to which he had ascribed in *Timur* and pleads for the liberal humanism to which he remained faithful for the rest of his life. In Sweden it became clear to Edschmid that the war was lost for Germany. After the armistice in November 1918, he continued to promote expressionism and also began to plead for reconciliation between Germany and France. In an essay written in 1919 for *Das Tribunal*, "Aufruf an die revolutionäre französische geistige Jugend" (An Appeal to the Revolutionary French Intellectual Youth), which was signed by many leading German expressionist writers, Edschmid gained international fame by calling for friendship between the two countries.

From 1919 to 1922 Edschmid edited *Tribüne der Kunst und Zeit,* a series of writings by modern German authors. The twenty-nine volumes in the collection include works by Schickele, Sternheim, Heinrich Mann, Gottfried Benn, Kurt Hiller, and Theodor Däubler. Edschmid's two manifestos on expressionism were published in the first volume. His activity as an editor and literary critic gained him the loyalty and friendship of these authors, many of whom worked in later years to extend his reputation.

Edschmid's last important expressionist work, *Die achatnen Kugeln* (The Agate Balls), appeared in 1920. The novel was a miserable failure—perhaps proving that an extended version of the author's hectic prose was impossible. Daisy Vaudreuil, Edschmid's first major woman character, frantically seeks adventure in the same manner as Raoul Perten, the hero of Edschmid's first story. In the character of Di Conti, Edschmid depicts a fanatical revolutionary doomed to failure. But the message of the book is less political than aesthetic. It is as if the author realized that his earlier excesses could not be maintained.

Edschmid wrote *Die achatnen Kugeln* in the last years of the war. By the time it was published he had already begun to distance himself from expressionism. He wrote in the essay "Bilanz 31 Dezember 1919": "Ich bin für die Leistung. Aber ich bin gegen Expressionismus, der heute Pfarrerstöchter und Fabrikantenfrauen zu Erbauung umkitzelt" (I am for achievement. But I am against expressionism, which today tickles ministers' daughters and industrialists' wives to their edification). Expressionism had lost its novelty and its shock value; by becoming generally accepted, it had become moribund.

In the mid 1920s Edschmid turned from writing about exotic scenes to seeing them at first hand. From about 1924 until 1941 he traveled almost constantly. He spent ten years in Italy, but also visited South America, the Near East, and Africa. The fruit of these journeys was a series of travelogues and fictional biographies written in the engaging and conversational style characteristic of his first articles for the *Frankfurter Zeitung*. Edschmid's later works are eminently readable and entertaining; they cannot be regarded as serious literature, although Edschmid received the Büchner Prize in 1927. He began to cultivate the image of the cosmopolitan literary gentleman and sportsman, a kind of German Hemingway. The novel *Sport um Gagaly* (1928) depicts Edschmid's new ideal: the Italian racer Passari, like Edschmid, excels in tennis while being highly literate and educated. Edschmid depicts Passari's affairs with the tennis player Gagaly Madosdy and her rival Pista Tossuth in the sophisticated and elegant world of upper-class Venice. The book was the first German novel to take sports as its central theme and gained Edschmid a special medallion for literature at the 1928 Olympic Games.

Throughout the 1920s Edschmid was an unofficial ambassador for the Weimar Republic. His support of the republic and the fact that he had once called President Paul von Hindenburg a mediocrity earned Edschmid the displeasure of the Nazis. In 1933 Edschmid's books were among those burned by German students, and he was forbidden to speak in public. His early expressionist works were spared, however, at least in the infamous blacklist published in the *Börsenblatt für den deutschen Buchhandel* in May 1933 to present "recommendations" to libraries of books that should be removed. Under Edschmid's name it states: "Alles außer Timur und Die sechs Mündungen" (Everything except *Timur* and *Die sechs Mündungen*). He was, however, able to continue writing, and he devoted himself to what became a five-volume study of Italy (1935-1948) in which travelogue, history, gossip, and anecdotes are skillfully combined.

In 1941 the Nazis forbade Edschmid to publish. He returned to Germany from Italy and spent the war years in Ruhpolding in Upper Bavaria. An account of his war experiences is contained in the autobiographical novel *Das gute Recht* (The Good Law, 1946). The novel describes in detail the frustrations and fears he had felt under the last years of fascism.

Edschmid returned to Darmstadt after the war and, as an untainted representative of the "Inner Emigration," played an influential role in the cultural life of the early Federal Republic of Germany. His postexpressionist work achieved much popularity, and he continued to write light novels, historical fiction, and travelogues. His assistance was decisive in the founding in 1949 of the Deutsche Akademie für Sprache und Dichtung (German Academy for Language and Writing), of which he became vice president. Edschmid was also influential in helping to found the new West German P.E.N. Club and was its secretary-general from 1950 to 1957. In 1955 he was awarded the Bundesverdienstkreuz and he received the Komtur Cross of Italy, the Goethe Plaque of Frankfurt, and the Goethe medallion of Hesse. In 1956 Palermo honored him with its first international prize. Throughout the 1950s Edschmid was also active in UNESCO.

With the renewed interest in expressionism in West Germany, Edschmid had some of his early works republished. In 1961 he wrote an account of the entire movement, *Lebendiger Expressionismus*, (Living Expressionism). He became honorary president of the West German P.E.N. Club in 1960 and honorary president of the Deutsche Akademie für Sprache und Dichtung in 1962. He died in Vulpera/Engadin, Switzerland, in 1966.

**References:**

Armin Arnold, *Prosa des Expressionismus* (Stuttgart: Kohlhammer, 1972);

Ursula G. Brammer, *Kasimir Edschmid: Bibliographie* (Heidelberg: Lambert Schneider, 1970);

Günther Engels, "Der Stil expressionistischer Prosa im Frühwerk Kasimir Edschmids," Ph.D. dissertation, Cologne University, 1952;

Hanns W. Eppelsheimer, "Zum 75. Geburtstag Kasimir Edschmids," *DASD-Jahrbuch* (1966): 141-143;

Susan B. Gaertner, "Kasimir Edschmid's 'Die sechs Mündungen': An Introduction and Translation," Ph.D. dissertation, Princeton University, 1974;

Helmut Liede, "Stiltendenzen expressionistischer Prosa: Untersuchungen zu Novellen von Döblin, Sternheim, Edschmid, Heym und Benn," Ph.D. dissertation, University of Freiburg im Breisgau, 1960;

Peter Pfaff, "Kasimir Edschmid," in *Expressionismus als Literatur*, edited by Wolfgang Rothe (Bern & Munich: Francke, 1969), pp. 701-716;

Kurt Pinthus, "Nachwort," in Edschmid's *Die sechs Mündungen* (Stuttgart: Reclam, 1965), pp. 123-134;

George W. Reinhardt, "Jehan Bodel, Gace Brule, and Gustave Flaubert in the Leprous Forest: On the French Sources of Kasimir Edschmid's 'Der aussätzige Wald,'" *Monatshefte*, 68 (1976): 60-69;

Günter Schab, ed., *Kasimir Edschmid: Ein Buch der Freunde zu seinem sechzigsten Geburtstag* (Düsseldorf: Bagel/Munich: Desch, 1950);

Frank Thieß, "So erlebten es Millionen: Über Kasimir Edschmid," *Prisma*, 1, no. 8 (1947): 49;

Lutz Weltmann, ed., *Kasimir Edschmid: Der Weg; die Welt; das Werk* (Stuttgart: Kohlhammer/Munich: Desch, 1955);

Henry Carl Werba, "Einflüsse von Nietzsches 'Zarathustra' auf das Bild des 'Neuen Menschen' in Edschmids frühen Prosawerken," Ph.D. dissertation, University of Connecticut, 1972.

# Hans Fallada
## (Rudolf Ditzen)
### *(21 July 1893-5 February 1947)*

Herbert Knust
*University of Illinois*

BOOKS: *Der junge Goedeschal: Ein Pubertätsroman* (Berlin: Rowohlt, 1920);

*Anton und Gerda: Ein Roman* (Berlin: Rowohlt, 1923);

*Bauern, Bonzen und Bomben: Roman* (Berlin: Rowohlt, 1931);

*Kleiner Mann—was nun? Roman* (Berlin: Rowohlt, 1932); translated by Eric Sutton as *Little Man—What Now?* (New York: Simon & Schuster, 1933; London: Baker, 1969);

*Wer einmal aus dem Blechnapf frißt: Roman* (Berlin: Rowohlt, 1934); translated by Sutton as *Who Once Eats out of the Tin Bowl* (London: Putnam's, 1934); translation republished as *The World Outside* (New York: Simon & Schuster, 1934);

*Wir hatten mal ein Kind: Eine Geschichte und Geschichten* (Berlin: Rowohlt, 1934); translated by Sutton as *Once We Had a Child* (London: Putnam's, 1935; New York: Simon & Schuster, 1936);

*Das Märchen vom Stadtschreiber, der aufs Land flog* (Berlin: Rowohlt, 1935); translated by Sutton as *Sparrow Farm* (London: Putnam's, 1937; New York: Putnam's, 1938);

*Altes Herz geht auf die Reise: Roman* (Berlin: Rowohlt, 1936); translated by Sutton as *Old Heart Goes on a Journey* (London: Putnam's, 1936); translation republished as *An Old Heart Goes A-Journeying* (New York: Simon & Schuster, 1936);

*Hoppelpoppel, wo bist du? Kindergeschichten* (Leipzig: Reclam, 1936);

*Wolf unter Wölfen: Roman* (Berlin & Stuttgart: Rowohlt, 1937); translated anonymously as *Wolf among Wolves* (New York: Putnam's, 1938);

*Der eiserne Gustav: Roman* (Berlin & Stuttgart: Rowohlt, 1938); translated by Philip Owens as *Iron Gustav* (London: Putnam's, 1940);

*Geschichten aus der Murkelei* (Berlin & Stuttgart: Rowohlt, 1938);

*Kleiner Mann, großer Mann—alles vertauscht; oder, Max Schreyvogels Last und Lust des Geldes: Ein heiterer Roman* (Stuttgart: Rowohlt, 1939);

*Hans Fallada (Ullstein)*

*Süßmilch spricht! Ein Abenteuer von Murr und Maxe* (Aalen: Stierlin, 1939);

*Der ungeliebte Mann: Roman* (Stuttgart: Rowohlt, 1940);

*Das Abenteuer des Werner Quabs* (Leipzig: Bohn, 1941);

*Damals bei uns daheim: Erlebtes, Erfahrenes und Erfundenes* (Berlin & Stuttgart: Rowohlt, 1941; edited by Lee Chedeayne and Paul Gottwald, Glenview, Ill.: Scott, Foresman, 1972);

*Heute bei uns zu Haus: Ein anderes Buch Erfahrenes und Erfundenes* (Berlin & Stuttgart: Rowohlt, 1943);

*Der Alpdruck: Roman* (Berlin & Weimar: Aufbau, 1947);

84

*Jeder stirbt für sich allein,* edited by Paul Wiegler
  (Berlin & Weimar: Aufbau, 1947);
*Der Trinker: Roman* (Hamburg: Rowohlt, 1950);
  translated by Charlotte Lloyd and A. L. Lloyd
  as *The Drinker* (London: Putnam's, 1952; New
  York: Didier, 1952);
*Ein Mann will hinauf: Die Frauen und der Träumer.
  Roman* (Munich & Konstanz: Südverlag,
  1953); republished as *Ein Mann will nach oben*
  (Reinbek: Rowohlt, 1970);
*Zwei zarte Lämmchen—weiß wie Schnee: Roman* (Han-
  nover: Fackelträger, 1953);
*Unge herr von Strammin,* translated into Swedish by
  Knut Stubbendorf (Stockholm: Bonniers,
  1954); original German version published as
  *Junger Herr—ganz groß: Roman* (Berlin, Frank-
  furt am Main & Vienna: Ullstein, 1965);
*Die Stunde, eh' du schlafen gehst: Roman einer Liebe*
  (Munich: Goldmann, 1954);
*Fridolin, der freche Dachs: Eine zwei-und vierbeinige
  Geschichte* (Frankfurt am Main: Scheffler,
  1955); translated by Ruth Michaelis-Jena and
  Arthur Ratcliff as *That Rascal, Fridolin* (Lon-
  don: Heinemann, 1959; New York: Pan-
  theon, 1959);
*Werkausgabe in 10 Bänden,* edited by Günter Caspar
  (Berlin & Weimar: Aufbau, 1962-  );
*Gesammelte Erzählungen* (Braunschweig: Rowohlt,
  1967); republished as *Lieschens Sieg und andere
  Erzählungen* (Reinbek: Rowohlt, 1973).

Hans Fallada, author of novels, short stories,
semifictitious memoirs, children's books, and essays
for newspapers and journals, is one of the most
popular German writers of this century, whose sporadic success during his lifetime has turned into
lasting posthumous appeal. Although from a fairly
well-to-do bourgeois background, he wrote
about—and for—the "little man," the common
people, with whom he was in close contact during
the various stages of his problem-ridden life. As an
agricultural assistant in the Prussian provinces; ac-
countant and inspector on several rural estates; inmate of sanatoria, asylums, and prisons; small-town
journalist; employee in many odd jobs; mayor of a
small community after Germany's collapse in 1945;
and champion of the downtrodden "man in the
street" in the metropolis of Berlin, Fallada was fellow companion, keen observer, and eloquent
chronicler of the masses of "small people" on the
social scale: petty bourgeoisie, laborers, low-rank-
ing employees, proletarians, farmers, and social
outcasts, with whose problems (especially during
the economic depression in the late 1920s and early

1930s) he was intimately familiar, and whose characters and idiom he captured in down-to-earth language. In addition to a number of important
Zeitromane (novels critically analyzing the age in
which he lived) portraying the dilemma of the underprivileged during the turmoil of the fading Weimar Republic, Fallada avoided censorship during
the Third Reich by writing novels and stories in a
lighter vein, entertaining and uncomplicated in
psychology and language. None of his writing,
however, is without echoes of his own troubled life
and personality.

Fallada's life, unusual as it may seem in its
disorderliness and its course of mishaps, also reflects characteristic reactions against the "orderli-
ness" of a declining bourgeoisie. Born Rudolf
Ditzen in Greifswald on 21 July 1893, he was the
third of four children of narrow-minded but up-
right citizens of the Wilhelminian empire. His
father, Wilhelm Ditzen, was an ambitious district
judge who later rose to Reichsgerichtsrat, the highest juridical position in Germany; his mother was
Elisabeth Lorenz Ditzen.

Unstable health, slow development, frequent
and almost fatal accidents, a complicated psyche,
and helplessness vis-à-vis social pressures and taboos contributed to Ditzen's vulnerability and unceasing difficulties. Changes of locality due to his
father's career moves, as well as his own lack of
academic success, caused the boy to attend various
schools. The first years at a Berlin Gymnasium under the harassing tutelage of harsh pedagogues led
to a mental crisis. He was transferred to another
school where he fared better. But a new crisis occurred in Leipzig, where his endeavor to meet his
father's expectations of accelerated training was cut
short by a near-fatal fall from his bicycle. He was
never to complete his formal education.

Ditzen's alienation from a sterile adult world
of principles, discipline, and bigotry led to depression, aberrant behavior, escapism, and pessimism.
Once he tried to run away from home and from
humiliation at school; frequently he sought refuge
in books of fantasy and adventure; later he joined
the youth movement Wandervogel and went on a
five-week excursion to Holland, only to find himself
an accident-prone and ridiculed outsider even
there. During his confused and unguided puberty
years he gave way to fixed ideas and suicidal emotions and was sent to a sanatorium in the country.
Seemingly recovered, he went back to school, this
time in Rudolstadt, where, wanting to become a
writer, he took an interest in modern literature.
But a literary contest and "death pact" with an

equally suicidal friend, Hanns Dietrich von Necker, led to a duel. Ditzen killed his friend, then shot himself twice, but survived and was confined in a psychiatric clinic in Tannenfeld, near Jena.

There he stubbornly resisted his aunt Adelaida Ditzen's attempts at therapy by instructing him in foreign languages, but indulged in a short-lived plan of translating works by Romain Rolland. Released in 1913, he took a series of agricultural jobs. At the outbreak of World War I he volunteered for military service but was quickly dismissed because of physical and mental unfitness. During the war he became successful as an authority on and distributor of seed potatoes. But his restlessness continued. A habitual smoker and drinker, he also began to take morphine; despite several treatments and partial recoveries he was never able to free himself completely from his addiction to narcotics.

Divided between a practical profession and his literary obsessions he put himself to the test, with the reluctant financial support of his father. Under the pseudonym Hans Fallada, taken from a sad tale by the Brothers Grimm and adopted to spare his parents embarrassment, he completed his first novel, *Der junge Goedeschal* (1920), the story of a young man's suffering during puberty. A thinly disguised autobiographical reckoning with the father who had dominated his life, the novel was written in imitation of expressionists such as Frank Wedekind, Walter Hasenclever, and Arnolt Bronnen, to whom generational conflict, including the problems of puberty and the hatred of fathers, had been a key issue. Distinct episodes from Fallada's unhappy youth are recognizable, and so are the symptoms of a split personality. To the fledgling author, this first book meant a breaking away from inhibiting fetters; to his parents it meant disgrace; to the public it meant very little.

Even less successful was Fallada's second expressionist novel, *Anton und Gerda* (1923), in which a young man, accompanied by a prostitute, escapes from the city to the country, but is put into a lunatic asylum by his parents. Fallada himself later rejected these first products, bought up the remaining copies, and destroyed them. (In recent criticism there have been attempts to rehabilitate these forgotten novels.)

His literary emancipation, then, was yet another defeat—he seemed unable to earn his living as a writer. Back in the provinces, drifting from one job to another, he became increasingly dependent on drugs and was sentenced to six months in jail for embezzlement. On his release he found

minor posts on estates in politically conservative Prussia. He wrote stories based on his experiences, in a new realistic style, for the journals *Tagebuch* and *Literarische Welt* in 1925. Still a drug addict, however, he was unable to continue to function in occupations he disliked. After a second embezzlement he turned himself in to the police, partly in despair, partly in the hope that imprisonment might free him from his addiction. He served his two-year sentence in the small industrial town of Neumünster.

When Fallada reentered society in 1928, he found himself at the bottom of the social ladder and in the midst of economic misery. In Hamburg, where he joined the Social Democratic party, he defrayed his living expenses by typing address labels for export firms. There he met Anna Issel, a healthy and practical girl from the working class; they were married in Neumünster on 5 June 1929. She was a stabilizing influence on him for a time; he idealized her in the "Lämmchen" figure of his writings.

Through connections in Neumünster Fallada found employment with a right-wing newspaper, for which he had to solicit advertising and subscriptions under humiliating circumstances and cover local events according to manipulated points of view. He also became a jack-of-all-trades for the city chamber of commerce and tourism. The milieu and the occurrences he observed—bribes and fraud, opportunistic intrigues, social and political clashes of town and country during a period of worsening conditions—became the subject of his first realistic novel. An intoxication with writing temporarily replaced his addiction to narcotics; he managed to turn personal experiences, compulsions, and inner conflicts into a creative process and a new identity. Ernst Rowohlt, whom he had met in 1920 and met again on the island of Sylt in 1930, gave him a position in his publishing house in Berlin. Rowohlt hoped that Fallada would use his spare time to write more novels which the firm could publish.

*Bauern, Bonzen und Bomben* (Farmers, Bigwigs and Bombs, 1931) is the story of a farmers' demonstration against excessive taxes and the threat of dispossession. Under their black flag the farmers march into Altholm (Neumünster). Their bloody clash with the police, whose superiors consider the rebellious movement more dangerous than the Communists or the Nazis, is followed by the trial of the protest leaders and the farmers' boycott of the town. The staff of the local newspaper is also involved in the political action and caught up in a

*Title page for Fallada's 1931 novel about a farmers' revolt*

thought in psychological rather than political terms: the small, weak, and hapless reporter Tredup and his tall and stronger colleague Stuff (as well as the vital town mayor, Gareis) may be seen as two sides of his own personality, assessed from a pessimistic and a wishful perspective. His writing style was radically different from that of his earlier novels: the action moves forward through quick, naturalistic, dynamic dialogue, in which Fallada captures linguistic idiosyncrasies of different social types. At dramatic high points, however, some expressionist images still flicker among the realistic descriptions.

Fallada and his wife "Suse" were able to trade their modest two rooms for better lodging in a Berlin suburb, and a son, Ulrich, was born on 14 March 1930. But in 1931 Fallada lost his position at Rowohlt's, and their financial situation worsened in

*Title page for Fallada's 1932 novel about the experiences of a young couple during the Depression*

devious network of conflicting interests. The highly autobiographical portrayal of contemporary events, which was prepublished in the illustrated journal *Kölnische Illustrierte*, paved the way to Fallada's fame. Sales and critical responses were encouraging. Kurt Tucholsky, writing for the liberal weekly *Die Weltbühne*, was among those who clearly saw the political implications of the novel. He agreed with Fallada's claim that this town could stand for a thousand others, with its gossip, greediness, ambitions, and political machinations, and that petty personal motives, shifty opportunism, and blackmail would betray genuine causes and lead to self-destruction. Tucholsky also foresaw that lack of ethical instinct, cowardly bending before ruthless powers, and haphazard chasing of quick profit would play into the hands of fascism, and he warned the book's author to be on his guard against political backlash. Fallada seems to have the deteriorating political climate. Fallada's next and most famous novel, *Kleiner Mann—was nun?* (1932; translated as *Little Man—What Now?*, 1933), appeared a year before Hitler's assumption of power. It depicts the grim prospects of a loving couple with a child amid the economic depression and brings out the existential insecurities of politically passive low-level employees as typical representatives of the "Kleinbürger," groping for sentimental private values as a last resort. (Fallada had read Siegfried Kracauer's important and influential sociological study *Die Angestellten*, 1930.)

Johannes Pinneberg, constantly threatened by unemployment, marries his pregnant girlfriend, who comes from a working-class milieu where he encounters something he has never experienced: political solidarity. A salesman in a Berlin clothing store, where nonfulfillment of a sales quota means the loss of his job and where cutthroat competition is worsened by his colleagues' intrigues, Pinneberg is finally fired and experiences his deepest humiliation when, poverty-stricken and hence socially unacceptable, he is pushed off the sidewalk by a policeman. The growing sense of the inevitability of the fate of the "small people," whose loss of income, exposure to stifling injustice, and paralyzing fear delivers them up to helpless misery, is interspersed with almost miraculous incidents of reprieve that temporarily stem the tide of ill fortune—a short-lived prospect of professional solidarity; deus-ex-machina interventions by helpful figures such as Pinneberg's mother, Pia, her lover Jachmann, Pinneberg's "noble" alter ego Heilbutt, and a cooperative landlord; the loving couple's sense of togetherness, their romantic feeling about a starry heaven over a peaceful river, and their enjoyment of their child "Murkel," private "things they cannot take away from us" and without which life would not be worth living. As much as this mixture of idyllic images, sentimentalism, and vague hope for change may appeal to the reader, these elements function as peaceful interludes rather than as solutions; they are drugs rather than medicine. Even the superior and more successful Heilbutt pursues nudism as a "diversion" from the "muck in Germany." The Nazis are ridiculed and Pinneberg plans to vote Communist next time, but he does not participate in political action. Fallada is criticizing the sociopolitical malaise of contemporary Germany; he is also questioning the values of the little man, which may not be sufficient to save him from destruction.

The success of the novel was instantaneous. Many newspapers had printed it serially; it was praised by critics; a radio play and a film version were made of it without delay; and it was translated into many languages. At last Fallada was his own man and could afford to buy a house. When Hitler's takeover triggered a huge exodus of those who were branded as undesirables, Fallada, because of what he considered his apolitical stance, did not fear a clash with the Nazis; but he was arrested and briefly held for his supposed affiliation with a "Jewish conspirator." Mental stress and drinking precipitated another breakdown. Unable to bring himself to go into exile abroad, Fallada withdrew to a farm he had acquired near Carwitz.

There he completed a novel he had started after his first imprisonment: *Wer einmal aus dem Blechnapf frißt* (1934; translated as *Who Once Eats out of the Tin Bowl*, 1934), the most noteworthy German "jail novel." Willi Kufalt, having been unjustly accused as a youth, reacts to a hostile environment by committing embezzlement. After five years behind bars he attempts to regain a foothold in society—only to land back in jail, where he finds a "home" that he had been denied outside prison walls. The novel's message is that a marked man has no chance of rehabilitation because of society's insensitivity, chicanery, and extortions, aggravated by unemployment. Indeed, "freedom" only leads to new enclosures and restrictions that make prison look attractive. When young Beerboom, like Kufalt an ex-convict and social failure, is turned away by the asylum where he seeks refuge, he cuts his throat. As in *Kleiner Mann—was nun?*, a sense of inevitability prevails, for each effort at reintegration with society falls short. The autobiographical aspects of the novel are obvious: the prison milieu, realistically portrayed in its demeaning effect on human behavior; the fear of stigmatization after release into society; the frustrating search for a job (Kufalt, like Fallada, types address labels in Hamburg, then is briefly employed by a small-town newspaper); the grasping attempts at founding a normal family relationship; the breakdown of all hope under suspicions, accusations, and arrest, causing the social outcast to accept the criminal role he had struggled to leave behind. In the brief preface to the novel Fallada sought to avoid Nazi censorship by declaring that times had changed for the better. As much as this statement was held against him by later critics, the preface did not change the thrust of his novel, nor did the Nazis like him any better for it.

In 1934 Fallada completed what he considered his best novel: *Wir hatten mal ein Kind* (1934; translated as *Once We Had a Child*, 1935). The title

*Fallada in 1936 (Ullstein)*

was prompted by the death of one of his twin daughters, born in 1933; but apart from this episode, a certain kinship with the main character, and the rural locale, there is little specific autobiography in the work. It is the story of a farmer, Johannes Gäntschow, whose stubborn and quarrelsome character leads to conflicts and decline: his marriage falls apart, he loses his child and his possessions, and he dies in solitude. The chroniclelike narrative, at times of striking poetic quality, blends legendary episodes, fantasies, and philosophizing excursions into the slowly unfolding plot. While Fallada pointed at affinities with Jean Paul and Wilhelm Raabe, others have suggested the influence of Knut Hamsun. Despite elements that must have appealed to Nazi ideology, such as northern myth, indictment of alienating city civilization in favor of a healthy country life and attachment to the soil, biological vitalism, and Nietzschean self-assertion, the book did not share the success of his previous novels but was critically attacked for its defeatism.

Suspected by the regime, irritated by criticism of his work, and pressed by property taxes, Fallada fell back into manic depression and apathy. Recovered from his collapse after treatment in a nerve

clinic, he attempted to secure his living by writing nonpolitical, journalistic novels of entertainment. One of these, *Altes Herz geht auf die Reise* (1936; translated as *Old Heart Goes on a Journey,* 1936), nonetheless triggered fierce attacks for ideological reasons; but a few years later, with radical changes imposed on the script, it was made into a movie. Among his lighter prose are also children's stories, such as *Hoppelpoppel, wo bist du?* (Hoppelpoppel, Where Are You?, 1936).

But in 1937 Fallada came out with another masterwork of topical impact, *Wolf unter Wölfen* (1937; translated as *Wolf among Wolves,* 1938), considered by many his most substantial book. It is certainly the most significant novel of social criticism to appear in Germany at that time. It portrays, in a wide panorama of turbulent events and desperate characters of various backgrounds, the economic and moral havoc created by inflation during the Weimar Republic. The many-faceted actions of the story, taking place during one day in 1923 and narrated brilliantly in a variety of techniques including newspaper reports and eyewitness accounts, branch out through the hectic city of Berlin and into the villages and country estates the author knew so well. From the narrative network emerge three main figures, former officers of a regiment, whose postwar lives intertwine. Cavalry Major von Prackwitz-Neulohe fails in his attempt to cultivate an estate leased to him and ends in bankruptcy and insanity. First Lieutenant von Studtmann, unsuccessful as chief receptionist in a Berlin hotel and unable to help his friend von Prackwitz-Neulohe in his crumbling existence, also withdraws into a sanatorium. Only Lieutenant Wolfgang Pagel, a gambler, is able to pull himself out of general disintegration, assume new social responsibilities, and find happiness with his beloved. Again, characters are contrasted in their weaknesses and strengths, but also in fine nuances of psychological development. A host of other figures and groups are shown in their economic hardship, their demoralized conditions, and their reckless struggle for an existence that keeps dissolving—each fighting alone for himself, each the other's enemy. The general atmosphere is one of depression, helplessness, hopelessness, despair. The novel sold rapidly, leaving the author between the satisfaction of popular success and the fear of adverse official reaction. But the book's reception in Nazi circles was split— there even was a short-lived interest in a film adaptation.

The attempt to lure the popular writer into ideological service came in the form of another film

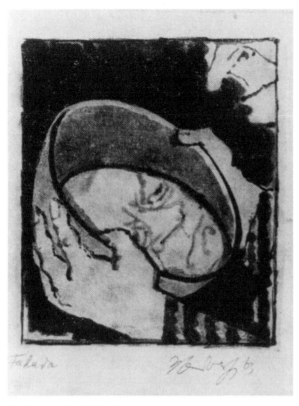

*Caricature of Fallada by Herbert Sandberg ( from the private collection of Herbert Sandberg; photo: Volk und Wissen Verlag Bildarchiv)*

offer. A company apparently backed by the ministry of propaganda proposed that Fallada write a manuscript dealing with German history between 1914 and 1933, to be adapted into a movie in which the celebrated actor Emil Jannings hoped to play a leading role. Under pressure, and working within imposed strictures, Fallada completed *Der eiserne Gustav* (1938; translated as *Iron Gustav*, 1940), the story of the disruption of a lower-class bourgeois family during the social decline after World War I. Old Gustav Hackendahl, a former Prussian cavalryman who now runs a horse-cab operation, has earned the epithet *Iron* because of the strict moral demands he has transferred from the military code to family order: hard work, a sense of duty, absolute uprightness, and submission to authority. But his unbending personality tyrannizes over his children, paralyzes their willpower, and turns them away. The oldest son secretly marries a seamstress, is cursed by his father, and dies at the front. Erich, Gustav's favorite son, turns from military officer to black market profiteer. His daughter Eva becomes a prostitute. His daughter Sophie forsakes the family for a more fashionable milieu. The youngest

son, Heinz, endowed with some of his father's qualities, manages to find a fairly idyllic existence with his girlfriend. Hackendahl himself, reduced to his last cab by inflation and competition from taxis, remains unchanged amid failure and humiliation and, shortly before his death, gains brief fame by making a trip with his cab to Paris. To the Nazis, who stalled the printing of the book—the film did not materialize—Fallada made concessions by letting the only son who succeeds in society join the Nazi party. While Fallada's hand was forced in some respects, the novel remains another realistic document of the time, weaving a unified plot out of the numerous episodic strands and culminating in the artful characterization of the title figure.

Tired of Nazi censorship, Fallada again withdrew into noncommittal subjects and wrote several novels for newspapers. *Kleiner Mann, großer Mann—alles vertauscht* (Little Man, Big Man—Everything Turned Around, 1939), which was first printed under the title "Himmel, wir erben ein Schloß" (Heavens, We Inherit a Castle) in the illustrated magazine *Die Dame*, deals with the little man's inability to manage sudden affluence (Fallada's own experience after his first literary success). *Der ungeliebte Mann* (The Unloved Man, 1940) is a moody narrative of problematic relations; the author's own marriage was deteriorating at the time, although another son, Achim, was born on 3 April 1940. *Ein Mann will hinauf* (A Man Wants Up), written in 1941 and published in book form in 1953, is the story of Karl Siebrecht, a young man who comes from a small town to seek his fortunes in Berlin, where he makes his way up from worker to manager of a transportation business. During this period Fallada also wrote more children's books as well as two books of memoirs in which he blended facts with fiction: *Damals bei uns daheim* (At Home with Us Then, 1941), a surprisingly carefree account of his youth before World War I; and the sequel, *Heute bei uns zu Haus* (At Home with Us Today, 1943), a portrayal of his life as a writer and family man. The love story *Zwei zarte Lämmchen—weiß wie Schnee* (Two Soft Little Lambs White as Snow), written in 1942, was published in 1953. Other nonpolitical works of Fallada's catered to the tastes of the Berlin newspapers *Berliner Illustrierte* and *Woche,* where they were first published. The lighthearted short novel *Die Stunde, eh' du schlafen gehst* (The Hour before You Go to Sleep), also written in 1942, first appeared as a book in 1954. The novel *Junger Herr—ganz groß* (Quite a Young Gentleman), a rural variation on the generation conflict theme, was written in 1943 and published as a book first in Swedish as *Unge herr von Strammin* (1954), then in German (1965).

In 1943 the Nazis attempted to enlist Fallada's services for a propagandistic report. He made a brief trip to France to collect information but never completed the assignment. Back in Carwitz, an encounter with a young widow, Ursula Losch, attractive but insecure, unstable, and addicted to alcohol and drugs, struck familiar chords in Fallada. His faltering marriage ended in divorce on 5 July 1944. More problems followed when, in a state of stress and confusion, he shot at his former wife, was tried for attacking her, and was confined in an institution for three and a half months. There, under the pretense of finishing an anti-Semitic work on the decline of a Jewish banking house, Fallada wrote an intensely personal, largely confessional novel, *Der Trinker* (The Drinker, 1950), whose main figure, the petty bourgeois Erwin Sommer, experiences loss of human relationships, divorce, social decline, addiction to alcohol, and destruction of his life down to hopeless seclusion in an institution, all described relentlessly in depressing detail. For its narrative realism and psychological insight into the unhappy state of outsiders and forlorn existences, this novel has been compared to Dostoyevsky's *The Gambler*.

Released from the sanatorium, Fallada, despite intentions of returning to his former wife, married Losch on 1 February 1945. They moved from Carwitz to Feldberg, which was occupied by the Russians at the end of the war. After delivering, at the behest of the Soviet commander, a speech on the "Day of Victory," Fallada was installed as mayor of Feldberg, but encountered great difficulties in the position. His experiences during this trying period are reflected in the novel *Der Alpdruck* (The Nightmare, 1947), an unsparing account of the Germans in 1945—including himself: Dr. Doll, the small-town mayor, with all his weaknesses, mistakes, hopes, and disappointments, is Fallada, despairing over the realization that the shambles of 1945 did not lead to a moral revival and a call to cooperative reconstruction, but produced a murky climate of cowardly and egoistic catch-as-catch-can, petty opportunism, shabby lies, continued meanness, and refusal of individual or joint responsibility. The novel, despite its faults, is a telling document of German demoralization in the postwar chaos but concludes with a cautious prediction of better times to come.

After another breakdown and treatment in a clinic, Fallada found emergency lodging for himself and his wife in destroyed Berlin. There the

*Fallada in 1946*

cultural official for East Berlin, Johannes R. Becher, aided Fallada and persuaded him to participate in efforts to revive intellectual life in the Russian zone of occupied Germany. Becher suggested that Fallada write a major novel dealing with the Nazi era, and despite exhaustion, illness, hospitalizations, and relapses into heavy use of narcotics, Fallada wrote his last and not his worst novel, *Jeder stirbt für sich allein* (Each Dies for Himself Alone), published posthumously in 1947. The novel, derived from actual Gestapo files and reading, in parts, like a detective story, is the tale of a married couple from the working classes, Otto and Anna Quangel, who—shaken by the death of their son—resist Nazi terror by secretly distributing subversive messages against the regime. It is a solitary, dangerous, and ultimately tragic endeavor of the old couple, who act for personal reasons rather than out of political ideology. The book may be Fallada's least autobiographical novel; nonetheless, it also reveals features and patterns familiar from his other works, including a disturbed father-son relationship, the "weak man-strong woman" constellation, the wavering Kleinbürger (petty bourgeois) mentality, the "solitary outsider" motif, and so forth, unmistakably betraying the author's own personality. The Gestapo agents and Nazi informers are drawn with precision, sometimes to the point of caricature. In the preface to the book, the author almost apologetically points out that the gloomy picture of torture and death, of jails and lunatic asylums simply corresponds to recent historical realities.

Fallada died on 5 February 1947 in the Charité Hospital in Berlin. The reception of his work since then is indicative of changing perceptions. Public interest in the works of this "people's author" was at first greater than scholarly interest in a writer who was not a deep thinker. During the two decades immediately following World War II, his novels of "entertainment" and his memoirs remained more popular than his novels of social criticism, which have gained increasing attention since the mid 1960s due to shifting economic and political conditions and a new historical awareness.

Serious research on Fallada first emerged in some non-German dissertations, but only since the 1970s has his writing become the object of steady and substantial inquiry. Apart from the common distinction between Unterhaltungsroman (light novel) and Zeitroman—to which may be added his "realistic" contribution to children's literature—movement-oriented critics have classified Fallada's writings as belonging to the postexpressionist period of Neue Sachlichkeit (New Objectivity)—a sober, factual realism, depicting the world and human problems from a seemingly detached, impersonal, often ironic perspective. But such objective "factuality"—be it through casual description of milieu, events, and behavior or through dialogues colored by dialect and jargon—can also enhance emotions released from restraint; and in the case of Fallada such dialectics occur frequently, ranging from a harsh reality, mostly perceived as fatalistic, to subjective, wish-dream escapism and a penchant for the idyllic.

Fallada's literary skills were praised by well-known authors of his time, including Tucholsky, Becher, Hermann Broch, Thomas Mann, Hermann Hesse, and Carl Zuckmayer; his lack of ideology and deficient political orientation, on the other hand, were criticized in various quarters. The Nazis had disliked his unheroic portrayal of figures from the Volk, especially from the country, even in books that appear to cater to the taste of the

regime. Marxist critics complained that while he certainly brought out the decline of the small bourgeoisie, he did not pay sufficient attention to the conditions and ethos of the working class. Other critics argued that the documentary quality of his work reveals more about the particularities of his pysche than about the facts of contemporary history. Many have expressed regret that his rational analysis fell short of his emotional reactions.

Despite several good biographies, further information from scattered sources is needed for a full understanding of his complicated life, his sometimes ambiguous political consciousness, and his public stands. In recent scholarship, psychological, historical, and sociological aspects of Fallada's work and its reception have been of major interest, and his dilemma under fascist dictatorship has been addressed repeatedly. The question of dichotomy or convergence of private experience and typical phenomena of the time continues to be a matter of curiosity and debate.

Comprehensive studies exist on recurring themes, motifs, constellations, and patterns in Fallada's work, such as the social outcast; the plight of the downtrodden and the victimization of the individual in a corrupt society; depression, unemployment, poverty, and the decay of morals after World War I; father-son conflicts; marriage problems; the role of woman, especially the idealized figure of "Lämmchen" and similar types as the "little" man's anchor or guardian angel; the juxtaposition of weak and strong figures or alter egos; patterns of dualism or schizoid dispositions; negative education, that is, lack of experience and of self-confidence, leading to isolation rather than social interaction. But dominating these themes are two major topics of comment, both derived from the title of Fallada's most successful novel and both frequently used as summary concepts in regard to the author and his oeuvre: one is a recurring social type, the "Kleiner Mann"—the characteristic representative of the lower middle class with which Fallada most identified, the Kleinbürger or petty bourgeois with all his limitations and yearnings; the other is the little man's apparently helpless attitude in the face of overpowering problems that seem without solution, expressed in the nagging question "Was nun?" (What is to be done?).

Fallada did not give any clear answers; he described what he observed. The questions he raised are symptomatic of the ills and the mentality of an epoch—but they are not limited to that epoch nor do they reflect strictly German conditions. His works appealed to millions by way of paperback editions and theater, film, or television adaptations. His books have been translated into over twenty languages. Generations of readers in Germany and abroad have recognized and been challenged by the problems he so obsessively described; they have been captivated by his yearning for peace, security, and private happiness; and they have been fascinated by his absorbing plots, compelling portrayals of milieu, masterful characterizations with subtle psychological insights, vivid imagery, and flexible language in a variety of realistic techniques. Not only was he an outstanding chronicler of his time, a seismographer of its social crises—he also was a sympathetic historian of human nature, a unique poet of the "little man."

**Biographies:**

Jürgen Manthey, *Hans Fallada in Selbstzeugnissen und Bilddokumenten* (Reinbek: Rowohlt, 1963; revised, 1983);

Alfred Gessler, *Hans Fallada: Sein Leben und Werk* (Berlin: Aufbau, 1972);

Tom Crepon, *Leben und Tode des Hans Fallada: Eine Biographie* (Halle & Leipzig: Mitteldeutscher Verlag, 1978);

Werner Liersch, *Hans Fallada: Sein großes kleines Leben. Biographie* (Berlin: Neues Leben, 1981).

**References:**

Johannes R. Becher, "Was nun? Zu Hans Falladas Tod," *Aufbau*, 3, no. 2 (1947): 97-101;

Harry Bergholz, "Hans Fallada's Breakthrough," *German Quarterly*, 29 ( January 1956): 19-24;

Leonhard Frank, *Hans Fallada* (Berlin: Volk & Wissen, 1962);

Hans Jürgen Frotscher, *Hans Fallada: Kleiner Mann—was nun?* (Munich: Oldenbourg, 1983);

Charlotte Heinrichs, "Wirklichkeit und Wirksamkeit des Dichters Hans Fallada," *Berliner Hefte*, 2, no. 4 (1947): 234-250;

Bernd Hüppauf, "Hans Fallada: 'Kleiner Mann—was nun?,' " in *Der deutsche Roman im 20. Jahrhundert, I: Analysen und Materialien zur Theorie und Soziologie des Romans*, edited by Manfred Brauneck (Bamberg: Buchner, 1976), pp. 209-239;

Karl Korn, "Moira und Schuld: Ein Bericht über neue Romane," *Die Neue Rundschau*, 49, no. 2 (1938): 603-616;

Claus Dieter Krohn, "Hans Fallada und die Weimarer Republik: Zur Disposition kleinbürgerlicher Mentalitäten vor 1933," in *Literaturwissenschaft und Geschichtsphilosophie:*

*Festschrift für W. Emrich*, edited by Helmut Arntzen and others (Berlin & New York: De Gruyter, 1975), pp. 507-522;

Jürgen Kuczynski, " 'Kleiner Mann—was nun?' oder Macht und Idylle," in his *Gestalten und Werke: Soziologische Studien zur deutschen Literatur* (Berlin & Weimar: Aufbau, 1969), pp. 350-358;

Helmuth Lethen, "Falladas 'Kleiner Mann—was nun?' und die bürgerliche Mittelstandtheorien," in his *Neue Sachlichkeit 1924-1932: Studien zur Literatur des weißen Sozialismus* (Stuttgart: Metzler, 1970), pp. 156-167;

Wilhelmus J. M. Loohuis, *Hans Fallada in der Literaturkritik. Ein Forschungsbericht* (Bad Honnef: Keimer/Zurich: Hebsacker, 1979);

Georg Lukács, *Deutsche Literatur im Zeitalter des Imperialismus* (Berlin: Aufbau, 1950), pp. 711-716;

Lukács, "Hans Fallada: Die Tragödie eines begabten Schriftstellers unter dem Faschismus," *Sammlung*, 3 (1980): 59-71;

Hanno Möbius, "Der Sozialcharakter des Kleinbürgers in den Romanen Falladas," in *Stereotyp und Vorurteil in der Literatur: Untersuchungen zu Autoren des 20. Jahrhunderts*, edited by James Elliot and others (Göttingen: Vandenhoeck & Ruprecht, 1978), pp. 84-110;

Renate Möhrmann, "Biberkopf, was nun? Großstadtmisere im Berliner Roman der präfaschistischen Ära: Dargestellt an Alfred Döblins 'Berlin Alexanderplatz' und Hans Falladas 'Kleiner Mann—was nun?,' " *Diskussion Deutsch*, 9 (1978): 133-151;

Ruth Römer, "Dichter des kleinbürgerlichen Verfalls: Vor zehn Jahren starb Hans Fallada," *Neue Deutsche Literatur*, 5, no. 2 (1957): 120-131;

Max Schroeder, "Hans Fallada: Zum Erscheinen seines nachgelassenen Romans 'Der Trinker,' " *Neue Deutsche Literatur*, 1, no. 12 (1953): 124-130;

Heinz J. Schueler, *Hans Fallada: Humanist and Social Critic* (The Hague & Paris: Mouton, 1970);

Harry Slochover, "Hauptmann and Fallada: Uncoordinated Writers of Nazi-Germany," *Accent*, 3 (Autumn 1942): 18-25;

Arrigo V. Subiotti, "Kleiner Mann—was nun? and *Love on the Dole*: Two Novels of the Depression," in *Weimar Germany: Writers and Politics*, edited by Alan F. Bance (Edinburgh: Scottish Academic Press, 1982), pp. 77-90;

Ulrike Theilig and Michael Töteberg, "Das Dilemma eines deutschen Schriftstellers: Hans

Fallada und der Faschismus," *Sammlung*, 3 (1980): 72-88;

Jürgen C. Thöming, "Hans Fallada: Seismograph gesellschaftlicher Krisen," in *Zeitkritische Romane des 20. Jahrhunderts: Die Gesellschaft in der Kritik der deutschen Literatur*, edited by Hans Wagener (Stuttgart: Reclam, 1975), pp. 97-123;

Thöming, "Soziale Romane in der Endphase der Weimarer Republik," in *Die deutsche Literatur in der Weimarer Republik*, edited by Wolfgang Rothe (Stuttgart: Reclam, 1974), pp. 212-236;

Kurt Tucholsky, "Bauern, Bonzen und Bomben," in volume 9 of his *Gesammelte Werke in 10 Bänden* (Reinbek: Rowohlt, 1976), pp. 168-175;

J. Williams, "Hans Fallada's Memoirs: Fact or Fiction?," *New German Studies*, 12 (1984): 21-35;

Livia Wittmann, "Der Stein des Anstoßes: Zu einem Problemkomplex in berühmten und gerühmten Romanen der Neuen Sachlichkeit," *Jahrbuch für Internationale Germanistik*, 14, no. 2 (1982): 56-78;

Rudolf Wolff, ed., *Hans Fallada: Werk und Wirkung* (Bonn: Bouvier, 1983);

H. A. Wyk, "Hans Fallada," *Living Age*, 344 (1933): 328-332.

**Papers:**
Although a Fallada archive exists at the Akademie der Künste (DDR) in East Berlin, many of Hans Fallada's papers are still scattered in private hands.

# Marieluise Fleißer
## (22/23 November 1901-2 February 1974)

### Peter Beicken
*University of Maryland, College Park*

BOOKS: *Fegefeuer in Ingolstadt* (Berlin: Arcadia Theaterverlag, 1926);

*Pioniere in Ingolstadt* (Berlin: Arcadia Theaterverlag, 1929);

*Ein Pfund Orangen und 9 andere Geschichten der Marieluise Fleißer aus Ingolstadt* (Berlin: Kiepenheuer, 1929);

*Mehlreisende Frieda Geier: Roman vom Rauchen, Sporteln, Lieben und Verkaufen* (Berlin: Kiepenheuer, 1931);

*Andorranische Abenteuer* (Berlin: Kiepenheuer, 1932);

*Karl Stuart: Trauerspiel in fünf Akten* (Munich: Desch, 1946);

*Avantgarde: Erzählungen* (Munich: Hanser, 1963);

*Abenteuer aus dem Englischen Garten: Geschichten* (Frankfurt am Main: Suhrkamp, 1969);

*Gesammelte Werke*, edited by Günther Rühle, 3 volumes (Frankfurt am Main: Suhrkamp, 1972);

*Stücke*, preface by Manfred Nössig (Berlin: Henschelverlag, 1976);

*Ausgewählte Werke in einem Band*, edited by Klaus Schuhmann (Berlin: Aufbau, 1979);

*"In die Enge geht alles," Marieluise Fleißers Gang in die innere Emigration, Fragment "Walper," Skizzen und zwei Briefe aus dem Nachlaß*, edited by Eva Pfister (Berlin: Friedenauer, 1984).

Marieluise Fleißer, an underrated author, is virtually unknown in the English-speaking countries. Fleißer achieved sudden prominence in the 1920s and suffered an equally sudden silencing when the Third Reich banned her books and forbade her to write, except for a few articles and stories in newspapers and magazines. Fleißer's struggle after World War II to regain the status she had enjoyed for a short time during the Weimar period was largely unsuccessful, and it was only toward the end of her life, from 1968 to her death in 1974, that she experienced a renaissance of sorts. During this period she revised many of her works for new productions of her plays and for the 1972 three-volume edition of her collected works.

Fleißer's name is closely associated with Ingolstadt, her hometown on the Danube north of

*Marieluise Fleißer (Ullstein)*

work, while centered around the provincialism and petty mentality of a small Bavarian town, nevertheless represents a cogent critique of the powers that dehumanize human societies. Whereas the prevalent social criticism during the Weimar period was informed by the Marxist analysis of alienation of the economic, social, and political conditions in society, Fleißer focused on the impact of societal pressures on the personal level. Her radical critique detected a "power play" between individuals and an ever present master-slave syndrome in the relationship between men and women.

Born on 22 or 23 November 1901 (sources give conflicting dates) to Heinrich and Anna Schmidt Fleißer, Marieluise Fleißer was an unwanted child; her father, a smith and owner of a hardware store, had wished for a boy. Yet, gifted and talented and determined to prove herself, Fleißer soon gained a privileged place within the family and won support for her educational ambitions. She was sent to a convent school, then to the University of Munich, where she entered the drama department then headed by the renowned Arthur Kutscher. Kutscher was a champion of the

Munich. It is a Catholic town with an illustrious history as an early trading center, university town, and garrison and served as the backdrop for most of Fleißer's works. Typically, these works explore the vicissitudes of the social life of a hypocritical people between the waning influence of religion and the rotten values of petty provincialism. Fleisser's harsh criticism of these alienating influences prompted an indignant reaction to her works; but, above all, it was her unfortunate fate of being manipulated into the crossfire between warring literary camps that caused her downfall at the end of the Weimar period. Even before the Nazis began stamping out her existence as a writer, she had collapsed from her struggles to become independent personally, professionally, and economically. By the end of 1932, after a disastrous romantic liaison, her economic situation had become so precarious, her health so deteriorated, and her confidence in her writing so eroded that she took refuge in Ingolstadt, where, despised and surrounded by hostility, she spent the rest of her life. The struggle of a woman writer to emancipate herself had ended in failure.

Fleißer's life is a paradigm case of the repressed female in a male-dominated society. Her

*The journalist Helmut Draws-Tychsen, with whom Fleißer had a disastrous relationship (Verlag Donau Kurier)*

*Fleißer (center) with the cast of her play* Pioniere in Ingolstadt, *Dresden, 1928 (Verlag Donau Kurier)*

playwright Frank Wedekind, an important influence on Bertolt Brecht. After a brief liberating and initiating relationship with Alexander Weicker, an adventurer of dubious character, Fleißer, who had been writing stories and essays to purge herself of the negative experiences she had had in the convent, was "transformed" by meeting two of the main figures of Munich's literary avant garde: Lion Feuchtwanger, on the brink of his successful career as novelist, and Brecht, who was just starting to revolutionize the German stage. Both men advised Fleißer to follow the new vein of writing, the Neue Sachlichkeit (New Objectivity). Feuchtwanger, in particular, called on Fleißer to relinquish her subjective and expressionistic beginnings. Obediently, she burned all of her youthful writings including an attack on the mental strictures of her "imprisonment" in the convent in an essay titled "Is Rebellion Sin?" She came to regret this act later, when she realized the extent to which the beginning of her serious writing was influenced by the men.

Fleißer's first published work was the autobiographical story "Meine Zwillingsschwester Olga" (My Twin Sister Olga, 1923), which was revised in 1969 as "Die Dreizehnjährigen" (The Thirteen-Year-Olds). The story treats the male-female relationship from the perspective of youths awakening to the crises of puberty under the pressures of both adult society and peer groups. Fleißer reveals the self-destructive aggressiveness prevalent in "youth packs" with their pecking orders and desire to beat down weaker members.

Challenged by Feuchtwanger's and Brecht's experiments on the stage, Fleißer conceived her first play, "Die Fußwaschung" (The Feet-Washing). The title was changed by Moriz Seeler, director of the Berlin avant-garde theater Junge Bühne, whom Brecht had pressured into producing the play, to *Fegefeuer in Ingolstadt* (Purgatory in Ingolstadt, 1926) because he needed a "catchier" title for promotional purposes. Thus Fleißer's intended allusion to the biblical ritual of washing feet was replaced by a much more apocalyptic title than she had in mind. The performance, a one-time Sunday matinee in 1924, was highly successful; the Berlin critics applauded the superb poetic qualities of Fleißer's play.

Fleißer had launched her career in Berlin, literary center of the Weimar Republic. The worldliness of the Berlin circles made her feel inferior, however; to soften her appearance as a provincial from the Bavarian countryside, she wore borrowed clothes. When her father forced her to leave the university in 1924 without a degree—supposedly because of financial problems but in reality because of his disapproval of her writing—Fleißer saw her chance for economic independence. With Brecht's assistance Fleißer signed with the Ullstein publishing house and began receiving a monthly income.

*Fegefeuer in Ingolstadt* was not performed again until a 1971 revision was produced by the Wuppertal theater. The play is a further exploration of the "youth pack." A group of lonely adolescents is driven by societal pressures and sexual repression either to insanity or to conformism. Olga, a pregnant teenager, is deserted by the cruel Peps and tries to drown herself and the unborn child in the river. She is saved by Roelle, the group's scapegoat, whose religious bent makes him a modern-day Christ figure, albeit a deranged one. Berotter, Olga's father, is a powerless patriarch weakened by the disrespect and aggressive counterattacks of his children. Roelle's mother, on the other hand, is a domineering woman whose possessiveness forces her child into the fold of the church, thus demonstrating the repressive and neurotic nature of misplaced mothering. Fleißer's poetically condensed language reflects the aggressive dynamics of beings who inhabit a Dantean purgatory without hope for redemption.

In her relationship with Brecht, Fleißer experienced both the inspiration and the authority of his mentorship. While Brecht led her on, admitting freely to his "career as a criminal" in matters of the heart, he directed her to write a play about the havoc created by visiting army engineers in Fleißer's hometown. This "Komödie in zwölf Bildern" (comedy in twelve pictures), *Pioniere in Ingolstadt* (Engineers in Ingolstadt, 1929), had an uneventful first performance in 1928 in Dresden, where it received mixed reviews. In 1929 Brecht, realizing the provocative potential of the play with its critique of the military, arranged for a Berlin performance, which he directed from behind the scenes ( Jacob Geis was the nominal director). Pursuing his radical Marxist goals, Brecht acted as an agent provocateur to annoy the police and the censors. Fleißer was forced to produce new and even more provocative material, and Brecht made revisions wherever he saw fit. His anticipation of the conflict with the officials proved to be correct. After the scandalous first performance the censors forced cuts of passages criticizing the military. Fleißer, realizing that Brecht had used her play and herself for political purposes, broke with this master of literary intrigue and cliquish infighting. In May of that year she fell into the hands of a reactionary journalist, Helmut Draws-Tychsen, to whom she got engaged—only to see her fortunes as a writer and independent woman take a ruinous turn.

*Pioniere in Ingolstadt* shows the all-pervasiveness of the master-slave syndrome in human life

*Fleißer in 1931 (photo by Lotte Jacobi, Ullstein)*

by focusing on the universality of love and exploitation. All human relations—social, professional, public, private, and intimate—are subject to the law of the users and the used. Above all, men are users of women: masters use their servant girls, lovers use their mistresses, soldiers use prostitutes; at the same time, these users get used by the women they believe they are exploiting: the prostitutes use their clients, the mistresses use their lovers, the servant girls use their masters to complete the vicious circle.

The play, staged in a pre-World War I setting for reasons of censorship, depicts the lawlessness and disorder caused in a small provincial town when a sex-hungry soldiery descends upon a complacent, corrupt citizenry. Fleißer shows that this seemingly orderly town is itself controlled by the exploitation principle. This point is made particularly obvious in Unertl's advice to his son Fabian to use their domestic Berta as a means to his sexual education. Berta, naively trying to escape the drudgery of her social condition, gives herself to love and throws herself into the arms of Korl, the most vicious of the army engineers, who passes on to her the humiliation to which he is subjected by his superiors. Berta's defloration only serves his self-gratification; she realizes that sexual contact under these conditions amounts to an absolute absence of love and mutual understanding.

Unlike her friend Alma, Berta is unable to exploit callously in return. Defending her sense of an unspoiled self and expressing her yearning for a life beyond the necessities of the brutal warfare between the sexes, she states: "I cannot live this way." It is a declaration of dignity in the face of a human hell. *Pioniere in Ingolstadt* goes beyond *Fegefeuer in Ingolstadt* to depict a human inferno. Yet in spite of its sexual frankness, its depiction of a brutish military, and its derision of middle-class life, the play has a comic intent: it exhibits the follies of people who are engrossed in a way of life that makes them both pitiful and ludicrous.

The master-slave syndrome, the exploitation of innocent, naively subservient, and lovingly dedicated girls and women, is at the center of Fleißer's first collection of short stories and first book publication, *Ein Pfund Orangen* (One Pound of Oranges, 1929). This volume received little praise from critics. Walter Benjamin, however, recognized the significance of these stories, which use language shifts to delineate the social movements of the characters, above all the masters and their servant girls. Woman is depicted as a servant without hope for mercy; love is shown as a merciless business transaction in which the women are powerless; symbolic fruits, the apple or the orange, signify innocent belief in a promised paradise. Fleißer's women, with their trust in magic, experience the loss of paradise every moment of every day.

From these negative fairy tales Fleißer, attacked by a hostile press and forced to litigate against defamations by the mayor of Ingolstadt (she won the case), turned to satire in her next play. Between travels with Draws to Sweden and Andorra, she mocked the infighting and the power structures of the Berlin literary cliques in *Tiefseefisch* (Deep Sea Fish, which was written in 1930 but not published until it was revised in 1972). The relationship of Elnis and Ebba (Gesine and Laurenz in the 1972 revision) depicts Fleißer's (Elnis/Gesine) exploitation by and dependence upon Draws-Tychsen (Ebba/Laurenz); Brecht (Wollank/Tütü) also appears. The Berlin critics reacted very unfavorably to two public readings of parts of the play, in which Fleißer exposed her dilemma as a woman writer caught in the firing line between opposing camps.

Ill advised by Draws-Tychsen to switch publishers from Ullstein to Kiepenheuer, Fleißer was forced to submit a novel within a year. In need of money and suffering under the pressure of producing by a deadline, Fleißer wrote her only novel, *Mehlreisende Frieda Geier: Roman vom Rauchen, Sporteln, Lieben und Verkaufen* (Flour Selling Frieda Geier: A Novel about Smoking, Sports, Love and Saleswomanship, 1931), which delves into the milieu of the Weimar proto-fascist petty bourgeoisie. The young tobacco shop owner Gustl Amricht, whose name originally served as the title of the novel, is a literary portrait of Josef ("Bepp") Haindl, a swimming champion in Ingolstadt, to whom Fleißer had been engaged in 1928. In renaming the novel, Fleißer shifted the focus from the male character to a traveling saleswoman and

Dust jacket for Fleißer's only novel, the story of the conflict between a domineering husband and an independent-minded wife

*Page from the manuscript for Fleißer's 1950 comedy in Bavarian dialect,* Der starke Stamm *(Verlag Donau Kurier)* her struggles to be a successful professional. Gustl initiates a relationship in which he attempts to dominate and subjugate Frieda, who resents his possessive behavior. She contrasts the patriarchal traditions of Europe with the liberated social conditions of America: "In America men and women work together." When Gustl rejects this principle of partnership and tries to force Frieda into subordination as a lover and assistant in his business, she leaves him. Gustl then drops back into the "pack," a gang that engages at the end of the novel in a brawl with another group, demonstrating the aggressive male behavior and violent resolutions of conflicts that became prevalent in the barroom politics of the Nazis.

While Fleißer succeeded in her novel in presenting a modern-day heroine capable of preserv-

*Fleißer in 1926 with her hometown sweetheart Josef ("Bepp") Haindl, whom she later married and who served as the model for the husband in* Mehlreisende Frieda Geier *(Verlag Donau Kurier)*

ing herself against exploitative social conventions and patriarchal pressures, she herself was not so strong. In 1932, after breaking her engagement to the irrational and dictatorial Draws-Tychsen, whom she labeled "der Dompteur" (the animal trainer), and attempting suicide, she moved back to Ingolstadt. In 1935 she married Haindl, who turned out to be a tyrant, imposing on her—contrary to his promise to allow her a certain amount of creative time for herself—household chores and duties in his tobacco shop. Her domestic situation, coupled with forced labor in war-related production in local factories, resulted in a nervous breakdown in 1938 and persistent ill-health thereafter. These problems are reflected in her moving autobiographical story "Eine ganz gewöhnliche Vorhölle" (A Quite Ordinary Hell, 1963, revised in 1972).

After the war Fleißer desperately tried to start anew as a writer, but two plays, the historical *Karl Stuart* (Charles Stuart, 1946), secretly written during the Third Reich, and the comedy in Bavarian dialect, *Der starke Stamm* (The Strong Tree, 1950), brought little success. In 1955 Fleißer, in despair, turned for help to Brecht, who suggested that she move to East Berlin to reestablish herself in the theater; but Fleißer felt compelled to remain with her husband, although she loathed their marriage. Only after Haindl's death in 1958 was she free, though exhausted and depleted in her creative energies, to resume her writing career. Among the works of the 1960s "Avantgarde" (1963) is the most impressive. This poetically dense work uses fictional characters to analyze Fleißer's relationship with Brecht, the genius and dominating figure of her Berlin experience. "Avantgarde" is an unmatched self-revelation of a woman who set out to liberate herself as a writer, only to find her attempts at emancipation foiled by powerful, radical, ruthlessly rational, and self-centered men. It is the story of woman as victim and as accomplice in her downfall, a scathing criticism of human exploitation and exploitability.

The commercial and critical response to "Avantgarde" was disappointing. Fleißer was regarded as Brecht's disciple but not as an original talent. A new generation of writers, however, including Rainer Werner Faßbinder, Franz Xaver Kroetz, and Martin Sperr, became her "sons" and promoted her works, which they both admired and also found useful for their radical purposes. In 1968 Faßbinder directed *Pioniere in Ingolstadt* in Munich in such a way that Fleißer considered withdrawing her permission for the performance, but she finally accepted the reinterpretation. Kroetz was instrumental in interesting the Suhrkamp publishing house in publishing a three-volume set of her collected works, and Fleißer spent the years from 1967 to 1972 in arduous rewriting of her plays, stories, and novel. Many critics have interpreted this need for revision as a sign of insecurity, rather than taking into account the fact that Fleißer, in order to come into her own, had to change the works of the Weimar period as they were conceived and written under the influence of her mentors Feuchtwanger and Brecht.

Her death in 1974 put an end to the tragically unfinished career of one of Germany's most gifted woman writers. She was at heart a true poet, a title that rightly adorns her tombstone in Ingolstadt.

**Biography:**
Sissi Tax, *Marieluise Fleißer: Schreiben, Überleben. Ein biographischer Versuch* (Basel: Stroemfeld/ Frankfurt am Main: Roter Stern, 1984).

**References:**
Peter Beicken, "Weiblicher Pionier. Marieluise Fleißer—oder Zur Situation schreibender Frauen in der Weimarer Zeit," *Die Horen,* 28 (Fall 1983): 45-61;

Susan L. Cocalis, " 'Weib ist Weib': Mimetische Darstellung contra emanzipatorische Tendenz in den Dramen Marieluise Fleißers," in *Die Frau als Heldin und Autorin. Neue kritische Ansätze zur deutschen Literatur,* edited by Wolfgang Paulsen (Bern & Munich: Francke, 1979), pp. 201-210;

Walter Dimter, "Die ausgestellte Gesellschaft: Zum Volksstück Horváths, der Fleißer und ihrer Nachfolger," in *Theater und Gesellschaft: Das Volksstück im 19. und 20. Jahrhundert,* edited by Jürgen Hein (Düsseldorf, 1973), pp. 219-245;

Donna L. Hoffmeister, *The Theater of Confinement: Language and Survival in the Milieu Plays of Marieluise Fleißer and Franz Xaver Kroetz* (Columbia, S.C.: Camden House, 1983);

Wend Kässens and Michael Töteberg, ". . . fast schon ein Auftrag von Brecht: Marieluise Fleißers Drama *Pioniere in Ingolstadt,*" in *Brecht-Jahrbuch* (Frankfurt am Main, 1976), pp. 101-119;

Kässens and Töteberg, *Marieluise Fleißer* (Munich: Deutscher Taschenbuchverlag, 1979);

Friedrich Kraft, ed., *Marieluise Fleißer: Anmerkungen, Texte, Dokumente* (Ingolstadt: Donau Courier Verlag, 1981);

Helmut Lethen, "Marieluise Fleißers *Mehlreisende Frieda Geier:* Kritik der sozialistischen Rettungstheorien," in his *Neue Sachlichkeit 1924-1932: Studien zur Literatur des "Weißen Sozialismus"* (Stuttgart: Metzler, 1970), pp. 168-175;

Günther Lutz, *Die Stellung Marieluise Fleißers in der bayerischen Literatur des 20. Jahrhunderts* (Frankfurt am Main, Bern & Cirencester, U.K., 1979);

Marsha Elizabeth Meyer, "Marieluise Fleißer: Her Life and Work," Ph.D. dissertation, University of Wisconsin-Madison, 1983;

Heidi Pataki, "Kritisches Lexikon: Marieluise Fleißer," *Neues Forum* (March 1973);

Eva Pfister, "Der Nachlaß von Marieluise Fleißer," *Maske und Kothurn,* 26 (1980): 293-303;

Pfister, " 'Unter dem fremden Gesetz': Zu Produktionsbedingungen, Werk und Rezeption der Dramatikerin Marieluise Fleißer," Ph.D. dissertation, University of Vienna, 1981;

Günther Rühle, ed., *Materialien zum Leben und Schreiben der Marieluise Fleißer* (Frankfurt am Main: Suhrkamp, 1973);

Angelika Spindler, "Marieluise Fleißer: Eine Schriftstellerin zwischen Selbstverwirklichung und Selbstaufgabe," Ph.D. dissertation, University of Vienna, 1980;

Barbara Stritzke, *Marieluise Fleißers Pioniere in Ingolstadt* (Frankfurt am Main & Bern: Lang, 1982);

Heidi Thoman Tewarson, *"Mehlreisende Frieda Geier: Roman vom Rauchen, Sporteln, Lieben und Verkaufen:* Marieluise Fleißer's View of the Twenties," *Germanic Review,* 60 (Fall 1985): 135-143;

*Text und Kritik,* special Fleißer issue, 64 (October 1979);

Elisabeth Wiesmüller, "Die kurze Frühprosa der Marieluise Fleißer: Untersuchungen zu Erzähltechnik, Stil und Thematik," Ph.D. dissertation, University of Innsbruck, 1980;

Gisela von Wysocki, "Die Magie der Großstadt— Marieluise Fleißer," *Die Fröste der Freiheit: Aufbruchphantasien* (Frankfurt am Main: Syndikat, 1980), pp. 9-22.

**Papers:**
Marieluise Fleißer's papers are in the Stadtarchiv (city archive), Ingolstadt, Bavaria, Federal Republic of Germany.

# Leonhard Frank
*(4 September 1882-18 August 1961)*

Reinhold K. Bubser
*University of Northern Iowa*

BOOKS: *Fremde Mädchen am Meer und eine Kreuzigung* (Munich: Delphin, 1913);

*Die Räuberbande: Roman* (Munich: Müller, 1914); translated anonymously as *The Robberband* (London: Davies, 1928; New York: Cape & Smith, 1929);

*Die Ursache: Eine Erzählung* (Munich: Müller, 1915); translated by Cyrus Brooks as *The Cause of the Crime* (London: Davies, 1928); translation republished as *Clamoring Self* (New York & London: Putnam's, 1930);

*Der Mensch ist gut* (Potsdam: Kiepenheuer, 1917);

*Die Mutter* (Zurich: Rascher, 1919);

*Hermann Büschler, der Stattmeister zu Schwäbisch-Hall* (Schwäbisch-Hall, 1922);

*Der Bürger: Roman* (Berlin: Malik, 1924); translated by Cyrus Brooks as *A Middle-class Man* (London: Davies, 1930);

*An der Landstraße: Erzählung* (Berlin: Rowohlt, 1925);

*Die Schicksalsbrücke: Erzählungen* (Berlin: Rowohlt, 1925);

*Im letzten Wagen: Erzählungen* (Berlin: Rowohlt, 1925); translated by Brooks as *In the Last Coach and Other Stories* (London: Lane, 1934); "Im letzten Wagen" revised as *Absturz: Novelle* (Leipzig: Reclam, 1929);

*Das Ochsenfurter Männerquartett: Roman* (Leipzig: Insel, 1927); translated by Brooks as *The Singers* (London: Grayson & Grayson, 1932; New York: Holt, 1933);

*Karl und Anna: Erzählung* (Berlin: Propyläen, 1927); translated by Brooks as *Carl and Anna* (London: Davies, 1929; New York: Putnam's, 1930); translation republished as *Beloved Stranger: The Story of Carl and Anna* (New York: Fischer, 1946); translation republished again as *Desire Me, and Other Stories* (New York: Triangle, 1947);

*Der Streber, und andere Erzählungen* (Berlin: Deutsche Buchgemeinschaft, 1928);

*Karl und Anna: Schauspiel in vier Akten* (Leipzig: Insel, 1928); translated by Ruth Langner as *Karl and Anna: A Drama in Three Acts* (New York: Brentano's, 1929);

*Bruder und Schwester: Roman* (Leipzig: Insel, 1929); translated by Brooks as *Brother and Sister* (London: Davies, 1930);

*Die Ursache: Drama in vier Akten* (Leipzig: Insel, 1929);

*Die Entgleisten: Filmnovelle* (Berlin: Hobbing, 1929);

(©*Nymphenburger Verlagshandlung, Munich*)

*Hufnägel: Schauspiel in drei Akten* (Leipzig: Insel, 1930);

*Von drei Millionen Drei: Roman* (Berlin: Fischer, 1932); translated by Brooks as *Three of the Three Million* (London: Lane, 1936);

*Traumgefährten: Roman* (Amsterdam: Querido, 1936); translated by Maxim Newmark as *Dream Mates* (New York: Philosophical Library, 1946);

*Gesammelte Werke in Einzelausgaben,* 7 volumes (Amsterdam: Querido, 1936-1949);

*Der Außenseiter: Komödie* (Basel: Reiß, 1937);

*Maria: Schauspiel* (Amsterdam: Querido, 1939);

*Mathilde: Roman* (Los Angeles: Privately printed, 1943; Amsterdam: Querido, 1948); translated by Willard R. Traska as *Mathilde* (London: Davies, 1948; New York: Simon & Schuster, 1948);

*Die Jünger Jesu: Roman* (Amsterdam: Querido, 1949);

*The Baroness,* translated by Brooks (London & New York: Nevill, 1950); original German version published as *Deutsche Novelle* (Munich: Nymphenburger Verlagshandlung, 1954);

*Links, wo das Herz ist: Roman* (Munich: Nymphenburger Verlagshandlung, 1952); translated by Brooks as *Heart on the Left* (London: Barker, 1954);

*Gesammelte Werke,* 6 volumes (Berlin: Aufbau, 1957-1959);

*Michaels Rückkehr* (Leipzig: Reclam, 1957);

*Schauspiele* (Berlin: Aufbau, 1959);

*Ruth* (Munich: Desch, 1960);

*Sieben Kurzgeschichten* (Berlin: Aufbau, 1961);

*Hans Fallada* (Berlin: Volk & Wissen, 1962);

*Leonhard Frank: Sein Leben und Werk* (Munich: Nymphenburger Verlagshandlung, 1962);

*Gesamtwerk,* 6 volumes (Munich: Nymphenburger Verlagshandlung, 1964);

*Das Porträt: Eine Berliner Erzählung um 1946* (Berlin-Friedenau: Friedenauer Presse, 1968);

*Die Summe,* edited by Martin Gregor-Dellin (Munich: Nymphenburger Verlagshandlung, 1982).

Hailed in the 1920s as one "of the greatest narrators of our time," today Leonhard Frank is not well known by younger German readers. But to those familiar with German literature between 1914 and 1933 his works are synonymous with criticism of the social, political, and educational institutions of the Wilhelminian empire and the Weimar Republic. Frank has been characterized as "a reliable observer of his time"; he was a pacifist

and a socialist—not an ideologue, but an altruist—who passionately fought against injustice, inhumanity, and intolerance. His novels were widely read and his plays were frequently and successfully performed on many stages before 1933, but during the Hitler years Frank became an exile for the second time in his life. The hiatus of his exile years and the prevailing literary conditions after 1945 precluded his works from again reaching the popularity that they had once enjoyed.

Frank was born on 4 September 1882 in Würzburg, in the Franconian region of the Main. He was the fourth child born to cabinetmaker Johann and Marie Bach Frank. After primary school he worked as an apprentice, bicycle mechanic, factory worker, chauffeur, housepainter, and helper in a clinic. Dissatisfied with the philistine environment of his hometown and seeking an opportunity for artistic endeavors, he left Würzburg in 1905 to immerse himself in the bohemian life of Schwabing, the university, cultural, and entertainment district of Munich, where he studied painting for six years. A book of his lithographs, *Fremde Mädchen am Meer und eine Kreuzigung* (Foreign Girls at the Sea and a Crucifixion), was published in 1913. The Café Stephanie in Munich was his university, Frank relates in his autobiographical novel *Links wo das Herz ist* (1952; translated as *Heart on the Left,* 1954).

In Schwabing he met the writers Oskar Maria Graf, Franz Jung, Karl Otten, and Erich Mühsam. Frank became an ardent student and follower of the influential psychoanalyst Otto Groß and adopted many of Groß's ideas, including rejection of the patriarchal society and social influences in the psychological development of the individual. In 1910 Frank went to Berlin, where he married Lisa Ertel on 4 February 1915 and started his writing career.

His first novel, *Die Räuberbande* (translated as *The Robberband,* 1928), was published in 1914. It established Frank as a novelist and received a distinguished literary prize, the Fontane Award. Set in Würzburg around 1900, *Die Räuberbande* has two segments. In the first part Frank depicts the adventures of twelve young men who are influenced by Karl May's immensely popular books about the white man's encounter with Indians in the Wild West. The young men emulate the heroic characters of these adventure stories and adopt their names, calling themselves "Oldshatterhand," "Winnetou," "Falkenauge" (Hawkeye), and "Rote Wolke" (Red Cloud). Their dreams lead them into valiant struggles in which the brave and magnanimous man overcomes all odds. As a handbook for

*Frank as a young man, circa 1902 (© Nymphenburger Verlags-
handlung, Munich)*

*(Lisa Ertel, whom Frank married in 1910 (© Nymphenburger
Verlagshandlung, Munich)*

their rebellion against adult society they have adopted Schiller's revolutionary drama *Die Räuber* (1781, translated as *The Robbers*, 1849). In their play-acting, in which they use names of characters from May's stories, they not only create an escape mechanism from the realities of poverty, social and political impotence, and paternal tyranny but also express their utopian hopes for the future. They look forward to a day of reckoning when the city will burn down and their mothers, fathers, teachers, and masters will perish. The fire will end the bigotry of their mothers, the insensitivity of their fathers, the brutality of their teachers, and the exploitation of their masters. In their dreams they reach America in a pirated ship; but in reality they merely play small pranks that annoy the citizens of Würzburg and commit petty thefts without great consequences. They hide their booty in a cave under the castle, which serves as their meeting place. Michael Vierkant ("Oldshatterhand") suffers from the severe punishment he receives at home and in school. As a result, he stutters, suffers from inhibitions and an inferiority complex, and has suicidal tendencies. Andreas Steinbrecher ("Winnetou") also wants to commit suicide to escape the beatings of his ruthless mother.

In the second part, the novel moves to the adult lives of the twelve "robbers." The noble aspirations and the nebulous dreams of their youth have given way to the same middle-class values for which they despised their parents and teachers. Only two of the twelve former "robbers" deviate from the norm. Steinbrecher chooses the life of a monk and Vierkant finds satisfaction as an artist. Nevertheless, the psychological damage Vierkant incurred in his youth continues to plague him in later life. Involved in an intrigue in Munich, he cannot cope with his anxieties and loneliness and commits suicide. (Frank resurrected the name Michael Vierkant for later works.)

Frank's literary career was soon interrupted by World War I. He went to Switzerland in protest against the patriotic calls for victory and heroic death and to escape persecution for his pacifist views. In exile he collaborated with René Schickele in editing the pacifist journal *Die Weißen Blätter* and wrote his second novel, *Die Ursache* (1915; translated as *The Cause of the Crime*, 1928). The book, an outcry against social and judicial injustice, focuses on the death penalty. Frank's collection of short stories, *Der Mensch ist gut* (Man Is Good, 1917), is a manifesto against war and for the belief in the ethical behavior of humanity. These themes coincide with the expressionist credo of the time, a call for an end to the war and for a reawakening of Man.

Even as a thirty-year-old man, the writer Anton Seiler in *Die Ursache* is haunted in his dreams by the physical abuse he endured in his school days. He is still obsessed by fear of his old teacher, whom he calls a "Repräsentant der Seelenzerstörer" (representative of the soul destroyers). Frank points out that the teacher acted only as a functionary of the whole society; consequently, he is not to be blamed as an individual but as a member of a larger social entity. Frank espouses his theory that the seeds of psychological deformation are implanted early in the child's life through the schools and their brutal education as well as the churches and their hypocritical teaching. When Seiler is sentenced to death for killing his former teacher, he accuses society of committing a murder that will spawn more crimes "denn alles Menschenblut ist göttlich miteinander verwandt" (because all human blood is related in a divine way). The death penalty, Frank argues, will not serve justice; on the contrary, it will help rationalize murderous acts by individuals.

After the war, Frank returned to Berlin. He received the Kleist Award in 1920 for *Der Mensch ist gut*. The death of his wife in 1923 is considered by many critics to mark the point at which Frank's writing began to deteriorate.

As in *Die Räuberbande*, the bourgeoisie is analyzed in *Der Bürger* (1924; translated as *A Middle-class Man*, 1930). Jürgen Kolbenreiher, a member of the upper middle class, feels repressed by his father. Even after the father's death, his omnipotent authority persecutes Jürgen: "In die Träume schickte die vergewaltigte Seele drohende Ungeheuer. Der Vater stand daneben" (Into his dreams the abused soul sent threatening monsters. His father stood next to them). Frank rejects the Marxist theory that a person's values are determined by his being part of a certain class; fathers oppress their children regardless of their membership in the lower or upper class: "Es gibt nicht nur eine herrschende Klasse und unterdrückte Klassen: es gibt auch eine jeweils herrschende Generation, die durch alle Klassen durchgeht" (There are not only a ruling class and oppressed classes; there is also an actual ruling generation, which goes through all classes).

Frank continued the account of the young men from the Robberband in *Das Ochsenfurter Männerquartett* (1927; translated as *The Singers*, 1932). The former juvenile delinquents are adults who have enjoyed some success in their professional lives. But the devastating economic plight of the

*One of Frank's lithographs from his 1913 collection* Fremde Madchen am Meer und eine Kreuzigung *(© Nymphenburger Verlagshandlung, Munich)*

Weimar Republic has caught up with them, causing them to become poor and unemployed like many of their fellowmen. Oskar Benommen is deep in debt and has lost his bakery and pub. Hans Lux has been phased out of his job as a railroad engineer just as he was about to be promoted to the highest job category. Georg Manger has lost his leather goods store. Along with Hans Wiederschein, an unemployed office clerk, they form a quartet in an effort to raise some money. Their desperate situation, however, takes a turn for the better just as the quartet is about to perform its first concert: Benommen is acquitted of the murder of the moneylender and gets his business back; Lux inherits a large sum of money from his aunt and can open a blacksmith shop; Manger marries the owner of a store. Only Wiederschein remains jobless.

*Das Ochsenfurter Männerquartett* depicts the life, traits, and viewpoints of the lower middle class in a small German town during the depression of the 1930s. The economic plight of the adult population is contrasted with the carefree life of the young: the adolescents enjoy a life full of love affairs, brazen pranks, and frivolous disrespect of customs and established authority. The adults hope for a better future based on ethics of honesty, diligence, and toughness.

Frank's short novel *Karl und Anna* (1927) received much acclaim both in its prose form and as a play. The play was first performed in 1929 in Berlin, staged by the then famous producer Leopold Jessner. The plot was based on a newspaper story about a soldier returning from the war to find his wife living with another man. Frank placed the story in the midst of the proletarian milieu with all its familiar conflicts and tragedies. Richard and Karl are in a Russian prisoner of war camp in Siberia. Richard describes his wife Anna in such detail that Karl falls in love with her. By chance, Karl is released from the camp half a year earlier than Richard. Anna had lost all hope of ever seeing her husband again, and when Karl, who resembles Richard, presents himself as her returning husband, she is totally confused. But having gained the intimate knowledge about her relationship with Richard, Karl deludes her into accepting him as her husband, and the question about his identity fades into the background. Gradually their love deepens. A letter from Richard reveals Karl's true identity, but the news can no longer alter the relationship of Karl and Anna. Anna is expecting Karl's child, and when Richard finally returns home, her love for Karl does not allow her to return to her former husband: "Ich kann nur noch mit ihm. . . . Ich kann's nicht anders mehr" (I can

only be with him. . . . I can't do it any other way).

Frank became a member of the Prussian Academy of Arts in 1928. On 22 October 1929 he married Elena Maquenne-Penswer. Berlin was Frank's "gefühlsgeladene Werkstatt" (emotional workshop) during the Weimar Republic, when his popularity among German readers was at its peak; but in 1933 Berlin and the rest of Germany became an extremely hostile place for anyone who was not in line with the prevailing fascist ideology. Frank's books were burned and he was forced into a second exile in Switzerland; from there he fled in 1937 to France, where he was placed in an internment camp. In 1940 he made his way through Spain and Portugal to the United States. While still in Switzerland he finished the novel *Traumgefährten* (1936;

*Woodcut by Frans Masereel for Frank's novel* Die Mutter *(1919)*

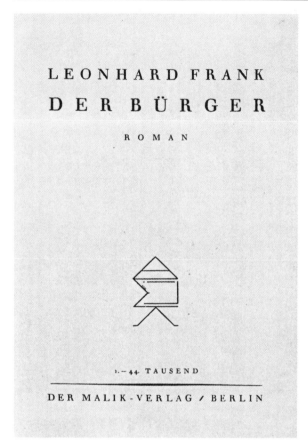

LEONHARD FRANK
DER BÜRGER

ROMAN

1.–44. TAUSEND

DER MALIK-VERLAG / BERLIN

*Title page for Frank's 1924 novel about a young man who is dominated by his father*

translated as *Dream Mates,* 1946). In the United States, Frank received support through one of the one-year scriptwriting contracts financed by Warner Bros. and coordinated through the Emergency Rescue Committee. In 1945 he sold the movie rights to his novella *Karl und Anna* to M-G-M. With this financial security, he left Hollywood, "diese ewig besonnte, lebensferne Hölle" (this eternally sunny hell divorced from reality), and moved to New York.

During his exile in the United States, he worked on several novels, among them *Die Jünger Jesu* (The Disciples of Jesus, 1949), *Deutsche Novelle* (1954; translated as *The Baroness,* 1950), *Links wo das Herz ist,* and *Michaels Rückkehr* (Michael's Return, 1957).

Frank wrote his autobiography in the form of a novel, *Links wo das Herz ist.* Although the author and the protagonist, Michael Vierkant, are identical, Frank fictionalizes other persons and events so that certain biographical and historical data are obscured. By and large, however, the novel closely

follows the stages in Frank's life. Vierkant is the fourth child of a carpenter who earns so little that he can barely support his wife and children. In school, Michael faces the same pedagogical adversities with which protagonists in Frank's previous novels have had to cope; the strict, dogmatic, and unrelenting educational methods of his teachers cause psychological damage beyond repair. Frank describes the methods as "Rohrstockpädagogie" (pedagogy with the rod) and *Seelenmord* (murder of the soul). The sensitive child starts to stutter, separates himself from his peers who tease him, and finally leaves school after seven years in a state of mental devastation. During his apprenticeship, he searches for new meaning in his life and discovers that painting affords him inner freedom and strength. Painting opens the way for Vierkant's career as a writer, and writing becomes a healing process for him. The psychological wounds of his youth are healed. The novel follows closely the facts of Frank's life, the vicissitudes he encountered as a writer and his hardships in exile. Characteristic of the exile experience is the loneliness of the writer in a foreign country: "Er trat auf die Straße und wurde verschluckt von New York, wo die Menschen einsamer sind als überall in der Welt" (He walked out onto the street and New York engulfed him, the city in which people are lonelier than anywhere else in the world). The novel not only presents a fictionalized account of Frank's life but also gives a review of German history from World War I to after World War II; it is almost a "who was who" of German politics and culture from 1914 to 1950.

In *Michaels Rückkehr,* Frank's last major prose work, Michael Vierkant returns to Germany to carry out revenge for the death of his sister at the hands of the Nazis. Vierkant feels that he has to gain justice on his own since the German courts are still, to a large extent, controlled by members of the former Nazi regime. Michael is sentenced to life imprisonment, but a girl who witnessed the trial falls in love with him, recognizing in Michael the person who had frequently appeared in her dreams. The love affair reminds the director of the prison of the passions of his youth. Realizing that he has spent his life in a meaningless occupation, he decides to retire and alter the course of his life. He arranges for Michael to escape, and Michael flees with his future wife to Italy.

The novel has been severely criticized for its superficial treatment of character and its failure to resolve the ethical problems it raises; the novel escapes into the realm of sociopolitical and erotic clichés, and the prison director's sudden conversion remains poorly motivated. Although Michael's self-administered justice may be justifiable from Frank's point of view, it nevertheless violates all legal and ethical principles of civilized states. Finally, Michael's escape from prison into an idyllic existence on the shores of Lake Maggiore turns a questionable melodrama into a farce. In Martin Glaubrecht's opinion, *Michaels Rückkehr* is a good example of the incredibility and banality in the plot design in Frank's later novels.

In 1950 Frank returned to Germany. His second marriage having ended in divorce, he married Charlotte London-Jäger on 29 May 1952. In 1955 he received the National Prize First Class for Art and Literature of the German Democratic Republic, and in 1957 he was awarded the Great Service Cross of the Federal Republic of Germany. He died in Munich on 18 August 1961.

No complete biography of Frank has been published which reliably relates his experiences to the artistic and intellectual development of his works. Many of the existing biographical descriptions have been extracted from the novel *Links, wo das Herz ist*. There are few documented accounts of Frank's family background, his youth, or his years in the bohemian circles of Munich between 1905 and 1910.

His literary production, on the other hand, has been subjected to substantial scrutiny. According to some critics, his work as a writer can be divided into three clearly discernible periods. The early period between 1914 and 1925 is characterized by formative intellectual, political, and socio-economic influences which had a lifelong effect on the self-educated writer. Between 1925 and 1945 Frank's feelings of resignation and discontent contributed to a weakening in his writing; many of the works of this period have been classified as bordering on junk literature. Gustav Schröder describes Frank's work between 1925 and 1945 as a "middle period" that was characterized by total disillusionment. The products of that period focus more on erotic than political themes and are less critical of society. After 1945 Frank returned to social criticism in his writings but retained some of the erotic themes.

One of Frank's major contributions to German literature lies in the sincerity of the message that his novels and plays convey. To Frank, social conditions are the chief causes of psychological phenomena: poverty, political impotence, unemployment, big-city life, corruption, and violence

*A scene from a Berlin performance of Frank's* Karl und Anna *in 1929 (© Nymphenburger Verlagshandlung, Munich)*

*Frank in 1929 (Ullstein)*

lead to irreparable psychological damage. Frank's prose and dramatic works create utopian models of thought and action as escape mechanisms. The utopian models are based on Frank's pantheistic view that man, animal, and nature are one and that nature can therefore serve as a yardstick for human actions. Frank incorporated anthropomorphic motifs into several of his novels. He believed that the souls of man and animal alike sense the cruelty inherent in daily life; as he wrote in *Der Mensch ist gut:* "Und das Pferd, getrennt von seinem Herrn, ganz verbunden mit den Menschen, schritt mit und blickte tief, kindlich und gut" (And the horse, separated from his rider but closely tied to humans, strode along and gazed piercingly, childlike and good). Throughout Frank's works there is a pas-

sionate longing for a new and better world expressed in visions of exotic landscapes ("Der Hut," 1928), of the "Wild West" (*Die Räuberbande*), and of a "simple city" (*Die Ursache, Der Mensch ist gut*). In all of these enticing places, life functions in accordance with "natural laws." Frank's visionary models are idyllic antipodes to the authoritarianism prevalent in all walks of life in the Germany of the 1920s. To a large extent his topics derive from current events or from personal experiences.

With his last books, *Die Jünger Jesu* and *Michaels Rückkehr*, Frank turned to a more optimistic outlook on mankind during the postwar period. With a renewed intensity he pictured the sociopolitical evolution of a new Germany in which the hope for a better future rested with the young peo-

*Painting of Frank by Gert Wollheim*

*Frank at his home in Berlin-Grunewald in 1930 (© Nymphenburger Verlagshandlung, Munich)*

*Page from the manuscript for* Mathilde (© *Nymphenburger Verlagshandlung, Munich*)

*Frank in 1928 (Ullstein)*

*A 1929 photo of the actress Lotte Jager, who became Frank's
third wife in 1952 (© Nymphenburger
Verlagshandlung, Munich)*

ple. Frank must have also known that after 1945 his novels and plays would never again be as widely known as they had been in the 1920s. His alter ego, Michael Vierkant, deduced that fact in his exile years; in *Links wo das Herz ist* he says: "In dieser Zeit, da der Leser in Deutschland unerreichbar war, wurde ihm klar, daß der Schriftsteller ganz zuletzt seiner selbst wegen schreibt, sich zur Freude und zur Qual, und weil er eben schreiben muß" (In this era, when the reader in Germany has become inaccessible, he realized that in the final analysis the writer writes only for himself, for his enjoyment and for his torment, and because he has to write).

**Bibliography:**
M. Rost and R. Geist, *Leonhard Frank: Auswahlbibliographie zum 100. Geburtstag* (Leipzig: Deutsche Bücherei, 1982).

**References:**
Hans Joachim Bähr, "Hugo Ball und Leonhard Frank," *Hugo Ball Almanach 1985/86* (Pirmasens: Stadtverwaltung, 1986);

Axel Eggebrecht, *Die literarische Welt*, 3, no. 44 (1927): 5;

Martin Glaubrecht, *Studien zum Frühwerk Leonhard Franks* (Bonn: Bouvier, 1965);

Therese C. Mathey, "Das Sozialkritische in den Werken Leonhard Franks," Ph.D. dissertation, University of Southern California, 1968;

Jennifer Michaels, "The Fiction of Leonhard Frank: A Survey," *International Fiction Review*, 8, no. 1 (1981): 47-52;

Gustav Schröder, "Zwischen Resignation und Hoffnung—Zur mittleren Schaffensperiode von Leonhard Frank," *Aufbau* (East Berlin), 13 (1957): 242-256.

**Papers:**
The Akademie der Künste der DDR, East Berlin, holds the Leonhard Frank Nachlaß and the Leonhard Frank archives. The Akademie der Künste Berlin, West Berlin, has a collection of papers and manuscripts by Frank. The Deutsches Literaturarchiv in Marbach has copies of the materials from the Nachlaß and archives at the Akademie der Künste der DDR.

# Friedrich Glauser

*(4 February 1896-8 December 1938)*

## H. M. Waidson

BOOKS: *Wachtmeister Studer: Kriminalroman* (Zurich & Leipzig: Morgarten, 1936);

*Matto regiert* (Zurich: Jean Christophe, 1936);

*Im Dunkel* (Basel: Gute Schriften, 1937);

*Die Fieberkurve: Wachtmeister Studers neuer Fall, Kriminalroman* (Zurich & Leipzig: Morgarten, 1938);

*Der Chinese: Wachtmeister Studers dritter Fall, Kriminalroman* (Zurich & Leipzig: Morgarten, 1939);

*Mensch im Zwielicht* (Zurich: Neue Schweizer Bibliothek, 1939);

*Gourrama: Ein Roman aus der Fremdenlegion* (Zurich: Schweizer Druck- & Verlagshaus, 1940);

*Krock & Co.: Wachtmeister Studers vierter Fall* (Zurich & Leipzig: Morgarten, 1941);

*Der Tee der drei alten Damen: Kriminalroman* (Zurich & Leipzig: Morgarten, 1941);

*Beichte in der Nacht: Gesammelte Prosastücke* (Zurich: Artemis, 1945);

*Gesammelte Werke*, edited by Hugo Leber, 4 volumes (Zurich: Arche, 1969-1974);

*Dada, Ascona und andere Erinnerungen* (Zurich: Arche, 1976).

PERIODICAL PUBLICATIONS: "Die Hexe von Endor," *Der kleine Bund* (Bern), 13 October 1929;

"Verhör," *Zürcher Illustrierte* (1 December 1933);

"Beichte in der Nacht," *National-Zeitung* (Basel), 6-13 January 1935;

"Der alte Zauberer," *Zürcher Illustrierte* (1 March 1935);

"König Zucker," *Zürcher Illustrierte* (19 June 1936);

"Die Begegnung," *Neue Schweizer Bibliothek*, 36 (1939).

Friedrich Glauser's literary reputation rests mainly on his seven novels; the first to be written, *Gourrama* (1940), describes life in the French Foreign Legion, while the other six are crime stories reflecting a realistic approach to everyday Swiss life in the 1930s. The novels are remarkable for their psychological insights and strong narrative tension.

Glauser was also a successful and fluent short story writer. His writing is clear and vigorous, yet is the product of an imagination that had to cope with many personal difficulties and experiences that were a constant threat to Glauser's mental stability.

Dr. Charles Pierre Glauser was a teacher of French at the Handelsakademie (commercial college) in Aussig, Bohemia, when he married Theresia Scubitz, the headmaster's daughter. The newlyweds moved to Vienna, where Charles Glauser had received a similar appointment to the one he had held at Aussig. Their son Friedrich was born on 4 February 1896. In the autobiographical *Mensch im Zwielicht* (Man in the Twilight, 1939), Glauser records the death of his mother when he was four-and-a-half in terms that make it clear that the loss was traumatic for him. After primary school, Glauser entered the Elisabeth Gymnasium in 1906. Gerhard Saner's biography refers to Glauser's father's misgivings about his son's truthfulness and honesty and describes the boy as a mediocre, apathetic student. Dissatisfied with the Vienna school, Charles Glauser transferred his son to the Landerziehungsheim (country educational home) Glarisegg at Thurgau, Switzerland, near Lake Constance, a boarding school run on Rousseauistic "principles of nature." Three years later, his father was asked to withdraw Glauser from the school, primarily because of the debts he was running up. After studying at the Collège de Genève, Glauser enrolled at Zurich University in 1916 as a student of chemistry.

Glauser spent very little time on chemistry. Instead, he became associated with the Dadaist circle of experimental artists and writers in Zurich. Here his literary talent began to find expression, and he received warm encouragement from Hugo Ball and Emmy Hennings. In January 1918 Glauser was declared incapable of managing his affairs and put under the care of a guardian. In June of that year he was arrested as a morphine addict after forging a prescription. Two months later he was interned in Münsingen mental hospital; he left after fourteen months and was for a time a member of an artistic and literary circle in Ascona, Switzerland. He made a suicide attempt while being held by the police at Bellinzona, Switzerland, in 1920 and underwent several more confinements in mental institutions. Glauser's idea of joining the French Foreign Legion was encouraged by his father. Glauser was in North Africa with the foreign legion from 1921 to 1923, and wrote to his father on 4 December 1922: "Selbst die Fremdenlegion hat mir nicht Übles angetan, trotz meinen Verzweiflungskrisen—im Gegenteil, ich glaube, daß ich vernünftiger geworden bin" (Even the foreign legion has not done me harm, in spite of my crises of despair—on the contrary, I believe that I have become more sensible).

After leaving the foreign legion with heart trouble in the spring of 1923, Glauser worked as a dishwasher in a Paris hotel. After an unsuccessful attempt to gain permission to go to the Belgian Congo, he worked in a coal mine at Charleroi, Belgium: he describes this phase of his life in *Im Dunkel* (In the Dark, 1937). He began taking drugs again, attempted suicide, and stayed on for a time as male nurse at the hospital where he had been treated. In May 1925 he returned to Switzerland, where he reentered Münsingen hospital. He wrote some short stories and sketches that appeared in the Bern newspaper *Der kleine Bund,* whose literary editor, Hugo Marti, had noticed Glauser's talent and had encouraged him. He began a relationship with Beatrice Gutekunst and took a job as a gardener's assistant. He wrote *Gourrama* (the title names a locality in Morocco where Glauser was stationed for a time) while studying to become a horticulturist. He was awarded a diploma by the Horticultural College of Oeschberg, near Bern, in 1931 but decided to choose writing rather than gardening as his occupation. After staying in several locations in France with Gutekunst, he arrived without notice in June 1932 at his father's home in Mannheim, where the latter was then teaching. Gradually Glauser became known for his writing, which had been published mainly in newspapers. In November 1937 his father, who had been supporting Glauser financially for many years, died. After the relationship with Gutekunst broke up, Glauser became involved with Miggi Senn and, finally, with Berthe Brendel, a nurse from Münsingen. On 8 December 1938, the eve of his marriage to Brendel, Glauser collapsed and died in Nervi, Italy. The last years of his life had been a period of major productivity.

Apart from the novel *Gourrama,* the foreign legion is featured in a number of Glauser's short stories. Saner quotes Martha Ringier, who took a particular interest in Glauser and his writing during the 1930s, as saying that the author was driven to the foreign legion by "ein Hunger nach neuen Menschen und fremdem Land" (a hunger for new people and a strange country). The new environment offered a fresh start, a flight from personal dissatisfaction, a removal of individual responsibility and the fear of failure and had the approval of his father.

The main action of *Gourrama* centers upon a group of soldiers under the command of Captain Chabert, "a quiet, decent man," but not a strong disciplinarian. After the troops return from an expedition against the Arabs, there is disorder and a shooting, and one man makes a revolutionary speech suggesting that they disband and live among the local people. Chabert eventually restores order, but subsequently he is suspended by higher authority. There are a number of short episodes giving realistic pictures of varied characters and of the monotony of their camp life. The character Lös, who is largely modeled on Glauser himself, has a relationship with the Arab girl Zeno; this affair is against regulations and has to take place clandestinely. After being arrested for misusing catering funds, he attempts to take his own life but is eventually released; he is last seen as a free but aimless man in Paris. *Gourrama* is full of descriptive material but does not have the fluency of style and deft presentation of action that characterize much of Glauser's subsequent work.

Having encountered many refusals from publishers with regard to *Gourrama,* Glauser turned to crime fiction (*Gourrama* was published posthumously in 1940). *Der Tee der drei alten Damen* (The Three Old Ladies' Tea Party) was completed in 1934 but not published until 1941. It is set in Geneva. Agents of Great Britain and the United States are in ruthless competition for the power to exploit the oil resources of an Indian princedom. Also involved are a mysterious sect and a psychiatric hospital.

The short story "Der alte Zauberer" (The Old Magician, 1935) and the five novels centering on the Bern police officer Jakob Studer exhibit Glauser's characteristic theme and manner. As he walks from the country railway station in a morning of autumn wind and rain, Studer is on his way to investigate the death of a farmer's wife. Studer is himself the son of an Emmental farmer: he has a fat red face, teeth that are stained brown from smoking, and a moustache that inspires confidence. He collects information in a relaxed manner as he visits the local inn and shows his strength of personality as he confronts the threatening figure and superstitious cast of mind of the farmer. Studer is a family man, between fifty and sixty years old. He was demoted due to a "bank affair" in Vienna some years ago and feels himself an outsider because of his refusal to compromise his convictions. He is anxious not to fail and even hopes for renown and possibly promotion if he can distinguish himself in an important case. He likes to speak in dialect though he uses standard German with his superiors and people he dislikes. He has a protective attitude to young women, and his chivalrousness amuses his wife. Glauser's criminals usually meet an untimely end, seldom finding punishment through the law. Only once, in *Matto regiert* (Matto Rules, 1936), does he fail to track down the criminal. Glauser was influenced by Georges Simenon, whom he described on one occasion as his teacher. He disclaimed any elite role as a writer: "Alle Leute wollen partout, daß ich ein Dichter sei. Und ich bin wirklich nur ein Handwerker, der im Schweiße seines Gehirns sein Metier lernt" (Everybody wants me above all to be a literary writer. And I am really only a craftsman who learns his job by the sweat of his brain).

Glauser had difficulty in getting *Wachtmeister Studer* (Police Officer Studer, 1936) accepted for publication, but once it started appearing as a newspaper serial it received acclaim. *Der kleine Bund* declared that the novel was far above the usual run of crime fiction and that its characterization was vivid and truthful: the characters were Bern people as they are encountered every day. Although Erwin Schlumpf, a disadvantaged orphan who is working at a nursery garden, is the prime suspect in the murder of the commercial traveler Wendelin Witschi, Studer knows better and takes an imaginative approach which leads to the final disclosure. The novel has unity of place and action, centering on the social situation in a village community during a span of five days. *Matto regiert* shows Studer endeavoring to fulfill his task of detection in an environment that is new to him—a psychiatric hospital, where he is investigating the murder of a porter. Dr. Ernst Laduner tells him as they enter the hospital premises: "Sie werden eingeführt ins dunkle Reich, in welchem Matto regiert" (You are being introduced to the dark realm where Matto rules); *Matto* (Italian for mad) is defined as "the spirit of madness." For a considerable time Studer is wary of Laduner; he wrongly mistrusts the latter's apparently casual approach and his unconventional view of human nature. Studer resists pressure from Dr. Herbert Kaplaun, a psychoan-

alyst, to give up his inquiries, and from this point on Studer shows more confidence in Laduner and in psychiatry. One of Glauser's aims in the novel is to inform the reader, as well as Studer, about the preoccupations and principles that underlie the running of a mental hospital.

*Die Fieberkurve* (The Temperature Curve, 1938), which has been criticized because of problems of plot construction, provides more glimpses of Studer's personal life and family than do other novels in the series. The complex action begins in Paris, where Studer is the guest of a French colleague; moves to Switzerland, where two mysterious deaths have occurred; and concludes at a foreign legion post in North Africa. *Der Chinese* (The Chinese Man, 1939) is set in a village which has suffered a decline in prosperity and where the advent of an orphanage and a nursery garden has not been welcomed. Studer has the task of investigating a series of mysterious deaths in the locality. The young people, who have little encouragement in their personal development in this environment, arouse Studer's concern and sympathy. *Krock & Co.* (1941) is a lighter work than *Der Chinese*, without as much serious emphasis on social issues and with a more unified plot. Attending his daughter's wedding at a country hotel, Studer finds himself professionally involved in the investigation of murder and suspicious financial dealings.

Some of Glauser's short stories are very effective, others are slight. "Die Begegnung" (The Encounter, 1939) concerns the distress and uncertainty facing a man who has recently been released from prison. In "Beichte in der Nacht" (Confession at Night, 1935) a nightclub is the background for one man's confidence to another concerning his wife's infidelity. "Verhör" (Interrogation, 1933) centers upon the conviction of a husband who has killed his wife's lover. Vienna is the scene of a murder in the early 1920s in "König Zucker" (King Sugar, 1936); crime is linked with irrational and supernatural factors in "Die Hexe von Endor" (The Witch of Endor, 1929).

Glauser is most accessible to readers in the Studer novels. Here he shows frequent concern for the social realities of his time and sympathizes with the outsiders and losers. An important factor in Glauser's creativity is the transformation of autobiographical experiences and the images of his past into narrative fantasy. Psychoanalysis, telepathy, magic, and witchcraft are shown as ways in which the human spirit can express itself, but reason usually triumphs in Glauser's fiction. The detective's concern for suffering humanity militates against the aggressiveness which is inherent in his role. Glauser's work combines a respect for law and order with sympathy for the lot of the suffering individual. Glauser's writing is clear, sincere, and often colorful.

**References:**
Eveline Jacksh, *Friedrich Glauser: Anwalt der* *Außenseiter* (Bonn: Bouvier, 1976);

Erhard Ruoss, *Friedrich Glauser: Erzählen als Selbstbegegnung und Wahrheitssuche* (Bern, Frankfurt am Main & Las Vegas: Lang, 1979);

Gerhard Saner, *Friedrich Glauser*, 2 volumes (Zurich & Frankfurt am Main: Suhrkamp, 1981).

# Oskar Maria Graf
*(22 July 1894-28 June 1967)*

Sheila K. Johnson
*University of Texas at Austin*

BOOKS: *Die Revolutionäre* (Dresden: Dresdner Verlag, 1918);

*Amen und Anfang: Gedichte* (Munich: Bachmair, 1919);

*Georg Schrimpf* (Konstanz: Saturne, 1919);

*Ua-Pua . . . ! Indianer-Dichtungen* (Regensburg & Leipzig: Habbel, 1921);

*Maria Uhden* (Leipzig: Klinkhardt & Biermann, 1921);

*Frühzeit: Jugenderlebnisse* (Berlin: Malik, 1922);

*Zur freundlichen Erinnerung: Acht Erzählungen* (Berlin: Malik, 1922);

*Georg Schrimpf* (Leipzig: Klinkhardt & Biermann, 1923);

*Bayerisches Lesebücherl: Weißblaue Kulturbilder* (Munich: Langes, 1924);

*Die Traumdeuter: Aus einer alten bayrischen Familienchronik* (Freiburg: Herder, 1924);

*Die Chronik von Flechting: Ein Dorfroman* (Munich: Drei Masken, 1925);

*Die Heimsuchung: Roman* (Bonn: Verlag der Buchgemeinde, 1925);

*Finsternis: Sechs Dorfgeschichten* (Munich: Drei Masken, 1926);

*Licht und Schatten: Eine Sammlung zeitgemäßer Märchen* (Berlin: Verlag der Neuen Gesellschaft, 1927);

*Wir sind Gefangene: Ein Bekenntnis aus diesem Jahrzehnt* (Munich: Drei Masken, 1927); translated by Margaret Green as *Prisoners All* (New York: Knopf, 1928);

*Wunderbare Menschen: Heitere Chronik einer Arbeiterbühne nebst meinen drolligen und traurigen Erlebnissen dortselbst* (Stuttgart: Engelhorn, 1927);

*Im Winkel des Lebens: Geschichten* (Berlin: Büchergilde Gutenberg, 1927);

*Das bayerische Dekameron* (Vienna: Verlag für Kulturforschung, 1928);

*Kalendergeschichten* (Munich & Berlin: Drei Masken, 1929; revised, Rudolstadt: Greifenverlag, 1957);

*Bolwieser: Roman eines Ehemannes* (Munich & Berlin: Drei Masken, 1931); translated by Margaret Goldsmith as *The Station Master* (London: Chatto & Windus, 1933); German version republished as *Die Ehe des Herrn Bolwieser* (Munich: Feder, 1964);

*Dorfbanditen: Erlebnisse aus meinen Schul- und Lehrlingsjahren* (Berlin: Drei Masken, 1932);

*Notizbuch des Provinzschriftstellers Oskar Maria Graf 1932: Erlebnisse, Intimitäten, Meinungen* (Basel, Leipzig & Vienna: Zinnen, 1932);

*Einer gegen alle: Roman* (Berlin: Universitas Deutsche Verlags-Aktiengesellschaft, 1932); translated anonymously as *The Wolf* (London: Dickson, 1934);

*Der harte Handel: Ein bayerischer Bauernroman* (Amsterdam: Querido, 1935);

*Der Abgrund: Ein Zeitroman* (London: Malik, 1936); revised as *Die gezählten Jahre* (Munich: Süddeutscher Verlag, 1976);

*Oskar Maria Graf (Ullstein)*

*Anton Sittinger: Roman* (London: Malik, 1937; New York, 1941);

*Der Quasterl* (Moscow: Iskra Revoljucii, 1938);

*The Life of My Mother: A Biographical Novel*, translated by A. van Eerden (New York: Howell, Soskin, 1940); German version published as *Das Leben meiner Mutter* (Munich: Desch, 1946);

*Das Aderlassen: Kalendergeschichten* (Weimar: Werden & Wirken, 1947);

*Unruhe um einen Friedfertigen: Roman* (New York: Aurora, 1947);

*Die Eroberung der Welt: Roman einer Zukunft* (Munich: Desch, 1949); republished as *Die Erben des Untergangs: Roman einer Zukunft* (Frankfurt am Main: Nest, 1959);

*Mitmenschen* (Berlin: Aufbau, 1950);

*Menschen aus meiner Jugend auf dem Dorfe: Drei Erzählungen* (Leipzig: Reclam, 1953);

*Der ewige Kalender: Ein Jahresspiegel* (New York, 1954);

*Die Flucht ins Mittelmäßige: Ein New-Yorker Roman* (Frankfurt am Main: Nest, 1959);

*An manchen Tagen: Reden, Gedanken und Zeitbetrachtungen* (Frankfurt am Main: Nest, 1961);

*Der große Bauernspiegel: Dorfgeschichten und Begebnisse von einst, gestern und jetzt* (Munich, Vienna & Basel: Desch, 1962);

*Altmodische Gedichte eines Dutzendmenschen*, anonymous (Frankfurt am Main: Nest, 1962); selections translated by Elisabeth Bayliss as *Old-Fashioned Poems of An Ordinary Man* (New York: Graf, 1967);

*Größtenteils schimpflich: Von Halbstarken und Leuten, welche dieselben nicht leiden können. Mitgeteilt und verfaßt von Oskar Maria Graf, Provinzschriftsteller derzeit wohnhaft in New York, USA* (Munich: Feder, 1962);

*Er nannte sich Banscho: Der Roman einer Gegend* (Berlin & Weimar: Aufbau, 1964);

*Gelächter von außen: Aus meinem Leben 1918-1933* (Munich: Desch, 1966);

*Bayrisches Lesebücherl: Von Früherszeiten bis heutzutag* (Hannover: Fackelträger, 1966);

*Reise in die Sowjetunion 1934*, edited by Hans-Albert Walter (Darmstadt & Neuwied: Luchterhand, 1974);

*Der Mord aus Zufall: Kriminalerzählungen*, edited by Herbert Greiner-Mai (Berlin: Das Neue, 1979).

"Verbrennt mich!" (Burn me!): two days after the infamous 10 May 1933 book burning at German universities, Oskar Maria Graf's enraged open-letter protest in the Vienna *Arbeiterzeitung* to the new Nazi regime carried the name of this Bavarian writer around the world via international news service. Graf's eloquent demand that his books not be included among the Third Reich's sanctioned "Blut- und Bodenliteratur" (blood and soil literature) is characteristic of this writer, whose works and life are full of conviction. Under threat of death in Germany, Graf was already in Viennese exile when he read that only one of his novels, *Wir sind Gefangene* (1927; translated as *Prisoners All*, 1928), had been condemned. Only after publication of his "Verbrennt mich!" letter was his entire oeuvre granted a special conflagration at the University of Munich. The Nazi propaganda machine, virtually drained of major contemporary literature, had been forced to usurp even non-Nazi works like Graf's harsh realistic portrayals of provincial and petty bourgeois life to help fill the sudden cultural void. Thus, Graf was compelled to disassociate himself publicly from the forces of oppression and false ideology against which his every instinct and literary product had cried out. Graf's ideas and political views were frequently out of step with the prevailing values of his age, and he had an almost perverse propensity for saying the right thing at the wrong time. As a consequence, Graf experienced during his lifetime only a relatively brief period during which his writing was accorded due recognition; this period began in the mid to late 1920s, the "golden twenties"—"gut versilberte" (nicely silverplated) years, in Graf's words—when his steady stream of contemporary novels and short stories sold well and were critically acclaimed in respected literary journals spanning much of the political spectrum. His early years of exile saw the publication of most of Graf's strongest novels, which received an enthusiastic reception among his fellow exiles. These exiles included Germany's best minds and literary talents: Thomas and Heinrich Mann, Johannes R. Becher, Lion Feuchtwanger, and Bertolt Brecht. In a poem honoring Graf's "Verbrennt mich!" letter, Brecht wrote that Graf was "Ein verjagter Dichter, einer der besten . . ."(A banished writer, one of the best . . .). But only before the "Verbrennt mich!" letter can one speak of a period of widespread popularity for Graf during his lifetime. Not until the 1970s did the name and works of Oskar Maria Graf begin to come to life again. The most concrete indicators of his current relevance and growing status are the three editions of his writings which began to appear in 1975. Munich's Süddeutscher Verlag has brought out fifteen volumes, with several more planned, including unpublished works from Graf's literary estate; the prestigious Büchergilde Gutenberg has published nine volumes of a critical edition; and dtv (Deutscher Taschenbuch Verlag) is licensed to publish the Süddeutscher Verlag works in paperback. Two biographies, one by Rolf Recknagel and one by Georg Bollenbeck, appeared in 1974 and 1985 respectively; a third, by Gerhard Bauer, will be brought out by the Süddeutscher Verlag in 1987. Several of Graf's works have been filmed, and scripts for others are awaiting production.

This long-overlooked exile with the trademark *Provinzschriftsteller* (provincial writer) on his calling cards and letterheads often referred to himself as a child of the nineteenth century. Oskar Graf was born on 22 July 1894 in the bucolic village of Berg on Lake Starnberg, a popular resort area south of Munich; he was the youngest of eleven children, nine of whom lived to adulthood. Graf's parents blended the old century and the new one: his mother, Theresa Heimrath Graf, came from a long-established local farm family; his father, Max Graf, had taken advantage of modern technology

to become a successful baker. Graf's writing combines elements of both centuries: his detailed, slowly unwinding narrative technique recalls those of earlier times, and his subject matter reflects the rural and metropolitan settings in which he lived. He was an insightful and sympathetic, yet critical observer of his contemporaries, especially of the common people; he was also a dynamic participant in the social and political developments of his times. The tyranny of a militaristic older brother who took over the household and family business after Graf's father died ended the twelve-year-old Oskar's relatively carefree childhood. Always an ardent reader, Graf left home for Munich shortly before he was seventeen, determined to make his way as a writer. Beyond basic schooling, however, his only training had been as a baker's apprentice; he was forced to take any job he could get, including elevator operator and sandwich man, and experienced firsthand the oppression of the urban proletariat. Naive and at the same time stimulated by the new ideas with which he was confronted in Munich, then the center of German culture, Graf became involved with anarchistic circles. By the outbreak of World War I he had established acquaintanceships with the local bohemians and leftist writers, including Georg Schrimpf and Franz Jung, and a few of his poems had been published in avant-garde and expressionistic journals such as *Die Aktion*. But, along with his whole generation, Graf—much less willingly than most—had to join the army in the summer of 1914. During the journey to the eastern front, his antimilitarism solidified into resistance; he refused to obey orders and eventually landed in an insane asylum because he laughed at every command and refused to talk. Released at the end of 1916, he returned to Munich, where he again "schuftete" (slaved) at menial jobs and wrote when he could. For obvious reasons, Professor Oskar Graf, an official war artist, paid him 500 marks to change his name; thereupon, Graf added Maria to his signature. The name was not an uncommon one in Catholic Bavaria, and Graf's admiration for Rilke made the alteration more appealing. In 1917 Graf, still something of a bumpkin, married Karoline Bretting, the jilted fiancée of a friend; a year later she bore Graf's only child, Annamarie, who was reared by his mother in Berg. Because Graf and his first wife had little in common they soon separated. Scraping together money from any source he could, from stipends provided by rich patrons to black marketeering and organizing wild parties for the local literati ("Bewegung!" and "Mehr Erotik!" [Action! and More eroticism!] were his advertising slogans), he was able to continue his writing, publishing two volumes of expressionist poetry as well as numerous short stories and essays. In 1919 Graf was involved in the leftist revolution and short-lived Räterepublik (soviet republic) in Bavaria. Also that year he met Mirjam Sacks, a student from a middle-class Berlin Jewish family, who was to share his difficult life and peregrinations until her death in 1959.

In the chaotic years following World War I, Graf gradually turned from the lyric mode—though he never completely abandoned it—and began concentrating on narrative prose, which was to remain his strongest métier. He made the first major step when, in need of money, he agreed somewhat reluctantly to let Wieland Herzfelde of the Malik Verlag publish one of his earliest attempts at extended prose narrative, a chronicle of his own life from 1911 through 1917. *Frühzeit: Jugenderlebnisse* (Early Times: Experiences of Youth, 1922) was in good company at the progressive Malik Verlag, which also published works by Else Lasker-Schüler, Upton Sinclair, and Georg Trakl. Although this book, as well as Graf's next several

prose works—historical novels and collections of proletarian and rural short stories—did not bring him overnight success, his reputation grew steadily, especially in southern Germany. Not, however, until *Frühzeit* was combined with Graf's account of the Munich revolution of 1918-1919 and republished under the title *Wir sind Gefangene* in 1927 did Graf's work receive acclaim throughout Germany, led by a detailed review by Thomas Mann. The book appeared in England as *Prisoners All* the next year, and in France in 1930. *Frühzeit* had already come out in two Russian translations and several editions in 1925; a Russian version of *Wir sind Gefangene* was published in 1928. In *Wir sind Gefangene* convention is largely abandoned. The perspective is both intensely personal, revealing Graf's ignoble as well as his idealistic motivations, and distanced; his controlled use of humor makes his criticism of himself and of his times especially effective. Graf becomes both subject and object of this work, as he does in all of his autobiographical writings. Furthermore, the historical period Graf treats in the book is fascinating in itself, and, through documentary inserts and his own eyewit-

*Nazi book-burning at the University of Berlin, 10 May 1933. Graf was outraged because his books were not included among those burned (Ullstein).*

ness testimony, Graf makes it live. His celebration of the leftist revolution in the closing chapters was to make *Wir sind Gefangene* anathema to the Nazis.

Graf rode the crest of his newfound popularity with three more books published in 1927: a collection of engaged, contemporary fairy tales, *Licht und Schatten* (Light and Shadows); a collection of short stories in a rural setting, *Im Winkel des Lebens* (In the Corner of Life); and another autobiographical volume dealing with his experiences from 1920 to 1923 as a rather bumbling producer in a Munich workers' theater, *Wunderbare Menschen: Heitere Chronik einer Arbeiterbühne nebst meinen drolligen und traurigen Erlebnissen dortselbst* (Wonderful People: A Light-hearted Chronicle of a Workers' Theater along with My Droll and Sad Experiences There). At the theater Graf had failed even to read *Trommeln in der Nacht* (Drums in the Night, 1923), which Bertolt Brecht had submitted to the theater, because the play had "too many characters for the fire regulations."

During the financially and professionally comfortable years before his exile, Graf had a book published every year except 1930, and three in 1932. His interest in politics was reflected in his active involvement in organizations fighting for freedom of expression and other human rights, as well as in his writing. He was never a member of a party, although he supported socialist causes; his focus was not on those who manipulated from the top but rather on those affected—used—by power politics. Humanitarianism, not tendentiousness, motivates and informs all his important works, which include the collection *Kalendergeschichten* (Calendar-Stories, 1929) and the novel *Bolwieser* (1931; translated as *The Station Master*, 1933). The former contains over 800 pages of Graf's short stories, old and new; those set in a rural milieu are generally more rounded and more convincing than the city stories. The use of dialect is so extensive that Graf included a dialect dictionary in the first edition; one of the reasons for his "renaissance" in the 1970s was a renewed interest in local dialect in German literature. *Bolwieser* became a further instrument of Graf's rediscovery when Rainer Werner Faßbinder filmed it in 1977. The book examines the petty bourgeoisie in a small German city: a stationmaster; his wife; and her two lovers, a butcher and a hairdresser. Petty power struggles, obsessions with sex and money, and political ignorance are incisively exposed, without the reader's losing sight of the fact that these characters are believable, pitiable human beings who are the victims of their own weaknesses. As Faßbinder's film

stresses, it was such weaknesses that facilitated Hitler's rise.

During this period, 1928 to 1932, Graf produced some of his most humorous books, most notably the notorious *Das bayerische Dekameron* (The Bavarian Decameron, 1928), which came close to destroying his reputation as a serious author. Still banned for sale to underaged readers in Austria at the end of the 1960s, *Das bayerische Dekameron* consists of hastily thrown together but well-recounted anecdotes of the sort Graf had long heard and told around the "Stammtisch" (table in a local inn reserved for cronies). The focus is country life; the flavor is crude but hearty; the themes are sex, practical jokes, and more sex. Graf, even in the best times short on cash, wrote the work in five weeks on commission from a publisher of risqué books. It has outsold his other works, appeared in a dozen editions, and has weathered all the changes in Graf's literary fortunes. Stemming from these years are two other books which are also basically humorous, but they are drawn from Graf's own experiences: *Dorfbanditen* (Village Bandits, 1932), stories drawing on his youth; and *Notizbuch des Provinzschriftstellers Oskar Maria Graf 1932* (Notebook of the Provincial Writer Oskar Maria Graf 1932,

*Painting of Graf by Rudolf Schlichter (Deutsche Fotothek, Dresden)*

1932), clever, satirical vignettes based on his observations and adventures in Munich and Berlin.

The last book by Graf published before he left Germany bears the title *Einer gegen alle* (One against All, 1932; translated as *The Wolf*, 1934), a blackly ironic twist of the phrase in the Weimar Republic Constitution: "One for all . . . all for one. . . ." The republic had clearly failed, and Graf integrates an account of this failure with the story of an individual destroyed by the war out of which the republic had been born. The novel is a condemnation of militarism, describing the plight of a veteran who cannot adjust to a peacetime environment in which people exhibit little more humanity than had the soldiers, who had been trained to kill in the war. Graf 's hope for a better Germany and a better world was to alternate for the rest of his life with the dark despair apparent in *Einer gegen alle*.

Life in exile was never easy, but Graf, the antinationalist, managed to keep growing as a writer in ever more foreign environments—first Austria, then Czechoslovakia, and finally America. He truly merits the appellation "Weltbürger" (citizen of the world) often conferred on him. In Vienna his "Verbrennt mich!" letter established him among anti-Hitler circles; working with Johannes R. Becher and Heinrich Mann, he was a central organizer of resistance writers in Austria. With Wieland Herzfelde, Anna Seghers, and Jan Peterson, he founded and edited *Neue deutsche Blätter*, an engaged literary journal of the highest quality which provided a forum for exiles from 1933 through 1935. Early in his stay Graf involved himself with the proletariat of the "red" quarter in the city, leaving Austria after the February 1934 workers' uprising was crushed by profascist forces.

Between early 1934 and the summer of 1938 Graf made his home in Brno, Czechoslovakia, and these uncertain times proved to be among his most productive: three of his most significant works were published and a fourth was begun. The short novel *Der harte Handel* (The Hard Deal), published in 1935 but completed in 1932, lays bare the harshness of life in a contemporary Bavarian farm setting. Ulrich Edel's 1978 film received much praise for capturing the brutal atmosphere Graf had depicted. *Der Abgrund* (The Abyss, 1936) deals with the history of Social Democracy in Germany and Austria and its demise in both countries; Graf concludes the novel with the crushing of the workers by Dollfuss in 1934, which he himself had experienced. The strength of *Der Abgrund* lies more in the characters Graf developed with historical hind-

*Drawing by Graf for the dust jacket of his novel* Anton Sittinger *(Verlag der Nation, Berlin)*

sight—the older generation of Social Democrats—than with the elaboration of his hope for a Socialist-Marxist future unbound to party structure. Nonetheless, the novel retains its power to bring this fateful time to life. The strongest of all his works written in Czechoslovakia is *Anton Sittinger* (1937), a novel in which Graf epitomizes, without slipping into stereotypes, the German philistine and his connection with the rise of Hitler. The postal inspector Sittinger and his south German world retain their credibility throughout, whether seen from the authorial perspective or that of the title character's inner monologues. The book's motto conveys Graf 's warning: "Menschen wie Sittinger gibt es in allen Ländern . . . in manchen Zeiten heißen sie 'du' und 'ich' " (There are people like Sittinger in every country . . . sometimes their names are "you" and "I").

In August 1934 Graf had traveled to Moscow to attend the First Congress of Soviet Writers; he recalled his six weeks there in the posthumously published *Reise in die Sowjetunion 1934* (Travels in the Soviet Union 1934, 1974). But four years later, when it became clear that he must again flee from the Nazis, he chose not to go back to the Soviet Union whose people he had found so vital and where many of his works had appeared; instead, he and Mirjam sailed to the United States, where two of his siblings had already become citizens. Graf took with him the half-finished manuscript of *Das Leben meiner Mutter* (1946; translated as *The Life of My Mother*, 1940), the book he called his "zweites Hauptwerk" (second major work) after *Wir sind Gefangene*. Despite its bulk, the appeal of the main characters in *Das Leben meiner Mutter* and the tangibility of its historical background (Bavaria between 1860 and 1934) have made it Graf's most popular work in Germany next to *Das bayerische Dekameron*. Graf completed *Das Leben meiner Mutter* in America, where he quickly established himself in the growing circle of German exiles streaming through New York, the city in which he was to live for the rest of his life.

Like Graf's other works, *Das Leben meiner Mutter* did not find a wide market in the United States. Although it first appeared in English translation in 1940 and was well received critically, the publisher soon went bankrupt. Graf continued to write, but the approach of war and the fact that Graf did not try to capture the American public but concentrated on a scattered German readership relegated his longer works to the "Schublade" (drawer). From the time he arrived in America Graf continued to be active in organizing exiled writers: he was, for example, cofounder of the German-American Writers' Association and president from 1938 to 1940, and president of the Aurora Verlag in 1944. He gave anti-Nazi lectures and readings of his works in universities and before German-speaking groups across the United States, and, working through various organizations, he was active in helping other exiles gain entry into America. He refused to learn English because he feared it would affect his writing. Graf was granted a divorce from his wife in June 1944, and he and Mirjam were married on 2 October.

Of Graf's novels published after the war, two are among the most important of his oeuvre: *Unruhe um einen Friedfertigen* (Unrest around a Peace-Lover, 1947) and *Die Flucht ins Mittelmäßige* (Escape into Mediocrity, 1959). The first offers a unique depiction of the development of pro-Nazi senti-ments among the rural populace. Set in southern Germany before and shortly after the Nazi take-over in 1933, this work constitutes the antithesis of the "Heimatkunst" (regional art) favored by Hitler. Julius Kraus is a village cobbler who wants only to live and let live; but he is a Jew and so is doomed to be a victim. Graf shows in this sensitively portrayed, understated character the fate not just of Jews in fascist Germany but of all those who choose not to fight against tyranny. "Ich [habe] mit der Zeit herausgebracht, daß die Menschen überall gleich sind und . . . man [sieht] sie in der Provinz schneller und leichter" (With time I [have] come to the conclusion that people are the same everywhere and . . . you can [see] them better in the provinces), wrote Graf in 1932. *Unruhe um einen Friedfertigen* illustrates this general thesis as well as its particular political insights. It is, for the most part, Graf's aesthetically best-formed novel.

Graf chose not to return to Germany because it was divided, directed from without, and run in large part by former Nazis, and because leftist exiles were not warmly welcomed by the government. His chances of gaining a postwar readership were, therefore, minimal; in any case, there was little market until the 1960s for the works of exiles generally. None of the novels and collections of short stories published before his death in 1967 attracted much attention. *Die Flucht ins Mittelmäßige* found its first major readership among those concerned with the renaissance of the writers of the Weimar Republic whose works had been banned and burned by the Nazis. Graf's dark portrayal of the lives of exiles has lasting worth as a document of the postwar era. In America, his outspoken advocacy of social justice, his pacifism modeled on Tolstoy and Gandhi, and his respect for Marx made him suspect in the cold war and Vietnam years. His intelligence and talent enabled him to capture in novels, short stories, and essays the essence of important developments in Germany and among Germans abroad during the first half of the twentieth century, often before Germans were willing to accept his insights or conclusions. A hastily assembled volume of his essays, speeches, and letters, *An manchen Tagen* (On Certain Days, 1961), evidences Graf's uniquely honest questioning of the world in which he lived and of his own ever evolving principles.

The final decade of Graf's life brought major developments. In 1958 he became a United States citizen and was thus able to travel abroad; in 1960 Wayne State University granted him an honorary doctorate and he became a founding member of

*Graf (right) and Bertolt Brecht in New York*

the Academy of Arts in West Berlin. Four years later, the East Berlin Academy of Arts made him a corresponding member. Graf married Dr. Gisela Blauner in 1962 and, in the same year, was given his first of two honoraria by the city of Munich, the city which now houses his literary estate at the Bayerische Staatsbibliothek. He died on 28 June 1967, and his ashes were interred in the Munich Bogenhausen Cemetery in 1968. Süddeutscher Verlag has commissioned H. F. Pfanner to edit a volume of selections from his literary estate. Oskar Maria Graf was a Bavarian Weltbürger (world citizen), a Catholic who believed in nothing except man's responsibility to nurture his fellowman, and a socialist who remained independent of any party. Beyond his ability to create unforgettable characters—his autobiographical writings being among his best—Graf will retain his relevance as a witness of his age who was able to make it live for posterity.

**Letters:**

*Oskar Maria Graf in seinen Briefen,* edited by Gerhard Bauer and H. F. Pfanner (Munich: Süddeutscher Verlag, 1984).

**Bibliography:**

H. F. Pfanner, *Oskar Maria Graf: Eine kritische Bibliographie* (Bern & Munich: Francke, 1976).

**Biographies:**

Rolf Recknagel, *Ein Bayer in Amerika: Oskar Maria Graf—Leben und Werk* (Berlin: Aufbau, 1974; revised, 1977);

Georg Bollenbeck, *Oskar Maria Graf: Mit Selbstzeugnissen und Bilddokumenten* (Reinbek: Rowohlt, 1985).

**References:**

Georg Bollenbeck, "Vom Exil zur Diaspora: Zu Oskar Maria Grafs Roman *Die Flucht ins Mittelmäßige*," in *Exilforschung: Ein internationales Jahrbuch,* 3 (1985): 260-269;

Wolfgang Dietz and H. F. Pfanner, eds., *Oskar Maria Graf: Beschreibung eines Volksschriftstellers* (Munich: Annedore Leber, 1974);

Günter Häntzschel, "Oskar Maria Graf: Writer of the People?," in *German Studies Review,* 9 (February 1986): 67-83;

Sheila K. Johnson, *The Critical Reception of Oskar Maria Graf's Prose Fiction* (Bonn: Bouvier, 1979);

Rolf Recknagel, "Oskar Maria Graf: Eine Renaissance," in *Exil: 1933-1945*, volume 2, edited

by Edita Koch (Maintal: Koch, 1984), pp. 55-70.

**Papers:**
Oskar Maria Graf's papers are in the Bayerische Staatsbibliothek, Munich.

# Felix Hartlaub
## (17 June 1913-? April 1945)

### Richard H. Lawson
#### University of North Carolina at Chapel Hill

BOOKS: *Don Juan d'Austria und die Schlacht bei Lepanto* (Berlin: Triltsch & Huther, 1939);

*Von unten gesehen: Impressionen und Aufzeichnungen des Obergefreiten Felix Hartlaub*, edited by Geno Hartlaub (Stuttgart: Koehler, 1950); expanded as *Im Sperrkreis: Aufzeichnungen aus dem zweiten Weltkrieg* (Hamburg: Rowohlt, 1955);

*Parthenope; oder, Das Abenteuer in Neapel* (Stuttgart: Deutsche Verlagsanstalt, 1951);

*Das Gesamtwerk: Dichtungen, Tagebücher*, edited by Geno Hartlaub (Frankfurt am Main: Fischer, 1955);

*Der Bundschuh: Ein Gemeinschaftsspiel* (Heppenheim: Privatdruck der Odenwaldschule, n.d.).

OTHER: Percy Ernst Schramm, ed., *Kriegstagebuch des Oberkommandos der Wehrmacht 1940-1945*, contributions by Hartlaub, 4 volumes (Frankfurt am Main: Bernard & Graefe, 1961-1965).

PERIODICAL PUBLICATIONS: "Mahad," *Kunstblatt der Jugend*, no. 6 (1928);

"Führerhauptquartier 1943/44," *Merkur*, 4 (April 1950): 370-384;

"Parthenope; oder, Das Abenteuer in Neapel," *Merkur*, 5 (February 1951): 152-168; (March 1951): 268-283; (April 1951): 353-371;

"Wolken über Paris: Tagebuchblätter aus dem Jahr 1941," *Merkur*, 6 (June 1952): 549-561;

"Wolken über Paris: Impressionen aus dem Besatzungsjahr 1941," *Die neue Rundschau*, 64, no. 4 (1953): 532-544;

"Der letzte Sonntag," *Rheinisch-Pfälzische Monatshefte für Kultur und Heimatspflege*, 5, no. 10 (1954);

"Mond und Pferde: Ein Nachtstück," *Jahresring 54: Ein Schnitt durch Literatur und Kunst der Gegenwart* (1954): 5-14;

"Die Reise des Tobias," *Merkur*, 8 (October 1954): 961-977; (November 1954): 1054-1067; (December 1954): 1138-1154;

"Berliner Tagebuchblätter 1935/36: Aus dem Nachlaß," *Akzente*, 2 (1955): 80-84, 179-183, 272-278;

"Briefe an N. N.," *Die neue Rundschau*, 67, no. 4 (1956): 671-698;

"Briefe und Tagebuchaufzeichnungen aus Neapel," *Merkur*, 10 (June 1956): 569-573;

"Hundegeschichte," *Texte und Zeichen*, 3 (July 1957): 348-350;

"Brueghels Affe: Ein Fragment," *Merkur*, 11 (November 1957): 1040-1057.

Felix Hartlaub's literary importance lies largely in the hypothetical—in what might have been had he lived beyond the age of thirty-one. On the basis of his precocious diction; his ability to transform visual experience into trenchant prose, whether cool or sensual; his breaking of syntax to reflect direct experience; and his early incorporation of filmic techniques into prose, his was one of the greatest and one of the most innovative talents of his generation. A trained historian, he was highly sensitive to the possibilities of interplay between professional language and literary language. Probably deriving from his sense of history is his "neg-

ative" or detached hero, who is buffeted by historical forces yet is capable of action and able to survive in spite of his fear and powerlessness. The distance insulating this hero from the historical forces working about him, as well as the distance between narrator and hero, give scope to a methodically devastating irony not far from cynicism. But how Hartlaub's already mature and sophisticated talent, his openness to innovation, would have further developed must unfortunately remain a matter of conjecture.

Felix Hartlaub was born in Bremen on 17 June 1913 to the art historian Gustav Friedrich Hartlaub and Félicie Meyer Hartlaub. A year after Felix's birth the family moved to Mannheim, where Gustav Friedrich became assistant director and, after World War I, director of the municipal art museum. Hartlaub, who had a younger sister and brother, attended the local Gymnasium (grammar school) and then, from 1928 to 1932, a progressive

residential school in nearby Heppenheim, in the Odenwald. His mother's death in 1930 was a severe blow. He traveled to Italy in 1931 and 1933. In the latter year the Nazis relieved his father of his post at the art museum.

Hartlaub studied romance philology and modern history at the University of Heidelberg in 1934, then transferred to Berlin, where in 1939 he received his doctorate in modern history. In that same year he was conscripted into the army. Field service in World War II alternated with assignments to the High Command and the Führer Headquarters as a military historian. His duty stations included Paris, Berlin, Romania, the Ukraine, East Prussia, and Berchtesgaden. In April 1945 he was assigned to the infantry in Berlin. After a visit with friends in the city on the eve of his reassignment, in the final stage of a deteriorating military situation, he set out for his new post. On the way he disappeared, apparently having been killed by Russian soldiers.

With the exception of surprisingly mature juvenile writings and his doctoral dissertation, *Don Juan d'Austria und die Schlacht bei Lepanto* (Don Juan of Austria and the Battle of Lepanto, 1939), Hartlaub's limited oeuvre was all published posthumously in a handful of books and in periodicals. None of his works has been translated into English. His literary remains consist of short narratives, sketches, notes, diary entries (tending to take the form of short expositions), and apparent plans for more far-reaching works after the war. Letters to family and friends also survive, as well as histories of certain World War II military operations that he wrote for the High Command.

Hartlaub's creative works, and to a noteworthy degree his letters and diaries as well, revolve about the highly sensitive observations of a loner and outsider, who in the creative works usually plays the role of a detached or negative hero. Hartlaub's style ranges from an exuberant lyricism to a highly disciplined, staccato quasi expressionism. There are indications that he was moving toward a synthesis of his disparate styles; his literary development was far from complete at his untimely disappearance. Brought up in an artistic environment, Hartlaub was also a self-taught graphic artist of no mean talent.

"Der verlorene Gott" (The Lost God) is a lavish drama, part verse and part prose. It was published in *Das Gesamtwerk* (The Collected Works, 1955), a single volume edited by Hartlaub's sister, Genovefa. Written at the Odenwald school in 1929, the drama reflects Hartlaub's study of history, the history of religion, and the interpretation of myth. The hero is the Emperor (the play was originally entitled *Emperor Julian*), who, in his wide-ranging but futile search for the lost pagan gods, holds together the otherwise centrifugal panoply of rich scene and vigorous action. As written, "Der verlorene Gott" is probably unstageable. Hartlaub later said that it flowed from "his clever and often enlightened boyhood dreams."

"Die Reise des Tobias" (The Journey of Tobias) was written in 1932, just after Hartlaub had completed his preparatory education, and published posthumously in *Merkur* in 1954. The lengthy novella fragment, based loosely on the Book of Tobit in the Apocrypha, was never completed, although Hartlaub wrote expansive notes sketching a variety of possible resolutions. Tobias is an autobiographical figure imbued with the youthful author's own concerns about confronting adult life. With an accompanying angel, Tobias, a merchant's son in a vaguely Middle Eastern milieu, travels to the caravansary of a business acquaintance of his father. Delayed by fever from undertaking the return trip, he becomes caught up in the domestic life of his host family and extends his

visit to attend the marriage of the daughter of the house.

From the beginning the atmosphere of the caravansary, although related in naturalistic detail, is suffused with an air of mystery and unreality which is evidently conducive to Tobias's even more fantastic personal visions. The daughter's prospective bridegroom dies—the second such untoward death in her young life. Tobias becomes infatuated with the girl, but the deaths of her two fiancés have placed her in danger of being adjudged a witch. Although his cause is aided by his angel, Tobias impresses the girl as a less than sufficient champion. The fragment ends with the angel losing his last vestige of divinity. Some of the projected endings embody a happy resolution for Tobias, the merchant's daughter, and the angel; others project an unhappy ending.

The insufficient champion or detached hero is encountered again in *Parthenope; oder, Das Abenteuer in Neapel* (Parthenope; or, The Adventure in Naples, 1951). Parthenope is an ancient name for Naples, from the Siren who was cast ashore there. Hartlaub wrote this novella in 1934, after a six-month stay in Italy, as an entry in a writing competition; thereafter, he submitted it in vain to several publishers.

The detached hero of the adventure is François Renaudet, a French artillery lieutenant posted to the Neapolitan Republic that was established in 1799 by the French occupiers. On his first night in Naples Renaudet strikes up a relationship with a well-situated pro-French courtesan and counts on an easy conquest. But Giovanna proves as sexually unattainable as she is politically ambiguous. Dropping her guise of a pro-French urban courtesan to reveal her true identity as a country girl who favors the Neapolitan monarchy, she betrays him to a mob in the countryside, and he is stabbed in the shoulder. Renaudet, on recovering from his wounds, refuses to swear to Giovanna's anti-French sympathies before a Neapolitan mob, and she is killed. Hartlaub combines his penchant for fantasy with his counterbalancing penchant for history.

"Berliner Tagebuchblätter" (Berlin Diary Pages) appears in *Das Gesamtwerk* with the subtitle "aus den Studienjahren 1935 bis 1938" (from the Student Years 1935 to 1938). In her notes Geno Hartlaub gives the dates, probably more correctly, as 1935 to 1939, Hartlaub's student years at the University of Berlin. His sense of isolation there, compounded by the prickly political situation and probably sharpened by the Nazi treatment of his father, is amply reflected in the diary. The entries

*Pen-and-ink drawing by Hartlaub at age thirteen*

dwell on such topics as the student's search for living quarters, scenes in the library, politically and ideologically oriented students, and a boulevard café at which the tables and chairs are moved outdoors at the end of April—prematurely, as it turns out. The style of the entries tends toward that of expressionism, although Geno Hartlaub reports that her brother actually had little interest in the literature of expressionism, preferring Hugo von Hofmannsthal, Heinrich von Kleist, Georg Büchner, and Friedrich Schiller.

"Tagebuch aus dem Kriege" (War Diary), also published in *Das Gesamtwerk*, covers the years 1939 to 1945. The entries, frequently self-contained prose sketches, are often undated and unordered. The fragmentary notes from Hartlaub's service in Rumania, for example, were written on loose slips of paper. The entries made in Paris reveal his typical isolation: keenly sensitive to everything that he sees and hears, he renounces the social life available to the conquerors, preferring to hang about in antiquarian bookstores. His irony is nicely exemplified in a sketch of la place Pigalle depicting a prostitute's dismay and disdain when she finds herself on the verge of being picked up by someone who is not a German soldier. Hartlaub's aloofness is reflected in his frequent references to himself in the third person. Material from "Tagebuch aus dem Kriege" was published in *Von unten gesehen* (As Seen from Below, 1950), which was expanded as *Im Sperrkreis* (In the Wave Trap [referring to a device for eliminating radio interference], 1955).

*Felix Hartlaub in seinen Briefen* (Felix Hartlaub in His Letters, 1958) contains selections from Hartlaub's letters from 1919 until 8 March 1945, just five or six weeks before his walk into oblivion. In addition to letters to members of his family, there are letters to Dr. Werner Meyer, the most inspiring of several inspiring teachers at the Odenwald school; Dr. Rudolph Kiewe, a friend from student days in Heidelberg and Italy; and Erna G., the mother of a school friend, a woman whom Hartlaub adored both romantically and, it appears, as a surrogate mother. His letters testify to his pervasive sense of aloneness as well as to an openness tinged but not overwhelmed by cynicism, and to a generosity of emotion. In his fiction he was apparently not yet sufficiently sure of himself to let the last-named quality emerge from under the protective cover of irony.

**Letters:**
*Felix Hartlaub in seinen Briefen,* edited by Erna Krauss and Gustav Friedrich Hartlaub (Tübingen: Wunderlich, 1958).

**References:**
Hans Egon Holthusen, "Der negative Held," *Merkur,* 5 (December 1951): 1179-1191;
Henri Plard, "Tout seul: La Conscience de la solitude chez Felix Hartlaub," *Études Germaniques,* 14 (April-June 1959): 128-147;
Max Rychner, "Felix Hartlaub," in his *Arachne: Aufsätze zur Literatur* (Zurich: Manesse, 1957), pp. 234-248;
Christian-Hartwig Wilke, *Die letzten Aufzeichnungen Felix Hartlaubs* (Bad Homburg, Berlin & Zurich: Gehlen, 1967).

# Ludwig Hohl

*(9 April 1904-3 November 1980)*

## H. M. Waidson

BOOKS: *Nuancen und Details,* 2 volumes (Zurich: Oprecht, 1939-1942);

*Nächtlicher Weg* (Zurich: Morgarten, 1943; revised, Frankfurt am Main: Suhrkamp, 1971);

*Die Notizen; oder, Von der unvoreiligen Versöhnung,* 2 volumes (volume 1, Zurich: Artemis, 1944; volume 2, Zurich: Artemis, 1954); Part II republished as *Vom Erreichbaren und vom Unerreichbaren* (Frankfurt am Main: Suhrkamp, 1972); Part VII republished as *Varia* (Frankfurt am Main: Suhrkamp, 1977); Parts I and XII republished as *Vom Arbeiten; Bild* (Frankfurt am Main: Suhrkamp, 1978); Part IX republished as *Das Wort faßt nicht jeden: Über Literatur* (Frankfurt am Main: Suhrkamp, 1980);

*Daß fast alles anders ist* (Olten & Freiburg: Walter, 1967);

*Bergfahrt* (Frankfurt am Main: Suhrkamp, 1975).

Ludwig Hohl's literary production is mainly in the form of short prose writings, either short stories or brief nonfiction pieces. The 1930s seem to have been his most productive period, but much of his work was published a number of years after its composition. Relatively little new writing by Hohl was published between 1945 and his death in 1980. His work gradually became known to a younger generation of Swiss writers in the last twenty years of his life, and his fiercely independent personality also contributed to his later reputation.

Hohl was born on 9 April 1904 in Netstal, Canton Glarus, Switzerland, to Arnold Hohl, a Protestant minister, and Magda Zweifel Hohl. After his primary education, Hohl went to the Gymnasium at Frauenfeld but left without completing the courses because of difficulties in his relationships with the school authorities. He studied privately for his school-leaving examination but failed in chemistry and physics. In October 1924 Hohl left for Paris, where he lived for seven years. During 1930-1931 he was in Vienna, and in the autumn of 1931 he went to Holland, where he lived for six years in poverty and isolation.

Xaver Kronig has maintained that almost all the important themes of Hohl's later writing are already touched upon in *Nuancen und Details* (Nuances and Details), a collection of observations and comments written between 1931 and 1935; these themes include work, death, art, education, and the middle-class philistine. Although Hohl did not wish his short prose pieces to be known as aphorisms, that term comes to mind in considering them. The pieces include maxims, notes, portraits, comments, questions, dreams, stories, parables, and personal memories. The first volume of *Nuancen und Details* was published in 1939, the second in 1942.

The central work to be published in Hohl's lifetime, *Die Notizen; oder, Von der unvoreiligen Versöhnung* (The Notes; or, Concerning the Not Overhasty Reconciliation), was written in Holland from 1934 to 1936. As Hohl said in 1955, "Dann, wie schon angedeutet, kam alles von selbst. *Die Notizen* sind geschrieben worden in einem während dreier Jahre fast unveränderten Zustand—welcher mir aus der Ferne als derjenige einer fortwährenden Glut, wie die Zeit einer einzigen Eruption erscheint" (Then, as already indicated, everything came of its own accord. *The Notes* were written in a state of mind that was unchanged for three years—which seems to me from the distance to be that of a continuous glowing fire, like the time of a single eruption).

The first volume of *Die Notizen* appeared in 1944, but only after Hohl had successfully brought a lawsuit did the Artemis-Verlag publish the second volume in 1954. As Hugo Loetscher wrote in a review in *Die Tat* (Zurich) at that time: "Sicherlich, Ludwig Hohl ist kein liebenswürdiger Autor, er wird sich nie ein breites Publikum erschreiben. Aber wir haben unbequeme Schriftsteller notwendig. . . . Unbequem ist er. Denn wenn man fragt, was er eigentlich sei: ein Dichter? Ein Philosoph? Ein Publizist? Ein Literat? Ein Aphorismen-Schreiber? Ein Kritiker? Wer könnte genau Antwort geben?" (Certainly, Ludwig Hohl is not an amiable author, he will never gain a large following from his writing. But we need uncomfortable authors. . . . He is uncomfortable. For when one asks what he actually is—a poet, a philosopher, a publicist, a man of letters, a writer of aphorisms, a critic—who could give an exact answer?).

*Die Notizen* consists of prose pieces arranged in twelve parts according to themes. In the preface to the second volume (Parts VII-XII) Hohl explains that he wishes this work to be understood as a unity, not as a collection of aphorisms. Part I, which contains fifty-one items, concentrates on the theme of work. In the first note Hohl writes about man's impulse to initiate creative activity, which has to be directed outwardly and at the same time to be an inner event. Note I, 18 is seen by Adrian Ewald Bänninger as providing a helpful approach to Hohl's work. It declares that human work activity of a world-changing kind is fulfilled in three stages: the initial "great idea" is dissolved into "small ideas," which lead to individual achievements ("small deeds"). Part II, "Vom Erreichbaren und vom Unerreichbaren" (Concerning the Attainable and the Unattainable), has 333 items. Its principal theme is the possibilities and limits of being human; II, 2 contains the statement that no human mind or spirit can exist without the will to change and to move toward what is better. Item II, 19 says that once light has begun to appear it can from then onward only increase. There is a basic optimism also in II, 80, where intelligence combined with talent and applied with will power are seen as always leading to achievements and discoveries. Effort is needed to pursue the way; Hohl refers to Goethe's *Faust* in this connection. Hohl's pieces in *Die Notizen* are not always of a consistent quality; the generalizations are sometimes sweeping and sometimes provocative. Part III, "Reden, Schwatzen, Schweigen" (Speaking, Chattering, Keeping Silent), criticizes frivolous chatter and silence and approves of true communication. Part IV, "Der Leser" (The Reader), contains comments on literature: for instance, a reader should be able to read both Proust and D. H. Lawrence, and he should approach German literature with a questioning, sharp, satirical attitude. Observations on art, in a wide sense, are collected in the section "Kunst." Hohl sees two basic factors in writing and art; while Katherine Mansfield and Goethe represent "Zartheit" (delicacy), Hölderlin, Michelangelo, and Dostoyevsky give expression to "das Gewaltige" (the violent). Literary and aesthetic themes appear again in Part VI, "Vom Schreiben"

(On Writing). Part VII, "Varia" (Odds and Ends), contains a wide variety of material. There are sketches of the author's environment in Holland; short stories on disparate themes; further calls for dedicated activity; appreciation of animals; support for the desire to be independent of the state, of the family, and of other people's opinions; and further references to literary stimuli. Part VIII, "Apotheker" (Pharmacist), is largely a collection of comments on the limited complacency of many philistines, including sharp criticisms of the Swiss—for instance, what Hohl considers the foolish attitude of German Swiss toward their dialects, for he feels that dialect is unproductive and uncreative. Part IX, "Literatur," contains further literary comment; in answer to the question which are the men of all ages to whom he must express gratitude, Hohl cites Goethe and Spinoza, then Heraclitus, Hölderlin, Bach, Montaigne, and Lichtenberg. In the short Part X, "Traum und Träume" (Dream and Dreams), the author recounts several of his dreams and comments on them. On the subject of death in Part XI, Hohl rejects the traditional Christian expectation of a life to come but seeks a positive response to death; after climbing up a difficult slope, a man looks down at the world and sees that not all was deception and vanity, that there can be meaningful action. Part XII, "Bild" (Picture or Image), is a sequence of observations and quotations that look back to earlier preoccupations in the work and offer hope or consolation in the face of death in dreams, imagination, happiness, knowledge, children, creative activity, and respect for life. Hohl quotes from a letter on the enhancement of personal life-style by Katherine Mansfield of 11 October 1922, declaring it to be "one of the most beautiful and most important letters":

> A new way of being is not an easy thing to *live*. Thinking about it, preparing to meet the difficulties and so on, is one thing, meeting those difficulties another. I have to die to so much; I have to make such *big* changes. . . .
>
> Were we positive, eager, real, alive? No, we were not. We were a nothingness shot with gleams of what might be. But no more. Well, I have to face everything as far as I can and see where I stand—what *remains*.

*Die Notizen* ends with reconciliatory comments about objects, people, the role of mankind, and personal fulfillment.

In 1937 a gift of money from his uncle enabled Hohl to return to Switzerland with his wife, the former Henriette Adelheid Charlotte von Mayenburg ("Lotte"), whom he had married on 7 March 1935. Both his father and his uncle believed that Hohl should find work and make himself financially independent, but he firmly refused to consider any profession other than writing. His father paid him a small allowance, and he was encouraged in his literary endeavors by the author Albin Zollinger until the latter's death in 1941.

Hohl's short stories are likely to be the most immediately accessible of his writings. A number of brief stories are included among the comments of *Nuancen und Details* and *Die Notizen*, but the central collection of stories is *Nächtlicher Weg* (Night Path), thirteen tales written mainly in the 1930s and published in Zurich in 1943. Hohl revised the texts, omitting some material, for the Frankfurt edition of 1971. Reviewers at the time of first publication described the author as a discoverer of hidden truths, a man whose strength lay in the minute observation of inner processes; a spirit of rebellion was noted in these stories, as well as remarkable beauties of language. Hohl was seen as a humanely motivated creator of characters whom life had left vulnerable. "Das Pferdchen" (The Little Horse) centers upon the collapse of a cart-horse from exhaustion in a Marseilles street. "Das Blatt" (The Leaf) presents a solitary man's preoccupation with a leaf that he has picked up. A painter's impoverished living conditions in Vienna are shown in "Und eine neue Erde . . ." (And a New Earth . . .); an artist's illness and death in a hospital are treated in "Optimismus" (Optimism). There is a hard, monumental feature in Hohl's portrayals of women in "Die Trinkerin" (The Drinker) and "Drei alte Weiber in einem Bergdorf" (Three Old Women in a Mountain Village). The outstanding story in the volume is "Nächtlicher Weg" (Night Path), where the protagonist tells of his encounter in a dream with a stranger who, from his slow, silent, swaying manner, may have needed help as he made his way on a freezing winter night from a café in the little town to the accommodation where he was staying. The protagonist has learned the next day that the body of a man who had died in the night has been found in a road. The man who has been listening to the account explains to the protagonist: "Der Mensch ist nicht universell, er kann nicht alles, nicht vieles tun; man wird ihn durch das Positive messen, das er geleistet hat" (Man is not universal, he cannot do everything, he cannot do much; he will be measured by the positive things he has achieved).

Hohl and Lotte were divorced on 8 March 1945. On 18 February of the following year he married Johanna-Katharina Fries; that marriage ended in divorce on 13 January 1948. Two months later, on 18 March, Hohl married Heidy Antoine; their daughter Adèle was born in 1949. Hohl underwent a second important creative phase at this time, producing a collection of papers he called "Von den hereinbrechenden Rändern" (Concerning the Edges That Are Giving Way); this work is currently being prepared for publication. Hohl's third marriage ended in divorce on 23 October 1951.

The Canton of Thurgau honored Hohl on his fiftieth birthday in 1954, the same year he moved into a basement apartment at rue David Dufour 8 in an inner-city block in Geneva. He married Erna Erika Tschanz on 21 November 1963. In 1965 he received a literary award from the Lions' Club.

The volume *Daß fast alles anders ist* (That Almost Everything Is Different, 1967) is described by the author as consisting of observations, dreams, and stories drawn from "Von den hereinbrechenden Rändern." The volume contains two short stories, "Vernunft und Güte" (Reason and Goodness) and "Polykrates," as well as shorter pieces. In one of the nonnarrative passages, entitled "Von den hereinbrechenden Rändern," Hohl argues that the center has lost the strength to renew itself and that something new will emerge at the edges of human experience; the dreamer of today will rule the land tomorrow.

In 1970 Hohl received a literary award from the Schiller Foundation; on 17 November of that year he was divorced again. His long story *Bergfahrt* (Mountain Climb) was first published in 1975, but the author explained that it had been started in 1926 and revised six times by 1940, and then had been left for over thirty years before he gave it its final form. The story concerns two young men who are undertaking an Alpine climb in the early summer during the first years of the twentieth century. Ull is more experienced than Johann, who fails to take Ull's advice about diet and sleeping arrangements. After a day is lost due to rainy weather, Johann loses the will to continue the climb. Ull angrily presses on alone; after losing his ice axe, he slips and meets his death. Johann also dies, much nearer the foot of the slope, after neglecting advice from a local farmer concerning the terrain. It has been suggested by Werner Fuchs that Ull and Johann are not to be seen as representatives of right and wrong attitudes, but as one person in his varied reactions to life; the mountain can be seen as a metaphor for right perception.

Hohl was awarded the Robert Walser Centenary Prize in 1978 and the Petrarca Prize in 1980. On 8 September 1980 he married Madeleine-Jeanne de Weiss. Less than two months later, on 3 November, he died.

*Die Notizen* remains the central published work of Hohl's career, though his short stories are probably more widely read. In a 1981 anthology of criticism edited by Johannes Beringer, Otto F. Walter refers to the precision of Hohl's language, its solemn intonation which has qualities of unmodernity and artifice; Hans Saner writes of the tragic quality of the tension between detail and totality in Hohl's writing: *Die Notizen* is an attempt to see the world whole, but what is offered is a multiplicity of small units; Carl Seelig comments that although Hohl's work is at times excessive in its generalizations and polemical facets, it is an extraordinary achievement, "a dazzling crystal collection of intellectual and spiritual insights into man's complex nature, life today, and the realm of dreams and death"; Friedrich Dürrenmatt says, "Hohl is necessary, we are fortuitous"; Adolf Muschg judges that "Hohl's work is great because it is a whole, a ruined and therefore true encyclopedia of intellectual and spiritual survival."

**References:**

Adrian Ewald Bänninger, *Fragment und Weltbild in Ludwig Hohls "Notizen"* (Zurich: Juris, 1973);

Johannes Beringer, ed., *Ludwig Hohl* (Frankfurt am Main: Suhrkamp, 1981);

Werner Fuchs, *Möglichkeitswelt: Zu Ludwig Hohls Dichtung und Denkformen* (Bern & Frankfurt am Main: Lang, 1980);

Xaver Kronig, *Ludwig Hohl: Seine Erzählprosa mit einer Einführung in das Gesamtwerk* (Bern & Frankfurt am Main: Lang, 1972).

**Papers:**

A major work by Ludwig Hohl, "Von den hereinbrechenden Rändern," is being prepared for publication. It is reported that there is also an extensive personal journal among Hohl's posthumous papers. Mme. Madeleine Hohl-de Weiss, Florimont 28, 1007 Lausanne, Switzerland, is in charge of the archives. A society for the promotion of Ludwig Hohl's work is being established in Zurich.

# Hans Henny Jahnn

*(17 December 1894-29 November 1959)*

Gerda Jordan
*University of South Carolina*

BOOKS: *Pastor Ephraim Magnus: Drama* (Berlin: Fischer, 1919);

*Die Krönung Richards III.: Historische Tragödie* (Hamburg: Hanf, 1921);

*Der Arzt; sein Weib; sein Sohn: Drama* (Klecken: Ugrino, 1922);

*Der gestohlene Gott: Tragödie* (Potsdam: Kiepenheuer, 1924);

*Medea: Tragödie* (Leipzig: Schauspiel, 1926);

*Perrudja: Roman,* 2 volumes (Berlin: Kiepenheuer, 1929);

*Der Einfluß der Schleifenwindlade auf die Tonbildung der Orgel* (Hamburg: Ugrino, 1931);

*Neuer Lübecker Totentanz* (Berlin: Fischer, 1931);

*Straßenecke: Ein Ort, eine Handlung* (Berlin: Kiepenheuer, 1931);

*Armut, Reichtum, Mensch und Tier: Ein Drama* (Munich: Weismann, 1948);

*Fluß ohne Ufer: Roman in drei Teilen. 1. Teil: Das Holzschiff* (Munich: Weismann, 1949); translated by Catherine Hutter as *The Ship* (New York: Scribners, 1961); *2.Teil: Die Niederschrift des Gustav Anias Horn nachdem er 49 Jahre alt geworden war,* 2 volumes (Munich: Weismann, 1949-1950);

*Spur des dunklen Engels: Drama* (Hamburg: Ugrino/ Munich: Weismann, 1952);

*Klopstocks 150. Todestag am 14. März 1953* (Mainz: Akademie der Wissenschaften und der Literatur, 1953);

*Über den Anlaß: Vortrag* (Munich: Weismann, 1954);

*13 nicht geheure Geschichten* (Hamburg: Rowohlt, 1954); translated by Gerda Jordan as *Thirteen Uncanny Stories* (Bern: Lang, 1984);

*Thomas Chatterton: Eine Tragödie* (Berlin & Frankfurt am Main: Suhrkamp, 1955);

*Die Nacht aus Blei: Roman* (Hamburg: Wegner, 1956);

*Jeden ereilt es* (Würzburg: Zettner, 1959);

*Aufzeichnungen eines Einzelgängers: Eine Auswahl aus dem Werk,* edited by Rolf Italiaander (Munich: List, 1959);

*Hans Henny Jahnn: Eine Auswahl aus seinem Werk,* edited by Walter Muschg (Freiburg: Walter, 1959);

*Die Trümmer des Gewissens—Der staubige Regenbogen: Drama,* edited by Muschg (Frankfurt am Main: Europäische Verlagsanstalt, 1961);

*Fluß ohne Ufer: Roman in drei Teilen. 3. Teil: Epilog* (Frankfurt am Main: Europäische Verlagsanstalt, 1961);

*Dramen,* 2 volumes (Frankfurt am Main: Europäische Verlagsanstalt, 1963-1965);

*Über den Anlaß und andere Essays* (Frankfurt am Main: Europäische Verlagsanstalt, 1964);

*Hans Henny Jahnn (Ullstein)*

*Perrudja II: Fragment aus dem Nachlaß*, edited by Rolf Burmeister (Frankfurt am Main: Heine, 1968);

*Ugrino und Ingrabanien: Fragment aus dem Nachlaß*, edited by Burmeister (Frankfurt am Main: Heine, 1968);

*Werke und Tagebücher*, edited by Thomas Freeman and Thomas Scheuffelen, 7 volumes (Hamburg: Hoffmann & Campe, 1974).

OTHER: "Entstehung und Bedeutung der Kurvenmensur für die Labialstimmen der Orgel," in *Bericht über den 1. Musikwissenschaftlichen Kongreß der Deutschen Musikgesellschaft in Leipzig vom 4. bis 8. Juni 1925* (Leipzig: Breitkopf & Härtel, 1926), pp. 71-77;

*Holloferniges: Märchen aus dem Retköz*, translated from Hungarian by Jahnn (Berlin & Zurich: Atlantis, 1940);

Aron Tamasi, *Ein Königssohn der Sekter: Roman*, translated from Hungarian by Jahnn (Leipzig: Payne, 1941);

"Mein Werden und mein Werk," in *Hamburger Jahrbuch für Theater und Musik 1948-49* (Hamburg: Toth, 1948), pp. 92-111;

"Vereinsamung der Dichtung: Vortrag," in *Minotaurus: Dichtung unter den Hufen von Staat und Industrie* (Wiesbaden: Steiner, 1953), pp. 247-265;

"Prinzipien der Freien Akademie in Hamburg," in *Neues Hamburg: X. Die Wiederaufrichtung Hamburgs 1945 bis 1955* (Hamburg: Hammerich & Leser, 1956), pp. 58-60.

PERIODICAL PUBLICATIONS: "Einige Elementarsätze der monumentalen Baukunst," *Kleine Veröffentlichungen der Glaubensgemeinde Ugrino*, 2 (March 1921): 5-46;

"Vincent Lübeck," *Hamburger Nachrichten*, 10 April 1922;

"Beitrag zu Dichter auf der Probe: Eine Umfrage des Leipziger Tageblatts," *Leipziger Tageblatt*, 16 April 1922;

"Die Orgel und die Mixtur ihres Klanges," *Kleine Veröffentlichungen der Glaubensgemeinde Ugrino*, 4 (1922): 37-68;

"Zum Kapitel: Gegen die moderne Orgel," *Zeitschrift für Instrumentenbau*, 5 (1 December 1924): 266-268;

"Die Orgel," *Melos: Zeitschrift für Musik*, 7/8 (15 February 1925): 391-398;

"Zur Medea," *Die Szene: Blätter für Bühnenkunst*, 2 (February 1926): 55-56;

"Orgelkonzert auf dem Dorfe," *Berliner Börsen-Courier*, 17 March 1926, p. 2;

"Ist der Denkmalschutz des klingenden Materials alter Orgeln zu fordern?," *Denkmalpflege und Heimatschutz*, 28 (1926): 111-114;

"Welche Forderungen sind an eine Orgel zu stellen?," *Die Bauwelt: Zeitschrift für das gesamte Bauwesen*, 41 (14 October 1926): 989-993;

"Orgelprobleme der Gegenwart," *Zeitschrift für Musik*, 10 (October 1926): 552-557;

"Ein Wozzek im Schreibtisch," *Hamburger Fremdenblatt*, 300 (30 October 1926): 17-18;

"Das Konterfei des dritten Richard," *Berliner Börsen-Courier*, 4 December 1926, p. 5;

"Die Reglementierung des freien Geistes," *Berliner Börsen-Courier*, 16 December 1926, p. 5;

"Beitrag zu der Rundfrage 'Die Lebensbedingungen der Schaubühne im Jahre 1927,'" *Die Szene: Blätter für Bühnenkunst* (January 1927): 6-7;

"Glosse zur siderischen Grundlage der Dichtkunst," *Die literarische Welt*, 2 (1927): 6;

"Alchimie des gegenwärtigen Dramas," *Die literarische Welt*, 26 (1927): 7;

"Orgelbauer bin ich auch," *Hamburger Anzeiger*, 139, First Supplement (17 June 1927);

"Spätgotische Umkehr," *Der Kreis: Zeitschrift für künstlerische Kultur*, 6/7 (June/July 1927): 305-311;

"Neue Wege der Orgel," *Die Musik: Monatsschrift*, 4 (1927/1928): 248-251;

"Henrik Ibsen und sein Land," *Berliner Tageblatt*, 20 March 1928;

"Die Wurstfinger des Herrn Lehrers," *Die literarische Welt*, 14/15 (1928): 4;

"Glossen zum Schicksal gegenwärtiger Dichtkunst," *Mitteilungen des Deutschen Schriftsteller-Verbandes* (September/October 1928): 16-19;

"Gedanken zu einer hamburgischen Festrede über Lessing," *Der Kreis: Zeitschrift für künstlerische Kultur*, 1 (1929): 7-10;

"Rechenschaft Kleistpreis 1928," *Der Kreis: Zeitschrift für künstlerische Kultur*, 3 (March 1929): 137-141;

"Zur Opernkrise," *Hamburger Nachrichten*, 27 April 1930;

"Der Dichter und die religiöse Lage der Gegenwart," *Der Kreis: Zeitschrift für künstlerische Kultur*, 7/8 (1930): 407-419;

"Modernes Theater," *Hamburger Fremdenblatt*, 28 October 1930;

"Wunderwerk Orgel," *Hamburger Fremdenblatt*, 38 (7 February 1931): 19;

"Ordnung und Unordnung," *Berliner Tageblatt*, 607, Fourth Supplement (25 December 1931);

"Vergessen und Freuen," *Der Kreis: Zeitschrift für künstlerische Kultur*, 1 ( January 1932): 24-29;

"Aufgabe des Dichters in dieser Zeit," *Der Kreis: Zeitschrift für künstlerische Kultur*, 5 (May 1932): 266-275;

"Vom Sinn des Essens und Trinkens," *Der Kreis: Zeitschrift für künstlerische Kultur*, 10 (October 1932): 549-553;

"Kleine Reise durch Kopenhagen," *Hamburger Fremdenblatt*, 231 (22 August 1933): 2;

"Die Insel Bornholm," *Atlantis: Länder/Völker/Reisen*, 3 (March 1941): 101-109;

"Von der Wirklichkeit," *Das Neue: Auswahl zeitgemäßer Stimmen*, 4 (1947): 50-70;

"Was ist vom Menschen zu erwarten?," *Das Neue: Auswahl zeitgemäßer Stimmen*, 5 (1947): 35-55;

"Reminiszenz," *Welt am Sonntag* (22 August 1948): 3;

"Die Abgründe vor uns," *Welt am Sonntag*, 1 (2 January 1949): 12;

"Antworten auf die Rundfrage 'Deutsche Schriftsteller zur deutschen Dramatik,' " *Programmheft der Hamburger Kammerspiele*, 1 (1951-1952): 14, 16;

"Requisiten des Theaters, zeitgemäße und mutige Worte," *Mindener Tageblatt*, 10 April 1953;

"Kleine Rede auf Hans Erich Nossack," *Sinn und Form: Beiträge zur Literatur*, 2 (1955): 213-219;

"Das schriftliche Bild der Orgel," *Abhandlungen der Braunschweigischen Wissenschaftlichen Gesellschaft*, 7 (1955): 132-170;

"Mozarts zweite Fassung der 'Gärtnerin aus Liebe,' " *Die andere Zeitung*, 4 (26 January 1956): 13;

"Der Dichter," *Die neue Gesellschaft* (April 1956): 43-54;

"Thesen gegen Atomrüstung," *Studenten-Kurier*, 7 (September 1957): 7;

"Der Mensch im veränderten Weltbild," *Blätter für deutsche und internationale Politik*, 12 (20 December 1957): 424-429;

"Freiheit—Frieden—im veränderten Weltbild," *Konkret: Unabhängige Zeitschrift für Kultur und Politik*, 2 (1958): 3;

"Am Schlagbaum vor dem Abgrund," *Vorwärts: Sozialdemokratische Wochenzeitung für Politik, Wirtschaft und Kultur*, 17 (April 1958): 1;

"Zwölf Jahre Warnungen vor der Atombombe," *Blätter für deutsche und internationale Politik*, 3 (20 May 1958): 353-357;

"Haben wir das neue Weltbild im Geiste bewältigt?," *Blätter für deutsche und internationale Politik*, 9 (25 September 1958): 699-708;

"Das Wort," *Blätter für deutsche und internationale Politik*, 5 (25 May 1959): 411-416.

Hans Henny Jahnn is probably the least known among the great German-speaking writers of the first half of the twentieth century, in his own country as well as elsewhere. He is rejected by many of those who do know of him because his ideas, presented in powerful dramatic and narrative prose, are provocative and disturbing; they explode the accepted bourgeois order of things and are offensive to a conventional mode of thinking. But one is hard put to deny their validity: Jahnn persistently preached pacifism, feared man's barbarism and opposed it with love of mankind, and fought materialism and a utilitarian life. His aim was to be absolutely truthful, but the truths he sought are not to be found on the surface of man but in his abysses, his errors, his suffering. And so he came to be known as the writer of the "Hölle des Fleisches" (hell of the flesh), as a rebel and a flagellant. Relatively few admiring scholars have taken him as their subject since Hans Wolffheim's *Hans Henny Jahnn: Der Tragiker der Schöpfung* (The Tragic Poet of Creation) appeared in 1966. Wolffheim pointed out that what Jahnn wanted to say does not lend itself to superficial reading—the superficial reader stumbles over coffins, nipples, and gore; and that Jahnn is still misunderstood, especially since some of the important critics of his time—among them Alfred Kerr, Julius Bab, Paul Fechter, and Kurt Pinthus—expressed open hatred in their reviews.

Jahnn was born on 17 December 1894 in Stellingen, a suburb of Hamburg, into a shipbuilder's family. As a boy he developed the technical and mathematical abilities that turned into an obsession with numbers and formulae, leading to passions for architecture, music, and organ building. From long hours spent at the newly opened Hagenbek Zoo he derived a compassion for captive animals. He was extremely pious, carrying a pocket edition of the New Testament wherever he went; he said of himself that he was the sort of Christian who frightens others. Puberty brought him inner turmoil; the world's cruelty and brutality troubled him greatly. This concern manifested itself in a number of early writings, among them a novel and a drama about Christ expressing his belief that a better world once existed and that it could return.

At the outbreak of World War I Jahnn succeeded in being recognized as a conscientious objector and immigrated to Norway with his friend Gottlieb Harms. There he found a world which became the background for many of his works: a rugged countryside which, in his imagination, was peopled with trolls and mythical beings. Here, too, he was exposed to the mysteries of architecture as they are revealed in ancient sacred buildings. Man, he realized, had erected buildings for the dead before he had constructed houses for the living.

Jahnn regarded the organ as an essential element of church structure and developed a passionate interest in music. He was able to construct an organ mathematically on paper and to hear its sound in his mind. The organ was to him the "gigantic flute of Pan," a legacy of ancient paganism, an instrument of cosmic harmony, representing that which had once existed, belonging to a god who "was perhaps not yet dead." Jahnn's repudiation of his youthful Christianity is expressed in his drama *Pastor Ephraim Magnus* (1919).

Upon his return to Hamburg after the war he restored at his own expense Arp Schnitger's seventeenth-century organ at St. Jacobi. He did away with the patchwork repairs of centuries, permitting the masterworks of the baroque to be heard as the composers had intended. Jahnn restored many other organs to their original state and contributed significantly to a movement to recover old organs of Europe and save them from oblivion. Organ building, not writing, provided his livelihood.

In 1920 Jahnn and several friends founded in Hamburg an altruistic community called Ugrino. Their program had the goals of preserving endangered works of art, fighting mass production and shoddy workmanship, and, in general, of reforming the world through art. These goals were inevitably destined to remain a dream for lack of disciples, but Ugrino's ideals were subsequently incorporated into Jahnn's writings. The permanent reminder of the community is the output of the Ugrino Publishing Company, which Jahnn and Harms ran jointly until its demise at Harms's death in 1931. Thanks to their efforts the complete works of Dietrich Buxtehude, Samuel Scheidt, and Vincent Lübeck were published and Mozart's opera *Die Gärtnerin aus Liebe* and the works of Carlo Guesaldo were made accessible to the public.

Jahnn's hopes for the betterment of mankind were dashed by the rise of Hitler, and he felt compelled to leave his country again in 1933. With his wife Ellinor, whom he married in 1922, and daughter Signe he settled in Bornholm, Denmark, and besides writing, practiced farming and horse breeding and experimented in hormone research. After World War II he returned to Hamburg and resumed his career as an organ builder. He became obsessed with fear of atomic warfare, which he called "betrayal by science," and he protested vociferously against the devastation of the entire creation which seemed possible since Hiroshima. Jahnn, who, according to his friend Werner Helwig, radiated cordiality and kindness, felt misunderstood and unable to help mankind to a way out of this "Spirale, die irgendwo in der Tiefe, in der größten Dunkelheit, endet" (spiral which ends somewhere in the depths, in greatest darkness). He died on 29 November 1959. In spite of several honors he received, including the Kleist Prize in 1920, the Lower Saxony Literature Prize in 1954, the Lessing Prize in 1956, and the presidency of the Freie Akademie der Künste (Free Academy of Arts) in Hamburg, he is not widely known. Jahnn's literary legacy includes several finished plays, manuscripts of fragments and designs of others, the novel *Perrudja* (1929), the trilogy *Fluß ohne Ufer* (River without Banks, 1949-1950, 1961), novel fragments, and numerous articles on a variety of topics. He began writing at the height of expressionism, but he did not share the early expressionists' belief in technology as the liberator of man. After the disillusionment of the abortive German revolutions of 1918-1919 many expressionists changed direction, but Jahnn continued on his chosen path. His works allude to the march of "civilization" into mass wars. He detested modern civilization, politics of any kind, the diminution of man's natural strengths and instincts brought about by the welfare state, the coercive systems of education and military service, and the gradual destruction of the free nature of men and animals. From the standpoint of nature, civilization is a crime; Jahnn compared it to the overloading of an organ with technical refinements that destroy it as a sacred instrument so that it no longer conveys the harmonious whole that was Jahnn's view of the universe.

He arrived at this view by way of his study of church architecture and organ music. The church and its organ must form a totality; architecture and acoustics must allow the organ its fullest development. Church and organ represent a sacred unity that must not be disturbed either by an imperfect space or by an imperfect instrument. Into this unity enter the living who worship in the church and the dead who lie buried beneath, so that the living are

*Design by Jahnn for the church for his utopian community, Ugrino (Frau Ellinor Jahnn, Hamburg)*

connected to the dead. Although the inception of this view lies in the Christian church, Jahnn, after leaving behind his adolescent religiosity, had no use for the idea of a personal God nor for Christianity: "Einen persönlichen Gott erfinden und ihn bemühen, um eine Lügenantwort bereit zu haben—das gelingt mir nicht mehr" (To invent a personal God and to trouble Him for a lying answer—I cannot do that any more); "Es ist der Sinn des Lebens, daß es darauf keine Antwort gibt. Alle Antworten, die der Mensch erfunden hat, sind schäbige Ausreden" (The meaning of life is that there are no answers. Any which man has invented are poor excuses). Religious consolation and assurances of Christian redemption only delude man into thinking that there is a better life to come, and so he neglects life on earth. Christianity is responsible for man's rejection of nature and for the evils of modern civilization, including the defamation of the most innocent of man's drives, the sex drive. Jahnn called the sex drive innocent because he believed it is not only the easiest to satisfy but also upsets the order of things the least; it is far less dangerous than the drive for power or even hunger. Jahnn observes nature and concludes that the drive to eat generates nothing but sorrow. Gustav expresses this idea in *Fluß ohne Ufer* as he watches the budding

of spring: "Und während sich das meinem Auge Wunderbare vollzieht, vermehren sich die Raubzüge aller Lebewesen gegen den Schwächeren, der gefressen wird.... Es ist Schicksal.... Es ist wie es ist, und es ist fürchterlich" (Before my eyes the miracle unfolds, while at the same time all living beings go out to prey against the weaker who will be devoured.... It is fate.... It is the way it is, and it is horrible). Everywhere Gustav sees copulation, multiplication, and death by being eaten. Every creature is part of this cycle. The singing of birds and the chirping of crickets are manifestations of the lust for begetting and, therefore, reminders of death. Nature is endless repetition. The opposite of eternal regeneration and destruction of organic matter is found in the realm of the dead, those who have passed through the cycle and become immortal spirit. The dead are among us; no house, no edifice is built without the help of the dead. Man is constantly in touch with them through their books and their works. The past lives within the present.

Jahnn was convinced that Christianity had obscured man's view of nature; pre-Christian man experienced the world directly, while modern man perceives it indirectly and distortedly through scientific laws. Ancient man's direct experience of nature is found in myth, which Jahnn understood to be man's first philosophical utterance and considered absolutely believable. Jahnn's fictional world, like that of the myths, is filled with archaic symbols, strange rites, and cruelties. Wolffheim maintains that Jahnn's work has so much in common with the Babylonian Gilgamesh epic that it could be considered a repetition of certain parts of it. There are occasional references in Jahnn's work to Gilgamesh; in the drama *Der Arzt; sein Weib; sein Sohn* (The Doctor; His Wife; His Son, 1922) the doctor says: "Es ist uns wie Engidu ergangen" (We fared like Engidu), and *Fluß ohne Ufer* also alludes to the epic. It furnished Jahnn a number of motifs: proximity to nature, the twin brothers, the exclusion of woman from a close male relationship, love between brother and sister, death and decomposition, and the desire to descend into the realm of the dead.

The motif of the twin brothers is the dominant one in Jahnn's work. It implies exactly what it meant in the Gilgamesh epic: overcoming the principle of creation through the spirit, especially in the homoerotic realm. The spirit contradicts the eternal process of becoming, which is the work of woman, of the goddess Ishtar. The motif of the twins can take various forms: the friendship of boys, its purest form; an organization of young men for a higher purpose; the subconscious attraction of two men in which one exerts a magnetic power over the other. Never is the homoerotic relationship of men purely a physical matter; it is the culmination of friendship, and the physical act, the "Ausschweifung" (excess) after years of love and devotion, serves the broadening of consciousness. The mingling of blood, symbolic for the complete readiness of one for the other, is an essential part of the relationship. A true brotherhood cannot be repeated; when one dies, the other remains alone. Women cannot enter into a twinship because women have no capacity for friendship. Jahnn's male characters fall in love, but their women are never admitted to the friendship of men. They are modeled after the seductress Ishtar, and they are ruled by the instinct of the matriarch and that of the courtesan. The first makes woman the epitome of the principle of creation, the other shows that she is incapable of a bond similar to that of the twins. Love is an object to her; it has nothing to do with the spirit, and she remains in the animal realm. Loyalty is not expected of her. Male and female are entirely separate and cannot understand each other.

Another of Jahnn's mythological motifs is that of brother and sister as sexual lovers. In the play *Der gestohlene Gott* (The Stolen God, 1924) he says: "Die alten Götter erstanden an der Liebe zwischen Bruder und Schwester, . . . man lehrte uns, daß wir Geschwister, und wir wünschen garnicht, es möchte anders sein" (The old gods descended from the love between brother and sister, . . . they have told us we are brother and sister, and we don't wish it otherwise). A variant of the love of brother and sister is that of mother and son, or its equivalent, the love of the older woman and the young man. Although in both the Gilgamesh epic and the Isis and Osiris myth one of the pair is destined to die, the Gilgamesh epic expresses only tragic hopelessness, while the Isis and Osiris myth points to the need for death and sacrifice as a prerequisite for something better. Many of Jahnn's works reflect variations on these two basic patterns.

In Jahnn's works death is an important part of the sacred order. Everything strives toward it; indeed, the ever present thought of death is the main motivation of the actions of the living. Jahnn is not so much concerned with dying itself as with what comes after death: decomposition. Flesh is the positive representation of life, of a person; man, therefore, has a desire to defy the law of decomposition. Man's attempt to check the dissolution of the body appears in his effort to achieve the opposite: hardening. Freezing the body serves this purpose, as do statue building and mummification. The statue or mummy means depersonalization; life and sexual function are excluded, but at the same time it is a step in creating an existence beyond life. A great tomb, a mountain grave, a rocky pit, a sarcophagus are other ways of trying to preserve man's positive form.

But these tombs are in vain if love has not made eternal those for whom they are intended. The kind of love Jahnn demands—and this is his ultimate message—is absolute, unconditional, unquestioning. Life without love is living death; only through love can eternity be achieved. Because life is horrible and tragic, the world is in need of pity, mercy, and love; since man is the highest being in the sacred order, he especially is called upon to love. Love overcomes the principle of decomposition by means of a human existence which, because of unconditional love, outlasts death.

Jahnn claims that literature since the ancient epics has missed the point of man himself; man has become a side issue. Civilization and technology have brought about a world of objects where man merely plays a role. Jahnn seeks to explore what man is, not what he does or feels. In the foreword to *Perrudja* he warns the reader that he will meet a new kind of man, a nonhero with strong qualities but not necessarily masculine ones, with no goals, no decision, no judgment, no heroism. It is perhaps man's attempt to lead a heroic existence that is at the root of his barbaric attitude, and from this attempt he derived the idea of right and wrong. Jahnn's man does not really know himself; he is influenced by all kinds of forces, impulses, and images, by different levels of consciousness that are often in conflict with one another. Man is a process, not a known quantity; therefore, he must be explored, not described. A typical Jahnn character is not consistent; his thoughts and feelings reverse and correct themselves and are newly evaluated. Jahnn tried to show man in a continuous metamorphosis and to lead him to an understanding of himself. He was convinced that man could understand himself only if he opened his soul to the total experience of his physical and spiritual existence without selection or resistance.

To present this kind of character, the writer must leave nothing out. In *Pastor Ephraim Magnus* Jahnn says: "Er muß dann doch beschreiben, was der tut, alles—selbst wie er seine Geschäfte erledigt und was er dabei denkt—was man überhaupt denken kann!—Und weshalb alles so ist, wie es ist und nicht anders" (He has to describe what he does, everything—even how he urinates and what he thinks when he does—what one can think altogether!—And why it is like that and not otherwise). Omission of anything is the same as a lie. Therefore, Jahnn observes exactly, and his observations include such data as the facts of metabolism and sexuality—in short, man's seemingly most insignificant daily activities—because what happens on the lower stratum has just as much effect on a person as that which is on the surface. Jahnn considers the fact that man is not a known quantity to be an optimistic view: since the soul is mutable, a point may be revealed at which he can be morally regenerated.

Jahnn depicts a cruel world; humor and playfulness are absent from his work. He began writing as an expressionist, and he retains expressionism's tendency toward terseness and compression. Scenes in his dramas and novels are austere and tense; explanatory detail and transitions are frequently missing. His prose sometimes reads like a scientific essay and at other times like lyric poetry, and his descriptions of nature are captivating. There is often a discrepancy between style and content: deeply stirring events are expressed in sober language, and the most banal subject matter in flowery tones.

Jahnn has no forerunner, belongs to no tradition which could explain his literary work; he defies classification. He studied music, not literature, and said that he did not read much, "daß ich mich durch Gelesenes nicht habe beirren lassen" (that I did not let myself be confused by reading). He saw it as the writer's calling to tell the truth and to fight against convention with its half-truths and lies. He did so alone, not belonging to any group.

Jahnn began as a playwright, and the issues of his novels are also found in his plays. With the exception of *Medea* (1926) they have had a precarious existence on stage, scandalizing public and critics alike.

*Pastor Ephraim Magnus*, for which he won the Kleist Prize, treats a number of the concerns Jahnn had all his life. Pastor Ephraim Magnus's three grown children, Ephraim, Jakob, and Johanna, witness their father's deathbed agony; he is literally putrefying while he is still alive. He advises his children to live life to the fullest, to love unconditionally or to suffer like Christ on the cross so that they will not decay in a like manner. The children begin by unmasking their loved ones as insincere; their love is not absolute. Jakob, seeking the life his father meant, indulges in excesses, and in search of ideals he cannot find he kills a girl and cuts her open to pursue them in her abdomen. After his execution Ephraim and Johanna entomb his body in the church crypt to prevent its decay. Ephraim, now a pastor, and Johanna endeavor to emulate a God-like existence through self-imposed suffering, culminating in Ephraim's blinding and castration at the hands of his sister to end their love for each other. But Jakob's remains are decomposing, a sign that Ephraim and Johanna have not succeeded. They turn to prayer. Ephraim squeezes his sister to death lest another man try to possess her. Probably the most outspoken and blunt of Jahnn's dramas, *Pastor Ephraim Magnus* nevertheless ends on an optimistic note. Ephraim's superior approaches him with a plan to enlarge the church building. He understands this opportunity as a sign from God to realize his own scheme for a new church that will house a tomb for Jakob, Johanna, and himself, one that prevents the decomposition of their remains. Bertolt Brecht staged the play in an abridged version, and it met a public totally unprepared for Jahnn's outcries. Critics called it "Erotomanendrama" (drama of an erotic maniac) and "Jauchenkübel" (bucket of dung water).

*Die Krönung Richards III.: Historische Tragödie* (The Coronation of Richard III: Historical Tragedy, 1921) focuses on man's vain search for inner peace and the power of pure love. When Elizabeth, the widow of Edward IV, tires of her young lover and has him castrated, Richard offers her marriage so that he will be king. Some of the courtiers consider him mad because they have witnessed his musings about the meaning of life and how to live so that one's soul will not rot. He is shaken by fears but hopes to have peace of mind after the removal of Elizabeth's sons. He orders them entombed alive so that nothing will disfigure their beautiful bodies and they will die at God's will. At the Tower the princes meet Elizabeth's discarded lover. The three boys overcome their fear of death through their love for one another, and they walk to their coffins serenely. Richard envies them; he has to face a new day alone and tormented. This play received almost no applause; the message of love went unnoticed. Critics called it Jahnn's "Schlachtplatte-historisch garniert" (butcher platter historically garnished).

Woman as Ishtar, the Isis and Osiris motif, and the twinship of boys is the topic of the play *Der Arzt; sein Weib; sein Sohn* of 1922. Dr. Mencke's wife has remained youthful while he has become impotent. She desires their son, but the boy, repelled by the idea of making love to his mother, sends her his own sexual partner, a youth his age. Afterward the boys wander off into the snowy countryside to die together. Whereas a woman can easily exchange sexual partners, boys completely devoted to one another are willing to make the ultimate sacrifice. Their icy entombment will preserve their remains.

In the drama *Der gestohlene Gott* of 1924, sixteen-year-old Leander has a double, Leonhard, who is also his best friend. Unknown to them they are half brothers through their father. Wendelin is in love with her brother Leonhard, but because such a relationship would be unnatural, Leander becomes her lover. Wendelin and Leonhard are cast out by their father, Wendelin because she is pregnant and Leonhard because he stood by her. They and Leander decide that there is no place on earth for them. Leonhard prepares a tomb for the lovers in an empty sarcophagus in the town's cathedral and buries them—"the lucky ones"—alive. He then writes to his father and Leander's mother, informing them that he has killed Leander and Wendelin, and commits suicide. His father is glad in the belief that his son, a murderer, has escaped.

Jahnn follows the story line of the Medea myth in his 1926 drama of the same name, but he changes the focus of Medea's revenge. She puts Jason to the test of his love for Kreusa by sending her a robe that causes Kreusa to decompose alive in front of Jason's eyes, and he turns away. Had he been able to embrace Kreusa in her rotten state, she would have been restored to him; but his love was not absolute. Medea kills her sons not to avenge the wrong done her by Jason but to save them from the evils of this world and to keep them pure and innocent. *Medea* is Jahnn's only play to be performed repeatedly and to be somewhat profitable, but it too earned unfavorable remarks from critics, such as "too much lust." Yet Medea clearly says: "Then at last love triumphed over lust," causing Wilhelm Emrich to remark: "Why don't people read carefully?"

Jahnn's first novel, *Perrudja*, published in 1929, exemplifies his conviction that man is an unknown quantity, something to be explored and not described. Perrudja has lived in the forest he owns since he was seventeen. One day a mysterious stranger makes his way to his hut, and from then on Perrudja has an inexhaustible supply of funds. While he has a fine house built, he gets to know the workmen and learns about the miseries of others. He decides he should be married, and Signe is the girl he wants and who wants him. But she will not break her engagement to a man she does not love. Signe's young brother Hein becomes Perrudja's steady companion, and Perrudja is appointed sheriff. One day the fiancé is killed while poaching elk; Perrudja denies to Signe that he had anything to do with the fiancé's death. At their wedding, however, Signe finds out that Perrudja has lied to her and she leaves him, saying that she could love a murderer but not a liar. Informed that he is the richest man in the world, Perrudja decides to buy some South Sea islands to liberate the exploited inhabitants. His wealth, however, is not money he can spend but consists of ships, factories, and buildings. Perrudja suffers guilt when he is shown all that he owns; he is frightened by the misery such wealth causes others. At a meeting of representatives of Perrudja's financial empire plans are made to establish a better world and a lasting peace. The boy from the mountains, the dreamer with no goals, has drifted into a mission that was not of his making. Without transition, the story turns to a boy named Pete, who was adored by all his friends until, through no fault of his, one friend drowns and another bleeds to death because of him. He becomes the chauffeur of a member of Perrudja's financial empire, and one day he becomes acquainted with a boys' association called

Golden Sevenstar. Signe, living alone in luxury, gives herself to her servant Ragnvald.

Jahnn planned to write several volumes to describe the realization of Perrudja's dreams, but the second volume, "Perrudja II," remained a fragment. The ideals of the Golden Sevenstar are explained; they are altruistic, like those of Ugrino. Besides swearing to love one another, the members are to fight the evils of capitalism: lack of permanence, waste, and desire for material goods. They advocate healthy bodies, the equality of all races, and the mixing of races. Perrudja is introduced to the association and participates in its plan to save the world. Hein at last is able to persuade his sister to return to Perrudja.

"Perrudja II" consists of a series of unconnected chapters and can be considered only a sketch for the larger work that was planned. Both the novel and the fragment display Jahnn's growing concern with the political situation in Germany in the late 1920s. Perrudja represents the antithesis of the new barbarism.

Jahnn used the form of the medieval morality play in *Neuer Lübecker Totentanz* (New Dance of Death in Lübeck, 1931). The characters appear and have their say; when the play was first performed in 1954, each speech alternated with a musical interlude added by Jahnn's adopted son Yngve Jan Trede. The theme is one of Jahnn's favorites: "Es ist wie es ist, und es ist fürchterlich" (It is the way it is, and it is horrible). Fat Death complains that the people have fatted him, but Skinny Death warns that he will return. A storm arises, showing that the forces of nature still prevail over man. The Poor Soul of the Good Man has suffered most; suffering is not in proportion to man's sins. The Hired Hand is satisfied with his work, the land is being prepared for spring, man and animal are eagerly awaiting summer. The Son has left the Mother, and she has become useless. That is the way it is and will be.

Hypocrisy as a trait of mankind out of touch with nature is the theme of the play *Straßenecke: Ein Ort, eine Handlung* (Street Corner: A Place, an Action, 1931). The Negro James exerts an animal attraction on white men and women alike; they vie for his favors, which he grants. Then, under social pressure, his lovers turn against him and join the crowd's call for lynching him because he seduced the whole neighborhood with the destructive energy of his blackness; they fear him. The mob pronounces him guilty; they want to see him torn apart, cut open, his eyes gouged out. James appears at a window, and the mob storms the house.

The characters in the play *Armut, Reichtum, Mensch und Tier* (Poverty, Wealth, Man and Animal, 1948), Jahnn's first work to be published after World War II, have good intentions, but they are simple hearts and act accordingly to their inescapable nature. The young Norwegian mountain farmer Manao spends the summer with Sofia, after which he returns to the mountains, having promised her a spring wedding. But by spring Sofia is in prison for killing her child. The villagers convince Manao that the child was not his, and he marries Anna, who is also a farmer. When Sofia is released, Manao leaves Anna on the farm with their two children and lives with Sofia. She tells him that the child was his, and that it was either Anna or her hired hand Gunvald, both of whom had attended the birth, who killed it. Sofia dies after a year of happiness with Manao. Meanwhile, Gunvald had returned to tell Anna that he will keep silent about her murder of Sofia's child in exchange for her bed. Manao returns to the farm to bury Sofia. He understands that Anna, now pregnant with Gunvald's child, has no soul. Anna confesses the murder of Sofia's child when she realizes that Manao is lost to her. Anna, like Ishtar of the Gilgamesh epic, is ruled by both maternal and courtesan instincts; she cannot be otherwise. And Manao, like Gilgamesh, refuses her renewed attempts at seduction.

Jahnn's magnum opus, the novel *Fluß ohne Ufer,* was written from 1934 to 1946 during his years on Bornholm. The first part, *Das Holzschiff* (The Wooden Ship, 1949), a mystery story, needed a tenth chapter; this final chapter turned into the 1,600-page *Die Niederschrift des Gustav Anias Horn nachdem er 49 Jahre alt geworden war* (The Notes of Gustav Anias Horn at Age Forty-Nine, 1949-1950) and the fragment *Epilog* (1961), tracing the fates of some of the characters. This novel cycle contains all of Jahnn's themes: the study of man as an unknown quantity, who acts on impulses he cannot fathom or is not aware of, who drifts, as if by accident, into discovering his special gifts; the male twinship that outlasts death; the Ishtar woman and her exclusion from a male relationship; the desire to overcome death; and man's closeness to nature, for which the rugged countryside of the north serves as a suitable backdrop.

The ship *Lais* in *Das Holzschiff* is built of wood; it is sturdy and solid and has red sails. It is no ordinary ship: there are strange passageways, walls are missing, a centrally located mechanism opens the locks on all cabin doors. No one knows its destination or its cargo. Rumors abound: is it carrying

*Painting of Jahnn by Karl Kluth, 1955 (Niedersächsische Landesgalerie)*

dynamite? Corpses? Besides the captain and crew it carries the captain's daughter Ellena; her fiancé, Gustav (Anias Horn); the mysterious Superkargo; and perhaps the ship's owner, but no one can be sure. Gustav becomes friendly with the crew and spends less time with Ellena, who is frequently seen in the company of Superkargo. One of the seamen, Alfred Tutein, warns Gustav of danger; soon after, Ellena disappears. Superkargo denies the accusations of foul play and helps Gustav look for her. During the search they discover that the hold is full of empty coffin-sized boxes, which are nailed to the floor. This discovery brings the crew close to mutiny. Gustav and Superkargo have explored the entire ship except for one space they cannot reach. The carpenter opens it with an axe and water gushes in. The crew and passengers escape in lifeboats, and as they watch the sinking ship, they see for the first time its figurehead is a woman. *Das Holzschiff* ends with nothing resolved.

About thirty years later, after Tutein's death, Gustav writes about his friendship and love for Tutein. *Die Niederschrift* begins shortly after the point where *Das Holzschiff* left off, describing events on the ship that rescued the survivors. Superkargo shoots himself and leaves his money to Gustav. Tu-

tein confesses to Gustav that it was he who murdered Ellena, and offers his own life in atonement. Instead on an impulse Gustav embraces and kisses him, and they swear eternal friendship. Tutein repays Gustav for sparing his life with advice in the ways of the world. They settle in a small South American town. Tutein begins a cattle trade and Gustav becomes intrigued by a mechanical piano and begins composing for it. The friends have arguments, always followed by reconciliation and a closer bond. Both undergo changes: Tutein reads and learns much; Gustav becomes more adroit, more worldly.

On a voyage to Africa Gustav meets a former seaman from the *Lais* who claims that the ship's figurehead kept it afloat until it was chopped by the axe and bled. Gustav wants to know more and writes to the seaman's friend, who is now the servant of the *Lais*'s owner.

Gustav and Tutein move to a small town in Scandinavia, where Gustav continues his study of music. A piece of birch bark reminds him of the dots on the rollers of the mechanical piano; he transforms them into notes, and becomes a great composer. Tutein is successful at horse trading and hires a man named Egil to help him. Egil's adoration of Tutein and Gustav's affair with Gemma bring about alienation between the friends. Tutein suggests the "excess," their sexual union. It takes place after days of silence, and they even drink each other's blood. They want to be of one flesh, and since their blood type is the same, they have their blood exchanged by an experiment-happy doctor. Gustav feels rejuvenated; Tutein is not well. Meanwhile, Egil and Gemma are married.

In Part II Gustav and Tutein are alone. They buy land in a remote region and build a house. Years pass during which they observe nature and the village folk, the eternal struggle for life and food and happiness, and realize how pointless it all is. One day Tutein comes home drenched; he has a chill and Gustav puts him to bed. Tutein knows that death is near, and he begs Gustav not to leave him to fetch a doctor. No one knows of Tutein's death; the villagers believe he went on a trip. Gustav embalms him—Jahnn gives a detailed description of the process—and puts him in a zinc container, which he places in a teak chest in the living room. In the years that follow Gustav finds some consolation in his music and his fame. One day he receives a response to the letter he had written to the seaman of the *Lais* from Ajax, the successor of the seaman in the service of the ship's owner. Ajax becomes Gustav's servant, but soon he is on the way to replacing Tutein. In a moment of closeness Gustav confides to Ajax the contents of the chest. Ajax helps Gustav bury it at sea; but now that he has a hold on Gustav, Ajax becomes brazen in his demands, and Gustav dismisses him. One evening, after a gathering with friends during which Gustav expounds on the nonexistence of God, death as the final end, the evils of so-called progress, and the fact that man is made useless by technology, Gustav has a vision of Tutein. Shortly thereafter someone comes to Gustav's house at night; he hears a shot, and stops writing. A statement of the court proceedings concerning Gustav's will informs the reader that his friend the veterinarian found him murdered. The brief retelling of the content cannot do justice to the novel. The strange events are developed slowly and logically. Compact, emotion-filled scenes alternate with lengthy yet lively impressions of nature and reminiscences.

The third part of the cycle, the fragment *Epilog*, was published posthumously. Nikolaj, Gustav's son by Gemma, is returning from visiting his father's grave when he meets a man who calls himself Tutein. From his speech and manner, the reader concludes that this man is Ajax; but he grad-

ually takes on the characteristics of the real Tutein. Ajax could not be Gustav's "twin," but he and Nikolaj are becoming friends when the fragment breaks off.

The elements of the action in the play *Spur des dunklen Engels* (Shadow of the Dark Angel, 1952) are taken from the First Book of Samuel in the Old Testament. David finds the meaning of life in the complete love and devotion of Jonathan. The play contains modern elements; for instance, David plays the piano, and Samuel lames David by shooting him in the foot with a gun.

In the tragedy *Thomas Chatterton* (1955) a boy genius represents his own poetry as the rediscovered poems of a historical personage, and he mixes truth and fancy beyond recognition in the manuscripts he copies as a legal apprentice. His external circumstances worsen; but he rejects all of the helping hands offered him, including that of the angel Aburiel, and commits suicide.

Jahnn originally planned the short prose piece *Die Nacht aus Blei* (Leaden Night, 1956) as a dream sequence within the novel *Jeden ereilt es*, but

*Bronze bust of Jahnn by Gerhard Marcks, 1957 (Galerie Rudolf Hoffmann, Hamburg)*

whereas he finished *Die Nacht aus Blei,* the novel to which it belongs remains a fragment. Matthieu finds himself suddenly alone in a strange, dark city—a dead city—and is drawn into an encounter with a black youth and a black woman. They are not Negroes; their skin is black because of lack of life. Matthieu flees. On the street he is accosted by a limping youth begging for his help. Matthieu is astounded because he recognizes his former self in the boy. They go to the boy's abode, a windowless hole deep beneath the city sewer, where he shows Matthieu the cause for his limp, a gaping wound in his abdomen. Matthieu is terrified, for this is precisely the wound that was inflicted on him fifteen years ago. He must help as he had been helped, but instead he plunges his fist into the boy's intestines, and he dies. Matthieu finds his way to the outside, and discovers that his friend Gari, who had left him suddenly the night before, has returned.

Helwig considers *Die Nacht aus Blei* Jahnn's "fürchterlichstes Werk" (most horrible work); it is about a state in which he found himself: desperate because he was unable to help mankind help itself. Matthieu sees himself as Gari saw him fifteen years before, but Gari was more fortunate in being able to help.

*Jeden ereilt es* (It Catches Up with Everyone, 1959) tells the story of Matthieu's wound. Matthieu is attacked by a horde of boys, one of whom opens his abdomen with a rusty pen knife and begins to poke around his intestines with dirty fingers. Gari, one of the gang, rescues Matthieu, takes him to the dirty shack he calls home, and bandages him. The boys are instantly attracted to one another, and the love between them lasts, much to the dismay of Matthieu's father. Years later Matthieu leaves his father's house and attaches himself to Gari. Since the novel remained a fragment, it is not clear how Jahnn planned to fit *Die Nacht aus Blei* into it; possibly the dream was intended to underline Matthieu's dependence on Gari.

Jahnn's concern with technology running amok dominated his work after 1945. It prompted the play *Die Trümmer des Gewissens—Der staubige Regenbogen* (Ruins of Conscience—The Dusty Rainbow), published posthumously in 1961. The scientist Jakob Chervat lives with his family in an isolated research compound. Although his son at age eighteen is bald and impotent and his new child is born deaf, mute, and blind, he does not realize the implications of his experimentation until a friend warns him. In hopes of a way out, Jakob joins a meeting of young people in the compound

who are united by a bond of love; but the meeting is interrupted by the authorities. During the confrontation, in which some are killed and others are wounded, Jakob commits suicide.

Hans Henny Jahnn's works are not widely read, but they should be. Though he was not a Christian, he nevertheless preaches a message of love—albeit hidden beneath a stark realism and embedded in lengthy prose—that could save mankind from itself.

**Letters:**
*Hans Henny Jahnn—Peter Huchel: Ein Briefwechsel 1951-1959,* edited by Bernd Goldmann (Mainz: Hase & Koehler, 1974).

**Bibliographies:**
Jochen Meyer, *Verzeichnis der Schriften von und über Hans Henny Jahnn* (Neuwied & Berlin: Mainzer Reihe XXI, 1967);
Meyer, "Hans Henny Jahnn: Kommentierte Auswahl-Bibliographie zu Hans Henny Jahnn," *Text und Kritik,* 2/3 (January 1980): 139-153.

**References:**
Henning Boetius, *Utopie und Verwesung* (Bern: Lang, 1967);
Russell E. Brown, *Hans Henny Jahnns 'Fluß ohne Ufer': Eine Studie* (Bern: Francke, 1969);
Knut Brynhildsvoll, *Hans Henny Jahnn und Henrik Ibsen: Eine Studie zu Hans Henny Jahnns Roman "Perrudja"* (Bonn: Bouvier, 1982);
Richard Detsch, "The Theme of the Black Race in the Works of Hans Henny Jahnn," *Mosaic,* 2 (1973/1974): 165-187;
Wilhelm Emrich, *Das Problem der Form in Hans Henny Jahnns Dichtungen* (Mainz: Akademie der Wissenschaften und der Literatur, 1968);
Thomas P. Freeman, "Structure and Symbolism in Hans Henny Jahnn's *Perrudja,*" Ph.D. dissertation, Stanford University, 1970;
Freie Akademie der Künste, ed., *Zeitgenosse Hans Henny Jahnn: Ist der Mensch zu retten?* (Hamburg: Freie Akademie der Künste, 1985);
Bernd Goldmann, *Hans Henny Jahnn: Schriftsteller, Orgelbauer, 1894-1959* (Mainz: Akademie der Wissenschaften und der Literatur, 1973);
Goldmann, *Hans-Henny-Jahnn-Woche* (Kassel: Stauda, 1981);
Jürgen Hansel, "Der Roman als Komposition: Eine Untersuchung zu den Voraussetzungen und Strukturen von Hans Henny Jahnns Erzählen," Ph.D. dissertation, University of Cologne, 1971;

Francis S. Heck, "Hans Henny Jahnn: Disciple of André Gide," *Research Studies*, 42 (1974): 36-43;

Werner Helwig, *Die Parabel vom gestörten Kristall* (Mainz: von Hase & Koehler, 1977);

Kurt Hock, "Untersuchungen zu Hans Henny Jahnns Roman *Perrudja* unter besonderer Berücksichtigung der Tierfigur," Ph.D. dissertation, University of Munich, 1976;

D. E. Jenkinson, "The Role of Vitalism in the Novels of Hans Henny Jahnn," *German Life and Letters*, 25 (1971/1972): 359-368;

Reimar Joswig, "Weltbewältigung zu Hans Henny Jahnns Roman *Fluß ohne Ufer*," Ph.D. dissertation, University of Freiburg im Breisgau, 1969;

Maria Kalveram, *Die Suche nach dem rechten Mann: Männerfreundschaft im literarischen Werk Hans Henny Jahnns* (Berlin: Argument, 1984);

Peter Kobbe, *Mythos und Modernität: Eine poetologische und methodenkritische Studie zum Werk Hans Henny Jahnns* (Stuttgart: Kohlhammer, 1973);

Hermann Josef Kraemer, "Hans Henny Jahnns Schlacht-Platte historisch garniert," *General-Anzeiger für Bonn und Umgebung*, 26/27 November 1960;

Michael Mahlstedt, *Erlösungsfigurationen in Hans Henny Jahnns "Perrudja"* (Hamburg: Lüdke, 1982);

Manfred Maurenbrecher, "Kritik an Kultur und Moral beim frühen Hans Henny Jahnn," Ph.D. dissertation, Freie Universität Berlin, 1977;

Hans Mayer, *Versuch über Hans Henny Jahnn* (Hamburg: Hoffmann & Campe, 1974);

Breon Mitchell, "Hans Henny Jahnn and James Joyce: The Birth of the Inner Monologue in the German Novel," *Arcadia*, 6, no. 1 (1971): 44-71;

Walter Muschg, *Hans Henny Jahnn: Eine Auswahl aus seinem Werk* (Freiburg: Walter, 1959);

Hans E. Nossack, "Nachruf auf Hans Henny Jahnn," *Deutsche Literaturkritik der Gegenwart*, 4 (1971): 502-509;

Reinhard Schmitt, *Das Gefüge des Unausweichlichen in Hans Henny Jahnns Romantrilogie "Fluß ohne Ufer"* (Göppingen: Kümmerle, 1969);

Jürgen Serke, "Hans Henny Jahnn: Vision vom Tod und Verwesung," in his *Die verbrannten Dichter* (Weinheim & Basel, 1977), pp. 176-189;

Jochen Vogt, *Struktur und Kontinuum: Über Zeit, Erinnerung und Identität in Hans Henny Jahnns Romantrilogie "Fluß ohne Ufer"* (Munich: Fink, 1970);

Rüdiger Wagner, *Der Orgelreformer Hans Henny Jahnn* (Stuttgart: Musikwissenschaftliche Verlagsgesellschaft, 1970);

Joachim Wohlleben, *Versuch über 'Perrudja': Literarhistorische Beobachtungen über Hans Henny Jahnns Beitrag zum modernen Roman* (Tübingen: Niemeyer, 1985);

Elsbeth Wolffheim, "Umgeben vom Blei der Trauer: Zu einer Werkausgabe Hans Henny Jahnns," *Frankfurter Hefte*, 30 (1975): 53-57;

Hans Wolffheim, *Hans Henny Jahnn: Der Tragiker der Schöpfung* (Frankfurt am Main: Europäische Verlagsanstalt, 1966).

**Papers:**

Hans Henny Jahnn's papers are in the Staats- und Universitätsbibliothek, Hamburg.

# Ernst Jünger

*(29 March 1895-    )*

Carl Steiner

*George Washington University*

BOOKS: *In Stahlgewittern: Aus dem Tagebuch eines Stoßtruppführers von Ernst Jünger. Kriegsfreiwilliger, dann Leutnant und Kompanieführer im Füsilier-Regiment "Prinz Albrecht von Preußen" (Hannov. Nr. 73)* (Hannover: Privately printed, 1920; revised, Berlin: Mittler, 1922); translated by Basil Creighton as *The Storm of Steel: From the Diary of a German Storm-Troop Officer* (London: Chatto & Windus, 1929; New York: Doubleday, Doran, 1929);

*Der Kampf als inneres Erlebnis* (Berlin: Mittler, 1922; revised, 1926);

*Das Wäldchen 125: Eine Chronik aus den Grabenkämpfen 1918* (Berlin: Mittler, 1925); translated by Creighton as *Copse 125: A Chronicle from the Trench Warfare of 1918* (London: Chatto & Windus, 1930);

*Feuer und Blut: Ein kleiner Ausschnitt aus einer großen Schlacht* (Magdeburg: Stahlhelm, 1925; revised, Hamburg: Hanseatische Verlagsanstalt, 1929);

*Das abenteuerliche Herz: Aufzeichnungen bei Tag und Nacht* (Berlin: Mittler, 1925); republished as *Das abenteuerliche Herz: Figuren und Capriccios* (Hamburg: Hanseatische Verlagsanstalt, 1938);

*Die totale Mobilmachung* (Berlin: Verlag für Zeitkritik, 1931);

*Der Arbeiter: Herrschaft und Gestalt* (Hamburg: Hanseatische Verlagsanstalt, 1932);

*Blätter und Steine* (Hamburg: Hanseatische Verlagsanstalt, 1934);

*Geheimnisse der Sprache: Zwei Essays* (Hamburg: Hanseatische Verlagsanstalt, 1934);

*Afrikanische Spiele* (Hamburg: Hanseatische Verlagsanstalt, 1936); translated by Stuart Hood as *African Diversions* (London: Lehmann, 1954);

*Auf den Marmorklippen* (Hamburg: Hanseatische Verlagsanstalt, 1939); translated by Hood as *On the Marble Cliffs* (London: Lehmann, 1947; New York: New Directions, 1947);

*Gärten und Straßen: Aus den Tagebüchern von 1939 und 1940* (Berlin: Mittler, 1942);

*Myrdun: Briefe aus Norwegen. Einmalige Feldpostausgabe für die Soldaten . . . in Norwegen* (N.p., 1943);

*Der Friede: Ein Wort an die Jugend Europas und an die Jugend der Welt* (Hamburg: Hanseatische Verlagsanstalt, 1945); translated by Hood as *The Peace* (Hinsdale, Ill.: Regnery, 1948);

*Atlantische Fahrt: Nur für Kriegsgefangene gedruckt* (London: Kriegsgefangenenhilfe des Weltbundes der Christlichen Vereine Junger Männer in England, 1947; republished as *Atlantische Fahrt* (Zurich: Arche, 1948);

Ernst Jünger

147

*Sprache und Körperbau* (Zurich: Arche, 1947; revised, Frankfurt am Main: Klostermann, 1949);

*Im Granit* (Olten, 1947);

*Ein Inselfrühling: Ein Tagebuch aus Rhodos, mit den sizilischen Tagebuchblättern "Aus der goldenen Muschel"* (Zurich: Arche, 1948);

*Strahlungen* (Tübingen: Heliopolis, 1949);

*Heliopolis: Rückblick auf eine Stadt* (Tübingen: Heliopolis, 1949);

*Über die Linie* (Frankfurt am Main: Klostermann, 1950);

*Das Haus der Briefe* (Olten: Vereinigung Oltner Bücherfreunde, 1951);

*Der Waldgang* (Frankfurt am Main: Klostermann, 1951);

*Am Kieselstrand: Gedruckt als Gabe des Autors an seine Freunde, Weihnachten 1951-Neujahr 1952* (Frankfurt am Main: Klostermann, 1951);

*Besuch auf Godenholm* (Frankfurt am Main: Klostermann, 1952);

*Drei Kiesel: Gedruckt als Gabe des Autors an seine Freunde, Weihnachten 1952-Neujahr 1953* (Frankfurt am Main: Klostermann, 1952);

*Ernst Jünger: Eine Auswahl,* edited by Arnim Mohler (Bielefeld, Hannover, Berlin & Darmstadt: Vehhagen & Klasing, 1953);

*Der gordische Knoten* (Frankfurt am Main: Klostermann, 1953);

*Das Sanduhrbuch* (Frankfurt am Main: Klostermann, 1954);

*Geburtstagbrief: Zum 4. November 1955* (Olten: Vereinigung Oltner Bücherfreunde, 1955);

*Die Herzmuschel* (N.p., 1955);

*Sonnentau: Pflanzenbilder* (Olten: Vereinigung Oltner Bücherfreunde, 1955);

*Am Sarazenenturm* (Frankfurt am Main: Klostermann, 1955);

*Rivarol* (Frankfurt am Main: Klostermann, 1955);

*Serpentara* (Zurich: Bösch-Presse, 1957);

*San Pietro* (Olten: Vereinigung Oltner Bücherfreunde, 1957);

*Gläserne Bienen* (Stuttgart: Klett, 1957; revised, Hamburg: Rowohlt, 1960); translated by Louise Bogan and Elizabeth Mayer as *The Glass Bees* (New York: Noonday, 1960);

*Mantrana: Einladung zu einem Spiel* (Stuttgart: Klett, 1958);

*An der Zeitmauer* (Stuttgart: Klett, 1959);

*Der Weltstaat: Organismus und Organisation* (Stuttgart: Klett, 1960);

*Ein Vormittag in Antibes* (Olten: Vereinigung Oltner Bücherfreunde, 1960);

*Sgraffiti* (Stuttgart: Klett, 1960);

*Werke,* 10 volumes (Stuttgart: Klett, 1960-1965);

*Fassungen* (Munich: Gotteswinter, 1963);

*Sturm* (Olten: Oltner Liebhaberdruck, 1963);

*An Friedrich Georg zum 65. Geburtstag* (Frankfurt am Main: Klostermann, 1963);

*Subtile Jagden* (Stuttgart: Klett, 1967);

*Annäherungen: Drogen und Rausch* (Stuttgart: Klett, 1970);

*Sinn und Bedeutung: Ein Figurenspiel* (Stuttgart: Klett, 1971);

*Die Zwille* (Stuttgart: Klett, 1973);

*Zahlen und Götter; Philemon und Baucis: Zwei Essays* (Stuttgart: Klett, 1974);

*Eumeswil* (Stuttgart: Klett, 1977);

*Siebzig verweht,* 2 volumes (Stuttgart: Klett-Cotta, 1980-1981);

*Aladins Problem* (Stuttgart: Klett-Cotta, 1983);

*Autor und Autorschaft* (Stuttgart: Klett-Cotta, 1984);

*Eine gefährliche Begegnung* (Stuttgart: Klett-Cotta, 1985).

OTHER: *Der Aufmarsch: Eine Reihe deutscher Schriften,* edited by Jünger, 2 volumes (Leipzig: Aufmarsch-Verlag-Gesellschaft, 1926);

*Die Unvergessenen,* edited, with contributions, by Jünger (Berlin: Andermann, 1928);

*Luftfahrt ist not!,* edited by Jünger (Leipzig: Rudolph, 1928);

*Der Kampf um das Reich,* edited, with contributions, by Jünger (Berlin: Andermann, 1929);

*Das Antlitz des Weltkrieges: Fronterlebnisse deutscher Soldaten,* edited by Jünger (Berlin: Neufeld & Henius, 1930);

*Krieg und Krieger,* edited by Jünger (Berlin: Junker & Dünnhaupt, 1930);

*Der gefährliche Augenblick: Eine Sammlung von Bildern und Berichten,* edited by F. Buchholz, introduction by Jünger (Berlin: Junker & Dünnhaupt, 1931);

*Hier spricht der Feind: Kriegserlebnisse unserer Gegner,* edited by Jünger (Berlin: Neufeld & Henius, 1931);

*Die veränderte Welt: Eine Bilderfibel unserer Zeit,* edited by E. Schultz, introduction by Jünger (Breslau: Korn, 1933);

A. Horion, *Käferkunde für Naturfreunde,* foreword by Jünger (Frankfurt am Main: Klostermann, 1949);

H. Speidel, *Invasion 1944: Ein Beitrag zu Rommels und des Reiches Schicksal,* foreword by Jünger (Tübingen: Wunderlich, 1949).

The soldier-philosopher, a combination with which ancient civilizations such as those of Greece and Rome were quite comfortable, has become a rarity in the modern age of progressive overspecialization. If one adds the categories of naturalist, writer, and essayist, one moves into even more rarified circles. Ernst Jünger, blending the courage of the soldier with the curiosity of the student of life forms, the skill and imagination of the literary stylist with the probing intellect of the researcher, is such an exceptional individual. What makes him even more special is the fact that he was still writing in his ninety-first year. He is the oldest German writer of stature, and his represents the longest life span of any major figure in the annals of German literature. To call him the doyen of twentieth-century German letters is indeed no exaggeration.

Born into the soaring Second German Reich, nurtured on its ideals of expansive nationalism and imperialism, he experienced as a soldier its last days of glory and its downfall and demise. He lived through the ill-fated Weimar Republic, in which he began to expand his role from soldier to student and lover of nature, writer, essayist, and political thinker. He braved and survived the twelve years of the Third Reich, with which he may have sympathized at first; but as soon as he became aware of the fatal flaws of its rulers, he turned intellectual critic if not outright enemy. He saw his homeland almost completely destroyed, tragically divided, and miraculously rebuilt. In the course of an active life that included extensive traveling, he was able to create a voluminous literary opus that is still not completed. Yet in spite of—or perhaps because of—his endeavors, he remains a controversial figure. His life, almost from the beginning, has been immersed in controversies paralleling those that have embroiled his nation.

Jünger was born in Heidelberg on 29 March 1895; soon after his birth, his family moved to Hannover. His father, Dr. Ernst Georg Jünger, a basically kind but authoritarian man, was well versed in the humanities but developed a liking for the sciences, and, like the father of the first German novelist of the modern era, Theodor Fontane, he became a chemist and apothecary. Unlike Theodor Fontane, Ernst Jünger never harbored any intention of entering his father's profession; nonetheless, he developed a considerable interest in and knowledge of the sciences later in life. Jünger's mother, Karoline Lampl Jünger, was called "Lily" by her husband; the lily was to become one of the most important symbols in Jünger's fiction. His mother was a beautiful, intelligent, cultured woman whose interests included literature and

such controversial issues as the emancipation of women.

Jünger was the oldest of seven children, of whom two died in childhood. His younger brother Friedrich Georg, nicknamed "Fritz," was also to become a well-known writer. The two brothers had a special relationship that lasted until Friedrich Georg's death in 1977. Otherwise, Ernst was much of a loner in his formative years. Highly intelligent, but a dreamer and underachiever in school, he very early developed a strong dislike for the established order. As a result, he and Friedrich Georg joined the Wandervögel (Boy Scouts), a group of middle-class youths banding together to escape what they perceived as a life of artificiality, bourgeois mediocrity, and decadence. Their aim was to find a new meaning in life through discussion, poetry, folk songs, and contact with nature on weekend hikes—very much in the mood of the then popular neo-romantic movement. Friedrich Georg Jünger described their shared feelings at the time in his book of remembrances *Grüne Zweige* (Green Branches, 1951): "Reisepläne beschäftigten uns. Die Unrast, der Wunsch, in eine sehr ferne Ferne zu gehen, der zugleich eine erste Regung von Selbständigkeit in sich birgt, setzte mir zu. Ernst wurde von diesem Wunsche sehr geplagt und entwickelte mir in dieser Zeit neue Pläne über Reisen in ferne Länder" (We were preoccupied with travel plans. I was troubled by unrest, by the desire to go to very distant lands, a wish which at the same time harbors a first impulse for independence. The desire tormented Ernst very much and caused him at that time to discuss with me plans for travel to far-away countries).

At the age of eighteen Jünger went to France, where he signed up for a five-year enlistment in the French foreign legion. His intent from the very beginning, though, was to desert from the legion once he had arrived in Africa, in order to assure himself of full freedom of action there. More than twenty years later, Jünger wrote an autobiographical novel based on his adventures, *Afrikanische Spiele* (1936; translated as *African Diversions*, 1954). In this somewhat romanticized version of his first attempt to gain independence from paternal supervision, Jünger tells the story of an adolescent, fascinated with danger and evil and filled with the hope of conquering all difficulties, who overcomes his earlier disappointments and disillusionment. The novel focuses on the two failed attempts by the narrator, Herbert Berger, to desert from the legion and on his encounter with the misfits and outcasts of society. It also marvels at the mysteries and natural wonders of parts of the Dark Continent. In real life, Dr. Jünger succeeded in having Ernst, who was still a minor, returned home. The magnanimous father promised to finance an extended excursion to Africa for Jünger once he had completed secondary school. Jünger agreed, but the outbreak of World War I in August 1914 intervened.

The nineteen-year-old Jünger enthusiastically signed up with the Seventy-third Hannoverian Fusiliers. Five days later he was allowed to take an emergency Abiturium (comprehensive examination) at his Gymnasium. After passing the examination, he enrolled at the University of Heidelberg. At the beginning of October he was inducted into his regiment, with which he served the entire four years of the war on the western front, advancing from cadet to first lieutenant and leader of elite assault troops; he received seven double wounds and was awarded the highest German medal of the time, the Pour le mérite, for exceptional bravery. His wish to leave his homeland and to face the challenges of the adventurous life had finally been realized, but the price and the pain were extremely high. The young warrior's first feelings of glory and enthusiasm soon gave way to an awareness of the reality of modern mass warfare. In his first book, *In Stahlgewittern* (1920; translated as *The Storm of Steel*, 1929), which became the most successful German book of its time and established the international fame of its author, Jünger conveyed the loss of illusion which was experienced by a whole generation of young German soldiers: "Nach kurzem Aufenthalt beim Regiment hatten wir alle Illusionen verloren, mit denen wir ausgezogen waren. Statt der erhofften Gefahren hatten wir Schmutz, Arbeit und schlaflose Nächte vorgefunden, zu deren Bezwingung ein uns wenig liegendes Heldentum gehörte" (After a short stay with the regiment, we lost almost all the illusions with which we had departed. Instead of the hoped-for dangers we found dirt, work and sleepless nights, which could only be overcome with a kind of heroism that was alien to us).

In spite of such pronouncements, Jünger neither denigrated war nor slighted the bravery of the soldier; occasionally he glorified both. In contrast to Erich Maria Remarque's international best-seller *Im Westen nichts Neues* (1929; translated as *All Quiet on the Western Front*, 1929) and other pacifistic books of the time, Jünger's book tells of the heroism of the warrior who is willing to sacrifice his life for his country and inspire his fellow soldiers. Jünger dedicated the book, which is written in diary form and

*Jünger as a young man (Sammlung Des Coudres, Hamburg)*

gives a personal account of trench warfare, to his fallen comrades in arms. Due to the strong antiwar sentiments in German publishing circles in the 1920s, he had difficulty in finding a publisher for the book; the first edition had to be printed privately.

Appearing in the heyday of German literary expressionism, the realistic matter-of-fact tone and the simple but artistic style of *In Stahlgewittern* anticipated the era of the Neue Sachlichkeit (New Objectivity). Yet one can also detect in this work the beginnings of what Volker Katzmann calls Jünger's "magic realism." Already in this text, the author's rendering of the devastating reality of modern war is marked by a sense of form and style reminiscent of eighteenth- and nineteenth-century classicism and romanticism. His other works of the 1920s were of similar nature and sentiment. *Der Kampf als inneres Erlebnis* (Combat as an Inner Experience, 1922) is an essay on the psychology of combat; *Feuer und Blut* (Fire and Blood, 1925) describes the German offensive on the Somme River of March 1917, again from a personal vantage point; *Das Wäldchen 125* (1925; translated as *Copse*

*125*, 1930) chronicles the trench warfare of 1918.

Jünger was among the first to portray the re-actions and emotions of a young, cultured Euro-pean trying to cope with modern warfare. He related not just the physical but also the psycho-logical effects of his experiences. The short novel *Sturm* deals with the feelings of a young leader when he must order his men to attack. Remarkable for its experimental form and style, the novel was published in installments in the daily *Hannoverscher Kurier* in 1923. The author had little recollection of the work later on; considered lost, it was found in 1960 and published in 1963. Its plot appears to be patterned somewhat after Rainer Maria Rilke's romanticized version of a soldier's life and death in war, *Die Weise von Liebe und Tod des Cornets Chris-toph Rilke* (1903; translated as *The Tale of the Love and Death of Cornet Christopher Rilke*, 1932). Longer and much less poetic in style than Rilke's popular tale, Jünger's account also ends with the death of the hero in battle. Nonetheless, the experiences of its main character, Lieutenant Sturm, are largely autobiographical. How important this character was to Jünger is attested to by the fact that when his essays which were later collected as *Das aben-teuerliche Herz: Aufzeichnungen bei Tag und Nacht* (The Adventurous Heart: Notations by Day and by Night, 1925) first appeared in the journal *Arminius*, they were published under the pseudonym Hans Sturm.

*Das abenteuerliche Herz* was published in a re-vised and expanded version in 1938 as a collection of sixty-three short prose pieces, which Gerhard Loose has characterized as "adventures of the spirit, as the heart, the organ of consummate cog-nition, understands them." Jünger's intention was to encompass and convey the whole external pic-ture as well as the inner core of the organic life of man, animal, and plant, a Goethean undertaking.

Yet the primary influence on Jünger's early works remained his war experiences. He continued his military service after November 1918 in the Reichswehr, a limited defensive force permitted the Weimar Republic by the Treaty of Versailles, until 1923. After his discharge, he studied biology in Leipzig and later in Naples, financing his school-ing through the sale of his books. On 3 August 1925 he married Gretha von Jeinsen, with whom he had fallen in love at proverbial first sight, and decided to end his academic pursuits and make a living as a writer. Gretha bore him two sons, Ernst Johann Friedrich Oskar and Alexander Joachim.

In 1927 Jünger moved to Berlin, where he became involved with a revolutionary movement which espoused a doctrine of "national bolshevism" aimed at linking Germany with Russia against the West. Jünger shared the movement's romantic no-tion of a hierarchical military state in which an elite force of workers and soldiers was to exercise su-preme power.

His fame as a writer of war experiences and as an officer and war hero made him not only the darling of some fringes of the political left but also a favorite of the right. As a result of his political flirtations with the extremist circles of the right, Jünger became a contributor and later also a coed-itor, well into the early 1930s, of the right-wing, antidemocratic political magazines *Standarte*, *Ar-minius*, *Widerstand*, *Der Vormarsch*, and *Die Kommen-den*. He also edited compilations dealing with World War I, including *Die Unvergessenen* (The Un-forgotten, 1928), *Der Kampf um das Reich* (The Struggle for the Empire, 1929), *Das Antlitz des Welt-krieges* (The Face of the World War, 1930), and *Krieg und Krieger* (War and Warrior, 1930).

Jünger's attempts to effect social change through the power of his pen and his intellect re-sulted in two important works: *Die totale Mobilma-chung* (Total Mobilization, 1931) and *Der Arbeiter: Herrschaft und Gestalt* (The Worker: Rule and Form, 1932).

*Die totale Mobilmachung*, written in Berlin in 1929 and 1930, advocates the total mobilization of society for total warfare. Peace is a time during which society has to go "all out" to prepare for war. Since the ideal of a permanent peace is an illusion, a futile dream to be abandoned, the notion of at-taining a life of ease and comfort is equally spu-rious. Such false hopes have to be replaced by a new willingness for service and sacrifice. Jünger envisaged the society of the future and its ruling class in the subsequent work *Der Arbeiter*, an essay of over 300 pages. While the worker as a type was considered downtrodden and exploited in the nineteenth century, the present age, according to Jünger, is in desperate need of developing a dif-ferent type, whose destiny is to become a leader and ruler. Unimpeded by prejudices, political the-ories, and divisions, the worker can determine the shape of society and the world. The ultimate goal is the "Ablösung der liberalen Demokratie durch den Arbeiterstaat" (replacement of liberal democ-racy by a workers' state). The worker is both build-ing block for and representative of the new order. To fulfill his destiny, he has to be militant and radical, a warrior and a destroyer. As a result of his radicalism and militancy, the old order will dis-integrate, giving life to a new world arising like a phoenix from the ashes of the moribund system. The worker, the progenitor of the new world, will then fully unfold his creative and constructive powers and become its actual builder. Jünger saw the worker not just as a member of a special class or social category but as a metaphysical being who appears to be not too distant a relative of Nietzsche's Übermensch (superman). Some thirty years after the appearance of *Der Arbeiter,* Jünger wrote an addition, titled "Maxima-Minima," to supplement and expand the earlier work and bring it up to date. This text contains new explanations about methodology as well as new insights and reflections.

With *Der Arbeiter,* Jünger reached the end of the first stage of his development as a writer of major importance. In all these early years, and in spite of his support for right-wing causes, he avoided party affiliations. He did not want to be bound by narrow party doctrines, especially those of the most forceful and powerful group of all, the National Socialist German Workers (Nazi) Party under Adolf Hitler. Jünger's stance vis-à-vis the Nazi movement in the 1920s and 1930s has been a topic of much investigation and deliberation, especially in connection with the reception of the author and his work after the demise of the Third Reich. The truth seems to be that Jünger, like Hitler, rejected the Weimar Republic and the democratic process. In their view, democracy was an ineffective form of government, lacking in authority if not in integrity. Both men criticized liberalism, the free press, the parliamentary system, the bourgeois mentality, and the exploitation of the workers and the public by unscrupulous capitalist entrepreneurs. Both propagated, in Roger Woods's words, "a blood-based community, and a state founded upon nationalism, socialism, authority, and a fitness to fight." Both proclaimed the supremacy of the will in partial adaptation of Nietzsche's vitalism and agreed with Oswald Spengler's contention that the inevitable decline of Western civilization could only be stopped by a unified nationalistic front within Germany asserting its supremacy.

Jünger's initial enthusiasm for National Socialism quickly gave way to disillusionment. The virulent anti-Semitism of the Nazis was a major stumbling block in Jünger's attempt to make common cause with the party. In the final analysis, Jünger acknowledged Hitler's effectiveness as an orator but rejected his claim to sole and supreme leadership of the envisaged conservative and nationalistic revolution. As a result, Jünger began to

distance himself from the Nazis and in time shunned all political affiliations. In 1927 he refused to run as a Nazi candidate for a seat in the Reichstag. After Hitler came to power in 1933, Jünger went so far as to write a letter of protest to the official newspaper and main propaganda organ of the Third Reich, *Der Völkische Beobachter,* for having published from his work without his permission; and he let the Deutsche Akademie der Dichtung (German Academy of Literature), the literary section of the prestigious Prussian Academy of Arts, know in unmistakable terms that he was not interested in demonstrating solidarity with the Nazi regime by accepting membership in the body.

When concerted efforts by the regime to make Jünger an adherent proved futile, he found himself more and more in a state of intellectual and professional isolation. On 12 December 1933 he and his family moved to Goslar. Three years later, they moved to Überlingen, and in April 1939 they established themselves in Kirchhorst.

Although Jünger was reinstated in the army at the beginning of World War II, he was given the rather lowly rank of captain, which was not at all commensurate with his previous record as a battlefield commander of elite troops and a war hero. Consequently, his years of service at the Westwall (Siegfried Line) and with occupation forces in France were rather undistinguished in light of his military potential. He saw relatively little battlefield action, spending most of the war years in Paris as a member of the staff of Generals Speidel and Stülpnagel with vague responsibilities, pursuing his private and intellectual interests. His novel *Auf den Marmorklippen* (On the Marble Cliffs, 1939) and the first part of his World War II diary, *Gärten und Straßen* (Gardens and Streets, 1942), were banned by government censors. Jünger's mood in 1940 can be gleaned from a letter to Alfred Kubin, with whom he had been in correspondence for many years: "Man reist heute lange, um einen Menschen zu sehen" (One has to travel far today to meet a genuine human being).

*Auf den Marmorklippen,* Jünger's first novel held together by a continuous story, established its author as one of the leading writers of the Innere Emigration, those authors who, instead of going into exile during the Hitler years, remained in Germany and published works that criticized fascism either openly or in symbolic and allegorical form. The group included Werner Bergengruen, Reinhold Schneider, Ernst Wiechert, and Hans Carossa. Even though Jünger's novel betrays many autobiographical features, it is essentially a denunciation and philosophical critique in allegorical form of the Nazi government. The surrealistic, futuristic novel relates the experiences of the anonymous narrator and his brother Otho, who leave military service and withdraw from a totalitarian organization called Mauretania to seek a peaceful life of contemplation and the pursuit of botanical and linguistic studies in a hermitage atop the marble cliffs of the lake of Marina. But their retreat is threatened by the charismatic leader of the Mauretanians, the Chief Ranger, who has come to power by spreading terror and fear. His aim is to reduce the social order to anarchy and primitivism, and ultimately to impose absolutist rule. The opposing forces, led by the Chief Ranger's principal opponent, Braquemart, a disciple of Nietzsche; Prince Sunmyra, the head of the conservatives; and Belovar, the protector of the farmers and herdsmen, are too divided and weak to ward off the destruction of the social order. The brothers are eventually drawn into the fighting and oppose the forces of the Chief Ranger openly. Although they are able to escape annihilation through the timely help of the narrator's son Erio, the child of a brief love affair, the atmosphere of impending doom and the symbolic ending hint that civilization will be destroyed. But there is hope, as in the ancient Germanic myth, that out of utter destruction new life will arise: the brothers leave for another shore after their hermitage is consumed in flames.

The novel is clearly a Zeit- und Schlüsselroman (novel of contemporary history and roman à clef ), describing the factional strife among the various political forces prior to Hitler's assumption of absolute power through ruthlessness and violence. It attacks the intelligentsia for their cowardly betrayal of the humanistic tradition and pillories the military for its equally cowardly neutrality during the struggle for power and its opportunistic declaration of loyalty to the victorious Führer. On the other side there appears Father Lampros, "the radiant one," the symbolic and heroic representative of Christianity. Beyond its references to the political scene of the 1920s and 1930s, *Auf den Marmorklippen* is a mythical conception of the history of humankind that shows the ultimate battle between the forces of good and evil.

*Gärten und Straßen* contains entries from as early as April 1939, when Jünger and his family had just moved from Überlingen on Lake Constance to Kirchhorst near Hannover; it conveys the tranquil picture of Jünger tending his garden and engaging in botanical studies. When the war began, he "took to some of the highways of Western Eu-

rope" as an officer of the German army.

Jünger was discharged from the army because of what was officially called "Wehruntüchtigkeit" (unfitness for service) in 1944, the same year his oldest son, Ernst, was killed in action in Italy. Jünger's dismissal was actually due to his suspected association with some of those involved in the plot to assassinate Hitler in July 1944. In April 1945 he was made commanding officer of the Kirchhorst District Volkssturm (people's militia), part of a last-ditch effort to summon to arms everybody who could possibly carry a rifle; Jünger ordered his men to put down their weapons.

During the period of denazification in Germany after the war, strong denunciations were made by literary critics of Jünger's nationalistic past. He was called a Nazi collaborator, and some demanded that he be tried as a war criminal. Typically, Jünger not only ignored these charges but refused to fill out the official denazification papers. This refusal led to a ban on the publication of his books in occupied Germany for several years. Yet Jünger, the ex-soldier and perennial adventurer, went even further, attacking the accusers by stating: "Nach dem Erdbeben schlägt man auf die Seismographen ein. Man kann jedoch die Barometer nicht für die Taifune büßen lassen, falls man nicht zu den Primitiven zählen will" (After the earthquake, people tend to attack the seismographs. However, they should not punish the barometers for the fact that there are typhoons, provided that they do not want to be counted among the primitives).

Jünger's *Der Friede: Ein Wort an die Jugend Europas und an die Jugend der Welt* (Peace: An Appeal to the Youth of Europe and to the Youth of the World, 1945; translated as *The Peace*, 1946), had originally been written between the winter of 1941 and the spring of 1942. Dissatisfied with this version as too personal, Jünger destroyed it and wrote a second, more political piece between July and October 1943. He had the manuscript read by fellow officers and superiors whom he could trust, among them Field Marshal Erwin Rommel. Conceived originally as an attempt to clarify the situation that the war had brought about and as an "Übung in Gerechtigkeit" (exercise in justice), Jünger intended to have the document printed and distributed in large quantities after the overthrow of the Nazi regime. Part one, "Die Saat" (The Seed), expounds prevailing philosophical ideas and envisages the achievement of peace. Part two, "Die Frucht" (The Fruit), develops a political program for peace that is to serve as a guideline not only

*Dust jackets for the German version (courtesy of Lilly Library, Indiana University) and the English translation of Jünger's futuristic allegory about the Third Reich*

for Europe but for the entire world. Before such a program can go into effect, the war has to end decisively: Germany has to suffer utter defeat. But if a lasting peace is to be achieved, everybody will have to benefit somehow: "Der Krieg muß von allen gewonnen werden" (The war has to be won by all). Jünger envisaged a culturally diverse but politically unified Europe as the ultimate goal, a political "Vaterland" of the various ethnic "Mutterländer," in which the worker was to play a central role by virtue of his constructive talents: "Die Erde muß für alle Brot haben" (The world must have bread for all). The creative forces thus released must include religion: peace cannot be secured unless it becomes a sacred compact to lessen violence, "zu trösten, zu mildern, Schutz zu verleihen" (to comfort, to mitigate, to grant protection). Only by these means could the forces of nihilism be banished. Ironically, Jünger's plan to have his treatise widely distributed among the German people after the collapse of the Hitler regime came to naught. Since his works were prohibited from publication in Germany by order

of the Allied occupation forces, only a limited number of copies came out illegally. The essay is significant not only as Jünger's political manifesto of the war years but also, along with such works as Wiechert's *Der Totenwald* (1945; translated as *The Forest of the Dead*, 1947), as one of the most courageous documents of resistance to the tyranny of the Third Reich.

In 1949 the publication restrictions on Jünger's works were lifted. That year he published his 900-page diary detailing his war experiences and his reflections on the three years of occupation of his homeland under the title *Strahlungen* (Emanations). The diary had been his only way, in a totalitarian state, to engage in meaningful discussion. Yet while writing it, he seems to have been disturbingly oblivious to the suffering that the regime he served was wreaking on the world. The first part of *Strahlungen* comprises the previously published *Gärten und Straßen*. Parts two and four are titled "Pariser Tagebuch" (Parisian Diary) and deal with his experiences in occupied Paris, where he associated with French writers, artists, and intellectuals such as Pierre Drieu la Rochelle; Jean Giraudoux; Jean Cocteau; Braque; Picasso; and Banine, who later wrote *Rencontres avec Ernst Jünger* (Encounters with Ernst Jünger, 1951). In Paris Jünger also read the Bible thoroughly for the first time because of his growing interest in religion. The third part of the diary, "Kaukasische Aufzeichnungen" (Caucasian Notes), relates a special mission by order of General Stülpnagel to the southern part of occupied Russia from October 1942 to February 1943 to provide a firsthand account of the German campaign there. Jünger was also looking for reliable fellow officers at the eastern front who might join him in a conspiracy against the Führer. Part five of the diary, "Kirchhorster Blätter" (Kirchhorst Journal), records Jünger's discharge from the army and command of the Kirchhorst District Volkssturm. The final part of the diary, "Jahre der Okkupation" (Years of Occupation), deals with the period from 1945 to 1948.

Jünger's second full-fledged novel, the futuristic *Heliopolis: Rückblick auf eine Stadt* (Heliopolis: Reflections on a City), also appeared in 1949. This ambitious epic work of universal scope deals with man's past and his possible future development. Heliopolis is an imaginary place, what Loose calls "a timeless prototype of a city," bearing no relationship to the ancient Egyptian city of that name. The novel is set in an epoch that postdates "the second nihilism" and the disappearance of the global workers' state. As in *Auf den Marmorklippen*, there are several opposing powers in the city. The Governor, an unscrupulous tyrant ruling on behalf of the extraterrestrial Regent, keeps the masses spellbound. His ultimate aim is "die Perfektion der Technik" (the perfection of technology). He is opposed by the Proconsul, who is supported by the army and conservative forces. The Proconsul strives for a "historische Ordnung" (historical order) and "die Vollkommenheit des Menschen" (the perfection of man). A third, smaller group is made up of the closely knit nihilistic Mauretanians, who adroitly exploit the standoff between the major powers. The protagonist, Lucius de Geer, commander of the war college, is a cultured humanist as well as a man of action. A diplomat, philosopher, teacher, and a skilled officer, as well as attractive to the opposite sex, he is the personification of the "adventurous heart." Intermittent acts of terror have taken the place of open warfare, yet a clash between the two main forces seems inevitable. Lucius is drawn into the action but tries to keep a measure of independence and follow the dictates

of his conscience. Hence, rather than persecuting the beautiful Budur Peri, as he is ordered to do, he saves her and falls in love with her, and she becomes his intellectual counterpart. This most exquisite female character that Jünger has ever conceived belongs to an outcast people, the Parsen, who, like the Jews in past ages, are subjected to constant persecution because of their aloofness and their beliefs. In the end, Lucius gives up his military and political ambitions and resolves to leave the violent and corrupt city of Heliopolis with Budur for the distant Hesperides, his original home.

Like *Auf den Marmorklippen*, this symbolic and allegorical narrative shows that Jünger's visions of the future are dystopian rather than utopian. But in both novels there is some hope at the end that man may be able to begin anew after the inevitable destruction of his civilization. As in the earlier novel, philosophical reflections and the exposition of ideas do more than fill out the framework of the narrative: they are the actual core of the work. Extraordinary figures such as Halder the painter, Ortner the poet, Serner the philosopher, and Father Foelix the enlightener open up significant aesthetic and philosophical questions to discussion in the manner of ancient symposia. These characters are joined by a geologist with philosophical inclinations and a historian, Orelli. Orelli represents the genuine scholar, who is not just in command of the facts but also possesses sensitivity and intuitive insight. They all act as mystagogues, verbalizing and clarifying de Geer's understanding of the eternal verities. Even though the hero falters in his political undertakings, he gains intellectually and spiritually. Clearly, Jünger has broken away from what Alfred von Martin calls the "heroic realism" and "heroic nihilism" of his early and middle years. He expresses belief in a "theological humanism" that celebrates free will and altruistic individualism, rejecting collectivism and the heartless worship of power.

In 1950 Jünger moved to the hamlet of Wilflingen in Württemberg, which has been his home ever since. A dedicated student of plant, animal, and insect life, his study of man always takes into account man's natural environment. In the reflective piece *Der Waldgang* (Walk through the Forest, 1951), he deals symbolically with the rootlessness of modern man, who has lost his homeland but is determined to transgress the metaphorical "Nullmeridian" (zero longitude) and to hold on to his newly gained freedom. This theme is expanded in the essayistic prose poem *Besuch auf Godenholm* (Visit on Godenholm, 1952). In this work, a phy-

*Index card for Jünger's insect collection (Sammlung Des Coudres, Hamburg)*

sician, representing modern man and his dilemma, is helped through a mental crisis by a mysterious magician on a Nordic island; the physician comes to the realization that "der Mensch trägt alles Nötige in sich" (Man carries all that is necessary within himself).

During the 1950s Jünger, who was already one of the most widely traveled German writers, undertook a series of extensive journeys. He continued his wanderings well into his ninth decade, visiting the Mediterranean, northern Europe, the Americas, the Canary Islands, Asia Minor, Ceylon, and the Far East. These experiences have led to the publication of more than a dozen travel books as well as countless reflections on faraway lands in his diaries and essayistic works. In the philosophical essay *Der gordische Knoten* (The Gordian Knot, 1953), he analyzes the areas of contact and contrast between East and West. Orient and occident are, he says, fundamentally separated from one another by their different attitudes toward freedom. Despotism is the inherent rule of the east; it tends to extinguish all impulses toward freedom. In the West, on the other hand, freedom remains deeply ingrained in man's psyche. Jünger refrains from giving specific definitions of freedom: "Sie führen zu unfruchtbarem Streit" (They lead to unproductive bickering). One of his most celebrated works in the travel genre is the 1955 diary of his journey to Sardinia, *Am Sarazenenturm* (At the Tower of the Saracens), which was awarded the literary prize of

the city of Bremen. Here the author learns among shepherds, hunters, fishermen, and gardeners that man is happy while living the simple, natural life but saddened when he forsakes nature for artificiality. In 1955 Jünger was awarded the Kulturpreis (Culture Prize) of the city of Goslar.

Jünger's complex science-fiction constructions in *Heliopolis* are greatly simplified in the short novel *Gläserne Bienen* (1957; translated as *The Glass Bees*, 1960). The plot of this work does not revolve around the fantastic mechanical insects of the title, which perform their task of nectar gathering by remote control; they merely serve as background. The story focuses on Captain Richard, a retired army officer who, having fallen on hard times, is forced to seek civilian employment. He is out of touch with the new age of automation; his world has disappeared. Put to a series of tests by the great Zapparoni, the industrial czar of modern automation, he is bound to fail. In the epilog to the second edition (1960), *Gläserne Bienen* is revealed to be a lecture given by Captain Richard in a seminar on historical topics, which one of the participants has published in drastically abbreviated form. Evidently, Jünger wished to deemphasize the novelistic aspect of the work in order to focus attention on the conflict between humanity and technology, sensitivity and automation. In peace as in war, the machine has made fallible man appear obsolete and useless. Perfection is no longer an ideal to be striven for, but an achieved reality, a perennial state of matter-of-factness. The altar on which it is worshipped is that of efficiency and productivity, the modern gods of man's industrial enterprises.

In 1959 Jünger received the Großes Bundesverdienstkreuz (Great Order of Merit of the Federal Republic of Germany) and became cofounder and coeditor of the periodical *Antaios: Zeitschrift für eine freie Welt.* In the same year the sequel to *Der Arbeiter, An der Zeitmauer* (At the Wall of Time), was published. Whereas the earlier essay was polemical in nature, dealing with the political issues of the age in a futuristic guise, *An der Zeitmauer* is concerned with metaphysics. Jünger has forsaken the role of political activist and become an objective observer of man and his institutions, a kind of detached prophet and cosmic visionary. A second volume of essays, *Sgraffiti,* appeared in 1960 as a follow-up to *Das abenteuerliche Herz.* The topics of discussion in *Sgraffiti* are nearly as broad as in the earlier volume, but there is a dearth of inventiveness; no fewer than fourteen pieces are given the title "Mosaik." These pieces present an interconnected pattern of short observations, personal commentary, aphorisms, and sayings.

Jünger's wife died in 1960. That year he received the Lituraturpreis des Bundesverbandes der deutschen Industrie (Literature Prize of the Federal League of German Industry) and produced an essay on global political structure, *Der Weltstaat: Organismus und Organisation* (The World State: Organism and Organization), as a sequel to *Der Friede.* Jünger contends that the national state determines the type of society it comprises, all the way down to the family unit. But even the great countries are limited in their freedom of action. Global decision-making is more and more a juggling act, especially since the world is divided into powerful western and eastern halves. The severity of the division is indicated by such slogans as "Cold War" and "Iron Curtain." Yet the two superpowers are much more alike than is generally believed; hence it would not be too farfetched to assume that these two halves are the casting-mold for the formation of a universal state. The possibility of its genesis augurs well for the prospect of ultimate world peace. The idea that the state is the source of all evil, is the core of anarchism. The anarchist in his purest form is one whose recollections go back to prehistoric, indeed premythical ages: he believes that man at that time already fulfilled his destiny. In this sense, anarchists are ultraconservatives who seek the salvation of society in its origins. Pure anarchists are almost an extinct species today; the present world is overrun by nihilists. Yet the anarchist has been

*Jünger in 1950 (Ullstein)*

instrumental in bringing about the great revolutions. His protests against the state and its institutions come from the heart. He shows us a better, more just, and more natural mode of existence. Today, the character of each state is determined by other states, which serve as models; but this has not always been true and need not be the case in the future. In an ideal state, which once existed in an insular or a similar type of secluded setting, no defensive or war-making forces are necessary. In it alone, the human organism, truly humane and freed from the coercive forces of organization, could appear in a more nearly pure form.

On 3 March 1962 Jünger married Dr. Liselotte Lehrer, an archivist and publisher's reader twenty-two years younger than he. During the decade following his second marriage Jünger again undertook extensive travels. He received the Immermann Prize from the city of Düsseldorf in 1964.

In 1970, at the age of seventy-five, Jünger produced a book about drugs and drug-taking entitled *Annäherungen: Drogen und Rausch* (Approach: Drugs and Intoxication). This book of some 500 pages is another of his travelogues, but this time the journey is an inward one in which he penetrates, in Loose's phrase, "the uncharted seas of the soul." Jünger was no novice in dealing with drugs: from 1918 to 1922 he had experimented with the mind-altering effects of ether, cocaine, opium, and hashish; thirty years later, he acquainted himself with mescaline, ololuiqui (a Mexican mushroom), and LSD. Scientific and literary sources, including Thomas De Quincey's *Confessions of an English Opium-Eater* (1822), Charles Baudelaire's *Les paradis artificiels* (1860), and Aldous Huxley's *The Doors of Perception* (1954), supplement his personal experiences in *Annäherungen*. In contrast to some of his literary predecessors, however, Jünger has never been addicted to drugs.

In the novel *Die Zwille* (The Slingshot, 1973) Jünger reminisces about his schooldays in Hannover and Braunschweig. But *Die Zwille* is less an autobiographical novel than a psychological study of the relationship between pupil and teacher. It is also an exposé of secondary education as well as of village and city life in the Wilhelminian era. The two protagonists, Clamor and Teo, are both endowed with certain traits of the author. Ten-year-old Clamor, the loner and dreamer who has lost his lowly parents, feels constantly threatened and considers himself a failure. Yet he desperately wants to belong, to be a member of a group. He shares these characteristics with Teo's father, the minister of Oldhorst, who has become his protector. Teo, on the other hand, is the exact opposite of both. Seven or eight years older than Clamor, he is as strong as his own father and Clamor are weak; consequently, he is cast in the role of lord and master over Clamor. The same hierarchical spirit prevails in the Gymnasium, where there is moreover a strong sense of antagonism and distrust between teachers and pupils. A prank conceived and directed by the domineering Teo results in the clumsy Clamor being nabbed and expelled from school, although it was really Teo who had shattered an unpopular vice principal's window with a slingshot. But the novel comes to a conciliatory ending. A benevolent art teacher to whom Clamor has become devoted takes the distraught youngster under his wing, giving him what he has needed most all along: parental love and understanding as well as sensitive preceptorship.

Jünger's next book, *Zahlen und Götter; Philemon und Baucis: Zwei Essays* (Numbers and Gods; Philemon and Baucis: Two Essays, 1974), deals with nothingness, chaos, creation, myths, and man's attempt to understand these concepts in mathematical terms. In the first essay, the author says that he subscribes to the Pythagorean principle: "Die Zahl ist das Wesen aller Dinge" (Numbers are the essence of all things). But Jünger modifies this notion by stating: "Die Zahl ist eine Erfindung: sie kommt im Universum nicht vor" (Numbers are an invention: they do not appear in the universe). Jünger discusses the special mystique and fascination of the number Null (zero). The second essay, "Philemon und Baucis," expounds the theme of death in the mythical and the technological worlds. It was written as a memorial to René and Blanka Marcic, two close friends who perished in an airplane crash in Belgium on 2 October 1971.

In 1977 the futuristic novel *Eumeswil* was published. It is cut from the same cloth as *Auf den Marmorklippen* and *Heliopolis* and is, in a sense, a sequel to both. The narrator of the new novel, Manuel Venator, is not a hunter or warrior, however, but a "Forscher" (researcher) and "Lauscher" (quiet listener). His main occupation is that of night steward in the Kasbah of Eumeswil, an imaginary place somewhere in the Near East. The government there seems to be dictatorial but not despotic. There is a ruling class, consisting of the Condor, the Consuls, and the Domo. Hunting appears to be one of the main pursuits of the rulers. Eumeswil also has a Luminar, a kind of time machine that is a relic from the days of high technology, which permits the narrator, who has been trained as a historian, to study images from the past. Venator calls himself an "Anarch," a term he defines not without humor as follows: "Der Anarch unterscheidet sich . . . vom Anarchisten, daß er einen ausgesprochenen Sinn für Vorschriften besitzt" (The anarch differentiates himself from the anarchist in that he has a pronounced fondness for regulations). In spite of all his occupations and callings, Venator, who is not quite thirty, is unimpressive. He is unheroic, subservient toward the ruling clique, dependent, and pleasant. He confesses: "Ich bin also dabei, als ob Eumeswil ein Traum, ein Spiel oder auch ein Experiment wäre" (I am thus part of it as though Eumeswil were a dream, a game or even an experiment). On the other hand, he is philosophical and playful. At the end, Venator is invited by the members of the ruling group to participate in a great hunt. Fearing the worst, he prepares himself for death; but he survives. His brother Martin, though, perishes in the retinue of the tyrants. (Jünger's own brother Friedrich Georg died the year the novel was published.)

This novel is more reflective than the two earlier works set in the future and displays considerable detachment from the woes of the future. Jünger finally seems to feel at ease in a world in which the hunger for equality has devoured personal freedom and conformity has supplanted individualism. All that is left for those indulging in the anachronistic pursuit of personal uniqueness is the power to disengage, to veer toward the anarchic, and above all to be playful. Here Jünger's versatile Manuel Venator shares some characteristics with Hermann Hesse's Magister Ludi, with Thomas Mann's doomed iconoclast Adrian Leverkühn, and even with Günter Grass's diabolic dwarf Oskar Matzerath.

At the age of eighty-five, Jünger directed the publication of the first volume of his diary, *Siebzig verweht* (Gone past Seventy). This volume, which was published in 1980, covers the period from 30 March 1965 to 12 December 1970. The fragmentary form of the diary and its focus on observations of the moment are part of the author's design, yet it is his ambition to be a cosmographer and to convey universals. Jünger continues here in a vein which he successfully employed in *Das abenteuerliche Herz,* focusing his gifts of observation with equal ardor on man and his artistic and technical products as well as on animals, flowers, and even minerals. His insights into the mysteries of organic and inanimate forms of creation are related in a style that only the wisdom acquired by many decades of observation and reflection can dictate. The entries were written in the garden or surrounding forests of his "Wilflingen Klause" (Wilflingen refuge); during sojourns in Rome, Portugal, the Canary Islands, Angola, and east Asia; or on ships or airplanes en route. "Ein Letzter aus Humboldts Schule" (one of the last of Humboldt's school), he notes while passing the coast of the island of Sokotra in the Indian Ocean. The reference is to Georg Schweinfurth, the explorer-scientist who gave an explanation of the island "aus den Fundamenten" (from the foundation upward). Jünger venerates Schweinfurth because in this extraordinary individual "treffen sich welt- und naturhistorische Einsichten als Frucht ausgedehnter Reisen und Studien" (philosophical and scientific insights come to fruition as a result of extended travels and studies). The same statement could be applied to Jünger himself. There are many personal letters to old friends and acquaintances such as Martin Heidegger and Henri Plard, reflections on philosophers and artists such as Nietzsche and Goya, letters to publishers such as Rowohlt and Klett. Jünger exposes a vast panoply of topics from the "drug scene" to fairy tales,

from World War I to the Portuguese involvement in Angola.

The second volume of *Siebzig verweht*, covering the period from 1971 to 1980, was published in 1981. Jünger has the reader witness and partake in his own development, a method he advocated in the preface to *Strahlungen*. Yet in contrast to the earlier journals, Jünger, chastened by old age, tries now to observe the highest standards of objectivity. He remarks: "Die abendländische Geschichtsschreibung eines Thukydides, eines Tacitus, eines Ranke hat ihre Grenzen, ihre Voraussetzungen. Sie hat ein Zentrum, von dem, wie von der Sternwarte von Greenwich aus, gemessen wird. Von daher wird das Geschehen in Geschichte transformiert. Der Begriff der Freiheit, vor allem der Willensfreiheit, zählt zu den Maßstäben. Das Schicksal wird durch den Willen, und zwar durch den Willen des Menschen, geformt. Der Historiograph prüft und beurteilt die Entscheidungen" (The western historiography of a Thucydides, a Tacitus, a Ranke has its limits, its presuppositions. It has a center, from which, as from the Greenwich observatory, measurements are taken. From there, occurrence is transformed into history. The concept of freedom, above all that of the freedom of the will, becomes one of the yardsticks. Fate is shaped by the will, that is, by the will of man. The historiographer checks and evaluates the decisions).

In volume two of *Siebzig verweht*, Jünger jots down his impressions of people, books, paintings, animals, plants, and landscapes as he encounters them. On some occasions his observations are compressed into aphorisms; at other times they set into motion chain reactions of reflections and associations, which, in spite of their multiple topics and themes, somehow converge at the end. His trips take him to Sardinia, Sicily, Malta, Tunisia, Corfu, Crete, Turkey, Liberia, and Sri Lanka and end in Wilflingen. Both volumes also contain direct and indirect social and political criticism. Jünger examines the age and its political and social developments in the same penetrating way in which he observes natural phenomena. These diaries, like Jünger's earlier ones, are timely documentation of an unfolding era.

*Aladins Problem* (1983), a volume of short aphoristic essays in four parts completed in Wilflingen on 6 January 1982, deals with the problem of the self. Part one focuses on personal confessions: "Nun bin ich kein Dichter; das muß ich zugeben, obwohl ich, 'was ich leide,' ausdrücken kann—freilich nur im Selbstgespräch" (After all, I am not a poet; that I must confess, although I can

*Jünger talking with Argentine author Jorge Luis Borges at Jünger's home in Wilflingen in 1982 (photo by Ricardo Bada)*

express "my suffering"—to be sure, only by talking to myself ). The narrator also reflects on his war experiences and on his close relationship with a senior fellow officer by the name of Jagello. In part two, he reminisces about his family, but also focuses on literature, philosophy, and religion: "Vor allem die Götter ändern sich. Entweder wechseln sie Gestalt und Gesicht, oder sie verschwinden ganz und gar" (Above all, the gods change. Either they alter their shape and face, or they disappear altogether). The third part deals in more detail with his friends, such as the ex-sculptor Kornfeld and the banker Sigi Jersson, whom he met at a Jewish cemetery. In the concluding fourth part, the narrator reflects on the themes of the brotherhood of all men, history, and nihilism. He explains the mysterious title of the book by establishing a relationship between himself and the Arabian fairy-tale figure of Aladdin: "Auch Aladin war ein erotischer Nihilist. Er begehrte die unerreichbare Prinzessin Budûr. . . . Und er berührte sie nicht als sie neben ihm lag. . . . Aladins Problem war die Macht mit ihren Genüssen und Gefahren" (Aladdin, too, was an erotic nihilist. He lusted for the unattainable princess Budûr. . . .

And he did not touch her when she lay by his side. . . . Aladdin's problem was power with its pleasures and dangers).

Jünger's latest collection of aphorisms and short essays, *Autor und Autorschaft* (Author and Authorship), appeared in 1984. Jünger, who calls these short compositions "notes," seems deeply concerned with the mark the creative writer leaves behind. The book begins with a reflection about the significance of Goethe's death for the history of thought and literature and ends with a maxim that states in its conclusion that "Verehrung und Liebe in hohen Graden sich ausschließen" (veneration and love are to a large extent mutually exclusive). In contrast to Goethe, Jünger does not feel that an author has to be loved to be esteemed.

On 29 March 1985 Jünger turned ninety. He celebrated his birthday by readying for publication his latest diaries and a new novel, *Eine gefährliche Begegnung* (A Dangerous Meeting), in which his skill as a storyteller is unimpeded by the passage of time. His keen eye for reality combines, as in his first books, with his classical sense of stylistic proportion and his romantic proclivity for adventure, wonderment, and the irrational forces of life. The plot takes the reader to the Paris of 1889, the year in which the Eiffel Tower was built. The young diplomat Gerhard zum Busche, nephew of the German ambassador, is drawn into an amorous relationship with Irene, a married woman of higher Parisian society. Her husband, Count Kargané, although no longer in love with her, takes this occasion to plot her murder. By chance, however, another woman of rather questionable reputation occupies the suite which Irene had used for past indiscretions and is murdered by mistake. Accused of the crime by the police, Kargané commits suicide. The story of the unfaithful wife and her equally unfaithful husband, who wants her dead and pays with his own life instead, is only outwardly an Alfred Hitchcock thriller. Jünger's inner theme is the superficiality, shallowness, and decadence of the pleasure-seeking society of the turn of the century. It was a world "die der Liebe und den heiteren Genüssen gewidmet war" (which was given to the pursuit of sex and pleasure)—a world not all that remote, the author implies, from our own time.

Without question, Jünger is one of the most prolific writers in modern German literature. His literary production includes diaries and travelogues, science fiction and futuristic novels, and political and philosophical essays and aphorisms on a wide variety of topics. But it could also be said that he is one of those authors who writes one or two basic books over and over again in ingenious variation. Ludwig Marcuse's description of Heinrich Heine as "armer Subjektivling" (pitiable chap immersed in his own subjectivity) could have been coined for Jünger. For the latter's depiction of the world, whether in diary form or through fiction, is always filtered through his overpowering ego. A confirmed individualist, he reacts to the drastically changing world of his long life with vigor, vehemence, and occasional scorn. His strong conservatism notwithstanding, however, there is a detectable development in his Weltanschauung through the years. The "heroic nihilism" of his early work, which found the highest values in nationalism, militancy, discipline, and defiance of death and glorified war as a mythical and metaphysical end in itself, gives way gradually to a cosmopolitan outlook that embraces the Western tradition of benevolent individualism, freedom of expression, and universal peace. In this drastically changed world view, the warrior and the worker—manifestations of the antibourgeois and antidemocratic "neuer Mensch" (new man), subordinating themselves to the demands of the collective

spirit—are replaced by the researcher and the teacher—the seeker and the conveyor of universal truths, acting to uphold the sanctity of benign individualism and constantly probing for inner meaning.

Jünger's style has been characterized by Joseph Peter Stern as a "fusion, perfect and unique . . . , of the language of the battlefield and the language of nature-study; . . . a fusion of command and aestheticism." The universal, almost Goethean quality of his style—which could be called "European"—results from his having synthesized not just "command and aestheticism" but also the essence of German and French culture as well as the stylistic fashions of the century from impressionism to existentialism and from neo-romanticism to surrealism.

As perhaps no other author, Jünger reflects nearly the entire development of the mainstream of German conservative intellectual and political thought of the twentieth century. Ironically, however, Jünger has always seen himself in the Nietzschean vein as a nonconformist and an antiestablishment writer. Again and again he points out the disproportion between nature and technology, the individual and the might of government, and sees in these disparities the unresolved if not insoluble, destructive, and even fatal debacle of our age.

The critical and analytical approach to Jünger's work has fluctuated over the decades from lavish praise and adulation to rejection and condemnation. Although critics of all persuasions have had to acknowledge the breadth and depth of his encyclopedic intellect, the largely political nature of his writing has made it almost impossible for a detached and impartial literary criticism to evolve. A truly objective interpretation of his voluminous, complex, and still incomplete literary opus will have to await the passing of time.

**Letters:**

*Ernst Jünger, Alfred Kubin: Eine Begegnung* (Frankfurt am Main, Berlin & Vienna: Propyläen, 1975).

**Bibliographies:**

Karl O. Paetel, *Ernst Jünger: Eine Bibliographie* (Stuttgart: Lutz & Meyer, 1953);

Hans Peter des Coudres, *Bibliographie der Werke Ernst Jüngers* (Stuttgart: Klett, 1970).

**References:**

*Ad hoc: Zum 75. Geburtstag Ernst Jüngers* (Stuttgart: Klett, 1970);

Heinz Ludwig Arnold, *Ernst Jünger* (Berlin: Steglitz, 1966);

Arnold, ed., *Wandlung und Wiederkehr: Festschrift zum 70. Geburtstag Ernst Jüngers* (Aachen: Georgi, 1965);

Banine, *Rencontres avec Ernst Jünger* (Paris: René Julliard, 1951);

Franz Baumer, *Ernst Jünger* (Berlin: Colloquium, 1967);

Max Bense, *Ptolemäer und Mauretanier oder die theologische Emigration der deutschen Literatur* (Cologne & Berlin: Kiepenheuer, 1950);

Karl Heinz Bohrer, *Die Ästhetik des Schreckens: Die pessimistische Romantik und Ernst Jüngers Frühwerk* (Munich & Vienna: Hanser, 1978);

Erich Brock, *Ernst Jünger und die Problematik der Gegenwart* (Basel: Schwabe, 1943);

Marcel Decombis, *Ernst Jünger: L'homme et l'oeuvre jusqu'en 1936* (Paris: Aubier, 1943);

*Farbige Saüme: Ernst Jünger zum 70. Geburtstag*, special issue of *Antaios*, 7 (1965);

Marjatta Hietala, *Der neue Nationalismus in der Publizistik Ernst Jüngers und des Kreises um ihn 1920-1933* (Helsinki: Suomalaison Tiedeakatemian Toimituksia, 1975);

Friedrich Georg Jünger, *Die Spiele: Ein Schlüssel zu ihrer Bedeutung* (Frankfurt am Main: Klostermann, 1953);

Volker Katzmann, *Ernst Jüngers magischer Realismus* (Hildesheim: Olms, 1975);

Arnim Kerker, *Ernst Jünger—Klaus Mann: Gemeinsamkeit und Gegensatz in Literatur und Politik* (Bonn: Bouvier, 1974);

Helmut Konrad, *Kosmos: Politische Philosophie im Werk Ernst Jüngers* (Vienna & Augsburg: Blasaditsch, 1972);

Gerhard Loose, *Ernst Jünger* (New York: Twayne, 1974);

Loose, *Ernst Jünger: Gestalt und Werk* (Frankfurt am Main: Klostermann, 1957);

Alfred von Martin, *Der heroische Nihilismus und seine Überwindung: Ernst Jüngers Weg durch die Krise* (Krefeld: Scherpe, 1948);

Arnim Mohler, ed., *Die Schleife: Dokumente zum Weg von Ernst Jünger* (Zurich: Arche, 1955);

Mohler, ed., *Freundschaftliche Begegnungen: Festschrift für Ernst Jünger zum 60. Geburtstag* (Frankfurt am Main: Klostermann, 1955);

Hans-Rudolf Müller-Schwefe, *Ernst Jünger* (Wuppertal: Barmen, 1951);

Gerhard Nebel, *Ernst Jünger und das Schicksal des Menschen* (Wuppertal: Marées, 1948);

Karl O. Paetel, *Ernst Jünger in Selbstzeugnissen und Bilddokumenten* (Reinbek & Hamburg: Rowohlt, 1962);

Paetel, *Wandlungen eines deutschen Dichters und Patrioten* (New York: Krause, 1946);

Hans Peter Schwarz, *Der konservative Anarchist: Politik und Zeitkritik Ernst Jüngers* (Freiburg: Rombach, 1962);

Joseph Peter Stern, *Ernst Jünger* (New Haven: Yale University Press, 1953);

Roger Woods, *Ernst Jünger and the Nature of Political Commitment* (Stuttgart: Heinz, 1982).

**Papers:**
Archives of Ernst Jünger's papers have been started by Hans Peter des Coudres in Hamburg and Karl O. Paetel in New York.

# Erich Kästner

*(23 February 1899-29 July 1974)*

## Herbert Knust
*University of Illinois*

BOOKS: *Herz auf Taille* (Stuttgart: Deutsche Verlagsanstalt, 1928);

*Emil und die Detektive: Ein Roman für Kinder* (Berlin: Williams, 1928); translated by May Massee as *Emil and the Detectives* (Garden City: Doubleday, Doran, 1930; London: Cape, 1931);

*Lärm im Spiegel* (Stuttgart: Deutsche Verlagsanstalt, 1929);

*Emil und die Detektive: Ein Theaterstück für Kinder* (Berlin: Chronos, 1930); translated by Cyrus Brooks as *Emil and the Detectives: A Children's Play in Three Acts* (London & New York: French, 1934);

*Ein Mann gibt Auskunft* (Stuttgart & Berlin: Deutsche Verlagsanstalt, 1930);

*Arthur mit dem langen Arm: Ein Bilderbuch*, by Kästner and Walter Trier (Berlin: Williams, 1931);

*Leben in dieser Zeit: Lyrische Suite in 3 Sätzen*, music by Edmund Nick (Berlin: Chronos, 1931);

*Fabian: Die Geschichte eines Moralisten* (Stuttgart & Berlin: Deutsche Verlagsanstalt, 1931); translated by Brooks as *Fabian: The Story of a Moralist* (New York: Dodd, Mead, 1932; London: Cape, 1932);

*Pünktchen und Anton: Ein Roman für Kinder* (Berlin: Williams, 1931); translated by Eric Sutton as *Annaluise and Anton: A Story for Children* (London: Cape, 1932; New York: Dodd, Mead, 1933);

*Das verhexte Telefon: Ein Bilderbuch*, by Kästner and Trier (Berlin: Williams, 1931);

*Der 35. Mai; oder, Konrad reitet in die Südsee* (Berlin: Williams, 1932); translated by Brooks as *The Thirty-fifth of May; or, Conrad's Ride to the South Seas* (London: Cape, 1933; New York: Dodd, Mead, 1934);

*Gesang zwischen den Stühlen* (Stuttgart & Berlin: Deutsche Verlagsanstalt, 1932);

*Pünktchen und Anton: Theaterstück* (Berlin: Chronos, 1932);

*Das fliegende Klassenzimmer: Ein Roman für Kinder* (Stuttgart: Perthes, 1933); translated by Brooks as *The Flying Classroom* (London: Cape, 1934);

*Emil und die drei Zwillinge: Die zweite Geschichte von Emil und den Detektiven* (Zurich: Atrium, 1934); translated by Brooks as *Emil and the Three Twins: Another Book about Emil and the Detectives* (London: Cape, 1935);

*Drei Männer im Schnee: Eine Erzählung* (Zurich: Rascher, 1934; edited by Clair Hayden Bell, New York: Appleton-Century-Crofts, 1934); translated by Brooks as *Three Men in the Snow* (London: Cape, 1935);

*Die verschwundene Miniatur; oder auch: Die Abenteuer eines empfindsamen Fleischermeisters* (Basel & Vienna: Atrium, 1935); translated by Brooks as *The Missing Miniature; or, The Adventures of a Sensitive Butcher* (London: Cape, 1936; New York: Knopf, 1937);

*Doktor Erich Kästners lyrische Hausapotheke: Ein Taschenbuch; enthält alte und neue Gedichte des Verfassers für den Hausbedarf der Leser* (Zurich: Atrium, 1936);

*Georg und die Zwischenfälle* (Basel: Atrium, 1938); republished as *Der kleine Grenzverkehr oder Georg und die Zwischenfälle* (Cologne: Kiepenheuer & Witsch, 1949); translated by Brooks as *A Salzburg Comedy* (London: Weidenfeld, 1950; New York: Ungar, 1957);

*Till Eulenspiegel: Zwölf seiner Geschichten frei nacherzählt* (Basel: Atrium, 1938); translated by Brooks as *Eleven Merry Pranks of Till the Jester* (London: Enoch, 1939); translated by Richard and Clara Winston as *Till Eulenspiegel, the Clown* (New York: Messner, 1957);

*Bei Durchsicht meiner Bücher: Eine Auswahl aus vier Versbänden* (Zurich: Atrium, 1946);

*Der tägliche Kram: Chansons und Prosa, 1945-1948* (Zurich: Atrium, 1948);

*Zu treuen Händen: Komödie*, as Melchior Kurtz (Hamburg: Chronos, 1948);

*Kurz und bündig: Epigramme* (Olten: Vereinigung Oltner Bücherfreunde, 1948);

*Die Konferenz der Tiere: Ein Buch für Kinder und Kenner. Nach einer Idee von Jella Lepman* (Zurich:

(Ullstein)

Europa, 1949); translated by Zita de Schauen-see as *The Animals' Conference*, based on an idea by Jella Lepman (New York: McKay, 1949; London: Collins, 1955);

*Das doppelte Lottchen: Ein Roman für Kinder* (Zurich: Atrium, 1949); translated by Brooks as *Lottie and Lisa* (London: Cape, 1950); translation republished as *Lisa and Lottie* (Boston: Little, Brown, 1951);

*Der gestiefelte Kater: Nacherzählt von Erich Kästner* (Zurich: Atrium, 1950); translated by the Winstons as *Puss in Boots: Retold by Erich Kästner* (New York: Messner, 1957);

*Des Freiherrn von Münchhausen wunderbare Reisen und Abenteuer zu Wasser und zu Lande: Nacherzählt* (Zurich: Atrium, 1951); translated by the Winstons as *Baron Munchhausen: His Wonderful Travels and Adventures* (New York: Messner, 1957);

*Die kleine Freiheit: Chansons und Prosa 1949-1952* (Zurich: Atrium, 1952);

*Die Schildbürger: Nacherzählt* (Zurich: Atrium, 1954); translated by the Winstons as *The Simpletons* (New York: Messner, 1957);

*Der Gegenwart ins Gästebuch: Gedichte* (Frankfurt am Main: Büchergilde Gutenberg, 1955);

*Die dreizehn Monate: Gedichte* (Zurich: Atrium, 1955);

*Eine Auswahl: Verse und Prosa* (Zurich: Atrium, 1956);

*Leben und Taten des scharfsinnigen Ritters Don Quichotte: Nacherzählt von Erich Kästner* (Zurich: Atrium, 1956); translated by the Winstons as *Don Quixote: Retold by Erich Kästner* (New York: Messner, 1957);

*Die Schule der Diktatoren: Eine Komödie in neun Bildern* (Zurich: Atrium, 1956);

*Menschen und andere Tiere*, by Kästner and Paul Flora (Munich: Piper, 1957);

*Als ich ein kleiner Junge war* (Zurich: Atrium, 1957); translated by Isabel and Florence McHugh as *When I Was A Little Boy* (London: Cape, 1959); translation republished as *When I Was a Boy* (New York: Watts, 1961);

*Rede zur Verleihung des Georg Büchner-Preises 1957* (Berlin: Dressler, 1958);

*Über das Nichtlesen von Büchern*, by Kästner and Flora (Frankfurt am Main: Börsenverein des deutschen Buchhandels, 1958);

*Gesammelte Schriften*, foreword by Hermann Kesten, 7 volumes (Zurich: Atrium/Berlin: Dressler/Cologne: Kiepenheuer & Witsch, 1959);

*Große Zeiten—kleine Auswahl*, edited by F. Rasche (Hannover: Fackelträger, 1959);

*Münchhausen: Ein Drehbuch* (Frankfurt am Main & Hamburg: Fischer, 1960);

*Notabene 45: Ein Tagebuch* (Zurich: Atrium, 1961);

*Gullivers Reisen: Nacherzählt* (Zurich: Atrium, 1961);

*Das Erich Kästner-Buch*, edited by Rolf Hochhuth (Gütersloh: Bertelsmann/Mohn, 1961);

*Wieso warum? Ausgewählte Gedichte 1928-1955* (Berlin: Aufbau, 1962);

*Das Schwein beim Friseur und anderes* (Berlin: Dressler, 1962);

*Der kleine Mann* (Zurich: Atrium, 1963); translated by James Kirkup as *The Little Man* (New York: Knopf, 1966);

*Von Damen und anderen Weibern*, edited by Alexander Blase (Hannover: Fackelträger, 1963);

*Das Erich-Kästner-Seemännchen*, edited by Erich Seemann (Recklinghausen: Seemann, 1963);

*Let's Face It: Poems*, translated by P. Bridgwater and others (London: Cape, 1963);

*Zwei Schüler sind verschwunden*, edited by J. C. Alldridge (London: Longmans, Green, 1966);

*Kästner ( fourth from left) in the artillery during World War I. His experiences in the army left him with permanent heart trouble and a lifelong distaste for militarism (Privat-Archiv Kästner)*

*Kästner für Erwachsene,* edited by Rudolf Walter Leonhardt (Frankfurt am Main & Berlin: Fischer, 1966);

*Warnung vor Selbstschüssen* (Berlin: Aufbau, 1966);

*Unter der Zeitlupe* (Freiburg: Hyperion, 1966);

*Der kleine Mann und die kleine Miss* (Zurich: Atrium, 1967); translated by Kirkup as *The Little Man and the Little Miss* (London: Cape, 1969); translation republished as *The Little Man and the Big Thief* (New York: Knopf, 1969);

*Kennst du das Land, wo die Kanonen blühn?,* edited by Walter Püschel (Berlin: Eulenspiegel, 1967);

*Gesammelte Schriften für Erwachsene,* 8 volumes (Munich: Droemer, 1969);

*Wer nicht hören will, muß lesen: Eine Auswahl* (Frankfurt am Main: Fischer, 1971);

*Friedrich der Große und die deutsche Literatur: Die Erwiderung auf seine Schrift "De la littérature allemande"* (Stuttgart: Kohlhammer, 1972);

*Der Zauberlehrling: Ein Roman-Fragment* (Ebenhausen: Voss, 1974);

*Das große Erich Kästner Buch,* edited by Sylvia List, foreword by Hermann Kesten (Munich & Zurich: Piper, 1975);

*Briefe aus dem Tessin* (Zurich: Arche, 1977);

*Mein liebes, gutes Muttchen, Du: Dein oller Junge. Briefe und Postkarten aus 30 Jahren,* edited by Luiselotte Enderle (Hamburg: Knaus, 1981).

OTHER: Kurt Tucholsky, *Gruß nach vorn: Eine Auswahl,* edited by Kästner (Stuttgart & Hamburg: Rowohlt, 1946);

*Pinguin: Für junge Leute,* edited by Kästner, volumes 1-4 (Stuttgart: Rowohlt, 1946-1949);

Erich Will-Halle, *Du und ich im Neuaufbau! Eine nachdenkliche Bilderfibel für große und kleine Kinder,* foreword by Kästner (Halle: Mitteldeutsche Verlag-Gesellschaft, 1947);

Hermann Kesten, *Glückliche Menschen: Roman,* foreword by Kästner (Kassel: Schleber, 1948);

Henry Meyer-Brockmann, *Satiren: Fünfzig Zeichnungen,* foreword by Kästner (Munich: Weismann, 1949);

James Matthew Barrie, *Peter Pan,* translated by Kästner (Berlin: Bloch, 1951);

165

T. S. Eliot, *Old Possum's Book of Practical Cats/Old Possums Katzenbuch: Englisch und Deutsch*, translated by W. Peterich, paraphrased by Kästner and others (Berlin & Frankfurt am Main: Suhrkamp, 1952);

Paul Hazard, *Kinder, Bücher und große Leute*, translated from French by H. Wegener, foreword by Kästner (Hamburg: Hoffman & Campe, 1952);

Paul Junker, ed., *Kindertage—Kinderseelen: Ein Bildwerk*, foreword by Kästner (Bonn: Athenäum, 1956);

*Heiteres von E. O. Plauen*, edited by Kästner (Hannover: Fackelträger, 1957);

Will-Halle, *Jetzt kommt's raus . . .*, foreword by Kästner (Berlin: Staneck, 1958);

*Deutscher Humor der Gegenwart in Wort und Bild: Heiterkeit in Dur und Moll*, edited by Kästner (Hannover: Fackelträger, 1958); enlarged as *Lachen, lächeln, schmunzeln: Deutscher Humor der Gegenwart in Wort und Bild, Verse und Prosa* (Hannover: Fackelträger, 1958); republished as *Heiterkeit in Dur und Moll: Deutscher Humor der Gegenwart in Wort und Bild* (Hannover: Fackelträger, 1959);

Bernd Lohse, ed., *Oh diese Katzen: Geschildert in vierunddreißig Fotos. Mit praktischen Ratschlägen von P. Leyhausen*, introduction by Kästner (Frankfurt am Main: Umschau, 1959);

*Heiteres von Walter Trier*, edited by Kästner (Hannover: Fackelträger, 1959);

*Heiterkeit kennt keine Grenzen: Ausländischer Humor der Gegenwart in Wort und Bild*, edited by Kästner (Hannover: Fackelträger, 1960);

Kesten, *Bücher der Liebe*, introduction by Kästner (Munich, Vienna & Basel: Desch, 1960);

Clara Asscher-Pinkhoff, *Sternkinder*, foreword by Kästner (Berlin: Dressler, 1961);

James Krüss, *Der wohltemperierte Leierkasten*, postscript by Kästner (Gütersloh: Mohn, 1961);

Helen Brun and others, *Buntes Berlin: Aquarelle und Federzeichnungen aus West-Berlin*, introduction by Kästner (Berlin-Schöneberg: Juncker, 1961);

*Heiterkeit braucht keine Worte: Humor der Welt im Bild*, edited by Kästner (Hannover: Fackelträger, 1962);

E. G. Linfield and E. Larsen, *England—vorwiegend heiter. Eine Literaturgeschichte des britischen Humors*, foreword by Kästner (Munich: Bassermann, 1962);

*Heiterkeit in vielen Versen*, edited by Kästner (Hannover: Fackelträger, 1965);

*Heiterkeit aus aller Welt*, edited by Kästner (Hannover: Fackelträger, 1968);

*Die lustige Geschichten-Kiste*, edited by Kästner (Munich: Betz, 1972).

Erich Kästner, one of the most popular German writers of the twentieth century, was a man of varied literary talents appealing to diverse audiences; he wrote poetry, novels, children's books, essays, chansons, plays, and film scripts. As a rationalist and moralist he saw himself in the tradition of the Enlightenment—averse to spurious "depth" but "devoted to three inalienable demands": genuineness of feeling, clarity of thought, and simplicity of expression. His language, the so-called Kästner tone, ranges from aggressive satire and provocative casual understatement to epigrammatic wit, ironic melancholy, and lighthearted humor. Having lived through two world wars, Kästner, a keen observer of human nature, was both a strongly autobiographical writer and a critical chronicler of his time, from the late Wilhelminian empire through the Weimar Republic and

*Kästner in 1930 (photo by Umbo, Ullstein)*

the Third Reich to the postwar Federal Republic. His wide international fame rests primarily on the countless translations of his children's books.

Born in Dresden, Kästner was the only child in an impoverished petty bourgeois family. The fact that he was the illegitimate son of a doctor named Zimmermann was a well-kept secret; other information about his youth is recorded, somewhat idyllically, in the selective autobiography of his childhood, *Als ich ein kleiner Junge war* (1957; translated as *When I Was A Little Boy,* 1959). His father, Emil Kästner, had had to give up his independent position as a master saddler and go to work in a luggage factory. Kästner's energetic, dedicated mother, Ida Amalia Augustin Kästner, determined to raise her son above a lower-class status, did menial work as a seamstress and hairdresser to augment the family's small income. She was the major educational force in his early years, taking him to the theater and on hiking tours and trips, and trying to pave his way in every respect. The devoted child, eager to fulfill her expectations, became a model son and a superior pupil at school, and remained strongly attached to her until her death.

Kästner's attraction to learning was boosted by his contact with several young teachers who, successively, rented a room from the Kästners. He decided to become a pedagogue and was admitted to a seminary for elementary teachers; but he was soon repelled by its authoritarian discipline and cultivation of submissiveness. Later he frequently criticized educational "barracks" run by incompetent teachers who stifled rather than nurtured children's fantasy and intellectual potential. His mother went through periods of exhaustion and depression and repeatedly left suicide notes, causing great anxiety for the boy. In 1914 she and her son were vacationing on the Baltic coast when their holiday was cut short by the Kaiser's order for mobilization. "The World War had begun, and my childhood had ended," Kästner concludes the memoirs of his youth.

In 1917 Kästner was drafted into the army, an utterly negative experience that only strengthened his antiauthoritarianism. Brutal "exercises" imposed by a sadistic officer left the young recruit with a permanent heart condition. In 1918 he welcomed the defeat that, as he saw it, prevented Germany from complete "militarization"; and in his subsequent poems, essays, and satires Kästner would never tire of attacking the militaristic tradition. As a young war veteran he was able to attend a Gymnasium, where he wrote his first poetry and graduated with distinction. With a scholarship

from the city of Dresden he enrolled in 1919 at the University of Leipzig, where he studied literature, theater, history, and philosophy.

Kästner also attended the University of Rostock during the 1921 summer semester and the University of Berlin during the 1921 winter semester. He was especially interested in the Enlightenment and planned a thesis on Lessing, but completed his doctorate at the University of Leipzig in 1925 with a study of the reception of Prussian King Frederick the Great's arrogant and ignorant views on German literature. (Kästner's dissertation, still unsurpassed five decades later, was published in 1972.) After his graduation, Kästner found well-paid employment as a journalist until, in 1927, one of his erotic-satiric poems caused a scandal leading to his dismissal. Like many talented young people of his time he went to cosmopolitan Berlin, where he quickly rose to literary fame.

He contributed poetry, essays, and theater critiques to the most significant liberal journals of the time, including the *Weltbühne,* and joined the company of progressive social critics of satirical bent, such as Kurt Tucholsky, Hermann Kesten, Robert Neumann, Walter Mehring, and Alfred Polgar. In quick succession, four volumes of balladesque poetry propelled his reputation: *Herz auf Taille* (literally, Heart on the Waist, 1928), *Lärm im Spiegel* (Noise in the Mirror, 1929), *Ein Mann gibt Auskunft* (A Man Gives Information, 1930), and *Gesang zwischen den Stühlen* (Singing Between the Chairs, 1932). In saucy, down-to-earth language and concise, artfully crafted rhymes with witty surprise effects Kästner comments provocatively on the public and private life of the petty bourgeoisie: its deadly routines, manipulation through power and money, unemployment, poverty, hunger, sexuality, strife, and many other topics from daily experience are surveyed in cool, ironical, sometimes melancholy manner, conveying disillusionment and skepticism but also hope against hope. He considered his poems Gebrauchslyrik (lyrics for everyday use) for those who were willing to look into the mirror, recognize themselves, and, perhaps, learn a lesson. But the lesson is not preached—it is implied through the critique and exposure of paradoxical social conditions and human behavior. Kästner's poignant lyrics about the small realities of life and their effects on man are notable not only as a sobering factual counterpoint to the subjective, emotional, visionary, and abstract projections of declining expressionism but also as prelude and counterpart to his major novel *Fabian: Die Geschichte eines Moralisten* (1931; translated as *Fabian: The Story of a Moralist,* 1932), which deals with similar themes and evokes similar effects in prose.

Upon a publisher's invitation Kästner wrote his first, most significant, and most popular children's book, *Emil und die Detektive* (1928; translated as *Emil and the Detectives,* 1930), which was quickly dramatized, turned into films, and translated into many languages. The successful experiment became a model for his subsequent children's books. This affirmative, idealizing, somewhat utopian adventure novel is a counterbalance to his biting critical satire, but it is not totally lacking in social criticism. Although capturing and addressing the mentality of youngsters, the short novel presents various relations between the adult world and a basically unspoiled children's world—with a variety of direct and indirect moralizing points. Emil, the son of a poor, hardworking widow, is carrying some money for his grandmother on the train from his small hometown to Berlin, but he falls asleep in his compartment and the money is stolen. Emil pursues the thief through the city and, with the help of a gang of children, captures him. The exciting event is featured in the news, and Emil and his young detectives gain not only fame but also a reward, for the thief turns out to be a long-wanted bank robber. Much of the story's humor and appeal

derive from the fact that the children's republic functions better than that of the grownups. Children set the precedent for good citizenship, displaying reason, a sense of justice, spontaneous helpfulness, initiative, and acceptance of responsibility.

In 1929 there followed a satirical critique of the contemporary city in Kästner's radio play *Leben in dieser Zeit* (Life in These Times), which was published in 1931. In 1930 he worked on film scripts, and the fast-changing "filmic" perspective became characteristic of his writing. Two more children's books appeared in the early 1930s: *Pünktchen und Anton* (1931; translated as *Annaluise and Anton,* 1932) and *Der 35. Mai* (1932; translated as *The Thirty-fifth of May,* 1933). These were overshadowed by his first and most significant novel for adults, *Fabian,* a bleak reflection of city life in the late 1920s with dim prospects for the future. During the economic crisis the thirty-two-year-old Fabian is fired from his job; he witnesses corruption of truth, perversion of love, chaos in politics, and solitude in human relations at all levels of society; and he falls from one disappointment to another. He loses his girlfriend, who for the sake of a career becomes the mistress of a film director; he loses his friend, who shoots himself because he believes the lie that

*Emil and his friends pursue through the streets of Berlin the thief who stole Emil's money in the 1931 film* Emil und die Detektive, *based on Kästner's 1928 novel*

*A scene from* Leben in dieser Zeit, *based on the 1929 radio play by Kästner, as performed at the Breslau City Theater in 1932 (Theaterwissenschaftliches Archiv Dr. Steinfeld)*

*Hans Albers in the title role in the 1943 film* Münchhausen, *for which Kästner wrote the screenplay. Although the film was allowed to be shown throughout Germany, Kästner's name was deleted from the credits because he had incurred Hitler's disapproval (Ullstein).*

*Cover for Kästner's 1934 sequel to* Emil und die Detektive
*(Lilly Library, Indiana University)*

his scholarly work has not been found acceptable; and he loses his own life in an attempt to save a drowning child because he cannot swim. (Ironically, the child swims to the bank unaided.) The original title rejected by the publisher, "Ein Gang vor die Hunde" (A Walk before the Dogs), would seem to support those who saw nothing but defeatism in his work. The new subtitle, *Die Geschichte eines Moralisten,* as well as the contradictions between the protagonist's observations and his behavior, raised questions about Kästner's own perspective. The overdrawn satirical scenes, seen mostly through Fabian's eyes, may be in line with the author's intended warning of the abyss to come. On the other hand, the somewhat sentimental sympathy created for the suffering victim seems to obscure the criticism of his passivity. The concluding advice, "Learn to swim," can hardly be taken as a serious call for opportunistic floating with the polluted trends of the time in order to survive; rather it sounds, however vaguely, like a provocation to greater practicality and activity in the conduct of moral people.

The year 1933 saw Kästner at the height of his Berlin success, but it also saw the beginning of Hitler's dictatorship. Kästner's books were burned by the Nazis because they were considered offensive to the "German spirit" and morally destructive, hence politically unreliable. But he did not go into exile, although he was twice interrogated by the Gestapo and was forbidden to publish in Germany. He declined an offer by the Nazis to launch an anti-emigrant newspaper in Switzerland. Instead, he published in Zurich a series of popular novels for entertainment, which shun the real issues of the day and escape into lighthearted daydream situations: role-playing, mistaken identities, and misunderstandings create comic suspense but are unproblematically resolved by love idylls, happy reunions, and lucky successes. The novels ignore social differences and do not touch political realities. In *Drei Männer im Schnee* (1934; translated as *Three Men in the Snow,* 1935), Kästner's ironical defense of "the millionaire as artistic motif" because of his social usefulness and because of the unsuitability of motifs such as burglary and robbery could hardly be taken as a serious statement on the contemporary political scene—at most it is an indication of the fairy-tale character of the story of a jobless young academic who is befriended by a humanistic millionaire and wins his daughter and his wealth. In *Die verschwundene Miniatur* (1935; translated as *The Missing Miniature,* 1936) a well-to-do butcher breaks out of his routine Berlin life, travels away to encounter humanity, and participates in an exciting hunt for a stolen painting, leading back to Berlin, "justice," family reconciliation for the butcher, and a happy ending for a responsible secretary and reliable insurance agent. (The film rights for these novels were quickly acquired by Hollywood.) *Georg und die Zwischenfälle* (George and the Untoward Incidents, 1938), republished in 1949 as *Der kleine Grenzverkehr* (Small Frontier Traffic; translated as *A Salzburg Comedy,* 1950), is escapist in theme and tendency: across the border in Austria (which was annexed by the Nazis in the same year the book appeared) a young bachelor commuting from Reichenhall to attend the Salzburg Festival finds a sweetheart who turns out to be a count's daughter. The only problem in the German Reich appears to be the tardiness of bureaucracy in regard to foreign money exchange, and even that triggers nothing but a social comedy. Kästner also published a politically defused selection from his earlier poetry under the title *Doktor Erich Kästners lyrische Hausapotheke* (Dr. Erich Käst-

*Sketch by Kästner of the Frauenkirche in his hometown of Dresden, 1944 (Privat-Archiv Kästner)*

*Kästner reunited with his parents, Emil and Ida Kästner, who survived the Allied firebombing of Dresden (photo by Fritz Eschen)*

# Der Mai

Im Galarock des heiteren Verschwenders,
das Blumenzepter in der schmalen Hand,
fährt nun der Mai, der Mozart des Kalenders,
aus seiner Kutsche grüßend, über Land.

Es überblüht sich, er braucht nur zu winken.
Er winkt! Und rollt durch einen Farbenhain.
Blaumeisen flattern ihm voraus, und Finken.
Und Pfauenaugen flügeln hinterdrein.

Die Apfelbäume hinterm Zaun erröten.
Die Birken machen einen grünen Knicks.
Die Drosseln spielen, auf ganz kleinen Flöten,
das Scherzo aus der Symphonie des Glücks.

Die Kutsche rollt durch atmende Pastelle.
Wir ziehn den Hut. Die Kutsche rollt vorbei.
Die Zeit versinkt in einer Fliederwelle.
O, gäb es doch ein Jahr aus lauter Mai!

Melancholie und Freude sind wohl Schwestern.
Und aus den Zweigen fällt verblühter Schnee.
Mit jedem Pulsschlag wird aus Heute Gestern.
Auch Glück kann weh tun. Auch der Mai tut weh.

Er nickt uns zu und ruft: "Ich komm ja wieder!"
Aus Himmelblau wird langsam Abendgold.
Er grüßt die Hügel, und er winkt dem Flieder.
Er lächelt. Lächelt. Und die Kutsche rollt.

*Manuscript for the poem "Der Mai" from Kästner's 1955 collection* Die dreizehn Monate *(Privat-Archiv Kästner)*

ner's Lyrical Medicine Cabinet, 1936). It is para-doxical that in 1942, after Hitler had seen scenes from the film *Münchhausen,* for which Kästner had written the script, the latter was forbidden to publish even abroad; whereas *Münchhausen,* with the famous Hans Albers in the starring role, as well as the 1930 screen version of *Emil und die Detektive,* continued to run successfully throughout Germany.

Kästner's heart condition had kept him from active service during World War II. At home he witnessed the bombardment of cities, the suicides and executions of friends, the despair of fellow beings, the insanity of relentless fanatics, and finally the total collapse of his country. His experiences during the last year of the war are recorded in his diary *Notabene 45* (1961). After the war he moved to Munich, where he was offered a leading post with the newspaper *Die neue Zeitung,* became a contributor to the cabarets *Die Schaubude,* founded in 1945, and *Die kleine Freiheit,* founded in 1951, and edited the children's journal *Pinguin.* Once again he participated actively, through various media, in the issues of the day, warning against the repetition of old mistakes and appealing for reason, freedom, and peace in postwar Germany, especially on behalf

of the young generation. In 1946 he visited his utterly destroyed birthplace, Dresden, where his parents had miraculously survived the Allied fire-bombing; his mother lived until 1951 and his father until 1957. He published selections from his earlier poetry in *Bei Durchsicht meiner Bücher* (On Perusing My Books, 1946), chansons and prose pieces in *Der tägliche Kram* (Everyday Odds and Ends, 1948), and epigrams in *Kurz und bündig* (Short and to the Point, 1948); his comedy *Zu treuen Händen* (In Loyal Hands), written under the pseudonym Melchior Kurtz, was published and performed in 1948. In 1949 two more children's books appeared. In *Die Konferenz der Tiere* (translated as *The Animals' Conference,* 1949), the first and last congregation of all the animals of the world uses more common sense on behalf of world peace, for the children's sake, than the countless and fruitless international conferences of adult politicians. In *Das doppelte Lottchen* (translated as *Lottie and Lisa,* 1950), originally written as a film treatment in 1942, reunited twins not only bury their differences but also set an example for the adult world by bringing their divorced parents back together. In divided postwar Germany, the theme of reunion was an especially topical issue.

*Scene from the premiere of Kästner's comedy* Die Schule der Diktatoren *in the Munich Kammerspiele, February 1957*
*(photo by Hildegard Steinmetz)*

The screen version of the novel received a film prize a year later.

Kästner was president of the West German P.E.N. Center from 1952 until 1962. In 1956 he received the literature prize from the City of Munich; a year later he was awarded the Büchner prize in Darmstadt. Kästner never married, but in 1957 a son, Thomas, was born to him by Fridine Siebert. Kästner wrote a children's novel, *Der kleine Mann* (The Little Man, 1963), and a sequel, *Der kleine Mann und die kleine Miss* (1967), for his son; but their relationship was never particularly close. In 1960 the International Board on Children's Books awarded Kästner the Hans Christian Andersen Medal. In 1964, on his sixty-fifth birthday, the Goethe Institute organized a Kästner exhibit that traveled through many countries. He received a literature prize and the Lessing Ring from the German Freemasons in 1968, and the Großes Verdienstkreuz (Distinguished Service Medal) of the Federal Republic of Germany in 1969. In 1970 and 1974 he was again honored by cultural prizes in Munich. Streets and schools were named after him in several cities. Kästner died on 29 July 1974 at the age of seventy-five. On 9 June 1975 the Erich Kästner Society was founded.

In spite of the popularity of Kästner's work—especially the stupendous international reception of his books for children—there have been relatively few learned and thorough investigations of his literary significance. The first studies, in the 1950s, came from outside Germany. With the increased importance of literary sociology in the late 1960s and early 1970s, accompanied by reevaluations of popular literature (which in Germany was traditionally called "trivial" literature), full-fledged scholarly studies of Kästner became more frequent. Particular attention was paid to such questions as the coherence of his works for adults and for children; the unity of pedagogic intent and artistic strategy; the writer's position under dictatorship; the fusion of autobiographical and historical elements; the relationship of satire and skepticism, pessimism and optimism; the political practicability of humanistic utopianism; and the paradoxes of literary taste as reflected in the reception of Kästner's works. To some readers and critics he has become a classic; to others he has increasingly become an object of debate. Both tendencies are a testimony of involvement in an author who was very much involved in his time.

**Biographies:**
Luiselotte Enderle, *Erich Kästner: Eine Bildbiographie* (Munich: Kindler, 1960);

Enderle, *Erich Kästner mit Selbstzeugnissen und Bilddokumenten* (Reinbek: Rowohlt, 1966; revised, 1984).

**References:**
Renate Benson, *Erich Kästner: Studien zu seinem Werk* (Bonn: Bouvier, 1973);

Kurt Beutler, *Erich Kästner: Eine literaturpädagogische Untersuchung* (Weinheim & Berlin: Julius Beltz, 1967);

Reinaldo Bossmann, *Erich Kästner: Werk und Sprache* (Curitiba, Brazil, 1955);

Elisabeth-Charlotte Breul, "Die Jugendbücher Erich Kästners," *Studien zur Jugendliteratur*, 4 (1958): 28-79;

Helmuth Kiesel, *Erich Kästner* (Munich: Beck, 1981);

Rex W. Last, *Erich Kästner* (London: Wolff, 1974);

Dieter Mank, *Erich Kästner im nationalsozialistischen Deutschland: 1933-1945; Zeit ohne Werk?* (Frankfurt am Main & Bern: Lang, 1981);

Werner Schneyder, *Erich Kästner: Ein brauchbarer Autor* (Munich: Kindler, 1982);

Egon Schwarz, "Die strampelnde Seele: Erich Kästner in seiner Zeit," in *Die sogenannten zwanziger Jahre*, edited by R. Grimm and J. Hermand (Bad Homburg: Gehlen, 1970), pp. 109-141;

Hans Wagener, *Erich Kästner* (Berlin: Colloquium, 1973);

Dirk Walter, *Zeitkritik und Idyllensehnsucht: Erich Kästners Frühwerk 1928-1933 als Beispiel linksbürgerlicher Literatur in der Weimarer Republik* (Heidelberg: Winter, 1977);

John Winkelman, *The Poetic Style of Erich Kästner* (Lincoln: University of Nebraska Press, 1957);

Winkelman, *Social Criticism in the Early Works of Erich Kästner* (Columbia: Univeristy of Missouri Press, 1953);

Rudolf Wolff, ed., *Erich Kästner: Werk und Wirkung* (Bonn: Bouvier, 1983).

# Martin Kessel
## (14 April 1901-   )

Peter C. Pfeiffer
*University of California, Irvine*

BOOKS: *Gebändigte Kurven: Gedichte* (Frankfurt am Main & Berlin: Kiepenheuer, 1925);

*Betriebsamkeit: Vier Novellen aus Berlin* (Frankfurt am Main: Iris, 1927); selections republished as *Eine Frau ohne Reiz: Drei Novellen aus Berlin* (Berlin: Kiepenheuer, 1929);

*Herrn Brechers Fiasko: Roman* (Stuttgart & Berlin: Deutsche Verlagsanstalt, 1932; revised, Frankfurt am Main: Suhrkamp, 1956);

*Romantische Liebhabereien: Sieben Essays nebst einem aphoristischen Anhang* (Braunschweig: Vieweg, 1938); revised as *Essays und Miniaturen* (Stuttgart & Hamburg: Rowohlt, 1947);

*Die Schwester des Don Quijote: Eine Malergeschichte* (Braunschweig: Vieweg, 1938); revised as *Die Schwester des Don Quijote: Ein intimer Roman* (Darmstadt, Berlin-Spandau & Neuwied: Luchterhand, 1959);

*Erwachen und Wiedersehen* (Berlin: Hugo, 1940);

*Aphorismen* (Stuttgart, Hamburg & Baden Baden: Rowohlt, 1948);

*Die epochale Substanz der Dichtung* (Mainz: Verlag der Akademie der Wissenschaften und der Literatur, 1950);

*Gesammelte Gedichte* (Hamburg: Rowohlt, 1951);

*Musisches Kriterium: Aphorismen* (Mainz: Verlag der Akademie der Wissenschaften und der Literatur, 1952);

*In Wirklichkeit aber . . . : Satiren, Glossen, kleine Prosa* (Berlin: Dressler, 1954);

*Eskapaden: Fünf Erzählungen* (Darmstadt, Berlin-Spandau & Neuwied: Luchterhand, 1959);

*Gegengabe: Aphoristisches Kompendium für hellere Köpfe* (Darmstadt, Berlin-Spandau, Neuwied: Luchterhand, 1960);

*Ironische Miniaturen* (Bonn: Privately printed, 1960; revised, Mainz: von Hase & Koehler, 1970);

*Kopf und Herz: Sprüche im Widerstreit* (Neuwied & Berlin-Spandau: Luchterhand, 1963);

*Lydia Faude: Roman* (Neuwied & Berlin-Spandau: Luchterhand, 1965);

*Alles lebt nur, wenn es leuchtet: Neue Gedichte* (Mainz: von Hase & Koehler, 1971);

*Ehrfurcht und Gelächter* (Mainz: von Hase & Koehler, 1974).

PERIODICAL PUBLICATIONS: "Romantische Selbstdurchdringung: Ein Selbstporträt," *Wort und Welt*, 3 (1948): 337-339;

"Mein erster Roman," *Jahresring* (1973/1974): 38-46.

Martin Kessel is a late-born child of German romanticism. His novels, books of aphorisms, poems, and essays treat the tension between inner ideality and the surrounding reality; stylistically, this tension is expressed through the use of a sa-

*Martin Kessel (Ullstein)*

tirical and ironically exaggerated realism filled with paradoxes and puns.

Born in Plauen in Saxony, Kessel studied German literature, philosophy, music, and art at the universities of Frankfurt am Main, Munich, and Berlin. In 1923 he received his Ph.D. with a dissertation on Thomas Mann's novellas. He has since been living as an independent writer in Berlin-Wilmersdorf. In the early 1920s Paul Hindemith introduced Kessel to the Novembergruppe, a circle of artists, architects, and theater directors which promoted modern concepts of the arts, held semipublic workshops, and organized exhibitions. It was then that Kessel began having essays and poetry published in various journals. An eye ailment kept Kessel from having to fight in World War II. He has generally avoided personal publicity, though in 1957 he joined Erwin Piscator, Wilhelm Lehmann, Hans Henny Jahnn and others in an open letter protesting the stationing of nuclear weapons in West Germany. On the whole, Kessel's relationship with his surroundings has been detached, almost eccentrically individualistic, a trait shared by the main characters in his novels. Even so his talents were quickly recognized. He received the Büchner Prize in 1954, the Fontane Prize in 1961 and the Große Bundesverdienstkreuz (Great Service Cross of the Federal Republic) in 1963. In spite of their critical acclaim, however, Kessel's works have failed to attract a wide reading public.

Kessel's major fictional work, *Herrn Brechers Fiasko*, was published in 1932. He completed the novel despite economic hardships and discouraging criticism from friends. In stature it surpasses such works as Erich Kästner's *Fabian: Die Geschichte eines Moralisten* (1931; translated as *Fabian: The Story of a Moralist*, 1932) and Hans Fallada's *Kleiner Mann, was nun* (1932; translated as *Little Man, What Now*, 1933). Like those novels, *Herrn Brechers Fiasko* is set in the Berlin of the 1920s. The main characters work in the advertising department of a media organization. A wide range of people are brought together by their function in the economic process: spinsters, members of the urban proletariat with high ambitions, a Jew who chooses to conceal his name for the sake of success, people from the provinces seeking to realize their dreams in the big city. They represent the new social archetype, the petty bourgeois clerical employee. The central conflict is between Max Brecher and Dr. Geist, who are childhood acquaintances. Endeavoring to preserve his personal integrity, Brecher protests both human alienation and the total socialization of the individual; he strives to keep his private life free

of the values of the marketplace. Dr. Geist, on the other hand, conforms to a mentality geared toward performance and production. His cynical principle "Ich tu, was getan werden muß, kommentarlos" (I do what has to be done, without comment) brings him dubious success: he is promoted to head the department and proceeds to fire Brecher, who was in sympathy with striking workers. Brecher becomes, as it were, a "Gespenst" (ghost), an unemployed man stripped of all social functions and purpose. It is Brecher's fiasco that gives meaning to this somewhat gloomy ending. The comical, sometimes grotesque manner with which Brecher clings to "old-fashioned" ideas makes the reader aware of the mechanisms at work behind Brecher's failure. A sentence at the end of the novel is an apt commentary on the whole: "An einer Sache, die glatt geht, ist nichts zu verstehen, höchstens alles zu bewundern" (There is nothing to understand about a matter that goes smoothly, at best, it's to be admired).

*Herrn Brechers Fiasko* is not solely a novel about white-collar workers. Beyond events in the office, one can observe the social and political climates of Germany during the 1920s. The reader is made aware of ever-increasing unemployment; hectic, vulgar hedonism; and class conflicts and the consequent political polarization, all presided over by an impotent political leadership. These problems are most clearly evinced in Brecher's regularly recurring monologues, which present images that contrast a superficial sanity with the growing irrationality in politics and everyday life. Germany appears as the state of the petits bourgeois, who gladly lose their identity in the anonymity of the masses and bow down to the "Nihilismus der Alltäglichkeit" (nihilism of banality). Kessel's novel gives an accurate depiction of the society of which Hitler was about to become dictator. Only months after its publication, *Herrn Brechers Fiasko* vanished from bookstores. For today's reader, it offers a fascinating account of the waning years of the Weimar Republic.

In contrast to the rapid progression of the earlier work, *Die Schwester des Don Quijote* (Don Quixote's Sister, 1938) flows calmly, interwoven with strands of subtle irony. Combining realism with references to fairy tales, the novel is Kessel's dirge to bourgeois society. It is the story of the young artist Theo Schratt, who is painting a portrait of the demonically beautiful Saskia Skorell. Only after Theo realizes that Saskia's aestheticism cloaks her inability to cope with modern life is he able to regain a sense of his self and finish the painting. Just as Cervantes in _Don Quixote_ conjures the vanished world of chivalry and thereby surrenders it to parody, Kessel depicts Saskia Skorell, "Don Quixote's sister," as a relic of the bourgeois epoch. The novel fails due to an idyllic strain that seems strangely out of place, a weakness also found in Kessel's short stories collected in _Eskapaden_ (1959).

In _Aphorismen_ (1948), Kessel wanted to give advice to his readers, as is clear from the headings in the first part of the book—for example, "Die Lust zu leben" (Joy of Living), "Vom Sinn des Lebens" (On the Meaning of Life). Because of their overt didactic intent, however, the aphorisms lose their edge. Only in _Gegengabe_ (Return Gift, 1960) does Kessel achieve the flexibility and freedom suitable for the aphoristic form. _Gegengabe_ touches on every sphere of life: critical reflections on language and art are juxtaposed with observations on everyday matters; political and moral maxims are mixed with comments on technology and private experiences. One theme running through the whole book has been the favorite subject of aphoristic literature since the time of the French moralists La Rochefoucauld and Chamfort: the laying bare of human vanities and social hypocrisies. By means of paradoxes, unusual metaphors, and parodies of common phrases, these aphorisms stimulate independent thought:

> "Es werde Licht, und es ward Licht!"—Das verblüfft nur, nichts daran überzeugt ("Let there be light, and there was light!"—This is perplexing, but not at all convincing).
> Die Waschmaschine ist das Symbol der demokratischen Öffentlichkeit (The washing machine is the symbol of the democratic public).
> Tatsachen werden eingeseift, Ideen rasiert (Facts are lathered, ideas shaved).

The reader must complete the aphorisms to grasp their meaning; the right margin of the book is unusually wide and invites the reader to jot down any thoughts that come to mind. A brilliant style, breadth of vision, and wit place _Gegengabe_ among the notable collections of aphorisms of the postwar era. The book is also a reminder that Kessel was a prolific abstract painter: it includes eight reproductions of his collages.

Yet another facet of Kessel's talent is his poetry. _Gesammelte Gedichte_ (Collected Poems, 1951) contains nature and lyric poems, as well as others which draw on the symbolist tradition. Kessel shows

that nature no longer serves as a source for readily available metaphors. The poem "Vertraute Weise" (Familiar Manner), for example, contrasts the moon as a natural phenomenon with _moon_ as a lyrical metaphor. The moon, like all of nature, indifferently looks down upon human longings and remains unattainable: "Was gilt's ihm, daß/ich wunder was/in seinem Antlitz lese" (What matters it to him that/I read a world/in his countenance).

In _Ironische Miniaturen_ (1960), a collection of 200 miniessays on the relationship between art and reality, the reader, politics, and ossified social structures, Kessel defends the autonomy of art against the infringement of doctrinaire ideologies. For him, art is the continuing attempt to impose order on a confusing reality and, thus, to build a counterreality. Art can, in this way, direct the reader or viewer toward new realizations not constrained by social or political opinions. In such a process, art makes use of those areas where the individual possesses an identity as yet unviolated. Kessel calls these areas the "Glückslöcher" (niches of happiness) of society. From them, strength for the future can flow, countering the petrification of the present. Autonomous art thereby receives a utopian impulse, which may affect reality.

Kessel's epigrammatic poetry, collected in _Kopf und Herz_ (Head and Heart, 1963), puts forward his conviction that even today the individual has the power to shape his own life. This point is addressed in the brief poem "Also": "Ermiß es!/ Wie es is/is es./Friß es!" (Judge it!/It is/as it is./Take it!) By no means is this poem a call to pure opportunism: it challenges the reader to look upon reality appraisingly, but then to be willing to take the consequences of this act of freedom, be they good or bad.

With _Lydia Faude_ (1965), Kessel caused a scandal in Berlin. He had obviously touched the narcissism and egomania of the daydreamers and undiscovered geniuses living in his neighborhood. The novel satirizes dilettantish idealism which crumbles in the face of crime and reality. In expectation of an enormous inheritance, Lydia indulges freely in plans to bring happiness to mankind, in which schemes she is actively supported by her pseudoartistic neighbors. By exploiting Lydia's grotesque disregard for reality, however, an international spy and drug-peddling ring cheats her out of the fortune. Lydia's cherished dreams evaporate while her pragmatic sister Alice, using the financial support of an admirer, opens a fashionable boutique. Kessel skillfully combines elements of the thriller and "higher" literary genres, thereby emphasizing the triviality of Lydia's idealized cultural aspirations. The language of the novel also supports this intention, drawing alternately on the jargon of the underworld, the Berlin dialect, and the elevated diction of classical drama. Kessel spoke of *Lydia Faude* as the "weibliche Gegenstück" (female counterpart) of *Herrn Brechers Fiasko*, but this description is not entirely accurate: the language in *Lydia Faude*, despite its satiric undercurrent, is gentler and less overtly reproachful than that in *Herrn Brechers Fiasko*. In addition, the emphasis has clearly been shifted in favor of Alice, the winner. Unlike Dr. Geist, she is a likeable figure whose success is not resented by anyone. Kessel also presents more clearly the positive influence the twisted ideals of the title figure have on the more pragmatic characters: Alice's clothing designs and her consequent success are inspired by the atmosphere created by Lydia; the exposure of the drug syndicate is set in motion by a lovesick young man whose passion Lydia does not reciprocate.

By the end of the 1960s Kessel's eye ailment had debilitated him to such an extent that he was practically unable to continue with his literary activities. He donated his unpublished works, including an unfinished novel, poems, short stories, and letters, to the Schiller Nationalmuseum in Marbach. His publications since then, apart from the poetry collection *Alles lebt nur, wenn es leuchtet* (Everything Lives Only When It Shines, 1971), are all revised versions of works that had appeared previously. *Ehrfurcht und Gelächter* (Reverence and Laughter, 1974) made Kessel's literary essays, which had been published in various periodicals, accessible once again. In a review, Hans Mayer praised the book's clarity of thought and precise language, calling it "Brot für freudige Leser" (bread to delight the reader). Kessel uses the biographies of Max Stirner, Christian Dietrich Grabbe, and Frank Wedekind as examples of how the insufficient separation of ideals and reality can bring about a personal disaster, a fiasco, but simultaneously be the source of all creative powers. After expounding on a variety of subjects ranging from Laurence Sterne and Nikolai Gogol to film, satire, and sports, Kessel finishes with an acknowledgment of life as "Dasein" (being), of the joy of life as an adventure that finds its highest expression in art.

The most striking feature of Kessel's best works is his view of life not as a martyrdom or a barren wilderness but as a gift and his ability to bring this view across to the reader in an unsentimental fashion. One can only hope that Wilhelm Emrich's wish for Kessel's eightieth birthday will be fulfilled: "Mögen Mit- und Nachwelt endlich seinen Rang begriefen" (May his contemporaries as well as his successors finally recognize his stature).

**References:**
Richard Drews, "Anläßlich eines Bandes Aphorismen," *Weltbühne*, 4 (1949): 388-389;

Wilhelm Emrich, "Literarisches Gewissen," *Der Tagesspiegel* (Berlin), 14 April 1981, p. 4;

Joachim Günther, "Martin Kessel 80," *Neue Deutsche Hefte*, 28 (1981): 221-223;

Hans Hennecke, "Martin Kessel," in his *Dichtung und Dasein* (Berlin: Henssel, 1950), pp. 238-241;

Wilhelm Lehmann, "Wie dem auch sei: Zu Martin Kessels Gesammelten Gedichten," in his *Sämtliche Werke*, volume 3 (Gütersloh: Mohn, 1962), pp. 319-321;

Hans Mayer, Review of *Ehrfurcht und Gelächter*, *Frankfurter Allgemeine Zeitung*, 31 August 1974;

Fritz Usinger, "Martin Kessel," in his *Miniaturen* (Merzhausen: Uhu-Presse Heizmann, 1980), pp. 145-150.

# Hermann Kesten
(28 January 1900-    )

## Helga Rudolf
*Marianopolis College*

BOOKS: *Josef sucht die Freiheit: Roman* (Potsdam: Kiepenheuer, 1927); translated by Eric Sutton as *Josef Breaks Free* (London: Constable, 1930);

*Admet: Ein Drama in zwei Akten* (Berlin: Kiepenheuer, 1928);

*Maud liebt Beide: Eine Komödie für die andern. Drei Akte* (Berlin: Kiepenheuer, 1928);

*Babel; oder, Der Weg zur Macht: Drama in drei Akten* (Berlin: Kiepenheuer, 1929);

*Die Liebes-Ehe* (Berlin: Kiepenheuer, 1929);

*Ein ausschweifender Mensch: Das Leben eines Tölpels: Roman* (Berlin: Kiepenheuer, 1929);

*Wohnungsnot; oder, Die heilige Familie: Schauspiel in drei Akten* (Berlin: Kiepenheuer, 1929);

*Einer sagt die Wahrheit: Komödie in drei Akten* (Berlin: Kiepenheuer, 1930);

*Glückliche Menschen: Roman* (Berlin: Kiepenheuer, 1931); translated by Edward Crankshaw as *Happy Man! A Novel* (London: Lane, 1935; New York: Wyn, 1947);

*Wunder in Amerika: Mary Baker Eddy*, by Kesten and Ernst Toller (Berlin: Kiepenheuer, 1931); translated as *Mary Baker Eddy* in *Seven Plays, by Ernst Toller* (London: Lane, 1935);

*Der Scharlatan: Roman* (Berlin: Kiepenheuer, 1932);

*Der Gerechte: Roman* (Amsterdam: De Lange, 1934);

*Ferdinand und Isabella: Roman* (Amsterdam: De Lange, 1936); translated by Crankshaw as *Spanish Fire: The Story of Ferdinand and Isabella* (London: Hutchinson, 1937); translation republished as *Ferdinand and Isabella* (New York: Wyn, 1946); German version republished in two parts; part 1: *Um die Krone: Der Mohr von Kastilien* (Munich: Desch, 1952); part 2: *Sieg der Dämonen, Ferdinand und Isabella: Roman* (Munich: Desch, 1953);

*König Philipp der Zweite: Roman* (Amsterdam: De Lange, 1938); translated by Geoffrey Dunlop as *I, the King* (London: Routledge, 1939; New York: Alliance, 1940); German version republished as *Ich, der König: Philipp der Zweite.*

(Ullstein)

*Roman* (Munich: Desch, 1950);

*Die Kinder von Gernika: Roman* (Amsterdam: De Lange, 1939); translated by Dunlop as *The Children of Guernica: A Novel* (New York: Alliance, 1939);

*Copernicus and His World*, translated by E. B. Ashton and Norbert Guterman (New York: Roy, 1945; London: Secker & Warburg, 1945); German version published as *Copernicus und seine Welt: Biographie* (Amsterdam: Querido, 1948);

179

*The Twins of Nuremberg: A Novel,* translated by Ashton and Andrew St. James (New York: Fischer, 1946); German version published as *Die Zwillinge von Nürnberg: Roman* (Amsterdam: Querido, 1947);

*Die fremden Götter: Roman* (Amsterdam: Querido, 1949);

*Casanova* (Munich: Desch, 1952); translated by James Stern and Robert Pick as *Casanova* (New York: Harper, 1955);

*Meine Freunde die Poeten* (Vienna & Munich: Donau, 1953; expanded, Munich: Kindler, 1959);

*Ein Sohn des Glücks: Roman* (Munich, Vienna & Basel: Desch, 1955);

*Mit Geduld kann man sogar das Leben aushalten: Erzählungen* (Stuttgart: Reclam, 1957);

*Oberst Kock und andere Novellen* (Amsterdam, 1957);

*Dichter im Café* (Munich, Vienna & Basel: Desch, 1959);

*Der Geist der Unruhe: Literarische Streifzüge* (Cologne & Berlin: Kiepenheuer & Witsch, 1959);

*Bücher der Liebe. Die Romane: Josef sucht die Freiheit; Glückliche Menschen: Die Kinder von Gernika; Die fremden Götter,* introduction by Erich Kästner (Munich, Vienna & Basel: Desch, 1960);

*Gotthold Ephraim Lessing: Ein deutscher Moralist* (Mainz: Verlag der Akademie der Wissenschaften und der Literatur, 1960);

*Die Abenteuer eines Moralisten: Roman* (Vienna, Munich & Basel: Desch, 1961);

*Filialen des Parnaß: 31 Essays* (Munich: Kindler, 1961);

*Die 30 Erzählungen* (Munich: Kindler, 1962);

*Lauter Literaten: Porträts, Erinnerungen* (Vienna, Munich & Basel: Desch, 1963);

*Gesammelte Werke in Einzelausgaben,* 13 volumes (Munich: Desch, 1966-1974);

*Die Zeit der Narren: Roman* (Munich: Desch, 1966);

*Die Lust am Leben: Boccaccio, Aretino, Casanova* (Munich: Desch, 1968);

*Ein Optimist; Beobachtungen unterwegs* (Munich, Vienna & Basel: Desch, 1970);

*Hymne für Holland* (Bonn: Kulturabteilung der königlichen niederländischen Botschaft, 1970);

*Ein Mann von sechzig Jahren: Roman* (Munich: Desch, 1972);

*Heine im Exil* (Cologne: Kölnische Gesellschaft für Christlich-Jüdische Zusammenarbeit, 1972);

*Revolutionäre mit Geduld* (Percha am Starnberger See: Schulz, 1973);

*Ich bin der ich bin: Verse eines Zeitgenossen* (Munich & Zurich: Piper, 1974);

*Ausgewählte Werke in 20 Einzelbänden,* 20 volumes (Frankfurt am Main: Ullstein, 1980-1984);

*Dialog der Liebe: Novellen* (Frankfurt am Main: Ullstein, 1981);

*Der Freund im Schrank: Novellen* (Frankfurt am Main: Ullstein, 1983).

OTHER: *24 neue deutsche Erzähler,* edited by Kesten (Berlin: Kiepenheuer, 1929);

*Neue französische Erzähler: Das Buch des jungen Frankreich,* edited by Kesten and Felix Bertaux (Berlin: Kiepenheuer, 1930);

Julien Green, *Leviathan,* translated by Kesten and Gina Kesten (Berlin: Kiepenheuer, 1930);

Emmanuel Bove, *Ein Verrückter,* translated by Kesten and Gina Kesten (Berlin: Kiepenheuer, 1931);

Jules Romain, *Der Kapitalist,* translated by Kesten (Berlin: Kiepenheuer, 1931);

Henri Michaux, *Meine Güter,* translated by Kesten and Gina Kesten (Berlin: Kiepenheuer, 1931);

Jean Giraudoux, *Die Abenteuer des Jérôme Bardini,* translated by Kesten and Gina Kesten (Berlin: Kiepenheuer, 1932);

*Novellen deutscher Dichter der Gegenwart,* edited by Kesten (Amsterdam: De Lange, 1933);

Ernst Toller, *Briefe aus dem Gefängnis,* edited by Kesten (Amsterdam: Querido, 1933);

René Schickele, *Heimkehr,* foreword by Kesten (Strasbourg: Brant, 1939);

Heinrich Heine, *Meisterwerke in Vers und Prosa,* edited by Kesten (Amsterdam: Forum, 1939);

John Gunther, *So sehe ich Asien!,* translated by Kesten (Amsterdam: De Lange, 1940);

*Heart of Europe: An Anthology of Creative Writing in Europe, 1920-1940,* edited by Kesten and Klaus Mann (New York: Fischer, 1943);

Heine, *Works of Prose,* edited by Kesten (New York: Fischer, 1943);

Heine, *Germany: A Winter's Tale,* edited by Kesten (New York: Wyn, 1944);

Stephen Vincent Benét, *Amerika,* translated by Kesten (New York: Overseas Editions, 1945);

*The Blue Flower: Best Stories of the Romanticists,* edited by Kesten (New York: Roy, 1946); German version published as *Die blaue Blume: Die schönsten romantischen Erzählungen der Weltliteratur* (Cologne: Kiepenheuer & Witsch, 1955);

Émile Zola, *The Masterpiece,* edited by Kesten (New York: Howell, Soskin, 1946);

Irmgard Keun, *Ferdinand,* foreword by Kesten (Düsseldorf: Droste, 1950);

E. B. White, *New York,* translated by Kesten (Frankfurt am Main: Fischer, 1954);

Kurt Tucholsky, *Man sollte mal. . . : Eine Auswahl*, edited by Kesten (Frankfurt am Main: Büchergilde Gutenberg, 1955);

Joseph Roth, *Werke in 3 Bänden*, edited by Kesten, 3 volumes (Cologne: Kiepenheuer & Witsch, 1956);

*Unsere Zeit: Die schönsten deutschen Erzählungen des zwanzigsten Jahrhunderts. Eine Anthologie*, edited by Kesten (Cologne: Kiepenheuer & Witsch, 1956);

Erich Kästner, *Gesammelte Schriften in sieben Bänden*, foreword by Kesten, 7 volumes (Frankfurt am Main: Büchergilde Gutenberg, 1958);

René Schickele, *Werke in 3 Bänden*, edited by Kesten and Anna Schickele, 3 volumes (Cologne & Berlin: Kiepenheuer & Witsch, 1959);

*Unsere Freunde, die Autoren*, introduction by Kesten (Munich, Vienna & Basel: Desch, 1959);

Nico Jesse, *Menschen in Rom*, introduction by Kesten (Gütersloh: Mohn, 1960);

Heinrich Heine, *Prosa*, edited by Kesten (Munich & Zurich: Droemer, 1961);

Gotthold Ephraim Lessing, *Werke*, edited by Kesten (Cologne & Berlin: Kiepenheuer & Witsch, 1962);

*Die wirkliche Welt: Realistische Erzähler der Weltliteratur. Eine Anthologie*, edited by Kesten (Cologne: Kiepenheuer & Witsch, 1962);

*Europa heute: Prosa und Poesie seit 1945. Eine Anthologie*, edited by Kesten, 2 volumes (Munich: Kindler, 1963);

*Deutsche Literatur im Exil: Briefe europäischer Autoren 1933-1949*, edited by Kesten (Vienna, Munich & Basel: Desch, 1964);

Klaus Mann, *Kindernovelle*, edited by Kesten (Munich: Nymphenburger Verlagshandlung, 1964);

*Ich lebe nicht in der Bundesrepublik*, edited by Kesten (Munich: List, 1964);

Joseph Roth, *Briefe 1911-1939*, edited by Kesten (Munich: Desch, 1970).

The twenty-eight-year-old Hermann Kesten received honorable mention at the awarding of the prestigious Kleist Prize in 1928 for his first novel, *Josef sucht die Freiheit* (1927; translated as *Josef Breaks Free*, 1930), the first of many honors that would be bestowed upon him for his achievements in literature. Kesten's fourteen novels and eight volumes of shorter works, including essays, biographies, short stories, and novellas, attest to his prodigious energies and also reveal a writer critical of his time, consistently outspoken in his defense of the freedom of the individual. He has edited anthologies of German and French authors; an exile himself during the Nazi period, he has organized the publications of other writers in exile. He has been an active member of many literary organizations, notably the German P.E.N. Club.

Kesten's energy has met with a somewhat mixed response. His works have gone through many editions and some have been translated into several languages, and he has been praised by such writers as Thomas Mann, Heinrich Mann, Alfred Döblin, Stefan Zweig, Erich Kästner, and Wolfgang Weyrauch; at the same time he has been treated with indifference by literary critics, who ignore him or mention him only as an essayist and editor and for his work in exile literature. An example of this indifference—particularly toward his novels—is that the only entries for Kesten in *Kindlers Literatur-Lexikon* are *Ein ausschweifender Mensch* (An Anarchist, 1929) and *Die Kinder von Gernika* (1939; translated as *The Children of Guernica*, 1939); even these are perhaps included only because Walter Benjamin and Thomas Mann wrote favorably about them. Kesten had to wait until 1980 to see his collected works published by the Ullstein Verlag in a series of twenty volumes; the last volume appeared in 1984. This definitive edition replaces an earlier publication by the Desch Verlag, which excluded Kesten's work before 1933.

Hermann Kesten, the second of three children, was born in Nuremberg on 28 January 1900 to the Jewish merchant Isidor Kesten and Ida Tisch Kesten. He first studied law and economics, then history, philosophy, and German literature, in Erlangen and Frankfurt. In 1923, after losing the manuscript of his dissertation on Heinrich Mann, he dropped his studies and traveled through Europe and Africa.

In 1926 the *Frankfurter Zeitung* and the journal *Jugend* published some of his short stories, essays, and novellas. In 1927 he became literary editor for the vanguard Kiepenheuer Verlag, a Berlin publisher specializing in antiwar literature. His success in this position coincided with his first success as a novelist. *Josef sucht die Freiheit* was written in a few weeks in 1927 and serialized in the *Frankfurter Zeitung* before being published in book form. Thirteen-year-old Josef Bar lives in one room with his promiscuous mother, two sisters, and a charming but thoroughly immoral uncle. When he learns their appalling secrets, he runs away to his socialist father under the illusion that he will now be free. The title of the novel announces Kesten's main concerns, which are expressed in his essays as well as in his fiction: personal freedom and integrity of the individual. This novel advocates freedom from the family; other works call for freedom from conventions, institutions, the church, and the state. In most of his novels Kesten describes deplorable social situations and abuse of power, particularly in dictatorships; but his characters seem only to a limited degree to be products of their milieu. They are above all products of their own weaknesses. In all the novels, and increasingly so in the later ones, there is a gap between the characters' ideals and the reality of their lives. A change of social systems will not solve the individual's problems; totalitarian systems, however, cause a deterioration in the individual's condition. This theme was to become the focus of Kesten's historical novels written in exile.

*Josef sucht die Freiheit* was intended as the first volume of a trilogy to be entitled "Das Ende eines großen Mannes" (The End of a Great Man). In the second volume, *Ein ausschweifender Mensch*, Bar, now twenty years old, tries to free himself from all social ties—to become "ein entschlossener Rebell" (a determined rebel). Kesten abandoned the idea of writing a third volume; apparently he could not envisage the end of his character.

In 1928 Kesten married Toni Warowitz, whom he knew from Nuremberg. During his Berlin years, Kesten met many writers, some of whom became his lifelong friends: among them were Kästner, Josef Roth, Ernst Toller, Klaus Mann, and Heinrich Mann. With Toller he wrote the play *Wunder in Amerika* (1931; translated as *Mary Baker Eddy*, 1935). He also wrote other plays, short stories, novellas, essays for newspapers and journals, and two novels. In the novel *Glückliche Menschen* (1931; translated as *Happy Man!*, 1935) Kesten depicts misery and corruption in the Weimar Republic. The question "What is happiness?" finds a sardonic answer: happiness is money, power, and high social standing—not love, as the hero, Max Blattner, had believed. "Unglück ist Talentlosigkeit, ist ein Charakterfehler, ist der Ruin der Menschheit" (Unhappiness is lack of talent, weakness of character, the ruin of mankind).

While his first novels had met with immediate success and were translated into several languages, the last novel of Kesten's Berlin period, *Der Scharlatan* (1932) was perceived as too complicated. Kesten, though he is at his satirical best, provides too many allusions, parodies, and paradoxes, too many details and characters. The novel deals with the "gewöhnlichsten Menschen von der Welt" (the most ordinary human being in the world), who has the ambition of forcing his will upon everybody

around him. The "charlatan" Albert Stifter achieves his goal through swindling, manipulation, and murder. The social and economic system of the Weimar Republic, together with the weaknesses of his victims, allow Stifter's rise to power. These were timely insights on the eve of Hitler's takeover.

As a literary editor, Kesten published works by Roth, Heinrich Mann, Franz Kafka, Gottfried Benn, and Anna Seghers. In the anthology *24 neue deutsche Erzähler* (24 New German Writers, 1929), he compiled stories by writers of the "Neue Sachlichkeit" (New Objectivity) movement. He also acted as an advocate for French literature: with his sister Gina, he translated works by Henri Michaux, Jules Romains, Jean Giraudoux, and Julien Green; he also edited the anthology *Neue französische Erzähler* (New French Writers, 1930).

Upon Hitler's rise to power, Kesten had to go into exile. On 2 March 1933 he read from his newest novel, *Der Gerechte* (The Just, 1934), on a Berlin radio station, then left Germany for Holland. His books were among those burned by the Nazis. Kesten was appointed literary editor of the newly founded German section of the Allert de Lange Verlag in Amsterdam, which developed under his guidance into a major publishing house for German writers in exile. In the years that followed, Kesten commuted between Amsterdam, Paris, and the refuge that Thomas and Heinrich Mann had established at Sanary-sur-Mer. He later rented a house in Nice which he shared with Heinrich Mann and Roth. He recorded some of their thoughts and conversations about their situations as exiles in *Filialen des Parnaß* (Branches of Parnassus, 1961). His most important achievement as an editor was the publication of Heine's *Meisterwerke in Vers und Prosa* (1939). In his own fiction, he abandoned the German scene from which he was cut off and turned to the history of Spain. The novels *Ferdinand und Isabella* (1936; translated as *Spanish Fire: The Story of Ferdinand and Isabella*, 1937) and *König Philipp der Zweite* (1938; translated as *I, the King*, 1939) depict the rise of Spain as a world power in the fifteenth and sixteenth centuries. Kesten describes the origin and development of a dictatorship in which the masses are oppressed by terror; the only escape from this totalitarian regime is exile. His novels serve as a diagnosis and prognosis of what was to happen to the Jews and to the opponents of Hitler's rule in Germany. King Philip states: "Der Einzelne ist gefährlich. Man muß den Einzelnen töten. Die Völker widerstehn nicht der Macht von uns Königen. Nur der Einzelne widersteht" (The individual is dangerous. One must kill the individual. The people do not resist the power of us kings. Only the individual resists). Hendrik Willem Van Loon offered a contemporary comment on *I, the King:* "It seems like the final word upon the hideous and age-old problem of man's tyranny over man. In writing this book, Hermann Kesten has done well by the country of his adoption. In addition, he has richly deserved the gratitude of those in every part of the world who still believe that the personal freedom and integrity of the individual are the beginning and end of happiness for a truly civilized people." These two novels are among Kesten's most important and most successful works. Both works appeared in many editions and were adopted by European book clubs. In 1952 Kesten divided *Ferdinand und Isabella* into two volumes, giving the first volume the title *Um die Krone: Der Mohr von Kastilien* (For the Crown: The Moor of Castile); the second volume was titled *Sieg der Dämonen, Ferdinand und Isabella* (Victory of the Demons, Ferdinand and Isabella, 1953). These volumes were afterward published along with *Ich, der König* (I, the King, 1950)—the new title of *König Philipp der Zweite*—as a trilogy.

Contemporary Spain is the setting for *Die Kinder von Gernika*, which depicts the suffering of children after the bombing of Guernica during the Spanish civil war. Thomas Mann declared this novel a high point in Kesten's writings but criticized the style as too elegant to be appropriate for its fifteen-year-old narrator.

After France declared war on Germany in September 1939, Kesten became an "undesirable alien" and was interned for five weeks in the concentration camps of Nevers and Colombes. He was able to leave France for New York in May 1940, and his wife and other family members followed shortly thereafter.

During his American exile Kesten divided his time between writing, translating, and editing. Seeing it as his responsibility to expose American readers to the great works of European literature, he undertook the publication in English of Heine's works, Émile Zola's *The Masterpiece* (1946), and of two anthologies: *Heart of Europe: An Anthology of Creative Writing in Europe, 1920-1940* (1943), which was coedited by Klaus Mann, and *The Blue Flower: Best Stories of the Romanticists* (1946). During the war Kesten and Thomas Mann acted as honorary advisers for the Emergency Rescue Committee; among the many European artists they helped to immigrate to the United States were Heinrich Mann, Alfred Döblin, Marc Chagall, and Bertolt Brecht.

The two novels written during Kesten's years in the United States are critical portrayals of their time. *The Twins of Nuremberg* (translation, 1946; original German version, *Die Zwillinge von Nürnberg*, 1947) tells the adventurous and at times grotesque story of a family against the background of German history between 1919 and 1945. Kesten later characterized the novel as a "Zeitbild eines aus den Fugen gegangenen Jahrhunderts mit lauter aus den Fugen gegangenen Typen" (portrayal of a century fallen to pieces with nothing but characters who have fallen to pieces). Through the device of separated twins, he is able to show simultaneously conditions inside Germany and among exiles in France, with emphasis on the latter. His own experience is rendered in detail in the description of the concentration camp at Colombes. *Die fremden Götter* (The Alien Gods, 1949) deals with a conflict caused by religious fanaticism. During the Nazi period a father who has rediscovered his Jewish faith tries in vain to convert or "free" his daughter from Catholicism. Kesten later commented that the gods destroy believers and their families and that religions created for peace are responsible for wars; in fact, gods turn into devils. The novel represents a powerful statement against "die anmaßenden Religionen" (the presumptuous religions).

Kesten returned to historical themes with two biographies, *Copernicus and His World* (translation, 1945; original German version, *Copernicus und seine Welt*, 1948) and *Casanova* (1952). For all his historical works he researched his topics thoroughly; he confesses that he enjoyed these studies so much that they sometimes made it hard for him to settle down to his task of writing. *Copernicus and His World*, which was adopted by book clubs and became a best-seller, concludes with chapters on Giordano Bruno and Isaac Newton. In *Casanova* Kesten recognizes the Italian adventurer as a brilliant writer who provided an exhaustive account of half a century. Kesten sees Casanova as one of the great representatives of world literature.

In 1949, shortly after becoming American citizens, Kesten and his wife visited Europe for the first time since 1933. Until 1977 the Kestens lived in modestly furnished apartments in New York and Rome. Kesten loves the anonymity of big cities and the impersonality of apartment buildings. As a result of his experiences he does not want to become too attached to his neighborhood; he always wants to be ready to move.

During and after World War II Kesten was a prominent spokesman for exile literature. Many exiled writers owe the publication of their works to Kesten, among them Roth, René Schickele, and Kurt Tucholsky. He collected several volumes of letters by European authors as documents of their experiences in exile. Again and again in his articles he returned to the problems of writers in exile. He still sees a need for this work, because "Zur Zeit des Dritten Reiches war die ganze deutsche Literatur im Exil, der deutsche Geist war im Exil" (At the time of the Third Reich the whole of German literature was in exile, the German intellect was in exile).

Kesten has collected his essays on literary, political, moral, and religious questions in six volumes. Particularly well received by German readers was *Meine Freunde die Poeten* (My Friends the Poets, 1953), nineteen portraits of authors to whom Kesten felt close, including Rabelais, Zola, and Mark Twain, as well as Kesten's contemporaries. Often considered Kesten's most beautiful book, the work contains a revealing portrayal of Heinrich Mann. More portraits are published in the volume *Lauter Literaten: Porträts, Erinnerungen* (Nothing but Literary Figures: Portraits and Reminiscences, 1963). *Dichter im Café* (Poets in Coffee-Houses, 1959) describes the history of famous cafés in Vienna, Munich, Rome, London, Paris, and Berlin which have been meeting places for writers and artists. Kesten has done much of his own writing in cafés, which, he says, provide a mixture of solitude and companionship needed by the artist.

Kesten's literary production since the 1950s includes several collections of short stories and novellas and four novels. All the volumes of short prose contain both new and earlier pieces. In the foreword to his edition of Roth's work, Kesten stated, "Die gesammelten Werke können einen Autor erschaffen, bekräftigen oder erledigen" (The collected works can create an author, can confirm or destroy him). His own collected works confirm Kesten as a writer in defense of truth, justice, and individual freedom. As he stated in his acceptance speech for the Büchner-Preis in 1974, "Ich habe nie um der Kunst willen geschrieben, sondern nur der Wahrheit wegen, oder wegen der Gerechtigkeit" (I have never written for arts' sake but only for truth or for justice). His work also documents his satiric talent and the sardonic humor with which he criticizes human weakness, particularly in its twentieth-century manifestations.

Kesten's novel *Ein Sohn des Glücks* (A Son of Good Fortune, 1955) depicts a modern version of Casanova, the adventurer and seducer. That the main character actually wants to be a decent, respectable person is typical of the gap between ideals and reality that has preoccupied Kesten throughout his writing. This novel, like most of Kesten's later works, contains many erotic details; love, sexuality, and eroticism play a role in his earlier novels but have become increasingly important. *Die Abenteuer eines Moralisten* (The Adventures of a Moralist, 1961), the story of a thirty-year love relationship, depicts life during the Third Reich.

When the novel *Die Zeit der Narren* (The Time of the Fools) appeared in 1966, parts of it had already been published as short stories: "Der Freund im Schrank" (The Friend in a Closet, 1957) and "Professor Kalb" (1962). The episodic structure of the novel reinforces the chaotic situation in postwar Germany against which the careers of three friends unfold. The story starts in 1949 and ends in 1965, the period of Germany's reconstruction, and shows the personal problems that result from too much success and a past that has not been assimilated. Kesten also touches on the problems faced by survivors of concentration camps. The author's critique of his era sometimes results in exaggerated statements, as in his polemic on the abolition of capital punishment in the Federal Republic of Germany: "The death penalty has been abolished since murder has officially spread in Germany. Every tenth larger family had at least one murderer among its members after 1945 who could have received the death penalty. Now capital punishment has been abolished. After the war, of course." Such comments, found particularly in his essays, earned him enemies among colleagues he attacked, including Ernst Jünger and Gottfried Benn.

In *Ein Mann von sechzig Jahren* (A Man of Sixty, 1972), which Cornelius Schnauber calls Kesten's "most mature and erotically wildest novel," four characters reveal their relationships with each other and indirectly reveal themselves. The background presents a summary of contemporary history of the last fifty years. The four monologue chapters expose the characters' feelings, experiences, and desires, particularly sexual desires. This emphasis on feelings and thoughts had not been so pronounced in any of Kesten's other works. In earlier works, especially in his short fiction, his failure to portray people's interior lives often made their actions seem strange, even grotesque. The female protagonist in *Ein Mann von sechzig Jahren* is typical of Kesten's image of women. Most of his female characters have particularly strong erotic appetites: in *Josef sucht die Freiheit* the mother and two sisters are shown as promiscuous; in *Die Kinder von Gernika* a mother can completely forget her family and indulge in her sexual desires. In *Ein Mann von sechzig Jahren* his view culminates in the statement: "Bei vielen Frauen sitzt ihre Seele in der Klitoris" (In many women their soul is located in their clitoris).

With this novel Kesten's writing has come to at least a temporary halt. An autobiography which he has been writing for years has not yet been published.

In 1972 Kesten became president of the German P.E.N. Club; he became honorary president in 1976. He is also a corresponding member of the Akademie der Wissenschaften und der Literatur (Academy of Sciences and Literature), Mainz; a member of the Deutsche Akademie für Sprache und Dichtung (German Academy for Language and Literature), Darmstadt; and a member of the Verband der deutschen Schriftsteller (Association of German Writers). After his wife died in 1977, he moved to Basel, where he now lives.

While Kesten's contribution as a novelist and moralist remains to be assessed, his accomplishments as an editor, critic, essayist, and biographer are undisputed. This fact is reflected in the many honors bestowed upon him, including the Culture Prize of the City of Nuremberg in 1954; the Premio Calabria in 1969; the Georg Büchner Prize in 1974; the creation of the Hermann Kesten Prize by the publishing house R. S. Schulz in 1975; the Culture Prize of the City of Dortmund and the Nelly Sachs Prize in 1977; honorary doctorates from the University of Erlangen-Nuremberg in 1978 and from the Free University of Berlin in 1982; and creation of the Hermann Kesten Medal by the German P.E.N. Club, awarded for outstanding work on behalf of persecuted authors, in 1985.

**References:**

Herbert Ahl, "Geist der Unruhe—Hermann Kesten," in his *Literarische Portraits* (Munich & Vienna: Langen-Müller, 1962);

Horst Bienek, "Hermann Kesten," in his *Werkstattgespräche mit Schriftstellern* (Munich: Hanser, 1962), pp. 152-163;

Paul E. H. Lüth, *Literatur als Geschichte: Deutsche Dichtung von 1885 bis 1947* (Wiesbaden: Limes, 1947), pp. 461-463, 526;

Marcel Reich-Ranicki, "Hermann Kesten und seine Essays," in his *Deutsche Literatur in Ost und West: Prosa seit 1945* (Munich: Piper, 1963), pp. 263-268;

Reich-Ranicki, "Immer noch im Exil," in his *Literarisches Leben in Deutschland. Kommentare und Pamphlete (1961-1965)* (Munich: Piper, 1965), pp. 262-269;

Cornelius Schnauber, "Hermann Kesten: Zuerst der Mensch, dann die Gesellschaft," in *Zeitkritische Romane des 20. Jahrhunderts: Die Gesellschaft in der Kritik der deutschen Literatur*, edited by Hans Wagener (Stuttgart: Reclam, 1975), pp. 146-166;

Walter Seifert, "Exil als politischer Akt: Der Romancier Hermann Kesten," in *Die deutsche Exilliteratur 1933-1945*, edited by Manfred Durzak (Stuttgart: Reclam, 1973), pp. 464-472;

Hans-Albert Walter, *Deutsche Exilliteratur 1933-1950* (Darmstadt & Neuwied: Luchterhand, 1972).

# Wilhelm Lehmann
*(4 May 1882-17 November 1968)*

David Scrase
*University of Vermont*

BOOKS: *Der Bilderstürmer: Roman* (Berlin: Fischer, 1917);

*Die Schmetterlingspuppe: Roman* (Berlin: Fischer, 1918);

*Weingott: Ein Roman* (Trier: Lintz, 1921);

*Vogelfreier Josef: Novelle* (Trier: Lintz, 1922);

*Der Sturz auf die Erde: Erzählung* (Trier: Lintz, 1923);

*Der bedrängte Seraph: Novelle* (Stuttgart, Berlin & Leipzig: Deutsche Verlagsanstalt, 1924);

*Die Hochzeit der Aufrührer* (Berlin: Fischer, 1934);

*Antwort des Schweigens* (Berlin: Widerstandsverlag, 1935);

*Der grüne Gott: Ein Versbuch* (Berlin: Müller, 1942);

*Entzückter Staub* (Heidelberg: Schneider, 1946);

*Verführerin, Trösterin und andere Erzählungen* (Heidelberg: Schneider, 1947);

*Bewegliche Ordnung: Aufsätze* (Heidelberg: Schneider, 1947; revised, Berlin & Frankfurt am Main: Suhrkamp, 1956);

*Bukolisches Tagebuch aus den Jahren 1927-1932* (Fulda: Parzeller, 1948);

*Noch nicht genug* (Tübingen: Heliopolis, 1950);

*Mühe des Anfangs* (Heidelberg: Schneider, 1952);

*Ruhm des Daseins: Roman* (Zurich: Manesse, 1953);

*Dichterische Grundsituation und notwendige Besonderheit des Gedichts* (Mainz: Akademie der Wissenschaften und der Literatur, 1953);

*Überlebender Tag: Gedichte aus den Jahren 1951 bis 1954* (Düsseldorf & Cologne: Diederichs, 1954);

*Der stumme Laufjunge: Vier Erzählungen* (Munich: Piper, 1956);

*Dichtung als Dasein: Poetologische und kritische Schriften* (Hamburg: Wegner, 1956);

*Meine Gedichtbücher: Zum fünfundsiebzigsten Geburtstag von Wilhelm Lehmann* (Frankfurt am Main: Suhrkamp, 1957);

*Erfahrungen mit Gedichten* (Mainz: Akademie der Wissenschaften und der Literatur, 1959);

*Kunst des Gedichts* (Frankfurt am Main: Insel, 1961);

*Abschiedslust: Gedichte aus den Jahren 1957 bis 1961* (Gütersloh: Mohn, 1962);

*(Ullstein)*

*Sämtliche Werke*, 3 volumes (Gütersloh: Mohn, 1962);

*Gedichte*, edited by Rudolf Hagelstange (Stuttgart: Reclam, 1963);

*Dauer des Staunens* (Gütersloh: Mohn, 1963);

*Der Überläufer* (Gütersloh: Mohn, 1964);

*Sichtbare Zeit: Gedichte aus den Jahren 1962-1966* (Gütersloh: Mohn, 1967);

*Gedichte*, edited by Karl Krolow (Frankfurt am Main: Suhrkamp, 1977);

*Michael Lippstock*, edited by David Scrase (Stuttgart: Akademischer Verlag, 1979);

*Gesammelte Werke in acht Bänden*, 3 volumes published (Stuttgart: Klett-Cotta, 1982-1985).

OTHER: Theodor Storm, *Meistererzählungen*, edited by Lehmann (Zurich: Manesse, 1956);

Alma Heismann, *Sonette einer Liebenden,* foreword by Lehmann (Heidelberg & Darmstadt: Schneider, 1957);

*Moritz Heimann: Eine Einführung in seine Werke und eine Auswahl,* edited by Lehmann (Wiesbaden: Steiner, 1960);

*Märchen der deutschen Romantik,* afterword by Lehmann (Düsseldorf & Cologne: Diederichs, 1960);

Oskar Loerke, *Gedichte,* edited by Lehmann (Frankfurt am Main: Fischer, 1968).

Wilhelm Lehmann was born in 1882, the same year as those giants of modernism James Joyce, Virginia Woolf, Georges Braque, and Igor Stravinsky. He died in 1968, the year of student revolt. Although he was a modern poet, he was too steeped in the German mystical tradition of Meister Eckhart, Jakob Böhme, Spinoza, Goethe, and the romantics to be far in advance of neoromanticism. As for politics, he was so far removed from the realities of state affairs as to remain an engaging *ingénu,* and the developments of 1968 were certainly as foreign to him as were the ominous trends and events of the years prior to 1914: on 3 August 1914 he wrote his mother, "Seit wann existiert dieser 'Panslawismus'?" (How long has this "pan-slavism" been around?). His long career as a writer was interrupted by both world wars, and he rose twice to considerable prominence only to fall twice into almost total oblivion. He enjoyed the esteem of such widely differing fellow writers as Hermann Hesse, Gottfried Benn, and Werner Kraft; he is now generally acknowledged one of the founders of German poetic Magic Realism; and yet—such is the esoteric nature of his work—he is read by only a few discerning kindred spirits. He was awarded some of Germany's highest literary prizes, including the Kleist Prize in 1923, the Lessing Prize in 1953, and the Schiller Prize in 1959. The development of German poetry over the past half-century and more would not have been the same without him, for his influence was crucial in the work of Elisabeth Langgässer, Günter Eich, Karl Krolow, Heinz Piontek, and Peter Huchel.

Lehmann was born in Puerto Cabello, Venezuela, in 1882. His father, Friedrich Lehmann, an iron merchant, was given to drink and womanizing; his mother, Agathe Wichmann Lehmann, the daughter of a doctor, was bent on bourgeois respectability and the outward trappings of material success. Lehmann grew up in Wandsbek in Schleswig-Holstein with his mother after his parents' early separation. An intelligent, capable, but some-times diffident schoolboy, he began writing poetry in his late teens; none of these juvenilia survive. His earliest extant poems stem from his student days and do not reveal great precocious talent. It is therefore all the more remarkable that his latent genius should have been recognized and nurtured by Moritz Heimann, a reader in the S. Fischer publishing house, who not only encouraged the aspiring poet but also served as a father figure and confidant. Heimann often dipped deep into his pockets to help Lehmann, who was chronically in financial trouble until well into his thirties.

Prior to his year at Berlin University in 1901-1902, during which his friendship with Heimann blossomed, Lehmann had studied at Tübingen in 1900 and at Strasbourg in 1900-1901. Although his studies lacked clear direction, a tendency toward language and philology is discernible. After Berlin Lehmann went to Kiel, where he obtained a doctorate in comparative linguistics in 1905. Upon graduation Lehmann became a schoolteacher at a series of public and private institutions. His first publications were scholarly in nature and appeared from 1906 to 1912 in philological journals. His love of Ireland, which inspired him to learn Gaelic, is manifested in a number of brief essays on Irish matters and a few short translations of Yeats. His linguistic interests were important for his later fiction and poetry.

In his first semester at Kiel, the shy and inhibited twenty-one-year-old Lehmann had fallen in love with Martha Wohlstadt, a woman of striking beauty some fifteen years his senior. They were married on 10 February 1906. They had two sons, Clemens Joachim and Berthold, the first of whom died in infancy. With Lehmann's passion for Frieda Riewerts, one of his older pupils, already aroused, he and Martha separated in 1911 and were divorced in 1912. Lehmann married Frieda on 2 October 1913, and in her he found a partner who took over all the tasks of a practical nature which had been beyond the capabilities of Lehmann and Martha. Lehmann's marriages are recounted faithfully in his fiction, from the ethereal lyricism of his first published story, "Cardenio and Celinde" (1912), to the more expressionistically inclined novels and longer tales of 1914 to 1934.

By 1914 Lehmann had been teaching for two years at the Freie Schulgemeinde Wickersdorf. By all accounts he was a good teacher, even though he regarded his profession as a mere means of livelihood, a necessary evil: teaching, he said in a letter to Heimann, was "meistens mit Holz auf Eisen schlagen" (usually a matter of beating iron with

*Lehmann with his father, Friedrich Lehmann, in Puerto Ca-bello, Venezuela, about 1884 (by permission of Agathe Weigel-Lehmann and Generalmusikdirektor Berthold Lehmann)*

*Lehmann's mother, Agathe Wichmann Lehmann (Deutsches Literaturarchiv Bild-Abteilung, Marbach am Neckar)*

*Lehmann's first wife, Martha Wohlstadt, shortly before their marriage in 1906. She was fifteen years older than Lehmann (by permission of Agathe Weigel-Lehmann and Generalmusik-direktor Berthold Lehmann).*

wood). A similar ambivalence was present in other facets of Lehmann's character: his insecurity in personal relationships was balanced by an unequivocal self-confidence in artistic matters; his perception of himself as lacking in love and destined for solitariness weighs against the view of those who knew him as a warm and caring individual; his awkwardness in social intercourse with adults contrasts with a relaxed and easy manner with children.

Lehmann was thirty-two at the outbreak of World War I. He postponed his military service for three years, and, despite the onerous duties connected with teaching in a private, progressive boarding school, he was able to write and publish four works of fiction before the end of the war. "Maleen," a novella written in 1913-1914 but not published until 1918, deals with the unhappy marriage of Jelden Galbraith and Maleen as Jelden attempts to both earn a living and pass his Staatsexamen, which will allow him to teach in the public

school system. This autobiographical, mundane, and superficial plot only thinly veils what now became the basic theme of Lehmann's work: the quest of a person alienated by our divided civilization for a "heile Welt" (unified world or Golden Age). "Maleen" contains stylistic elements which became typical of his fiction for a time: the arbitrary introduction of fairy-tale names and episodes, dreamlike visions, and extremely graphic metaphors.

By June 1914 Lehmann had completed his next novella, *Der bedrängte Seraph* (The Troubled Seraph), and within a year Efraim Frisch had published it in his important journal *Der neue Merkur;* it appeared in book form in 1924. *Der bedrängte Seraph* covers much of the same biographical material as "Maleen" with the character Lachnit Bittersüß corresponding to Lehmann. Bittersüß flees his unhappy domestic situation, however, and at the end of the story marries Joneleit Kemter, a

*Lehmann in 1906 (Deutsches Literaturarchiv Bild-Abteilung, Marbach am Neckar)*

189

*Frieda Riewerts, one of Lehmann's pupils, around 1908. She became Lehmann's second wife in 1913 (by permission of Agathe Weigel-Lehmann and Generalmusikdirektor Berthold Lehmann).*

Michael is called away to the war and is killed by a sniper. His death coincides with the birth of his and Johanna's child, however, and is to be seen as a release into the oneness of cosmic unity rather than as a tragic curtailment of a meaningful life on earth.

By this time Lehmann was quietly attracting the attention of literary Berlin, some of whose critics and writers he met through the Donnerstags-Gesellschaft (Thursday Club). One of these acquaintances, E. R. Weiß, privately and bitterly attacked "Michael Lippstock" for its bizarre imagery. The attack came to Lehmann's attention, and, with Heimann's encouragement, he purged his writing of such excrescences in favor of sober, balanced description. Heimann also urged Lehmann to produce something bigger, and his next three works were—in terms of their length, at least—full novels.

*Der Bilderstürmer* (The Iconoclast, 1917) reflects Lehmann's experiences at the Freie Schulgemeinde Wickersdorf, where he and a few of his

*Lehmann (left) with Moritz Heimann, a reader in the S. Fischer publishing house who served as his father figure and confidant, and an unidentified pupil at Lehmann's school in Wickersdorf circa 1913 (Deutsches Literaturarchiv Bild-Abteilung, Marbach am Neckar)*

sturdy farmer's daughter modeled on Frieda Riewerts. *Der bedrängte Seraph* relies less on autobiographical material than "Maleen" and brings into prominence the central problem of Bittersüß's quest for integration into the cosmos. The work, as Hans Dieter Schäfer puts it, "besitzt in der Metapherfügung eine größere Sicherheit" (is much more confident in its arrangement of metaphors), and is superior to "Maleen" both as a work of fiction and as a web of lyrical imagery.

Lehmann's use of lyrical images as bearers of his fiction's underlying philosophical message reaches an extreme, indeed often bizarre intensity in his novella "Michael Lippstock," which was written in 1914-1915 and published in *Die neue Rundschau* in 1915. Again, the work is largely autobiographical. By now, it would appear, Lehmann had exorcised the ghost of Martha, for she does not appear in the work. Michael Lippstock (Lehmann) does meet his Frieda, however, in the form of Johanna Rothmond. The newly married

*Lehmann in Wickersdorf circa 1915, around the time of the writing of the autobiographical novella "Michael Lippstock" (Deutsches Literaturarchiv Bild-Abteilung, Marbach am Neckar)*

colleagues found themselves in deep opposition to the ideas of the school's founder and sometime head, Gustav Wyneken. Wyneken's views are voiced in the novel by Magerhold, while Lehmann's allies Martin Luserke and Rudolf Aeschlimann are portrayed in the characters Gilbert Mannhardt and Raffael Rinroth; Lehmann's counterpart in the novel is Beatus Leube. The novel deals with the establishment of a progressive boarding school and the ensuing pedagogical and philosophical disagreements among the faculty. Leube and his cohorts view the world subjectively and imaginatively, whereas Magerhold champions the "objektive Geist" (objective intellect) and sees existence in rational, intellectual terms. Leube attempts to find ultimate truth by means of concrete images and specific natural phenomena; Magerhold storms straight to the absolute with no need for images as intermediaries.

*Der Bilderstürmer* received enthusiastic reviews. Oskar Loerke, who was then becoming Lehmann's closest friend, called him an "Erzähler, in dem sich ein großer Dichter ankündigt" (a writer of fiction, in whom a great poet is announced).

Oscar Bie, the longtime editor of *Der neue Rundschau,* was equally complimentary. The young Kurt Pinthus, whose epoch-making anthology of expressionist poetry *Menschheitsdämmerung* (1920) was soon to appear, spoke of "eine neue Ausdrucksmöglichkeit zur Darstellung äußerer und innerer Ereignisse" (a new possibility for the expression of outer and inner events). Given Lehmann's distinctly lyrical talent, Pinthus was of the opinion that the author would remain "eine einmalige Erscheinung" (a unique phenomenon). Lehmann was also heartened by Alfred Döblin's warm response to the work, which was communicated to him personally.

When Lehmann's next novel, written in 1916-1917, was published by the S. Fischer Verlag in 1918, Lehmann had been drafted and was seeing action on the western front. *Die Schmetterlingspuppe* (The Chrysalis) is less often and less obviously autobiographical than his previous works. The hero, Stanislaus Loeski, resigns from his teaching position and travels to Ireland in search of an ideal community where people and nature live in harmony. Although there are indications that such a unified world is still possible in the magical and

*Gustav Wyneken, founder of the Freie Schulgemeinde Wickersdorf and the model for Magerhold in Lehmann's* Der Bilderstürmer *(by permission of Helene Aeschlimann)*

myth-laden landscape of Ireland, Loeski does not find it. He returns bitterly disappointed to Germany, where he unsuccessfully searches for such harmony by working on a farm. Distraught, he kills himself.

All of Lehmann's works to this point are stories of quest. "Maleen" ends with the certainty that one must break with a stultifying past and set off in search of the "heile Welt." The fitting end to this search seems in *Der bedrängte Seraph* to be love and in "Michael Lippstock" to be death as a means of absorption into the cosmos. Beatus Leube's quest in *Der Bilderstürmer* leads him to an ideal educational establishment and a clash with its leader; but at the end, he and Friederike Wesendonck seem destined for a meaningful and unified communal existence in the village of Hollebüttel as they bring up their own and Magerhold's child after the latter dies a violent death. *Die Schmetterlingspuppe* differs markedly from all of Lehmann's previous works in

that there is no suggestion of any possible resolution. This lack of hope probably reflects Lehmann's pessimistic view of life at a time when war was raging and he expected to be drafted and killed at any moment. His response to the war, in contrast to that of many of his literary contemporaries, had never been enthusiastic or patriotic, and when he found himself fighting around Verdun and Cambrai in the last months of the war he determined to desert. His first attempt failed when he lost his bearings and was picked up by one of his own patrols. The second attempt saw him safely taken prisoner by Canadian troops and incarcerated in a British prisoner-of-war camp in France until the end of 1919. After his release, he left the Freie Schulgemeinde Wickersdorf for a job at a less progressive boarding school, the Landschulheim am Solling in Holzminden.

*Weingott,* his next book, does not reflect these events but is Lehmann's most purely fictional novel. Written in 1920-1921 and published in 1921 by the provincial publisher Friedrich Lintz, it tells the story of the history professor Karl Johannes Weingott, whose Weltanschauung corresponds to Lehmann's and, therefore, to that of the heroes of the previous works. The theme of the novel is spelled out in the opening sentence: "Der süße Geist der Gestaltung und der grauenvolle Geist der Gestaltlosigkeit liegen immer miteinander im Kampf" (The sweet spirit of form and the dreadful spirit of formlessness are continually locked in battle). Like Leube in *Der Bilderstürmer,* Weingott advocates a harmony between man and nature—a harmony which, since it no longer exists, must be shaped and formed through a unifying "Blick" (gaze, scrutiny) and which comes through association with concrete images rather than grand abstractions. This idea is examined through the relationships between two sets of characters: those who espouse "Gestaltung" (form) include Weingott, Tieftrunk the musician, Endlicher the botanist, Liebetraut the philosopher, and Marggraf the deranged student; those who favor abstraction are the history professor Dürrlitz and his students Killisch, Bratengeier, Schwink, Lühne, and Bökenstein—their very names attest to the torpid superficiality and deadly infertility of the group. As in *Die Schmetterlingspuppe,* the hero dies, and the divisive forces of abstraction seem victorious. But, as in "Michael Lippstock," Weingott's death is less a severance from life than an absorption into a unified cosmos; and, as in both "Michael Lippstock" and *Der Bilderstürmer,* there is a child pointing to the future.

*Lehmann (left) with his Wickersdorf colleague Willy Bezner during World War I. Lehmann later deserted from his unit and had himself taken prisoner by Allied troops in order to escape the fighting (Deutsches Literaturarchiv Bild-Abteilung, Marbach am Neckar).*

In *Weingott*, then, there is consolidation of the qualities prevalent in Lehmann's earlier works. The quest for a "heile Welt" is central; the role of nature, and imagery taken from nature, is essential; the interplay of human beings is tangential at most; the dialectical engagement of semantic, character, seasonal, and imagistic polarities is omnipresent; and the lyrical tone continues to overwhelm the narrative, fictional qualities. The importance of the overtly autobiographical continues to decline, although some events are taken directly from Lehmann's life. The use of metaphor is more subdued than in "Michael Lippstock" and *Der Bilderstürmer*. The book is more balanced and more unified than its predecessors. But, because of its style, its lack of narrative interest, and its intense lyricism, it was not likely to appeal to a broad readership—especially since the recent war seemed to have finally destroyed that age in which people needed books in order to fill an excess of leisure time. Samuel Fischer's parting words to Lehmann when publisher and poet went their separate ways were en-

tirely accurate: "Für Ihre Bücher haben die Menschen jetzt keine Zeit mehr" (People do not have time for your books anymore).

Lehmann's next two works were the novella *Vogelfreier Josef,* written and published in 1922, and the story *Der Sturz auf die Erde* (The Fall to Earth), written in 1922-1923 and published in 1923. Published in provincial Trier, they were hardly noticed by the critics, and even Heimann's and Loerke's responses were muted.

Conscious of the material benefits a public school would provide, Lehmann moved in 1923 to Eckernförde on the Baltic coast of Schleswig-Holstein. Any hope that life at a public school rather than a private boarding school would be quieter and less demanding of his time and energy proved ill-founded. Lehmann was seized upon by an ambitious director as confidant, amanuensis, and sounding board for new ideas. The resulting frustrations were set down in a bleak, lengthy novel that, when it finally appeared in 1953, was entitled *Ruhm des Daseins* (The Glory of Existence), but was

193

*Cover illustration by A. Paul Weber for Lehmann's 1935
collection of poetry*

which incorporates the harrowing months of his military service, desertion, and captivity as well as many details of his childhood years. Nuch, the hero, is a shy boy brought up by his mother in a strict and respectable bourgeois setting that he hates. His search for a harmonious existence within nature is thwarted by his mother, his pedantic schooling, his disastrous marriage, his more successful second marriage, the war, his subsequent imprisonment, and the postwar society into which he finds it impossible to integrate. Finally, after one of his many "desertions"—flights into solitary communion with nature—he dies. The close correlation of biography and fiction in this work may be verified by comparing it with Lehmann's autobiographical tract *Mühe des Anfangs* (Early Trials, 1952). Most publishers approached before 1933 praised *Der Überläufer* but regretted that the hero's desertion was not acceptable for a bourgeois and patriotic readership. The more crucial factors were left unstated: the work was, typically, intensely lyrical, relatively short on plot, and too demanding. After 1933 Lehmann no longer tried to find a publisher for the novel, knowing that its "un-German" tone precluded the possibility of publication in Nazi Germany. The novel was finally published in 1962 when Lehmann's collected works came out in celebration of his eightieth birthday; it appeared separately in 1964.

Lehmann's next book of fiction, *Die Hochzeit der Aufrührer* (The Marriage of the Agitators), appeared in 1934. Just prior to the publication of this book, he had begun to write poetry again. Throughout the 1920s his long, solitary walks through the fields and woods and along the waters around Eckernförde yielded poetic fruit of rare quality. Unlike his youthful attempts, these poems were not only deeply felt but were written with consummate artistry in impressively controlled form. Published in journals and newspapers, they attracted a considerable following among younger writers such as Eich, Langgässer, Huchel, and Krolow even before their appearance in book form as *Antwort des Schweigens* (The Answer of Silence) in 1935. This slim volume is generally regarded as the best of Lehmann's collections of poems; it contains lyrics that bear eloquent witness to the poet's ability to describe in terse and strikingly new images nature's less spectacular events. There are mythic intrusions, though not so many as in later poems, and the "heile Welt," if not observed in nature, is invariably achieved through the poem. The book received a bad review in the nationalistic periodical *Das innere Reich* but was well received by younger

originally given the more informative title "Der Provinzlärm." (The Provincial Scandal). *Ruhm des Daseins* again depicts the struggle of a hero, Asbahr, as he strives for a meaningful existence as part of nature. He is frustrated in large part because of his profession as a schoolteacher and especially because of the frenetic, fiercely intellectual, and unimaginative director of the school, Lupinus. It proved impossible for years to find a publisher for the novel, but the author's regret was tinged with relief, since he was well aware of the scandal his harshly accurate portrayal of his pompous, puerile colleagues would cause in the conservative community of Eckernförde.

From 1924 to 1927 Lehmann was working on his longest novel, *Der Überläufer* (The Deserter),

*Lehmann in later years (Sigbert Mohn Verlag, Gütersloh)*

poets with no political axes to grind, such as Krolow: "Ich . . . fand mich nach der Lektüre benommen vor Verwunderung und Bewunderung" (After reading this volume . . . I was beside myself with amazement and admiration).

In 1934-1935 Lehmann's eyes, which had never been strong, were threatened by an infection and subsequent detached retina. After several months in the hospital Lehmann emerged blind in his right eye.

Lehmann had, like many public servants, taken the precaution of joining the Nazi party as early as May 1933, yet his diary entries reveal how abhorrent he found the party's ideology. Although never explicitly forbidden to write, he found himself on a list of authors publishers were urged to avoid because *Antwort des Schweigens* had been published by the vehement anti-Nazi Ernst Niekisch's Widerstandsverlag. Despite this semi-proscription, his second collection of poems, *Der grüne Gott* (The

Green God), was published by Otto Müller in 1942. A few more poems were published individually in the few journals and newspapers still printing literature of quality during the later war years. At the end of the war, Lehmann found publishers suddenly receptive to his work, and his various poem collections, together with some minor fiction pieces and other short prose, appeared in rapid succession, establishing Lehmann as one of the most important German poets of his generation. After his retirement from teaching in 1947 he traveled throughout Germany giving poetry readings, and his poems and essays were published in most of the influential journals and newspapers of West Germany. He was a founding member of the Deutsche Akademie für Sprache und Dichtung (German Academy for Language and Literature) in Darmstadt and the recipient of numerous honors and awards, including the Großes Verdienstkreuz des Verdienstordens der Bundesrepublik Deutschland (Great Order of Merit of the Service Order of the Federal Republic of Germany). In the 1960s Lehmann was again forgotten; only about 900 copies of his 1962 collected works were sold. After almost half a year of illness he died in November 1968.

**Biographies:**

Heinz Bruns, *Wilhelm Lehmann: Eine Chronik* (Kiel: Mühlau, 1962);

Hans Dieter Schäfer, *Wilhelm Lehmann: Studien zu seinem Leben und Werk* (Bonn: Bouvier, 1969);

David Scrase, *Wilhelm Lehmann: A Critical Biography*, Part I (Columbia, S.C.: Camden House, 1984).

**References:**

Oskar Loerke, "Literarische Chronik," *Die neue Rundschau*, 28 (1917): 1284-1285;

Kurt Pinthus, "Der Bilderstürmer," *Zeitschrift für Bücherfreunde*, new series 9 (1917-1918): 421-422;

Werner Siebert, *Gegenwart des Lyrischen: Essays zum Werk Wilhelm Lehmanns* (Gütersloh: Mohn, 1967).

**Papers:**

Wilhelm Lehmann's unpublished diaries and correspondence are in the Deutsches Literaturarchiv, Marbach.

# Klaus Mann
### (18 November 1906-21 May 1949)

Ilsedore B. Jonas
*Carnegie-Mellon University*

BOOKS: *Vor dem Leben: Erzählungen* (Hamburg: Enoch, 1925);

*Anja und Esther: Ein romantisches Stück in sieben Bildern* (Berlin: Oesterheld, 1925);

*Der fromme Tanz: Das Abenteuerbuch einer Jugend* (Hamburg: Enoch, 1926);

*Kindernovelle* (Hamburg: Enoch, 1926); translated by Lambert Armour Shears as *The Fifth Child* (New York: Boni & Liveright, 1927);

*Revue zu Vieren: Komödie in drei Akten* (Berlin: Oesterheld, 1926);

*Heute und Morgen: Zur Situation des jungen geistigen Europas* (Hamburg: Enoch, 1927);

*Rundherum: Ein heiteres Reisebuch*, by Mann and Erika Mann (Berlin: Fischer, 1929);

*Gegenüber von China: Komödie in sechs Bildern* (Berlin: Oesterheld, 1929);

*Abenteuer: Novellen* (Leipzig: Reclam, 1929);

*Alexander: Roman der Utopie* (Berlin: Fischer, 1929); translated by Marion Saunders as *Alexander: A Novel of Utopia* (New York: Brewer & Warren, 1930);

*Das Buch von der Riviera*, by Mann and Erika Mann (Munich: Piper, 1931);

*Auf der Suche nach einem Weg: Aufsätze* (Berlin: Transmare, 1931);

*Treffpunkt im Unendlichen: Roman* (Berlin: Fischer, 1932);

*Kind dieser Zeit* (Berlin: Transmare, 1932);

*Flucht in den Norden: Roman* (Amsterdam: Querido, 1934); translated by Rita Reil as *Journey into Freedom* (New York: Knopf, 1936; London: Gollancz, 1936);

*Symphonie Pathétique: Ein Tschaikowsky-Roman* (Amsterdam: Querido, 1935); translated by Hermon Ould as *Pathetic Symphony: A Novel about Tchaikovsky* (London: Gollancz, 1938; revised, New York: Allen, Towne & Heath, 1948);

*Mephisto: Roman einer Karriere* (Amsterdam: Querido, 1936); translated by Robin Smyth as *Mephisto* (New York: Random House, 1977);

*Vergittertes Fenster: Novelle um den Tod des Königs Ludwig II. von Bayern* (Amsterdam: Querido, 1937);

*Escape to Life*, by Mann and Erika Mann (Boston: Houghton Mifflin, 1939);

*Der Vulkan: Roman unter Emigranten* (Amsterdam: Querido, 1939);

*The Other Germany*, by Mann and Erika Mann, translated by Heinz Norden (New York: Modern Age, 1940);

*The Turning Point: Thirty-Five Years in This Century* (New York: Fischer, 1942; London: Gollancz, 1944; revised, New York: Weiner, 1984); German version published as *Der Wendepunkt: Ein Lebensbericht* (Frankfurt am Main: Fischer, 1952);

*André Gide and the Crisis of Modern Thought* (New York: Creative Age, 1943; London: Dobson,

*Klaus Mann (Ullstein)*

1948); German version published as *André
Gide: Die Geschichte eines Europäers* (Zurich:
Steinberg, 1948); revised as *André Gide und die
Krise des modernen Geistes* (Munich: Nymphen-
burger Verlagshandlung, 1966);

*Prüfungen: Schriften zur Literatur,* edited by Martin
Gregor-Dellin (Munich: Nymphenburger
Verlagshandlung, 1968);

*Heute und Morgen: Schriften zur Zeit,* edited by Gregor-Dellin (Munich: Nymphenburger
Verlagshandlung, 1969);

*Die Heimsuchung des europäischen Geistes: Aufsätze,* edited by Gregor-Dellin (Munich: Deutscher
Taschenbuch-Verlag, 1973);

*Abenteuer des Brautpaars: Die Erzählungen,* edited by
Gregor-Dellin (Munich: Edition Spangen-
berg, 1976);

*Woher wir kommen und wohin wir müssen: Frühe und
nachgelassene Schriften,* edited by Gregor-Dellin (Munich: Edition Spangenberg, 1980);

*Mit dem Blick nach Deutschland: Der Schriftsteller und
das politische Engagement,* edited by Michel
Grunewald (Munich: Edition Spangenberg,
1985).

OTHER: *Anthologie jüngster Lyrik,* edited by Mann
and Willi R. Fehse, introduction by Stefan
Zweig (Hamburg: Enoch, 1927);

*Anthologie jüngster Prosa,* edited by Mann, Erich
Ebermayer, and Hans Rosenkranz (Berlin:
Spaeth, 1928);

*Anthologie jüngster Lyrik: Neue Folge,* edited by Mann
and Fehse, introduction by Rudolf G. Binding
(Hamburg: Enoch, 1929);

*Heart of Europe: An Anthology of Creative Writing in
Europe 1920-1940,* edited by Mann and Her-
mann Kesten (New York: Fischer, 1943); re-
published as *The Best of Modern European
Fiction,* introduction by Dorothy Canfield
Fisher (Philadelphia: Blakiston, 1944).

Klaus Mann was not only one of the most
versatile and productive members of the younger
generation of German exile writers but also an author of truly international stature. He is known
primarily for his novels and essays and his biographical portraits of significant historical or artistic figures. Like the novels he wrote during his
exile, his autobiographical writings deal to a large
extent with the problems of the emigration. The
best known of all his books is his most controversial
one: *Mephisto* (1936; translated, 1977), a political
satire which many regard as a brilliant roman à
clef. Through its stage adaptation for the Théâtre

du Soleil in Paris and a successful film version, this
work has reached large audiences throughout the
world.

An early opponent of fascism, Mann was
among the first writers to go into exile. He became
a naturalized citizen of Czechoslovakia in 1937 and
of the United States in 1943. While in exile, he
founded and directed two prestigious journals, *Die
Sammlung* in Amsterdam and *Decision: A Review of
Free Culture* in New York. These journals may be
considered his most important contributions to the
fight against the Third Reich and to the preservation of humanistic values.

Klaus Heinrich Thomas Mann was born in
Munich in 1906, the second of six children of
Thomas and Katia Mann. Between 1906 and 1918
Mann spent his summers in the spacious family
home in Bad Tölz in Upper Bavaria, known to
readers of his first book of memoirs, *Kind dieser Zeit*
(Child of This Time, 1932). While attending the
Wilhelmsgymnasium in Munich, the fourteen-
year-old boy, even then a staunch admirer of the
literary successes of his father and of his uncle,
Heinrich Mann, wrote in his diary: "I must, must,
must become famous."

At the outbreak of the Bavarian Revolution
in November 1918, and with the collapse of the
German Empire of Kaiser Wilhelm II, Mann found
himself in a country plagued by political unrest,
general disillusionment, and the disintegration of
all moral and social values. It was during these troubled times that he first showed an interest in the
stage. Together with his sister Erika, who was a
year older than he, and their friend Richard
("Ricki") Hallgarten, he formed an amateur theatrical group in his hometown. Because their parents believed that conditions in postwar Munich
could not fail to exercise a negative influence, the
two older Mann children were sent away to a Landschulheim, a progressive boarding school in the
country. From April until July 1922 Klaus and Erika attended the Bergschule Hochwaldhausen in
the Röhn mountains not far from Fulda, but Klaus
could not endure the atmosphere of the school.
His parents tried an even more prestigious institution, Odenwaldschule Oberhambach near Heppenheim an der Bergstrasse in the vicinity of
Heidelberg, founded and directed by the well-
known liberal and progressive educator Paulus Geheeb; but Klaus stayed less than a year.

After his return home in the summer of 1923,
Mann was educated by a private tutor. Yearning
for freedom and adventure—not unlike the character Bert in his father's story "Disorder and Early

Sorrow" (1926)—he mingled with people from all walks of life, actors and dancers as well as the children of great writers and artists such as Hugo von Hofmannsthal, Carl Sternheim, Bruno Walter, and Frank Wedekind.

In 1924 Mann decided to devote himself to writing. To the end of his life he was enabled to do so through a monthly stipend from his parents. By September 1924 he was settled in Berlin, where his first story, "Nachmittag im Schloß" (An Afternoon in the Castle), had appeared in the *Vossische Zeitung* on 3 May. Writing anonymously, he contributed theater reviews to *Zwölf-Uhr-Mittagsblatt* and critical essays to *Die Weltbühne.* He and Erika joined Pamela Wedekind and the actor Gustaf Gründgens in forming a theater ensemble; the group performed Mann's first play, *Anja und Esther,* which opened in Hamburg on 20 October 1925. *Anja und Esther* deals with the emotional and psychological problems and conflicts of a group of adolescents in crisis. Its setting, a home for delinquent children, strongly resembles Odenwaldschule, and the character of Der Alte (The Old Man) is satirically modeled after Geheeb.

In 1925 Mann undertook his first major trip abroad, traveling to England, France, Italy, and North Africa. His first book of short stories, *Vor dem Leben* (Before Life), was published the same year. Some of these vignettes, written in a lyrical, dreamlike style, deal with the enigmatic figure of Caspar Hauser—the foundling of noble birth depicted in Jakob Wassermann's 1908 novel—with whose fate Mann felt an intense emotional involvement.

The following year saw the publication of his first full-length novel, *Der fromme Tanz* (The Devout Dance). Set chiefly in Berlin and Paris, the book relates many of the author's experiences during his adolescent crisis. Mann considered his generation a "dancing" one, with the dance taking place on top of a volcano above an abyss; he described the young people of his time as uprooted, forlorn, and pessimistic about their future.

During the same year Mann's *Kindernovelle* was published; a translation appeared in the United States under the title *The Fifth Child* in 1927. The widow of a famous philosopher lives with her four children in seclusion in a village in the Bavarian Alps. One day a young man, an admirer of the philosopher, introduces himself; he becomes the friend of the children and the lover of their mother. After a time he disappears as suddenly as he came, while she awaits in a spirit of exaltation the birth of her fifth child. *The Fifth Child* received a mixed reaction in the American press. "Confused in ideas, formless in structure, anticlimactic in its final impression," wrote Arthur Herman in his review in the *New York Evening Post;* he added, however, that the scenes of the children playing at their imaginative games are quite convincing.

From the very beginning, critics were unusually harsh with Mann. Although his father's prestige granted him certain advantages and helped him to get into print, his name soon proved a handicap. Endless comparisons were made between his youthful writings and the mature achievements of the master storyteller Thomas Mann. Thus, the playwright Bertolt Brecht asked jokingly in an essay: "The whole world knows Klaus Mann, the son of Thomas Mann. By the way, who is Thomas Mann?" The satirical journal *Simplicissimus* published a cartoon showing Klaus Mann saying to Thomas Mann: "You know, of course, Papa, that geniuses never have highly gifted sons. Therefore, you are no genius." Knowing of the difficulties his son was experiencing, Thomas Mann autographed a copy of his novel *Der Zauberberg* (1924; translated as *The Magic Mountain,* 1927) for him with the dedication: "To my respected colleague—his promising father."

*Mann in 1925 (Ullstein)*

Thomas Mann und sein Sohn Klaus (Th. Th. Heine)

„Du weißt doch, Papa, Genies haben niemals geniale Söhne, also bist du kein Genie."

*Cartoon from the magazine* Simplicissimus, *1925. Klaus Mann is saying to Thomas Mann: "You know, of course, Papa, that geniuses never have highly gifted sons. Therefore, you are no genius."*

Mann's second play, *Revue zu Vieren* (Four in a Revue, 1926), was first performed by his own group in Leipzig on 21 April 1927. It was less successful than his previous play. On 7 October 1927 Klaus and Erika, posing jokingly as "the literary Mann twins," set sail on a trip around the world. During their tour of the American continent they lectured at several universities, including Columbia, Harvard, and Princeton, and met H. L. Mencken and Max Reinhardt in New York and Greta Garbo, Upton Sinclair, Ernst Lubitsch, and Emil Jannings in Beverly Hills. There were also reunions with old friends from Europe, such as Hallgarten and Eva Herrmann. Continuing their journey until July 1928, they visited the Hawaiian Islands, Japan, Korea, and the Soviet Union. Upon their return to Germany, they coauthored a charming travel book, *Rundherum* (Round About, 1929), based on their trip. A result of his visit to the East was Mann's third play, *Gegenüber von China* (Op-

posite China, 1929), which was first performed in Bochum on 27 January 1930.

Mann's second novel, *Alexander*, was published in Germany in 1929 and in translation in the United States the following year. Mann portrays Alexander the Great as an inspired man who dreams of unifying the world and making it happy under his rule. "A centrifugal force—irrational and irresistible—seemed to impel Alexander away from the heart of Europe, outward, into the vastness of Asia," Mann said in his autobiography. "Awestruck and enchanted, I followed him on his maniac venture." In 1931 Mann and his sister produced a second travel account, *Das Buch von der Riviera* (The Book of the Riviera).

Mann's novel *Treffpunkt im Unendlichen* (Meeting Place in Infinity, 1932) is a work of transition from the early romantic stories to the more realistic Emigrantenroman (novel of emigration) for which he is best known. Written and published a year before Hitler's rise to power, it is characterized by a feeling of anxiety and oppression on the part of the author, who had been afraid as early as 1931 that the worsening political situation might lead to his own forced departure from Germany. The two main characters—Sebastian, a writer, and his mistress Sonja, a successful actress—bear a strong resemblance to the author and his sister; the principal antagonist, the ambitious dancer Gregor Gregori, is clearly modeled after Gründgens. The complex, high-strung Richard Darmstaedter also resembles Mann in many ways. Darmstaedter's life ends with his suicide on the Côte d'Azur after the breakup of a homosexual relationship.

In his slim 1932 volume of memoirs, *Kind dieser Zeit,* Mann reports with insight and understanding the problems he confronted in his youth: the crisis of the middle class, the chaos and uncertainty of the postwar years, and his conflicts with the older generation in general and with his father in particular.

On 13 March 1933 Mann left Nazi Germany for Paris, then moved on to Amsterdam. He spent much of the next five years in these two cities not far from the German border, visiting and revisiting such favorite places as Prague, Zurich, and Budapest, where he underwent treatment in a sanatorium for drug addiction. After he lost his German citizenship in November 1934, the Dutch authorities provided him with identification papers as a stateless person until he was granted citizenship in Czechoslovakia in March 1937.

In Amsterdam Mann founded the journal *Die Sammlung* with the help of the German-born publisher Fritz H. Landshoff. *Die Sammlung* was issued in an edition of 3,000 copies between September 1933 and August 1935 by Querido Verlag. Under the sponsorship of André Gide, Aldous Huxley, and Heinrich Mann, this journal—often considered the best literary journal in German at the time—was intended both to introduce the greatest literary talents among the emigrants to the European public and to project a message of hope to those left behind in Nazi Germany. Its contributors included Brecht, Jean Cocteau, Benedetto Croce, Albert Einstein, Christopher Isherwood, Ernest Hemingway, Ernst Bloch, Else Lasker-Schüler, and Boris Pasternak. But several of the writers Mann most wanted to have among his contributors, including Stefan Zweig, declined his invitation, fearing the loss of their German reading public. Even Thomas Mann, then in exile in Switzerland, refused to collaborate with his son on the advice of his publisher, Gottfried Bermann Fischer. Fischer

kept the S. Fischer Verlag in operation in Berlin until 1935, thus enabling Thomas Mann's books to be published in Germany during the first years of the Nazi regime. Under pressure from Joseph Goebbels's Ministry of Propaganda, Fischer objected to the participation of any of his leading authors, including Alfred Döblin and René Schickele in addition to Thomas Mann, in Klaus Mann's venture. "No one of the great names," Klaus Mann complained in a letter to Zweig on 15 September 1933, "is willing to identify himself with those who are fighting. Heinrich Mann is almost the only exception." His father finally declared his solidarity with German writers in exile in "Ein Brief von Thomas Mann" (A Letter from Thomas Mann) in the *Neue Zürcher Zeitung* of 3 February 1936; but Klaus Mann had been forced to discontinue his journal the year before because of financial difficulties.

Mann's novel *Flucht in den Norden,* which was published in Amsterdam in 1934 and as *Journey into Freedom* in London and New York in 1936, was inspired by a trip to Finland Mann and Erika had taken in 1932. A young woman, a Communist, has fled Nazi Germany with her brother and a friend. Intending to join other exiles in Paris in their activities against the Hitler regime, she first travels to Finland, where she falls in love with a man who is unable to understand her political concerns. In the end, she reluctantly leaves her lover to rejoin her comrades in their fight against the Nazis.

The critical reception of *Journey into Freedom* was mixed. Both British and American reviewers found fault with the quality of the translation. Graham Bell suggested in the *New Statesman and Nation* that "the whole thing might have sounded better in German." In the *New York Herald Tribune,* David Ilden considered Mann's theme "an old and powerful one, and one particularly appropriate to the times and conditions with which he deals. His novel, however, is but an indifferent play upon it, and as a story it is singularly dull and amateurish, at least in the English translation." More positive was the reaction of Alfred Kazin; who noted in the *New York Times* that the author "avoided tempting opportunities to go dramatic and heart-wringing. His novel is not extraordinary, but it is well-made and moving, and not its least value is its indication of the dangers and exaltations involved in living thoughtfully in such a world as ours."

The last of Mann's novels to appear in the United States during his lifetime was written in German, despite its French title, *Symphonie Pathétique.* Published in Amsterdam by Querido Verlag in 1935, the translation came out in New York in 1948 under the title *Pathetic Symphony: A Novel about Tchaikovsky*. Mann said in his autobiography that he had long been attracted to the nineteenth-century Russian composer: "I wrote his story because I know all about him. Only too intimately versed in his neurasthenic fixations, I could describe his aimless wanderings, the transient bliss of his elations, the unending anguish of his solitude. . . . He was uprooted, disconnected: that's why I could write his story." The American critic Herbert Kupferberg, writing in the *Herald Tribune*, felt that the novel "makes no particularly outstanding contribution to the ample literature on Tchaikovsky," but admitted that "those who like to read about him will find 'Pathetic Symphony' a leisurely and skillful retelling of a familiar story." Far more critical was Gretchen Finletter's review in the *Saturday Review of Literature*: "When Klaus Mann superimposes his own thoughts and conversations as belonging to Tchaikovsky, he achieves a book which has neither the reality of a creation of character nor the reality of an honest biography." The most favorable review appeared in the *New Yorker*: "In addition to presenting all the verifiable facts of the composer's life, the author attempts to give some idea by means of frequent interior monologues of what the hero was thinking about when he sat down at the piano."

In 1936 Mann's *Mephisto: Roman einer Karriere* (Mephisto: Novel of a Career) appeared in Amsterdam. The novel deals with the life of a talented but vain and ruthless actor who attains a position of power and influence during the Third Reich. Within a short time of its publication, this "satirical-political novel," as the author called it, became the most controversial of all of Mann's books. Its central character, Hendrik Höfgen, bears an unmistakable resemblance to Gründgens, who had been married to Erika Mann from 1926 to 1929 and had been one of Mann's closest friends. When the novel was serialized in the *Pariser Tageszeitung*, the editors referred to it as a roman à clef. Mann vehemently took issue with this term: "It was *not* my purpose to tell the story of a particular person when I wrote 'Mephisto.' It was my purpose to portray a *type*, and along with it the various milieus, the sociological and intellectual preconditions which made its success possible in the first place." Many years later, however, Mann admitted that he had indeed intended to portray Gründgens in this novel: "Gustaf Gründgens, hitherto a flamboyant champion of Communism, made a staggering career under the auspices of Field Marshal Hermann Göring. Before long Gustaf was appointed manager of the State

Theater and thus became the leader of theatrical life in the Third Reich. I visualize my ex-brother-in-law as the traitor par excellence, the macabre embodiment of corruption and cynicism. So intense was the fascination of his shameful glory that I decided to portray Mephisto-Gründgens in a satirical novel. I thought it pertinent, indeed, necessary to expose and analyze the abject type of the treacherous intellectual who prostitutes his talent for the sake of some tawdry fame and transitory wealth."

After World War II Mann tried in vain to have the book reprinted in West Germany, but his efforts failed as long as Gründgens was alive. Gründgens died in 1963, long after Mann's death in 1949; but in 1971, at the end of a ten-year lawsuit brought by Gründgens's adopted son Peter Gorski-Gründgens, the highest court in the Federal Republic of Germany barred the publication of *Mephisto* in the country. In the German Democratic Republic, on the other hand, the book had been published by Aufbau Verlag in Berlin in 1956. It was only after a long court battle and the appearance of two books documenting the controversy that a paperback edition was published in 1981 by Edition Spangenberg in Munich. *Mephisto* became an immediate best-seller. A stage version by the French writer Ariane Mnouchkine was successfully performed by the Théâtre du Soleil in Paris and also abroad. Istvan Szabo's Hungarian-German film, with Klaus Maria Brandauer playing the German actor who sells his soul to the devil, won the Academy Award for Best Foreign Film in 1981.

Most of the reviews appearing at the time of the novel's publication in the United States in 1977 were positive. "Mann's portrait of evil is sinister and expert, the story is fascinating" was the commentary of *Publishers Weekly*. Inge Judd, writing in the *Library Journal*, called the book "a complex, fast-paced novel in a successful translation." The reviewer for *Booklist*, on the other hand, thought that the novel had not withstood the passage of time: "Most of the pertinent associations unfortunately won't connect except in a very general way for modern readers; moreover, the period has been so well documented in recent film and literature that the shock value has worn pretty thin."

Mann's novella *Vergittertes Fenster* (Barred Window, 1937) is an intimate portrayal of Bavaria's King Ludwig II, Richard Wagner's most generous patron, in the last stages of insanity. According to Mann, Ludwig was "a royal martyr and madman whose sombre glamor had seized my imagination when I was still a child. I remembered what the nurses and cooks had told us about his tragedy, rather than what I had subsequently read in historic reports and treatises. His prodigious castles—monumental whims scattered all over Bavaria—belonged to the mythic language of my childhood."

In the fall of 1936 Klaus and Erika Mann returned to the United States for a four-month lecture tour, traveling from coast to coast to warn the American public against the danger of fascism in Europe and describing conditions in Nazi Germany. During a third stay in the United States from September 1937 to February 1938, one of Mann's most successful lectures, "A Family against a Dictatorship," dealt with the activities and political involvement of his own family. In June and July 1938, Klaus and Erika reported on the Spanish Civil War in a series of articles in the *Pariser Tageszeitung.*

On 25 September 1938 Mann finally immigrated to the United States. Dividing his time between New York and his parents' home in Princeton, New Jersey, he soon accepted a suggestion from Houghton Mifflin for a book to be written with his sister. *Escape to Life* (1939), a collection of sketches written in English, gives a vivid picture of immigrants to the United States, such as Einstein, Reinhardt, and Rudolf Serkin, who had suf-

fered under Hitler's regime. The volume opens with an epigraph by Dorothy Thompson: "Practically everybody who in world opinion has stood for what was currently called German culture prior to 1933, is now a refugee."

In 1939 Querido Verlag in Amsterdam published *Der Vulkan: Roman unter Emigranten* (The Volcano: A Novel among Emigrants), in which Mann attempted to create a panoramic view of life among German emigrants between 1933 and 1938. A chronicle of the author's own generation and a study of the history and sociology of German emigration, the novel reports the fates of a number of lonely, homeless, uprooted exiles driven into an uncertain future in a foreign land. The characters seem to be intended more as types than as portraits of individuals; nevertheless, the central character, Martin Korella, a frustrated writer who gradually loses confidence in his talent, bears a striking resemblance to the author. The novel concerns Korella's attempt to write a novel about the problems of emigration set in Paris, Prague, Zurich, Amsterdam, and New York. In the end, Korella commits suicide after losing his battle against drug addiction, while the central female character, Marion von Kammer—modeled after Erika Mann—becomes an inspiration to everyone around her be-

*Mann and his sister Erika, with whom he traveled extensively and coauthored several books*

cause of her strength of character. She is able to adjust to adverse conditions and eventually finds happiness at the side of an intellectual who loves and understands her. The strange figure of Kikjou, inspired by Cocteau, especially impressed Thomas Mann. Writing from the Netherlands on 22 July 1939, he congratulated his son on the novel: "Since I have had it, I have written various people to call their attention to the book seriously and to ask them to do something for it because it is really a first-rate thing which is only too naturally being neglected by a world caught up in stupidity and malice." The following day he added: "I read it through all the way, with emotion and gaiety, enjoyment and satisfaction, and more than once with deep sympathy. For a long time people did not take you seriously, regarded you as a spoiled brat and a humbug; there was nothing I could do about that. But by now it cannot be denied that you are capable of more than most—this is the reason for my satisfaction as I read; and my other feelings had their good reasons also."

The following year, *The Other Germany*, a collection of lectures on Nazi Germany given by Klaus and Erika Mann in the United States since 1937, was published. "Europe's Youth," the authors stress in their foreword, "has taken to the battlefields lest 'wicked Germany' become the tyrant of the Continent and of the world. First and foremost it is a determined struggle in self-defense—this is its most urgent aspect; but the victory over evil will have true meaning only if the good subsequently will succeed in organizing itself wisely and for all time."

The book's critical reception in the United States was far from enthusiastic. "The organization of their material is not faultless," wrote Shepard Stone in the *New York Times*. "It isn't too much to say that Erika and Klaus Mann still have a great deal to learn from their father." No less severe was the judgment of Toni Stolper, writing in the *Saturday Review of Literature*, who concluded that "the two gifted young writers would be well advised if they could spare some time from explaining things to Americans for a thorough study of the origins of Western liberties. Perhaps it would detract something from their trusting faith in the existence today of the 'Other Germany.' "

Since December 1939 Mann had been thinking about founding a political-literary journal in the United States. For several months Mann and his friends proposed titles for the journal, from "Solidarity," "Zero Hour," and "Cross Road" to "New World"; in the end, they agreed on *Decision:*

*A Review of Free Culture.* In the first issue, which appeared in January 1941, Mann stated the journal's purpose: "Social programs, the tenets of philosophy, ethics and aesthetics, the moral import of history, the implications of scientific developments, the aims and the practice of pedagogy—all these must be re-analyzed and tested in the light of recent events. And, above all, the unquenchable flame of creative writing must be permitted to burn on. Young story-tellers want to mirror and clarify the conditions of our life. The mysterious solace and lament of poetry remain as indispensable now as a thousand years ago."

Mann succeeded in winning important writers and artists as contributors to his new magazine, among them Cocteau, Zweig, Walter, Sherwood Anderson, Stephen Vincent Benét, Janet Flanner, Heinrich Mann, W. Somerset Maugham, and Muriel Rukeyser. But the number of subscribers remained extremely limited—at no time were there more than 2,000 subscriptions out of 5,000 copies printed—and by the end of the first year, the future of *Decision* was in doubt. The last issue, for January/February 1942, contained Thomas Mann's essay "Richard Wagner and the *Ring of the Nibelungen*." Notwithstanding the fame of its contributors and Thomas Mann's efforts to raise funds for the expensive venture—donations had been received from Thomas Quinn Curtiss, Bruno Frank, Max Ascoli, and Erich von Kahler—the financial difficulties had proven insurmountable. This failure was one of the greatest disappointments in Klaus Mann's entire career, and for a while he was in a state of deep depression.

As a kind of therapy, Mann completed in June 1942 his autobiography, *The Turning Point*, which he had begun the previous summer. Written in English, it was published in September by L. B. Fischer in New York. This self-analysis was intended, according to Mann's diary of 11 August 1941, "to tell the truth, the whole truth, and nothing but the truth. To tell my own story. To tell the story of an intellectual in the period from 1920 to 1940—a character who spent the best time of his life in a social and spiritual vacuum; striving for a true community but never finding it; disconnected, restless, wandering; haunted by those solemn abstractions in which nobody else believes—civilization, progress, liberty. To tell the story of a German who wanted to be a European; of a European who wanted to be a citizen of the world. Of an individualist equally opposed to standardization and anarchy."

Of all his books published in the United States, this one received the most critical acclaim. Charles Neider in the *New Republic* hailed it as an autobiography "which is, in the best sense, original and charming and which is the detailed account of Klaus Mann's quest for what was necessary to him and his own pattern." In the *Saturday Review of Literature*, Leo Lania considered Mann at his best in this work when describing his childhood and family life, whereas he found those chapters less successful "in which the author tries to give an interpretation of the political and social evolution of the period between the two wars and of the postwar generation." W. C. Kernan, writing in the *Churchman*, considered Mann a penetrating observer: "what he sets forth is not so much his own life as it is the life of his generation." Like other critics, Kernan praised the portrayal of Thomas Mann in the book: "One sees the rich, mellow personality of this great literary master first in Munich, then in exile near Zurich and later at Princeton. The reader leaves Klaus Mann preparing to enlist in the American Army, eager to fight for the return of the civilized Europe which he appreciated so keenly." The German version of *The Turning Point*, *Der Wendepunkt*, which appeared in Frankfurt in 1952, had been revised and greatly expanded by Mann between 1947 and 1949.

In the summer of 1942, while waiting in the Pacific Palisades, California, home of his parents for his induction into the United States Army, Mann wrote *André Gide and the Crisis of Modern Thought* (1943). In the *New York Herald Tribune Weekly Book Review*, Albert Guérard praised the book because of the author's "personal acquaintance, talent, sympathy. He sends us back to the works of Gide with clearer sight and a more understanding heart. I do not believe that genuine criticism could have a higher purpose." Ernst Boyd in the *New York Times* considered the book an "excellent study" and was convinced that "this distinguished son of a distinguished father is obviously not to rest on the laurels of a family name, but is achieving his own destiny in a most original fashion." The reviewer for the *New Yorker* called the book an "admiring but perceptive study of a great master, in which his subtle relation to his period is admirably demonstrated." Margaret Meagher, writing in *Catholic World*, pointed out Mann's "remarkable command of English and . . . unusually rich, wide-ranging vocabulary for a foreigner." Although she admitted that "his acquaintance with modern European literature seems to be considerable," she deplored his lack of solid learning in

attributing a volume of confessions to St. Thomas Aquinas.

On 6 September 1942 Mann reported in New York for a physical examination, but was rejected by the army. For several weeks he was in a state of deep depression. Finally, on 14 December he was examined again and accepted. After basic training in New Jersey and Arkansas, Mann was transferred in April 1943 to the First Mobile Radio Broadcasting Company stationed in Maryland, where he was promoted to staff sergeant. When his company was sent to Europe on 1 May, he had to stay behind because he was not yet a U.S. citizen; he had hoped to be naturalized in Baltimore on 30 April, but was suspected by the F.B.I. of being homosexual and a "fellow traveler." He was transferred to a unit at Camp Crowder, Missouri, where he was given a public relations assignment, contributing articles to the camp newspaper and lecturing to soldiers and civilians. On 25 September the thirty-six-year-old Klaus Henry Mann—as he was called on his naturalization certificate—became a U.S. citizen in the Circuit Court of Newton County, Missouri. On 24 December his fondest wish was fulfilled when he was sent overseas, landing on 2 January 1944 in Morocco. Assigned to the psychological warfare

*Mann in 1949 (Thomas Mann Archiv, Zurich, Switzerland)*

branch of military intelligence, Mann took part in the invasion of Italy; one of his comrades, Peter Viereck, recalled that he behaved "with competence and bravery." He spent most of the summer of 1944 in Rome. On 10 August he applied for a discharge from the army, hoping to be allowed to do newspaper or radio work as a civilian in the U.S. occupation zones of Germany or Austria, but his request was turned down. On 31 December the first of some forty-five articles he had written within a six-month period appeared in the official army newspaper, *Stars and Stripes*. It was as a staff writer for the paper that he was sent to occupied Germany early in May 1945—his first visit to his former homeland since 1933. He saw his parents' Munich home, half destroyed by bombs, and interviewed Jannings, Field Marshal Göring, and the composer Richard Strauss.

After his discharge from the army on 28 September 1945, a period of disappointments and emotional instability began. Mann was unsuccessful in having his play *Der siebente Engel* (The Seventh Angel, 1945) performed in Europe; he also found it difficult to reestablish himself as a writer, feeling estranged from both his native country and his adopted one. Early in 1946 he started translating his monograph on Gide into German, revising parts of it. *André Gide: Die Geschichte eines Europäers* (André Gide: The Story of a European) appeared in Zurich in 1948.

During 1946 and 1947 Mann delivered lectures in German and English on American literature and culture in Germany, Switzerland, Denmark, Sweden, the Netherlands, and other countries. Returning to the United States, he settled in Santa Monica, not far from his uncle Heinrich's and his parents' Pacific Palisades homes. In March 1948 he traveled to Prague. Upon his return to the United States, the death wish that had been with him for most of his adult life became increasingly stronger. On 11 July 1948 he made a suicide attempt that was widely reported in the American press. Several of his friends, among them Vicki Baum, tried to give him moral support. "Don't do it," Sinclair wired him, "you have written fine books and you can do a most important job in helping to interpret Europe to America and vice versa." In August, Mann's old friend Landshoff secured for him a part-time position with the Bermann Fischer/ Querido Verlag in Amsterdam, but in his restlessness Mann gave up the job after a few months.

Early in 1949 Mann returned to Europe. Deeply disturbed by the increasing discord between the ideologies of East and West, he made a last desperate plea to the European intellectuals to bring about progress and harmony among peoples in his essay "Europe's Search for a New Credo," which appeared in the journal *Tomorrow* in June 1949.

Lonely, unhappy, and frustrated, he took an overdose of sleeping pills in Cannes on 21 May 1949. He is buried in the Cannes cemetery.

His old friend Isherwood, to whom he had dedicated *Symphonie Pathétique*, remembered him as "bitterly lonely, despite his many friends and the affection of a large, closely-knit family. A wanderer himself, he was temperamentally drawn to other wanderers, the confused, the lost, the astray. I believe that he helped many of them, but they could give him little in return. He found no permanent companion on his journey. Klaus had fought and worked so hard, achieved so much, inspired so many people by his example. In forty years, he had suffered and experienced enough for a long lifetime. No wonder if he grew utterly weary. He had certainly earned the right to take his rest."

**Letters:**

*Briefe und Antworten*, edited by Martin Gregor-Dellin, 2 volumes (Munich: Edition Spangenberg, 1975);

"André Gide—Klaus Mann, Ein Briefwechsel," edited by Michel Grunewald, *Revue d'Allemagne*, 4 (1982): 581-682.

**Bibliography:**

Michel Grunewald, *Klaus Mann 1906-1949: Eine Bibliographie* (Munich: Edition Spangenberg, 1984).

**Biographies:**

Uwe Naumann, *Klaus Mann mit Selbstzeugnissen und Bilddokumenten* (Reinbek: Rowohlt, 1984);

Michel Grunewald, *Klaus Mann 1906-1949* (Bern & Frankfurt am Main: Lang, 1985).

**References:**

Peter T. Hoffer, *Klaus Mann* (Boston: Twayne, 1978);

Frederic Kroll and Klaus Täubert, *Klaus-Mann-Schriftenreihe*, 3 volumes (Wiesbaden: Edition Blahak, 1976-1979);

Erika Mann, ed., *Klaus Mann zum Gedächtnis* (Amsterdam: Querido Verlag, 1950);

Berthold Spangenberg, *Mephisto: Die Entscheidung des Bundesverfassungsgerichts und die abweichende Richtermeinung* (Munich: Edition Spangenberg, 1971);

Eberhard Spangenberg, *Karriere eines Romans: Mephisto, Klaus Mann und Gustaf Gründgens* (Munich: Edition Spangenberg, 1982);

Rudolf Wolff, ed., *Klaus Mann: Werk und Wirkung* (Bonn: Bouvier, 1984);

Stefan Zynda, *Sexualität bei Klaus Mann* (Bonn: Bouvier, 1986).

**Papers:**

Klaus Mann's papers were donated by his mother, his brother, and his sisters in 1973 to the City Library of Munich. Its rapidly growing Klaus-Mann-Archive contains his books and manuscripts, his personal library, translations of his works, his private correspondence, and a pictorial record of his life. The correspondence concerning his journal *Decision* is in the Yale University Library. His private diaries are still being kept under lock and key by his heirs.

---

# Agnes Miegel
*(9 March 1879-26 October 1964)*

Katharina Aulls
*McGill University*

BOOKS: *Gedichte* (Stuttgart: Cotta, 1901; revised and enlarged as *Frühe Gesichte* (Stuttgart: Cotta, 1939);

*Balladen und Lieder* ( Jena: Diederichs, 1907);

*Gedichte und Spiele* ( Jena: Diederichs, 1920);

*Geschichten aus Alt-Preußen* ( Jena: Diederichs, 1926);

*Heimat: Lieder und Balladen*, edited by Karl Plenzat (Leipzig: Eichblatt, 1926);

*Die schöne Malone: Erzählung* (Leipzig: Eichblatt, 1926);

*Gesammelte Gedichte* ( Jena: Diederichs, 1927);

*Spiele* ( Jena: Diederichs, 1927);

*Die Auferstehung des Cyriakus; Die Maar: Zwei Erzählungen*, edited by Plenzat (Leipzig: Eichblatt, 1928); republished as *Das Osterwunder; Die Maar: Zwei Erzählungen* (Leipzig: Eichblatt, 1936);

*Kinderland: Heimat- und Jugenderinnerungen*, edited by Plenzat (Leipzig: Eichblatt, 1930);

*Dorothee; Heimgekehrt: Zwei Erzählungen* (Königsberg: Gräfe & Unzer, 1931); enlarged as *Noras Schicksal: Erzählungen* (Königsberg: Gräfe & Unzer, 1936);

*Heinrich Wolff* (Königsberg: Gräfe & Unzer, 1932);

*Herbstgesang; Neue Gedichte* ( Jena: Diederichs, 1932);

*Die Fahrt der sieben Ordensbrüder* ( Jena: Diederichs, 1933);

*Der Vater: Drei Blätter eines Lebensbuches* (Berlin: Eckart, 1933);

*Kirchen im Ordensland: Gedichte* (Königsberg: Gräfe & Unzer, 1933); enlarged as *Ordensdome: Gedichte* (Königsberg: Gräfe & Unzer, 1941);

*Weihnachtsspiel* (Königsberg: Gräfe & Unzer, 1934);

*Gang in die Dämmerung: Erzählungen* ( Jena: Diederichs, 1934);

*Die Mutter: Dank des Dichters*, by Miegel, J. Wittig, and others (Berlin: Eckart, 1934);

*Die Schlacht von Rudau: Eine Szenenfolge* (Königsberg: Landesverein für freie Volksbildung und Wohlfahrtspflege in Ostpreußen, 1934);

*Der Augenblick: Sechs Erzählungen*, by Miegel, Otto Gmelin, and others (Berlin: Eckart, 1935);

*Das alte und das neue Königsberg* (Königsberg: Gräfe & Unzer, 1935);

*Deutsche Balladen* ( Jena: Diederichs, 1935);

*Unter hellem Himmel* ( Jena: Diederichs, 1936);

*Katrinchen kommt nach Hause: Drei Erzählungen*, edited by Plenzat (Leipzig: Eichblatt, 1936);

*Audhumla* (Königsberg: Gräfe & Unzer, 1937); republished as *Herden der Heimat* (Königsberg: Gräfe & Unzer, 1944);

*Das Bernsteinherz: Erzählungen* ( Jena: Reclam, 1937);

*Und die geduldige Demut der treuesten Freunde . . . Nächtliche Stunde mit Büchern* (Ebenhausen: Langewiesche-Brandt, 1938);

*Meine alte Lina* (Hannover: Feesche, 1938);

*Viktoria: Das Erlebnis des Feldwebels Schmidtke* (Leipzig: Gesellschaft der Freunde der Deutschen Bücherei, 1938);

*Herbstabend: Eine Novelle um die heilige Elisabeth zu ihrem 700. Todestag 1931* (Eisenach: Privately printed, 1939);

*Ostland: Gedichte* ( Jena: Diederichs, 1940);

*Im Ostwind: Erzählungen* ( Jena: Diederichs, 1940);

*Wunderliches Weben: Zwei Erzählungen* (Munich: Langen & Müller, 1940);

*Hausbuch der deutschen Jugend,* by Miegel, Josef Weinheber, and Bruno Brehm, edited by August Friedrich Velmede (Berlin: Junge Generation, 1941);

*Die gute Ernte* (Berlin: Junge Generation, 1942);

*Mein Bernsteinland und meine Stadt* (Königsberg: Gräfe & Unzer, 1944);

*Du aber bleibst in mir: Flüchtlingsgedichte* (Hameln: Seifert, 1949);

*Die Blume der Götter: Erzählungen* (Düsseldorf: Diederichs, 1949);

*Der Federball: Erzählungen* (Düsseldorf: Diederichs, 1951);

*Die Meinen: Erinnerungen* (Düsseldorf: Diederichs, 1951);

*Ausgewählte Gedichte* (Düsseldorf: Diederichs, 1952);

*Gesammelte Werke,* 7 volumes (Düsseldorf: Diederichs, 1952-1955, 1965);

*Truso: Geschichten aus der alt en Heimat* (Düsseldorf: Diederichs, 1958);

*Mein Weihnachtsbuch: Gedichte und Erzählungen* (Düsseldorf: Diederichs, 1959; enlarged, 1978);

*Heimkehr: Erzählungen* (Düsseldorf: Diederichs, 1962);

*Gedichte, Erzählungen, Erinnerungen* (Düsseldorf & Cologne: Diederichs, 1965);

*Gedichte und Prosa,* selected by Inge Diederichs (Düsseldorf: Diederichs, 1977);

*Gedichte aus dem Nachlaß,* edited by Anni Piorreck (Cologne: Diederichs, 1979);

*Alt-Königsberger Geschichten* (Düsseldorf: Diederichs, 1981);

*Es war ein Land: Gedichte und Geschichten aus Ostpreußen,* edited by Ulf Diederichs and Christa Hinze (Cologne: Diederichs, 1983).

OTHER: *Ostpreußens Bernsteinküste,* foreword by Miegel (Königsberg: Gräfe & Unzer, 1934).

(*Ullstein*)

Agnes Miegel, who wrote the most gripping ballads in early modern German literature, started her career as a poet but later turned to writing short prose works. Her poems and stories appeared in every German school reader and are still being published in new collections. Miegel was deeply rooted in her birthplace, the "Bernstein Küste" (coast of the amber stone) along the Baltic Sea, and her beloved city of Königsberg (now Kaliningrad, U.S.S.R.). This easternmost corner of the German Empire provides the setting for much of her work, which portrays the magic of its people, its history, and its myths. She was thought of as the voice and heart of East Prussia.

Agnes Miegel was born in Königsberg on 9 March 1879 to Gustav Adolf and Helene Wilhelmina Miegel. She was the only child of a middle-class merchant and grew up mostly among adults. When she was fifteen, her parents sent her to a boarding school in Weimar, the city of Goethe, where she was swept up in an atmosphere of enthusiasm for theater and music and started to write poetry in her journals. After a year she was brought home; her ambitious parents wanted her to become an artist and enrolled her in painting classes. Miegel failed to become a painter, but benefited from the training she received in precise observation. She continued to write poems and found the courage to send them to Carl Busse, a respected author and critic, who encouraged her.

In 1898 she went to Paris for several months with a friend. Upon her return she stopped in Berlin to meet a prospective editor, the acclaimed poet Börries von Münchhausen. Seventeen of her ballads and thirteen of her lyric poems appeared in the 1901 issue of his *Göttinger Musenalmanach*. Münchhausen encouraged Miegel to send her work to the famous Cotta publishing house in Stuttgart.

In 1900 Miegel went back to Berlin to be trained as a pediatric nurse. After completing the course, she caught scarlet fever while working in the children's ward. She recuperated at Apelern, the country estate of the Münchhausens, and then went back home, never to practice nursing again. In Berlin she had met Lulu von Strauss und Torney, another young poet and writer of ballads, who was to remain a lifelong friend. Miegel returned to Königsberg with a copy of her first book of poems, *Gedichte* (1901), just published by Cotta.

The collection contains sixty-three poems and twenty-seven ballads. Many of the love poems catered to the contemporary sentiment of "sacred eroticism," but others have a unique personal tone. Some audaciously disregarded taboos: in "The Prayer of a Young Maiden," a girl prays that God will let her lover die if he marries someone else. Miegel's love of her home country runs through many poems, which reveal both dark prophetic visions and a clear sense of reality. The ballads combine simplicity and a compelling rhythm with mythical dimensions. All of the ballads are about historical figures; titles include "Mary Stuart," "Cleopatra," and "The Duchess of Burgundy." Collectively these early poems capture the essence of her later work: immediacy of feeling in the lyrical poetry, and objective detachment and deft craftsmanship in the ballads.

Miegel now found the provinciality of her hometown depressing. Accepting the invitation of a friend who taught German at a boarding school in Bristol, she escaped to England in the fall of 1902. While carrying out the duties of housemother and making frequent visits to London, Miegel devoted much time to writing poetry. While in England she wrote some of her best ballads, in-

*Miegel in 1901, the year her first volume of poetry was published (©1981 by Eugen Diederichs Verlag, Cologne)*

cluding "Jane," "Lady Gwen," and "Die Nibelungen."

In April 1904 she went to Berlin to study for a teaching degree, planning to return to England as a certified teacher; but she soon began to harbor doubts about her vocation. Shortly before completing her degree she became ill and went home; her parents sent her to the Bavarian mountains to recuperate. During her convalescence she frequently visited friends in Munich who exposed her to the city's literary and artistic scene, where she felt utterly out of place. Toward the end of 1906 Miegel was abruptly called home when her mother was put into a mental hospital, where she died three years later. For the following ten years Miegel took care of the household of her father, who was going blind. In letters to friends, Miegel often expressed the frustration she felt in her oppressive situation. But she continued to write.

In 1907 Miegel's *Balladen und Lieder* (Ballads and Songs) was published. The book's twelve lengthy ballads were considered by critics to be of

*Title page by F. H. Ehmcke for Miegel's second collection of poems*

near classical perfection. Some of them, such as "Schöne Agnete" (Beautiful Agnete), have folkloristic elements; three are "nature ballads" that conjure up the world of ancient nature spirits. Some critics called "Die Mär vom Ritter Manuel" (The Tale of the Knight Manuel) *the* best example of a true ballad. The lyrical poems in the collection show maturity; the personal and highly emotional poems of her previous book have given way to more refined and delicate works filled with a sense of resignation.

In 1916 Miegel was awarded the Kleist Prize as the best living German poet. Otherwise the World War I years were marked by the death of her father, frequent illnesses, and a sense of despair and sadness caused by the war. Miegel was depressed by being cut off from the rest of Germany when Western Prussia became part of Poland following the German defeat.

During the thirteen "lost years" of caring for her parents her creative work almost came to a standstill, but in 1920 a small collection of twenty-six poems and five negligible dramatic fragments

was published as *Gedichte und Spiele* (Poems and Plays). The poems reveal a new awareness and perception of self: Miegel looks at herself from a distance and points out the dichotomy of her dual identity as a member of the bourgeois, on one hand, and an artist, on the other. The poems also express the pain she felt when forced to renounce her youth; many of them are full of mourning for lost love. The tone of the collection is one of sadness and ultimate resignation. Some poems are deeply religious; others reveal a newly found identification with her home city, now isolated and vulnerable; still others deal with war and death. Although this volume marked the end of her ballad writing, Miegel continued to be known, through her ballads, as "The Voice of East Prussia."

In 1920 Miegel became a journalist for the *Ostpreußische Zeitung*, covering cultural events. She soon became editor of the "Culture and Literature" section, for which she wrote a weekly column entitled "Childhood Memories." She received an honorary doctorate from the University of Königsberg in 1924. In 1926 health problems forced her to resign from the newspaper.

*Geschichten aus Alt-Preußen* (Stories from Old Prussia), a collection of four stories based on historical facts and myths, was published in 1926. The first story, "Die Fahrt der sieben Ordensbrüder" (The Journey of the Seven Knights of the Teutonic Order), set in Old Prussia and about seventy pages in length, is her longest piece of prose writing and is regarded as her major prose work and was published separately in 1933. Seven knights of the Teutonic Order get lost on a stormy winter night and ask to follow an old man, who is on his way to the residence of the dying Christianized ruler of the pagan natives. After briefly paying tribute to the ruler in the hall where his family is assembled, the knights are fed and assigned sleeping quarters in one of the storehouses. Preparations for the traditional pagan death rites are going on in the kitchen, the baking house, the bathhouse, and the stables. Servants move in and out of the darkness and view the knights either with suspicion or with signs of devotion. Orders are shouted in various Slavic and Baltic tongues. The gates are opened to admit a stream of local peasants assembling for the wake and funeral. As the night progresses, the ritualistic shrieks of the two widows cut through the air (though a Christian, the ruler still took a second wife), the horses and dogs of the dead ruler are turned loose, and chants demand sacrifice for the dead. Miegel briefly sketches and illuminates some faces and happenings, but for the most part leaves the reader (and the knights) in the dark, creating an eerie atmosphere and a premonition of horror to which some of the knights succumb. The next morning the knights find the whole family of the deceased ruler, his servants, and his animals slaughtered. As the knights ride away into a glistening winter morning, they see the residence go up in smoke.

The second story, "Landsleute" (Local People), set during the migration of the Goths, deals with the selling and ravaging of women during tribal wars. It does not reach the level of intensity and symbolic depth of the first tale, but it is a powerful example of storytelling based on history and myth. The next two stories, "Engelkes Buße" (Engelke's penitence), about the raids of the Tartars, and "Der Geburtstag" (The Birthday), about settlers in East Prussia from Salzburg, are lighter in character and move on a more personal level. In all the stories, Miegel's clear and succinct language, sprinkled with expressions unique to East Prussia, has a special flavor. Dialogue alternates with narrative prose that has not lost its balladesque quality.

The book met with great popular success; more than forty newspapers reviewed or mentioned it, with one reviewer writing: "Her first book of prose has become the history book of East Prussia." But it never caught the attention of the literary critics. During the same year other stories that had previously appeared in newspapers were published under the title *Die schöne Malone* (The Beautiful Malone).

The title story concerns a young German woman who has moved to East Prussia with her family and disappears the day before her wedding. The local non-Christian population knows that she has gone to live with "the big father" and will return someday. She does so three generations later to help her family, then disappears forever during a violent lightning storm—a manifestation of "the big father." The saga portrays the supernatural from the perspective of the local people, who accept it in a matter-of-fact way.

*Gesammelte Gedichte* (Collected Poems, 1927) contains twenty-eight of Miegel's previously published ballads; twenty-nine lyrical poems, of which only five are new; and twenty-two new poems about East Prussia. The collection was even reviewed in the *New York Times;* the review concluded: "so stirring a hymn is this, so magnificent a cosmic revelation, that it alone would be sufficient to stamp Agnes Miegel as the greatest German poetess of our time."

Miegel's fiftieth birthday in 1929 was officially celebrated by the city of Königsberg. Newspapers all over Germany honored her work, especially her ballads and poems about East Prussia. Her poetic praise of her homeland and its traditions and history fit in with the political ideology of the rising Nazi party. Each year from 1930 to 1940 saw the publication of individual stories, story collections, new poems, and commissioned work, usually by small publishers. None of the prose works published during these years reaches the depth and mythic quality of "Die Fahrt der sieben Ordensbrüder." They are lighter in tone and are more like the stories published after the war.

Among them there is a collection of eight historical tales, *Gang in die Dämmerung* (Walk in the Twilight, 1934), that portrays small but unusual events. Some are set in ancient times, others draw upon myths of East Prussia. The underlying theme of most stories in the collection is the main character's vision of future happenings. The characters are more clearly defined than in Miegle's earlier works. The most popular of them, "Das Lösegeld" (The Ransom Money), describes the return of East Prussian girls and women bought back from the Tartars who had stolen them during raids ten years previously. Miegel sketches a welcome gone wrong: the cultural shock of the old couple who expect to embrace their young girl but are faced with a mature, fat woman with three children, in the company of a pregnant friend. Christian mores clash with the pagan values of the freed hostages. The women cope with the situation better than the parents, because they have to concentrate their energies on taking care of the children. There is much inner truth to this sensitive portrayal of the reactions of humans locked into rigid cultural beliefs.

In many other stories published during this decade the theme of returning home is elaborated again and again. They show the love of the protagonists for their family members and describe the memory of, or nostalgia for, their hometowns in East Prussia. Other stories are about family events or small happenings that are lovingly told. Visionary aspects and mythical significance are absent. All in all, they are charming and well-written little stories that make for pleasant reading. They are the kind of stories suited to be read under the Christmas tree. Miegel also wrote five short dramas, but they were unsuccessful.

In 1933 Miegel was elected a member of the Prussian Academy of the Arts, newly organized by the Nazi party. She received the Herder Prize in 1936. The Nazis used her poems for nationalistic propaganda, and she joined the party in 1937. She praised the Führer in a hymn; it was published in *Ostland: Gedichte* (1940) with five other nationalistic hymns that poured forth with great pathos her love and support for the fatherland. On her sixtieth birthday Miegel's first volume of poetry, which already had gone through nineteen editions, was revised and enlarged as *Frühe Gesichte* (Early Visions). She was now called "Mother East Prussia."

During World War II Miegel read her poetry throughout Germany. Her work continued to receive literary awards including the Goethe Prize of the city of Frankfurt in 1940. She escaped the hard realities of war until August 1944, when Königsberg was bombed. In December she held her last public reading, beginning with her new poem "Abschied von Königsberg" (Farewell to Königsberg). In February 1945 she was ordered to leave the city and became one of two million East Prussian refugees. She lived in a refugee camp in Denmark until October 1946; then she and her housekeeper-

companion of over twenty years returned to Germany to live on the country estate of the Münchhausen family in Apelern.

At sixty-seven Miegel felt that her talent had undergone an "Altersevolution" (old-age-evolution). Withdrawing from the world of great events and strong emotions, her poetry focused on small events, depicted with the simplicity of the folk song. Her work at this time reveals a higher level of insight into life and a deep faith in God.

In 1949 she and her companion moved into two furnished rooms in Bad Nenndorf, near Hannover. The same year *Du aber bleibst in mir* (But You Remain in Me), a small volume of poems she had written as a refugee, was published; it began with "Farewell to Königsberg." The book sold out immediately. Miegel later got an apartment of her own in Bad Nenndorf, where she received many visitors, mostly exiles from East Prussia who had known and admired her before the war.

Miegel's collection of five stories, *Die Blume der Götter* (The Flower of the Gods, 1949), reaches beyond her homeland. The stories deal with both historical and fictional events. "Der Ruf" (The Call) is set in ancient Greece; "Der Rosenbonbon" (Rose Candy) takes place in Hungary and Romania during the time of the Hapsburg Empire; "Die Quelle" (The Spring) concerns the Albigensian religious sect during the Middle Ages; "Apotheose" (Apotheosis) deals with the court of Catherine the Great; and the title story relates an event in the life of the German romantic poet Chamisso. These stories lack the dark, mythical dimension of the stories in *Geschichten aus Alt-Preußen*. Events are narrated with a precision of observation and a continuity that leaves no gaps for speculation and conjecture. The collection offers light and pleasant reading. Another collection of stories, *Der Federball* (The Badminton Birdie), was published in 1951. A serene mood prevails in all four of these stories.

In 1952 Miegel began editing her collected works, which were published in six volumes from 1952 to 1955; a seventh volume appeared in 1965, after her death. During the last years of her life she received many honors, among them the literary prize of West Prussia in 1962. She held her last public reading in 1958 but continued writing until her death in Bad Salzuflen on 26 October 1964.

Miegel enjoyed much of her success during the restoration of Germany after World War II. To expatriates her work became a symbol of East Prussia, a country, a people, and a tradition lost forever. Miegel's poems and stories helped nostalgic readers to recapture their past. Thus, it was

*Miegel in 1940 (Ullstein)*

the emotional rather than the literary value of her work, and the myth of "Mother East Prussia" that she perpetuated, that brought Miegel back into the limelight.

**References:**
Paul Fechter, *Agnes Miegel. Eine preußische Frau* (Berlin: Frundsberg, 1933);

Harold Jensen, *Agnes Miegel und die bildende Kunst* (Leer: Rautenberg, 1982);

Erhard Krieger, *Agnes Miegel: Leben und Werk* (Bad Homburg: Das Viergespann, 1959);

Inge Meidinger-Geise, *Agnes Miegel und Ostpreußen* (Würzburg: Holzner, 1955);

Anni Piorreck, *Agnes Miegel: Ihr Leben und ihre Dichtung* (Düsseldorf: Diederichs, 1967);

Karl Plenzat, *Agnes Miegel: Werden und Werk* (Leipzig: Eichblatt, 1938);

Ruth Maria Wagner, ed., *Leben, was war ich dir gut* (Munich: Gräfe & Unzer, 1966);

Margaret Woodbridge, "Keywords and the language of Agnes Miegel," Ph.D. dissertation, Columbia University, 1942.

---

# Alfred Neumann
### (15 October 1895-3 October 1952)

## Christopher L. Dolmetsch
*Marshall University*

BOOKS: *Die Lieder vom Lächeln und der Not: Gedichte* (Munich: Müller, 1917);

*Die heiligen: Legendäre Geschichten* (Munich: Müller, 1919);

*Neue Gedichte* (Munich: Müller, 1920);

*Rugge: Ein Buch Erzählungen* (Munich: Müller, 1920);

*Magister Taussig: Erzählung* (Berlin: Deutsche Buchgemeinschaft, 1923);

*Die Brüder: Roman* (Stuttgart: Deutsche Verlagsanstalt, 1924);

*Lehrer Taussig* (Ludwigsburg: Deutscher Volksverlag, 1925); translated by A. H. King as "Schoolmaster Taussig" in *King Haber and Other Stories* (New York: King, 1930);

*Der Patriot: Erzählung* (Stuttgart: Deutsche Verlagsanstalt, 1925); translated by Cyrus Brooks as *The Patriot* (London: Davies, 1929); translation republished in *King Haber and Other Stories*;

*Der Teufel: Roman* (Stuttgart: Deutsche Verlagsanstalt, 1926); translated by Huntley Paterson as *The Devil* (New York: Grosset & Dunlap, 1926); translation republished as *The Deuce* (London: Heinemann, 1928);

*König Haber: Erzählung* (Stuttgart: Engelhorn, 1926); translated by Marie Busch as "King Haber" in *King Haber and Other Stories*;

*Der Konnetabel* (Munich: Müller, 1927);

*Der Patriot: Drama in fünf Akten* (Stuttgart: Deutsche Verlagsanstalt, 1927); translated and adapted by Ashley Dukes as *The Patriot: A Play in Three Acts* (New York: Boni & Liveright, 1928); translation republished as *Such Men Are Dangerous* (London: Gollancz, 1928);

*Rebellen: Roman* (Stuttgart: Deutsche Verlagsanstalt, 1927); translated by Paterson as *The Rebels* (New York: Knopf, 1929);

*Königsmaske: Drama in fünf Akten* (Stuttgart: Deutsche Verlagsanstalt, 1928);

*Frauenschuh: Tragikomödie in vier Akten und einem Nachspiel* (Stuttgart: Deutsche Verlagsanstalt, 1929);

*Guerra: Roman* (Stuttgart: Deutsche Verlagsanstalt, 1929); translated by Paterson as *Guerra* (New York: Knopf, 1930);

*Der Held: Roman eines politischen Mordes* (Stuttgart & Berlin: Deutsche Verlagsanstalt, 1930); translated by Paterson as *The Hero: The Tale of a Political Murder* (New York: Knopf, 1931);

*Die Brautauktion, Spiel in drei Akten nach einem Goldoni-Thema* (Berlin: Arcadia, 1931);

*Haus Danieli: Schauspiel in vier Akten* (Stuttgart: Deutsche Verlagsanstalt, 1932);

*Narrenspiegel: Roman* (Berlin: Propyläen, 1932); translated by Trevor and Phyllis Blewitt as *The Mirror of Fools* (New York: Knopf, 1933);

*Marthe Munk: Eine Erzählung* (Wuppertal-Barmen: Plaut, 1933);

*Kleine Helden: Erzählungen* (Paris: Europäischer Merkur, 1934);

*Sais: Ein Rätselbuch* (Vienna: Saturn, 1934);

*Neuer Caesar: Roman* (Amsterdam: De Lange, 1934); translated by Eden and Cedar Paul as *The New Caesar* (London: Hutchinson, 1934); translation republished as *Another Caesar* (New York: Knopf, 1935);

*Königin Christine von Schweden* (Amsterdam: De Lange, 1935); translated by Barnard Balogh as *The Life of Christina of Sweden* (London: Hutchinson, 1935);

*Rätsel-Dichtungen* (Vienna: Saturn, 1935);

*Tunkal: Neue Rätsel-Dichtungen* (Vienna: Saturn, 1935);

*Delphi: Neue Rätsel-Dichtungen; Lösungen* (Vienna: Saturn, 1936);

*Kaiserreich: Roman* (Amsterdam: De Lange, 1936); translated by the Pauls as *The Gaudy Empire*

(New York: Knopf, 1937); translation republished as *Man of December: A Story of Napoleon III and the Fall of the Second Empire* (London: Hutchinson, 1937);

*Rhodus: Neue Rätsel-Dichtungen; Lösungen* (Vienna: Saturn, 1937);

*Die Goldquelle: Roman* (Amsterdam: De Lange, 1938);

*Die Volksfreunde* (Amsterdam: De Lange, 1940); translated by Nora Wydenbrück and Neumann as *The Friends of the People* (London & Melbourne: Hutchinson, 1940; New York: Macmillan, 1942); German version reprinted in limited edition (Stockholm: Neuer Valley, 1948); republished as *Das Kind von Paris* (Zurich: Fretz & Wasmuth, 1952);

*War and Peace*, by Neumann, Erwin Piscator, and Guntram Prüfer, translated by Ashley Dukes (N.p., 1941); German version published as *Krieg und Frieden: Nach dem Roman von Leo Tolstoi für die Bühne nacherzählt und bearbeitet von A. Neumann, E. Piscator und G. Prüfer* (Hamburg: Rowohlt, 1955);

*Gitterwerk des Lebens* (Los Angeles: Privately printed, 1943);

*Es waren ihrer sechs: Roman* (Stockholm: Neuer Verlag, 1944); translated by Anatol Murad as *Six of Them* (London: Hutchinson, 1945; New York: Macmillan, 1945);

*Gesammelte Werke*, 2 volumes (Stockholm: Neuer Verlag, 1949-1950);

*Dostojewski und die Freiheit: Eine Rede* (Amsterdam: De Lange, 1949);

*Der Pakt: Roman* (Stockholm: Neuer Verlag, 1950); translated by Ransom L. Taylor as *Look upon This Man* (London & New York: Hutchinson, 1950); translation republished as *Strange Conquest* (New York: Ballantine, 1954);

*Viele heißen Kain: Erzählung* (Stockholm: Neuer Verlag, 1950);

*Alfred Neumann: Eine Auswahl aus seinem Werk*, edited by Guy Stern (Wiesbaden: Steiner, 1979).

OTHER: *Alt- und neufranzösische Lyrik in Nachdichtungen*, edited and translated by Neumann (Munich: Recht, 1922);

Alphonse Marie Louise de Lamartine, *Girondisten und Jakobiner: In Porträts*, edited and translated by Neumann (Munich: Allgemeine Verlagsanstalt München, 1923);

Alfred de Musset, *Die beiden Geliebten: Erzählungen und Komödie*, translated by Neumann (Munich: Müller, 1924);

de Musset, *Gesammelte Werke*, translated by Neumann, 5 volumes (Munich: Müller, 1925);

*Aus fremden Landen: Nachdichtungen französische, englische und italienische Lyrik*, translated by Neumann (Vienna: Saturn, 1935);

Armand Godoy, *Passionsdrama: Nachdichtung*, adapted by Neumann (Vienna: Saturn, 1935);

Godoy, *Marcel: Nachdichtung*, adapted by Neumann (Vienna: Saturn, 1936);

Godoy, *Marien-Litanien: Nachdichtung*, adapted by Neumann (Vienna: Saturn, 1936);

Godoy, *Hosianna zum Sistrum: Nachdichtung*, adapted by Neumann (Vienna: Saturn, 1937);

Godoy, *Rom: Nachdichtung*, adapted by Neumann (Vienna: Saturn, 1937).

PERIODICAL PUBLICATIONS: "Autobiographische Skizze," *Blätter der Bücherstube am Museum Wiesbaden*, 3 (1927): 6-7;

"Selbstdarstellungen deutscher Dichter, III: Alfred Neumann," *Die literarische Welt*, 6 (7 November 1930): 1;

"Alfred Neumann über sich selbst," *Der Freihafen*, 13 (1930-1931): 52-53.

In a time of lesser literary genius Alfred Neumann surely would have achieved the enduring recognition he deserves; unfortunately for him, his work was overshadowed by that of such renowned contemporaries and associates as Thomas Mann, Leonhard Frank, Lion Feuchtwanger, and Franz Werfel. Still, while Neumann is, in the words of one scholar, "verschollen und vergessen" (gone and forgotten), he was highly acclaimed during his lifetime. This reputation was built on his prolific contributions as a novelist, dramatist, and screenplay writer, and to a lesser degree as a poet, short story writer, and essayist.

Neumann came, in his own words, "aus reichem Hause, wilhelminischer Bourgeoisie" (from a rich house of the Wilhelmine middle class). He was born into the Jewish family of Wolff and Malvina Joseph Neumann in the provincial town of Lautenburg, West Prussia (now in Poland), and his family moved to Berlin within a few years of his birth. His father, a highly successful entrepreneur in the lumber business, saw to Alfred's traditional, strict, university-oriented education. He attended schools in Berlin and Rostock, graduating in the latter city in 1912. What Neumann called his "emancipation" came when he traveled to Munich to study art history and history. The Munich of the early years of the century fired his creative imagination. He ambitiously set out to make contact with

people connected with the burgeoning cultural life of the city; one of those he met was Georg Müller, a publisher and patron of struggling authors. Müller brought Neumann into contact with Efraim Frisch, a young editor and reader for Müller's firm, who was among the first to recognize and encourage Neumann's literary talent.

At the outbreak of World War I Neumann was conscripted. He saw action only briefly in a field artillery unit before he was wounded in 1915, and it was while recuperating in a military hospital in Augsburg that he began writing poetry. Judged unfit for further military service, he returned to Munich in 1917 and submitted his first slender volume of poems to Müller. *Die Lieder vom Lächeln und der Not* (Songs of Laughter and Despair) was published that year. Müller died in December 1917, but his influence on Neumann's life and work lingered long after the publisher's death; in fact, he married Müller's adopted daughter Katharina (Kitty) Schatzberger-Müller in 1924, after a first impetuous marriage in 1922 to a Swiss dancer named Martina was quietly dissolved. Kitty Neumann was, in the words of the writer, "das Geschenk, das das persönliche Leben erhalten hat" (the gift that nurtured my personal life).

Neumann remained in Munich until 1920, earning his living principally as the dramatic advisor to the famous repertory theater of Otto Falkenberg. This experience served to school him in the arts of acting and dramatic production, crafts he applied in later years as a dramatist and writer of film scripts.

In 1920 Neumann resumed his studies, this time in Geneva, where he received a degree in 1921 in romance language and literature. His interest in French language, literature, and culture led him to dabble in translations of Alfred de Musset and to write a dissertation on de Musset, Stendhal, and Flaubert.

By 1921 Neumann had resolved to become a free-lance writer. He established two residences, in Munich and in Fiesole, near Florence. Living in what his *New York Times* obituary was to call "circumstances of dire poverty," Neumann produced several short stories and his first major novel, *Der Teufel* (1926; translated as *The Devil*, 1926), for which he was named corecipient of the prestigious Kleist Prize in 1926. This work was translated into at least twelve languages and is reputed to have sold 300,000 to 400,000 copies.

A single thematic thread runs through many of Neumann's works, whether fiction, poetry, essay, or film script: his fascination—one might almost say obsession—with the demonic nature of power and guilt. As Neumann expressed it in 1930: "Es geht um die uralte Spannung zwischen Tat und Gewissen. Es geht immer darum. Es geht immer um die Schuldfrage" (It is a matter of the ancient tension between deed and conscience. It is always about that. It is always about the question of guilt). Twenty years later, in response to an inquiry about his work, Neumann again stressed his involvement with this theme: "Es ist mein ewiges Thema, das Sie in allen meinen Büchern finden können: die Psychologie der Macht, die Moraltheologie gegen das Böse, das mit der Machtlust identisch ist" (It is my eternal theme, which you can find in all of my books; the psychology of power; the moral theology against evil which is identical with the lust for power).

This theme surfaces in his earliest novel. Like most of Neumann's prose works, *Der Teufel* deals with a specific historical situation: in this case, the play for power by the parvenu Oliver Necker, from his improbable rise from the barber's trade in Ghent to his exalted position as advisor and confidant to King Louis XI. Three major motifs link Louis's fortunes and fate to those of the brazen upstart Necker: love, intrigue, and death. The love story is that of the sordid triangle in which Louis takes Anne, Oliver's beautiful wife, as his mistress. Her premature death so outrages her husband that he vows to see the king defeated at the hands of his powerful enemies. Intrigue is found in both men's indefatigable skill in outwitting and destroying those opposed to their close collaboration. In the words of Louis Kronenberger in his review for the *New York Times*, "Neumann proves his feeling for the Zeitgeist in contrasting the modernity of minds such as were Louis's and Oliver's—which were not medieval minds at all, but, both of them, great bourgeois minds—with the surviving medievalism of the common people, who could see in Oliver only the incarnation of the devil." The death motif emerges toward the middle of the book: fearing for his life, Louis shuts himself off from everyone except his trusted ally Necker. Oliver exploits the king's anxiety, gradually assuming the role of head of state. Upon Louis's death the minister's offenses quickly lead to his execution.

Although some critics judged *Der Teufel* to be too long and wordy, Neumann's style was typical of that prevalent in Germany at the time. He had overcome a proclivity toward the mannerisms of the expressionist style and wrote in the predominant German prose style of the 1920s, the Neue Sachlichkeit (New Objectivity).

From 1925 through 1934 Neumann was a productive and successful author. No fewer than seven novels, five short stories, two screenplays, and five dramas appeared. His 1926 screenplay of his story *Der Patriot* (1925; translated as *The Patriot*, 1929) became his first contribution to the film industry; produced by the renowned director Ernst Lubitsch for Paramount Pictures in 1928, *The Patriot* won Neumann an Academy Award and gained him instant recognition among Hollywood's movie moguls.

*Der Patriot*, like *Der Teufel*, is loosely based on historical fact. The old Count Peter von der Pahlen conspires with a small group of Russian nobles to overthrow the despotic Czar Paul and replace him with his son, Alexander. The coup d'état receives the blessing of Alexander, provided his father's life is spared. Pahlen pledges his own life that no harm will befall the old czar. When Paul's room is stormed and the vengeful intruders kill the wicked monarch, Pahlen realizes that he must die by his own hand to preserve his honor.

*Neumann in 1932, the year of publication of his novel*
Narrenspiegel *(Ullstein)*

In America *Der Patriot* first appeared in a 1930 anthology of Neumann stories, along with *Lehrer Taussig* (translated as "Schoolmaster Taussig") from 1925 and *König Haber* (translated as "King Haber") from 1926. Neumann's work was becoming familiar to a select readership, and reviewers began to compare such "new" works to his previous publications. One reviewer stated: "Where . . . 'King Haber' and 'The Patriot' are merely clever experiments, striking a paradoxical note in their treatment of human character, 'The Devil' is a piece of literature because the note it strikes is truly mystical."

Despite the success of the film version of *Der Patriot*, Neumann did not give in to the temptation to concentrate on writing screenplays. Rather, he continued to produce and publish prose works, among them *Rebellen* (translated as *The Rebels*, 1929) in 1927; *Guerra* in 1929; *Der Held* (translated as *The Hero*, 1931) in 1930; *Narrenspiegel* (translated as *The Mirror of Fools*, 1933) in 1932; and a biographical study, *Königin Christine von Schweden* (translated as *The Life of Christina of Sweden*, 1935), written in 1934 and published in 1935.

*Rebellen* deals with the revolutionary movement in Italy between 1830 and 1848 as mirrored in conditions in the Grand Duchy of Tuscany. This story unfolds on a grander scale than Neumann's earlier works. Relationships are more complex: Princess Corleone becomes the mistress of the Grand Duke for the sake of the secret societies of the Camorra, who are plotting the forthcoming rebellion; yet all the while, she loves the leader of the rebels, the dashing and handsome Gasto Guerra. He, in turn, is embroiled in disputes involving his sister and his fellow conspirators. Reviewers, by now comfortable with Neumann's precise historical vignettes, tended to find *The Rebels* diffuse and obscure. Gabriele Reuter admonished the author in the *New York Times:* "Alfred Neumann: Control your fine gifts and do not indulge in too many subtle complications and insinuations, lest the great lines of the action disappear under the confused network of details. Your fine art must not be permitted to freeze into mannerism!"

The sequel to *Rebellen, Guerra,* which continued the story of the Tuscan uprising through 1848, received far more praise from American critics. One reviewer noted: "At all events, there is a strong parallel between the two cases [Germany of the Metternich era and revolutionary Italy] which may serve to explain some of the book's popularity in Germany. For the rest, it is a well-written, mature and leisurely account of the part played by the Car-

bonari in Tuscany in 1848. The whole is told with grace and energy and is couched in a style that is both dignified and attractive."

In contrast to *Rebellen* and *Guerra, Der Held* represented a major change in both mood and setting for Neumann. Called by one reviewer "a horrifying and fantastic modern psychological novel," it concerns a political murder. The radical prime minister of a postwar European country is assassinated by the nationalistic ex-army officer Hubert Hoff. The killer is so tormented by his deed that he feels he must immerse himself in the past of his victim. Overwhelmed by guilt, Hoff is driven to confess first to the widow, then to his landlady, and finally to the chief of police, who produces evidence that he cannot possibly be guilty. Noting that *Der Held* "can never appeal to a wide audience," one reviewer nonetheless stressed that it is "an awesome and stirring book, which pushes ahead into new and yet unrealizable forms of human experience." With this work Neumann proved himself a master of the art of the modern novel of crime and suspense, just as with *Der Teufel* he had won recognition in the field of historical fiction.

The last of Neumann's novels published in Weimar Germany was *Narrenspiegel*. Set in sixteenth-century Germany, it is the lighthearted tale of Duke Heinrich of Liegnitz, a Falstaffian character who shares little of Sir John's magnetism or—in the words of *New York Times* reviewer Louis Kronenberger—his "wayward lovableness." A rogue who bullies, abuses, and preys upon all who seek to serve and assist him, Heinrich is the ultimate scoundrel. Yet, unlike Neumann's earlier historical villains, his German ruffian is not so much intimidating as annoying. Nonetheless *Narrenspiegel* was favorably compared to *Der Teufel*. In a revealing letter to his publisher Neumann said he wrote the work

because I wanted to fight against the general and my personal depression, and because in hard and bad times there is always one tragi-comic feeling in place—gallows humor.

Because in the Falstaffian magic of the fat belly and the inflated life much more than in dreary materialism and the triumph of eating and drinking there is—vital strength.

Because in a volcanic and misanthropic world like ours, and in the tragi-comedy of the hero, who is half Falstaff and half Don Quixote, one positive force succeeds against a thousand negative ones—the will to live.

Because the cheerlessness of the world, the animosity of a barbaric and murderous time, the swamps and fogs of a gloomy soul, idiotic adventures, war and pestilence, death and the devil, all are conquered by—joy of living.

Because we need this gallows humor, vital strength, will to live and joy of living just as my fat Duke Heinrich needs his quantities of wine.

The advent of the Nazi regime in 1933 forced Neumann to leave Germany for his Villa San Mariana at Fiesole, where he assumed he would be left in peace to continue his writing. He had just completed *Neuer Caesar* (translated as *Another Caesar*, 1935), the first book in a historical-novel trilogy; owing to the ban placed on his works in Germany, the book was published in Amsterdam by Allert de Lange in 1934. In Italy he commenced work on the second volume, *Kaiserreich* (translated as *The Gaudy Empire*, 1937), which was published in Holland in 1936. The final volume, *Die Volksfreunde*, was composed while Neumann was living in Nice in 1939. This work had just been printed by de Lange in May 1940 when the occupying German forces confiscated and destroyed the entire press-run. Thus its first licensed appearance was in an English translation, *The Friends of the People*, later that year, and the first German copies did not circulate until 1948. It became widely available in Germany only when it was reprinted in 1952 under a new title, *Das Kind von Paris*.

*Neuer Caesar* traces the controversial rise of Louis Napoleon Bonaparte, a sallow, whispering, little man lacking perceptible heroism or demonstrable genius, who emerges from nowhere to shake the throne of a powerful dynasty and pervert the course of a triumphant revolution. He is, in the words of *New York Times* reviewer R. L. Duffus, "a small man forced—one may say hypnotized—by circumstances into playing a role for which he is not fitted." Critics said, as they had of his earlier historical novels, that Neumann seemed to be at his best when describing the highly complex and emotionally charged personal relationships and intrigues of royal personages and their subjects. The work is a splendid documentary in which Neumann fills the historical gaps with his own fantasy.

*Kaiserreich* continues the story of Louis Napoleon after his accession to power. The volume begins with the fall of the Second Republic and dwells on the events surrounding the new Empire: the Crimean War; the Austro-Sardinian War; the rise of Bismarck and Prussia; the Danish War; the Napoleonic empire in Mexico; the rise and subtle influence of Offenbach, Morny, Thiers, Clemenceau, and Gambetta; the Franco-Prussian War; the fall of the Second Empire; and the death of Louis Napoleon.

*Die Volksfreunde* reexamines the Franco-Prussian War through the eyes of participants in the Paris Commune of 1870-1871. This time the central figures of the story are not royalty, nor even the usual historical "greats," but common folk: Pierre Cagnocle, a sixteen-year-old boy, and Léonie Léon, a woman twice his age with whom the lad is smitten. As in the preceding two works, however, Neumann weaves into *Die Volksfreunde* a prodigious number of real historical events and figures. Although these works are little read today, all three of them became, upon publication in translation, best-sellers in the United States and Great Britain and were featured selections of book clubs.

Plans for a second filming of *Der Patriot* brought Neumann to Paris in 1937. Eager to capitalize on this renewed interest in his first film script, he composed a second, this one based on the Rasputin story, which he titled *Tragédie Imperiale*. It too was soon filmed in Paris, and Neumann found himself a film celebrity among the French. His intention to settle in Paris was thwarted by increasing anti-German sentiments there. He spent most of the summer of 1938 with friends and artistic associates near Zurich. He was invited by other German literary exiles to join them in Nice, and upon his arrival in September he cabled his wife in Fiesole, instructing her to hastily and inconspicuously pack a few belongings and join him. Kitty Neumann was detained by Italian authorities at the border while her husband waited impatiently on the French side. Only thanks to the intervention of sympathetic officials was she at last permitted to cross into France.

In the south of France Neumann found safe haven among fellow German literati Feuchtwanger, Werfel, and Heinrich Mann. For nearly two years he was able to live and work in relative peace and security, and at times he seemed almost oblivious to the war raging elsewhere in Europe. By failing to grasp the seriousness of the situation when his own comfort and safety seemed assured, Neumann came close to becoming yet another victim of the Holocaust. By the winter of 1940 Nice was no longer considered safe; many German exiles had already crossed the Atlantic to America and others followed daily. On 24 December Neumann noted in his diary that it might be necessary for him and his wife to exit France illegally. But on 10 January 1941 they were permitted to leave France

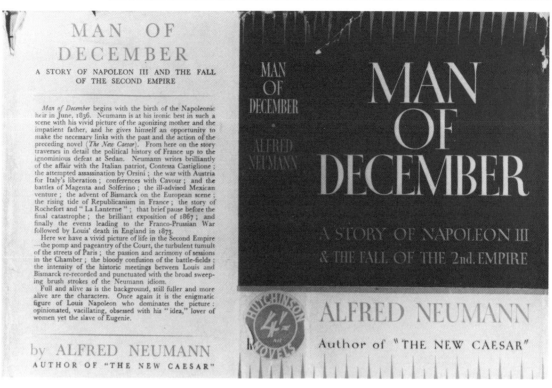

MAN OF
DECEMBER

A STORY OF NAPOLEON III AND THE FALL
OF THE SECOND EMPIRE

*Man of December* begins with the birth of the Napoleonic heir in June, 1856. Neumann is at his ironic best in such a scene with his vivid picture of the agonizing mother and the impatient father, and he gives himself an opportunity to make the necessary links with the past and the action of the preceding novel (*The New Caesar*). From here on the story traverses in detail the political history of France up to the ignominious defeat at Sedan. Neumann writes brilliantly of the affair with the Italian patriot, Contessa Castiglione; the attempted assassination by Orsini; the war with Austria for Italy's liberation; conferences with Cavour; and the battles of Magenta and Solferino; the ill-advised Mexican venture; the advent of Bismarck on the European scene; the rising tide of Republicanism in France; the story of Rochefort and " La Lanterne "; that brief pause before the final catastrophe; the brilliant exposition of 1867; and finally the events leading to the Franco-Prussian War followed by Louis' death in England in 1873.

Here we have a vivid picture of life in the Second Empire—the pomp and pageantry of the Court, the turbulent tumult of the streets of Paris; the passion and acrimony of sessions in the Chamber; the bloody confusion of the battle-fields; the intensity of the historic meetings between Louis and Bismarck re-recorded and punctuated with the broad sweeping brush strokes of the Neumann idiom.

Full and alive as is the background, still fuller and more alive are the characters. Once again it is the enigmatic figure of Louis Napoleon who dominates the picture: opinionated, vacillating, obsessed with his "idea," lover of women yet the slave of Eugenie.

by ALFRED NEUMANN
AUTHOR OF "THE NEW CAESAR"

Dust jacket for the 1937 British edition of the English translation of Neumann's 1936 novel Kaiserreich

and settle in America under the special powers granted by President Roosevelt to the Emergency Rescue Committee.

The Neumanns arrived in New York on the steamer *Excambio* on 17 February. Their stay on the East Coast was brief, since Neumann had decided to accept an offer from Jack Warner of Warner Bros. Pictures in Hollywood and was eager to get started in his new assignment. The second film version of *Der Patriot,* under the title *The Mad Emperor,* had just opened to rave reviews in New York, and Neumann was confident that Warner—"Jack" as he was told to call him—would have more than enough work for him to do upon his arrival.

Hollywood in the 1940s was teaming with foreign literary talent, most of whom had been promised unlimited opportunities in the film business. The vast majority were mere retainees, paid a subsistence and asked not to loiter about or even contact their respective studios. Neumann, with one Oscar to his credit already, thought his fortunes would be different. When the situation proved otherwise, he wrote in bitter disappointment to his friend and fellow exile Hermann Kesten: "Man ist zwar—aus ursprünglich mildtätigem Herzen—als *writer* angestellt und wird dafür gezahlt: aber das, was man beruflich und verträglich schreibt, wird

nicht *gelesen*" (One is indeed employed—by an originally charitable heart—as a *writer* and is paid to be such: but what one professionally and contractually writes is not *read*).

Despite his legitimate complaint, Neumann was, in the end, far luckier than most of his compatriots. Warner Bros. did eventually accept one of his stories for a film that was made in 1943 and released two years later under the title *Conflict.* In this story, which probably owes its inspiration to *Der Held,* Richard Mason (played in the film by Humphrey Bogart) is driven to the brink of self-destruction by his guilt over having murdered his wife. The murder was committed so skillfully that it has left no leads for the police to follow. The crime is solved only when Mason proves unable to suppress a gnawing fear that his wife has somehow survived. Inevitably the nerve-shattered killer is drawn back to the scene of his crime, where he is caught. Although *Conflict* does not rival the suspense films of Alfred Hitchcock, it is a clever tale and displays Neumann's interest in subjects that were not strictly historical in nature.

Several more film scripts and stories followed before Warner quietly allowed Neumann's contract to expire; none of these works was turned into a finished film. On the other hand, several other major studios, including RKO, 20th Century-Fox, and Columbia Pictures, did express interest in Neumann's work, leading in 1944 to the filming of *None Shall Escape*, for which Neumann received his second Academy Award nomination. While some critics branded this film "bombastic" and "overblown," its virtue lay in its depiction of Nazi ideology as the collective product of individual frustrations and prejudices with no central purpose. It is the story of a German schoolteacher who is banished from a Polish village for social and sexual improprieties, only to return as a Nazi official.

*The Return of Monte Cristo*, released in 1945, and *Matto Regiert* (Matto Rules), a 1946 Swiss production written in collaboration with Leopold Lindtberg, were less successful than Neumann's earlier films. One of his most ambitious screenplays, "Alfred Nobel," was written in 1946 at the request of actor Paul Muni. Neumann later said of this work: "Ich tat es und halte es für meine beste Filmarbeit. Dies ist vielleicht der Grund, daß der Film noch nicht gemacht wurde" (I did it and consider it to be my best film work. This is perhaps the reason why the film has not been made yet).

In spite of his involvement with the Hollywood film industry, most of Neumann's time in California was devoted to working on what became his last two completed novels, *Der Pakt* (The Pact) and *Es waren ihrer sechs* (There Were Six of Them). *Der Pakt* is about the nineteenth-century American freebooter and megalomaniac William Walker, whose story had first attracted Neumann's attention in New York when he chanced to borrow Laurence Greene's *The Filibuster: The Career of William Walker* (circa 1937). Soon thereafter, Neumann turned the Walker story into a screenplay which Warner immediately rejected, apparently without reading it. Neumann commenced his novel by using the text of his screenplay. Two years into the project, in 1943, he permitted his friends and compatriots Ernst Gottlieb and Felix Guggenheim to contract with Pacific Press, a small Los Angeles firm, for the publication of two chapters of the unfinished book as *Gitterwerk des Lebens* (Trelliswork of Life). The pressrun was limited to 250 copies, 150 of them bound in leather and inscribed by the author. Neumann interrupted the writing of *Der Pakt* on several occasions to pursue other movie and literary endeavors. The book was published in Stockholm in 1950. Ransom L. Taylor immediately translated it into English as *Look upon This Man*. A second American edition, inexplicably retitled *Strange Conquest*, was published by Ballan-tine Paperback Books in 1954 and included in the firm's category of westerns.

The first part of the novel recounts Walker's short-lived career in Baja California, where he heads a self-styled provincial republic; is arrested and acquitted of all charges by an amazingly sympathetic jury; and, in the process, reveals to the reader his origins and earliest exploits. The second half of the novel describes Walker's conquest of Nicaragua as the leader of a ragtag army of ex-convicts and mercenaries. His earlier idealism has by now vanished and been replaced by a demonic obsession and greed. The defeat of Walker's forces, his ignominious deportation to the United States, and his arrest and execution following his return to Nicaragua contribute to what the *New York Times* called an "engrossing account of a career which cannot be overdramatized."

*Es waren ihrer sechs*, published in Stockholm in 1944 and translated the following year as *Six of Them*, was Neumann's only attempt in prose to come to terms with the evils of the Hitler dictatorship. Since American press censorship had made it almost impossible for European exiles to stay informed about covert anti-Nazi organizations in their homelands, Neumann decided to write a novel about the arrest and execution in 1943 of key student and faculty members of the Munich-based Weiße Rose (White Rose) conspiracy. With the magazines *Time*, *Nation*, and *Aufbau* and a few essays and editorials as his main sources of information, Neumann laboriously reconstructed the probable activities of the clandestine organization. To insure a high degree of accuracy he examined available documents on the Nazi Peoples' Courts, corresponded with several prominent academic refugees who had established contact with White Rose members, and even sought answers to technical questions pertaining to one conspirator's artificial limb. The result is, in the words of Walter A. Berendsohn, "einer der besten Dichtungen über das grosse grauenvolle Motiv" (one of the best works of fiction about this huge gruesome motif).

Neumann's "six" are allowed to tell their own story, which in turn conveniently lets the reader forgive the author for any factual errors or omissions; thus, for example, the protestor's leaflet reproduced in the book is not the actual Munich text but an approximation based on *Time*'s rough translation. Yet even though he lacked many details of the tragic events surrounding Hans and Sophie Scholl, Professor Kurt Huber, and their comrades, Neumann's version of the story captures, in an unusually succinct and dramatic style, much of the tension that characterized the events in Munich. The end of the novel suggests that these martyrs did not die in vain: as the assembled students of the university are told about the execution of the six conspirators, they are showered from the auditorium's airshafts with more leaflets denouncing the government. Neumann concludes the work: "The Security Department, prepared for every eventuality, succeeded in arresting the students active on the roof. There were six of them."

During the war years Alfred and Kitty Neumann became close friends with many of the famous German refugees living in Southern California, including Bruno and Lotte Walter, Bruno and Elizabeth Frank, Franz and Alma Werfel, Fritz Lang, Peter Lorre, and Walter Slezak. Among their American friends were Edward G. Robinson, Sidney Greenstreet, and Alexis Smith. But no relationship was dearer or more enduring for the Neumanns than their friendship—going back to the Munich days—with Katja and Thomas Mann. Indeed it has been intimated that Thomas Mann's greatest American accomplishment, *Doktor Faustus* (1947), owes much of its inspiration and outlook to Neumann's patient advice. Their friendship did not wane with time, as was to happen among so many former exiles, but remained vital to the end.

In October 1946 the Neumanns became American citizens. At his naturalization hearing Neumann surprised his examiner when, in response to an inquiry about his recent work, he mentioned his interest in the life of William Walker. The judge responded, "And who is he?" After Neumann's thorough reply, the stunned judge exclaimed, "My God, you know American history better than I do!"

After the completion of *Der Pakt*, Neumann traveled to Europe and lectured at universities in Sweden, Norway, Denmark, Holland, Belgium, Switzerland, and Italy; he was the first postwar German "guest" at several prominent institutions. One of his lectures, *Dostojewski und die Freiheit: Eine Rede* (Dostoyevski and Freedom: A Speech), published in Amsterdam in 1949, is ostensibly a discourse on the life of Dostoyevski, but its parallels to Neumann's own life and experiences are unmistakable. At the end of the piece Neumann echoes the Russian novelist's desperate lament: "Wir sind ein geschlagenes Volk! Alles ist zerbrochen in uns! Darum schreien wir so in der Nacht!" (We are a beaten people! Everything in us is shattered! Thus we cry out so in the night!).

Back in Fiesole in 1949 Neumann worked on his last two prose works, which remain unfinished and unpublished. "Franziscus; oder, die Versöhnung" (St. Francis; or, The Reconciliation) was to have been a historical novel about a German cleric who disobeys the rules by hearing the confessions of his fellow internees in a Nazi concentration camp. "Georg Meister," left as a 143-page manuscript at Neumann's death, is a roman à clef about a German publisher. Originally given the punning working title "Die Meistersinger," it was based principally on Neumann's recollections of Georg Müller.

Late in his life Neumann devoted increasing amounts of his time to helping younger writers gain recognition. Among his disciples was Hans Werner Richter, one of the founders of the writers' association Gruppe 47. Neumann also kept in touch with his old literary colleagues, especially Thomas Mann, Frank, and Kesten. But by the summer of 1951 Neumann was so ill he virtually ceased all serious literary activity. He died in Lugano, Switzerland, on 3 October 1952, just twelve days before his fifty-seventh birthday. A few days before his death Thomas Mann had dedicated a public reading in Zurich to his friend, emphasizing "die reine, noble Kunstarbeit . . . in der er sein Dasein befestigte, ein Mehrer des Gutens" (the pure and noble work of art . . . from which he derived his existence; one who multiplies goodness).

By the 1960s Neumann had become a forgotten figure in most literary and scholarly circles. His historical prose was not considered sufficiently "engagiert" (politically committed) to warrant the attention afforded newer works of fiction by Günter Grass, Heinrich Böll, or Martin Walser. Nor was he dubbed a "literary genius" like his contemporaries the Manns, Alfred Döblin, and Hermann Hesse. Neumann subscribed to the notion that history is often shaped by obsessed and highly unscrupulous individuals who rise to great power, fortune, and fame, only to fall victim to their own greed and blind ambition. His perceptiveness, no less than his literary genius, merits greater attention than it has received in the recent past.

**Letters:**

*Thomas Mann und Alfred Neumann: Briefwechsel,* edited by Peter de Mendelssohn (Heidelberg: Schneider, 1977).

**References:**

"Alfred Neumann nicht 'heimgekehrt,' " *Aufbau* (New York), 16 (10 February 1950): 6;

Walter A. Berendsohn, " 'Es waren ihrer sechs' von Alfred Neumann: Ein Querschnitt durch das Dritte Reich," in *Germanische Streifzüge: Festschrift für Gustav Kolén,* edited by Gert Mellbourn, Helmut Müssener, Hans Rossipal, and Birgit Stott (Stockholm: Almqvist & Wiksell, 1974), pp. 20-33;

Doris Brett, "Alfred Neumanns Romane: Exil als Wendepunkt," Ph.D. dissertation, University of Cincinnati, 1975;

"Heimgekehrt," *Aufbau* (New York), 16 (13 January 1950): 8;

Ferdinand Kahn, "Alfred Neumann liest im Jewish Club of 1933," *Aufbau* (New York), 13 (9 May 1947): 24;

Kurt Lubinski, "Alfred Neumanns 'anderes' Deutschland," *Aufbau* (New York), 11 (16 November 1945): 11;

Ludwig Marcuse, "Erinnerung an Alfred Neumann," *Aufbau* (New York), 18 (24 October 1952): 9;

Anatol Murad, "Alfred Neumann 50 Years Old," *Aufbau* (New York), 11 (9 November 1945): 18;

Walter H. Perl, "Gespräch mit Alfred Neumann," *Aufbau* (New York), 12 (16 August 1946): 20-21;

Kurt Pinthus, "Ein Meister des historischen Romans: Zum Tode Alfred Neumanns," *Aufbau* (New York), 18 (10 October 1952): 7;

Frederick Porges, "Alfred Neumanns Europa-Eindrücke," *Aufbau* (New York), 16 (3 November 1950): 26;

Klaus Schröter, "Der Historische Roman," in *Exil und innere Emigration,* edited by Reinhold Grimm and Jost Hermand (Frankfurt am Main: Athenäum, 1972), pp. 111-151;

Guy Stern, "Alfred Neumann," in *Deutsche Exilliteratur seit 1933,* edited by John M. Spalek and Joseph Strelka, volume 1: *Kalifornien* (Bern: Francke, 1976), pp. 542-570;

Stern, "Das Amerikabild der Exilliteratur: Zu einem unveröffentlichten Filmexposé von Alfred Neumann," in *Amerika in der deutschen Literatur,* edited by Sigrid Bauschinger, Horst Denkler, and Wilfried Malsch (Stuttgart: Reclam, 1975), pp. 323-328;

Stern, "Erfolg in Hollywood: Der Ausnahmefall von Alfred Neumann," in *Deutsches Exildrama und Exiltheater: Jahrbuch für Internationale Germanistik,* edited by Wolfgang Elfe, James Hardin, and Gunther Holst, volume 3 (Frankfurt am Main: Lang, 1977), pp. 36-45;

Ransom L. Taylor, "Literatur im Exil: Alfred Neumann (Special Report)," *German Quarterly,* 45 (November 1972): 800-806.

**Papers:**

The majority of Alfred Neumann's papers are in the manuscript departments of the Stadtbibliothek München (City Library of Munich) and in the Akademie der Künste (Academy of Arts) in Berlin. A small number of documents pertaining to his American exile are at the University of Southern California, the University of Texas-Austin, and the Library of the Academy of Motion Picture Arts & Sciences in Hollywood. See also *Guide to the Archival Materials of the German-Speaking Emigration to the United States after 1933,* edited by John M. Spalek (Charlottesville: University Press of Virginia, 1978), pp. 673-675.

# Erich Maria Remarque

## Charles W. Hoffmann
### *Ohio State University*

BIRTH: Osnabrück, 22 June 1898, to Peter Franz and Anna Maria Remark.

EDUCATION: Catholic Teachers' Seminary, Osnabrück, 1915-1916, 1919.

MARRIAGES: 14 October 1925 to Jutta Ilse Zambona; divorced 1930 or 1931; remarried 1938 (?); divorced 1951. 25 February 1958 to Paulette Goddard.

AWARD: Großes Verdienstkreuz (Great Order of Merit) of the Federal Republic of Germany, 1967.

DEATH: Locarno, Switzerland, 25 September 1970.

BOOKS: *Die Traumbude: Ein Künstlerroman* (Dresden: Schönheit, 1920);
*Im Westen nichts Neues* (Berlin: Propyläen, 1929); translated by A. W. Wheen as *All Quiet on the Western Front* (Boston: Little, Brown, 1929; London: Putnam's, 1929);
*Der Weg zurück* (Berlin: Propyläen, 1931); translated by Wheen as *The Road Back* (Boston: Little, Brown, 1931; London: Putnam's, 1931);
*Three Comrades*, translated by Wheen (Boston: Little, Brown, 1937); original German version published as *Drei Kameraden* (Amsterdam: Querido, 1937);
*Flotsam*, translated by Denver Lindley (Boston: Little, Brown, 1941; London: Hutchinson, 1941); German version published as *Liebe deinen Nächsten: Roman* (Batavia: Querido/Stockholm: Bermann-Fischer, 1941);
*Arch of Triumph*, translated by Lindley and Walter Sorell (New York & London: Appleton-Century, 1945; London: Hutchinson, 1946); original German version published as *Arc de Triomphe: Roman* (Zurich: Micha, 1946);
*Der Funke Leben* (Cologne: Kiepenheuer & Witsch, 1952); translated by James Stern as *Spark of Life* (New York: Appleton-Century-Crofts, 1952);

*Erich Maria Remarque (Ullstein)*

*A Time to Love and a Time to Die*, translated by Lindley (New York: Harcourt, Brace, 1954); original German version published as *Zeit zu leben und Zeit zu sterben* (Cologne: Kiepenheuer & Witsch, 1954);
*Der schwarze Obelisk: Geschichte einer verspäteten Jugend* (Cologne: Kiepenheuer & Witsch, 1956); translated by Lindley as *The Black Obelisk* (New York: Harcourt, Brace, 1957; London: Hutchinson, 1957);
*Der Himmel kennt keine Günstlinge* (Cologne: Kiepenheuer & Witsch, 1961); translated by Richard and Clara Winston as *Heaven Has No Favorites* (New York: Harcourt, Brace & World, 1961); translation republished as *Bobby Deerfield* (Greenwich, Conn.: Fawcett, 1961);

*Die Nacht von Lissabon* (Cologne: Kiepenheuer &
Witsch, 1963); translated by Ralph Manheim
as *The Night in Lisbon* (New York: Harcourt,
Brace & World, 1964; London: Hutchinson,
1964);

*Schatten im Paradies* (Munich: Droemer Knaur,
1971); translated by Manheim as *Shadows in
Paradise* (New York: Harcourt Brace Jovanovich, 1972);

*Full Circle*, translated by Peter Stone (New York:
Harcourt Brace Jovanovich, 1974).

It is sometimes claimed that next to the Bible,
Erich Maria Remarque's *Im Westen nichts Neues*
(1929; translated as *All Quiet on the Western Front*,
1929) has sold more copies than any other book in
history. Whether that claim is true or not, the enormous popularity of this best-seller has made the
name Remarque a household word for over half a
century; and without much question that name is
recognized by more readers around the world than
that of any other modern German writer. For serious observers of literature he does not rank with
Thomas Mann, Heinrich Böll, or Bertolt Brecht;
but generations of young people continue to form
their attitudes toward war from *Im Westen nichts
Neues*, and it is difficult to find a literate person
anywhere who has not read the novel.

In spite of such success, however, Remarque
is not very well known today if one considers not
just *Im Westen nichts Neues* but the whole of his output. Readers who consider themselves fans because
of this first book are often surprised to learn that
it was followed by ten more novels. This surprise
is in turn surprising, for when the later works first
appeared, several of them were also best-sellers;
and from the 1930s through the 1960s the appearance of "a new Remarque" was a major publishing event—especially outside of Germany,
where the author's reputation was never as high as
it was abroad.

His books have appeal on several counts.
They are generally well-crafted novels with clear
plot lines; they are easy to read; and they mix adventure, suspense, social comment, and some violence with a central love story. At the same time,
they were clearly intended as documents of their
age, telling in presumably realistic fashion what was
happening to Germans in the chaotic 1920s, during
the Hitler years and the war, and in exile. No doubt
it was Remarque's vivid chronicling of at least one
side of the German experience in this momentous
century that once made up a major part of the
appeal for non-German readers; and his episodic

*Remarque in 1918, shortly after the end of World War I
(Ullstein)*

style and his use of the first person and the present
tense gave several of the later novels the same appearance of eyewitness authenticity that *Im Westen
nichts Neues* had had.

Remarque lived a colorful life, and most of
his works are autobiographical, though seldom in
much more than an incidental way. His protagonists like to recall boyhood haunts and pleasures
that were also Remarque's own: they, too, collected
butterflies and read Schopenhauer, Nietzsche, Jack
London, Hölderlin, and Thomas Mann. Streets
and houses where the author lived and places
where he worked appear again and again in the
novels; and characters are often named directly
after or modeled in thinly disguised fashion on
people he had known. Recognizing such real-life
references increases one's enjoyment of the works
and, perhaps, one's sense of their authenticity,
though it is not necessary for understanding the
novels themselves. In the infrequent interviews he
granted, Remarque always insisted that the events
of his life were not important for his fiction and

that, like any decent novelist, he wanted to be known for the latter. Nevertheless, Remarque was a successful, famous, and colorful man.

He was born in Osnabrück on 22 June 1898 as Erich Paul Remark. He later took the middle name Maria from his mother, Anna Maria Remark, and the spelling *Remarque* from French ancestors. His father, Peter Franz Remark, was a bookbinder and the family, which included two sisters, was poor. By the time Remarque left for the army the family had had to move some eleven times, and yet the clearly autobiographical reminiscences of his later heroes suggest that his childhood was happy. He was close to his mother, less so to his father, and fond of roaming the streets of Osnabrück and exploring the nearby countryside. His early education was Catholic, and at the time he was drafted he was preparing for a career as an elementary school teacher. His interest in music, which is so well documented in the novels, began in these early years—Remarque played both the organ and the piano and gave lessons in the latter. At the age of sixteen or seventeen he also made his first attempts at writing: essays, poems, and the beginnings of an eminently forgettable novel. Finished later and published in 1920 as *Die Traumbude* (The Dream Room or Dream Den), this first novel was written in a flowery art nouveau style and was an embarrassment to Remarque after he turned seriously to literature. To his great relief, the Ullstein publishing house bought up and destroyed the unsold copies when it published *Im Westen nichts Neues* a decade later.

Although some of his own war experiences are reflected in *Im Westen nichts Neues*, Remarque did not, like his hero Paul Bäumer, volunteer enthusiastically for military service. He was drafted in November 1916; and, because his mother was seriously ill (she died in September 1917), he was given frequent leave to visit her at home and was not sent to France until the following summer. Nor did he see much fighting or frontline service. In the battle of Flanders in July his unit was attacked by the British; and while carrying a wounded comrade back from the attack, Remarque suffered shrapnel wounds which sent him to a hospital in Germany. There he spent most of the rest of the war recuperating, writing music, and working on *Die Traumbude*.

In 1919 he returned to school to finish his teacher training and for a little over a year served as substitute teacher in several small-town schools near Osnabrück. Accused of lack of cooperation with the local authorities and of having played a

*Front wrapper for Remarque's classic antiwar novel (Ullstein)*

role in the revolutionary Spartacist movement—he steadfastly denied the latter charge—he was in constant trouble during his brief teaching career and in 1920 decided that the education of the nation's youth was better left in other hands. He turned to a variety of odd jobs which are mirrored in the later novels, especially in *Der schwarze Obelisk* (1956, translated as *The Black Obelisk*, 1957): he was an itinerant peddler, a salesman for a gravestone firm, an organist in an insane asylum, and an advertising copywriter. In 1925 he moved to Berlin, where he edited the magazine *Sport im Bild* and began to establish a reputation for high living, fancy clothes, hard drinking, and as an aficionado of automobile racing. He married his first wife, the actress Jutta Zambona, in 1925. He made a second literary start with the story "Stationen am Horizont" (Stations on the Horizon), which was serialized in the sports journal for which Remarque was working but was never published in book form.

*Remarque discussing with producer Carl Laemmle the details of the filming of* Im Westen nichts Neues *in 1929 (Ullstein)*

*Nazis demonstrating against the premiere of the film* Im Westen nichts Neues *in Berlin in December 1930 (Ullstein)*

*Im Westen nichts Neues* was written in a few months in 1927, but Remarque was not immediately able to find a publisher. Ullstein eventually decided to bring out the work, and it appeared first in serial form during November and December 1928 in the *Vossische Zeitung*. Book publication followed in January 1929, and *Im Westen nichts Neues* proved to be an instant best-seller. Within three months a half million copies were sold in Germany, and the book was quickly translated into fourteen languages. A year after publication the figure had jumped to a million copies at home and the number of translations to twenty-three, not counting a half dozen pirated editions. After eighteen months the worldwide sales totalled three-and-a-half million copies.

Such phenomenal and immediate success was spurred by the fact that the publishers aggressively promoted the book with a media campaign that might not seem unusual today but that was unprecedented in the 1920s. But the main reason was that readers ten years after the Armistice found their own perceptions of the Great War confirmed by Remarque's portrayal of a new kind of war which seemed to mark a turning point in man's history. Remarque allows this theme to emerge indirectly and without much direct editorial comment.

Paul Bäumer, eighteen years old and fresh from school at the beginning of the novel, is sent after skimpy but brutal basic training to the trenches in France. The plot consists of Paul's experiences at the front, at home on leave, and in the hospital where he twice recuperates from wounds. The novel ends with his death just before the cessation of hostilities, on a day when all is otherwise "quiet on the front." What happens between the beginning and the end is divided almost exactly into two halves. In the first half the action takes place largely behind the lines; the fighting is only sporadic; and Paul and the other soldiers spend much of their time thinking about home, school, and what life might be like after the war is over. This half ends with the first great battle, and the second half begins with Paul's subsequent leave at home. After he returns to France, the book depicts unrelieved fighting. Most of the main characters die in quickening succession, and life is reduced to a primitive struggle for survival where instinct is crucial and reason meaningless, reaction and luck are everything, and thinking or planned action are at best irrelevant and at worst disastrous.

This construction of the novel mirrors the actual course of the war, in which the German troops had to fight against the growing material superiority of the Allies, though Remarque does not really present the conflict as war between Germans and Allies. The battles are almost never identified and dates are rarely given; he writes of "the troops over there" more often than he does of the French or the British or the Americans, for they are not the real enemy. Speaking in a foxhole in no-man's-land to the Frenchman he has killed, Paul blames the carnage on the desire for profit and on "national interest" as defined by authorities and institutions on both sides. Little men ruled by forces over which they have no control, those doing the fighting are *all* victims and have too much in common to be enemies. The rhythm established by the book's structure also underlines the theme of the lost generation, to whom *Im Westen nichts Neues* is dedicated. In the beginning the young recruits are still closely tied to the past; and in their conversations with the older soldiers, who look forward to returning to jobs and family, they struggle to imagine a future for themselves. When Paul is home on leave, he realizes that the war has cut him and his comrades off from a past that is forever lost; and back at the front he recognizes that the war has made concern for the future meaningless. The only thing that counts is the present and surviving from one moment of that present to the next. Survival becomes increasingly more difficult as the book progresses and the technological nature of the war is made more evident. From the start Remarque stresses that living or dying has little to do with one's prowess as a soldier, except as "prowess" is equated with conditioned reflex. Death comes from afar in the artillery shells and the bombs; and as the trenches offer less and less refuge from the other side's new tanks and airplanes and its better guns, survival becomes little more than a matter of chance.

*Im Westen nichts Neues* is, of course, a book about the war, but in its insistence that life has been reduced to reaction and instinct it goes beyond the war. Remarque means more than just the trenches when he has Paul say that "das Leben ist nur auf einer ständigen Lauer gegen die Bedrohung des Todes,—es hat uns zu denkenden Tieren gemacht, um uns die Waffe des Instinktes zu geben,—es hat uns mit Stumpfheit durchsetzt, damit wir nicht zerbrechen vor dem Grauen, das uns bei klarem, bewußtem Denken überfallen würde . . ." (life is simply one continual watch against the menace of death;—it has transformed us into unthinking animals in order to give us the weapon of instinct—it has reinforced us with dullness, so that we do not go to pieces before the horror which would overwhelm us if we had clear, conscious thought . . .). Nowhere in the novel is the real meaning of the war brought home to Paul more clearly than in the military hospital where he is recovering from his wounds: the war is a new outbreak of man's inherent primitivism and makes a lie of his belief in culture and civilization and progress. "Wie sinnlos ist alles, was je geschrieben, getan, gedacht wurde, wenn so etwas möglich ist! Es muß alles gelogen und belanglos sein, wenn die Kultur von Jahrtausenden nicht einmal verhindern konnte, daß diese Ströme von Blut vergossen wurden, daß diese Kerker der Qualen zu Hunderttausenden existieren. Erst das Lazarett zeigt, was Krieg ist" (How senseless is everything that can ever be written, done, or thought, when such things are possible. It must be all lies and of no account when the culture of a thousand years could not prevent this stream of blood being poured out, these torture-chambers in their hundreds of thousands. A hospital alone shows what war is). A. F. Bance points out that *Im Westen nichts Neues* "is a novel of Weimar Germany," written not immediately after the war but in the late 1920s, when "the individual became fully aware of his limited freedom of action in the face of social, industrial and political forces." It would be going too far to suggest that Remarque's intention was to present World War I as a metaphor for what has happened to man in the twentieth century, yet the theme of the individual struggling against but clearly determined by forces beyond his control—technology, institutions, politics, social conventions, disease, death—remained central in his later work. So did the importance of chance and accident and of the one thing that retains its positive value in the novel: comradeship. Finally, the straightforward, relatively unadorned, realistic style of *Im Westen nichts Neues*, with its division into succinct short episodes and a heavy reliance on conversation, remained characteristic of Remarque's writing.

Despite the instant acclaim that greeted the novel, its appearance also caused a tidal wave of controversy—which did nothing to harm book sales. While most of the early critics and reviewers praised *Im Westen nichts Neues* as the ultimate antiwar statement, others attacked its view of the war, its inherent pacifism, its "outrageous" popularity, the quality of the writing, and Remarque himself. His role in the war, and thus the authenticity of his portrayal of it, were called into doubt. Even the author's identity was questioned in a book-length satire, *Hat Erich Maria Remarque wirklich gelebt?* (Does Erich Maria Remarque Really Exist?), and

Remarque's novel was blasted as both mediocre writing and bad propaganda. The most outspoken revilers were the Nazis, by 1930 the second most important party in the nation. Literally everything about *Im Westen nichts Neues*, but particularly its pacifism and its "defamatory" picture of the German soldier, aroused their ire. Late in 1930, when Lewis Milestone's American film version played in Berlin, Nazi gangs roughed up spectators waiting in line for tickets and disrupted performances. In a Germany buffeted by the shock waves of the stock market crash, precariously close to civil chaos, and already ruled in large measure by emergency decree, the film was banned as too controversial and a threat to law and order. The Nazis' ultimate verdict was pronounced in 1933 when *Im Westen nichts Neues* was one of the first books to be burned publicly. Propaganda Minister Joseph Goebbels himself consigned it to the flames with the words: "For his literary betrayal of the soldiers of the First World War and so that our people may be educated in the spirit of truthfulness, I give to the flames the writings of Erich Maria Remarque."

Remarque was not on hand to see the novel so honored. After his unprecedented first success he was able to devote himself exclusively to writing, and he had immediately begun work on a sequel. But he recognized that the political reaction to *Im Westen nichts Neues* had made him a marked man; and in 1931, after finishing *Der Weg zurück* (1931; translated as *The Road Back*, 1931) and making sure that his money was out of the country, he left Germany. He bought a villa in Porto Ronco in Switzerland and lived both there and in France until 1939, when he left Europe for the United States. Sometime during the early 1930s he divorced his wife (sources disagree as to the date) but subsequently remarried her so that she could remain in Switzerland and avoid having to return to Hitler's Germany. In 1938 the Third Reich took away his citizenship.

*Der Weg zurück* takes up where *Im Westen nichts Neues* ended: on the battlefields of France in the final days before the Armistice. All of the principal characters are veterans of the trenches; some of them are known to the reader from *Im Westen nichts Neues* but most, including the narrator, Ernst Birkholz, are new. The book traces their return from France and their attempts to get a footing in a world which they find alien and hostile. Some seek this footing in reestablished relationships with parents, wives, friends, or school, others in jobs and new commitments. Most are unsuccessful: two commit suicide; one disappears with a wife who had been unfaithful while he was away and with whom there can now be no more love; another is sent to prison for murder; and the few who manage to find a niche in the postwar world do so by becoming profiteers and opportunists.

Though the fact is not made explicit, the novel is set in the Osnabrück to which Remarque himself returned after demobilization. The time span is kept indefinite: not long before the end it is mentioned that the characters were at the front "a year ago"; but there is also reference to the rapidly falling value of the mark, which suggests that the work ends closer to 1923. In any event, the novel is set primarily in 1919 and 1920, the fateful years when the seeds of the ultimate death of Weimar democracy and the victory of fascism were sown. These were months of civil strife, of unsuccessful revolution both from the left and from the right, of economic deprivation, of acrid division on national goals and national identity, of humiliation from the peace treaty, and of groping experimentation with a new form of democratic government for which there was neither the necessary tradition nor sufficient popular support. This historical background is all part of *Der Weg zurück*, and the novel is a fascinating chronicle of the period.

Historical event is not really the issue, however, for Remarque is primarily interested in private concerns. His theme is the inability of the lost generation to function in the civilian world, and it is made abundantly clear that this failure stems from the war. The characters' values and motivations, their actions, and their reactions to the current situation are all determined by their wartime experience. "Halt die Ohren steif, Junge, der Krieg ist noch nicht zu Ende" (That's right, keep smiling, lad; the war's not over yet), "Aber für den Frieden? Taugen wir dazu? Passen wir Überhaupt noch zu etwas anderm, als Soldaten zu sein?" (But for peace? Are we suitable? Are we fit for anything but soldiering?), "Wir sind immer noch Soldaten, ohne es gewußt zu haben" (We are soldiers still without having been aware of it), "Wir haben den Krieg noch in den Knochen. . . . Wir werden ihn auch nie mehr los" (We have the war in our bones still. . . . Yes, and we'll never get it out again)—these quotations taken from various places in the novel could be multiplied many times over. In *Im Westen nichts Neues* the past had been wiped out; the future did not exist; the present was all that was real. In *Der Weg zurück* it is only the past that counts; and as much as the veterans struggle against the past and lament the fact that they have been permanently crippled by it, they continually affirm its signifi-

cance. The horrors of the war must not be glossed over or forgotten, they tell their teachers, their parents, the court, and a troubled society that would like to get back to business as usual; otherwise the sacrifices and the losses will have been in vain. But their stubborn clinging to the wartime past makes *Der Weg zurück* as much a novel of resentment as the commitment to a new beginning that Remarque claimed he wanted it to be.

This commitment is nowhere more evident than in his continuing emphasis on the one thing that had remained a positive value in the otherwise pessimistic *Im Westen nichts Neues:* comradeship. In the sequel the pronoun *wir* (we) is by far the most important one, and it means "we, the veterans" vis-á-vis "them, the rest of the world." The characters are scarcely home before they seek each other out, and only when they are together do they feel a sense of belonging and a bit of hope. As some adjust and others disappear, as social distinctions and civilian ties gradually erode the old solidarity from the front, Birkholz sees that the one positive thing which the war had given him is now lost: "Alles andere ist kaputgegangen im Kriege, aber an die Kameradschaft hatten wir geglaubt. Und jetzt sehen wir: was der Tod nicht fertiggebracht hat, das gelingt dem Leben: es trennt uns" (All else went west in the war, but comradeship we did believe in; now only to find that what death could not do, life is achieving; it is driving us asunder). The inability to fit into civilian life confirms his feeling that he and his friends are ruined, that they are helpless to do much about the problems that now confront them, and that others are responsible for making it so.

Remarque had not intended for *Der Weg zurück* to be quite the pessimistic work that it is. "We want to begin once more to believe in life," he said in correspondence when he was working on the novel, and its title means not just "the road back" to postwar Germany but explicitly "the road back to life." For a time Ludwig Breyer, a veteran who has recognized that the real enemy is not the past but the reactionary trend of the present, seems to be on the right road. And in the novel's brief epilogue, which is—uncharacteristically for Remarque—filled with metaphors, Birkholz assures the reader that he will find his way back to vital living just as surely as "ein Baum oder die atmende Erde" (a tree or the breathing earth) do every spring. But Breyer has committed suicide; Birkholz has suffered a nervous breakdown; and the overwhelming prior evidence of the book argues for skepticism that the lost generation can ever find new meaning.

As in the case of *Im Westen nichts Neues,* it is well to remember that *Der Weg zurück* was written a decade after the period it depicts and to ponder what the text reveals about German thinking in the late 1920s and early 1930s. The conviction that private identity is determined by external factors and that the individual is powerless to do much but react to the social, economic, and political forces that impinge on him is characteristic of the last years before Hitler. This conviction turned out to have fatal consequences; and some early critics, hitting on this point, blamed Remarque for not warning openly of the dangers in such thinking. The left particularly criticized the novel for dwelling so exclusively in the realm of private fate and for failing to pay sufficient attention to the historical context. Remarque himself considered *Der Weg zurück* a better novel than *Im Westen nichts Neues* and was disappointed when it did not sell as well. Reviewers abroad, especially in the United States, tended to agree with the author; but German critics generally found the work repetitive in style, lacking in focus, given to sentimentality and sensationalism (a

charge Remarque would hear again and again), and poorly written.

Remarque's next novel, *Drei Kameraden* (1937; translated as *Three Comrades,* 1937) spans the years from the inflation of 1923 to the end of the decade. The book was begun in Berlin, finished in Switzerland after he had emigrated, and published by the Querido Verlag in Amsterdam, by this time the leading publisher for the works of German writers in exile.

The three comrades of the title—the narrator Robert Lohkamp, Otto Köster, and Gottfried Lenz—run an auto repair shop and garage. The novel is made up of a series of episodes in which they confront the economic problems of the times and the institutions and values of the society in which they live—or, one might better say, in which they do their best to exist *despite* these "values," for Lohkamp and his friends are outsiders. They vehemently reject the demands of normal living, which they consider false, meaningless, and stupid, and insist instead on living according to a self-determined code that brings them into constant conflict with the rest of their world. To make ends meet they also use as a taxi a magnificent old souped-up car named Karl, which functions almost

*(From left) Franchot Tone, Margaret Sullavan, Robert Taylor, Robert Young, and Lionel Atwill in the 1938 M-G-M film of Remarque's* Three Comrades, *with screenplay by F. Scott Fitzgerald and Edward B. Paramore*

as a fourth comrade in the novel. A fifth comrade is Patricia Hollmann, a glamorous but fragile woman with whom Lohkamp falls in love. The tale of this love, from hesitant first approach to Pat's death from tuberculosis at the end, gives the novel its plot; and this use of a love story to provide the principal action and structure—which marks a distinct break from the two earlier, essentially all-male books—sets the model for the rest of Remarque's writing.

Like Remarque's previous novels, *Drei Kameraden* is a first-person narrative, told this time in the past tense. The plot is once more developed in episodes which are strung together loosely and can often stand as semi-independent stories. Characterization and dialogue remain more important than action, relationships more important than historical background. While the role of the war in making the principal characters what they are is now less decisive, it still gets a major share of the blame for their unwillingness to adjust, their lack of purpose, their indifference, and even—in the case of Pat—for their inability to survive: chronic malnutrition during the war years is responsible for her frailty and ultimate death. The basic tone of this book, like that of the earlier ones, is pessimistic. Lenz is murdered by a rival political group after a rally which he attends more out of curiosity and for the excitement than out of conviction. Karl is sold to pay for Pat's stay in the sanatorium even though it is clear that this sacrifice of the means of the comrades' livelihood will do nothing but buy a few more days together for her and Lohkamp. Lohkamp and Köster are left at the end with no particular reason, and surely without the wherewithal, to go on living.

In a number of ways, however, *Drei Kameraden* points ahead to the author's later works more than it does back to his earlier ones. Themes, motifs, and settings that would become Remarque trademarks are developed here: the fascination of his characters with auto racing and fast cars, the prodigious amounts of alcohol they drink and the number of pages they spend doing it, the conspicuous role played by a colorful but often seamy variety of social outcasts and misfits as secondary characters. Much more significant is Remarque's building the action around an intense but doomed love story, and Pat Hollmann is the first of a kind of heroine for which he would become famous. Like Patricia ("Patrice" in the German version), several of these heroines have names which are strange to the German ear; they are beautiful but usually not in the way their world customarily de-

fines beauty; they are passionate but at the same time aloof, fragile, and somehow even artificial. They are different from other women and seem to come, as Remarque says about Pat, "from another world." In this "foreignness" they are fit lovers for outsiders like Lohkamp and Remarque's other loners. They have a greater willingness to belong to the society around them than do the men; but they also recognize that because of illness or personality or (in the later novels) external circumstance, they will never belong. Though not necessarily resigned to their fate, they accept their feelings of separateness and loneliness and their need for a like partner. These qualities are also characteristic of Remarque's male protagonists in his later novels.

Shortly before Pat dies she has an exchange with Lohkamp which states the view of existence that drives most of Remarque's later figures. After reviewing their brief time together and granting that it has brought a happiness he never really expected to find, Lohkamp says of life, "Die Einzelheiten sind wunderbar, aber das Ganze hat keinen Sinn. Als wenn es von einem Irren gemacht ist, dem auf die wunderbare Vielheit des Lebens nichts anderes eingefallen ist, als es wieder zu vernichten" (The details are wonderful, but the whole has no sense. As if it had been made by a madman who could think of nothing better to do with the marvelous variety of life that he had created but to annihilate it again). Pat replies, "Doch, Liebling, mit uns, das hat er schon gut gemacht. Besser gings gar nicht. Nur zu kurz. Viel zu kurz" (Anyway, darling, he hasn't done so badly by us. That couldn't have been better. Only too short. Far too short). Remarque's characters are isolated and alone either because they reject the expectations and life-style of the world around them or because they are forced (by exile, internment, or war) to live as outsiders. They seek companionship, usually with others who also rebel against the accepted values. But they do not believe that happiness can be found and do not trust it when it does sometimes come, because they "know" that ultimately happiness, like life itself, will not last. They are convinced that chance is more important than their own planned actions, and their perception of life's brevity leads them to pessimism and resignation. They drink to avoid confronting reality. They welcome risk and danger as ways of combating stagnation, and the fast pace at which they live helps them to avoid confronting existential fear. Their cynicism is often a cover for inner hurt, their flippancy for insecurity. They long to have something—or, more frequently, someone—to believe in, but their hope for success is outweighed by the conviction that the world in which they live offers only the shakiest basis for trust and confidence.

Because *Drei Kameraden* was published by an émigré press, the original German version did not receive much attention, but Remarque's name was enough to get a good reception for the English translation in the United States. The *New York Times* reviewer said: "I found Remarque's novel the most moving, the hardest to put down, that I have read in a long time. He is that rarity, a born storyteller with something to say." In 1938 M-G-M made a movie of the work for which F. Scott Fitzgerald wrote the significantly changed film script (his only screen credit) and with an all-star cast including Robert Taylor as Lohkamp, Franchot Tone, Robert Young, and Monty Woolley; Margaret Sullavan was nominated for an Academy Award for her portrayal of Pat. Though the film did not fare well at the box office, it helped prepare the way for the American phase of the author's exile.

Remarque wrote three novels that depict most vividly the fate of those who fled from the Nazis and their persecution as stateless persons in the countries where they sought refuge. Remarque himself experienced little of their misery: his stay in Switzerland was legal and relatively comfortable; and he seems to have had no great trouble in getting to the United States once it became clear that war in Europe was inevitable. President Roosevelt himself saw to it that the author of *All Quiet on the Western Front* was allowed legal entry under the immigrant quota. From 1939 to 1942 Remarque lived in Hollywood, where he had a celebrated affair with Marlene Dietrich, a close friendship with Greta Garbo, and working associations with Charlie Chaplin, Cole Porter, Fitzgerald, and Ernest Hemingway. He applied for American citizenship in 1941; in 1942 he moved to New York, where he maintained a residence until his death, although after the war he spent a part of each year in his villa in Switzerland.

The war years were not without tragedy: in 1943 the Nazis executed his youngest sister Elfriede for her involvement with the White Rose resistance group, and Remarque was convinced that the fact that she was his sister had something to do with her death. But exile in America was good to him, and he suffered few of the disappointments that were the general rule for German authors living in the United States during the Hitler years. Far from being unknown, he was celebrated in America; he moved in exciting circles; he had money;

he continued to write and to enjoy success with his work.

Remarque's fourth novel, *Flotsam*, appeared in a serial version in English translation in *Collier's* magazine in 1939, and Remarque spent another year revising the text for its book publication in 1941; the German version, *Liebe deinen Nächsten*, was published the same year. It is episodic and made up in large part of dialogue, but it differs from most of Remarque's earlier work in that it is a third-person narrative with frequent flashbacks. This style was dictated by the fact that the novel has two central heroes, rather than one, and an omniscient narrator was needed to report their separate fates. The one who is followed most closely is Ludwig Kern. In his early twenties, he has fled from Germany to Austria after his Jewish father was forced out of his pharmacy and imprisoned. From older and more seasoned refugees Kern learns the hazardous business of living without papers in a foreign country which is hostile toward the émigrés from across the border. He learns the most from Josef Steiner, who had earlier escaped from a concentration camp and has been in Austria long enough to be thoroughly familiar with the tricks of survival, the best ways of avoiding police and bureaucracy, and the elaborate networking which enables the refugees to keep in contact and to provide each other what meager help they can. Kern's and Steiner's paths cross frequently but they are never together long, for the nature of living in exile is that one is always on the move, always essentially in hiding, and regularly separated from others by deportation or imprisonment. Though this isolation now stems not from choice but from circumstance, Remarque's refugees are thus, once again, outsiders who know that relationships can only be temporary and that existence itself is constantly threatened.

The title page of *Flotsam* bears the motto "To live without roots takes a stout heart," to which the author might well have added "and continued good luck." Most of the characters who people his émigré novels soon run out of one or the other or both, but Kern is an exception. In Vienna he falls in love with Ruth Holland, a Jewish student at the university until the imminent German annexation of Austria forces her, too, into exile. Ruth and Kern make their way to Switzerland, and eventually to Paris; at the end of the novel, after all sorts of perils, they secure visas and ship tickets for immigration to Mexico, where they hope to begin a new life together. The money that makes this escape (and the happy ending unusual for Remarque) possible comes from Steiner. He has gone to Berlin to be with his dying wife; knowing that return to Germany means almost certain death, he has left the money he had set aside for his own passage abroad for Kern. Steiner is apprehended in Berlin by an SS officer who is his longtime enemy; and in a final, satisfying gesture he kills the officer by pushing him out of the hospital window and plunging to death with him.

Such incidents are the stuff of melodrama, and in *Flotsam* Remarque pulls out all the stops. The novel is essentially a thriller, and its basic story is less memorable than is the endless series of escapes, illegal border crossings, arrests, imprison-

ments, beatings, acts of persecution, and betrayals. Readers today are likely to be most impressed by the portraits of the other refugees with whom the protagonists come in fleeting contact: Jews, political émigrés who have to worry not just about the local authorities but also about German spies and Gestapo agents, White Russians who have already lived in exile for two decades, and a host of others. All live a hand-to-mouth existence; all survive from one day to the next with the conviction that they are merely "corpses on parole."

*Flotsam* was not particularly popular, either as a book or as the movie *So Ends Our Night* (1941); but the novel *Arch of Triumph*, first published in 1945 in English translation and republished in German as *Arc de Triomphe* in 1946, was another instant best-seller and reached worldwide sales of nearly five million copies. *Arch of Triumph* also has a large cast and a wealth of journalistic detail that is at times confusing. Its characters philosophize a great deal—and when Remarque lets his characters do that, he becomes pretentious and they do not ring true. There is more than a touch of the soap opera in the central love story, and the role played by coincidence taxes the reader's credulity. But the novel is far better artistically than *Flotsam*. The plot is less diffuse; the things that happen to the principal actors are not there just for their own sake but add up to a larger meaning for a culture on the verge of collapse. The novel is set in Paris in the months immediately preceding the fall of France and concludes at the moment of occupation. The characters live with the growing realization that an end is just ahead and, since the Parisians are unwilling and the exiles are unable to do anything but watch it come, with a paralyzing fatalism.

In *Arch of Triumph* the surface story takes on a metaphoric quality that Remarque's work had not had since *Im Westen nichts Neues*. The novel is about Ravic (his current name, anyway, thanks to the false passport he holds), once a successful surgeon in Germany, who earns his meager and illegal keep by checking the health of the whores in a brothel and by doing "ghost operations" for Parisian surgeons who take the credit for his work and all but a fraction of the money. At the beginning of the book he prevents another classic Remarque heroine, Joan Madou, from committing suicide; and the story of the love that soon develops between them is the main thread of the narrative. It is not an easy love and both know it will not last, but for a time at least it gives them a reason to go on living in a world that is coming apart around them. At the end Joan leaves Ravic and is shot by a jealous new

*Charles Boyer and Ingrid Bergman in the 1948 United Artists film of Remarque's* Arch of Triumph

lover; unable to save her, Ravic watches her die in the hospital. With the only thing that has given his life some brief meaning now gone, Ravic stays in Paris to be arrested and presumably to be sent to a concentration camp by the Nazi invaders.

Ravic is the most complex, least one-dimensional hero Remarque had created to this point. "A stranger everywhere," he is, to be sure, much like his predecessors in believing that the only thing that really counts in a threatened and transitory world is the intensity with which one can live the moment. But though he essentially remains a cynic, Ravic does change and things other than self and survival become important to him. Though he tries to get over it quickly—usually with Calvados, the apple brandy made famous by the novel—it matters to him when a patient dies; and when a difficult operation is successful he is pleased not only with his own skill but also because of the saved life. He can go out of his way to help others, and at one point doing so leads to his arrest and deportation to Switzerland. Above all, he changes as a result of his love for Joan. At the beginning of the tale Ravic is burned out, utterly without hope, and capable of emotion only when he dreams of exacting revenge on Haake, the Gestapo man who tortured him and sent him to a concentration camp in 1933. With Joan he learns that there are other feelings which can at least help to fill his spiritual vacuum and are worth having even if one is doomed to lose them. Amazed that he is jealous when she has left him, he discovers that he is "nicht mehr wie ein Toter auf Urlaub mit Kleinem Zynismus, Sarkasmus und etwas Mut, nicht mehr kalt; lebendig wieder, leidend meinetwegen, aber offen wieder den Gewittern des Lebens, zurückgeboren in seine schlichte Gewalt!" (no longer like a dead man on furlough with his small cynicism, sarcasm, and portion of courage, no longer cold: alive again, suffering if you like, but again open to all the thunderstorms of life, reborn into its own simple strength!). This "rebirth" is not strong enough to give him the will to resist his eventual betrayal to the Germans, but it brings a precarious sort of fulfillment that none of Remarque's earlier heroes had achieved—not even Kern, who survives at the end of *Flotsam* but is pale as a character compared to Ravic. Ravic also experiences fulfillment in revenge: just before the fall of the city he kills Haake; after the deed he feels at peace, as he had not since before their first encounter years ago—"leicht und gelöst . . . als wenn ein Schloß von seiner Vergangenheit abgefallen wäre" (easy and as if a padlock had fallen from his past). So great is this sense of

finished business that Ravic decides not to flee again when the Germans reach Paris but to suffer whatever comes his way: "Er hatte Rache gehabt und Liebe. Das war genug. Es war nicht alles, aber es war so viel, wie ein Mann verlangen konnte. Er hatte beides nicht mehr erwartet" (He had had revenge and love. That was enough. It was not everything, but it was as much as a man could ask for. He had not expected either one again).

As had been the case with each of Remarque's four previous novels, a Hollywood film version of *Arch of Triumph* followed soon after book publication, starring Ingrid Bergman as Joan, Charles Boyer as Ravic, and Charles Laughton as Haake. Even with this cast the film was a box office failure. It emphasized the love story to the virtual exclusion of all else and failed particularly to capture the desperate atmosphere of existence in exile which the novel had depicted so vividly. Remarque would return a third time to this subject in *Die Nacht von Lissabon* (1963; translated as *The Night in Lisbon*, 1964), but not until nearly twenty years later. First he wrote a novel about the more immediate past in Germany, a task which necessitated considerable research. There was a gap of seven years—a long silence for Remarque—between *Arch of Triumph* and his next work, *Der Funke Leben* (translated as *Spark of Life*), which appeared both in German and in English in 1952.

*Der Funke Leben* is the author's literary tribute to the suffering and determination of the victims of the concentration camps. The novel is set in a camp in Germany called Mellern and in a town in a valley below the camp; it begins in March 1945 and ends after the camp has been liberated by American troops. Like *Flotsam* and *Arch of Triumph*, it is written in the third person so that the author can trace the fates of a number of characters. The principal focus is on an inmate who is called "509" throughout and is not identified by name until well into the work. But the reader also gets to know a number of other prisoners and several of their SS guards—especially the camp commandant, Neubauer, whose complex personality is developed more fully than that of any other character in the book. In some respects the structure recalls that of *Im Westen nichts Neues:* the central figure is less a binding force than elsewhere in Remarque's works, and the plot is less important than the individual episodes which it ties together.

German critics have long contended that the subject of the concentration camps is all but impossible to treat effectively in fiction. The historical facts familiar to everyone from eyewitness accounts, pictures, and newsreels, it is argued, have left an impact that literature cannot hope to match. Fact is so vividly real that fiction is certain to seem a pale imitation; and unless the horror is presented through stylization and metaphor, literary treatments run the dangers of trivializing atrocity and of sensationalism. In *Der Funke Leben* Remarque in no way departs from his usual stark realism, and some of his descriptions of life and especially of death in Mellern certainly earn the charge of sensationalism. Mellern is not an extermination camp, but a forced-labor camp; it has no gas chambers, but it does have a crematorium which is kept busy day and night. Death, brutality, and terror are depicted on every page, and some of the descriptions seem to be there for their own gruesome sake rather than because they are needed to make the book's point.

These flaws are not fatal, however, for Remarque's theme is that death and horror will end and life will return, even for the skeletal inmates of Mellern. The first event in the book is an Allied bombing raid on the town below the camp, and thus from the beginning the prisoners have a sign that their liberation may be coming closer. This and other signs gradually kindle in them a new "spark of life" and a hesitant determination to survive a while longer. The spark causes 509, who has been in the camp for ten years and is near death when the story opens, to defy the SS by refusing to "volunteer" for medical experiments; his example leads his young friend Bucher to refuse as well. The two are savagely tortured and given up for lost by the rest; but their return, just barely alive, is a further indication that holding out may yet be worth the effort. Plans are made to take over the barracks when the Americans arrive; Bucher and Ruth Holland from the women's camp begin to think of a life not separated by barbed wire but together; and the Communist prisoners talk of a new political order for Germany once the Nazis are gone.

Although 509 is touched by the growing determination of the others to live and begins to remember a name and a past he had all but forgotten, he dies in a senseless bloodbath staged by the SS hours before the camp is liberated. By killing one of the most sadistic guards who is shooting prisoners as they try to escape a burning building, however, he saves the lives of many more inmates. This is a melodramatic and not exactly happy ending, yet 509 accomplishes something no other Remarque protagonist does: he comes to believe that betterment may be possible, at least for others, and he is willing to act for the common good. In a sense,

Steiner had done the same thing in *Flotsam;* but his leaving money for Kern was a private deed, done as a contingency, and the reader knows nothing beyond the fact that it will enable Kern to escape Europe. In 509 Remarque portrays for the only time a central character whose actions have a demonstrated positive effect on others that lasts beyond his own death. Dozens of fellow prisoners live to see freedom as a result of his death, particularly Bucher. The book's final pages tell of his leaving Mellern with Ruth: the spark fanned by 509 has sprung to life in their new beginning.

While he was writing *Der Funke Leben* Remarque was also working on a novel he called *Zeit zu leben und Zeit zu sterben* (Time to Live and Time to Die). Published first in English translation in

*Remarque (seated) with John Gavin in a scene from the 1958 Universal film of Remarque's* A Time to Love and a Time to Die

1954 with the not-quite-literal title *A Time to Love and a Time to Die*, it is a novel with clear echoes of *Im Westen nichts Neues:* this time the story is of a soldier who falls in love while home on leave from the Russian front at the end of World War II and who dies when he returns to the battlefield. Like *Im Westen nichts Neues*, the book begins and ends at the front, and many of the themes and motifs of the first novel are repeated: the all-important role of chance, the ruling of the world by inhumanity and unreason, the soldiers' realization that the war is lost and they are lost with it. Unlike Paul Bäumer, however, the hero, Graeber, cannot escape despair in comradeship, for in *Zeit zu leben und Zeit zu sterben* Remarque has again created a lone protagonist who is at odds with most of his surroundings. Nor can Graeber fall back on instinct, since—at least at the end—he is much more aware than Paul had been of what is happening to him and what it means. Above all, the books differ in that here Remarque uses a love story to structure the main plot: four-fifths of the novel is devoted to Graeber's three-week furlough; and though his love for Elisabeth Kruse does not develop until nearly a week of the leave is over and ends with his death a few days after his return to Russia, the love story is what the book is about.

In many ways this is a typical Remarque love: although Elisabeth is a more wholesome and normal heroine than many of the others, the "life" together of the two characters is again brief, intense because they know it will be brief, and lived essentially in isolation from the world around them. There is something new here, however: their isolation from others has a strongly underlined idyllic quality, and they share an eagerness to make their love last even as they recognize that it is not likely to do so. In the book's early sections the word *Verzweifelung* (despair) is used again and again to characterize Graeber's attitude toward his existence; yet by the end of his leave he and Elisabeth have married, talk of having a child (a most unusual notion for Remarque characters), and dream of normalcy and permanence once the war is over. This, of course, is not to be. Back at the front, Graeber is soon forced to realize that, strong though his love for Elisabeth is, "es reichte nicht weit genug. Es rührte sein Herz, aber es hielt ihn nicht. Es versank, es war ein kleines Privatglück, es konnte sich nicht halten in dem endlosen Moor des allgemeinen Elends und der Verzweifelung" (it could not extend far enough. It touched his heart but it did not hold him. It was swallowed up; it was a small, private happiness that could not support itself in the limitless morass of general misery and despair).

In good Remarque fashion his death is both dramatic and ironic. After killing a fanatical German comrade who is about to gun down a group of Russian civilians, Graeber is himself shot by one of the Russians whom he has freed. Christine R. Barker and R. W. Last, who are among the best critics of Remarque's work, find "at least a suggestion of hope for the future" in this death, since Graeber "has come to realize the necessity for involving himself in wider issues than his own personal survival." They also conclude that, because Elisabeth may be pregnant, the novel "marks a huge advance on the bleak negativity" of *Im Westen nichts Neues* and other earlier works. There is truth in this judgment and one does hear faint echoes of expressionism's symbolic "new man" optimism in the hint that Graeber may be survived by the child he and Elisabeth discussed when they talked of the future. But Graeber's last word on his leave demonstrates that Remarque has not mellowed very much: "Es war zu kurz gewesen, und das andere war zu lang. Es war ein Urlaub gewesen; aber das Leben eines Soldaten rechnet nach der Zeit an der Front und nicht nach Urlauben" (It had been too short and the other was too long. It had been a furlough; but a soldier's life is reckoned by his time at the front and not by furloughs).

The best part of *A Time to Love and a Time to Die* is not the central story but the picture of life in Germany during the late days of the Third Reich. When Graeber arrives home he finds destruction and loss, distrust and fear everywhere. The physical destruction from the bombing is bad, but worse is the destruction of old values and relationships under Nazi rule. Pervasive fear is both the result of this rule and the tool it uses to maintain control as its power crumbles. As he had done in *Der Funke Leben*, the author stresses that the bulk of Hitler's support came not from gangsters or unusually evil people but from everyday Germans. As a major source of the regime's tyranny he cites its passion for organization, its manipulation of a normal respect for authority and institutions, its overburdening bureaucracy.

There is a final tie between *Im Westen nichts Neues* and *A Time to Love and a Time to Die* in the fact that the later work once again made Remarque the subject of controversy. Written, as were all his novels, in German, it appeared first in English translation; publication in Germany followed the same year, but only after the author had made a number of changes in the text. Critics claimed that these changes amounted to censorship forced on

Remarque by his German publisher and were intended to blunt the potential political impact of the novel. It was charged that the publisher was afraid that the original version would stir up memories which German readers of the 1950s were trying hard to forget and even that the book's depiction of Nazi tyranny could embarrass the many former Nazis who held powerful positions in the Federal Republic. Remarque dismissed the criticism as an unfounded attack on his publisher and maintained, as he had always done, that his novels were not political. It is possible, however, that the furor helped to rule out any plans he may have had of returning to Germany.

Actually, he probably had no such plans. The firm conviction that "you can't go home again" is expressed in one way or another in every one of his novels; besides, Remarque liked living in a country which had been good to him, especially in New York. He had become an American citizen in 1947; and though he made occasional trips to Germany during the postwar years, they were always short. After 1945 he spent part of the year in New York and part in his villa in Switzerland or in Italy until, in the last years of his life, illness kept him entirely in Europe.

Although Remarque is known almost exclusively as a novelist, he did try his hand briefly at dramatic forms during his later years and did so with considerable success. In 1955 he wrote the screenplay for an Austrian movie, *Der letzte Akt* (The Last Act), about Hitler's final days in the bunker of the Chancellery in Berlin, which was based on the book *Ten Days to Die* (1950) by Michael A. Musmanno, one of the American judges at the Nuremberg Trials. Directed by G. W. Pabst, the film played to large audiences and favorable reviews in its English version, *Ten Days to Die*. Two years later Remarque was also persuaded by Universal Studios to write the screenplay for Douglas Sirk's Hollywood adaptation of *A Time to Love and a Time to Die;* this script was the only work he ever wrote in English. Except for a few scenes, his script was not actually used in the film. In the movie, however, the author himself played the secondary but important role of a former schoolteacher with whom Graeber discusses the war and the meaning of Nazism for Germany, and his acting was praised by the critics as more convincing than the performances turned in by the stars, John Gavin and Lilo Pulver. In 1956 Remarque wrote a drama for the stage, *Die letzte Station* (The Last Station), which played successfully both in Germany and on Broadway; it was never published in German, but an English translation, *Full Circle*, appeared in 1974.

After *Zeit zu leben und Zeit zu sterben* Remarque wrote four more novels, but none of them broke significant new ground. Two return to settings and themes familiar from earlier novels and are among his more effective works; the other two are clearly his weakest books. *Der schwarze Obelisk* (translated as *The Black Obelisk*, 1957), published in 1956 and set in the inflation year 1923, belongs in the former category. The most autobiographical of all Remarque's novels and the one in which the historical background is most precisely documented, it depicts a small German city in a time of reviving nationalism and rising anti-Semitism, of unemployment, and above all of racing inflation—"der große Ausverkauf des Sparers, des ehrlichen Einkommens und der Anständigkeit" (the great sellout of thrift, honest effort, and respectability). From his postwar vantage point Remarque sees in this combination the fertile soil from which National Socialism was able to grow.

There is another doomed love story, though this time it is depicted with a lighter touch that is in keeping with the book's satirical intent. *Der schwarze Obelisk* has a greater measure of humor than one finds in Remarque's other works; but it is very black humor, for the main concern of the novel is death. The narrator, Ludwig Bodmer, works for a gravestone company, and the black obelisk of the title is a monument which is too costly to sell and which functions throughout the book as a fairly heavy-handed symbol of death. Although at the end it is finally sold, the inflation is brought under control, and Bodmer leaves for a new life as a journalist in Berlin, fear of "the great dark," with which the author's protagonists had wrestled ever since *Im Westen nichts Neues*, is what makes the characters what they are and is the issue that drives the plot.

*Der schwarze Obelisk* is a rambling narrative, the individual episodes of which are better than the story itself. The principal settings, which include a whorehouse and an insane asylum as well as the office and sales lot of the tombstone firm, are bizarre, and the secondary characters are colorful, some of them grotesquely so. The best feature of the book is the uncertain atmosphere it captures of loss and struggle and change in one of the decisive years of the 1920s.

In 1958 Remarque married the film star Paulette Goddard. After 1960 he spent more and more of his time in Italy and at his villa in Switzerland, returning less frequently to the United States as increasing ill health made overseas travel more dif-

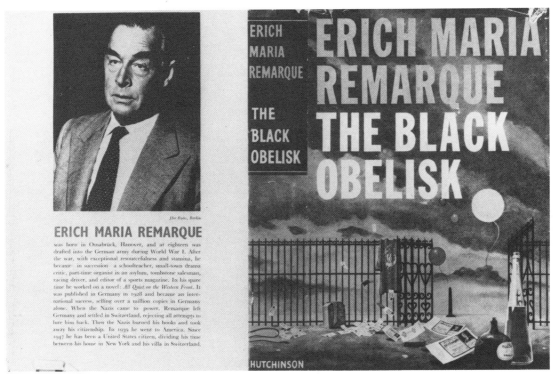

ERICH MARIA REMARQUE

was born in Osnabrück, Hanover, and at eighteen was drafted into the German army during World War I. After the war, with exceptional resourcefulness and stamina, he became—in succession—a schoolteacher, small-town drama critic, part-time organist in an asylum, tombstone salesman, racing driver, and editor of a sports magazine. In his spare time he worked on a novel: *All Quiet on the Western Front*. It was published in Germany in 1928 and became an international success, selling over a million copies in Germany alone. When the Nazis came to power, Remarque left Germany and settled in Switzerland, rejecting all attempts to lure him back. Then the Nazis burned his books and took away his citizenship. In 1939 he went to America. Since 1947 he has been a United States citizen, dividing his time between his home in New York and his villa in Switzerland.

*Dust jacket for the 1957 British edition of the English translation of Remarque's most autobiographical novel,* Der schwarze Obelisk *(1956)*

ficult. Aside from his health, he lived comfortably and enjoyed a life that was quiet in comparison to the fast pace of his earlier years.

German reviewers could always be counted on to greet the appearance of a new Remarque novel with the charge that he had written "yet another" overly sentimental book that was ridden with clichés. This criticism was often undeserved, but it was certainly appropriate for *Der Himmel kennt keine Günstlinge* (1961; translated as *Heaven Has No Favorites*, 1961), and for once most of the foreign critics agreed. The characters were universally seen as Hollywood caricatures of real people and the story as far-fetched. The author's habit of repeating and even of quoting himself, which is evident in all his books, was found to be particularly annoying here, and his penchant for facile philosophizing was held to have gone beyond all bounds of good taste. Remarque himself apparently had a different opinion of the novel's worth, since he dedicated it "to Paulette Goddard Remarque"; and his readers must have disagreed, too, for the book sold better than any work since *Arch of Triumph*.

Attention is fairly evenly divided between Clerfayt, a professional racing car driver, and Lillian Dunkerque, but for a change the heroine is really the principal character. The first third of the story is set in a sanatorium where she awaits death, the rest in Paris, Venice, and glamorous stops on the racing circuit where she seeks to spend the time she has left in adventure and fast living with Clerfayt. She is attracted to him because his life-style represents vitality, risk, and intensity. When he starts to talk of settling down and of the future, she hears bourgeois stagnation—"the prison of mediocrity"—and realizes that she must break with him. In a typically ironic ending the author makes this action unnecessary: Clerfayt is killed in a crash and Lillian dies soon after returning to the sanatorium. The novel ends with the judgment that "sie glücklich gewesen sei, soweit man einen Menschen jemals glücklich nennen Könne" (she had been happy, insofar as any human being can ever be called happy).

*Die Nacht von Lissabon*, published in 1963 and a year later in English as *The Night in Lisbon*, is the last work Remarque finished and a far better novel than its predecessor. In it the author returns to subjects and techniques which had worked well for him in the past: to the time of Nazi persecution and the fate of those who fled from it, to suspense, and to the first-person narrative with its sense of

*Remarque with his second wife, the actress
Paulette Goddard (Ullstein)*

for long. The core of the novel is, as always, a tragic love story.

The only new feature is the framing structure the author employs. The narrative present, Lisbon in 1942, is only a small part of the book. The essential matter is the tale of how he got to Lisbon told by "Josef Schwarz" (the passport is again false) to the unnamed narrator, himself a German emigrant, during the course of a long night in one refugee bar after another. The first-person flashback is a technique Remarque had tried before but never to the extent that it is used here. The need to compress the story so that it could be related in a single night makes this book shorter than Remarque's other novels, and the writing is much tighter; together with the considerable restraint with which Schwarz's tale is developed, these qualities make *Die Nacht von Lissabon* one of Remarque's better novels.

In 1967 Remarque was awarded the Großes Verdienstkreuz (Great Order of Merit) of the Federal Republic of Germany. In 1968 his postwar German publishers, Kiepenheuer & Witsch and Kurt Desch, issued a slim volume of tributes to mark his seventieth birthday; in it his friend and fellow novelist Hans Habe praised Remarque as "the last *grandseigneur* of literature." But discussion of his work virtually ceased. Though slowed by several heart attacks, the author continued to work quietly on his last novel, *Schatten im Paradies*, right up to his death in the hospital at Locarno on 25 September 1970 at the age of seventy-two. After a Catholic funeral he was buried in the cemetery above the village of Porto Ronco.

His death was prominently noted in newspapers around the world, but neither the obituaries nor the reawakened critical comment that followed them did anything to change the well-established views of Remarque and his place in literature. In Germany he was still described as the successful (and therefore suspect) writer of popular thrillers and pulp love stories, abroad as the chronicler of German destiny from 1914 through 1945. Everywhere he remained, above all, the author of *Im Westen nichts Neues*.

*Schatten im Paradies* confirms much of the criticism given his other books over the years and is virtually a compilation of the author's weaknesses: superficiality, pretentiousness, stereotyped characters, an unlikely plot with inconsistencies and too many coincidences, sentimentality, and sensationalism. In addition there is artistic bad taste in the somewhat lurid eroticism which invades the love story and which had been absent from the earlier

immediacy and authenticity. German reviews were mixed but generally much more favorable than reviews of Remarque's previous novel had been; and though it was feared that the reading public would resent being reminded of the Nazi past, the book actually contributed to the public discussion of that past which had begun to take place in the early 1960s. The novel sold some 900,000 copies in Germany and was a modest best-seller abroad as well.

There is nothing very new about *Die Nacht von Lissabon*. Those who knew *Flotsam* and *Arch of Triumph* were long since familiar with its motifs and the events it describes: the inhuman treatment suffered by the émigrés, the impossibility of living without papers or work, the never-ending cycle of imprisonment and release or escape, accident and bad luck. (The *New York Times* reviewer, who felt that *Die Nacht von Lissabon* was Remarque's best book, called it "almost a manual of underground refugee existence.") The tone is somber; the overall mood is hopeless; the atmosphere is charged with suspense that is only rarely relieved, and then never works. Published in 1971 and a year later in English translation as *Shadows in Paradise*, the novel pleased no one, not even longtime Remarque fans; one should keep in mind, however, that it was not a finished piece and that the author would surely have changed it a good deal had he lived. The draft he was working on when he died was complete, but Remarque was notorious for rewriting and tinkering with his manuscripts.

Remarque's intention in the novel was to follow the émigrés to America. Both *Flotsam* and *Die Nacht von Lissabon* end at the moment of departure for the promised land overseas; in *Schatten im Paradies,* which was clearly meant to be a sequel to *Die Nacht von Lissabon,* the reader is told that life in "paradise" is not really so different for the émigrés from what it was elsewhere, that paradise does not exist. The protagonist, Robert Ross, and the many other displaced Germans with whom he comes in contact in New York and Los Angeles suffer no physical brutality and are free of the old persecution. They work; they can earn money, some of them a lot of it; and they are allowed the pursuit

of private happiness. But though they are no longer dead men on leave, they remain outsiders. The weight of the past is too great to permit them any real trust in other people or in permanence, any real hope for fulfillment and a future.

Although the book is less autobiographical than has generally been claimed, there is obviously much of Remarque's own experience in it, and the style reminds one as much of the diary as it does of the novel. More important than the plot is the author's desire to document what it was like for "us refugees" who managed to reach a shadowy paradise that could not live up to its promise.

The constant underlying theme for Remarque, as for so many other writers of his generation, was the breakdown of Western civilization and order that World War I brought to the surface of European consciousness and that the following decades served to substantiate, especially in Germany. Lacking the belief of earlier ages in something absolute to fall back on in the face of such dissolution, Remarque found himself with few alternative responses. On the one hand there was

*Remarque at his villa on Lake Maggiore, near the village of Porto Ronco, Switzerland (Ullstein)*

*The Remarques inside their Swiss villa*

anarchy, nihilism, and despair. At the other end of the scale there was political ideology, but for Remarque ideology was the enemy and not a solution. Somewhere in the middle there was the individual self, and this is what he wrote about. The characters in his novels are essentially always alone; and though they seek to escape isolation in the companionship of others like themselves or in love, the attempt is born of panic and is successful only in the short run. If external circumstances and political events have not done so already, death can always be counted on to make sure that success does not last. Because living is a brief and hazardous undertaking, Remarque's characters prize the intensity of the moment above all else, for it, at least, is real .

This Remarque—the cultural pessimist—and the other Remarque who wanted to write popular and entertaining novels did not always get along well with each other. Three or four of the novels that resulted from their collaboration, however, will remain vivid documentation of the desperate times they depict and moving statements of the power of the human spirit to endure and conquer such times.

**Biographies:**

Franz Baumer, *E. M. Remarque* (Berlin: Colloquium, 1976);

Christine R. Barker and R. W. Last, *Erich Maria Remarque* (London: Wolff, 1979);

Alfred Antkowiak, *Erich Maria Remarque: Leben und Werk* (Berlin: Das Europäische Buch, 1983).

**References:**

A. F. Bance, "*Im Westen nichts Neues:* A Bestseller in Context," *Modern Language Review,* 72 (April 1977): 359-373;

Hans-Werner Baum, "E. M. Remarque und seine Zeitromane," *Der Bibliothekar,* 11 (1957): 509-604;

S. E. Cernyak, "*The Life of a Nation:* The Community of the Dispossessed in Erich Maria Remarque's Emigration Novels," *Perspectives on Contemporary Literature,* 3, no. 1 (1977): 15-22;

"The End of the War? A Correspondence between the Author of *All Quiet on the Western Front* and General Sir Ian Hamilton," *Life and Letters,* 3 (November 1929): 399-411;

*Erich Maria Remarque zum 70. Geburtstag am 22. Juni 1968* (Cologne: Kiepenheuer & Witsch, 1968);

M. Feldmann, "Gespräch mit C. [*sic*] M. Remarque," *Europäische Rundschau,* 1, no. 2 (1946): 228-230;

Armin Kerker, "Zwischen Innerlichkeit und Nacktkultur: Der unbekannte Remarque," *Die Horen,* 96, no. 1 (1974): 3-23;

Hermann Kesten, "Gedenkwort für Erich Maria Remarque," *Deutsche Akademie für Sprache und Dichtung Darmstadt: Jahrbuch 1970* (1971): 99-102;

Manfred Kuxdorf, "Mynona versus Remarque, Tucholsky, Mann, and Others: Not So Quiet on the Literary Front," in *The First World War in German Narrative Prose,* edited by Charles H. Genno and Heinz Wetzel (Toronto: University of Toronto Press, 1980), pp. 71-92;

Frédéric LeFèvre, "An Hour with Erich Remarque," *Living Age,* 339 (December 1930): 344-349;

Helmut Liedloff, "Two War Novels: A Critical Comparison," *Revue de Littérature Comparée,* 42 (July-September 1968): 390-406;

P. J. Middleton, "The Individual, Society, and the Contemporary Background in the Novels of Erich Maria Remarque," Ph.D. dissertation, University of Southampton, 1969;

Hanns-Gerd Rabe, "Erich Maria Remarque 1898-1970," *Niedersächsische Lebensbilder*, 8 (August 1973): 193-211;

John F. Riddick, "Erich Maria Remarque: A Bibliography of Biographical and Critical Material, 1929-1980," *Bulletin of Bibliography*, 39, no. 4 (1982): 207-210;

Helmut Rudolf, "Helden in der Krise: Zu Erich Maria Remarques Emigrationsromanen," *Arbeiten zur deutschen Philologie*, 2 (1966): 83-93;

Hubert Rüter, *Erich Maria Remarque: "Im Westen nichts Neues." Ein Bestseller der Kriegsliteratur im Kontext* (Paderborn: Schöningh, 1980);

Helena Szépe, "Der deklassierte Kleinbürger in den Romanen Erich Maria Remarques," *Monatshefte*, 65 (Winter 1973): 385-392;

Harley U. Taylor, "Autobiographical Elements in the Novels of Erich Maria Remarque," *West Virginia University Philological Papers*, 17 (1970): 84-93;

Taylor, "Humor in the Novels of Erich Maria Remarque," *West Virginia University Philological Papers*, 29 (1983): 38-45;

Pawel Toper and Alfred Antkowiak, *Ludwig Renn; Erich Maria Remarque: Leben und Werk* (Berlin: Volk & Wissen, 1965);

Robert Van Gelder, "An Interview with Erich Maria Remarque," in his *Writers and Writing* (New York: Scribners, 1946), pp. 377-381;

Hans Wagener, "Erich Maria Remarque," in *Deutsche Exilliteratur seit 1933. I: Kalifornien*, edited by John M. Spalek and Joseph Strelka (Bern: Francke, 1976), pp. 591-605;

Irene Wegner, "Zur Rezeption der Romane Erich Maria Remarques," in *Erzählte Welt: Studien zur Epik des 20. Jahrhunderts*, edited by Helmut Brandt and Nodar Kakabadse (Berlin: Aufbau, 1978), pp. 384-399.

# Ina Seidel
### (15 September 1885-2 October 1974)

JoAnn Stohler Bennett
*Chatham College*

BOOKS: *Gedichte* (Berlin: Fleischel, 1914);

*Neben der Trommel her: Gedichte* (Berlin: Fleischel, 1915);

*Das Haus zum Monde: Roman* (Berlin: Fleischel, 1917);

*Weltinnigkeit: Neue Gedichte* (Berlin: Fleischel, 1918; enlarged, 1921);

*Hochwasser* (Berlin: Fleischel, 1920);

*Lebensweg* (Chemnitz: Gesellschaft der Bücherfreunde, 1921);

*Das Labyrinth: Ein Lebenslauf aus dem 18. Jahrhundert* (Jena: Diederichs, 1922); translated by Oakley Williams as *The Labyrinth* (London: Lane, 1932; New York: Farrar & Rinehart, 1932);

*Sterne der Heimkehr: Eine Junigeschichte* (Stuttgart, Berlin & Leipzig: Deutsche Verlagsanstalt, 1923);

*Das wunderbare Geißleinbuch: Neue Geschichten für Kinder, die die alten Märchen gut kennen* (Stuttgart & Gotha: Perthes, 1925);

*Die Fürstin reitet: Erzählung* (Berlin & Leipzig: Deutsche Verlagsanstalt, 1926);

*Neue Gedichte* (Berlin & Leipzig: Deutsche Verlagsanstalt, 1927); enlarged as *Die tröstliche Begegnung: Dichtungen* (Leipzig: Gesellschaft der Freunde der Deutschen Bücherei, 1932);

*Brömseshof: Eine Familiengeschichte* (Berlin & Leipzig: Deutsche Verlagsanstalt, 1928);

*Renée und Rainer* (Leipzig: Gesellschaft der Bibliophilen, 1928);

*Der vergrabene Schatz: Drei Erzählungen* (Berlin: Deutsche Buchgemeinschaft, 1929);

*Die Brücke und andere Erzählungen*, edited by Regina Tieffenbach (Leipzig: Quelle & Meyer, 1930);

*Das Wunschkind: Roman* (Stuttgart & Berlin: Deutsche Verlagsanstalt, 1930); translated by G. Dunning Gribble as *The Wish Child* (London: Lane, 1935; New York: Farrar & Rinehart, 1935);

*Das Geheimnis: Eine Geschichte von Sachen allein, mit einem Hund und einer Kinderstimme am Schluß.*

*Zwei Erzählungen* (Berlin: Warneck, 1931);

*Der Weg ohne Wahl: Roman* (Stuttgart & Berlin: Deutsche Verlagsanstalt, 1933);

*Dichter, Volkstum und Sprache: Ausgewählte Vorträge und Aufsätze* (Stuttgart & Berlin: Deutsche Verlagsanstalt, 1934);

*Luise, Königin von Preußen: Ein Bericht über ihr Lehen* (Königstein & Leipzig: Eiserne Hammer, 1934);

*Meine Kindheit und Jugend: Ursprung, Erbteil und Weg* (Stuttgart & Berlin: Deutsche Verlagsanstalt, 1935);

*Spuk in des Wassermanns Haus: Novellen. Mit einem autobiographischen Nachwort* (Leipzig: Reclam, 1936);

*Gesammelte Gedichte* (Stuttgart & Berlin: Deutsche Verlagsanstalt, 1937);

*(Ullstein)*

*Lennacker: Das Buch einer Heimkehr* (Stuttgart & Berlin: Deutsche Verlagsanstalt, 1938);

*Unser Freund Peregrin: Aufzeichnungen des Jürgen Brook. Eine Erzählung* (Stuttgart & Berlin: Deutsche Verlagsanstalt, 1940);

*Achim von Arnim* (Stuttgart: Cotta, 1944);

*Bettina* (Stuttgart: Cotta, 1944);

*Clemens Brentano* (Stuttgart: Cotta, 1944);

*Drei Dichter der Romantik; Clemens Brentano, Bettina, Achim von Arnim* (Stuttgart: Deutsche Verlagsanstalt, 1944);

*Die Vogelstube: Drei Aufsätze* (Iserlohn: Holzwarth, 1946);

*Familie Mutz: Ein Bilderbuch von Eugen Osswald. Verse von Ina Seidel* (Wiesbaden: Scholz-Mainz, 1947);

*Gedichte: Eine Auswahl* (Stuttgart: Deutsche Verlagsanstalt, 1949);

*Osel, Urd und Schummei: Fragmente einer Kindheitsgeschichte* (Gütersloh: Bertelsmann, 1950);

*Das Tor der Frühe: Roman einer Jugend* (Stuttgart: Deutsche Verlagsanstalt, 1952);

*Die Geschichte einer Frau Berngruber: Erzählung* (Gütersloh: Bertelsmann, 1953);

*Die Versuchung des Briefträgers Federweiß: Erzählung* (Munich: Nymphenburger Verlagshandlung, 1953);

*Die Orange*, by Seidel and Heinrich W. Seidel (Düsseldorf: Hoch, 1954);

*Das unverwesliche Erbe: Roman* (Stuttgart: Deutsche Verlagsanstalt, 1954);

*Dank an Bayern* (Starnberg: Jägerhuber, 1955);

*Der vergrabene Schatz: Erzahlung* (Munich: Piper, 1955);

*Der verlorene Garten* (Braunschweig: Werkkunstschule Braunschweig, 1955);

*Die Fahrt in den Abend: Erzählung* (Stuttgart: Deutsche Verlagsanstalt, 1955);

*Gedichte: Festausgabe zum 70. Geburtstag der Dichterin* (Stuttgart: Deutsche Verlagsanstalt, 1955);

*Dank an Rudolf Alexander Schröder* (Munich: Rudolf Alexander Schröder-Gesellschaft, 1958);

*Michaela: Aufzeichnungen des Jürgen Brook* (Stuttgart: Deutsche Verlagsanstalt, 1959);

*Drei Städte meiner Jugend* (Stuttgart: Deutsche Verlagsanstalt, 1960);

*Berlin, ich vergesse dich nicht!* (Berlin: Staneck, 1962);

*Dresdener Pastorale* (Hamburg: Furche, 1962);

*Vor Tau und Tag: Geschichte einer Kindheit* (Stuttgart: Deutsche Verlagsanstalt, 1962);

*Quartett: Vier Erzählungen* (Stuttgart: Deutsche Verlagsanstalt, 1963);

*Die alte Dame und der Schmetterling: Kleine Geschichten* (Stuttgart: Deutsche Verlagsanstalt, 1964);

*Ricarda Huch: Rede zum 100. Geburtstag* (Munich: Hanser, 1964);

*Frau und Wort: Ausgewählte Betrachtungen und Aufsätze* (Stuttgart: Deutsche Verlagsanstalt, 1965);

*Lebensbericht 1885-1923* (Stuttgart: Deutsche Verlagsanstalt, 1970);

*Sommertage: 2 Erzählungen* (Heilbronn: Salzer, 1973);

*Aus den schwarzen Wachstuchheften* (Stuttgart: Deutsche Verlagsanstalt, 1980).

OTHER: *Herz zum Hafen: Frauengedichte der Gegenwart,* edited by Seidel and Elisabeth Langgässer (Leipzig: Voigtländer, 1933);

Willy Seidel, *Der Tod des Achilleus und andere Erzählungen,* edited by Seidel (Stuttgart & Berlin: Deutsche Verlagsanstalt, 1936);

*Deutsche Frauen: Bildnisse und Lebensbeschreibungen,* introduction by Seidel (Berlin: Steiniger, 1939);

*Dienende Herzen: Kriegsbriefe von Nachrichtenhelferinnen des Heeres,* edited by Seidel and Hanns Großer (Berlin: Limpert, 1942);

*Briefe der Deutschen aus einem Jahrhundert,* introduction by Seidel (Leipzig: Reclam, 1943);

Heinrich Wolfgang Seidel, *Aus dem Tagebuch der Gedanken und Träume,* edited by Seidel (Munich: Piper, 1946);

*Clemens und Bettina: Geschwisterbriefe,* edited by Seidel (Munich: Piper, 1948);

Thomas Wolff, *Briefe an die Mutter,* translated by Seidel (Munich: Nymphenburger Verlagshandlung, 1949);

Andreas Gryphius, *Gedichte,* edited by Seidel (Stuttgart: Klett, 1949);

Heinrich Wolfgang Seidel, *Drei Stunden hinter Berlin: Briefe,* edited by Seidel (Gütersloh: Bertelsmann, 1951);

*Heinrich Wolfgang Seidel: Jugendbriefe,* edited by Seidel (Gütersloh: Bertelsmann, 1952);

*Heinrich Wolfgang Seidel: Briefe, 1934-1944,* edited by Seidel (Berlin: Eckart, 1964).

In a lecture to a group of Munich students in 1933, "Der Dichter und sein Volk" (The Poet and His People), Ina Seidel compared the poet to a priest: like the priest, the poet not only bears the suffering of others but is also a guardian of a culture's most sacred inheritance: language. Despite the cultural, political, and intellectual turmoil of her time, Seidel reveals in this lecture, as in all her works, both confidence in the power of the written word and reverence for the task of the writer to

preserve the language, culture, and values of his people. For Seidel, who is often viewed as a representative Protestant writer, these values were not merely the tenets or dogma of any one religious, political, or intellectual movement; they were the inherent connections of man to nature, mother to child, brother to sister, and generation to generation. The task of the writer was to articulate and preserve these ties, and "das Erlebnis ins Wort zu heben und warnend, mahnend, preisend, anfeuernd in seinem Werk dem Volk den Spiegel vorzuhalten, den wahrhaft magischen Spiegel, in dem das Geschehen zu Gestalt gerinnt—den Spiegel der zur Tafel wird, aus der spätere Geschlechter Größe und Heldentum der Vergangenheit so gut erkennen wie ihre Schwäche und ihren Verfall" (to elevate experience into words, and with caution, warning, and praise, to hold up a mirror to the people, that truly magical mirror in which events take form—the mirror which becomes a tablet in which later generations can recognize the greatness and heroism of the past as well as their weaknesses and their decline). The mirror Seidel holds up in her writing is indeed a magical one, which reflects not only a historical image of a time and its problems but also the invisible ties connecting every era to its past and to the future.

Seidel's life and work are characterized by her interest in her own family history, which she claimed could be traced back to the fourteenth century. Her father's ancestors were clergymen, doctors, scholars, and writers, and represented to Seidel a tradition of dedication to humanity and to the spiritual world. Her grandfather, Heinrich Alexander Seidel, a minister and the author of Christian epics and songs, and her uncle, Heinrich Seidel, the author of the humorous adventures of Leberecht Hühnchen, exemplified this tradition. Her maternal ancestors, the merchant family Loesevitz, also represented a tradition of dedication to scholarly and artistic pursuits. Writing was, she felt, a natural vocation for her and for her brother Willy. In her autobiographical writings *Meine Kindheit und Jugend* (My Childhood and Youth, 1935), *Drei Städte meiner Jugend* (Three Cities of My Youth, 1960), *Vor Tau und Tag* (In the Dewy Morn, 1962), and *Lebensbericht 1885-1923* (Life Story 1885-1923, 1970), Seidel details not only her own life but also the story of her ancestors, whose personalities and experiences are often echoed in her fiction.

Seidel was born in Halle on 15 September 1885 to Dr. Hermann Seidel and Emmy Loesevitz Seidel. Soon after her birth, the family moved to Braunschweig. Her mother encouraged her, Willy, and their sister Annemarie in the arts and introduced the children to the world of fairy tales and to the tales of Brentano, Storm, Twain, and Poe; Willy went on to become a writer of exotic tales and was often called "the German Kipling"; Annemarie grew up to be an actress. Seidel revered her father as a scholar and as a doctor concerned with both the body and the soul, and he imparted to her a love of nature that characterizes many of her works. The gifts of rare and exotic animals and birds which her father brought his children from his travels made an impression on the young girl which is evident in much of her writing. In *Osel, Urd und Schummei* (1950), for example, the Chinese nightingale that Hermann Seidel brought his children appears as a symbol for the mysteries of childhood and for the bonds between parents and children. The theme of childhood mysteries recurs throughout Seidel's works.

For Seidel, childhood represented an experience of immediacy, a direct relationship to God, nature, and the family. The wonders of childhood, she claimed, can only be recaptured by an adult through art or religion. Her life and work can be seen as an attempt to recapture this experience. Many of the themes that dominate her works—her reverence for the past and for the continuity of history, her celebration of the family, and her love of nature and of God—are deeply rooted in her childhood. The memories of childhood would always remain especially poignant for Seidel, since the circumstances of her father's death brought this period of her life to an abrupt end.

When Seidel was twelve, her father committed suicide in despair over an official investigation of his professional competency. Her mother took the children to Marburg, and then to Munich to live with their maternal grandmother and stepgrandfather, the Egyptologist and writer of historical novels Georg Ebers. Seidel spent her adolescence and early adult years in the Munich of the early twentieth century, a city alive with cultural and intellectual activity. Seidel later described herself at this time as typical of her generation: though energetic and intellectual, she lacked a sense of direction. Due to the prominence of her family, she knew many of the leading intellectual and artistic figures of the time, but considered herself merely an onlooker, an observer of the great minds and movements of the era. In a sense, Seidel remained an observer throughout her life, and her art centered around her own spiritual world.

In 1907 Seidel married her cousin, Heinrich Wolfgang Seidel, a minister and writer. In 1907

the couple moved to Berlin, and in 1908 their first child, a daughter, was born. The birth left Seidel with a handicap that impaired her movements for the rest of her life, and she began to write in an attempt to recover from her depression over the injury. In the beginning of her career, she turned to Lulu von Strauß und Torney and the circle surrounding Börries von Münchhausen for encouragement in her literary endeavors. Although she received a confirmation of her talent from von Strauß und Torney, it was Agnes Miegel who offered the young writer the greatest support. Miegel, whose ballads Seidel admired for their mysterious and supernatural flavor, became a lifelong friend and was an important influence on Seidel's early works.

From 1914 to 1923 the Seidels lived in the village of Eberswald, where their son Georg, who became a novelist under the pseudonym Simon Glas and a critic under that of Christian Ferber, was born in 1919; in 1923 they moved back to Berlin. Relatively isolated in Eberswald from the events of World War I and the political and economic upheaval of the postwar years, Seidel was able to dedicate herself to writing and had several volumes of poetry published in quick succession: *Gedichte* (Poems, 1914), *Neben der Trommel her* (Here beside the Drum, 1915), and *Weltinnigkeit* (World Intimacy, 1918). Her early poetry is noted for its celebration of nature and of motherhood and for its pantheistic mysticism. Her first novel, *Das Haus zum Monde* (The House on the Moon, 1917), raises the question of reincarnation in a manner which the author later considered superficial.

Although Seidel dismissed her own tales of reincarnation, claiming that she did not possess the supernatural gift she admired in Miegel, she retained her interest in the spiritual world. The four novels that form the basis of her literary reputation, *Das Labyrinth* (1922; translated as *The Labyrinth*, 1932), *Das Wunschkind* (1930; translated as *The Wish Child*, 1935), *Lennacker* (1938), and *Das unverwesliche Erbe* (The Incorruptible Legacy, 1954), present a gallery of portraits that grants the reader a glimpse into a spiritual world complete in itself and into a tradition which survives the turmoil of past and present eras. Characters from one novel reappear in other works as memories, ancestors, or characters in their own right. Each of the novels, although treating different times and problems, remains a part of a larger whole which mirrors the sustaining ties between the generations.

Seidel began work on her masterpiece and most successful novel, *Das Wunschkind*, in 1914 and

*Seidel in 1933 (Ullstein)*

completed it sixteen years later. In researching the history of Mainz for the novel, she became fascinated with the eighteenth-century explorer, scholar, and revolutionary Georg Forster, whose life story she developed into the psychological novel *Das Labyrinth*. Forster is led by his tyrannical father into the labyrinth which leads inexorably to his death; the father becomes in his son's eyes the minotaur who stands at the end of the labyrinth and waits to devour his victim. Forster's childhood is brought to an abrupt end when his father discovers that the boy is able to read and forces him to become a slave to his vainglorious scholarly ambitions. Georg suffers throughout his travels with his father in Russia and on Captain Cook's second voyage to the South Seas, for he yearns to be merely a child and to rest in his mother's arms. The mysterious bond between mother and son, a hallmark of Seidel's works, is destroyed by the demands of the father. Forster does manage to escape his father's control, but the minotaur becomes the monster within himself: he remains trapped by the demands of his wife, the expectations of the world, and his own image of himself as the "great Forster." He dies miserably in Paris, abandoned by his wife and

children. He dies, however, as a servant of the French Revolution, realizing that "wenn wir Geopferten werden zu Opfernden, so haben wir heimgefunden ins Herz der Dinge und Gottes" (when we sacrificial victims become those who have sacrificed, we have found our way home to the heart of things and of God). Forster dies not as a victim but as a sacrifice to an ideal that will survive; he dies, Seidel suggests, a free man.

*Das Labyrinth* is the story of one man. For Seidel, however, no man is ever truly alone, for every man is connected by history, by family, or merely by chance to the lives of others. Seidel's novels reflect these connections both thematically and stylistically. Shortly before his death, Forster happens upon the funeral procession in Mainz of a small child, the son of Hans Adam and Cornelia Echter von Mespelbrunn. This incidental scene in *Das Labyrinth* forms the introduction to *Das Wunschkind*. In this novel, women become the sustaining thread in the labyrinth of history. Women play a decisive role in Seidel's fiction: as a woman living remote from the battlefield, the image she evokes of war is not a picture of death and destruction but a testimony to the strength of the wives and mothers left behind.

*Das Wunschkind* centers around Cornelia, who, having lost her first son, conceives a child on the eve of her husband's departure for battle in the Napoleonic Wars. Her husband never returns, and the entire novel is overshadowed by the certainty that Christoph, the wish child, will also encounter his father's fate. Cornelia raises Christoph, who is her life and comfort, as well as Delphine, the beguiling, coquettish daughter of her sister and a mysterious French officer. Cornelia is transformed from a woman numbly accepting her grief into a caring nurse, and finally into a matriarch who revitalizes the estate her Prussian father relinquished to her. The second half of the novel explores Christoph's ill-fated love for Delphine, his cousin who was raised as his sister. Christoph misunderstands the nature of the bond between them, the bond between siblings which appears repeatedly throughout Seidel's works. Christoph falls in battle at the conclusion of the novel; but he dies a happy man, never knowing the disappointment and defeat that the women are left to bear. In the final lines of the novel Seidel pays tribute to women as the mothers who give life, who preserve traditions and values, and who will extinguish war: "Aber der Tag wird kommen—und er muß kommen—da die Tränen der Frauen stark genug sein werden um gleich einer Flut das Feuer des Krieges für ewig zu löschen" (But the day will come—and it must come—when the tears of women will be strong enough to extinguish like a flood the fire of war forever).

Although *Das Wunschkind* was Seidel's most successful novel, it was *Lennacker* which earned her the reputation of the Protestant writer of her age. Hans Jacob Lennacker, a soldier and a medical student, visits his last remaining relative and learns that each of his twelve paternal ancestors was a Protestant clergyman. Lennacker falls ill, and in his dreams during the twelve holy nights of Christmas the history of the Protestant church is unfolded: each of the twelve chapters is the story of one of the hero's ancestors and of the time in which he lived. The novel, though a vivid chronicle of the Protestant faith, revolves around Lennacker's recognition of his own spiritual heritage and of the strength of the Christian values that are still valid despite the horrors of World War I. Lennacker realizes that "die Urmacht des Christentums wird immer von neuer Gestalt werden" (the primal force of Christianity will always assume new forms). Religion, as Seidel presents it, is not dogmatic or restricted to any one confession but is a primal force which weathers history; it is yet another tie, perhaps the strongest tie, of man to his past and future.

*Lennacker* has been viewed as symptomatic of Seidel's retreat from a confusing present into the past and her own spiritual world. *Unser Freund Peregrin* (Our Friend Peregrin, 1940), the author's most successful shorter novel, can be seen as the completion of this inward turn. Influenced by the death of her brother Willy in 1934, *Unser Freund Peregrin* is a lyrical story of the mystical connections between brother and sister. The children's union is symbolized by their devotion to the poetry of Peregrin, a distant ancestor of the pair; Seidel modeled Peregrin on Novalis. Gregor and Tania admit the story's narrator, Jürgen Brook, into their secret world. The novel relates Jürgen's search, many years after Tania's death and Gregor's disappearance, to find their Peregrin and to recapture the mystery of childhood.

The year 1934 had been marked not only by Seidel's brother's death but also by her husband's retirement from the church in protest against the politicization of religion and their move to Starnberg in Upper Bavaria, where Heinrich Wolfgang Seidel died in 1945. Inspired by a romantic idealism and national pride, Seidel paid homage to Hitler in poems honoring his birthday. Basically apolitical and ignorant of the atrocities of the Third Reich, the author initially viewed the Nazis as a revitalization of the Germanic past and tradition. Seidel did not immediately express her reactions to World War II, but fell silent and did not produce a major work for nearly a decade. In 1949, however, she published an edition of Andreas Gryphius's poetry. She may have found in the baroque poet's works both a mirror of her own despair and disillusionment over the war and an affirmation of the historical strength of her own faith.

*Das unverwesliche Erbe* recounts the maternal lineage of Hans Jacob Lennacker. Lennacker is the great-grandson of Christoph and Delphine, the ill-fated lovers of *Das Wunschkind*, who reappear as memories of a treasured past in *Das unverwesliche Erbe*. Elisabeth, Lennacker's grandmother, converts to her husband's Protestant faith, but her life is marred by guilt and depression until she returns to the Catholic religion. Although Seidel's presentation of the problem of a mixed marriage is intricate and sympathetic, the novel emerges as a celebration of the primal powers of Christianity.

Seidel's final novel, *Michaela* (1959), which takes place during World War II, is an attempt to examine the question of guilt. Although the work has been criticized as too idyllic and for failing to come to terms with the questions it raises, the final image of the novel may serve as a supreme example of Seidel's work and world view: a minister offers communion to both Protestant and Catholic troops, including the soldiers who have caused his daughter's death. In the midst of a battle, Seidel portrays the conciliatory hand, the hand which upholds the tradition that binds generations, religions, and nations together. The author is again holding up the magical mirror which is the tool of a writer, and which reflects the invisible ties she saw.

Seidel was admitted to the Prussian Academy of Arts in 1930 and the Bavarian Academy of Fine Arts in 1948. She was awarded the Goethe Medal in 1932, the Grillparzer Prize of the City of Vienna in 1941, the Wilhelm Raabe Prize of the City of Braunschweig in 1948, and the Great Art Prize of North Rhine-Westphalia in 1958. She died on 2 October 1974, celebrated by her contemporaries as the upholder of the nineteenth-century tradition. Her works were successful and well received, and she was heralded as the Protestant writer and woman writer of her era. The poetic realism of her writing has led many critics to consider Seidel a disciple of Theodor Storm; more often, however, she is viewed as the literary descendant of Annette von Droste-Hülshoff and the most recent representative of a small but important group of German women writers. Seidel employed many traditionally feminine themes, but she did not write specifically for or about women. Her celebration of the feminine, like her emphasis on faith, is a celebration of the unifying principles of life and of human history.

**References:**
Hans Brandenburg, "Ina Seidel," *Die Neue Literatur,* 32 (1931): 358-367;

Simon Glas (Georg Seidel), *Die Seidels: Geschichte einer bürgerlichen Familie* (Stuttgart: Deutsche Verlagsanstalt, 1956);

Karl August Horst, *Ina Seidel: Wesen und Werk* (Stuttgart: Deutsche Verlagsanstalt, 1956);

Hans Jaeger, "Die Lebensgestaltung im Werk Ina Seidel," in his *Essays on German Literature 1935-1962* (Bloomington: Indiana University Department of Germanic Languages, 1968), pp. 13-34;

Jaeger, "Weib und Erde: Studie zu Ina Seidels Lyrik," *Germanic Review,* 6 (1931): 266-293;

Mary MacKittrick, "Weltinnigkeit: An Introductory Study of Ina Seidel," *Monatshefte für deutschen Unterricht,* 30 (1938): 83-93;

Clementina di San Lazaro, *Ina Seidel: Eine Studie* (Stuttgart: Metzler, 1938);

Margarete Schulenburg, *Stellung und Bedeutung der Frau in den Romanen von Ina Seidel* (Würzburg-Aumühle: Triltsch, 1938);

Gabriele Thoens, "Aufklärungskritik und Weiblichkeitsmythos: Die Krise der Rationalität im Werk Ina Seidel," Ph.D. dissertation, University of Freiburg, 1984.

**Papers:**
Ina Seidel's papers are in the Deutsches Literaturarchiv, Marbach, West Germany.

# Carl Sternheim
*(1 April 1878-3 November 1942)*

Edson M. Chick
*Williams College*

BOOKS: *Der Heiland: Komödie in einem Aufzug* (Hamburg: Hoffmann & Campe, 1898);

*Judas Ischariot: Die Tragödie vom Verrath* (Dresden & Leipzig: Pierson, 1901);

*Fanale!* (Dresden & Leipzig: Pierson, 1901);

*Auf Krugdorf: Schauspiel in zwei Akten* (Berlin: Entsch, 1902);

*Vom König und der Königin: Tragödie in fünf Aufzügen* (Schandau: Petrich, 1905);

*Ulrich und Brigitte: Ein dramatisches Gedicht* (Düsseldorf: Müllern & Lehneking, 1907);

*Don Juan: Eine Tragödie* (Leipzig: Insel, 1909);

*Die Hose: Ein bürgerliches Lustspiel* (Berlin: Cassirer, 1911); translated by Eric Bentley as *The Underpants: A Middle-Class Comedy* (New York: Doubleday, 1957);

*Die Kassette: Komödie in fünf Aufzügen* (Leipzig: Insel, 1912); translated by Maurice Edwards and Valerie Reich as *The Strongbox,* in *Anthology of German Expressionist Drama,* edited by Walter H. Sokel (New York: Doubleday, 1963);

*Bürger Schippel: Komödie in fünf Aufzügen* (Leipzig: Insel, 1913); translated by M. A. L. Brown as *Paul Schippel Esq.: A Comedy,* in *Scenes from the Heroic Life of the Middle Classes: Five Plays* (London: Calder & Boyars, 1970), pp. 23-75;

*Busekow: Eine Novelle* (Leipzig: Wolff, 1914); translated by Eugene Jolas as "Busekow," *Transition,* no. 1 (1927): 36-56;

*Der Snob: Komödie in drei Aufzügen* (Leipzig: Insel, 1914); translated by J. M. Ritchie and J. D. Stowell as *The Snob,* in *Scenes from the Heroic Life of the Middle Classes,* pp. 145-193;

*Der Kandidat: Komödie in vier Aufzügen nach Flaubert* (Leipzig: Insel, 1914);

*1913: Ein Schauspiel in drei Aufzügen* (Leipzig: Wolff, 1915); translated by Ritchie as *1913: Play in Three Acts,* in *Scenes from the Heroic Life of the Middle Classes,* pp. 195-244;

*Das leidende Weiß: Drama nach Friedrich Maximilian Klinger* (Leipzig: Insel, 1915);

*Der Scharmante: Lustspiel mit Benutzung einer fremden Idee* (Leipzig: Wolff, 1915);

*Carl Sternheim (Ullstein)*

*Napoleon: Eine Novelle* (Leipzig: Wolff, 1915);
*Die drei Erzählungen* (Leipzig: Wolff, 1916);
*Tabula Rasa: Ein Schauspiel* (Leipzig: Wolff, 1916);
*Meta: Eine Erzählung* (Leipzig: Wolff, 1916);
*Der Geizige: Komödie in fünf Aufzügen nach Molière* (Leipzig: Wolff, 1916);
*Mädchen* (Leipzig: Wolff, 1917);
*Perleberg: Komödie in drei Aufzügen* (Leipzig: Wolff, 1917);
*Posinsky: Eine Erzählung* (Berlin: Hochstem, 1917);
*Ulrike: Eine Erzählung* (Leipzig: Wolff, 1918);
*Chronik von des zwanzigsten Jahrhunderts Beginn*, 2 volumes (Leipzig: Wolff, 1918);
*Vier Novellen: Neue Folge der Chronik vom Beginn des zwanzigsten Jahrhunderts* (Berlin: Hochstem, 1918);
*Prosa* (Berlin-Wilmersdorf: Verlag der Wochenschrift Die Aktion, 1918);
*Die Marquise von Arcis: Schauspiel in fünf Aufzügen nach Diderot* (Leipzig: Wolff, 1919); translated and adapted by Ashley Dukes as *The Mask of Virtue: A Comedy in Three Acts* (London: Gollancz, 1935; New York & Los Angeles: French, 1935);

*Die deutsche Revolution* (Berlin-Wilmersdorf: Verlag der Wochenschrift Die Aktion, 1919);
*Europa: Roman*, 2 volumes (volume 1, Munich: Musarion, 1919; volume 2, Munich: Wolff, 1920);
*Der entfesselte Zeitgenosse: Ein Lustspiel* (Munich: Wolff, 1920);
*Berlin; oder, Juste Milieu* (Munich: Wolff, 1920);
*Fairfax: Eine Erzählung* (Berlin: Rowohlt, 1921); translated by Alfred B. Cutter as *Fairfax* (New York: Knopf, 1923);
*Tasso; oder, Kunst des Juste Milieu: Ein Wink für die Jugend* (Berlin: Reiß, 1921);
*Manon Lescaut: Ein Schauspiel* (Munich: Drei Masken, 1921);
*Libussa, des Kaisers Leibroß (Memoiren)* (Berlin-Wilmersdorf: Verlag der Wochenschrift Die Aktion, 1922);
*Der Abenteurer: Drei Stückchen von ihm* (Munich: Drei Masken, 1922);
*Der Nebbich: Ein Lustspiel* (Munich: Drei Masken, 1922);
*Gauguin und van Gogh* (Berlin: Die Schmiede, 1924);
*Das Fossil: Drama in drei Aufzügen* (Potsdam: Kiepenheuer, 1925); translated by Ritchie as *The Fossil: Drama in Three Acts*, in *Scenes from the Heroic Life of the Middle Classes*, pp. 245-285;
*Oscar Wilde: Sein Drama* (Potsdam: Kiepenheuer, 1925);
*Lutetia: Berichte über europäische Politik, Kunst und Volksleben 1926* (Berlin, Vienna & Leipzig: Zsolnay, 1926);
*Die Schule von Uznach; oder Neue Sachlichkeit: Ein Lustspiel in vier Aufzügen* (Berlin, Leipzig & Vienna: Zsolnay, 1926);
*John Pierpont Morgan: Ein Schauspiel* (Brussels: Privately published, 1930);
*Kleiner Katechismus für das Jahr 1930/31: Für die in Verwirrung heranwachsende deutsche Jugend aber auch für Ältere beiderlei Geschlechts, die ihn brauchen können* (Starnbergersee: Privately published, 1930);
*Vorkriegseuropa im Gleichnis meines Lebens* (Amsterdam: Querido, 1936);
*Aus dem bürgerlichen Heldenleben*, 2 volumes (Berlin: Aufbau, 1947); translated by Brown and others as *Scenes from the Heroic Life of the Middle Classes*;
*Das dramatische Werk*, 2 volumes (Berlin: Aufbau, 1948);
*Gesamtwerk*, edited by Wilhelm Emrich and Manfred Linke, 10 volumes (Neuwied: Luchterhand, 1963-1976).

OTHER: Ottomar Starke, *Schippeliana: Ein bürgerliches Bilderbuch,* foreword by Sternheim (Leipzig: Wolff, 1917).

PERIODICAL PUBLICATIONS: "Vincent van Gogh," *Hyperion,* no. 11/12 (1910): 110-113;
"Molière, der Bürger," *Blätter des Deutschen Theaters* (Berlin), no. 17 (13 April 1912): 259-260;
"Molière," *Berliner Tageblatt,* 14 April 1917;
"Kampf der Metapher," *Berliner Tageblatt,* 21 July 1917.

Best known as one of Germany's three or four leading expressionist playwrights, Carl Sternheim was also a serious and successful writer of stories, essays, pamphlets, and one novel, all of which belong in the canon of German expressionist writings. He created an idiosyncratic prose style more dynamically expressive than that of any of his contemporaries as a vehicle for his radical, sometimes inconsistent views on the origins and catastrophic development of early twentieth-century Europe. Both his life and his works give unequaled insight into the mind and behavior of the middle classes, into the decay of Western culture, and into the

*Dust jacket for an English translation of Sternheim's satirical comedies (Lilly Library, Indiana University)*

causes of two world wars. He pillories his own bourgeois vices and cast of mind and, because of his fanatical honesty, often throws his ideological principles into question.

William Adolph Carl Francke was born in Leipzig to Rosa Marie Flora Francke, a Lutheran, on 1 April 1878, almost two years before her marriage to Jacob Sternheim, a Jewish merchant, banker, and publisher. After the wedding, Jacob Sternheim recognized his son and a baby daughter, Marie, as legitimate offspring, and the family settled in Hannover. In 1884 they moved to Berlin, where young Carl attended grade school and Gymnasium.

It was in the upper-middle-class, plush upholstered salons and in the Bellealliance Theater belonging to his uncle that Sternheim gathered his first impressions. He was deeply influenced by the newspaper publisher Hans Maske, by well-to-do school friends and their families, by the universal admiration for the Prussian military in dress uniform, by Bismarck and Kaiser Wilhelm II—in short, by the showy, sometimes fraudulent, nouveau riche world of fin de siècle Berlin. Sternheim's particular idol was Ernst von Schwabach, a young dandy of great wealth, coowner of the Bleichröder banking house, inhabiter of a castle and hunting preserve in Silesia, a person of impeccable taste and cultivation who was the first to urge Sternheim to study French literature. A second model was his own father, a powerful, overfed, tyrannical, high-living entrepreneur and speculator.

The young Sternheim had two dreams. The first was to lead the heightened dramatic life made possible by high social standing, political and financial power, and sexual success: a fantasy that, more in its sinister than in its pleasurable implications, forms the groundwork for several of his plays and stories, including *Der Snob* (1914; translated as *The Snob,* 1970), *1913* (1915; translated, 1970); "Vanderbilt" (1918), and *Europa* (1919-1920). His second ambition, seemingly incompatible with the first, was to become a great poet. By the age of fourteen he was composing dramas and writing verse. Unlike his coevals, many of whom shared his devotion to the muse, he was able to pursue this career throughout his life, undistracted by the need to work for a living. His father supported him until, in 1907, he married the heiress Thea Bauer, whose seemingly boundless wealth enabled him to realize his dreams.

The year 1907 was the watershed of Sternheim's formative years and the end of what he termed the "terrible decade" of his life. The decade

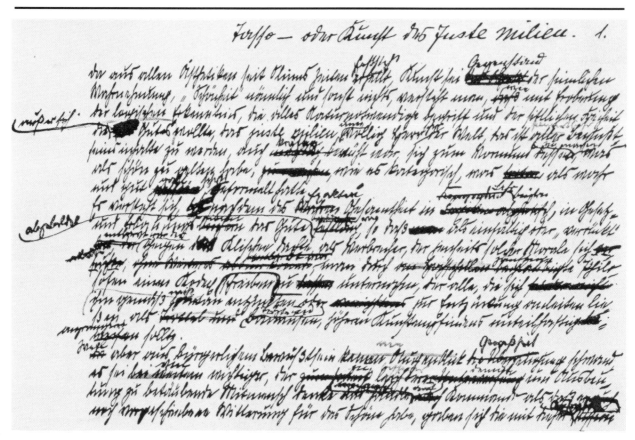

*Part of a manuscript page for an essay by Sternheim (Albert Soergel and Curt Hohoff,* Dichtung und Dichter der Zeit *[Düsseldorf: Bagel, 1961-1963])*

began in 1897, when he converted to Protestantism, graduated from the Gymnasium, and began his university studies. Then followed ten restless years of moving from city to city; enrolling at the universities of Munich, Göttingen, Leipzig, Jena, and Berlin; marriage in a Roman Catholic ceremony to Eugenie Hauth in 1900; separation from her in 1904; and the painful delay before he and Thea could obtain divorces and remarry. It was a time of psychic strain and frequent nervous breakdowns—diagnosed by Sternheim and some doctors as the consequence of a syphilitic infection—requiring convalescence in sanatoriums. The most severe of these breakdowns occurred in Freiburg in 1906 and resulted in a waitress leaping in terror from his hotel window. She broke both legs, and Sternheim was spared a trial when he became a patient for three months at the university clinic. He experimented with the philosophies of Darwin and Haeckel, Nietzsche, and Heinrich Rickert, the neo-Kantian. He was greatly distressed by his failure to gain recognition as an artist, try as he might to find the right formula. Only one of his early plays was

performed, and those that were published were printed at his—that is, at his father's—expense. It took him years of fighting writer's block before he completed even a preliminary version of *Don Juan* (1909), a play that he thought would be his *Faust* but proved a disastrous failure in the theater.

His early writings, which include a few prose vignettes, were generally in the neoromantic vein and dealt with the problem of the artist or with religious figures. In Nietzschean fashion, they were admiring of the exceptional individual, and they posited life as a kind of mystical force informing all human values and expressing itself most often in erotic terms.

The will to power, the economics of human energy, unfettered egotism, and obsessive eroticism remain dominant themes through all of Sternheim's work. The great change that took place around 1907 was more personal and aesthetic. On 14 July 1906 he and Eugenie were divorced by a decree that gave their son Carlhans into her custody. In the following year came Thea's divorce from Arthur Löwenstein, and she and Sternheim were married on 13 July. She had to leave her two children with her first husband, who eventually, in 1912, renounced his claim to Dorothea, the younger of the two and her child by Sternheim.

Sternheim's second marriage brought relative stability to his life. In 1908 Thea bore him a son, Klaus, and with her constant affection she gave him the emotional support he depended on to lead a sane and productive existence. Also in 1908, with her inheritance of roughly two million marks, she financed the construction of a palatial mansion—Bellemaison—to his specifications in Höllriegels-kreuth near Munich; over the years she purchased a large collection of paintings, most of them by Vincent van Gogh. The same year he founded the literary magazine *Hyperion* with the publicist and actor Franz Blei.

Thea had spent her school years in Belgium, and it was at her urging, reinforced by the recommendation of Blei, that he began seriously to look to the French literary tradition—Molière, Flaubert, and later Maupassant—for models to emulate. In the years 1907 to 1909 Sternheim changed from a neoromantic aesthete to a politically conscious, activist writer. Also at Blei's suggestion, he turned from legendary, bigger-than-life characters to a contemporary social reality populated by unexceptional, representative bourgeois figures drawn from his personal acquaintances, including himself, with the aim of becoming, like Molière, a homeopathic physician to the body of his age. Since around 1905 he had been striving to free his writing from neoromantic lyricism, with its addiction to figurative language. Inspired in part by what he perceived in works of great painters, especially Raphael and van Gogh, he was working to develop a terse, dynamic, intentionally unpoetic prose style.

The products of this reorientation, starting with *Die Hose* (1911; translated as *The Underpants*, 1957) and embracing the plays written between 1911 and 1914, later collected under the title *Aus dem bürgerlichen Heldenleben* (1947; translated as *Scenes from the Heroic Life of the Middle Classes*, 1970), earned him his long-sought recognition as Germany's leading playwright.

This success was poisoned for Sternheim by his growing feeling of estrangement from his public and from Germany in general. His essay on van Gogh (1910), while primarily a statement of aesthetic principle, opens with an unvarnished confession of disgust with German culture as it had been perverted over the course of the nineteenth century. In particular, the second paragraph of the essay, easily misread as an unqualified rebuke to

the entire nation, aroused the anger of the right wing and made Sternheim the target of jingoist attacks in the press. As late as 1915 it was cited by the Berlin censor as grounds for banning his more serious plays from public performance.

In 1912 the collapse of his father's business enterprise, together with a marital crisis—Thea discovered a list he had kept of his sexual conquests—made him all the more irritable as he increasingly despaired of Germany, Kaiser Wilhelm, and the cynical cultural establishment, which in this case was largely synonymous with Max Reinhardt's theater chain, where most of Sternheim's dramas saw their world premiere and where in 1912 *Don Juan* failed dismally on opening night. The Sternheims had to sell some paintings in order to pay his father's creditors; they also sold Bellemaison, later purchasing a small estate, Claircolline, in La Hulpe near Brussels.

Though he never ceased to write for the theater, these events had a dampening effect on Sternheim's dramatic productivity; on the other hand, they hastened the development of the narrator. Late in 1912 he began to concentrate his energies on novellas and stories, excited by the discovery, as he told Thea, that this kind of writing was altogether different from play writing: "Hier kann nichts gedacht werden, muß alles gefühlt sein" (Here there can be nothing cerebral, everything must be felt). Immediacy and intensity of feeling are the prime characteristics of *Busekow* (1914; translated, 1927), which, like several pieces to follow, was published in *Die Weißen Blätter*, one of the leading literary journals of the time. In 1918 *Busekow* reappeared in a volume of Sternheim's stories titled *Chronik von des zwanzigsten Jahrhunderts Beginn* (Chronicle of the Beginning of the Twentieth Century).

This first novella displays all the traits of the half dozen or so serious and ambitious stories Sternheim published between 1913 and 1918. Christof Busekow, whose sole reason for existing is loyalty and service to the kaiser, is too nearsighted and slow of mind to qualify as a Prussian soldier and so has to take second best and serve as a Berlin traffic policeman. He is rescued from his empty, henpecked existence by the love of a streetwalker. Their ecstatic union brings both of them fulfillment in the broadest sense: she actualizes her tendency to religious mysticism, and he is transformed into an even better, more devoted, but no longer servile public servant. His feelings of self-importance find their expression in the carrying out of his calling as policeman, which Sternheim calls his "eigene

*Sternheim in 1928 (Ullstein)*

Nuance" (special nuance). Overwhelmed by the news that he has fathered a child, he loses contact with reality and is killed, appropriately and ironically, when run over by a car while directing traffic in front of the royal theater.

Like all of Sternheim's early stories, this one has an extremely narrow focus: all is seen and felt by the nearsighted, inarticulate Busekow; all of the significant action takes place within the mind of the banal hero. When Sternheim speaks of the importance of feeling for the creative process, he means that these stories are born of great feats of empathy. Busekow reveals nothing of his experience to the outside world; it emerges only in the privacy of Gesine's room and in their intense erotic excitement. The major difference between the dramas and the stories is that in the stories Sternheim gives the reader less of the world; society plays only a shadowy role as a repressive, devitalizing force. The characteristic decisive turn in the central figure usually coincides with a sexual experience that gives life fresh intensity and meaning; in self-surrender the individual finds new sources of vital energy. In ways that are often comic or satiric—Busekow ex-

presses his rapture by playing the national anthem with one finger on the piano and singing along—and scarcely visible from the outside, Sternheim's unheroic heroes escape the bonds of conformity; seize control of their lives; assert their will to power, often in destructive but not evil ways; and either come to a violent end or settle into a congenial milieu somewhere on the fringes of society—in a madhouse, in the East Indies, in a home for the aged.

*Busekow* was reprinted in 1916 with "Napoleon"—the title character is a master chef, not the emperor—and "Schuhlin," about a mediocre musician who ruthlessly exploits a young couple, in the volume *Die drei Erzählungen* (The Three Stories). This book received the prestigious Fontane Prize, being cited for its craftsmanship and stylistic innovation. At Blei's suggestion, Sternheim accepted the honor but gave the cash to the then little-known Franz Kafka in recognition of the excellence of *Der Heizer* (The Stoker, 1913) and "Die Verwandlung" (1915; translated as *The Metamorphosis*, 1937).

*Ulrike* (1918) was the last of Sternheim's major novellas, the last of his works to create a public furor, and one of several stories using World War I as background. Its heroine, a repressed Prussian aristocrat, is so overwhelmed by her experiences as a nurse in a military hospital that she sheds the last vestiges of her authoritarian, Calvinist heritage, loses herself in sexual passion, lets her naked body be painted to match her primitive state of mind, and dies bearing the child of her artist lover. Appearing in the last year of the war, *Ulrike* aroused the indignation of patriots and authorities. All copies were confiscated by the Leipzig district attorney, who charged Sternheim and his publisher with purveying pornography. The case was decided in favor of the defendants in the more liberal atmosphere of June 1919.

*Ulrike* shows the linguistic compression which increasingly characterized Sternheim's later writings. In them and in revisions of early ones, he developed what he called his phenomenological approach, focusing on the given and eliminating all moral or political preconceptions. This approach is one aspect of Sternheim's "Kampf der Metapher" (war on metaphor), his battle against the transfiguration and consequent diminution of reality. Like others of his generation, including Hugo von Hofmannsthal and Rainer Maria Rilke, he looked to the graphic arts for guidance and inspiration, and it was the painting of van Gogh that suggested ways to give his prose greater density, sharp contours,

*Portrait of Sternheim by Ernst Ludwig Kirchner (reproduced by permission of Roman Norbert Ketterer, Campione d'Italia, Lago di Lugano)*

lives the ideologies of her age—Kantian, Hegelian, and ultimately Marxian—so completely that she loses her personal identity. Carl Wundt (the wounded one) is her opposite number: mature, objective, cynical. Their love affair is brief because she is totally and suicidally committed to the cause of socialism. She dies in a street riot, grotesquely raped by the jackboot of a Dutch soldier. Wundt, revolted by the moral and intellectual corruption around him, retires to an island in what is now called Indonesia because "Europa was dead." In the last work published during Sternheim's lifetime, *Vorkriegseuropa im Gleichnis meines Lebens* (Prewar Europe as Figured by My Life, 1936), he carries both tendencies to new extremes by trying to make his sometimes trivial personal experience stand for the major currents of recent history.

The course of Sternheim's life after 1914 had become even more erratic than it was before. In August of that year he left Belgium to present himself for induction but was found not fit for military service. Dismayed by World War I and the mindless chauvinism of most Germans, he suffered a worsening series of nervous collapses. Driven by war, postwar inflation, and deteriorating health, he moved in and out of sanatoriums from Belgium to Switzerland, then to Dresden, then back to Switzerland, and finally, after some months in London in 1934-1935, again to Brussels. His chronic irritability forced his children out of the house and led to a divorce from Thea in 1927. In 1930 he married Pamela Wedekind, the actress daughter of Frank Wedekind, but the union lasted only four years. On their accession to power in 1933 the Nazis banned all of his writings, cutting off his main sources of income; he was obliged to sell off paintings and other valuables to survive. His last eight years, spent in isolation, were an unremitting decline with frequent blackouts and spells of depression. To judge from his letters, death must have been a welcome guest in Brussels on 3 November 1942.

Throughout his life Sternheim represented the opposition, cultivating a provocative stance to the point of self-contradiction and paradox. He made immoderate demands on himself as well as on others. The ambiguity of his work arises from his own ambivalence about Germany and Europe: he conducted a bitter campaign against Wilhelmine culture and at the same time affirmed its values in his work and way of life; he preached the virtues of ruthless egoism and dreamed of a utopian socialist idyll. Though many who knew him agree that he had a split personality, there has never been a

energy, and maximum expressive force. Stark juxtaposition, visual imagery, one-syllable words, alliteration, removal of adjectives and adverbs, even—in the latest revisions—omission of articles, commas, and conjunctions are designed to affront the reader's expectations and convey a sense of extreme plasticity and vigor.

After 1918 Sternheim seems to have lowered his sights and to have drawn more and more on his narrow private experience. He produced either frivolous and often very funny satiric stories, such as *Fairfax* (1921), or works weighed down by disquisitions on freedom and the downward course of Western civilization. An example of the latter is the novel *Europa*, in which an analysis of European social and intellectual history at the outset of the twentieth century is presented through the actions and ruminations of plainly allegorical figures. Europa is a Dutch woman persuaded of the necessity and power of systematic thought. She absorbs and consensus about the quality of Sternheim's work or about how it is to be interpreted. One school sees in him an ironic satirist; the other believes him to be the prophet of an amalgam of vitalist and individualist ideas. He espoused strong views on politics and society and, on the other hand, claimed to be a totally objective, "phenomenological" writer. The common denominator in all of these contradictions is the passionate moral impulse behind everything he wrote. Sternheim's work continues to be vigorous, topical, and controversial; it still excites theater riots and scholarly polemics.

**Letters:**
"Carl Sternheim: Briefe," edited by L. M. Fiedler, *Hofmannsthal Blätter*, 4 (Spring 1970): 243-254;

"Carl Sternheim: Briefe an Franz Blei," edited by Rudolf Billetta, *Neue deutsche Hefte*, 18, no. 3 (1971): 36-69.

**Bibliography:**
Rudolf Billetta, *Sternheim-Compendium: Carl Sternheim, Werk, Weg, Wirkung* (Wiesbaden: Steiner, 1975).

**Biography:**
Manfred Linke, *Carl Sternheim* (Reinbek: Rowohlt, 1979).

**References:**
R. Beckley, "Carl Sternheim," in *German Men of Letters*, edited by Alex Natan, volume 2 (London: Wolff, 1963), pp. 131-154;

Bernhard Budde, *Über die Wahrheit und über die Lüge des radikalen, antibürgerlichen Individualismus: Eine Studie zum erzählerischen und essayistischen Werk Carl Sternheims* (Frankfurt am Main: Lang, 1983);

Colette Dimic, "Das Groteske in der Erzählung des Expressionismus," Ph.D dissertation, University of Freiburg im Breisgau, 1960;

Friedrich Eisenlohr, "Der Fall Ulrikes," *Die Aktion*, 8 (27 July 1918): 373-374;

Wilhelm Emrich, "Carl Sternheims 'Kampf der Metapher' und für die 'eigene Nuance,'" in his *Geist und Widergeist* (Frankfurt am Main: Athenäum, 1965), pp. 163-184;

Hans Kaufmann, *Krisen und Wandlungen der deutschen Literatur von Wedekind bis Feuchtwan-*

ger (Berlin: Aufbau, 1966), pp. 280-293, 325-329, 338-341;

Robert Musil, "*Busekow,*" *Neue Rundschau*, 25 (1914): 848-850;

Lothar Peter, *Literarische Intelligenz und Klassenkampf: Die Aktion 1911-1932* (Cologne: Pahl-Rugenstein, 1972);

Herbert W. Reichert, "Nietzsche und Carl Sternheim," *Internationales Jahrbuch für die Nietzsche-Forschung*, 1 (1972): 334-352;

Hans Schwerte, "Carl Sternheim," in *Deutsche Dichter der Moderne*, edited by Benno von Wiese (Berlin: Schmidt, 1965), pp. 420-434;

W. G. Sebald, *Carl Sternheim: Kritiker und Opfer der Wilhelminischen Ära* (Stuttgart: Kohlhammer, 1969);

Walter H. Sokel, *The Writer in Extremis* (Stanford: Stanford University Press, 1964), pp. 62, 108, 121-123;

Wolfgang Wendler, *Carl Sternheim: Weltvorstellung und Kunstprinzipien* (Frankfurt am Main: Athenäum, 1966);

Wendler, ed., *Carl Sternheim* (Darmstadt: Luchterhand, 1980);

Rhys W. Williams, *Carl Sternheim: A Critical Study* (Bern: Lang, 1982);

Williams, "Carl Sternheim's Debt to Flaubert: Aspects of Literary Relationship," *Arcadia*, 15 (1980): 149-163;

Williams, "Carl Sternheim's Image of Marx and his Critique of the German Intellectual Tradition," *German Life and Letters*, new series 32, no. 1 (1978/1979): 19-29;

Williams, "Carl Sternheim's Image of van Gogh," *Modern Language Review*, 72, no. 1 (1977): 112-124;

Williams, "Carl Sternheim's *Tasso; oder, Kunst des Juste Milieu:* An Alternative History of German Literature," *Modern Language Review*, 75, no. 1 (1980): 123-147;

Williams, "From Painting into Literature: Carl Sternheim's Prose Style," *Oxford German Studies*, 12 (1981): 139-157;

Arnold Zweig, "Versuch über Sternheim," in his *Essays*, volume 1 (Berlin: Aufbau, 1959), pp. 246-275.

**Papers:**
Sternheim's papers are preserved in the Deutsches Literaturarchiv, Schiller Nationalmuseum, Marbach, West Germany.

# B. Traven
*(3 May 1882? or 5 March 1890?-26 March 1969?)*

## Wulf Koepke
*Texas A&M University*

See also the B. Traven entry in *DLB 9, American Novelists, 1910-1945.*

BOOKS: *Das Totenschiff: Die Geschichte eines amerikanischen Seemanns* (Berlin: Büchergilde Gutenberg, 1926); translated by Eric Sutton as *The Death Ship* (London: Chatto & Windus, 1934); English version by Traven, revised by Bernard Smith (New York: Knopf, 1934);

*Der Wobbly* (Berlin & Leipzig: Buchmeister, 1926); republished as *Die Baumwollpflücker* (Berlin & Leipzig: Buchmeister, 1929); translated by Eleanor Brockett as *The Cotton-Pickers* (London: Hale, 1956; New York: Hill & Wang, 1969);

*Der Schatz der Sierra Madre* (Berlin: Büchergilde Gutenberg, 1927); translated by Basil Creighton as *The Treasure of the Sierra Madre* (London: Chatto & Windus, 1934); English version by Traven, revised by Smith (New York: Knopf, 1935);

*Der Busch: Erzählungen* (Berlin: Büchergilde Gutenberg, 1928); republished as *Der Banditendoktor: Mexikanische Erzählungen* (Frankfurt am Main: Fischer, 1955);

*Land des Frühlings* (Berlin: Büchergilde Gutenberg, 1928);

*Die Brücke im Dschungel* (Berlin: Büchergilde Gutenberg, 1929); English version by Traven, revised by Smith as *The Bridge in the Jungle* (New York: Knopf, 1938);

*Die weiße Rose,* translated by Rudolf Dörwald from Traven's English manuscript (Berlin: Büchergilde Gutenberg, 1929); translated anonymously as *The White Rose* (London: Hale, 1965); translated by Donald J. Davidson as *The White Rose* (Westport, Conn.: Hill, 1979);

*Der Karren* (Berlin: Büchergilde Gutenberg, 1931); enlarged as *Die Carreta* (Berlin: Universitas, 1953); translated by Creighton as *The Carreta* (London: Chatto & Windus, 1935; New York: Hill & Wang, 1970);

*Regierung* (Berlin: Büchergilde Gutenberg, 1931); translated by Creighton as *Government* (Lon-

*B. Traven (?)*

don: Chatto & Windus, 1935; New York: Hill & Wang, 1971);

*Der Marsch ins Reich der Caoba: Ein Kriegsmarsch* (Zurich: Büchergilde Gutenberg, 1933); translated anonymously as *March to Caobaland* (London: Hale, 1961; New York: Dell, 1963);

*Die Troza* (Zurich: Büchergilde Gutenberg, 1936); republished as *Trozas: Roman* (Frankfurt am

Main: Europäische Verlagsanstalt, 1959);

*Sonnen-Schöpfung: Indianische Legenden* (Zurich: Büchergilde Gutenberg, 1936); translated anonymously as *The Creation of the Sun and the Moon* (New York: Hill & Wang, 1968; London: Muller, 1971);

*Die Rebellion der Gehenkten: Roman* (Zurich: Büchergilde Gutenberg, 1936); translated by Charles Duff as *The Rebellion of the Hanged* (London: Hale, 1952); English version by Traven (New York: Knopf, 1952);

*Ein General kommt aus dem Dschungel* (Amsterdam: De Lange, 1940); translated by Desmond Vesey as *General from the Jungle* (New York: Hill & Wang, 1954);

*Macario: Eine Novellette,* translated by Hans Kauders from Traven's English manuscript (Zurich: Büchergilde Gutenberg, 1950); translated by R. E. Lujan as *Macario* (Boston: Houghton Mifflin, 1971);

*Der dritte Gast und andere Erzählungen* (Berlin: Volk & Welt, 1958);

*Aslan Norval: Roman* (Munich, Vienna & Basel: Desch, 1960);

*Stories by the Man Nobody Knows: Nine Tales* (Evanston, Ill.: Regnery, 1961);

*Khundar: Das erste Buch Begegnungen* (Egnach, Switzerland: Clou, 1963);

*The Night Visitor, and Other Stories* (New York: Hill & Wang, 1966; London: Cassell, 1967);

*Erzählungen,* edited by Werner Sellhorn (Zurich: Limmat, 1968);

*The Kidnapped Saint and Other Stories,* edited by Rosa Elena Lujan and Mina C. and H. Arthur Klein (New York: Hill, 1975);

*Das Frühwerk* (Berlin: Guhl, 1977);

*To the Honorable Miss S... and Other Stories,* translated by Peter Silcock (Westport, Conn.: Hill/Sanday, Orkney, U.K.: Cienfuegos Press, 1981);

*Werkausgabe,* 15 volumes (Zurich: Diogenes, 1982).

B. Traven won instant fame in 1926 when the newly founded book club of the German Printers Union, Büchergilde Gutenberg, published *Das Totenschiff* (translated as *The Death Ship,* 1934). It was a story of outcasts on a ship condemned to sink in the next storm, a story both realistic and romantic, both pessimistic and full of vibrant vitality. It was a story betraying leftist leanings and intense empathy with the suffering lower classes, but at the same time revealing his decidedly individualistic, even anarchistic bent. This and his other early books made Traven, like Jack London, a favorite author of young readers, and one of the models

for German and European proletarian literature.

Readers, critics, and the media were intrigued by the mysteries surrounding the identity of the elusive author. His manuscripts came from Mexico, with post office box return addresses. Biographical inquiries were never answered. Who was B. Traven? is a question still awaiting a definitive answer. The question has also been raised whether the B. Traven who submitted such exciting manuscripts was really their author, or whether they were written by another person—or by several persons. The theory of an "Erlebnisträger" (experience carrier) holds that a person other than Traven must have provided the authentic experiences for these books, either as oral narration or a written draft: while the early Traven books are first-person narratives and have elements of autobiographical storytelling, chronology precludes that Traven could have had most of these experiences firsthand.

A man who sometimes called himself Hal Croves and sometimes used the name Traven Torsvan, who had the copyright to B. Traven's works, and who died in Mexico City in 1969, claimed to be an American born in or near Chicago in 1890 of parents of Scandinavian ancestry. This claim has generally been dismissed; it is believed that he was a German. The East German Traven scholar Rolf Recknagel has provided proof—to the extent that proof can be provided—that another of Traven's many aliases was Ret Marut. Marut was an actor and occasional stage director in Germany whose not very successful career can be traced from 1907 to 1914; in official documents he claimed to be an American, born in San Francisco in 1882. He was employed in many provincial theaters from the Ruhr area to Saxony and Danzig. He ended up in Düsseldorf and left the stage in the early part of World War I, applying unsuccessfully for an American passport. He lived with the actress Elfriede Zielke and had a daughter, Irene, born in 1912. In 1917 the first issue of the magazine *Der Ziegelbrenner,* edited and published by Marut and Irene Mermet, appeared; a novel, *An das Fräulein von S...* (1916), plays, and poems were published under pseudonyms including Richard Maurhut, Helmuth Guhn-Moyn, and Arthur Terlehn by otherwise nonexistent publishing houses. *Der Ziegelbrenner* was so violently antiauthoritarian and antiwar that it is surprising that the vigilant Bavarian censorship allowed it to appear at all. Its readership was small, in part because Marut refused to market his product. After the Bavarian revolution of November 1918, Marut participated in the new socialist state. He was an anarchist and close in spirit to one of

*Photograph of Ret Marut, generally believed to be one of the
aliases used by the man who later called himself B. Traven,
from the files of the United States Department of State*

*British mug shot of Ret Marut (Ullstein)*

*1902 photo of Otto Feige, who is thought by some investigators to be the real B. Traven. Others believe Traven to have been the illegitimate son of Kaiser Wilhelm II.*

the leading minds of the revolution, Gustav Landauer. During the short last phase of socialism in Bavaria, the Räterepublik of April 1919, Marut was a press censor. Next in line to be executed, he escaped the firing squads of the victorious Freikorps on 1 May 1919. He went into hiding but continued to publish *Der Ziegelbrenner* until 1921.

At the end of 1922, Marut disappeared from Germany. An investigation by a BBC team in the late 1970s identified Marut as one Otto Feige, born on 23 February 1882 in Schwiebus, east of Frankfurt an der Oder, now called Swiebodzin and part of Poland. Feige was apprenticed to a locksmith and served in the German army from 1902 to 1904. The BBC team dismisses the legend that Marut may have been an illegitimate son of Germany's last emperor, Wilhelm II.

In 1923 Marut was in prison in London for illegal entry and was refused visas to Canada and the United States. In 1925 B. Traven began sending manuscripts from Mexico.

Between 1926 and 1930 Traven Torsvan acted as a photographer on scientific expeditions

in Chiapas. In 1930 he moved to Acapulco and lived on a small property called Cashew Park. He must also have been in Mexico City and San Antonio, Texas, at times. He moved away from Acapulco in 1948, after being identified by the journalist Luis Spota, and apparently lived in Mexico City until his death. In 1957 he married his literary agent, Rosa Elena Lujan. Their last house was on the Rio Mississippi.

For the time being one must assume that, with one possible exception, Traven's works were written by one person, identical with the man who died in 1969. Most of these works appeared between 1925 and 1940. A late novel, *Aslan Norval*, published under the name B. Traven in 1960, is so different in content and style and of such inferior quality from the other works that it seems to be from another pen.

*Das Totenschiff* stands out as the only book, other than *Aslan Norval*, not dealing with Mexico. Gerard Gales, an American sailor, misses his ship in Antwerp and is left behind without identification papers. No country will accept him, and no ship will take him without proper papers. After numerous adventures with the police and bureaucracies in Belgium, Holland, France, and Spain, Gales ends up as a stoker on the *Yorikke*—a ship deliberately sent out by its owners to sink in a storm for the insurance money. Before the *Yorikke* goes down, Gales is shanghaied to another ship, the *Empress;* but it, too, is wrecked, and Gales is the only survivor. There is a strain of strong vitality in the book, of surviving against all odds.

*Das Totenschiff* was the second novel to be written under the name B. Traven; the first serialized in the Social Democratic paper *Vorwärts* in 1925 was *Die Baumwollpflücker* (translated as *The Cotton-Pickers*, 1956). It was published in book form as *Der Wobbly* after *Das Totenschiff* in 1926 and was republished under its original title in 1929. It was followed by the novels *Der Schatz der Sierra Madre* (translated as *The Treasure of the Sierra Madre*, 1934) in 1927 and *Die Brücke im Dschungel* (translated as *The Bridge in the Jungle,* 1938) and *Die weiße Rose* (translated as *The White Rose,* 1965) in 1929. In 1928 Traven published a travel book on Chiapas, *Land des Frühlings* (Land of Spring). All of these books sing the praise of the Indians living in accordance with nature and condemn the white man for his greed and exploitation of the Indians and for the artificiality of his life. *Die Baumwollpflücker* views the exploitation of the Indian cotton pickers from the perspective of a "Wobbly," a member of the left-wing American trade union Industrial Workers of the World. While resistance against the capitalists, whose headquarters are in the United States, proves to be futile in spite of temporary victories, a rebellious spirit is generated which might lead to future actions. Gales, the American Wobbly who witnesses the sense of solidarity of the Mexicans, begins to consider Mexico his home: he loves the land and feels close to the soil. Becoming part of the land, of nature, is the real blessing for Traven's lonely white men who are alienated from their own society.

The three men in *Der Schatz der Sierra Madre* have already found out that there is no way to escape from the pits of society through regular work, so they decide to dig for gold in the mountains. They are successful, but with the growing treasure their problems increase: fear of attacks from outside and suspicions among themselves. The most difficult problem proves to be transporting the sacks of gold dust from the mountains

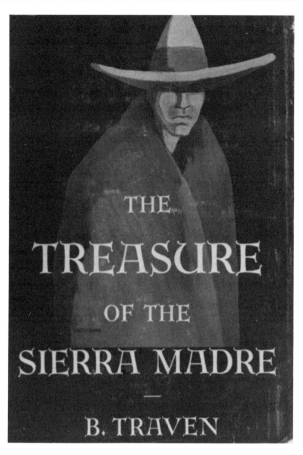

*Dust jacket for the English translation of Traven's novel about three gold seekers in the Mexican mountains (Lilly Library, Indiana University)*

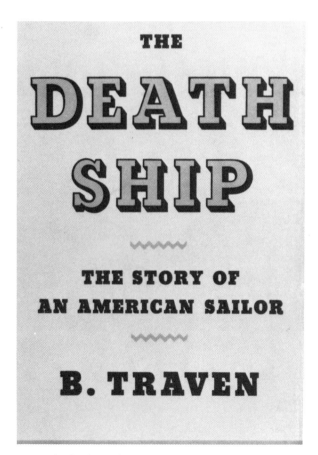

*Dust jacket for the English translation of Traven's first published novel (Lilly Library, Indiana University)*

to town. One of the men, Dobbs, is murdered by Mexican bandits, but ironically not for his gold: the killers throw the gold dust away and keep the sacks. The others fulfill their dream of living a peaceful life of plenty in a totally unexpected way: Howard is accepted by the Indians as a miracle healer and lives among them as an honored wise man, joined by his surviving comrade, Curtin. It is not the exploitation of the land for greed that brings about happiness, but helping and healing suffering fellow humans.

The conclusions of the following novels are less optimistic. In *Die weiße Rose* an American oil company tries to buy a Mexican hacienda situated in the middle of an oil field. The owner, however, does not want to sell; for him, land is the real value, while money is dangerous and will not last. The fight against the all-powerful oil company is eventually lost, and the owner dies. (The film made from this novel in 1963 turns the ending around:

*(Facing camera, from left) Walter Huston, Humphrey Bogart, and Tim Holt in the 1948 Warner Bros. film of* The Treasure of the Sierra Madre. *Hal Croves, who may have been Traven under yet another name, was present during the filming.*

instead of the novel's vague hope of defeating the American capitalists sometime in the future, the film ends with the nationalization of oil production in Mexico under Cárdenas in 1938.)

*Die Brücke im Dschungel* presents the conflict of the two cultures in a different way. Gales visits a friend in an Indian village. During a festival, a boy drowns near the bridge in the jungle. Most of the text is devoted to the search for the boy, the mourning of the community, and the funeral. The narrator is struck both by the elementary solidarity and communal feeling of the village and the disastrous inroads made by Western civilization. At his funeral, the boy is dressed in a cheap sailor's suit that could be found in department stores in the United States or Europe. The narrator feels that this costume cheapens the entire ceremony and calls into question the authenticity of the Indians' rituals and emotions.

The publishing histories of *Das Totenschiff, Der Schatz der Sierra Madre,* and *Die Brücke im Dschungel* serve to deepen the mystery surrounding their author. The three novels were first published in German and were translated into English for publication in London. But manuscripts for all three, *in English,* were sent by Traven to Alfred A. Knopf in New York. Even though both Ret Marut and Traven Torsvan claimed to be American by birth, these manuscripts—with their odd sentence structures, malapropisms, and unsuccessful attempts at American idioms—appeared to have been translated into English from German. All were heavily revised by Bernard Smith, a Knopf editor, for publication in the United States.

Traven was attracted by the communal living in the self-governing Indian villages. Recknagel and Michael Baumann have demonstrated the decisive influence of the nineteenth-century anarchist philosopher Max Stirner's ideas on Traven, who rejected government and argued for a voluntary association of free and self-reliant individuals. Government is unnatural; it is synonymous with oppression and the stifling of individual vitality. Justice and solidarity are not achieved by enforced rules of equality. In spite of his empathy with human suffering, and as much as he acted as a spokesman for the oppressed proletariat, Traven was not a socialist. But he came closer than before to socialist positions on economy in his travel book *Land des Frühlings.* Traven was apparently a member of a scientific expedition set up to report to the Mexican government on conditions in Chiapas, the "backward" southernmost state of Mexico, in 1926. Traven evidently left the group and went off on his own, traveling by mule with the help of a native servant. *Land des Frühlings* contains a vivid description of this remote and exotic region as well as numerous ideas on how to improve the conditions of the inhabitants, including proposals for the modernization of agriculture. Traven advocates calling in the government to organize the modernization effort and to break up the holdings of the large landowners.

During this period of enormous activity and productivity Traven also wrote his best-known short stories. After being published in newspapers and magazines, they were collected in 1928 under the title *Der Busch* (The Jungle). In "Der Nachtbesuch im Busch" (The Night Visitor in the Jungle), the narrator, Gales, lives in a jungle hut. He agrees to guard the hut of his learned neighbor while the latter is away. This odd scholar seems to know more about the pre-Columbian civilization than anybody else does, but as soon as he finishes

*Dust jacket for the third of Traven's cycle of six novels about Indians enslaved to work in the timber camps in the Mexican jungle (Lilly Library, Indiana University)*

*Dust jacket for the English translation of Traven's novel about the death of an Indian boy (Lilly Library, Indiana University)*

a manuscript, he destroys it. He knows that the outside world will never understand. Gales immerses himself in books about Indians. The past comes alive when, out of an overgrown temple, an Aztec prince appears who wants to enlist Gales's help against attacks by pigs. Gales is drawn into a realm between dream and reality. When his neighbor returns, Gales takes a train into the deepest part of the jungle, leaving the train at night to immerse himself fully in the land. Most of the stories are told in a humorous tone. They denounce capitalism and the Catholic church, but they are less a plea for social change than studies of the Indian mentality. The stories highlight Indian superstitions and their sense of honor as well as their radically different idea of property. They also demonstrate the irreconcilable differences in mentality between white people—North Americans in particular—and the Mexican Indians. The setting of these stories is a Mexico with an unstable government, antigovernment guerrillas and gangs, police brutality, village priests maintaining their rule of superstition, and, most of all, with countless modes of surviving against great odds. The plots are not always original, but the tone of the stories is unmistakably authentic, and the details penetrate into the daily lives of these people.

Traven's earlier novels and stories are works of an author who wants to gain recognition and popularity. In spite of the author's physical distance from his markets, he seemed to have a good sense of what would sell in Germany. On the other hand, he refused to permit his publishers' most common advertising practices. This contradictory attitude toward the market reveals a man who was hungry for recognition but wanted to gain it outside the capitalist system. Later Traven would change this attitude and permit anything that made money.

Around 1930 Traven embarked on the great project of his writing career. In Chiapas he had come across traces of the once-flourishing mahogany trade. These trees, with their very hard wood, had to be cut in the jungle, then moved to the nearest waterway, where they could be collected and brought down the rivers to the ocean. This back-breaking work was performed by Indians who were forced into camps (*monterias*) for debts or minor crimes. Discipline in the camps was severe; cruel punishment was inflicted for any transgression or attempt at rebellion. The most lucrative times had been the late nineteenth and early twentieth centuries, during the rule of the dictator Porfirio Díaz. Traven returned repeatedly to the area for more studies, until he was ready to write the cycle of his six "Caoba" (mahogany) novels: *Der Karren* (1931), which was revised as *Die Carreta* (1953; translated as *The Carreta*, 1935); *Regierung*

(1931; translated as *Government*, 1935); *Der Marsch ins Reich der Caoba* (1933; translated as *March to Caobaland*, 1961); *Die Troza* (1936); *Die Rebellion der Gehenkten* (1936; translated as *The Rebellion of the Hanged*, 1952); and *Ein General kommt aus dem Dschungel* (1940; translated as *General from the Jungle*, 1954). Andres Ugaldo, a young Tseltal Indian, is the central character in the series. Shortly after his marriage, his happiness is interrupted when he has to go to a *monteria* for the debts of his father. The camp management makes its cruelty clear when the workers march into Caobaland; it becomes even more brutal once they start their work. Andres and some comrades, notably Celso and the schoolteacher Martin Trinidad, bring with them a spirit of rebellion. Brutal punishments, such as cutting off ears, provoke all the woodcutters and *carreta* (cart) drivers, and "the rebellion of the hanged" finally breaks out. (The nickname "the hanged" is taken from one of their punishments: hanging all night by their feet.) The rebellion, well prepared by Andres's group, succeeds. The Indians in their isolated jungle region do not know the revolution of 1911 has taken place and Díaz has been expelled from the country. The little army marches out of the jungle; it has to learn military tactics and discipline and must find more powerful weapons. Its battle cry is "*Tierra y libertad*" (land and freedom). It defeats several police and army units; its strength increases, and the population is on its side. The end, however, is strangely ambiguous: while the rebels are founding their utopian commune, Solipaz (Sun and Peace), they are finally told that the system they are fighting is already gone. But whether the revolution has really succeeded and

*Dust jacket for the English translation of Traven's novel about the revolt of the Indians in the mahogany camps (Lilly Library, Indiana University)*

brought happiness for the Mexican people is in doubt, even if the days of the Díaz oppression are over. Traven seems less optimistic than ten years before about the future of Mexico.

He also must have been watching events in Europe with alarm and dismay. When the Büchergilde Gutenberg was taken over by the Nazis in 1933, he followed the old management into its Zurich exile, thus cutting himself off from his German readers. After his agent, Josef Wieder, quarreled with the Büchergilde, Traven had his last Caoba novel published by the exile firm Allert de Lange in Amsterdam, where the book appeared shortly before the Germans occupied Holland.

Traven's last Mexican work, *Macario* (1950; translated, 1971), is a skillful adaptation of "Gevatter Tod" (Godfather Death), the German folk tale written down both by the Brothers Grimm and by Ludwig Bechstein, whose version seems to have been the model used by Traven. The poor woodcutter Macario has one wish in life: to be able to eat a whole turkey by himself. His wife finally fulfills this wish. Macario withdraws into the jungle to enjoy his feast. Before he can start to eat, however, three figures appear who want to share his meal: the devil, Jesus Christ, and death. He cannot refuse death, who grants him miracle healing power for a limited amount of time. Macario's new life, with all its brilliance and its tragic end, is described in detail. But all is revealed to be a dream. When Macario's wife searches for him, she finds him dead; he has finished half of his turkey, while the other half is intact, evidently having been offered to a guest at the meal.

Traven's works went through many editions, and the author made many changes. In the postwar editions, he deleted allusions to German conditions, as if to cut his last ties with Germany. Only after World War II did he allow his books to appear in Spanish for Mexican readers. Hal Croves, who insisted that he was Traven's translator, collaborated on most scripts of films made from Traven novels. While his suggestions were generally considered very good, he usually quarreled with the directors when he was present during the filming of the novels, especially *The Treasure of the Sierra Madre* (1948) in 1947. He was short and slender, shy but strong-willed and stubborn, and hard to get along with. After World War II he intensified his efforts to create and maintain a "Traven legend," fabricating a biography and viciously attacking in his "B.T. Mitteilungen" (B.T. Announcements) anyone who contradicted him—especially those who suspected his identity as Ret Marut.

While Ret Marut's literary output is interesting, it is hardly that of a writer to be remembered. Traven came into his own when he wrote about the outcast sailors of the "death ship" and the Indians of Mexico. His literary models—Jack London and, to a lesser degree, Joseph Conrad—are outside the German literary tradition. Traven's style is unpolished; his German is as full of Americanisms as his English is of Germanisms. He gives the

*Photograph by Traven of the cabin in the jungle where he claimed to have written some of the stories collected in* Der Busch *(1928)*

impression of a man of little education writing spontaneously. But that impression is deceptive: he knows his craft. It is possible that he wrote rapidly and revised little, but the image of the rough proletarian writer is a carefully created one. Truth and fiction intermingle both in his books and in his life. Traven's works are neither high literature nor trivial adventure stories; they do not conform to the normal categories of literary evaluation. This may be one reason Germanists have been reluctant to examine Traven's works; more Traven scholars can be found outside the German-speaking countries than inside.

Traven's popularity continues unabated. While the interest in the biographical mysteries will fade, it may become clearer with time that he was a remarkable writer. His writing is hauntingly realistic, yet it expounds a vitalistic and anarchistic philosophy, and symbols and leitmotifs are skillfully woven into these seemingly artless stories. He condensed the essence of his beliefs about the Indians into an imitation of a Mayan legend, *Sonnen-Schöpfung* (1936; translated as *The Creation of the Sun and the Moon*, 1968), a myth of a modern man who is a creator, is not alienated from nature, and is an integral part of his community. Traven believed, at least at times, that the future belonged to peoples like the Mexicans, uncorrupted by capitalism and living in communes without government. He may have been a dreamer, but he conveyed his dreams in powerful images.

**Bibliography:**

E. R. Hagemann, "A Checklist of the Works of B. Traven and the Critical Estimates and Biographical Essays on Him, Together with a Brief Biography," *Papers of the Bibliographical Society of America*, 53 (1959): 37-67.

**References:**

Michael L. Baumann, *B. Traven: An Introduction* (Albuquerque: University of New Mexico Press, 1976);

Johannes Beck, Klaus Bergmann, and Heiner Boehncke, eds., *Das B. Traven Buch* (Reinbek: Rowohlt, 1976);

Donald O. Chankin, *Anonymity and Death: The Fiction of B. Traven* (University Park: Pennsylvania State University Press, 1975);

Karl S. Guthke, "Das Geheimnis des Jahrhunderts entdeckt—und rätselhafter denn je: B. Traven," in his *Erkundungen: Essays zur Literatur von Milton bis Traven* (Bern, Frankfurt am Main & New York: Lang, 1983), pp. 337-370;

Gerd Heidemann, *Postlagernd Tampico: Die abenteuerliche Suche nach B. Traven* (Munich: Blanvalet, 1977);

Frederik Hetmann, *Der Mann, der sich verbarg: Nachforschungen über B. Traven* (Stuttgart: Klett, 1980);

Hubert Jannach, "B. Traven—An American or German Author?," *German Quarterly*, 36 (Fall 1963): 459-468;

James L. Kastely, "Understanding the 'Work' of Literature: B. Traven's *The Death Ship*," *Mosaic*, 18, no. 1 (1985): 79-96;

Heribert Körner and Ernst-Ulrich Pinkert, "Prinzip Utopia: Nicht Eldorado. B. Travens Roman *Die weiße Rose*," *Text und Kontext*, 12 (1984): 330-348;

Peter Lübbe, "Das Revolutionserlebnis im Werk von B. Traven," Ph.D. dissertation, University of Rostock, 1965;

Winfried Pogorzelski, *Aufklärung im Spätwerk B. Travens* (Bern, Frankfurt am Main & New York: Lang, 1985);

Jonah Raskin, *My Search for B. Traven* (New York: Methuen, 1980);

Rolf Recknagel, *B. Traven: Beiträge zur Biografie* (Leipzig: Reclam, 1966; revised, Berlin: Guhl, 1977);

Armin Richter, *Der Ziegelbrenner: Das individualistische Kampforgan des frühen B. Traven* (Bonn: Bouvier, 1977);

Judy Stone, *The Mystery of B. Traven* (Los Altos, Cal.: Kaufmann, 1977);

Will Wyatt, *The Secret of the Sierra Madre: The Man Who Was B. Traven* (New York: Harcourt Brace Jovanovich, 1985).

# Kurt Tucholsky

*(9 January 1890-21 December 1935)*

Herbert Knust
*University of Illinois*

BOOKS: *Rheinsberg—ein Bilderbuch für Verliebte* (Berlin: Juncker, 1912);

*Der Zeitsparer: Grotesken,* as Ignaz Wrobel (Berlin: Reuss & Pollack, 1914);

*Fromme Gesänge,* as Theobald Tiger (Charlottenburg: Lehmann, 1919);

*Träumereien an preußischen Kaminen,* as Peter Panter (Charlottenburg: Lehmann, 1920);

*Die verkehrte Welt in Knüttelversen dargestellt,* as Kaspar Hauser (Berlin: Vereinigte Internationale Verlagsanstalten, 1922);

*Ein Pyrenäenbuch* (Berlin: Die Schmiede, 1927);

*Mit 5 PS* (Berlin: Rowohlt, 1928);

*Das Lächeln der Mona Lisa* (Berlin: Rowohlt, 1929);

*Deutschland, Deutschland über alles: Ein Bilderbuch von Kurt Tucholsky und vielen Fotografen,* assembled by John Heartfield (Berlin: Neuer Deutscher Verlag, 1929); translated by Anne Halley as *Deutschland, Deutschland über alles: A Picture-Book* (Amherst, Mass.: University of Massachusetts Press, 1972);

*Schloß Gripsholm* (Berlin: Rowohlt, 1931);

*Lerne lachen ohne zu weinen* (Berlin: Rowohlt, 1931);

*Gruß nach vorn: Eine Auswahl,* edited by Erich Kästner (Stuttgart: Rowohlt, 1946);

*Na und—? Eine Auswahl,* edited by Mary Gerold-Tucholsky (Hamburg: Rowohlt, 1950);

*Zwischen Gestern und Morgen: Eine Auswahl aus seinen Schriften und Gedichten,* edited by Gerold-Tucholsky (Hamburg: Rowohlt, 1952);

*Und überhaupt . . . : Eine neue Auswahl,* edited by Gerold-Tucholsky (Hamburg: Rowohlt, 1953);

*Panter, Tiger & Co.: Eine neue Auswahl aus seinen Schriften und Gedichten,* edited by Gerold-Tucholsky (Hamburg: Rowohlt, 1954);

*Nachher* (Darmstadt: Büchner, 1956);

*Das Wirtshaus im Spessart* (Darmstadt: Büchner, 1956);

*The World Is a Comedy: A Tucholsky Anthology,* translated and edited by Harry Zohn (Cambridge, Mass.: Sci-Art, 1957);

*Kurt Tucholsky (Ullstein)*

*Man sollte mal . . . : Eine Auswahl,* edited by Hermann Kesten (Frankfurt am Main: Büchergilde Gutenberg, 1957);

*Kurt Tucholsky haßt-liebt in Prosastücken, Gedichten und Briefen,* edited by Gerold-Tucholsky (Hamburg: Rowohlt, 1957);

*Gesammelte Werke 1907-1932,* edited by Gerold-Tucholsky and Fritz J. Raddatz, 3 volumes (Reinbek: Rowohlt, 1960-1961, 1967);

*Kurt Tucholsky: Eine Auswahl,* edited by Egon Schwarz (New York: Norton, 1963);

*Morgen wieder—?,* edited by Raddatz (Frankfurt am Main: Büchergilde Gutenberg, 1964);

*Ausgewählte Werke,* edited by Raddatz, 2 volumes (Reinbek: Rowohlt, 1964);

265

*Von Rheinsberg bis Gripsholm* (Hamburg: Rowohlt, 1966);

*Wenn die Igel in der Abendstunde: Gedichte, Lieder und Chansons,* edited by Raddatz (Reinbek: Rowohlt, 1968);

*What if—? Satirical Writings,* translated by Zohn and Karl F. Ross (New York: Funk & Wagnalls, 1968);

*Politische Justiz,* edited by Martin Swarzenski (Reinbek: Rowohlt, 1970);

*Politische Texte,* edited by Raddatz (Reinbek: Rowohlt, 1971);

*Christopher Columbus,* by Tucholsky as Panter and Walter Hasenclever, manuscript translated by M. Spalter and G. E. Wellwarth in *German Drama between the Wars,* edited by Wellwarth (New York: Dutton, 1972);

*Literaturkritik,* edited by Raddatz (Reinbek: Rowohlt, 1972);

*Schnipsel,* edited by Gerold-Tucholsky and Raddatz (Reinbek: Rowohlt, 1974);

*Gesammelte Werke 1907-1932,* edited by Gerold-Tucholsky and Raddatz, 10 volumes (Reinbek: Rowohlt, 1975);

*Die Q-Tagebücher 1934-1935,* edited by Gerold-Tucholsky and Gustav Huonker (Reinbek: Rowohlt, 1978);

*Kurt Tucholsky 1890-1935: Ein Lebensbild,* edited by Richard von Soldenhoff (Berlin: Quadriga-Verlag Severin, 1985).

Kurt Tucholsky—poet, storyteller, literary journalist, and critic—left behind a voluminous oeuvre that bears witness to his courageous commitment and unusual creativeness as a writer during one of Germany's most difficult epochs. He was feared as a satirical chronicler of the Weimar Republic, praised as the wittiest poet of the Berlin dialect, liked for his refreshing and melancholy tales of love and companionship, and admired for his passionate and uncompromising fight for truth, justice, freedom, and peace. His love-hate relationship to Germany, born of wounded idealism, has been compared to that of other great satirists, such as Heinrich Heine or Tucholsky's contemporary George Grosz, whose acid, graphic attacks on the culprits and ills of their times parallel Tucholsky's own eloquent criticism. But Tucholsky is not just a German phenomenon: the increasing public attention he has received since the war, at home and abroad, shows that the various voices in which he has spoken are widely recognized and that the humanistic values for which he stood are of constant concern in an insecure world.

Born in 1890 in Berlin, the bustling capital of the expansive Wilhelminian Empire and increasingly a cosmopolitan center of intellectual life, Tucholsky was the oldest of three children of well-to-do Jewish parents. He felt close to his art-loving and humorous father, Alex Tucholsky, who died prematurely in 1905; but his relationship with his mother, Doris, was strained, gradually grew into conflicts, and may have contributed to his troubled relationships with women in his later years.

After elementary school in Stettin (now Szczecin, Poland), where his parents lived for a while and where Tucholsky became attached to the Baltic seascape, he attended Gymnasium in Berlin. In retrospect, he had little good to say about his teachers, and some of his literary attempts as a schoolboy reveal the traces of a rather chauvinistic education. After delayed progress and changes from one school to another, the sensitive and vulnerable Tucholsky, aided by private tutoring, finally graduated in 1909.

Initially thinking of a practical, "safe" profession, Tucholsky began to study law in Berlin, went to Geneva for a semester in 1910, then returned to Germany to finish his studies at Jena. Yet he was less interested in his academic discipline—which, after a refusal of his dissertation, finally gained him the doctorate in 1915—than in his literary pursuits.

*Ulk,* the satirical supplement to the journal *Berliner Tageblatt,* had published Tucholsky's first brief story, ridiculing the Kaiser's lack of culture, in 1907. In 1912 the short novel *Rheinsberg—ein Bilderbuch für Verliebte* (Rheinsberg—A Picture Book for Lovers) brought him his first big success as a writer. It is the simple story of two young lovers, Wolfgang and Claire, who escape from boring everyday life in Berlin to idyllic Rheinsberg in the country. Pretending to be married, they spend three happy, carefree days visiting the castle of Frederick the Great, going for boat rides on a lake, taking a carriage ride through the woods, enjoying walks through parks and meadows, shopping, going to the movies, and sharing their love for each other. Their relationship is expressed through charming playfulness and witty dialogues, on Claire's part in funny yet poetic childlike nonsense language; they tease each other and quarrel affectionately. They have amusing encounters with peculiar members of bourgeois society, all somehow tied down by their habits, mental burdens, or other limitations; by contrast, Claire and Wolfgang appear uniquely free and exuberant in their spirited imaginativeness, lighthearted playacting, and happy enjoyment of their togetherness during

*Tucholsky (at left) with his sister Ellen; his mother, Doris; his brother Fritz; his father, Alex; and his grandmother in 1898*
*(Kurt-Tucholsky-Archiv, Rottach-Egern)*

their temporary respite from responsibility. Yet amid the fleeting impressionistic scenes there are also melancholy notes: the awareness that all must end, and the realization that even in intensive and harmonious encounters between lovers there remains a yearning for ultimate fulfillment. Still, it is Tucholsky's least burdened book and, as he said later, it captured the happier times of his youth. The manuscript was declined by several publishers because the theme of free love, although never explicit, was considered risqué; but the story quickly became a classic. Its continuing success lies in its appeal to the young, who periodically rebel against the drabness of an increasingly complicated and routine life beset by restrictions, but just as much in its evocation of happy memories among those who are no longer young.

Tucholsky had been active as a political journalist since 1911; by 1913 his lively critical contributions, mostly essays on the Berlin theater scene, were appearing in the renowned avant-garde weekly *Die Schaubühne*, founded by Siegfried Ja-

cobsohn. For the sake of variety in perspective and tone, Tucholsky began to write under several pseudonyms in addition to his own name: Ignaz Wrobel, Peter Panter, Theobald Tiger, and Kaspar Hauser. This intellectual disguise appealed to his many-faceted character as well as his personal modesty.

Tucholsky was drafted in 1915 and served on the eastern front in administrative posts behind the lines. His observations of military arrogance, exploitation of patriotism, and blindly nationalistic propaganda fueled his satiric spirit, which broke loose after the war in *Die Weltbühne*, the politically emancipated new format of the former *Schaubühne*, in attacks on the reactionary forces that were striving violently to regain control in the new Weimar Republic. Tucholsky devoted thirteen years to *Die Weltbühne*, which became the foremost left-wing weekly of its time and presents, largely through his countless contributions, the most interesting and dynamic political and cultural chronicle of the Weimar Republic. His more than 1,800 short, spirited

*Siegfried Jacobsohn, founder of the weekly* Die Schaubühne, *where many of Tucholsky's early writings appeared. Tucholsky continued to write for the journal, renamed* Die Weltbühne, *after World War I, and briefly assumed the editorship after Jacobsohn's death in 1926 (Kurt-Tucholsky-Archiv, Rottach-Egern).*

pieces ranged from sharp aggressiveness to disarming humor; from crisp ironic wit to skepticism and melancholy sentiments; from straightforward essays, insinuating parables, parodistic sketches, and sarcastic dialogues to pointed documentaries, spicy lyrics, provocative ballads, and memorable witty aphorisms. His themes varied widely, and his criticism was openly aimed at dubious institutions, traditions, public events, and prominent figures. Among his critiques of the ills of the republic, his condemnation of militarism is frequent and fierce in such biting essays as "Militaria," "Krieg" (War), "Neuer Militarismus" (New Militarism), "Unser Militär" (Our Military), "Preußenhimmel" (Prussian Heaven), "Offiziere" (Officers), "Mordkommission" (Hit Squad), "Deutschland, ein Kasernenhof" (Germany, a Barrack-Square), "Hepp hepp, hurra," and "Das Buch von der deutschen Schande" (The Book of German

Shame). Tucholsky took pride in the fact that *Die Weltbühne* was one of the first papers to attack systematically the German officer mentality—a mixture of brutality, stupidity, arrogance, and lack of civil courage. In addition to warning of corrupt military jurisdiction, he suggested the transformation of the Reichswehr into a reliable people's army.

As a trained lawyer, Tucholsky exposed with particular urgency the perversion of justice for reactionary ends. Allegorically, he portrayed "Justitia" as a callous slut. Tucholsky visited trials during the aftermath of the Spartakus uprising and was clearly on the side of the defendants, whose hopeless legal position before a prejudiced jury he reflects in the satirical essay "Wie benehme ich mich als Mörder" (How to Behave as a Murderer). He also produced statistical evidence of the counterrevolutionary bias of the judiciary. Tucholsky's ominous statement that Germany was no longer the land of "Dichter und Denker" (poets and thinkers) but of "Richter und Henker" (judges and hangmen) points to a conspiracy of law, business, military, church, and educators and finds expression in such prophetic satirical pieces as "Deutsche Richtergeneration 1940" (German Judicial Generation 1940). In addition to criticism, he also offers constructive suggestions for legal reform.

The tenacious obsession with endless stifling laws and bylaws in the service of an old order typifies the uniformed bureaucracy, which Tucholsky calls "die Beamtenpest" (the plague of officials) at large. Tucholsky depicts civil servants, including police officers, as inflexible, irresponsible, and inhumane—much like the military caste. He connects these traits to the instinctive servility of the German people, who bow and scrape before uniforms, titles, and medals. Slavish servility is a frequent metaphor in Tucholsky's satirical arsenal; it takes one of its wittiest forms in the story "Der Hund als Untergebener" (The Dog as Subordinate): in a hierarchical chain of German subjects each one below can be treated like a dog—even a dog can be so treated, "weil auch er aus Deutschland ist" (because it, too, is German).

Nor did business escape the acid pen of Tucholsky, who had to resort to a temporary job in a bank for a living in 1923. He attacks employers as hard-boiled exploiters and industrialists as ruthless profiteers; in "Die Herren Wirtschaftsführer" (Their Lords, the Economic Leaders), he uses strong invective against capitalist entrepreneurs. Among the victims of big business he counts not only the economically disadvantaged but also—as

*Dust jacket for Tucholsky's 1919 collection of satirical verses,
written under one of his pseudonyms (Lilly Library,
Indiana University)*

*Dust jacket for a 1928 collection of Tucholsky's magazine ar-
ticles. The title is a play on words:* PS *stands for both*
Pferdestärke *(horsepower) and* Pseudonyme *(pseudonyms).*

*Tucholsky in his student days (Kurt-Tucholsky-Archiv, Rottach-Egern)*

*Tucholsky in 1915, the year he was drafted into the German army. He never saw combat, but his experiences during the war made him an outspoken opponent of militarism (Kurt-Tucholsky-Archiv, Rottach-Egern)*

in "Bilder aus dem Geschäftsleben" (Pictures from Business Life)—the employees who are turned into robots by their daily office routines. In a series of seventeen "Wendriner" stories he portrays a Jewish businessman, both loathsome and likeable, comparable to Heinrich Mann's "Untertan" (vassal) Diederich Hessling or Sinclair Lewis's George F. Babbit. The opportunistic Wendriner is satirically revealed through skillfully handled interior monologue to be a rather complex individual of dubious morals, a common "Spießer" (philistine) rather than a big-time entrepreneur.

In his criticism of the church Tucholsky did not attack religion but its abuse by the clergy. Under the sign of the cross mankind was driven to war by those in power. The church, by catering to the state, betrayed and violated the Christian message and even condoned political murder. In his *Briefe an eine Katholikin* (Letters to a Catholic Woman, 1969) he defends himself against the charge of blasphemy and criticizes the practice of priests inciting soldiers to kill, falsifying the word of love into the word of the state.

Tucholsky distrusted the ideological stance of the extreme left almost as much as that of the extreme right. He always was on the side of the underdog; but, as he once stated, his dislike of the tormentors was far greater than his love for the tormented. But it was the bourgeoisie that was most guilty of bringing about the decline of the republic, he felt; for without the bourgeoisie's sympathy for authoritarianism, neither the generals nor the Communists nor eventually the National Socialists would have been able to destroy democracy.

Apart from his satirical writings in journals and newspapers, Tucholsky also gained popularity through his ballads and chansons, which were set to music by well-known composers and sung in the thriving Berlin cabarets; he himself wrote the music for some of his lyrics. With the renewed interest in the "Roaring Twenties" during the 1960s, the songs reemerged; they are still in today's repertoires. No other writer surpassed his skill in using witty Berlin dialect for literary purposes. Collections of his works quickly became popular: in 1914 the grotesques of *Der Zeitsparer* (The Time Saver), in 1919 his volume of poetry *Fromme Gesänge* (Pious Songs), and in 1920 his "bourgeois fairy tales" in *Träumereien an preußischen Kaminen* (Reveries by Prussian Firesides).

In 1920 he married Else Weil, whom he had known since his student days, but they soon separated. In 1924 they were divorced and Tucholsky married Mary Gerold, whom he had met during his military service in Romania. As a correspondent for several leading journals in Berlin and Prague he was able to go to Paris, as he had long planned, to "rest from his fatherland." But although he felt the relief of detachment from frustrations in Germany, became an ardent Francophile, and was quite productive in the new milieu, his writing—either in comparisons of conditions in France with those in Germany or in direct statements on issues in the country from which he had fled—shows that Germany's political and social problems continued to plague him. When Hindenburg became president after Ebert's death, a dismayed Tucholsky predicted the end of the German republic, and his political writing, especially against rising National Socialism and militarism, became even more aggressive. In 1926 his mentor and friend Jacobsohn died; Tucholsky temporarily accepted the editorship of *Die Weltbühne* but passed it in 1927 to the pacifist writer Carl von Ossietzky.

In 1927 *Ein Pyrenäenbuch* (A Book of the Pyrenees), based on a 1925 trip through southern France and northern Spain, was published. It is a unique travel book in a double sense, for Tucholsky's observation of the land and his insight into the social and psychological characteristics of its people triggers a "journey through himself" which reveals at least as much about his personal convictions as about the Pyrenees. A bullfight leads to questions about mores; an excursion to Biarritz inspires sociological reflections; crossing the border evokes thoughts on national separations; a visit to monasteries suggests provocative queries about Christian customs; a Basque ball game is viewed from comparative ethnic and cultural perspectives. In connection with various stations of his journey he recalls passages from books, friendships, and previous experiences; injects philosophical, cultural, and political aperçus; and gives way, time and again, to disturbing memories of Germany. Of particular interest is his report on Lourdes, with profound observations about the individual and the mass, faith and psychosis, and the business of salvation. Tucholsky contrasts his own daydreams of mass congregations for world peace and mass protests against political mass murder with the private hopes of the masses of pilgrims. The book was hailed as a humanistic travelogue and a primer of international understanding at a time when fascism was advancing.

In 1928 Tucholsky's wife returned to Berlin. Although they remained separated, they continued corresponding. As a desperate and angry outcry against the worsening political situation, Tucholsky

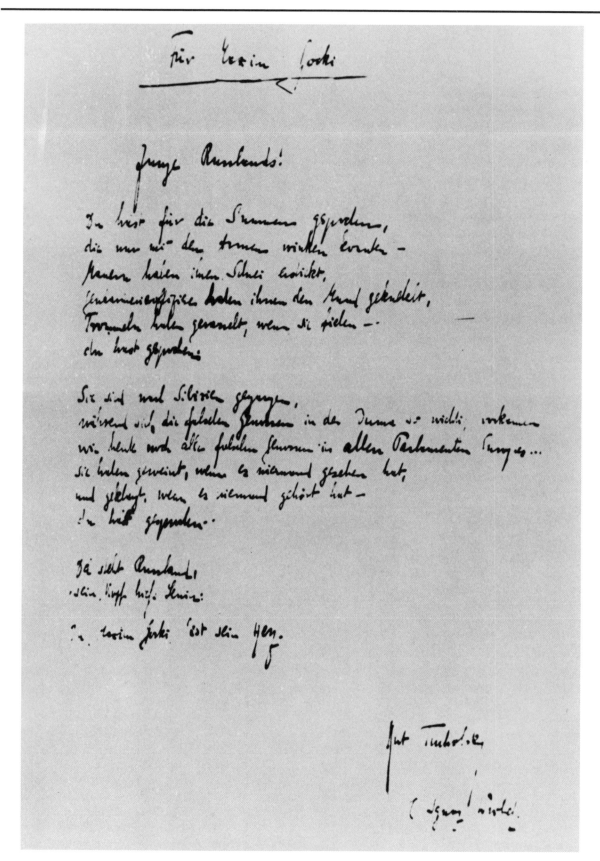

*Manuscript for Tucholsky's poem "Für Maxim Gorki"*

published collections of his previous journal pieces in *Mit 5 PS* (With 5 Pseudonyms or 5 Pferdestärke [Horsepower], 1928) and *Das Lächeln der Mona Lisa* (Mona Lisa's Smile, 1929), followed by his fiercest and most controversial book, *Deutschland, Deutschland über alles* (1929), illustrated with John Heartfield's photomontages. Tucholsky had repeatedly argued for the realistic impact of annotated tendentious photography, and this bitter satirical volume summarizes, through its combination of text and revealing pictures of the contemporary scene, all of his frustrations with and criticism of unjust and dangerous sociopolitical conditions in a declining Germany.

*Tucholsky with his wife, Mary Gerold-Tucholsky, whom he married in 1924. He divorced her in 1933 to spare her harassment by the Nazis (Kurt-Tucholsky-Archiv, Rottach-Egern)*

*Poster advertising a public reading by Tucholsky from his writings (Kurt-Tucholsky-Archiv, Rottach-Egern)*

But by this time, an increasingly skeptical Tucholsky was already beginning to retreat. He suffered from the realization that his work, though "successful," remained without effect. In 1929 he withdrew to Hindås in Sweden, which provided the setting for his last major book, similar in theme and popularity to his first. *Schloß Gripsholm* (Gripsholm Castle, 1931) is another short novel about a brief, happy summer vacation. Again there is an escape from the bustling big city of Berlin, this time to an ancient Swedish castle in a quiet little seaside town. Again the simple adventures and the erotic companionship of a man—Peter, nicknamed "Daddy"—and a woman—Lydia, nicknamed "the Princess"—are portrayed playfully and humorously. There is a tribute to the vitality of Plattdeutsch, the north German dialect, and Lydia's whimsical games with language add to the lighthearted spirit of the holiday. A visit by Daddy's longtime friend, the scurrilous Karlchen, and then

*Dust jacket for a 1929 collection of Tucholsky's satirical pieces
(Kurt-Tucholsky-Archiv, Rottach-Egern)*

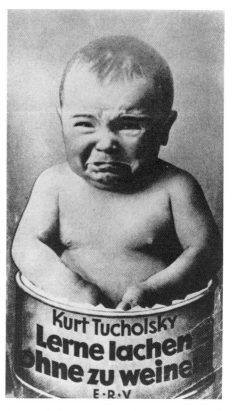

*Dust jacket for the last collection of Tucholsky's writings published during his lifetime (1931)*

*Dust jacket for Tucholsky's fiercest attack on social and political conditions in the Weimar Republic. The book, published in 1929,
was heavily illustrated with photographs by John Heartfield.*

*Scene from the unsuccessful play* Christoph Columbus *by Tucholsky and Walter Hasenclever, as performed in Leipzig in 1932*

by Lydia's attractive young girlfriend Billie leads to new congenial constellations, witty reflections, and amorous escapades. A counterpoint story is woven into the plot: Frau Adriani, a nasty, dictatorial woman, exercises her abusive power over a nearby children's home, instilling fear and tears among the girls entrusted to her, and evokes, in a memorable passage, a pessimistic vision of mankind's bestial cruelty since ancient times. The friends save a desperate child from Frau Adriani's tyranny, and the political connotations of the episode give way to skeptical notions about "Zeit"—both in the sense of "time" and of "the times" catching up with life and putting an end to rare moments of happiness. This last significant work of Tucholsky's, while again blending joyful togetherness and melancholy reflection, is much more complex than *Rheinsberg* and also more broadly and subtly autobiographical. Daddy, the narrator, resembles Tucholsky in his close but tentative relationships with women; his praise of friendship; and his philosophical observations—mostly in the form impressionistically abbreviated "Schnipsel" (splinters of thought) like those in Tucholsky's other works.

In late 1932 Tucholsky fell silent. His work, including a last volume of collected pieces entitled *Lerne lachen ohne zu weinen* (Learn to Laugh without Crying, 1931) as well as a play, *Christoph Columbus* (1932; translated as *Christopher Columbus*, 1972), coauthored by Walter Hasenclever, no longer found a public. In 1933 his books, along with those of many other contemporary writers, were burned by the Nazis, and his German citizenship was revoked. He divorced his wife to spare her harassment by the Nazis. Tucholsky had claimed that satire was entitled to do anything for a worthwhile cause; now the resigned exile not only admitted that satire had limits but saw no point in writing at all. His lifelong literary activities, his warnings, his criticism of corruption, and his appeal to reason had not helped to prevent the arrival of Hitler, and he could see that the worst phase of German history was beginning. An isolated, ailing, and despairing Tucholsky was intent on dissociating himself from everything German, but the letters and diary notes written during his last years bear witness to his deep indignation and bitterness. In December 1935 he took poison and died two days later. He lies buried

*Tucholsky's grave in Mariefred Cemetery near Gripsholm. Tucholsky committed suicide in December 1935 (Kurt-Tucholsky-Archiv, Rottach-Egern)*

in Mariefred Cemetery near Gripsholm.

After World War II, Tucholsky's defamation by the Nazis gave way to a renaissance that turned his books, anthologies, and editions of collected works into best-sellers. This public interest was not equally matched by Tucholsky scholarship. His great versatility has received varied responses from historians, political scientists, journalists, and literary critics. Different Tucholskys were perceived by posterity: some favored the charming humorist and witty songwriter, others the aggressive political satirist, still others the ironic sentimentalist. A recurring focus of inquiry was Tucholsky as a Jewish phenomenon, but also—especially in the United States—the supposed analogy between the position of left-wing intellectuals such as Tucholsky during the Weimar Republic and their radical pacifist counterparts in America in the 1960s. Apart from general assessments in journals, literary histories, and monographs, a number of dissertations and specialized studies have emphasized particular as-

pects of Tucholsky's work, such as his polemics on various subjects, his forms of protest, his literary criticism, his theater critiques, his role on the *Weltbühne,* his political development, the periodization of his work, his image of France, his strategy of enlightenment, his satirical role-playing, his connections with other writers, and his reception by various segments of society. While these contributions have increased our understanding of Tucholsky's complexity, systematic scholarship has only just begun, and even basic questions about his life and his work are still awaiting thorough investigation.

**Letters:**
*Politische Briefe,* edited by Fritz J. Raddatz (Reinbek: Rowohlt, 1969);
*Briefe an eine Katholikin 1929-1931* (Reinbek: Rowohlt, 1969);
*Ausgewählte Briefe 1913-1935,* edited by Mary Gerold-Tucholsky and Raddatz (Reinbek: Rowohlt, 1972);
*Briefe aus dem Schweigen 1932-1935: Briefe an Nuuna,* edited by Gerold-Tucholsky and Gustav Huonker (Reinbek: Rowohlt, 1977);
*Unser ungelebtes Leben: Briefe an Mary,* edited by Raddatz (Reinbek: Rowohlt, 1982).

**Bibliography:**
Petra Goder-Stark, *Das Kurt-Tucholsky-Archiv* (Marbach: Deutsche Schillergesellschaft, 1978).

**Biographies:**
Klaus-Peter Schulz, *Kurt Tucholsky in Selbstzeugnissen und Bilddokumenten* (Reinbek: Rowohlt, 1959; revised, 1979);
Hans Prescher, *Kurt Tucholsky* (Berlin: Colloquium, 1959);
Fritz J. Raddatz, *Tucholsky: Eine Bildbiographie* (Munich: Kindler, 1961);
Karl Kleinschmidt, *Kurt Tucholsky: Sein Leben in Bildern* (Leipzig: Enzyklopädie, 1961; revised, 1964);
Gerhard Zwerenz, *Kurt Tucholsky: Biographie eines guten Deutschen* (Munich: Bertelsmann, 1979).

**References:**
Irmgard Ackerman, ed., *Kurt Tucholsky: Sieben Beiträge zu Werk und Wirkung* (Munich: Text & Kritik, 1981);
Heinz-Ludwig Arnold, ed., *Text und Kritik,* special Tucholsky issue, 29 (1971);

Anton Austermann, *Kurt Tucholsky: Der Journalist und sein Publikum* (Munich & Zurich: Piper, 1985);

Hans J. Becker, *Mit geballter Faust: Kurt Tucholskys "Deutschland, Deutschland über alles"* (Bonn: Bouvier, 1978);

Istvan Deak, *Weimar Germany's Left-Wing Intellectuals: A Political History of the Weltbühne and its Circle* (Berkeley & Los Angeles: University of California Press, 1968);

Marianne Doerfel, "The Origins of a Left Intellectual: Kurt Tucholsky, the Romantic Conservative," *Oxford German Studies*, 7 (1972-1973): 119-142;

Bryan P. Grenville, *Kurt Tucholsky: The Ironic Sentimentalist* (London: Wolff, 1981);

William John King, "Tucholsky's *Q-Tagebücher*," *German Life & Letters*, new series 33 (October 1979): 61-65;

Hans Mayer, "Der pessimistische Aufklärer Kurt Tucholsky," *Akzente*, 14, no. 1 (1967): 73-84;

Helmut Mörchen, "Anmerkungen zur Tucholsky-Forschung," *Zeitschrift für deutsche Philologie*, 9, no. 2 (1980): 298-305;

Harold Lloyd Poor, *Kurt Tucholsky and the Ordeal of Germany 1914-1935* (New York: Scribners, 1968).

**Papers:**
Kurt Tucholsky's papers are at the Kurt-Tucholsky-Archiv of the Deutsche Schillergesellschaft, Marbach, and at the Tucholsky-Archiv, Rottach-Egern.

# Fritz von Unruh
## (10 May 1885-28 November 1970)

Ulrich R. Froehlich
*Appalachian State University*

BOOKS: *Offiziere: Ein Drama* (Berlin: Reiß, 1911);

*Louis Ferdinand, Prinz von Preußen: Ein Drama* (Berlin: Reiß, 1913; New York: Oxford University Press, 1933);

*Vor der Entscheidung: Ein Gedicht* (Berlin: Reiß, 1914);

*Ein Geschlecht: Tragödie* (Leipzig: Wolff, 1917);

*Opfergang* (Berlin: Reiß, 1919); translated by C. A. McCartney as *Way of Sacrifice* (New York: Knopf, 1928);

*Platz: Ein Spiel; Zweiter Teil der Trilogie Ein Geschlecht* (Munich: Wolff, 1920);

*Rosengarten* (Darmstadt: Darmstädter Theater, 1921);

*Stirb und Werde: Eine Ansprache zur Frankfurter Goethewoche* (Frankfurt am Main: Englert & Schlosser, 1922);

*Stürme: Ein Schauspiel* (Munich: Wolff, 1922);

*Vaterland und Freiheit: Eine Ausprache an die deutsche Jugend* (Berlin: Schneider, 1923);

*Reden* (Frankfurt am Main: Frankfurter Societäts-Buchdruckerei, 1924);

*Flügel der Nike: Buch einer Reise* (Frankfurt am Main: Frankfurter Societäts-Buchdruckerei, 1925);

*Heinrich aus Andernach* (Frankfurt am Main: Frankfurter Societäts-Buchdruckerei, 1925);

*Bonaparte: Ein Schauspiel* (Frankfurt am Main: Frankfurter Societäts-Buchdruckerei, 1927); translated by Edwin Björkman as *Bonaparte: A Drama* (New York: Knopf, 1928);

*Phaea: Eine Komödie* (Berlin-Wilmersdorf: Bloch, 1930);

*Zero: Eine Komödie* (Frankfurt am Main: Societäts-Verlag, 1932);

*Politeia*, edited by Ernst Adolf Dreyer (Paris & Vienna: Bergis, 1933);

*Europa erwache! Rede gehalten am Europa-Tag in Basel, 17. May 1936* (Basel: Verlagsgenossenschaft der Europa-Union, 1936);

*Seid wachsam! Eine Goethe-Rede* (Frankfurt am Main: Kramer, 1945);

*The End Is Not Yet: A Novel of Hatred and Love; of Darkness and Light; of Despair and Hope; of Death and Life; of War and a New Courage*, translated by Willard R. Trask (New York: Storm, 1947);

*Fritz von Unruh*

original German version, *Der nie verlor: Roman von Haß und Liebe, Dunkelheit und Licht, Verzweiflung und Hoffnung, von Krieg und einem neuen Mut* (Bern: Hallwag, 1948);

*Friede auf Erden! Peace on earth!* (Frankfurt am Main: Kramer, 1948);

*Rede an die Deutschen: Mit einem Geleitwort von Eugen Kogon* (Frankfurt am Main: Verlag der Frankfurter Hefte, 1948);

*The Saint: A Novel,* translated by Trask (New York: Random House, 1950); original German version, *Die Heilige: Roman* (Braunschweig: Kleine, 1952);

*Fürchtet nichts: Roman* (Cologne: Comel, 1952);

*Wilhelmus, Prinz von Oranien: Drama* (Cologne: Comel, 1953);

*Duell an der Havel: Schauspiel* (Berlin-Charlottenburg: Krüger, 1954);

*Mächtig seid ihr nicht in Waffen: Reden* (Nuremberg: Carl, 1957);

*Der Sohn des Generals: Roman* (Nuremberg: Carl, 1957);

*Dramen: Bonaparte, Louis Ferdinand, Bismarck, Offiziere, Phaea* (Nuremberg: Carl, 1960);

*Wir wollen Frieden: Die Reden und Aufrufe 1960/61* (Düsseldorf: Monitor, 1961);

*Im Haus der Prinzen* (Frankfurt am Main: Societäts-Verlag, 1967);

*Friede in den USA? Ein Traum* (Ulm: Gerhard Hess, 1967);

*Odysseus auf Ogygia* (Frankfurt am Main: Societäts-Verlag, 1968);

*Kaserne und Sphinx* (Frankfurt am Main: Societäts-Verlag, 1969).

Fritz von Unruh was one of the most prominent dramatists of the German expressionist movement. Like other expressionists, he directed strong, passionate language against war and inhumanity and constructed in his writings a visionary world of global brotherhood, love, and peace. Unruh's dramas and public speeches drew large audiences in pre-Nazi Germany. But the messages he conveyed, warning against a radical nationalism, did not suit the ideology of the Third Reich. After Hitler seized power Unruh's works were banned, his property was confiscated, and he had to flee through several European countries before he finally found asylum in America.

Unruh's literary production in prose can be seen as a direct consequence of the difficulties he faced in putting his plays on the stage in America. His novels carry the same polemic thrust as his dramas: the vision of a new humanity is portrayed in sharp distinction to Germany's most recent past. Reminiscences of war and totalitarian governments give Unruh's novels a strong autobiographical component. In style and content Unruh remained true to his expressionist heritage, which once aided his rise to prominence but caused sharp criticism when those literary values were no longer in vogue.

Fritz Wilhelm Ernest von Unruh was born on 10 May 1885 in Koblenz. His father, Karl von Unruh, was a colonel of infantry in the Prussian army. Unruh was educated in a cadet corps at Plön together with the sons of the emperor. His conflicts with the Prussian army mentality caused an early suicide attempt. Unruh's autobiographical novel *Der Sohn des Generals* (The General's Son, 1957) describes this school as the prototype of a concentration camp. The dichotomy between state and citizen is the theme of Unruh's early plays. After his drama *Offiziere* (Officers) was produced by Max Reinhardt at the Deutsches Theater in Berlin in 1911, Unruh relinquished his military commission and became a free-lance writer. Two years later he completed another drama, *Louis Ferdinand, Prinz von Preußen* (Louis Ferdinand of Prussia). Since it depicts the fall of the Prussian monarchy, the play was banned by the emperor William II. Even so, Reinhardt and Walther Rathenau planned a performance of the play to commemorate the twenty-fifth anniversary of the Freie Volksbühne in Berlin, but the outbreak of World War I put an end to this effort.

Unruh enlisted in the cavalry, but the initial euphoria of victory soon dissipated and Unruh was converted to pacifism. His dramatic antiwar poem *Vor der Entscheidung* (Before the Decision, 1914) was circulated in the trenches. It is a vehement plea for humanity, peace, brotherhood, and love. The poem projects a new world in which individuals reject all militant tendencies. Unruh was court-martialed for "impairing the fighting spirit of the troops," but the commanding general found that "the heroic battle of all soldiers was the main topic of the poem" and Unruh was acquitted.

Before the end of the war Unruh completed *Ein Geschlecht* (A Race, 1917), the first in a projected trilogy of verse plays. The drama is dedicated to his brother Erich, "born 1888, died in battle 1915." The critic Julius Bab labeled Unruh's language "fieberhaft überfüllt" (feverishly saturated) and called *Ein Geschlecht* an "aus allen geistigen und künstlerischen Formen gequollenes Produkt" (product swollen with all sorts of intellectual and artistic forms).

Unruh's first novel, *Opfergang* (1919; translated as *Way of Sacrifice*, 1928), describes a suicide mission during the battle of Verdun. Published in France as *Verdun* (1923), it was one of the first postwar German novels to be translated into French. Unruh was awarded the Kleist Prize in 1915, the Bodmer Prize in 1917, and the Grillparzer Prize in 1922.

Unruh was one of the best-known dramatists of the literary movement known as expressionism; his plays, like those of his contemporaries, are characterized by a pronounced flamboyance and emo-

*Lithograph by Willy Jaeckel illustrating Unruh's* Ein Geschlecht *(1917)*

tionalism. For Unruh literature served as a means to an end; writing and politics always constituted a whole. He wrote to generate commitment to his ideals: accountability to God, the preservation of human dignity, and love for one's fellow man. Constantly in his works a new social order is envisioned and the dramatis personae are transformed to fit into this new system.

After the war Unruh was one of the founders of the Republican party and won a seat in the Reichstag in 1924. "Euch fehlt der Schauder vor dem geschlachteten Menschen!" (The butchery of humans fails to horrify you!). Unruh called out to students during his campaign. He received the Schiller Prize in 1926. The growing power of the Nazis caused Unruh to warn an audience of 24,000 people against Hitler and Nazism on 18 January 1932 in the Berlin Sports Palace. This address, entitled "Die Front des Reiches" (The Forward Line of the Reich), called for an "eiserne Front" (iron front) against war and fascism.

While he continued to give public addresses, Unruh also worked on new plays. The premiere of the comedy *Zero* (1932) under the direction of Alvin Kronacher caused a scandal. When the line "Deutschland will Raum" (Germany needs space) drew the response "Dann wird es untergehn! Auf dem Potsdamer Platz werden Schafe weiden!" (Then it will perish! Sheep will graze on Potsdamer Platz!), pandemonium broke out in the Frankfurt Theater; fascist campaign songs were heard in the audience: "Heute gehört uns Deutschland, morgen die ganze Welt!" (Today we command Germany, tomorrow the entire world!) Unruh's right of lifetime residence in the Frankfurter Rententurm (Frankfurt Home for Retirees) was canceled and the comedy was immediately prohibited. Unruh retired to his home in Zoagli in northern Italy, where he began writing the novel *Der nie verlor* (1948; translated as *The End Is Not Yet*, 1947), which was not completed until he was in exile in America in 1945.

On a visit to Switzerland in 1932, Unruh attempted to warn the younger generation, in two elaborate speeches, against the fascist ideology. In the first speech, he sees the basis for the downfall of the Weimar Republic in the fact that it had failed to recognize the youthful desire for heroism: "So sei ihr Gewicht voll in die Waagschale der Gegenseite, der Reaktion, gefallen und habe jetzt das meiste zum Sieg der Hitlerleute beigetragen, die es verstanden hätten, sich ein Monopol auf die Jugend und die mystische Opfersehnsucht zu sichern" (Consequently it threw its full weight to the

opposition, to the reactionaries, having thus contributed most to the success of the Hitler people who had the skill to assure for themselves a monopoly over the youth and the mystic longing for sacrifice). In the second speech, "Rede an die europäische Jugend" (Address to European Youth), he says: "Ich kann euch keine Wimpel und Fähnchen versprechen, kein Räuber- und Gendarmspiel im Großen, kein Marschziel auf irgendeinen äußeren Feind, Unser Exerzieren beginne im Nein! zur Lüge, im Ja! zur Wahrheit, im Nein! zur Lust, im Ja! zur Liebe, in der Absage an den Zweifel, in der Hingabe an den Glauben" (I cannot promise you pennants and banners, no cops and robbers games on a large scale, no marching orders to some external enemy. Let us begin our routine by saying No! to lies, Yes! to truth, No! to pleasure, Yes! to love, by renouncing doubt, by dedication to faith). Unruh goes on to name Romain Rolland, René Schickele, Hermann Hesse, Stefan Zweig, Franz Werfel, Thomas Mann, and Henri Barbusse as writers who speak the language of peace.

On 5 May 1933 Unruh was ousted from the Prussian Academy of the Arts after he refused to sign the loyalty oath that had been distributed by Gottfried Benn. His stay in Italy lasted less than three years. In 1935 Italian fascists raided his house in Zoagli after Unruh refused to support Mussolini. He fled across the border to distant relatives in Menton, France, and then to Arcachon, always being required to register and always subject to police supervision.

In 1938 Unruh was officially expatriated as a traitor to his country, and his property was confiscated. The concept of "staatenlose Emigranten" (émigrés without country) finds especially poignant expression in his paintings; his collection includes several self-portraits bearing the title *Homeless*.

Unruh made several trips to Paris, where he met Otto von Habsburg, Prince August Wilhelm of Prussia, who had escaped from Germany, as well as other political émigrés. He continued working on *Der nie verlor*, which incorporates persons he encountered during his flight. In the summer of 1939 Unruh was interned in Camp Libourne on the Dordogne. During his internment he wrote several essays about life in the camp that were to be incorporated in an elaborately projected series of autobiographical novels. These manuscripts, along with other notes, pen and ink sketches, and poems Unruh carried with him in a footlocker, had to be left behind when the French opened the gates of the camp at the time of the German invasion. In May 1952 this footlocker was shipped by French

*Manuscript page for Unruh's play* Heinrich aus Andernach *(1925)*

*Cover for Unruh's autobiographical comedy, published in 1930*
*(Lilly Library, Indiana University)*

authorities to Unruh's brother Kurt von Unruh in Roding, West Germany.

The French minister for foreign affairs, Eduard Daladier, interceded personally on Unruh's behalf. It was probably due to his influence that two passports with the pseudonyms Fred Onof and Frederique Onof were issued on 22 July 1940, enabling Unruh and his wife to flee across the Spanish border. The American consul in Malaga issued two emergency visas, and, by way of Lisbon, the Unruhs arrived at Ellis Island in New York harbor on 10 August. In the eyes of the American authorities both were "enemy aliens." Aside from their financial plight, their immediate concern was how to legitimize themselves as immigrants. Albert Einstein, then at Princeton, wrote letters of recommendation for Unruh, as did Thomas Mann, who was living in Brentwood, California.

During the initial years of his American exile Unruh began friendships with Stefan Zweig and the Austrian writer Johannes Urzidil and continued his relationship with Mann. He also entered into correspondence with Einstein.

The financial support that Unruh received during this period was meager. Contributions from the Emergency Rescue Committee and the American Committee for Christian Refugees, Inc., were not enough to live on. Beginning in 1942 the New York exile magazine *Aufbau* published poems and essays by Unruh that may have contributed somewhat to his support, and he gave talks for the American Association of Teachers of German in Ohio, Philadelphia, and New York as well as readings from his works at the New York New World Club (1946). All of these activities could have yielded only a modest income.

From his earliest youth, Unruh had expressed his ideas in painting as well as writing. Since his literary production did not hold out much commercial promise, he turned to the sale of his paintings and produced several in rapid succession. The art dealer Otto Kalir, who had befriended Unruh, exhibited twenty-five of his paintings in the Galerie St. Etienne in New York in November 1947. Not a single item was sold during the exhibit; but some of the paintings must have been sold privately, since Unruh later claimed to have had a large turnover.

Erwin Piscator, a friend from Unruh's youth who had also immigrated to New York by way of France, had developed the Dramatic Workshop, which was associated with the New School for Social Research, into a well-known theatrical school; its faculty included Tennessee Williams, Hans Rehfisch, Kurt Pinthus, John Gassner, and Carl Zuckmayer. A few of Unruh's dramas, including *Phaea* (1930), were performed at the school as experiments, but they were never able to make the transition to public production. Alvin Kronacher, the former director of the Leipzig Theater, did attempt to put *Phaea* on the commercial stage, but discord between author and director caused the project to be dropped.

The dramas Unruh wrote during the earlier period of his exile were neither produced nor published. They include "Das Schiff " (The Boat, 1940), "Miss Rollschuh" (Miss Rollerskate, 1941), "Die Geheimmappe des Generals" (The Secret Briefcase of the General, 1942), "Gefängnis" (Prison, 1946), and "Friedrich der Große: Amerika" (Frederick the Great: America, 1949). Unruh's

*Unruh in 1930 (Ullstein)*

correspondence with various New York publishers indicates that commercial considerations, as well as the poor quality of the English translations, prevented the publication of his works. His lack of access to the theater moved him to direct his efforts to the novel.

*Der nie verlor*, begun in Italy in 1932, was completed in 1945. The first chapters are a poetically imaginative flashback to Unruh's experiences at the battle of Verdun; as the Nazi movement progressed during the writing of the novel, Unruh expanded the scope of his work to include Hitler and his commanding officers. The author himself appears as the unknown soldier, Uhle, confronting the Antichrist, Hitler. The basic theme of the work is given in a preamble:

> Concerning hate and love,
> despair and hope, death and life,
> concerning war and a new courage.

The plot of the novel serves only to sketch the personalities of the characters. Instead of a continuity of action or an interplay of intrigues, there is description and analysis of the persons involved, who are presented in a deliberate black-and-white

fashion with no subtle gradations. All of the characters are complete persons, not subject to any further development. The chaos of the Hitler regime is shown in a series of episodes that leap from scene to scene, seeking to grasp the fanatical frenzy of the Nazis. The Hitler figure is exaggerated to the extreme in burlesque fashion, and Unruh even provides elaborate accounts of the sodomistic practices of the Nazi leadership.

The few reviews that the novel received directed vehement criticism against its unrealistic portrayal of the Nazis. The *Tagesspiegel* of 26 August 1947, under the "Europas Walpurgisnacht" (Europe's Walpurgis Night), said that the novel constituted the embittered memoirs of an author whose books had been burned, who had been stripped of his citizenship, who had lived in exile for ten years and who, "verzehrt von der Flamme seines Zorns gegen die monströse Gangsterbande, die sein Land in Ruinen verwandelte und die ganze Welt mit Krieg überzog" (consumed by flames of indignation against the monstrous gangster hordes that had laid his country into ruins and enveloped the entire world in war), was incapable of writing a temperate novel. Thus developed a "Hexengebräu fast unvorstellbarer Schreckensszenen, gespielt von offensichtlich Wahnsinnigen" (witches' brew of unimaginable horror scenes, enacted by obvious madmen). Nowhere in the entire book do the Nazi leaders appear to be mentally stable; Hitler's rantings "lassen im Leser nicht die Vorstellung aufkommen, er könne jener Energie, die dieser Dämon Jahr um Jahr der Ausdehnung seiner Macht widmete, fähig gewesen sein" (do not allow the reader to imagine that he [Hitler] might have been capable of the energy that this demon year after year dedicated to the extension of his power). Unruh was also severely taken to task for his stylistic peculiarity of mixing descriptive elements with dialogue. In 1949 *Die neue Zeitung* attacked this mannerism, which constantly recurs in Unruh's writing: "'Beg pardon . . . he adjusted his shirt collar.'— 'Jees! so overpoured Therese, wounded in her religious feelings, a pot-full of bubbling chicken by the spoonful with its own fat . . .'—'You European people! Miss Gloria painting her lips.'—'Man . . . Egath polishes his monocle. Are you willing? The situation demanded it!' . . . A hundred examples could be cited. Their total number is the distinguishing style characteristic of Unruh's dramatic prose and incidentally an insight for the deeply troubled reader."

Unruh's efforts to publish *Der nie verlor* led him to the German-American Alexander Gode von

Aesch, whose support he was to enjoy until his death. Gode von Aesch worked for the Thomas Crowell Publishing House until September 1946, when he became independent under the name Storm Publishers. In 1947 Unruh's novel, translated under the title *The End Is Not Yet*, became the first work published by the new house; it almost ruined the firm.

During a trip to Switzerland in 1948, Unruh laid the groundwork for a German edition of *Der nie verlor*. The Hallwag publishing firm in Bern published the work in 1948, but realized after meager sales that most German readers were not willing to concern themselves with "Vergangenheitsbewältigung" (coping with the past) in a literary work; besides, the pathos of Unruh's language had long since ceased to be fashionable. The French translation, *Ce n'est pas encore la fin* (1951), was also unsuccessful.

The need for a social renewal was subsequently formulated by Unruh in the visionary novel *Die Heilige*, which was published in English translation by Random House in 1950 as *The Saint* and in the original German two years later. The work opens with a quotation from Balzac: "Facts are nothing. They do not exist. Nothing is left for us but ideas." The novel portrays the conflict between an atheistic painter and Saint Catherine of Sienna, who fights for his soul but experiences carnal love with him. This novel was also unsuccessful; the review in the *Saturday Review of Literature* was typical of the critical reaction: "The serious intent of Fritz von Unruh, whatever it may be, cannot be questioned. But his novel of 'sacred and profane love' is not plausible. Character and story are infantile. And the spuriously romantic manner of the writing is so bloated that there is neither form nor grace nor taste."

Random House declined to publish Unruh's next novel, *Fürchtet nichts* (Fear Not), citing the poor sales record of *The Saint;* it was published in Germany in 1952. The novel is set in eighteenth-century St. Petersburg under the reign of the czarina Anna Ivanovna. The freedom fighter Count Galitzin is favored by the czarina but rejects her advances because of her tyranny. He is demoted to court jester and ultimately banished to Siberia as a revolutionary. The structure and dramatic dialogue of the novel once again reflect Unruh's style as a dramatist.

In the meantime, Germany had remembered the author in exile. The city of Braunschweig bestowed the Wilhelm Raabe Prize in 1946, and when the city of Frankfurt am Main celebrated the cen-

tennial of the convocation of the National Assembly in the Paulskirche on 18 May 1948, Unruh was invited to give the official address. His *Rede an die Deutschen* (Address to the Germans) begins with an autobiographical sketch: the painful departure of a Prussian officer from his caste. Then it traces the road of the German people to the catastrophe: "Und als dann der Besessene vom Obersalzberg die deutsche Kriegsaxt in die Wurzel des Weltfriedens hieb, da begriff ich dies ist die Niederlage von uns 'guten,' von allen, deren Wort keine Einheit mehr war mit der Tat" (And when that Possessed One from the Obersalzberg chopped with his battle ax into the very roots of world peace, I comprehended: this means the defeat of us 'People of Good Will,' of all those whose word no longer corresponded to their deed). Unruh alludes to his warnings prior to the bloodletting, and recognizes "was sich viele selbst in der stillsten Zelle ihrer Selbsterkenntnis noch immer scheuen, einzugestenen, nämlich: wie schlecht wir es machten, als wir noch handeln konnten" (what many, even in the deepest recesses of their self-awareness, still fear to admit, and that is: how badly we behaved when there was still time to act). He calls out to the Germans in this speech—during which, according to eyewitnesses he almost fainted several times but continued despite the advice of his doctor—to resist the seducers, no matter in what gilded goblets they might serve the red wine of temptation: "Widerstehen wir, wenn uns ewige Kompromißler und Ablaßkrämer unserer Epoche das Gewissen wieder einlullen und uns korrumpieren wollen" (Let us resist, whenever compromisers and dealers in indulgences of our epoch once again lull our consciences to sleep and try to corrupt us).

Since a recording of the speech has been preserved, it is easy to verify the verbal power of the sixty-three-year-old Unruh. His voice resounds in the church interior: "Hinweg mit ihnen! Das ganze Rudel der Mitläufer und Beamten, Professoren und Generäle, die gestern pro Hitler und vorgestern pro Weimar und vorvorgestern pro Kaiser waren!—und heute schon wieder mit den Zonenbefehlshabern liebäugeln—hinweg mit ihnen! Auch mit jenen, die von draußen hereinreisen und plötzlich schmeicheln 'keiner ist schuld, ihr wart alle unter Zwang,' Hinweg mit dem ganzen Geschmeiß, das uns das Recht auf unsere Zerknirschung, das uns die Pflicht zu unserer Erneuerung, das uns die Hoffnung auf Gnade fortschwatzen will, weil es das politische Schachspiel der Gegenwart—schon wieder mal—erheischt" (Let them begone! The whole pack of fellow travelers and bureaucrats, professors, and generals, who yesterday were pro-Hitler and the day-before-yesterday pro-Weimar and the day-before-the-day-before-yesterday pro-Kaiser!—and today are already flirting with the Zone commanders—let them begone! Away as well with those who enter from beyond and of a sudden flatter: 'No one is to blame, you were all being coerced.' Away with the whole crowd that wants to talk us out of our prerogative to feel crushed, out of our obligation to renew ourselves, out of our hope for mercy, because the contemporary game of politics once more demands it thus). Unruh demands that the Germans declare themselves as of a mind with Luther, who said: "Here I stand, I cannot do otherwise!" Unruh was awarded the Goethe Prize on this occasion.

Unruh's drama *Wilhelmus, Prinz von Oranien*, which premiered in 1953 at the Frankfurter Großes Haus, presents an event from the War of Liberation of the Netherlands. The play suffers from several flaws: besides the linguistic style, which obscures the clarity of the ideas being presented, there are too many flowery phrases of French, Italian, Spanish, and Latin origin, a feature frequently found in Unruh's later works. The reaction to the first performance made it apparent that Unruh could hardly expect any subsequent productions of this drama. Another drama that did not survive beyond a first performance was *Duell an der Havel* (Duel on the Havel), which premiered in 1954 at Wiesbaden; in this play, a visit to Frederick the Great by an American trade delegation is made the occasion for a contrast of freedom-loving, youthful America with authoritarian Prussia. In spite of these failures, the author was awarded the Great Service Cross of the Federal Republic in 1955. He returned to America the same year. A year later he settled on the French Riviera, where he completed *Der Sohn des Generals* (1957).

Unruh constantly urged Piscator, who had returned to Dillenburg, to produce his dramas. The correspondence in the 1950s and 1960s between Unruh and Piscator is filled with Unruh's constant, often bitter accusations that his plays were deliberately being ignored, while the dramas of others—his irritation is directed particularly against Gerhart Hauptmann—were being staged. Piscator replied that Unruh's style was outdated, a comment which reflected the critical consensus that Unruh was something of a literary fossil.

Unruh's later work was dominated by a far-reaching literary undertaking: the series of eight autobiographical novels which he had begun in the internment camp in France and which was never

*Bust of Unruh by Wilhelm Lehmbruck*

completed. *Der Sohn des Generals* began the projected cycle; the volume describes the author's years as a cadet at the officers' training camp, which he calls a "caning hell." The style of this work is noticeably better than that of his earlier novels; the difficult metaphors and supercharged expressions are largely absent.

Even though Unruh's works were rejected as outmoded, his best-known dramas were published in a new edition in 1960 by the Hans Carl publishing house in Nuremberg. This volume, *Dramen*, includes *Bonaparte*, *Louis Ferdinand*, *Bismarck*, *Offiziere*, and *Phaea*. Unruh returned to America in 1961 and settled in Atlantic City; when his house was destroyed by a flood in 1962 he moved back to Germany and for the rest of his life lived on the family estate at Diez. He received the Kogge Literature Prize in 1963 and the Carl von Ossietzky

Medal in 1966; in 1967 he was made an honorary member of the German Academy for Language and Literature.

Unruh's novel *Friede in den USA? Ein Traum* (Peace in the USA? A Dream), about his exile in America, passed through the hands of German publishers for ten years before being published in 1967. The review in *Die Zeit* said that the images of Hieronymus Bosch that the character Uhle frequently refers to may have been the model for Unruh's representation of reality in the novel. The language in the novel is faulted for failing to blend American phraseology and slang expressions into the German.

Two years before Unruh's death his last drama, *Odysseus auf Ogygia* (Odysseus on Ogygia, 1968), was performed as a reading at the Berlin Academy of Art. In this drama Odysseus is not the Homeric hero but a man who has attained insight. On the island of Ogygia, Odysseus, the conqueror of Troy, is made aware of the criminal nature of war by the sight of the remains of the Trojan horse, which has washed ashore. Feelings of guilt erupt with the recollection of the horrors that had been committed in the name of the gods. Unruh's Wandlungsdrama (drama of conversion) ends in a utopian vein. Odysseus declines to return home with his son to Ithaca for more spilling of blood. Zeus orders Hermes, the messenger of the gods, to accompany the son, but Odysseus decides to try, with the help of the nymph Calypso, to speed ahead of the two in order to prevent more murder. The homage that Unruh received after the reading was an expression of respect for the high moral quality of his personality.

*Kaserne und Sphinx* (The Barracks and the Sphinx, 1969) appeared one year before the author's death as the third and last volume of his projected autobiographical novel series; it once again demonstrates the shortcomings which had largely been eliminated in the first two volumes, *Der Sohn des Generals* and *Im Haus der Prinzen* (In the House of the Princes, 1967). The *Frankfurter Allgemeine Zeitung* reported that the expressionistic affectations of Unruh's earlier writings had reasserted themselves, and said that whereas the boundaries between realism and symbolism, indignation and fascination, and lust and ardor were blurred, they became unmistakably apparent between art and trash.

Unruh died in Diez on 28 November 1970. George Zivier, who had written several articles about his life and works for *Der Tagesspiegel*, said

of him in a necrology: "The homecoming Fritz von Unruh was pressed ever more urgently into a leading role of an intellectual anti-Hitler German. He was drafted for distinguished manifestations and along with many other honors, was presented with the Goethe Prize in the Paulskirche in Frankfurt in 1948. But the role as the personification of a good conscience did not suit him as well as it seemed. Unruh's protestations against force and suppression, his constant intercession for moral law in the Kantian sense, his intense battle cry on behalf of cleanliness and social justice—all that essentially contradicted the nature of a traditional German, into which the rebelling elements would like to have molded him."

**References:**

Heinrich Bitsch, "The Fritz von Unruh Society," *Books Abroad,* 29 (Spring 1955): 164-165;

Reinhold Breuer, "Fritz von Unruh: Portrait of a Poet," *Books Abroad,* 25 (Summer 1951): 220-222;

Alexander Gode von Aesch, "Fritz von Unruh," *Germanic Review,* 23 (April 1948): 149-154;

Ina Götz, *Tradition und Utopie in den Dramen Fritz von Unruhs* (Bonn: Bouvier, 1975);

Edith J. R. Isaacs, "Fritz von Unruh: Hero, Apostle, and Poet," *Theatre Arts,* 31 (February 1947): 33;

Alvin Kronacher, *Fritz von Unruh* (New York: Schick, 1946);

Walter F. Mainland, "Fritz von Unruh," in *German Men of Letters,* edited by Alex Natan, volume 3 (London: Wolff, 1964), pp. 153-175;

Friedrich Rasche, ed., *Fritz von Unruh: Rebell und Verkünder; Der Dichter und sein Werk* (Frankfurt am Main: Büchergilde Gutenberg, 1965);

Guenther E. Salter, "Christian Symbolism and Concepts in Fritz von Unruh's Works," Ph.D. dissertation, Vanderbilt University, 1970;

Walter H. Sokel, *The Writer in Extremis: Expressionism in Twentieth-Century German Literature* (Stanford: Stanford University Press, 1959);

Judith Taylor, "Death as Escape and Rebirth in Fritz von Unruh's *Ein Geschlecht,*" *Germanic Review,* 44 (March 1969): 110-120.

**Papers:**

Fritz von Unruh's letters, papers, and manuscript materials can be found in the Storm Archives, State University of New York at Albany, and the Deutsches Literaturarchiv, Schiller-Nationalmuseum, Marbach, West Germany.

# Ernst Wiechert

*(18 May 1887-24 August 1950)*

## Klaus Thoenelt
*George Washington University*

BOOKS: *Die Flucht: Roman,* as Ernst Barany Bjell
   (Berlin: Deutsche Verlagsanstalt, 1916);
*Der Wald: Roman* (Berlin: Grote, 1922);
*Der Totenwolf: Roman* (Regensburg: Habbel & Nau-
   mann, 1924);
*Die blauen Schwingen: Roman* (Regensburg: Habbel
   & Naumann, 1925);
*Die Legende vom letzten Wald* (Regensburg: Habbel,
   1925);
*Der Knecht Gottes, Andreas Nyland: Roman* (Berlin:
   Grote, 1926);
*Der silberne Wagen: Novellen* (Berlin: Grote, 1928);
*Die kleine Passion: Roman* (Berlin: Grote, 1929);
*Die Flöte des Pan: Novellen* (Berlin: Grote, 1930);
*Jedermann: Geschichte eines Namenlosen* (Munich:
   Langen-Müller, 1932);
*Die Magd des Jürgen Doskocil: Roman* (Munich: Lan-
   gen-Müller, 1932); translated by Eithne Wil-
   kins and Ernst Kaiser as *The Girl and the
   Ferryman* (London & New York: Pilot Press,
   1947);
*Das Spiel vom deutschen Bettelmann* (Munich: Langen-
   Müller, 1933);
*Die Majorin: Eine Erzählung* (Munich: Langen-
   Müller, 1934); translated by Phyllis and Trev-
   or Blewitt as *The Baroness* (New York: Norton,
   1936; London: Allen & Unwin, 1936);
*Der Todeskandidat; La Ferme morte; Der Vater: Drei
   Erzählungen* (Munich: Langen-Müller, 1934);
*Der Kinderkreuzzug* (Berlin: Grote, 1935);
*Der verlorene Sohn: Schauspiel* (Munich: Langen-
   Müller, 1935);
*Hirtennovelle* (Munich: Langen-Müller, 1935);
*Von den treuen Begleitern* (Hamburg: Ellermann,
   1936);
*Der Dichter und die Jugend* (Mainz: Werkstatt für
   Buchdruck, 1936);
*Das heilige Jahr: Fünf Novellen* (Berlin: Grote, 1936);
*Wälder und Menschen: Eine Jugend* (Munich: Lan-
   gen-Müller, 1936);
*Eine Mauer um uns baue* (Mainz: Werkstatt für Buch-
   druck, 1937);
*Atli der Bestmann; Tobias: Zwei Erzählungen* (Berlin:
   Grote, 1938);

*Ernst Wiechert (Ullstein)*

*In der Heimat* (Munich: Piper, 1938);
*Vom Trost der Welt* (Mainz: Werkstatt für Buch-
   druck, 1938);
*Das einfache Leben: Roman* (Munich: Langen-Müller,
   1939); translated by Marie Heynemann as *The
   Simple Life* (London: Nevill, 1954);
*Der ewige Stern: Eine Adventsgeschichte* (Mainz: Werk-
   statt für Buchdruck und Verlag, 1940);
*Demetrius und andere Erzählungen* (Zurich: Scientia,
   1945);
*Der Dichter und seine Zeit: Rede, gehalten am 16. April
   1935 im Auditorium Maximum der Universität
   München* (Zurich: Artemis, 1945);

287

*Der Totenwald: Ein Bericht* (Zurich: Rascher, 1945); translated by Ursula Stechow as *The Forest of the Dead* (London: Gollancz, 1947);

*Die Jerominkinder: Roman*, 2 volumes (Munich: Desch, 1945-1947); translated by Robert Maxwell as *The Earth is Our Heritage* (London & New York: Nevill, 1951);

*Rede an die deutsche Jugend, 1945* (Munich: Zinnenverlag, 1945);

*Totenmesse* (Zurich: Rascher, 1945);

*Der weiße Büffel; oder, Von der großen Gerechtigkeit* (Zurich: Rascher, 1946);

*Der brennende Dornbusch* (Zurich: Arche, 1946);

*An die deutsche Jugend: Drei Reden und ein Aufsatz* (London: World's Alliance of the Young Men's Christian Associations War Prisoners' Aid, 1946);

*Über Kunst und Künstler: Aus einer ungesprochenen Rede* (Hamburg: Ellermann, 1946);

*Märchen*, 2 volumes (Zurich: Rascher, 1946);

*Okay; oder, Die Unsterblichen: Eine ernsthafte Komödie in drei Aufzügen* (Zurich: Artemis, 1946);

*Erzählungen* (Düsseldorf: Schwann, 1947);

*Die Gebärde; Der Fremde* (Zurich: Arche, 1947);

*Rede an die Schweizer Freunde* (Zurich: Rascher, 1947);

*Der große Wald* (Olten: Vereinigung Oltner Bücherfreunde, 1947);

*Jahre und Zeiten: Erinnerungen* (Zurich: Rentsch, 1948);

*Das zerstörte Menschengesicht: Rede an der Goethe-Feier in Stäfa (Zurich) am 22. IX. 1947* (Olten: Vereinigung Oltner Bücherfreunde, 1948);

*Der Richter* (Zurich: Arche, 1948);

*The Poet and His Time: Three Addresses*, translated by Irene Taeuber (Hinsdale, Ill.: Regnery, 1948);

*Das Antlitz der Mutter: Eine Bilderfolge* (Zurich: Arche, 1949);

*Die Mutter: Eine Erzählung* (Zurich: Arche, 1949);

*Missa sine nomine: Roman* (Munich: Desch, 1950); translated by Heynemann and Margery B. Ledward as *Missa sine Nomine* (London: Nevill, 1953); translation republished as *Tidings* (New York: Macmillan, 1959);

*Ernst Wiechert: Lebensworte aus seinem Schrifttum*, edited by Adolf Wendel (Zurich: Rascher, 1950);

*Der Exote: Roman* (Munich: Desch, 1951);

*Es geht ein Pflüger übers Land: Betrachtungen und Erzählungen*, edited by Lilje Wiechert (Munich: Desch, 1951);

*Vom bleibenden Gewinn: Ein Buch der Betrachtung* (Zurich: Arche, 1951);

*Die letzten Lieder* (Zurich: Arche, 1951);

*Meine Gedichte* (Munich: Desch, 1952);

*Gesegnetes Leben: Das Schönste aus den Werken des Dichters*, edited by Gerhard Kamin (Vienna: Desch, 1953);

*Am Himmel strahlt der Stern: Ein Weihnachtsbuch* (Vienna: Desch, 1957);

*Fahrt um die Liebe: Erzählung* (Zurich: Arche, 1957);

*Sämtliche Werke*, 10 volumes (Munich: Desch, 1957);

*Briefe an einen Werdenden, and Ein deutsches Weihnachtsspiel*, edited by Sumner Kirshner (Pullman: Washington State University Press, 1966);

*Häftling Nr. 7188; Tagebuchnotizen und Briefe*, edited by Kamin (Munich: Desch, 1966);

*Regina Amstettin; Veronika; Der einfache Tod; Die Magd: 4 Novellen* (Munich: Desch, 1969);

*Der Vogel Niemalsmehr: 12 Märchen* (Berlin & Vienna: Ullstein, 1973).

OTHER: Willy Fries, *Die Fischer: Eine Geschichte in Bildern*, introduction by Wiechert (Zurich: Rascher, 1934);

Walter Engelhardt, *Ein Memelbilderbuch*, introduction by Wiechert (Berlin: Grenze & Ausland, 1935);

*Von Mutter und Kind: Bilder alter und neuer Meister*, introduction by Wiechert (Leipzig: Seemann, 1937).

Ernst Wiechert was a famous teacher and writer whose books were essentially extensions of his classes. Wiechert's collected novels, short stories, fairy tales, plays, lectures, and poetry total approximately 10,000 pages, of which only a few major novels and some short stories and speeches are of lasting interest. His language, rich in imagery and evocative of landscape and man's paradise regained in nature, engages the reader in a dialogue whose central topic is Germany. Like Thomas Mann, Wiechert saw Germany's role as mankind's educator through Goethean Bildung (self-realization). Also like Mann, Wiechert felt that the German preference for power politics over Bildung since the time of Bismarck constituted a national self-betrayal that was the cause of both world wars. But unlike Mann in *Der Zauberberg* (1924; translated as *The Magic Mountain*, 1927) and in *Doktor Faustus* (1947; translated as *Doctor Faustus*, 1948), Wiechert did not limit himself to an analysis of German inauthenticity. Wiechert's goal was to impart Bildung to his students and readers in order to strengthen individualism in an anti-individualistic society.

Ernst Emil Wiechert was born on 18 May 1887 in the county of Sensburg, East Prussia. His father, Emil Martin Wiechert, was a royal forester who loved the woods and knew long passages of the Bible by heart; his mother, Henriette Andreae Wiechert, was a hardworking, deeply religious, melancholic woman who committed suicide in 1912. Wiechert grew up in the solitude of the East Prussian woods with no books other than the Bible. His experience of nature was religious in character; nature was a realm not subject to human incoherence and unpredictability. This childhood experience was to affect his entire life. Wherever he traveled, Wiechert was at home in nature. The skills he learned from his father—forestry, hunting, fishing, and gardening—were never mere hobbies but were different approaches to nature.

In his Gymnasium and university years at Königsberg from 1898 to 1911, Wiechert learned to approach nature with a special awareness his studies of German, English, and philosophy imparted to him. He viewed the world of nature and of letters as a unity, and came to a Goethean understanding of Bildung. This early experience of Bildung was confirmed when, in 1906, he lived as a private tutor with the family of Baron von Grotthuss on an estate outside Königsberg. The baron and his family were highly educated aristocrats whose daily life was rooted in the arts and letters. Thus, Wiechert not only experienced Bildung as an adventure of the mind in his student years, he also learned in the baron's family how to make Bildung a way of life. Even though he never used the term *Bildung* for the way of life he wanted to live, teach, and write about, his entire works consist of ever varying presentations of the quest for Bildung. From the early 1930s on, he describes applied Bildung as a Goethean tradition and a preeminently German task.

When Wiechert received the Staatsexamen diploma (a degree required for high school teachers) in 1911, he was not yet a conscious disciple of Goethe. As an underpaid teaching assistant he taught German and English at Königsberg gymnasia from 1911 to 1914, rebelling against the narrow-mindedness of his colleagues and dreaming about a writing career. In 1912 he married a forester's daughter, Meta Mittelstädt against the wishes of his father. The marriage proved to be a mismatch. Wiechert describes Meta in the second part of his autobiography, *Jahre und Zeiten* (Years and Times, 1948), as a conventional woman whose lack of comprehension of his rebellious views led to a separation in the late 1920s.

*Wiechert and his wife in Bavaria*

In Wiechert's own judgment, the books he wrote during his first marriage were worthless. A new life, he states in his autobiography, was called for to write books of lasting value. Like Goethe, Wiechert attributes male creativity to the influence of a liberated woman who can free the man from the chains of self-inflicted absurdity. "Der Mann unserer Zeit," Wiechert wrote at the end of his life, "hat mit Denken und Planen und Tun nichts zustande gebracht als die beiden Kriege, die die Erde zerstört haben, indes unter den Kellern in den Ruinen die Frauen immer noch das Ewige bewahrt haben . . ." (The male of our time, with all his intelligence, his planning and his busyness, has achieved nothing but the two wars that have destroyed the earth, whereas in the cellars underneath the ruins women, unceasingly, have preserved that which is eternal . . .).

Wiechert's evaluation of his early books is accurate. In four successive novels he treats only one theme: rebellion against all aspects of German middle-class conventionalism. Wiechert's rebel figures destroy Bildung instead of establishing it. To them, the experience of arts and letters and of nature is ultimately not liberating but depressing and, in some instances, leads to destruction and even suicide. A narcissistic and therefore purely aesthetic approach leads to a perception of nature as devoid of values. Nature, thus viewed, becomes a secluded realm of soulless, primordial beauty where man is a wolf to other men and crime is of no consequence.

Wiechert's early heroes walk a thin line between a redeeming nature and a man-devouring, monstrous deathscape. They perceive both, yet are unable to take roots in a *terre humaine*, a humanized nature, and finally wander off into the depersonalized anonymity of a homeless wilderness. In Wiechert's first novel, *Die Flucht* (The Escape, 1916), Peter Holm, a suppressed, rebellious high school teacher in a small Prussian town, resigns his position out of disgust with the obtuse pettiness of his colleagues; he returns to the woods where he was born and raised, attempts to write a great book, and, realizing his failure as a writer, "escapes" through suicide. Repeated presentations of Holm's self-avoidance are mirrored by descriptions of nature as an unfeeling realm of timeless winter. Although the author provides a sympathetic treatment of Holm's perversion of Bildung, Wiechert is not Holm and the latter's escape is not his own.

World War I intensified Wiechert's rejection of self-avoiding conventionalism. Inducted in 1914, he fought on the western front, was promoted to lieutenant, and returned to Königsberg in 1918 a stranger to his wife and to most of his colleagues. Wiechert was less disillusioned with war than with the society for which he had risked his life: like many demobilized German soldiers, he felt that the nation had been undeserving of his spirit of sacrifice.

In *Der Wald* (The Woods, 1922), Captain Henner reacts to the loss of his illusion by engaging in crime. Forced by postwar legislation to grant the public access to his huge estate, he sets fire to his house and woods and, sought by the police, treks off into the anonymity of a primitive wilderness, never to be seen again.

The hero of *Der Totenwolf* (The Death Wolf, 1924), Wolf Wiedensahl, attempts to transform German society by waging a terroristic "holy war" against Western materialism that ends with his death. The novel, which Wiechert later called "eine Krankheit" (a disease), brought him the favor of the still-small Nazi party. The first edition of the book appeared with a swastika on its cover, by all accounts with Wiechert's consent. It must be remembered, however, that Wiechert does not approve of his heroes' perversion of Bildung; it is therefore possible he felt that his theme, an illusion

leading to terrorism, was appropriately represented by the swastika.

Wiechert's fourth novel, *Die blauen Schwingen* (The Blue Wings, 1925), refers to a childhood experience of the author's. In the first part of his autobiography, *Wälder und Menschen* (Forests and People, 1936), he describes the mysterious behavior of a blue-winged eagle that he could never catch and could hardly ever sight. In the novel, a young musician, Harro Bruckner, cannot win the love of Maja; she is his constant illusion. Upon losing this illusion, he wanders off into the woods "als gehe er aus seinem Vaterland in das Elend" (as if he were leaving his fatherland to wander off into exile). This inconclusive outcome suggests an ultimate anonymity that is literally beyond words: the hero vanishes from the view of the reader as if he had never existed.

The heroes of *Die Flucht, Der Wald, Der Totenwolf,* and *Die blauen Schwingen* are seeking Bildung, but they are diverted by illusions and lose their identities and often their lives. Johannes, the protagonist of *Die kleine Passion* (The Little Passion, 1929), is not a self-destructive rebel but a victim of rebellion and anarchy. He is a sensitive boy, persecuted by his father, a thief and counterfeiter; by the school authorities; and, finally, by the entire town. His high school teacher, Dr. Luther, represents for the first time in Wiechert's work unadulterated Bildung. He virtually adopts Johannes, saving the boy's sanity in an insane society and imparting to him his own ability to heal. *Jedermann* (Everyman, 1932) is a sequel to *Die kleine Passion.* A pervasive social insanity generates the catastrophe of World War I, and Johannes, now a youth in his twenties, is inducted and sent to the western front where he becomes Everyman. War is the great equalizer; every soldier in any army shares Johannes's fate, the dehumanizing role of killing and expecting to be killed. In *Jedermann* Wiechert describes World War I very much as Erich Maria Remarque does in *Im Westen nichts Neues* (1929; translated as *All Quiet on the Western Front,* 1929). "Sie werden," Wiechert writes about the soldiers, "nach Gewehren gezählt, nicht nach Namen, Intelligenzen, sittlichen Kräften" (They count only insofar as they carry guns; their names, their intelligence, and their ethical consciousness are irrelevant). Johannes experiences the torn-up landscape of war as a "Wildnis des Primitiven" (wilderness of primitivity) where mass death is dispensed with assembly-line precision. Mass death makes no exceptions; it engulfs its makers, and insanity turns against itself. In *Die kleine Passion* and

*Jedermann* Wiechert's early experience of Bildung in Baron Grotthuss's family resurfaces. Bildung is not achieved in total rebellion, nor does it call for social submission; it is a form of self-realization that helps others to find their identities and bestows a spiritual nobility on those who live it. At the end of the war, Johannes returns to Germany as a figure who represents Bildung: the healed has become a healer.

In these two novels, while Bildung seems to be the only answer to all final human questions, this answer is still a privilege of the educated. In *Die Magd des Jürgen Doskocil* (1932; translated as *The Girl and the Ferryman*, 1947) Wiechert attempts to demonstrate that Bildung is available to everyone. Martha, a poor ferryman's wife, kills a Mormon priest, Mr. McLean, who is about to murder her husband because she refuses to become the priest's mistress. Mr. McLean is a fanatic and a powerful dictator, and while the entire community blindly submits to him, Martha's love for her husband generates an inner certitude in her that transcends even Christ's orders announced to her by the priest. The court recognizes that Martha has killed to save her husband's life and imposes a minimal penalty. At the end of the novel Martha and the ferryman recultivate their field, which the community had destroyed on the priest's order. While in *Die kleine Passion* and *Jedermann* authenticity generates love, in *Die Magd des Jürgen Doskocil* love generates authenticity and hence consciousness. In Bildung, thought and action are interdependent, each generating the other. In *Die Magd des Jürgen Doskocil* the official churches, represented by the Mormon priest, not only prevent but destroy self-realization.

Wiechert said that his relationship with Paula Marie Junker inspired him to write *Die kleine Passion*, *Jedermann*, and *Die Magd des Jürgen Doskocil*. He probably met Paula Marie, a highly cultured married woman, in 1928. According to Wiechert's account, their relationship so scandalized Königsberg that the high school administration threatened to transfer him to a provincial town. Wiechert resigned his teaching post, but the Prussian secretary of education offered him a new position in Berlin. Wiechert accepted and moved with Paula Marie to the German capital. In 1931 Wiechert's wife Meta died; Paula Marie obtained a divorce, and she and Wiechert were married in August. Wiechert was then forty-four years old and internationally known as a teacher-author who taught students and readers that Germany was still the proverbial "Land der Dichter und Denker" (the country of poets and thinkers). Wiechert's conviction that his mission

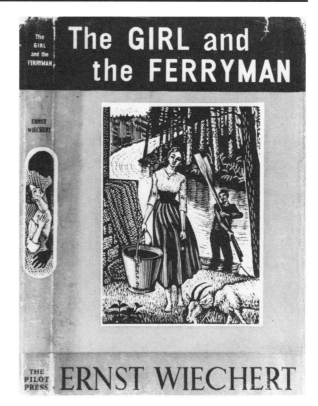

Dust jacket for the English translation of Wiechert's 1932 novel Die Magd des Jürgen Doskocil, *about the triumph of love over religious fanaticism*

was to teach Bildung and his increasing disenchantment with the Prussian Untertan (underling) mentality led to his final resignation from teaching in 1933. He felt he could better fulfill his calling by leaving Prussia and dedicating his time to writing. He moved to Bavaria—first to Ambach, by the Lake of Starnberg, then into a farmhouse near Munich called Hof Gagert.

In 1933 Wiechert began to criticize National Socialism publicly. While the Nazis had initially supported his cultural nationalism, they did not agree with the substance of this nationalism. Similarly, the Nazis were at first supportive of Wiechert's love for nature but later called it an undesirable form of individualism. In his autobiography, Wiechert notes that in 1933 he realized that to live with integrity in Nazi Germany was far harder than to die with integrity. In this situation, Wiechert rediscovered Goethe "auf unverlierbare Weise" (in an irrevocable way). From then on, he associated Bildung with Goethe, who had developed the concept in his Wilhelm Meister novels (1797-1828).

*Wiechert in the garden of his home, Hof Gagert, in 1934*

In *Die Majorin* (1934; translated as *The Baroness*, 1936), Michael Fahrenholz has spent twenty years as a soldier, first with the German army in World War I, then with the French Foreign Legion in Africa. He returns to the East Prussian countryside a rootless, embittered man, devoid of human feelings and resentful of war and peace alike. His father believes Michael dead and, upon his return, cannot accept him as his son. The baroness attempts to heal Michael of his restlessness and hires him as a hunter on her estate. Resentful of the baroness's compassion, he tries to possess her sexually; frustrated in his advances, he shoots at poor people collecting wood in the baroness's forest and kills one of her beautiful swans. His repeated attempts to leave the baroness and wander off into anonymity fail, precisely because he cannot possess her; he experiences for the first time a form of love that cannot be reduced to sex. After trying for months to avoid the acceptance of an I-Thou relationship, he learns how to farm and is asked by

the baroness to move into her castle as manager of the estate. He wavers, but finally accepts. He has reached a degree of authenticity that makes sexual relationships irrelevant; for this reason, the reader never learns whether or not Michael slept with the baroness. Michael has discovered his identity, and the twenty years he spent as an anonymous Everyman fade into oblivion.

In this novel Wiechert again describes two contrasting conceptions of nature. As a hunter, Michael perceives nature as a wilderness where he may kill the baroness's swan without consequences; as estate manager, Michael lives in a humanized nature. As in Goethe's *Wilhelm Meister* novels, it is a woman who is capable of healing the male of his self-inflicted absurdity. In a little-known play, *Das Spiel vom deutschen Bettelmann* (The Play of the German Beggar, 1933), the hero, Hiob (Job), represents Germany before World War I. Hiob, power-hungry and heedless of his true calling, starts the war; after his defeat, he asks the victors for a second chance to follow his authentic vocation. The victors, embodied in a soulless Pontius Pilate figure, throw Hiob in jail, where he dies. The message of the play is that the Allies are responsible for the failure of the Weimar Republic. In the equally unknown—and equally bad—play *Der verlorene Sohn* (The Prodigal Son, 1935), Wiechert revises his verdict. The prodigal son, who represents the authentic Goethean Germany, is drawn into World War I by his older brother, who stands for imperial Germany between 1870 and 1914. Both brothers are killed in the war, yet their mother believes that the prodigal son will return one day and build an authentic Germany. The message now is that Germany alone is to blame for the war and its consequences. The Nazis suggested that Wiechert write a sequel in which National Socialism would be represented by the returning prodigal son. Wiechert's refusal to comply may have been his first unequivocal rejection of what he later called the incarnation of the "Massenseele" (the soul of the masses).

Both dramas confirm Wiechert's later assertion that, from the early 1930s on, he had seen the roots of Nazism in Germany's preference for power politics over Goethean thought during the Bismarck era. Wiechert's 1935 address to the students of the University of Munich, published in 1945 under the title *Der Dichter und seine Zeit* (translated in *The Poet and His Time*, 1948), represents a courageous, unequivocal public rejection of Nazi Germany in the name of a suppressed Goethean Germany. Wiechert states that the German citizens had only one alternative to the "Boxerethos" of National Socialism, Goethe's "Ehrfurcht" (reverence for one's own self ). The speech was smuggled to Moscow, where excerpts were printed as documents attesting to German resistance against the Nazi regime. Wiechert was not arrested after giving this lecture because the Nazis still hoped that the author of *Der Totenwolf* might give thought to his previous discontent with Western materialism and write a pro-Nazi novel. Instead, he wrote an essay highly critical of the regime, *Von den treuen Begleitern* (On the Loyal Companions, 1936), which states that a nation contemptuous of its only loyal companions, the poets and writers, is doomed.

In 1937 Wiechert read his story *Der weiße Büffel; oder, Von der großen Gerechtigkeit* (The White Buffalo; or, Final Justice, 1946) at a literary meeting in Cologne. Vaseduva, a personification of the suppressed authentic Germany, is imprisoned by Murduk, a tyrant modeled on Hitler. Haunted by the idea that his petty bourgeois mentality may become visible behind his contrived image of grandeur, Murduk can rule only if all the people live in fear of him. He executes Vaseduva, who dies as fearlessly as he lived. Vaseduva's death so intensifies Murduk's feelings of insufficiency that he decides to become a Vaseduva figure himself. He relinquishes the country's leadership to his liberal son and embarks on a pilgrimage of self-realization. The Nazis suppressed the story, but Wiechert did not heed the warning.

When Wiechert protested against the continued detention of pastor Martin Niemöller in Nazi concentration camps in an outspoken letter to the Bavarian Nazi authorities in 1938, he was finally arrested and deported to the Buchenwald concentration camp. *Der Totenwald* (1945; translated as *The Forest of the Dead*, 1947) gives an account of his experiences. The theme of the book is the immeasurable cultural and spiritual distance that separates Hitler's Germany from Goethe's Germany, as symbolized by the contrast of Buchenwald with the nearby town of Weimar. Weimar had become the center of Nazi writers' conventions, and the oak tree under which Goethe had sat with Charlotte von Stein stood within the confines of the camp. Every evening, Wiechert, ill and exhausted, walked to this tree, which became for him the symbol of old Germany's fate in Hitler's Reich and, by implication, of the futility of his own inner emigration. The Nazis released Wiechert after a few months of forced labor. After his release he had to meet with Propaganda Minister Joseph Goeb-

bels, who assured him that any further criticism of National Socialism would bring about his physical extinction.

Though under close Gestapo surveillance, Wiechert risked his life one more time by writing *Das einfache Leben* (1939; translated as *The Simple Life*, 1954), which was published through an oversight by the party censors. Even though bookstores were no longer allowed to put Wiechert's books on display, 250,000 copies of the novel were sold. *Das einfache Leben* represents a total rejection of National Socialism. Thomas von Orla, a naval officer in World War I, realizes that an ever faster pace of life produces a depersonalizing superficiality on all levels of human relations. He concludes: "Wir bringen unsere Jahre zu wie ein Geschwätz" (We spend our years as a tale that is told). People can conceive of themselves only as objects; they are alternately possessed by a dehumanizing rationalism and an equally dehumanizing bestiality and are thus ruled by machine and animal alike. Orla's family is no exception: his wife be-

*Wiechert and unidentified boy in Wiechert's study at Hof Gagert*

*Page from the secret diary Wiechert kept while confined at the Buchenwald concentration camp in 1938 (Verlag Kurt Desch)* comes a drug addict, and his son, who wants to be commander in chief of the new German navy, literally and figuratively walks over corpses to achieve his goal. Orla retreats to a small island on a Masurian lake, where he becomes a fisherman and a writer. Orla not only rebuilds his own life but, like Dr. Luther in *Die kleine Passion*, he becomes a twentieth-century Wilhelm Meister who heals the wounds of time. His cabin becomes the meeting place of a growing classless community. Intellectuals and fishermen, aristocrats and their servants group around Orla and live "das einfache Leben." As opposed to "*a* simple life," Wiechert's phrase "*the* simple life" refers to that specific form of human simplicity that originates in the consciously established unity of subject and object—in short, in Bildung. The community represents the authentic, inner Germany that is manifest in Goethe's *Faust* (1805-1832) and Schubert's songs. While this Germany may be physically destroyed, it will be, as Orla puts it, forever true.

Wiechert considered *Das einfache Leben* his best book because in no other work did he present National Socialism's "Gegenbild" (counterimage) as convincingly. Wiechert's images of a dehumanized society whose gods are the machine and the animal corresponds to Thomas Mann's analysis of National Socialism in *Doktor Faustus:* Adrian Leverkühn, Mann's Faust figure, pledges his soul to the devil in exchange for the devil's powers of rationalism and animalism—the ice of intellect and the fire of mass ecstasy. Partaking in both, Leverkühn lives in hell on earth—as German society does in Wiechert's *Das einfache Leben.*

Wiechert's next book, the first volume of the two-volume novel *Die Jerominkinder* (1945-1947; translated as *The Earth is Our Heritage*, 1951), was automatically rejected by the censors in the early 1940s. Thereafter, Wiechert kept silent and, mindful of Nazi unpredictability, slept with a loaded gun under his pillow: he says in his autobiography that he was ready to commit suicide rather than face another term of imprisonment.

When Germany surrendered and the American army moved into Bavaria in May 1945, Wiechert believed that his inner emigration had helped prepare the ground for a rebirth of Goethe's Germany. But American denazification methods seemed to favor the same organizational and technical talents that had been emphasized by the Nazis. In an open letter to the American military administration of Bavaria entitled "The Rich Man and Poor Lazarus" (1945), Wiechert describes his disappointment with America's approach to denazi-

*Painting of Wiechert by Leo von König*

fication and Germany's resentful reaction to democratic freedom. He concludes with the statement that Americans are naive and incapable of comprehending the real cultural and spiritual issues at stake. When Nazi circles in Bavaria published only the anti-American part of the letter and claimed Wiechert's name for their purposes, Wiechert wrote a second, "Vom Wolf und dem Lamm" (On the Wolf and the Lamb, 1946), refuting the Nazis' claim that he had always sided with them. After receiving many insulting and threatening letters, Wiechert decided to leave Germany and settle in Switzerland.

In the two years between his decision to emigrate and his actual emigration in 1948, Wiechert wrote the second volume of *Die Jerominkinder*. While the first volume reads like a sequel to *Das einfache Leben*, the second volume betrays Wiechert's increased concern with the lack of consciousness of identity in postwar Germany. In the first volume, Jons Ehrenreich Jeromin, a poor worker's son, grows up in Sowirog, a small East Prussian town, and then experiences the horror of World War I. Wounded, he returns home and becomes a physician. In the second volume Jeromin founds a classless community and discusses the theory of Bildung with his educated friends, the teacher Stilling and the estate owner Herr von Balk. The result of these discussions is that it is not enough to follow one's heart instinctively; the heart must be consciously recognized as a mediating agency reconciling intellect and primitive drives.

In Switzerland, Wiechert established himself in the Rütihof near Ürikon by the Lake of Zurich. His constant concern was still Germany. The Bewältigung der Vergangenheit (overcoming of the [Nazi] past) seemed possible to Wiechert only on an individual basis. Thus, in his last novel, *Missa sine nomine* (1950; translated, 1953), he attempts to assert man's power over the cause-and-effect, assembly-line automatism of history. The vicious circle of social Darwinism, Wiechert asserts, can be broken by the recognition of man's faculty of self-renewal. Amadeus von Lijecrona, a young Prussian aristocrat, has survived four years of detention in concentration camps. After the German defeat he returns to a small estate in West Germany owned by his two brothers, who were officers in Hitler's army. His heart is so filled with hatred that he cannot live under the same roof with his brothers, so he moves into a small cabin. As the years pass, he gradually recaptures his lost faith in man. While the official Aufbau (the economic rebuilding of Germany) takes place with Hitler's voice still loudly speaking in the builders, Amadeus transforms Hitler's voice in himself into Goethe's voice. Barbara, a young woman who has remained a fanatical National Socialist and is pregnant by a Nazi terrorist, attempts to have Amadeus murdered by some of her Nazi friends. The wounded Amadeus is lying helplessly on the ground when Barbara arrives to witness the end of her enemy. Amadeus's appeal to Barbara's love for her unborn child first startles, then transforms her. She realizes that her life-denying hatred was, deep down, an unconscious quest for love. As soon as she realizes her error, she begins to take care of Amadeus and he takes care of her. The novel was translated into many languages and was widely read, especially in France, but most German critics felt that its message was unrealistic.

Wiechert corresponded with authors such as Reinhold Schneider, Werner Bergengruen, and Hermann Hesse, and he had lifelong relationships with the Goethe scholar Eduard Spranger, the musician Wilhelm Kempff, the painter Leo von König, and especially with Dr. Max Picard, the author of *Hitler in uns selbst* (1945; translated as *Hitler in Our Selves*, 1947). Wiechert's real friends, however, were his students and readers. Many of them vis-

ited him frequently and corresponded with him until his death at the age of sixty-three on 24 August 1950. Erich W. Isenstead, for instance, who had left Germany in 1933 and returned in 1945 as an American army officer, spent numerous evenings in Wiechert's house in Bavaria, as he had done twenty years earlier in Berlin, and protected Wiechert from postwar hardships as best he could. Wiechert was not a misanthropic loner but an educator in the Socratic sense; he wanted to cultivate dialogue rather than appear in the limelight of literary gatherings.

Wiechert was a fascinating storyteller engaging the reader in dialogue and trying to teach him the Goethean art of living. He fully subscribed to Goethe's statement: "Wir wissen von keiner Welt als im Bezug auf den Menschen; wir wollen keine Kunst als die ein Abdruck dieses Bezugs ist" (We do not conceive of a nonanthropomorphic world, and the only art we value is anthropomorphic).

**Bibliographies:**
Siegfried B. Puknat, "Wiechert Bibliography," *Monatshefte für deutschen Unterricht*, 43 (December 1951): 409-413;
Guido Reiner, *Ernst-Wiechert-Bibliographie*, 3 volumes (Paris: Selbstverlag, 1972-1976).

**Biographies:**
Hans Ebeling, *Ernst Wiechert: Der Weg eines Dichters* (Berlin: Grote, 1937);
Helmut Olesch, *Ernst Wiechert* (Wuppertal: Müller, 1949);
Hans-Martin Plesske, *Ernst Wiechert* (East Berlin: Union, 1967).

**References:**
Jean-Jacques Anstett, "Ernst Wiechert théologien," *Etudes Germaniques*, 7 (January-March 1952): 7-24;
Lydia Baer, "A Study of Wiechert with Special Reference to Jens Peter Jacobsen and Rilke," *Modern Language Quarterly*, 5 (December 1944): 469-480;
Arnold Bergstraesser, " 'Das einfache Leben': Zu dem Roman von Ernst Wiechert," *Monatshefte*, 38 (May 1946): 293-297;
Hildegard Chatellier, "Ernst Wiechert im Urteil der deutschen Zeitschriftenpresse 1933-1945," *Recherches Germaniques*, 3 (1973): 153-195;
Kurt Desch, ed., *Bekenntnis zu Ernst Wiechert: Ein Gedenkbuch zum 60. Geburtstag* (Munich: Desch, 1947);

Hans Ebeling, *Ernst Wiechert: Das Werk des Dichters* (Wiesbaden: Limes, 1947);

Jürgen Fangmeiner, *Ernst Wiechert: Ein theologisches Gespräch mit dem Dichter* (Zurich: Theologischer Verlag, 1976);

Willi Fehse, "Bekämpft—geliebt—gelitten: Ernst Wiechert zum 25. Todestag," *Der Literat,* 17 (1975): 178-179;

Maurice Fraigneux, *Littérature héroique: Tolstoi—Péguy—Wiechert—Malraux—Bernanos* (Brussels: Goemaere, 1958);

John R. Frey, "Ernst Wiecherts Werk seit 1945," *German Quarterly,* 22 ( January 1949): 37-46;

Max Frisch, "Stimmen eines anderen Deutschland? Zu den Zeugnissen von Wiechert und Bergengruen," *Neue Schweizer Rundschau,* 13 (1945-1946): 537-547;

Reinhold Grimm, "Im Dickicht der inneren Emigration," in *Die deutsche Literatur im Dritten Reich,* edited by Horst Denkler and Karl Prümm (Stuttgart: Reclam, 1976), pp. 406-426;

Carl Helbling, "Alles meinige trage ich bei mir," *Neue Züricher Zeitung,* 26 May 1950;

Werner Hollman, "Ethical responsibility and Personal Freedom in the Works of Ernst Wiechert," *Germanic Review,* 25 (February 1950): 37-49;

Erich W. Isenstead, "Ernst Wiechert," *American German Review,* 14 (April 1948): 7-8;

Marianne R. Jetter, *The Island Motif in the Prose Works of Ernst Wiechert* (Vancouver: Continental Book Centre, 1957);

Gerhard Kamin, ed., *Ernst Wiechert: Der Mensch und sein Werk* (Munich: Desch, 1951);

Sumner Kirshner, "A Bibliography of Critical Writing about Ernst Wiechert," *Librarium,* 7 (1964): 59-67;

Kirshner, "Some Documents Relating to Wiechert's 'Inward Emigration,' " *German Quarterly,* 33 ( January 1965): 38-43;

Emil Müller, "Die Motive für die Verhaftung Ernst Wiecherts," *Stuttgarter Zeitung,* 23 February 1971;

Henry Nannen, "Die Wandlungen Ernst Wiecherts," *Weser Kurier,* 3 August 1947;

Carol Petersen, "Dank und Gruß an Ernst Wiechert: Offener Brief eines Schülers zum 60. Geburtstag des Dichters," *Telegraf,* 18 May 1947;

Petersen, "Ernst Wiechert," in *Christliche Dichter im 20. Jahrhundert,* edited by Otto Mann (Bern: Francke, 1968), pp. 349-359;

Hans-Martin Plesske, "Der Zauberklang des Jenseits: Ernst Wiechert und die Musik," *Musica,* 8 (October 1954): 425-427;

Siegfried B. Puknat, "Max Picard and Ernst Wiechert," *Monatshefte,* 42 (December 1950): 371-384;

Arno Schirokauer, "Zu Wiecherts 'Totenwald,' " *Die neue Rundschau,* 58 (Summer 1947): 348-352;

Reinhold Schneider, "Die Leidenschaft des Glaubens: 'Missa sine nomine,' ein Roman als letztes Vermächtnis Ernst Wiecherts," *Die Neue Zeitung,* 8 August 1951;

Oskar Seidlin, "Begegnung mit Ernst Wiechert," *German Quarterly,* 19 (November 1946): 270-273;

Horst-Johannes Tümmers, "Eine Insel als Ort ersehnter Einsamkeit: Der Autor von 'Das einfache Leben' ist heute fast vergessen," *Kölner Stadt-Anzeiger,* 31 December 1981;

Hansgeorg Zollenkopf, "Unser Lehrer Ernst Wiechert," *Hamburger Freie Presse,* 17 May 1947.

**Papers:**

Manuscripts of Ernst Wiechert's early novels are located in the Ernst Wiechert Archiv, Museum Haus Königsberg, Duisburg, Federal Republic of Germany.

# Paul Zech

*(19 February 1881-7 September 1946)*

Ward B. Lewis
*University of Georgia*

BOOKS: *Das schwarze Revier* (Elberfeld, 1909; revised, Berlin-Wilmersdorf: Meyer, 1913; revised, Munich: Musarion, 1922);

*Waldpastelle: Sechs Gedichte* (Berlin-Wilmersdorf: Meyer, 1910); revised and enlarged as *Der Wald* (Dresden: Sibyllen, 1920);

*Gedichte: Paul Zech, August Vetter und Friedrich Kerst* (Elberfeld: Bergische Druckerei und Verlagsanstalt, 1910);

*Das frühe Geläut: Gedichte,* by Zech, Christian Grunewald, Ludwig Fahrenkrog, and Julius August Vetter (Berlin-Wilmersdorf: Meyer, 1911);

*Rainer Maria Rilke* (Berlin: Borngräber, 1912); revised and enlarged as *Rainer Maria Rilke: Der Mensch und das Werk* (Dresden: Jess, 1930);

*Schollenbruch: Gedichte* (Berlin-Wilmersdorf: Meyer, 1912);

*Fanale: Gedichte der rheinischen Lyriker,* by Zech, Richard M. Cahén, Johannes Kuhlemann, Paul Mayer, Bruno Quandt, and Robert R. Schmidt (Heidelberg: Saturn, 1913);

*Schwarz sind die Wasser der Ruhr: Gesammelte Gedichte aus den Jahren 1902-1910* (Berlin-Wilmersdorf: Druckerei der Bibliophilen, 1913);

*Die Sonette aus dem Exil* (Berlin-Steglitz: Officina Serpentis, 1913; enlarged, Berlin: Zech, 1948);

*Die eiserne Brücke: Neue Gedichte* (Leipzig: Weißen Bücher, 1914);

*Der schwarze Baal: Novellen* (Leipzig: Weißen Bücher, 1917; revised, 1919);

*Helden und Heilige: Balladen aus der Zeit* (Leipzig: Drugulin, 1917);

*Gelandet: Ein dramatisches Gedicht* (Laon: Révillon-Presse, 1918; revised, Munich: Roland, 1919);

*Vor Cressy an der Marne: Gedichte eines Frontsoldaten namens Michel Michael* (Laon: Révillon-Presse, 1918);

*Der feuerige Busch: Neue Gedichte (1912-1917)* (Munich: Musarion, 1919);

*Das Grab der Welt: Eine Passion wider den Krieg auf Erden* (Hamburg & Berlin: Hoffmann & Campe, 1919);

*Die Gedichte an eine Dame in Schwarz* (Munich: Musarion, 1920);

*Das Ereignis: Neue Novellen* (Munich: Musarion, 1920);

*Golgatha: Eine Beschwörung zwischen zwei Feuern* (Hamburg & Berlin: Hoffmann & Campe, 1920);

*Das Terzett der Sterne: Ein Bekenntnis in drei Stationen* (Munich: Wolff, 1920);

*Verbrüderung: Ein Hochgesang unter dem Regenbogen in fünf Stationen* (Hamburg & Berlin: Hoffmann & Campe, 1921);

*Paul Zech in 1913, drawing by Ludwig Meidner (Schiller-Nationalmuseum, Marbach am Neckar)*

298

*Omnia mea mecum porto: Die Ballade von mir* (Berlin: Rowohlt, 1923);

*Die ewige Dreieinigkeit: Gedichte* (Rudolstadt: Greifenverlag, 1924);

*Das Rad: Ein tragisches Maskenspiel* (Leipzig: Schauspiel-Verlag, 1924);

*Die Reise um den Kummerberg: Erzählung* (Rudolstadt: Greifenverlag, 1924);

*Das trunkene Schiff: Eine szenische Ballade* (Leipzig: Schauspiel-Verlag, 1924);

*Steine: Ein tragisches Finale in sieben Geschehnissen* (Leipzig: Schauspiel-Verlag, 1924);

*Der Turm: Sieben Stufen zu einem Drama* (Leipzig: Schauspiel-Verlag, 1924);

*Erde: Die vier Etappen eines Dramas zwischen Rhein und Ruhr* (Leipzig: Schauspiel-Verlag, 1925);

*Die Geschichte einer armen Johanna* (Berlin: Dietz, 1925);

*Peregrins Heimkehr: Ein Roman in sieben Büchern* (Berlin: Dietz, 1925);

*Das törichte Herz: Vier Erzählungen* (Berlin: Dietz, 1925);

*Die Mutterstadt; Die unterbrochene Brücke: Zwei Erzählungen* (Kempten & Munich: Kösel & Pustet, 1925);

*Ich bin Du; oder, Die Begegnung mit dem Unsichtbaren: Roman* (Leipzig: Wolkenwanderer-Verlag, 1926);

*Rainer Maria Rilke: Ein Requiem* (Berlin: Officina Serpentis, 1927);

*Das Baalsopfer* (Hamburg: Deutsche Dichter-Gedächtnis-Stiftung, 1929);

*Rotes Herz der Erde: Ausgewählte Balladen, Gedichte, Gesänge,* edited by Walther G. Oschilewski (Berlin: Arbeiterjugend-Verlag, 1929);

*Morgenrot leuchtet! Ein Augsburger Festspiel für Einzelstimmen, Sprech-, Tanz- und Bewegungschöre* (Augsburg: Heber, 1930);

*Neue Balladen von den wilden Tieren* (Dresden: Jess, 1931); revised as *Balladen von den Tieren* (Berlin: Zech, 1949);

*Berlin im Licht; oder, Gedichte linker Hand,* as Timm Borah (Berlin: Rabenpresse, 1932);

*Terzinen für Thino* (Berlin: Rabenpresse, 1932);

*Das Schloß der Brüder Zanowsky: Eine unglaubwürdige Geschichte* (Berlin: Rabenpresse, 1933);

*Bäume am Rio de la Plata* (Buenos Aires: Transmare-Verlag, 1935);

*Neue Welt: Verse der Emigration* (Buenos Aires: Quadriga, 1939);

*Ich suchte Schmied . . . und fand Malva wieder* (Buenos Aires: Editorial Estrellas, 1941);

*Stefan Zweig: Eine Gedenkschrift* (Buenos Aires: Quadriga, 1943);

*Die schwarze Orchidee: Indianische Legenden* (Berlin: Zech, 1947);

*Occla, das Mädchen mit den versteinerten Augen: Eine indianische Legende* (Frankfurt am Main: Schauer, 1948);

*Paul Verlaine und sein Werk* (Berlin: Zech, 1949);

*Kinder vom Paraná: Roman* (Rudolstadt: Greifenverlag, 1952);

*Das rote Messer: Begegnungen mit Tieren und seltsamen Menschen* (Rudolstadt: Greifenverlag, 1953);

*Die Vögel des Herrn Langfoot: Roman* (Rudolstadt: Greifenverlag, 1954);

*Die grüne Flöte vom Rio Beni: Indianische Liebesgeschichten* (Rudolstadt: Greifenverlag, 1955);

*Die Ballade von einer Weltraumrakete* (Berlin-Friedenau: Trias, 1958);

*Abendgesänge und Landschaft der Insel Mara-Pampa* (Kronenburg: Zech, 1960);

*Die ewigen Gespräche: Deutsche Variationen nach Themen von Charles Péguy* (Berlin: Zech, 1960);

*Die Sonette vom Bauern* (Berlin: Zech, 1960);

*Venus Urania: Sieben Gesänge für Mirjam* (Berlin: Daphnis-Presse, 1961);

*Hymnen von den zwölf Fenstern: Gedichte* (Berlin-Friedenau: Zech, 1965);

*Die Häuser haben Augen aufgetan: Ausgewählte Gedichte,* edited by Manfred Wolter (Berlin & Weimar: Aufbau, 1976);

*Deutschland, dein Tänzer ist der Tod: Ein Tatsachen-Roman,* edited by Helmut Nitzschke (Rudolstadt: Greifenverlag, 1980);

*Menschen der Calle Tuyutí: Erzählungen aus dem Exil,* edited by Wolfgang Kießling (Rudolstadt: Greifenverlag, 1982);

*Vom schwarzen Revier zur Neuen Welt: Gesammelte Gedichte,* edited by Henry A. Smith (Munich & Vienna: Hanser, 1983);

*Michael M. irrt durch Buenos Aires: Aufzeichnungen eines Emigranten. Roman,* edited by Nitzschke (Rudolstadt: Greifenverlag, 1985);

*Von der Maas bis an die Marne: Ein Kriegstagebuch* (Rudolstadt: Greifenverlag, 1986).

OTHER: Léon Deubel, *Die rot durchrasten Nächte: Gedichte,* translated by Zech (Berlin: Officina Serpentis, 1914);

Stéphane Mallarmé, *Nachmittagstraum eines Fauns,* translated by Zech (Berlin: Privately printed, 1914);

Émile Verhaeren, *Die wogende Saat,* translated by Zech (Leipzig: Insel, 1917);

Hans Ehrenbaum-Degele, *Gedichte,* introduction by Zech (Leipzig: Insel, 1917);

Mallarmé, *Herodias: Ein Fragment,* translated by Zech (Berlin: Privately printed, 1919);

Honoré de Balzac, *Tante Lisbeth,* translated by Zech, 2 volumes (Berlin: Rowohlt, 1923);

*Der Mann am Kreuz: Geschichten zeitgenössischer Erzähler von Rhein und Ruhr,* edited by Zech (Berlin: Zentralverlag, 1923);

Arthur Rimbaud, *Erleuchtungen: Gedichte in Prosa,* translated by Zech (Leipzig: Wolkenwanderer-Verlag, 1924);

Christian Dietrich Grabbe, *Werke in Auswahl,* edited by Zech, 2 volumes (Berlin: Volksbühnen-Verlag, 1925);

Henry-Marx, *Triumph der Jugend: Ein Schauspiel in drei Akten,* translated by Zech (Leipzig: Schauspiel-Verlag, 1925);

Rimbaud, *Das Werk,* translated by Zech (Leipzig: Wolkenwanderer-Verlag, 1925); revised as *Das gesammelte Werk* (Leipzig: Wolkenwanderer-Verlag, 1927);

Rimbaud, *Das trunkene Schiff: Ballade,* translated by Zech (Bochum: Schacht, 1928);

François Villon, *Die Balladen und lasterhaften Lieder des Herrn François Villon,* translated by Zech (Weimar: Lichtenstein, 1931);

Friedrich Hölderlin, *Hiperión; o, El eremita en Grecia,* introduction by Zech (Buenos Aires: Emecé Editores, 1946);

Louise Charly Labé, *Die Liebesgedichte einer schönen Lyoneser Seilerin namens Louize Labé,* translated by Zech (Berlin: Zech, 1948; revised, Rudolstadt: Greifenverlag, 1956);

Rimbaud, *Das Herz unter der Soutane,* translated by Zech (Lorch & Stuttgart: Bürger, 1948);

Jorge Icaza, *Huasipungo: Ruf der Indios,* translated by Zech (Rudolstadt: Greifenverlag, 1952);

Balzac, *Gesammelte Werke,* translated by Zech (Hamburg: Rowohlt, 1952);

Rimbaud, *Sämtliche Dichtungen,* translated by Zech (Munich: Deutscher Taschenbuch Verlag, 1963);

*Altfranzösische Liebeslieder,* translated by Zech (Berlin: Friedenauer, 1965).

In the autobiographical notes accompanying Paul Zech's contributions to the famous verse anthology *Menschheitsdämmerung* (The Dawn and Dusk of Mankind, 1920), edited by Kurt Pinthus, the poet writes of the self-imposed challenge that caused him to leave school to work for two years in the coal mines and steel mills of the Ruhr, Belgium, and northern France. The attitudes which were fostered at that time by Zech's identification with the working class remained with him throughout his life. In the early days his prose depicted aspects of the existence he had known in the mills and mines; but even in his advanced years, when the author found himself encapsulated in an alien culture, his sympathies continued to be expressed for the subjects of exploitation.

Zech's socialistic impulses were infused initially with a Christian religiosity that was associated with vitalism and a reverent awe of nature. These attitudes evolved as did his writing, reflecting at turns his pastoral inclinations, the features of Worker's Poetry, the styles of expressionism and the New Objectivity, and various combinations of all of these. His work is by no means uniformly excellent; it provides, however, a fascinating variety of styles and themes which Zech employed during a lifetime of incredible productivity.

After moving from West Prussia, where he was born in Briesen near Thorn in 1881, Zech, the son of a teacher, attended school in Wuppertal-Elberfeld. In 1904 he married Helene Siemon. His first literary efforts were verse and included *Waldpastelle* (Forest Pastel, 1910), an idealized sylvan reflection of the area. Five additional verse collections, as well as translations of French poetry, followed from 1912 to 1914.

At the behest of Else Lasker-Schüler, a lifelong friend, Zech moved to Berlin when he was in his early thirties. His activities there included freelance writing, editorship of the journal *Das neue Pathos* irregularly from 1913 to 1920, and, later, employment in the municipal library. He was drafted in 1915 and served in Russia and France. In 1916 he was injured by a grenade and gas poisoning; as a result, he developed a heart condition from which he suffered for the rest of his life. In 1917 Zech turned to prose, recalling in *Der schwarze Baal* (Black Baal) his experiences in the mines and mills. Borrowing for the title the image of a Semitic deity favored by the expressionists, he describes the industrial scene—cables, chains, rails, cogged wheels, the humming of belts, the whine of drills, sparks, smoke, and steam from engines and chimneys. This kind of language is usually associated with the genre of Worker's Poetry, where it constitutes a paean to the joy of labor. Here Zech employs the vocabulary in prose; there is not a hint of joy, however, in *Der schwarze Baal.*

The term *demonic* was used by some critics to describe these seven tales. Pinthus characterized the work as a gigantic fresco painted with merciless objectivity to depict a realm of horror. The reader hears the cry of embittered and desperate people suffering deprivation in their most basic human needs. Baal or Satan is the agent of industrial accidents and death, events which sometimes befall a victim as retribution for a misdeed in his past. The character Nervil Munta, for example, pays for his murder of a strikebreaker when, before the eyes of the dead man's brother-in-law, he loses his balance and falls into the teeth of gigantic cogwheels. A miner who had strangled a comrade attempts to escape in an elevator which is yanked into the bowels of the earth by the claw of Satan. The death of a boy in a dynamite blast evokes terrible subterranean laughter; his fearful mother had forbidden him access to the mines where her husband died, but the father's spirit has claimed the boy's life from below. A hint of Zech's radical politics is evident in the tale of an anarchist, an engineer who destroys a mining complex to prevent the intervention of strikebreakers. Differences that had divided the workers are forgotten, and they unite, causing the anarchist to remark that his deed, although a crime, was honorable.

In 1918 Zech received the Kleist Prize for young writers. Zech's pacifistic drama *Gelandet* (Landed) dates from this year, and writing in the same vein continued in the years that followed.

*Das Grab der Welt: Eine Passion wider den Krieg auf Erden* (The World's Grave: A Passion against War on Earth, 1919) reflected Zech's attitudes and those of the expressionists during the final years of World War I. It was written in 1918, but its appearance was delayed for a year by military censors. Although the novel concludes with an expressionistic religious vision entitled "In the Beginning Was Peace," the body of the text consists of something very different. In a series of unconnected episodes narrated by a German infantry soldier on the western front, encampment, march, and terrible destruction are depicted. An impassioned description of carnage emerges—a grenade tears a soldier's body to bits, a field is strewn with the mangled corpses of humans and horses, a landscape is cluttered with wrecked and abandoned equipment.

The style and content resemble those of Erich Maria Remarque's *Im Westen nichts Neues* (translated as *All Quiet on the Western Front*), a novel that would appear a decade later. Zech's work, however, is less directly polemical than Remarque's. Profuse and lyrical descriptions of the country—the music of wind in the treetops, apple picking in gardens, views along the roadside—suggest that nature's beauty continues eternally despite the ravages of war. The author borrows from the palette of van Gogh to juxtapose vivid swatches of color, setting

the black of a roof against the blue of the sky, the white of a gable before yellows and vermilions in the background. A sense of youthful adventure and the invigorating and uplifting influence exerted by nature upon the soldiers dilute the pacifistic and antimilitaristic tone of the work.

Bearing the erroneous designation "novella," as did several of Zech's collections, *Das Ereignis* (The Event) appeared in 1920. It consists of nine sketches in which the author's prose often attains a lyrical quality—especially in passages depicting sexual ecstasy, of which there are many. The dominant figures are women: a lustful and devious widow; a girl who seduces a Bible-thumping clergyman; frigid, deceitful wives; and prostitutes. The settings include an industrial town on the lower Rhine; Belgian coal mines; and France under occupation during World War I, a scene populated by country girls and their German lovers. Representative of the collection is the tale "Jadwig," bearing the name of a Czech-born Jewess who serves both the French resistance forces and the occupying German troops as the town whore. A German officer for whom she has shown open contempt is charged with transporting her to a lazaret; when he attempts to assault her sexually, she repels him by exposing her disgustingly diseased body. Upon a bridge he looks to one side, allowing her to slip beneath the water and drown herself; later he pleads guilty before the authorities to her murder.

Two new verse collections also appeared in 1920, and the following three years saw a drama, an expanded edition of an early collection of poems, a new book of poetry, and a two-volume translation of Balzac. One or two new titles a year was average for Zech, and these often included a translation or a monograph dealing with a poet's life and works.

The zenith of Zech's productivity was reached in 1924, when he served as editor of the journal *Das dramatische Theater.* Four of his plays were published that year, including one dealing with the life of Rimbaud that would be directed on the Berlin stage by Erwin Piscator two years later. A prose translation of Rimbaud's poetry also appeared, as well as a collection of Zech's own verse and a prose work. The latter, *Die Reise um den Kummerberg* (Travels about the Mountain of Grief ), consists of twenty-six autobiographical sketches narrated in the first person. The author describes the sleepy peasant village on the Polish border where he was born, recalls a week as the guest of Lasker-Schüler, and indicts Wuppertal, the mountain of grief, for its destructive philistine influence. Employing a sparse, direct style consisting of short sentences and sentence fragments to achieve a staccato effect, Zech writes in language which the critics characterized variously as boldly original or insufferably affected. Light-and-color imagery creates a brilliant aura, and a strangely archaic quality is conveyed by Old Testament references. An impressionistic style renders scenes in fleeting glimpses with obscured details: movement in the city during a heavy rain; the teeming streets of Rotterdam and activity about the port; the proletariat inhabiting industrial towns; sights and sounds around the Potsdamerplatz in Berlin. A lyrical outpouring of joy and vitalism in the style of expressionism celebrates a country landscape and its creatures in the summer.

Zech attained his greatest popularity as a prose author in 1925 with a work that was promoted by a book club. *Die Geschichte einer armen Johanna* (The Story of a Poor Johanna) regaled feminine devotees of romance with the tale of a simple, almost homely, seamstress alone in the world; having "fallen," she discovers the life of a courtesan and pursues it with zest until overtaken by sickness and old age. Neglected and bedridden, she dies coughing blood like Camille, fulfilling her

*Woodcut by Willi Geißler for* Der Mann am Kreuz (The Man on the Cross), *a collection of stories edited by Zech in 1923*

fate "erzengelgleich, in frommster Erhabenheit" (like an archangel in the most pious grandeur). The wide audience reached by this novel felt that the work was a profound expression of the author's love and sympathy toward a victim of society. Less gracious voices characterized the work as sentimental kitsch. In this novel the smallest scenes are described minutely and often verbosely. Ecstatic outbursts, along with impressionistic, lyrical, and often vague philosophizing, accompany titillating sensuality. Johanna is not only a particular character; she is a representative of thousands of her sisters and a symbol of the Eternal Feminine as it exists through time and across cultural boundaries.

*Peregrins Heimkehr* (Peregrin's Return Home, 1925), on the other hand, achieved critical success but not nearly the popular reception accorded *Johanna*. Zech was hailed as a creator of poetic and stormy prose, an artist of language that is energetic and creative. The novel was found to be explosive in its intensity and power, suspenseful, and magically poetic. The musical prodigy Peregrin Schniewindt never overcomes his infatuation for his childhood sweetheart Mareija Wülfrath, an emancipated woman opposed to his denial of her equality, scornful of his purely physical regard for her, and determined to equal his success in her own career as a singer. Before her goal is achieved, Peregrin dies of a stroke without ever having possessed her. Driven by self-hate and guilt Mareija destroys her voice with chemicals and subjects her body to the sexual ravages of Rhenatus—a figure who emerges from nowhere, bearing a name derived from a pseudonym of the author. Moments of ecstasy inspired by music and eroticism are reflected in the grammatical convolutions of expressionism; the style is awkward and self-conscious at times, and the tone is often sentimental. A fashionable literary theme, criticism of the secondary school system, is incorporated in the novel through the character of Mareija's father, Professor Andreas Wülfrath.

The prose collection *Das törichte Herz* (The Foolish Heart, 1925) contains two pieces which drew particular attention. The title story recalls *Die Geschichte einer armen Johanna* in a plot that is not tragic but sad and sentimental, concerning two people who cannot bring themselves to surmount convention and confess their love. Their lives follow separate paths until the couple are united in death. A characteristic theme, the life of hardship and danger, returns in "Das Bergwerk" (The Mine Pit). Critics praised the author for his creative use of language and for the social conscience he revealed in his Marxist sympathies. Here Zech goes far beyond his customary regard for detail with a minute representation of the squalor, misery, disease, and deprivation faced by a married couple sharing a barrack with a dozen other workers. The work is in the tradition of Jack London and Upton Sinclair.

Throughout his life Zech was quite secretive; moreover, his self-disclosures were often disingenuous and contradictory. One has, therefore, to be cautious in lending credence to autobiographical details he provided. Zech's social democratic political sympathies were, however, no secret, and in 1932 a verse collection, *Berlin im Licht* (Berlin in the Light), subtitled *Gedichte linker Hand* (Poems of the Left Hand), appeared under the pseudonym Timm Borah. Zech was arrested in April 1933 and held briefly in Spandau Prison. Four months later he fled into exile and by December had joined his brother in Buenos Aires. Left behind in Berlin were his wife; two children; and Zech's companion since 1921, the actress and singer Hilde Herb, who committed suicide six years later.

Exile was a period of voluntary isolation for Zech. Supported in the early years by his brother and friends as well as by funds from acquaintances in the United States and meager royalties and honoraria, he wrote most prolifically. Sometimes employing pseudonyms, he contributed essays, satires, poems, and stories to the leading German-language newspaper, *Das Argentinische Tage- und Wochenblatt*, as well as to the Yiddish *Di Presse* and, after 1943, to the important exile journal *Deutsche Blätter*, published in Santiago, Chile.

During the late 1930s and early 1940s, after the financial help of his brother was withdrawn, Zech became more dependent on the charity of others. He obstinately refused to adapt himself to the ways of his host country and to the style of a city he heartily disliked. Advancing age hastened the deterioration of his health, and he suffered a fatal stroke on 7 September 1946 at the entrance to his residence.

Only four works were published during the exile years, but many other titles appeared posthumously. Nevertheless, it has been estimated that even now only one third of Zech's exile writing has seen print.

One group of works deals with materials purportedly gathered among the Indians. In the epilogue to *Die grüne Flöte vom Rio Beni* (The Green Flute of Rio Beni, 1955), the author relates that he traveled for years among South American tribes after mastering their dialects in order to collect their tales and legends. It has been ascertained, however, that Zech traveled very little, probably learned no Indian dialects, and employed as his sources two German-language collections of such tales. The eighteen love stories in *Die grüne Flöte* treat tribal customs, rites, and ceremonies dealing with magic and good and evil spirits. Tragic love provides the explanation for the color of a flower or of the setting sun, for the sighing and groaning of trees in the wind, and for the resemblance of a blossom to the human ear.

*Das rote Messer: Begegnungen mit Tieren und seltsamen Menschen* (The Red Knife: Encounters with Animals and Strange Humans, 1953) also belongs to this group of Zech's prose works. Here he provides what he calls eyewitness accounts of Bolivian Indians seized by fear of the black wasp; cannibals fishing in the Amazon; the damage and injury inflicted by grasshopper swarms, ant infestations, piranhas, and poisonous snakes; and German settlers living in the hinterlands.

German immigrants figure prominently in three prose works from Zech's exile years. German settlers in Zech's fiction are industrious, tenacious, and ruthless in the face of adversity. Their lot is precarious since an unsuccessful harvest may plunge them to the level of an Indian, a creature without rights. Quick to ally themselves with new immigrants are the Creoles, who are proud of their European extraction and "whiter" than the whites. They teach hatred of the Indians, who are exploited as peons by the few wealthy families who own practically all the property and control the economy.

*Ich suchte Schmied . . . und fand Malva wieder* (I Was Looking for Schmied . . . and Found Malva Again, 1941) was Zech's only novel published during his life in exile. Here he details the geography of Paraguay and Uruguay and levels social criticism at the Creoles for their domination of the Indians. The narrator, finding himself in Paraguay in 1933, seeks Rudolf Schmied, a writer whom he had known thirty years earlier in Berlin. During the course of the search he meets the Creole woman Malva, upon whom he forces his sexual attentions. Long after the discovery of Schmied the narrator witnesses the death of a woman from a poisonous bite; it is Malva, whose spirit is captured in the love tales of *Die grüne Flöte*, which are related by her mother.

Much more socially critical is *Kinder vom Paraná* (Children of Paraná, 1952), which treats the relationship between the races in Paraguay as reflected in the friendship between Cayru, an Indian boy, and Anne-Marie Coßmann, the daughter of a German settler. Through the years of childhood and puberty and into their late teens the two explore themselves and each other while concealed on their secret island, a paradise of innocence removed from the corruption and racism of the adult world. The novel moves between scenes of increasing intimacy and intervening periods of separation enforced by the girl's parents out of anxiety over her awakening sexuality as well as outrage and disgust at her relationship with an Indian. Detailed, realistic descriptions are given of a puma hunt, crab fishing, and Indian customs and tales in a matter-of-fact style far removed from the lyrical effusions evoked by nature in the author's early work. The novel concludes with the departure of the seventeen-year-old girl for school in Buenos Aires; unknown to her, the boat on which she rides swamps the canoe of Cayru in water infested with piranha.

The central figure of *Die Vögel des Herrn Langfoot* (Mr. Langfoot's Birds, 1954) is a German immigrant in Argentina. Zech relates in a light and very readable style his amusing and ribald adventures inspired by the multitude of birds which, according to the German idiom, inhabit the head of someone who does not think straight. Turning his back on commercial undertakings in Buenos Aires, such as selling razor blades and shining shoes, Langfoot rides the rails into the hinterlands in search of work in the fields and mines. He copulates joyously with large-bosomed women of all ages, nationalities, and races while he moves around the edges of the German colony. Finally, back in the city, he finds a highly paid position in a German-owned weaving mill.

A collection of stories, sketches, and autobiographical pieces appeared in 1982 as *Menschen der Calle Tuyutí: Erzählungen aus dem Exil* (People of Tuyutí Street: Tales from Exile). The title story depicts the life of a poor Indian family in a slum on the outskirts of Buenos Aires. Carlos Chaca is driven from his home by his daughter to gain room for the man she takes to live with her and her children. The intruder then kills Chaca to gain the shed the old man inhabits to use it for a smokehouse. A common theme in Zech's exile works that appears in *Menschen der Calle Tuyutí* is the sexuality of Indian girls and women: they are driven mad with desire by the Pampero, the wind from the pampas, behaving grotesquely in their animal responses. Themes from earlier days are recalled in the strike of tannery workers, the entrance of strikebreakers, and preparations for revolution. Ten scenes from the "well-aired city," as Zech calls

Buenos Aires, consist of sketches of its inhabitants and their manners as observed on a streetcar and on the streets. An indictment is leveled at the city for its lack of social conscience. Personal reflections recall prewar Germany and express the author's longing for Berlin. Longer pieces detail the misery of Indians and their gradual extermination in the Gran Chaco during a war between Paraguay and Brazil manipulated by Standard Oil and Royal Dutch Oil. The only story not set in South America describes the life of a Chinese laborer who works for the revolution; his wife's belief in religion's power to improve their lot reveals itself as futile.

Zech's major prose work, a significant contribution to the genre of exile literature, is the novel *Deutschland, dein Tänzer ist der Tod* (Germany, You Are Dancing with Death, 1980). Begun in Germany in February 1933, the unfinished manuscript accompanied Zech to Buenos Aires and was probably completed in 1937. The title of the work is a variation of the last line of a 1918 poem by Zech in which he admonished Berlin to come to its senses rather than indulge in excess and depravity while young men were being destroyed on the battlefields. In the novel Germany is similarly warned against abandoning herself to the treacherous allurements of fascism. The novel reveals the terror and repression embodied in the Third Reich. Instead of a unified plot there is a series of episodes involving a handful of characters, each of whom reappears from time to time to demonstrate the response of individuals as they confront the growing strength of fascism. Zech displays the behavior characteristic of various types of persons: intellectuals distant from reality, too irresolute or cowardly to acknowledge the dangers of fascism and draw the consequences; opportunists who turn at the prospect of increased business and profits from the Social Democratic party to the Nazis; pacifists, socialists, and Communists who, for self-preservation, unite to pursue a common goal in the Unity Front; brutal storm troopers who commit atrocities. The second part of the book concentrates on internal resistance to the Third Reich: the organization of cells and the distribution of propaganda; the arrest, torture, and escape of resistance fighters; the advisability of using terrorism as a weapon; defections by some Nazis to the underground; condemnation of exile authors for failing to inform the world about the evils of fascism; the flight of the central figure, Grätz, into exile.

For the most part, Zech employs the objective documentary style of Remarque and Anna Seghers that conveys the impression of factual reporting. A failure to preserve consistency, however, results in vague philosophizing, stilted conversations, tendentiousness, literary gossip, and digressions. The novel remains, nevertheless, a bold statement of the author's naive optimism which extended well into the 1930s.

Concurrently with his work on *Deutschland, dein Tänzer ist der Tod,* Zech occupied himself with another extensive exile novel, which he probably concluded about a year later, in 1938 or 1939: *Michael M. irrt durch Buenos Aires: Aufzeichnungen eines Emigranten* (Michael M. Goes Astray in Buenos Aires: Notes of an Emigrant, 1985). The name Michael M. or Michael Michel was a pseudonym which had been employed by Zech in the past. Zech assumes the fiction that he has edited the notes of Michael M., thereby establishing a distance between himself and the text which lends an air of historical objectivity. Simultaneously he indulges his characteristic reluctance to divulge anything about himself, for Michael M. is not identical with Zech. The first three chapters of the novel consist of third-person narration by the editor to introduce the reader to the central figure. Michael M.'s arrival in Buenos Aires in September 1938 is described, then a flashback depicts events five years earlier when he fell under the suspicion of the authorities and was dismissed from his position as chief justice. The last of these introductory chapters describes his leave-taking from his lover Michaeline, who is remembered with loneliness and longing throughout the novel. This character was based on Hilde Herb. The rest of the novel is told in the first person as Michael relates his impressions of Buenos Aires—its noise, heat, and humidity, and the sleeplessness, headaches, and heart problems it induces. The text bristles with resentment toward the German-speaking colony from which he isolates himself because of their condescension and the "bolshevistic fragrance" they fancy he brings to their nostrils and toward authors whom he regards as having reached accommodation with the Third Reich—Gottfried Benn, Hans Fallada, Ernst Lissauer, and the Arbeiterdichter (worker-writers) Heinrich Lersch, Max Barthel, and Karl Bröger.

The novel is studded with colorful episodes as Michael encounters other exiles such as Heinrich Rehberger, a former book printer living as a tramp; Anne Hous, a beautiful young Jewish widow who rises to the inner circles of high society thanks to her gifts as a pianist; and a liberal Swiss newspaper editor (based on Ernesto Alemann) who gives the hapless Michael a chance to prove himself as a writer, an opportunity at which he fails and thereby

initiates a two-week period of severe depression. Michael's decline reaches a nadir early on, and his status is maintained at this point until relieved by occasional episodes which revive hope for the prospects of his writing. He sustains himself as a peddler with his wares about his neck until he is invited to write an exile novel in a competition sponsored by the American Guild for German Cultural Freedom. When his finances are terminated, however, he returns to a state of deepest depression and peddles cigarettes to avert utter ruin. A position as a multilingual secretary for 150 pesos a month rescues him from this social station, and he experiences a renewed sense of human dignity; at the conclusion of the book he avows in the present tense his determination to maintain himself in this state continuously.

During the postwar years and into the 1960s Zech did not regain the readership he once enjoyed, notwithstanding the efforts of his son Rudolf and the continuing support of his early publisher, Greifenverlag. Exhibitions of Zech's books, manuscripts, letters, photos, and wood and linoleum cuts were held at archives and museums in Marbach, Wuppertal, Dortmund, and Berlin, but his name caused barely a stir.

During the 1970s the situation began to change. *Der schwarze Baal* and the verse collection *Die eiserne Brücke* (The Iron Bridge, 1914) were made available once more by Kraus Reprint in 1973, and the drama *Gelandet* (1918) was added six years later. In the intervening period the first Zech scholarship appeared—an annotated bibliography, a study of his drama, and a work treating Zech in Argentinean exile. In 1976 the Aufbau publishing house brought forth an edition of his poetry gleaned from a dozen collections. In 1980 *Deutschland, dein Tänzer ist der Tod* appeared in both East and West Germany; the next year saw new editions of *Kinder von Paraná* and *Die grüne Flöte,* and *Menschen der Calle Tuyutí* appeared in 1982. One more title was published in 1983, and in that year Zech's translation of François Villon reached its seventeenth edition. In 1985 the collected letters of Zech and Stefan Zweig were published, as was *Michael M. irrt durch Buenos Aires.* The fortieth anniversary of Zech's death was observed in 1986 by the appearance of his World War I diary *Von der Maas bis an die Marne* (From the Maas to the Marne). The Zech "boom" shows every sign of continuing.

**Letters:**

*Stefan Zweig/Paul Zech: Briefe 1910-1942*, edited by Donald D. Daviau (Frankfurt am Main: Fischer, 1986).

**Bibliography:**

Ward B. Lewis, *Poetry and Exile: An Annotated Bibliography of the Works and Criticism of Paul Zech* (Bern: Lang, 1975).

**References:**

Donald G. Daviau, "Paul Zech as an Interpreter and Mediator of South America," in *Kulturelle Wechselbeziehungen im Exil—Exile Across Cultures*, edited by Helmut F. Pfanner (Bonn: Bouvier Verlag Herbert Grundmann, 1986), pp. 164-179;

Alfred Hübner, *Das Weltbild im Drama Paul Zechs* (Bern: Lang, 1975);

Fritz Hüser, ed., *Paul Zech* (Dortmund: Städtische Volksbüchereien/Wuppertal: Stadtbibliothek, 1961);

Wolfgang Kießling, "Phantastisches und Realistisches: Paul Zech," in his *Exil in Latein Amerika* (Frankfurt am Main: Rödenberg, 1981), pp. 324-352;

Ward B. Lewis, " 'Die Ballade von einer seligen Sommerversöhnung': Notes to an Unpublished Poem by Paul Zech," *Modern Language Notes*, 88 (April 1973): 574-581;

Lewis, "The Path of the Wheel in the Lyric Poetry of Paul Zech," *South Atlantic Bulletin*, 38 (November 1973): 54-61;

Lewis, "The Poet and the Tower: A Development in the Imagery of Paul Zech," *German Life & Letters*, new series 24 ( January 1971): 174-182;

Arnold Spitta, *Paul Zech im südamerikanischen Exil 1933-1946* (Berlin: Colloquium, 1978).

**Papers:**

Paul Zech's papers are held by the Schiller-Nationalmuseum, Marbach, and the Akademie der Künste, West Berlin.

# Carl Zuckmayer
## (27 December 1896-18 January 1977)

Hans Wagener
*University of California, Los Angeles*

BOOKS: *Kreuzweg: Drama* (Munich: Wolff, 1921);

*Der fröhliche Weinberg: Lustspiel in drei Akten* (Berlin: Propyläen, 1925);

*Der Baum: Gedichte* (Berlin: Propyläen, 1926);

*Ein Bauer aus dem Taunus und andere Geschichten* (Berlin: Propyläen, 1927);

*Schinderhannes: Schauspiel in vier Akten* (Berlin: Propyläen, 1927);

*Katharina Knie: Ein Seiltänzerstück in vier Akten* (Berlin: Propyläen, 1929);

*Kakadu-Kakada: Ein Kinderstück* (Berlin: Propyläen, 1929);

*Der Hauptmann von Köpenick: Ein deutsches Märchen in drei Akten* (Berlin: Propyläen, 1930); translated by David Portman as *The Captain of Köpenick: A Modern Fairy Tale in Three Acts* (London: Bles, 1932); translated by Carl Richard Mueller as *The Captain of Köpenick*, in *German Drama between the Wars*, edited by George E. Wellwarth (New York: Dutton, 1974), pp. 179-296;

*Die Affenhochzeit: Novelle* (Berlin: Propyläen, 1932); translated by F. A. Beaumont as "Monkey Wedding," *Argosy*, 23 (March 1938): 53-69;

*Gerhart Hauptmann: Rede zu seinem siebzigsten Geburtstag, gehalten bei der offiziellen Feier der Stadt Berlin* (N.p., 1932);

*Eine Liebesgeschichte* (Berlin: Fischer, 1934);

*Der Schelm von Bergen: Ein Schauspiel* (Berlin: Propyläen, 1934);

*Salwàre; oder, Die Magdalena von Bozen: Roman* (Berlin: Fischer, 1935; Vienna: Bermann-Fischer, 1936); translated by Moray Firth as *The Moon in the South* (London: Secker & Warburg, 1937); translation republished as *The Moon Rides Over* (New York: Viking, 1937);

*Ein Sommer in Österreich: Erzählung* (Vienna: Bermann-Fischer, 1937);

*Herr über Leben und Tod* (Stockholm: Bermann-Fischer, 1938);

*Pro Domo* (Stockholm: Bermann-Fischer, 1938);

*Second Wind,* translated by Elizabeth Reynolds Hapgood, with an introduction by Dorothy

*Carl Zuckmayer (photo by Sven Simon, Bonn)*

Thompson (New York: Doubleday, Doran, 1940; London: Harrap, 1941);

*Carlo Mierendorff: Porträt eines deutschen Sozialisten* (New York: Selbstverlag, 1944; Berlin: Suhrkamp, 1944);

*Der Seelenbräu: Erzählung* (Stockholm: Bermann-Fischer, 1945);

*Des Teufels General: Drama in drei Akten* (Stockholm: Bermann-Fischer, 1946); translated by Ingrid G. and William F. Gilbert as *The Devil's General*, in *Masters of German Drama*, edited by H. M. Block and R. G. Shedd (New York: Random House, 1962), pp. 911-958;

*Gesammelte Werke*, 4 volumes (Stockholm: Bermann-Fischer, 1947-1952);

*Die Brüder Grimm: Ein deutscher Beitrag zur Humanität* (Frankfurt am Main: Suhrkamp, 1948);

*Barbara Blomberg: Ein Stück in drei Akten mit Vorspiel und Epilog* (Amsterdam & Vienna: Bermann-Fischer, 1949);

*Der Gesang im Feuerofen: Drama in drei Akten* (Frankfurt am Main & Berlin: Fischer, 1950);

*Die langen Wege; Ein Stück Rechenschaft: Rede* (Frankfurt am Main: Fischer, 1952);

*Ulla Winblad; oder, Musik und Leben des Carl Michael Bellman* (Frankfurt am Main & Berlin: Fischer, 1953);

*Engele von Loewen: Erzählungen* (Zurich: Classen, 1955);

*Das kalte Licht: Drama in drei Akten* (Frankfurt am Main: Fischer, 1955);

*Fünfzig Jahre Düsseldorfer Schauspielhaus, 1905-1955* (N.p., 1955);

*Ein Blick auf den Rhein: Rede, gehalten bei der feierlichen Verleihung der Würde eines Doktor honoris causa der Philosophischen Fakultät der Universität Bonn am 10. Mai 1957. Mit einer Einführungsrede von Benno von Wiese und Kaiserswaldau* (Bonn: Hanstein, 1957);

*Die Fastnachtsbeichte: Eine Erzählung* (Frankfurt am Main: Fischer, 1959); translated by John and Necke Mander as *Carnival Confession* (London: Methuen, 1961);

*Ein Weg zu Schiller* (Frankfurt am Main: Fischer, 1959);

*Gedichte* (Frankfurt am Main: Fischer, 1960);

*Gesammelte Werke*, 4 volumes (Frankfurt am Main & Berlin: Fischer, 1960);

*Hinein ins volle Menschenleben*, edited by Franz Theodor Csokor (Graz & Vienna: Stiasny, 1961);

*Die Uhr schlägt eins: Ein historisches Drama aus der Gegenwart* (Frankfurt am Main: Fischer, 1961);

*Festrede zum vierhundertjährigen Bestehen des Humanistischen Gymnasiums in Mainz, gehalten am 27. Mai 1962* (Mainz: von Zabern, 1962);

*Ein voller Erdentag: Zu Gerhart Hauptmanns hundertstem Geburtstag* (Frankfurt am Main: Fischer, 1962);

*Eine Weihnachtsgeschichte* (Zurich: Arche, 1962);

*Geschichten aus vierzig Jahren* (Frankfurt am Main: Fischer, 1963);

*Three Stories*, edited by D. Barlow (London: Oxford University Press, 1963);

*Das Leben des Horace A. W. Tabor: Ein Stück aus den Tagen der letzten Könige* (Frankfurt am Main: Fischer, 1964);

*Als wär's ein Stück von mir: Horen der Freundschaft* (Frankfurt am Main: Fischer, 1966); translated by Richard and Clara Winston as *A Part of Myself* (London: Secker & Warburg, 1970; New York: Harcourt Brace Jovanovich, 1970);

*Meisterdramen* (Frankfurt am Main: Fischer, 1966);

*Scholar zwischen gestern und morgen: Ein Vortrag gehalten in der Universität Heidelberg anläßlich seiner Ernennung zum Ehrenbürger am 23. November 1967* (Heidelberg: Brausdruck, 1967);

*Meistererzählungen* (Frankfurt: Fischer, 1967);

*Carl Zuckmayer: Eine Auslese*, edited by Wolfgang Mertz (Vienna & Heidelberg: Überreuter, 1968);

*Memento zum zwanzigsten Juli 1969* (Frankfurt am Main: Fischer, 1969);

*Auf einem Weg im Frühling: Erzählung; Wiedersehen mit einer Stadt: Aus dem Stegreif erzählt* (Salzburg: Residenz, 1970);

*Über die musische Bestimmung des Menschen: Rede zur Eröffnung der Salzburger Festspiele 1970*, edited by Max Kaindl-Hönig, with English translation by Richard Rickett and French translation by Martha Eissler (Salzburg: Festungsverlag, 1970);

*Stücke meines Lebens: Mit persönlichen Einleitungen des Autors* (Frankfurt am Main: Büchergilde Gutenberg, 1971);

*Henndorfer Pastorale* (Salzburg: Residenz, 1972);

*Der Rattenfänger: Eine Fabel* (Frankfurt am Main: Fischer, 1975);

*Aufruf zum Leben: Porträts und Zeugnisse aus bewegten Zeiten* (Frankfurt am Main: Fischer, 1976);

*Werkausgabe in zehn Bänden, 1920-1975*, 10 volumes (Frankfurt am Main: Fischer, 1976);

*Gedichte* (Frankfurt am Main: Fischer, 1977);

*Einmal, wenn alles vorüber ist: Briefe an Kurt Grell, Gedichte, Dramen, Prosa aus den Jahren 1914-1920* (Frankfurt am Main: Fischer, 1981).

RECORDINGS: *Als wär's ein Stück von mir; Des Teufels General*, read by Zuckmayer (Preiserrecords PR 3187, 1968);

*Ein Stück von mir; Gedichte*, read by Zuckmayer (Exlibris EL 12249, 1975).

OTHER: Karl Otto Paetel, *Deutsche innere Emigration: Anti-nationalsozialistische Zeugnisse aus Deutschland*, contributions by Zuckmayer and Dorothy Thompson (New York: Krause, 1946);

Ödön Horváth, *Ein Kind unserer Zeit*, commemorative speech by Zuckmayer (Vienna: Berglandverlag, 1951);

Gerhart Hauptmann, *Herbert Engelmann: Drama in vier Akten*, completed by Zuckmayer (Munich: Beck, 1952);

W. Krauss, *Das Schauspiel meines Lebens: Einem Freund erzählt*, introduction by Zuckmayer (Stuttgart: Goverts, 1958);

I. Engelsing-Malek, *Amor Fati in Zuckmayers Dramen*, foreword by Zuckmayer (Konstanz: Rosgarten, 1960).

Until 1966, when his autobiography *Als wär's ein Stück von mir* (translated as *A Part of Myself*, 1970) appeared, Carl Zuckmayer was known mainly as the author of highly successful plays. He had been one of the most popular playwrights of the Weimar Republic and, next to Bertolt Brecht, he was the most widely performed dramatist in West Germany after World War II. His comedy *Der fröhliche Weinberg* (The Merry Vineyard, 1925), with its blunt realism, had been hailed as the end of expressionism in drama. *Der Hauptmann von Köpenick* (1930; translated as *The Captain of Köpenick*, 1932), an excellent example of neorealism in drama and probably Zuckmayer's best play, was a sharp attack on Prussian militarism which was to brand the author as an irreconcilable enemy of National Socialism. After the war, *Des Teufels General* (1946; translated as *The Devil's General*, 1962), about a general who reluctantly aligns himself with the Third Reich out of his love for flying, mirrored the conflict of many Germans and placed its author in the forefront of German dramatists of the postwar era. His subsequent plays, however, were not as successful, since Zuckmayer did not change his humanistic world view or his dramatic techniques to conform to the latest developments in German drama. But in the 1960s Zuckmayer achieved literary fame with the publication of his autobiography, which soon became a best-seller in Germany. Furthermore, the two editions of his collected works in 1960 and 1976, as well as the collections of his stories and short novels which were published in 1963 and 1967, made it clear that Zuckmayer was not only one of the best German dramatists of the twentieth century but also an important author of prose fiction. Several of his novellas, such as *Der Seelenbräu* (The Soul Brew, 1945) and *Die Fastnachtsbeichte* (1959; translated as *Carnival Confession*, 1961), are masterpieces which achieved high sales in paperback editions.

Carl Zuckmayer was born on 27 December 1896 in Nackenheim to Carl and Amalie Friedericke Auguste Goldschmidt Zuckmayer; his father owned a factory in nearby Mainz that produced caps for wine bottles. His grandfather on his mother's side was originally Jewish, but in his youth he had converted to Catholicism, a religion that Zuckmayer embraced throughout his life. Zuckmayer spent a happy childhood in and around Mainz, where he attended the local public schools, including the humanistic Gymnasium. With the outbreak of World War I in August 1914 he enlisted in the German army. His initial patriotic enthusiasm soon gave way to disillusionment and pacificistic ideas; these were expressed in his first published poems, which appeared in the magazine *Die Aktion* in 1917. By the end of the war he had become a lieutenant. He enrolled at the University of Frankfurt, then at the University of Heidelberg, but abandoned his studies to turn to writing. A youthful marriage to Annemarie Seidel in 1920 ended in divorce in less than a year.

Success did not come easily. His first play, *Kreuzweg* (Crossroads, 1921), which was written in the expressionist style, closed after three performances in Berlin, and Zuckmayer, who had moved to the capital, had to take a series of odd jobs in order to survive. After working during the summer of 1922 in a mine in Norway, he finally obtained a position as a Dramaturg (literary advisor) with the municipal theater in Kiel; but he was fired after his adaptation of Terence's *The Eunuch* was closed by the police on grounds of obscenity. In 1925 Zuckmayer and Brecht were employed by Max Reinhardt's Deutsches Theater in Berlin.

Zuckmayer never completed his remarkable first piece of prose fiction, "Sitting Bull: Ein Indianer-Roman" (Sitting Bull: An Indian Novel), which he wrote in 1924-1925, because his literary creed changed while he was working on it. It was first published in his *Gesammelte Werke* (Collected Works, 1960). Although he makes use of historical facts about Custer's last stand of 1876, it is the fictional world of James Fenimore Cooper and Karl May that determines the characters and atmosphere of the fragment. In the tradition of European literature, Zuckmayer contrasts the noble savages with the decadent whites who rape the Indian women and slaughter the buffalo. In its style the work not only attempts to emulate the narrative characteristics of Indian tales and ancient epics but also betrays the author's proximity to literary expressionism at this time in his career. Zuckmayer's depiction of man's symbiosis with nature in the

*Scene from the premiere of Zuckmayer's comedy* Der Fröhliche Weinberg *at the Theater am Schiffbauerdamm, Berlin, 22 December 1925. The play was hailed as the end of expressionism in drama.*

character of his Indian hero as well as in the only positively drawn white protagonist, the hunter Florymont, has parallels with the poems in his collection *Der Baum* (The Tree, 1926).

In 1925 Zuckmayer married the Austrian actress Alice Herdan, who had a two-year-old daughter, Michaela, from a previous marriage. A daughter, Winnetou, was born in 1926. That year, following the success of *Der fröhliche Weinberg,* for which he received the Kleist Prize, Zuckmayer was able to purchase a summer home, the Weismühl, in Henndorf, Austria, near Salzburg.

Zuckmayer's fascination with life in its most basic forms and his belief in the basic goodness of man find expression in his collection of stories *Der Bauer aus dem Taunus und andere Geschichten* (A Farmer from the Taunus and Other Stories, 1927). "Die Geschichte vom Tümpel" (The Story of a Pond) borrows many metaphorical elements from his lyrical poetry. It is the minute description of the annual life cycle of a pond, a story of eating and being eaten and the seemingly endless breeding of insects, larvae, batrachians, and other small animals engaged in the struggle for survival. A former student of zoology, Zuckmayer believed in the goodness of all forms of life, no matter how small. This story documents the influence on him of Darwin, through the works of Ernst Haeckel, and of

the vitalism of Friedrich Nietzsche and Hans Driesch. The idea of the victoriousness of life in spite of defeat and death is also found in "Ein paar Brocken Erde" (A Few Lumps of Earth). In this story, an American farmer fights for his land, which the government has designated as an inundation area for the Mississippi River. At the end of the story the farmer dies, but his corpse serves as nourishment for innumerable insects and other small animals.

The theme of the triumph of life is central to several stories for which World War I serves as the background. In "Geschichte von einer Geburt" (Story of a Birth), which Zuckmayer claimed was based on an actual experience of his, three exhausted soldiers at the western front assist an animalistic farm girl in giving birth. The birth is an event of elemental power in which the forces of life overcome the surrounding atmosphere of death. In the title story, "Der Bauer aus dem Taunus," a farmer who has been invalided out of the army leaves his young pregnant wife to return to the Russian front. While there, he saves the child he had had with a Russian woman. With a relentless survival instinct, and against all odds, he succeeds in bringing the child home to his wife, who welcomes her husband and the other woman's child with open arms and without question. The story

testifies to the innate goodness of the simple people, shows that national boundaries are mere arbitrary lines of demarcation, and, again, reflects the
triumph of life over the forces of war.

In another story in the collection, "Die Geschichte einer Entenjagd" (The Story of a Duck
Hunt), a Norwegian wife keeps a visiting foreigner's lack of hunting skills secret by covering up for
his lie about some ducks, thereby placing humanity
and affection over manliness. Thus, again, Zuckmayer expresses his affirmation of life and the basic
goodness of human nature.

In 1929 Zuckmayer received both the Georg
Büchner Prize and the Heidelberg Festival Performance Prize. The following year he had one of
his greatest theatrical successes with the comedy
*Der Hauptmann von Köpenick*, about an ex-convict's
struggles with the Prussian bureaucracy. He continued to express his creed of the goodness of man
in his stories published during the 1930s. In "Eine
Weihnachtsgeschichte" (A Christmas Story), published in the *Vossische Zeitung* in 1931 and in book
form in 1962, the plot of "Geschichte von einer
Geburt" is transferred to the environment of a
large city. On Christmas Eve 1929, a delicately built

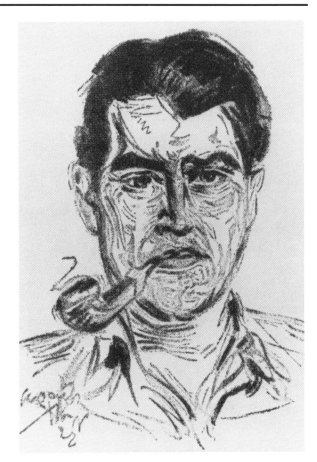

*Lithograph of Zuckmayer by Emil Stumpp*

young foreign woman gives birth in the back room
of a Berlin pub, where the innkeeper and a group
of hardened taxi drivers help her to regain her
strength. The original Christmas story is repeated
in the modern environment of the seemingly un-
caring large city; even in a time of economic crisis,
people lend a helping hand.

The sentimentality which this story derives
not only from its use of Berlin dialect but also from
its biblical overtones is missing in *Die Affenhochzeit*
(1932; translated as "Monkey Wedding," 1938). A
painter, who cannot think of giving away one of
his own works, gives a rhesus monkey to his lawyer
friend as a wedding present. The animal causes
utter confusion, so the friend is happy when a lady
whose son has recently died takes it home. Zuckmayer tries to contrast the natural sincerity and
enthusiasm of the artist with the arrogant display
of materialism and self-interest of the Berlin
bourgeoisie, but this social criticism is only implicit.
The life-style of the painter and his bohemian acquaintances—perhaps a depiction of the life-style
of Zuckmayer and his circle of friends at that

*Zuckmayer in 1928 (Ullstein)*

*Dust jacket for Zuckmayer's 1930 comedy attacking Prussian militarism (Lilly Library, Indiana University)*

time—is unconvincing as a positive model.

　　Following Hitler's rise to power in 1933, performances of Zuckmayer's plays were forbidden in Germany. Zuckmayer and his family stayed in involuntary exile in their summer home in Austria, where they enjoyed a few idyllic years until Hitler annexed the country in 1938. During these years, Zuckmayer made a number of trips to London to work on screenplays for films produced by Alexander Korda.

　　Zuckmayer's last book to appear in Germany before censorship of the Third Reich took effect was *Eine Liebesgeschichte* (A Love Story). Following the burning of the Reichstag on 27 February 1933, the Ullstein publishing company stopped serializing the novella in its *Berliner Illustrierte Zeitung;* only after Zuckmayer's angry protests was the serialization resumed. The Fischer firm published the work in book form the next year. The story deals

with the clash of love and soldierly honor in Prussian history. Cavalry Captain Jost Fredersdorff falls in love with his friend's mistress, a former opera singer. When his request for permission to marry her is denied by his superiors, he seeks and is granted a discharge from the army; but when the battle-hardened soldiers of his old squadron spurn him, he shoots himself to death. Fredersdorff's existence cannot be separated from his social class or from his experiences as a soldier; human existence cannot be based on love alone, no matter how absolute it may be.

　　Zuckmayer's last work to be published in Austria before its annexation by the Third Reich was the novel *Ein Sommer in Österreich* (A Summer in Austria, 1937), originally conceived as a film script, in which a group of eccentric Englishmen, who try

*Dust jacket for Zuckmayer's comic 1932 novella about the confusion caused when a monkey is given as a wedding present (Lilly Library, Indiana University)*

*Dust jacket for Zuckmayer's melodramatic 1938 novel dealing
with the subject of euthanasia (Lilly Library,
Indiana University)*

mother-in-law. Their child is born with severe brain damage and will probably never develop normally. For Norbert and his mother the child is a social embarrassment, and Norbert coldly advocates euthanasia. Lucile takes the child to a monastery in northern France, where she falls in love with Raymond, a country doctor who represents all the qualities of feeling and caring that Norbert lacks. When the child dies, Lucile tries to run away with Raymond to America; but on the way to the harbor Raymond dies in a train accident. Norbert, whose character has changed, reunites with his wife and forgives her. The story, with its soap-opera twists and reversals, is ultimately unconvincing; but in his rejection of euthanasia, which was gaining a macabre actuality in Germany at that time, Zuckmayer demonstrates that his world view is diametrically opposed to that of the Nazis.

All of Zuckmayer's stories of the 1930s are action-packed and have a clear story line; but his only full-length novel of this time, *Salwàre; oder, Die Magdalena von Bozen* (1935; translated as *The Moon in the South,* 1937), has neither of these qualities. It is never clear whether the characters are real or mere projections of the narrator's imagination. The meager plot does not develop in a logical manner and is interrupted by long conversations. The narrator, the painter Thomas Stolperer, visits his friend Firmin, a nobleman, in his castle near Bozen. Firmin is always in the company of his sister Magdalena, who has a mysterious relation to the moon. She rejects Stolperer's advances because she is soon to be married to the Italian Mario. Stolperer leaves the spiritual atmosphere of the castle and takes up residence in the valley, where he has an affair with the sensuous Mena. Firmin and his sister die in a mountain-climbing accident; Stolperer's relationship with Mena comes to an end, and after a trip to Africa he returns to his home in the north to begin painting again.

Mena is an abbreviation for Menega, the local dialect form for Magdalena. This identity of names indicates that the spiritual, mythical Magdalena and the sensuous, earthly Mena are opposites who complement each other, representing two aspects of woman. The opposite spirits of the two women are mirrored in the atmospheres surrounding them: the intellectuality, spirituality, fruitless discussions, and decadence in the castle are contrasted with the common and vile elements in Mena's environment: her brother is a smuggler and her father is a fence. It seems that Stolperer must disassociate himself from both in order to be able to work again in the cool atmosphere of the north.

to emulate the customs of the native population, rent a castle in Austria. In the end, after a great deal of confusion, several pairs of lovers find each other. Mistaken identities, the invention of nonexistent lovers, wrong perceptions—all the ingredients of a situation comedy—are employed in order to create a spirit of careless gaiety diametrically opposed to the political developments of the time. The book does not rise above the type of novel which is serialized in provincial newspapers and has not been reprinted in Zuckmayer's collected works.

Love is also the theme of *Herr über Leben und Tod* (Master of Life and Death, 1938), which, in its melodramatic plot, also betrays its origin as a film treatment. The famous surgeon and heart specialist Norbert marries Lucile, the daughter of a poor French nobleman. He takes her home to London, where her life is made miserable by an overbearing

The novel's strength is in its descriptions of nature, especially the depictions of the mountains at night. The lengthy conversations rarely arrive at a conclusion and are devoid of clear statements; only now and then are Zuckmayer's ideas about the interconnection of all life mentioned. Europe appears as an old, decadent continent, while America stands as a symbol of youthfulness and hope. The book lacks concrete references to the time in which it was written: the fact that Magdalena's fiancé is a fascist, for example, is not incorporated into the political or philosophical discussions. In its lack of concreteness, the novel resembles Thomas Mann's *Der Zauberberg* (1924; translated as *The Magic Mountain*, 1927), but it lacks the lucidity of Mann's work. It was not successful either in German or in English translation.

In *Pro Domo* (1938) Zuckmayer reflects upon his life in relation to the political situation at that time. In 1938 he immigrated with his family first to Switzerland and, in the following year, to the United States by way of Cuba. Soon after his arrival in the United States, he wrote another autobiographical account, *Second Wind* (1940), which was only published in English. In *Second Wind*, Zuckmayer is not, as in *Pro Domo*, looking back in order to clarify the present situation; he is looking forward with a view to conquering life in the New World. The epilogue reads like a manifesto: "The dream of today, the deed of tomorrow, is the creation of a new world entity in which the outworn, decayed contradictions of society will be merged and equalized. It must be the creation of a new synthesis between labor and value, between raw material and finished product, between matter and form—or to go back to the ever-lasting formula, between nature and spirit. . . . This is the true and only meaning of all revolutions, including that of our times: to restore the natural relationship of man to organic life whenever it has been disturbed or destroyed."

*Second Wind* contains a story, "Angela of Louvain," which was published here for the first time; the German version, "Engele von Loewen," first appeared in 1955 as the title story in a collection. In a bar in Brussels at the end of World War I the narrator meets a girl who sells cigarettes. Because of her angelic innocence, she is being protected from the customers' advances by the other girls who work there. The narrator learns that she had met a young German soldier in the village where she was staying with her aunt; three years later, he had returned as a lieutenant and won her love. Now, at the end of the war, she is persecuted by her countrymen for her fraternization with the enemy. She and her lover, who has come to look for her, are saved by returning Belgian troops. The story is written in a realistic manner; Zuckmayer was intimately familiar with the atmosphere of World War I, with the Belgian villages, as well as with the boisterous gaiety in the bars of Brussels. But amid this chaotic atmosphere, the heroine possesses the attributes of a saint, thus adding hagiographic characteristics to the story. Engele's innocent, absolute love for the enemy soldier proves itself in the middle of an absolutely hostile environment. The story expresses Zuckmayer's belief in the possibility of the survival of humaneness in a world of evil, as well as his belief in the reconciliation of nations.

Zuckmayer's attempts to establish himself as a writer in the United States failed. He soon gave up a position as a screenwriter for Warner Bros. in Hollywood because the working conditions were not to his liking. After a short, unsuccessful stay in New York, in 1941 he leased a farm near Barnard, Vermont, which he worked until 1946.

In the 1945 novella *Der Seelenbräu*, Zuckmayer creates an idyllic picture of an Austrian village based on Henndorf. A new teacher, the young Franz Haindl, comes to Köstendorf and falls in love with Clementin. The relationship is opposed by her uncle, the rich brewer Matthias Hochleithner, an enormous man with an unbridled zest for life. A second man with whom Haindl comes into conflict is the unsophisticated village priest, "the soul brew," whom he offends with his modern taste in music. But at the end, both older men, because of their basic goodness and conciliatory spirit, accept Haindl and approve of his marrying Clementin. The conflict between the old and the new, Zuckmayer is saying, can be overcome by the right spirit of goodness and humor.

Zuckmayer spent 1946 and 1947 in Germany and Austria as a civilian employee of the American military government, preparing reports on the cultural situation in those countries. His play *Des Teufels General*, written during his exile in America but accurate in its portrayal of life in the Third Reich, was performed more than 3,000 times between 1946 and 1950. In 1948 Zuckmayer received the Gutenberg Plaque. From 1951 to 1958 he alternated his residence between Woodstock, Vermont, and Europe. He was awarded the Goethe Prize of the City of Frankfurt am Main in 1952, the Great Order of Merit of the Federal Republic of Germany with Star and the Vienna Culture Prize in 1955, an honorary doctorate of literature from Dartmouth

*A scene from the premiere of Zuckmayer's anti-Nazi play* Des Teufels General *at the Schauspielhaus Zurich, 1946*

College in 1956, and the Literature Prize of the Rhenish Palatinate and an honorary doctorate of philosophy from the University of Bonn in 1957. In 1958 he settled in Saas-Fée, Switzerland.

In the 1959 novella *Die Fastnachtsbeichte*, set during the last days of the Mainz carnival season in February 1913, a man in the uniform of the Mainz dragoons enters the confessional booth in the cathedral. Before he can mutter the introductory formula of confession, he is stabbed to death with a knife of Italian origin. What begins as a detective story, however, does not end as one; Zuckmayer is not interested in bringing the murderer to justice but in revealing a web of guilt that entangles all the individuals involved. Consequently, it is not the police who are in authority in the case, but a humane and understanding canon, who decides that while the various characters may not have broken any law, they all bear a moral guilt for which they must atone. The theme of the tightly woven novella, which is reminiscent of Heinrich von Kleist's novellas in its analytic construction, is that life must be lived in spite of guilt, by accepting responsibility for one's fellow men. In 1960 Zuckmayer received the Great Austrian State Prize for his collected works.

The mellow, reflective attitude expressed in *Die Fastnachtsbeichte* came to full fruition in Zuck-

mayer's great success of the 1960s, his 1966 autobiography, *Als wär's ein Stück von mir*. The earlier autobiography, *Second Wind*, forms the basis for many chapters of the book; the story of his exile in America and his return to Europe after the war has been added, along with anecdotes about his encounters with many celebrities of German cultural life, particularly of the Weimar Republic. But the most important difference is in the author's perspective: he is no longer looking forward to life as a challenge but backwards, examining the course of his life and the lessons he has learned. Time and again, he finds support for his credo: the importance of human ties and the necessity of restoring the interconnection of all creation. Hence, *Als wär's ein Stück von mir* contains the culmination of the author's message, which he had presented repeatedly in his dramas and in his narrative prose. Zuckmayer's views did not substantially change during his career as a writer. His humanism may seem old-fashioned today, but for him it was the quintessence of his life and his work.

In 1967 Zuckmayer was made an honorary freeman of the University of Heidelberg and was awarded the Insignia of the Order Pour le mérite for Science and Art. He died on 18 January 1977 in Visp, Switzerland.

315

*Zuckmayer's home in Saas-Fée, Switzerland, where he moved in 1958*

**Letters:**

*Späte Freundschaft in Briefen: Carl Zuckmayer, Karl Barth,* edited by Hinrich Stoevesandt (Zurich: Theologischer Verlag, 1977); translated by Geoffrey W. Bromiley as *A Late Friendship: The Letters of Carl Zuckmayer and Karl Barth* (Grand Rapids, Mich.: Eerdmans, 1982).

**Bibliography:**

Arnold John Jacobius and Harro Kieser, *Carl Zuckmayer: Eine Bibliographie 1917-1971* (Frankfurt am Main: Fischer, 1971).

**Biographies:**

Ludwig Emanuel Reindl, *Zuckmayer: Eine Bildbiographie* (Munich: Kindler, 1962);

Thomas Ayck, *Carl Zuckmayer in Selbstzeugnissen und Bilddokumenten* (Reinbek: Rowohlt, 1977).

**References:**

Arnold Bauer, *Carl Zuckmayer* (Berlin: Colloquium, 1977);

*Fülle der Zeit: Carl Zuckmayer und sein Werk* (Frankfurt am Main: Fischer, 1956);

Barbara Glauert, Siegfried Mews, and Siegfried Sudhof, eds., *Carl Zuckmayer '78: Ein Jahrbuch* (Frankfurt am Main: Fischer, 1978);

Alice Herdan, *Die Farm in den Grünen Bergen* (Hamburg: Toth, 1949);

Marianne Kesting, "Carl Zuckmayer: Zwischen Volksstück und Kolportage," in her *Panorama des zeitgenössischen Theaters: 58 literarische Porträts* (Munich: Piper, 1969), pp. 278-283;

Rudolf Lange, *Carl Zuckmayer* (Velber: Friedrich, 1969);

Siegfried Mews, *Carl Zuckmayer* (Boston: Twayne, 1981);

Wolfgang Paulsen, "Carl Zuckmayer," in *Deutsche Literatur im 20. Jahrhundert,* edited by Otto Mann and Wolfgang Rothe, fifth edition (Munich: Francke, 1967), pp. 332-361;

Sheila Rooke, "Carl Zuckmayer," in *German Men of Letters,* volume 3, edited by Alex Natan (London: Wolff, 1964), pp. 209-233;

Siegfried Sudhof, "Carl Zuckmayer," in *Deutsche Dichter der Gegenwart: Ihr Leben und Werk* (Berlin: Schmidt, 1973), pp. 64-82;

Hans Wagener, *Carl Zuckmayer* (Munich: Beck, 1983).

**Papers:**
A great number of Carl Zuckmayer's papers, manuscripts, letters, and other documents are available at the Deutsches Literaturarchiv, Marbach, West Germany.

---

# Hermynia zur Mühlen
*(12 December 1883-19 March 1951)*

Lynda J. King
*Oregon State University*

BOOKS: *Was Peterchens Freunde erzählen: Märchen* (Berlin: Malik, 1921);

*Der kleine graue Hund: Märchen* (Berlin: Vereinigung Internationaler Verlagsanstalten, 1922);

*Der Rosenstock: Märchen* (Berlin: Vereinigung Internationaler Verlagsanstalten, 1922);

*Der Spatz: Ein Märchen* (Berlin: Vereinigung Internationaler Verlagsanstalten, 1922);

*Der Tempel: Roman* (Berlin: Vereinigung Internationaler Verlagsanstalten, 1922);

*Der blaue Stahl*, as Lawrence H. Desberry (Stuttgart: Wagner, 1922);

*Licht* (Contance: See, 1922);

*Märchen* (Berlin: Vereinigung Internationaler Verlagsanstalten, 1922); translated by Lydia Gibson as *Fairy Tales for Workers' Children* (Chicago: Daily Worker Publishing Co., 1925);

*Warum?: Ein Märchen* (Berlin: Vereinigung Internationaler Verlagsanstalten, 1922);

*Ali, der Teppichweber: Fünf Märchen* (Berlin: Malik, 1923);

*Der Deutschvölkische: Eine Erzählung* (Berlin: Vereinigung Internationaler Verlagsanstalten, 1924);

*Der rote Heiland: Novellen* (Leipzig: Die Wölfe, 1924);

*Schupomann Karl Müller* (Berlin: Vereinigung Internationaler Verlagsanstalten, 1924);

*Das Schloß der Wahrheit: Ein Märchenbuch* (Berlin-Schöneberg: Malik, 1924);

*Ejus: Ewige Jugend und Schönheit*, as Desberry (Jena: Neue Welt, 1925);

*An den Ufern des Hudson*, as Desberry (Jena: Neue Welt, 1925);

*Kleine Leute: Eine Erzählung* (Berlin: Vereinigung Internationaler Verlagsanstalten, 1925);

*Abenteuer in Florenz*, as Desberry (Vienna & Berlin: Agis, 1926);

*Die weiße Pest: Ein Roman aus Deutschlands Gegenwart*, as Traugott Lehmann (Berlin: Vereinigung Internationaler Verlagsanstalten, 1926);

*Lina: Erzählung aus dem Leben eines Dienstmädchens* (Berlin: Vereinigung Internationaler Verlagsanstalten, 1926);

*Der Muezzin: Märchen* (Berlin: Verlag der Jugendinternationale, 1927);

*Die Söhne des Aischa: Märchen* (Berlin: Verlag der Jugendinternationale, 1927);

*Said, der Träumer: Ein Märchen* (Berlin: Verlag der Jugendinternationale, 1927);

*Im Schatten des elektrischen Stuhls*, as Desberry (Baden-Baden: Merlin, 1929);

*Der Fememord in New York*, as Desberry (Jena: Neue Welt, 1929);

*Ende und Anfang: Ein Lebensbuch* (Berlin: Malik, 1929); translated by Frank Barnes as *The Runaway Countess* (New York: Cape & Smith, 1930);

*Es war einmal . . . und es wird sein: Märchen* (Berlin: Verlag der Jugendinternationale, 1930);

*Das Riesenrad: Roman* (Stuttgart: Engelhorn, 1932); translated by Margaret Goldsmith as *The*

*Hermynia zur Mühlen in 1926 with Wieland Herzfelde, foun-
der of the Malik Publishing Company (Malik Publishing
Company archives)*

*Wheel of Life* (London: Barker, 1933; New
York: Stokes, 1933);

*Nora hat eine famose Idee: Roman* (Bern: Gotthelf,
1933);

*Schmiede der Zukunft: Märchen* (Berlin: Verlag der
Jugendinternationale, 1933);

*Reise durch ein Leben: Roman* (Bern: Gotthelf, 1933);
translated by Phyllis and Trevor Blewitt as *A
Life's Journey* (London: Cape, 1935);

*Ein Jahr im Schatten: Roman* (Zurich: Humanitas,
1935); translated by Ethel K. Houghton and
H. E. Cornides as *A Year under a Cloud* (London: Selwyn & Blount, 1937);

*Unsere Töchter, die Nazinen: Roman* (Vienna: Gsur,
1935);

*Fahrt ins Licht: Sechsundsechzig Stationen* (Vienna:
Nath, 1936);

*We Poor Shadows* (London: Muller, 1943);

*Kleine Geschichten von großen Dichtern: Miniaturen*
(Vienna: Stern, 1945);

*Little Allies: Fairy and Folk Tales of Fourteen Nations*
(London: Alliance, 1945);

*Came the Stranger* (London: Muller, 1946); German
version published as *Als der Fremde kam* (Vienna: Globus, 1947);

*Eine Flasche Parfüm: Ein kleiner humoristischer Roman*
(Vienna: Schönbrunn, 1947);

*Guests in the House* (London: Muller, 1947);

*Der kleine graue Hund und andere Märchen* (Ober-
hausen: Asso, 1976);

*Die Märchen der Armen* (Leipzig: Zentralantiquariat
der Deutschen Demokratischen Republik,
1982; Wiesbaden: Ausgabe für Fourier Verlag, 1982);

*Der Spatz: Märchen,* edited by Manfred Altner (Berlin: Kinderbuchverlag, 1984).

TRANSLATIONS: Upton Sinclair, *König Kohle*
(Zurich: Internationaler Verlag, 1918);

Sinclair, *Jimmy Higgins* (Potsdam: Kiepenheuer,
1919);

Sinclair, *Ein Hundert Prozent: Roman eines Polizeispit-
zels* (Berlin: Malik, 1921);

Sinclair, *Prinz Hagen: Ein phantastisches Schauspiel in
vier Aufzügen* (Berlin: Malik, 1921);

Sinclair, *Der Liebe Pilgerfahrt* (Potsdam: Kiepenheuer, 1922);

Sinclair, *Man nennt mich Zimmermann* (Berlin: Malik,
1922);

Sinclair, *Das Haus der Wunder* (Prague: Orbis,
1922);

Sinclair, *Das Buch des Lebens* (Berlin: Malik, 1922);

Sinclair, *Der Sumpf* (Berlin: Malik, 1923);

Sinclair, *Der Fassadenkletterer: Drama* (Leipzig: Die
Wölfe, 1924);

Sinclair, *Der Parademensch: Eine Studie über ameri-
kanische Erziehung* (Berlin: Malik, 1924);

Sinclair, *Nach der Sintflut: Ein Roman aus dem Jahre 2000*
(Berlin: Malik, 1925);

Sinclair, *Die Wechsler* (Berlin: Malik, 1925);

Sinclair, *Der Industriebaron* (Berlin: Malik, 1925);

Sinclair, *Die Metropole* (Berlin: Malik, 1925);

Sinclair, *Die Hölle: Drama in vier Aufzügen* (Berlin:
Malik, 1925);

Sinclair, *Präsident der U.S.A.: Roman aus dem weißen
Haus* (Berlin: Universum Bücherei, 1927);

Sinclair, *Petroleum* (Berlin: Malik, 1927);

Sinclair, *Die goldene Kette; oder, Die Sage von der Freiheit
der Kunst* (Berlin: Malik, 1927);

Sinclair, *Samuel, der Suchende* (Berlin: Malik, 1928).

PERIODICAL PUBLICATIONS: "Junge-
Mädchen-Literatur," *Die Erde,* 1 (August
1919): 473-474;

"Tod dem Bourgeois," *Die Erde,* 1 (November
1919): 632;

"Bekenntnis eines ehrlichen Bourgeois," *Der Revolutionär,* 1, no. 19 (1919): 16-17;

"Die Räterepublik im Himmel," *Der Revolutionär*, 1, no. 19 (1919): 26-28;

"Der lästige Ausländer," *Die Rote Fahne* (22 September 1920);

"Zerrissene Stiefel," *Die Rote Fahne* (16 December 1921);

"Das Lied der Treppen," *Die Rote Fahne* (1 January 1922);

"Der rote Heiland," *Die Rote Fahne* (16 April 1922);

"Der Tod des Boris Ossipowitsch Lunin," *Die Rote Fahne* (30 September 1922);

"Die Affen und die Peitsche," *Die Rote Fahne* (26 October 1922);

"Sonnenaufgang," *Die Rote Fahne* (7 April 1923);

"Sonntagspredigt," *Proletarische Heimstunden*, no. 6 (1924): 173-174;

"Das blutende Herz," *Der Knüppel*, 3 (1 May 1925): 3;

"Der Traumhändler," *Proletarische Heimstunden*, no. 16 (1925): 341-342;

"Der Wetterhahn," *Arbeiter Zeitung* (Vienna), 16 April 1933, p. 17;

"Freundinnen," *Das Kleine Blatt* (Vienna), 14 May 1933, p. 3;

"Der achzigste Geburtstag des Zeitungskönigs," *Arbeiter Zeitung*, 28 September 1933, p. 4;

"Das harmlose Thema," *Neue Deutsche Blätter*, 1, no. 2 (1933-1934): 126-128;

"Der Angeklagte lächelte: Eine Skizze aus dem dritten Reich," *Der Kuckuck* (4 February 1934): 4;

"Estella," *Pariser Tageblatt*, 18 February 1934, pp. 3-4;

"Jeremiade einer Asphaltliteratin," *Der Simplicus* (Prague) (15 March 1934): 9;

"Der Vater," *Deutsche Freiheit* (Saarbrücken), 22 March 1934;

"Anstandsbücher von gestern und heute," *Pariser Tageszeitung*, 14 March 1937, p. 4;

"Eine Bio-Bibliographie," *Das Wort*, 2 (April/May 1937): 184-185;

"Die Senora," *Die Zeitung* (London), 1 April 1941, p. 3;

"Miss Brington," *Die Zeitung*, 10 November 1941, p. 3;

"Das verschlossene Zimmer," *Die Zeitung*, 16 January 1942, p. 6;

"Die Bauern von Poitou," *Die Zeitung*, 5 June 1942, p. 6;

"Die Schwalbe," *Freie Tribüne* (London), 5 (December 1943): 8-10;

"Holländischer Frühling," *Zeitspiegel* (London), 8 April 1944, p. 5;

"Hinter der Maske," *Zeitspiegel*, 13 December 1944, pp. 7-8;

"Flüchtlinge: Eine Legende," *Zeitspiegel*, 13 December 1944, pp. 7-8;

"Der Ausflug," *Kunst und Wissen* (London) (February 1946): 31-34;

"Pferde-Mobilisierung: Eine Skizze aus den Septembertagen, 1938," *Die Woche* (24 February 1946): 8;

"Das Wort: Eine Legende," *Die Woche* (17 March 1946): 6;

"Der Sohn des Piraten," *Die Woche* (11 August 1946): 8;

"Wien: 12. März 1938," *Österreichisches Tagebuch*, 4 (March 1949): 16-18.

In 1943, during Hermynia zur Mühlen's exile in England, a commentator predicted that her works would become standards in postfascist Austria, and in 1948 another commentator wrote that she was the best-known progressive woman author writing in the German language; but despite the postwar republication of her works, the Austrian-born writer's name was soon forgotten. A major factor influencing zur Mühlen's reception was the situation in the cultural and scholarly arena after World War II. In Austria the newly awakened search for a national identity, influenced by conservative cultural politicians who came to control the literary scene after 1950, drew its impetus from the monarchy and largely ignored the interwar period. In addition, scholars and critics of German-language literature turned away from works designed to illuminate a specific historical era, favoring instead those considered more universal.

Zur Mühlen's reception was affected by these trends. A dedicated socialist, she considered literature an instrument for uncovering the causes of injustice in society and for seeking a just order based on socialist principles. She believed that the unpopularity of her works in postwar Austria was due to their critical focus on the social and political issues of the interwar period and complained about official response to them—including censorship—in a 1948 letter to the Communist Vienna city councilman for cultural affairs, Viktor Matejka.

Recent developments in German literary scholarship have again affected response to zur Mühlen's work. The shift toward examining literature in relation to its historical context and toward the exploration of the interaction of textual and extratextual elements in the literary work has stimulated interest in her life and writings. New research into the history and literature of the Weimar Republic has also contributed to this scholarly attention, which has been paralleled by the reissue of several of zur Mühlen's works.

Zur Mühlen tried to unite her socialist ideals with a positive attitude toward certain elements of traditional culture in her works, especially in those not designed as propaganda. This task represented a unification of the two distinct segments of her life, before and after her conversion to socialism around 1917. In her well-received autobiography *Ende und Anfang* (1929), she described her life before that turning point as having been lived in a beautiful, well-tempered, and fragrant greenhouse, her words for the world of Austria-Hungary's highest nobility, into which she was born Hermine Isabella Maria Folliot de Crenneville-Poutet in 1883.

Zur Mühlen was always aware of the positive values she had learned in this world: her appreciation of tradition, culture, and beauty, as well as the sense of social justice and respect for others she had first been taught—long before her encounter with socialism—by her unusually liberal family. But she was attracted to socialism because it was designed not to right individual wrongs, as members of her family had tried to do, but to change the entire social structure through collective effort; if this change meant the end of her own class, so be it.

Zur Mühlen was also conscious of negative aspects of her early environment, such as the aristocrats' ignorance of the real world. This ignorance caused them to stand helpless before practical problems; they hid their helplessness behind a disdain for the practicality they associated with the bourgeoisie. Many impoverished aristocrats foundered when forced to seek mundane occupations after World War I; zur Mühlen portrays such incidents in some of her best fiction. On the other hand, the least successful aspect of her writing—negative stereotyping of the bourgeoisie—stems as much from her own upper-class contempt for the middle-class mentality as from her political principles.

Upon coming of age, the young woman refused to settle for the conventional existence of an Austrian countess and sought a more fulfilling life, but she was woefully unprepared for the quest. After several abortive attempts at alternative lifestyles, she married a German Baltic landowner, Baron Victor zur Mühlen, on 16 June 1908. She never adjusted to life in the Baltic social and intellectual wilderness, and the marriage was plagued with heated arguments about the inhumane treatment of the native farm laborers by the German

landholders. After a few years she left her husband and later divorced him.

During part of World War I, zur Mühlen lived in Switzerland, where she was first exposed to organized political movements through exiled revolutionaries and anarchists. The Russian Revolution convinced her that the Bolshevik movement was the cause she needed to give meaning to her life, and she joined the Communist party of Germany in 1919. Some time in the 1920s she married the Hungarian translator Stefan Klein, and they resided in Frankfurt until 1933. That marriage, like her first, was childless.

During her early years in Germany, zur Mühlen's personal goals were completely subordinated to those of the Communist party. Although she was first recognized for translations of Russian, French, English, and American leftist writings, especially of Upton Sinclair's works, around 1920 she began to make an impact on leftist circles with her fairy tales, stories, articles, story collections, and novels, including socially critical detective thrillers. Her involvement in Communist party affairs made her the target of official persecution, which began in 1921 with police surveillance. Charges of literary treason were brought against her for *Schupomann Karl Müller* (Policeman Karl Müller, 1924); although the charges were dropped, a memorandum in zur Mühlen's file warned that the novel could motivate readers to direct political action, so effectively did its author use literature to dramatize Communist propositions.

The works that made zur Mühlen famous in the 1920s were fairy tales and fables that combined fantasy, social criticism, and a Communist moral; these tales were a component in the drive by Communist literary figures to create a new "proletarian-revolutionary" literature, including children's literature, in the 1920s. Denouncing traditional "bourgeois-apologetic" children's stories, Communist pedagogues like E. Hoernle entrusted to the new stories the mission of awakening proletarian-revolutionary class consciousness in young readers, while heightening identification with the party and dramatizing working-class solidarity. Zur Mühlen's stories in this mold were, as Karl-Markus Gauß puts it, "Kleinkunstwerke" (miniature works of art) and "zählten zum Besten und Originellsten in der proletarisch-revolutionären Literatur der zwanziger Jahre" (were among the best and most original [works] of the proletarian-revolutionary literature of the twenties).

Zur Mühlen's children's stories generally follow a single pattern: the main figures, who are

*Two illustrations by George Grosz for zur Mühlen's first book of socialist fairy tales,* Was Peterchens Freunde erzählen *(1921)*

clearly identified with the working class and belong to a collective, struggle to end exploitation by capitalist figures and succeed, through a combination of individual initiative and the unified action of the collective, in establishing a just and harmonious society. In "Die rote Fahne" (The Red Flag, 1930), for example, a ship carrying a group of emigrants from nations traditionally at odds sinks, and the survivors make their way to an island ruled by a creature which tyrannizes and exploits them. When a group of young people joins across national barriers, the creature discovers their growing solidarity and has them shot. The action backfires as the remaining castaways are united under the bloody shirt of one of the dead youngsters, the red flag of the title; they fight and overthrow the oppressor.

Although zur Mühlen's stories contain many features of traditional fairy tales, the author's intention of transmitting a revolutionary lesson necessitated breaking with other traditional elements. Earlier tales either neglected to explain the events portrayed or did so in a naive way; but in these stories exact explication was necessary to guide readers to the "correct" conclusion, requiring longer passages than those found in conventional

tales. The orthodox contraposition of good and evil is modified to fit the socialist mold, with the good characters associated with exploited workers and the evil ones with capitalist exploiters.

Response to zur Mühlen's fairy tales has generally been positive both among Communists reviewing them upon their first appearance and among Marxist scholars of the 1970s and 1980s, her main critical audiences. Some criticism has, however, been focused on the problems arising from her attempts to depict the vastly complicated conflicts of capitalist society in a literary form directed to naive readers. She intentionally reduced these conflicts to a level of intelligibility suited to children, but the resulting picture is at times so simplistic that the fictional situation no longer corresponds to the historical one, thus negating the text's value for the revolutionary cause. Indeed, how best to balance comprehensibility, entertainment, and revolutionary enlightenment for an audience lacking literary training was one of the thorny problems of the search for a new leftist literature in the 1920s, and the discussion of zur Mühlen's texts was part of this debate.

Zur Mühlen's relationship with the Communist party had eroded by the early 1930s and she left its ranks, apparently over the issue of worker solidarity, a main theme of her fiction. Along with other intellectuals, she was alarmed both by the party's increasingly rigid policy against those who sympathized with leftist goals but refused to submit completely to party doctrine and by the ever widening rift between the Social Democratic and Communist parties. She seems to have expressed her views openly, putting herself at the center of the controversy and prompting Communist party stalwart Johannes R. Becher to attack her, while H. Guilbeaux defended her independent stance against unnamed party functionaries in his review of her memoirs in *Die Weltbühne*, a leftist intellectual journal that opposed Communist policy.

In 1933 zur Mühlen joined the stream of exiles from Nazi Germany, going first to Vienna, then Prague, and finally to England. In late 1933 Wieland Herzfelde singled her out as an example of courage in the face of Nazi barbarism. In his Prague-based journal *Neue Deutsche Blätter*, Herzfelde printed an eloquent letter to her German publisher in which she refused, despite financial hardship, to renounce her anti-Nazi writings, a position Herzfelde contrasted with that of several leading writers, among them Thomas Mann. During her years outside Germany zur Mühlen published several novels, some originally in English; contributed to émigré periodicals; wrote radio plays; and translated. She also participated in the Free Austrian Movement in England.

A new phase in zur Mühlen's career began after she turned away from the Communist party and from what she later called her propagandistic works. From 1932 to 1935 she wrote a series of autobiographical novels set against the backdrop of the historical situation from 1900 to the mid 1930s; the best parts of these novels portray women's struggle for personal emancipation. The interweaving of private and public issues in *Reise durch ein Leben* (1933; translated as *A Life's Journey*, 1935) and *Unsere Töchter, die Nazinen* (Our Daughters the Nazis, 1935) is typical of zur Mühlen's writing after 1932. *Reise durch ein Leben*, the most obviously autobiographical of her novels, depicts the personal struggles of Erika against the restricting conventions of the aristocratic environment into which she was born and then against those of the middle-class world into which she chooses to marry. The author's prejudice against the middle class is evident in her depiction of the objectionable bourgeois family members, who are allowed only a hint of human qualities; this stereotypical portrait, reminiscent of her fairy tales, is the major weakness of the book. Erika sees the flaws in both of her worlds, but she is not strong enough to take control of her life and choose an alternative, so she submits to the authorities and conventions of each until a sudden emotional stimulus sends her into flight. But because she does not soberly weigh the changes she makes, Erika inevitably ends up in yet another restrictive environment, that of revolutionary socialists in Switzerland. Even though her decision to join the revolutionary cause is partly emotional, Erika could contribute to the revolution while finding a real goal for herself; but the revolutionaries reject her because their conventions do not allow for a comrade of Erika's background. Unable to contradict the verdict of an authority figure, this woman becomes a wasted resource, one less person of goodwill fighting for justice.

Unlike zur Mühlen's earlier works, which admitted no doubt about Communist politics, her skepticism is evident in *Reise durch ein Leben*, written during her disillusionment with the party. Erika is not the strong, extraordinary woman breaking through all barriers to emancipate herself, like the

*Sketch of zur Mühlen by B. F. Dolbin, circa 1929*

main character in zur Mühlen's 1922 novel *Der Tempel*, nor is the wisdom of the revolutionary leadership above reproach; even now, however, zur Mühlen never questions socialist ideals themselves. Reviewers generally praised the novel; Fritz Rosenfeld believed that its artistic portrayal of a real woman's struggle for independence and its insight into the times would find an echo among many readers.

In *Unsere Töchter, die Nazinen* (1935), serialized in 1934 in the exile newspaper *Deutsche Freiheit*, personal issues serve as a backdrop for political concerns in a specific time and place, 1933-1934 in a German village on the Austrian border. The author's bitterness has subsided, replaced by hope for the future mixed with a still critical view of leftist factionalism. One of several contemporary accounts of Nazi Germany written by émigrés, this novel has received the most scholarly attention of zur Mühlen's novels and was republished in 1979. While other émigré novels show individuals' lives after the National Socialist takeover without an overall perspective on the process leading up to the takeover, zur Mühlen focuses on this process. As in her fairy tales, her aim is to give comprehensible dimensions to an extraordinarily complex historical process. She focuses on three young women representing different classes, and their involvement in the same series of events in the village. In order to supply readers with a multidimensional view of these events and of the historical situation, she employs three first-person narrators: the mothers of the three women, chronicling their daughters' actions. Zur Mühlen does not try to be objective by giving good arguments for the actions of all three women: while the author stands on the side of the aristocratic and working-class women, the middle-class representative is predictably egotistical and materialistic. For other novels of the same period, such as *Nora hat eine famose Idee* (Nora has a Wonderful Idea, 1933) or *Ein Jahr im Schatten* (1935; translated as *A Year under a Cloud*, 1937), the author created positive middle-class characters, but *Unsere Töchter, die Nazinen* is the most polemically antibourgeois of her post-1932 works.

Through the two nonbourgeois daughters, zur Mühlen presents her views on the attraction of National Socialism for idealistic young women. Both turn to the Nazis after disillusionment with other attempts to find their life's goal: working-class Toni rejects the infighting and broken promises of the leftists, and artistocratic Claudia embraces Nazism as a surrogate religion. Toni's and Claudia's personal reasons for joining this revolu-

tionary movement are similar to those Erika displayed when she wanted to join the socialist revolution. As the ultimate authority, with the consummate authority figure in the Führer, National Socialism has enormous appeal for confused and disappointed women. But zur Mühlen intended to stimulate resistance with this novel, so these two women are stronger than Erika, and after logically weighing the evidence, they decide to pull away from Nazism. Claudia dies for the now-united leftist front, but Toni lives to work for the overthrow of Nazi tyranny, which, it is implied, is imminent.

The Austrian fascist authorities, goaded by Nazi pressure, banned the novel almost immediately after it appeared, effectively silencing most critical response. One reviewer did express the hope that zur Mühlen would eventually produce *the* Austrian novel, which would demonstrate the unity of conservative and socialist thinking that the reviewer believed zur Mühlen embodied in her aristocratic and socialist sides. This hope was not fulfilled, but zur Mühlen continued to write novels providing insight into the social and political issues of her time.

Zur Mühlen moved somewhat closer to the Communist party in the mid 1930s, when it initiated the People's Front, an attempt at a unified antifascist movement among exiles; but she never rejoined the party. After World War II zur Mühlen, who was in precarious health, remained in England. She died in Radelts, Hertfordshire, on 19 March 1951.

**References:**

Manfred Altner, "Wer war Hermynia zur Mühlen?," *Die Weltbühne*, 52 (27 December 1983): 1649-1650;

M. Freiberger, "Gesellschaftliche Wirklichkeit und kindliche Phantasie," *Kürbiskern*, no. 1 (1974): 51-67;

Karl-Markus Gauß, "Der lange Weg nach Hertfordshire: Zum hundertsten Geburtstag von Hermynia zur Mühlen," *Wiener Tagebuch*, December 1983, pp. 24-26;

"Hermynia zur Mühlen gestorben," *Die Presse* (Vienna), 22 March 1951, p. 4;

Wieland Herzfelde, "Briefe, die den Weg beleuchten," *Neue Deutsche Blätter*, 1, no. 3 (1933-1934): 129-139;

Edwin Hoernle, "Etwas über Erzählungen, Fabeln und Märchen," *Das proletarische Kind*, 2, no. 1 (1922): 16-19;

F. Hubalek, "Hermynia zur Mühlen: Zum Tode einer großen Frau und Dichterin," *Arbeiter Zeitung,* 21 March 1951, p. 4;

Lynda J. King, "The Woman Question and Politics in Austrian Interwar Literature," *German Studies Review,* 6 (February 1983): 75-100;

Hanno Möbius, "Revolutionäre Märchen der zwanziger Jahre," *Kürbiskern,* no. 2 (1971): 267-270;

Rudolf Popper, "Hermynia zur Mühlen zum sechzigsten Geburtstag," *Zeitspiegel,* 11 December 1943, pp. 7-8;

Eva Priester, "Hermynia zur Mühlen zu ihrem fünfundsechzigsten Geburtstag," *Österreichisches Tagebuch,* 3 (December 1948): 28;

Sigrid Schmid-Bortenschlager, "Thema Faschismus," *Zeit und Geschichte,* 9 (October 1981): 1-17;

Herbert Staud, "Zum hundertsten Geburtstag von Hermynia zur Mühlen," *Mitteilungen des Instituts für Wissenschaft und Kunst* (Vienna), 38, no. 4 (1983): 94-96;

W. Sternfeld, "Hermynia zur Mühlen: Zu ihrem sechzigsten Geburtstag," *Freies Deutschland,* 3 (January 1944): 28.

# Books for Further Reading

Baumgart, Reinhard. *Aussichten des Romans oder hat Literatur Zukunft? Frankfurter Vorlesungen.* Munich: Deutscher Taschenbuch Verlag, 1970.

Bennett, Edwin K. *A History of the German Novelle,* second edition, edited by H. M. Waidson. Cambridge: Cambridge University Press, 1961.

Berman, Russell A. *The Rise of the Modern German Novel: Crisis and Charisma.* Cambridge & London: Harvard University Press, 1986.

Bithell, Jethro. *Modern German Literature 1880-1950,* third edition. London: Methuen, 1963.

Borcherdt, H. H. *Geschichte des Romans und der Novelle in Deutschland.* Leipzig: Weber, 1926ff.

Bosmajian, Hamida. *Metaphors of Evil: Contemporary German Literature and the Shadow of Nazism.* Iowa City: University of Iowa Press, 1979.

Chick, Edson. *Dances of Death: Wedekind, Brecht, Dürrenmatt and the Satiric Tradition.* Columbia, S.C.: Camden House, 1984.

Childs, David. *Germany since 1918.* New York: Harper & Row, 1970.

Closs, August, ed. *Introductions to German Literature,* 4 volumes. London: Cresset Press, 1967-1970.

Craig, Gordon A. *Germany 1866-1945.* New York: Oxford University Press, 1978.

Duwe, Wilhelm. *Ausdrucksformen deutscher Dichtung vom Naturalismus bis zur Gegenwart: Eine Stilgeschichte der Moderne.* Berlin: Erich Schmidt Verlag, 1965.

Esslin, Martin. *Brecht: A Choice of Evils.* London: Heinemann, 1965.

Garland, H. B. *A Concise Survey of German Literature.* London: Macmillan, 1971.

Garland, Henry and Mary. *The Oxford Companion to German Literature.* Oxford: Clarendon Press, 1976.

Gray, Ronald. *The German Tradition in Literature, 1871-1945.* Cambridge: Cambridge University Press, 1965.

Grunberger, Richard. *The 12-Year Reich: A Social History of Nazi Germany 1933-1945.* New York: Holt, Rinehart & Winston, 1979.

Hamburger, Michael. *From Prophecy to Exorcism: The Premises of Modern German Literature.* London: Longmans, 1965.

Hamburger. *Reason and Energy: Studies in German Literature.* London: Weidenfeld & Nicolson, 1970.

Hatfield, Henry. *Modern German Literature: The Main Figures in Context.* Bloomington: Indiana University Press, 1968.

Heller, Erich. *The Disinherited Mind: Essays in Modern German Literature and Thought*. Cambridge: Bowes & Bowes, 1952.

Jones, M. S. *Der Sturm: A Focus of Expressionism*. Columbia, S.C.: Camden House, 1984.

Kracauer, Siegfried. *From Caligari to Hitler: A Psychological History of the German Film*. Princeton: Princeton University Press, 1947.

Kunisch, Hermann. *Die deutsche Gegenwartsdichtung*. Munich: Nymphenburger Verlag, 1968.

Kunisch, ed. *Handbuch der deutschen Gegenwartsliteratur*. Munich: Nymphenburger Verlag, 1965; second edition, 1969-1970.

Langer, Lawrence. *The Holocaust and the Literary Imagination*. New Haven: Yale University Press, 1975.

Lukács, Georg. *Die Zerstörung der Vernunft*. Berlin: Aufbau, 1954.

Mosse, George L. *Nazi Culture: Intellectual, Cultural and Social Life in the Third Reich,* translated by Salvator Attanasio and others. New York: Grosset & Dunlap, 1966.

Natan, A., ed. *Swiss Men of Letters: Twelve Literary Essays*. London: Oswald Wolff, 1970.

Pascal, Roy. *The German Novel*. Manchester: Manchester University Press, 1956.

Reed, Donna K. *The Novel and the Nazi Past*. New York & Bern: Peter Lang, 1985.

Ringer, Fritz K. *The Decline of the German Mandarins: the German Academic Community, 1890-1933*. Cambridge: Harvard University Press, 1969.

Robertson, J. G. *A History of German Literature,* sixth edition, edited by Dorothy Reich. Edinburgh & London: Blackwood, 1970.

Soergel, A., and Curt Hohoff. *Dichtung und Dichter der Zeit,* 2 volumes. Düsseldorf: Bagel, 1961-1963.

Sokel, W. H. *The Writer in Extremis: Expressionism in Twentieth-Century German Literature*. Stanford: Stanford University Press, 1959.

Viereck, Peter. *Metapolitics: From the Romantics to Hitler*. New York: Capricorn, 1941.

Viereck. *Metapolitics: The Roots of the Nazi Mind,* second edition. New York: Capricorn, 1965.

Waidson, H. M. *The Modern German Novel: A Mid-Twentieth Century Survey*. London & New York: Oxford University Press, 1959.

Ziolkowski, Theodore. *Dimensions of the Modern Novel: German Texts and European Contexts*. Princeton: Princeton University Press, 1969.

# Contributors

Katharina Aulls.................................................................*McGill University*

Peter Beicken..........................................*University of Maryland, College Park*

JoAnn Stohler Bennett ................................................*Chatham College*

Reinhold K. Bubser ...........................................*University of Northern Iowa*

Edson M. Chick .......................................................*Williams College*

Christopher L. Dolmetsch ...........................................*Marshall University*

Ulrich R. Froehlich...........................................*Appalachian State University*

Charles W. Hoffmann .............................................*Ohio State University*

Sheila K. Johnson ...........................................*University of Texas at Austin*

Ilsedore B. Jonas ...........................................*Carnegie-Mellon University*

Gerda Jordan.................................................*University of South Carolina*

Lynda J. King.....................................................*Oregon State University*

Herbert Knust.....................................................*University of Illinois*

Wulf Koepke.................................................*Texas A&M University*

Richard H. Lawson...........................*University of North Carolina at Chapel Hill*

Ward B. Lewis ...................................................*University of Georgia*

Ursula R. Mahlendorf .........................*University of California, Santa Barbara*

Siegfried Mews .........................*University of North Carolina at Chapel Hill*

Gerlinde F. Miller ...............................................*University of Illinois at Chicago*

Hans-Christian Oeser ...........................................*University College, Dublin*

Peter C. Pfeiffer ...........................................*University of California, Irvine*

Helga Rudolf .....................................................*Marianopolis College*

David Scrase .................................................*University of Vermont*

Carl Steiner .................................................*George Washington University*

Robert G. Sullivan.................................................*McGill University*

Klaus Thoenelt ...........................................*George Washington University*

Hans Wagener.................................*University of California, Los Angeles*

H. M. Waidson ...........................................*Swansea, United Kingdom*

Gerhard H. Weiss .................................................*University of Minnesota*

# Cumulative Index

*Dictionary of Literary Biography*, Volumes 1-56
*Dictionary of Literary Biography Yearbook*, 1980-1985
*Dictionary of Literary Biography Documentary Series*, Volumes 1-4

# Cumulative Index

**DLB** before number: *Dictionary of Literary Biography*, Volumes 1-56
**Y** before number: *Dictionary of Literary Biography Yearbook*, 1980-1985
**DS** before number: *Dictionary of Literary Biography Documentary Series*, Volumes 1-4

## A

# B

## C

# F

# I

# J

# K

Cumulative Index

# N

# Q

# S

## Y

## Z